The Color of
LAW

GREAT LAKES BOOKS

A complete listing of the books in this series can be found online at
wsupress.wayne.edu

The Color of LAW

Ernie Goodman, Detroit, and the
Struggle for Labor and Civil Rights

STEVE BABSON, DAVE RIDDLE, AND DAVID ELSILA

Wayne State University Press
Detroit

14 13 12 11 10 5 4 3 2 1

Library of Congress Cataloging-in-Publication Data

Babson, Steve.
The color of law : Ernie Goodman, Detroit, and the struggle for labor and civil rights / Steve Babson, Dave Riddle, and David Elsila.
    p. cm.
Includes bibliographical references and index.
ISBN 978-0-8143-3496-6 (cloth : alk. paper)
1. Goodman, Ernest, 1906–1997.   2. Lawyers—Michigan—Detroit—Biography.
3. Civil rights—United States—History—20th century.   I. Riddle, Dave.   II. Elsila,
Dave.   III. Title.
KF368.G594B33 2010
340.092—dc22
[B]
2010011104

∞

Grateful acknowledgment is made to the Goodman family for the generous support of the publication of this volume.

For ordering information plus video, photos, links and updates on the issues central to Ernie Goodman's life, go to erniegoodman.com.

Designed by Walter Schwarz
Typeset by Westchester Book Group
Composed in Grotesque MT and Life

Contents

Preface

"How do you go about choosing a client?"
Said the Michigan Bar to Ernie, one day.
"Do you look for someone grossly defiant,
Or someone with whom the Left is pliant,
Or corporate clients who know how to pay?"

"I fight for those in need," Ernie said;
"I fend for those who've no more hope,
Sold on the block for so much a head,
The poor, the black, and those called red,
And anyone else at the end of his rope."

Hal and Esther Shapiro, *A Tribute to Ernest Goodman* (1980)

This is a book about the people and the social forces that have changed our society over the last century, told through the story of Ernie Goodman, the Detroit lawyer and political activist who played such a unique role in the struggle for social justice.

There is much in the story of Goodman's life that speaks to activists today and the lawyers who represent them. Racial discrimination and class oppression, as Goodman well knew, do not openly declare themselves as injustice. Rather, when prejudice is well established, it takes on a legal coloring, codified in statutes and court rulings that justify inequality and uphold the status quo. Often enough, it is the thick, timeworn varnish of legal precedent that smothers innovation and gives power and privilege the sheen of legitimacy: owners can dismiss long-term employees and move jobs elsewhere because the common law has "always" favored the master's deed of ownership (however recent) over the servants' sweat equity. Until the last third of the twentieth century, the color of law was also uniformly white: racial segregation was the norm and courts routinely upheld the separate and inferior treatment of minorities. At moments of crisis, when precedent was no longer compelling and protesters demanded change, it was the thin veneer of legal rationalization that gave cover to an underlying tyranny: as Goodman came to know, even the most peaceful demonstrators could be arrested for "disturbing the peace," giving the color of law to police actions that nullified the Bill of Rights.

Goodman wrestled with these many moments when the law was at odds with changing conceptions of social justice, when, at times, even the semblance of legality was stripped away and all that remained was the blatant injustice of lynch law or the police riot. The questions he had to address at these moments in his career are no less compelling today. How does an attorney committed to social justice make a living when the people he or she represents are so often the ones least able to pay for representation? When these dispossessed people confront laws that perpetuate injustice, how does a lawyer sworn to uphold the legal system represent social movements that so often have to break the law in order to change it? And when do threats to national security become such a clear and present danger that they warrant suspension of the very constitutional rights we claim as our birthright?

There are no simple answers to these questions today, and in Goodman's time it was all the harder to come to terms with these issues when government leaders branded dissenters as un-American, targeting them for harassment in their professional and personal lives. Goodman persevered nevertheless, and his life demonstrates the human and ethical qualities that helped him survive as a partisan of social justice.

We have many people to thank for assisting us in chronicling this story. Goodman himself wanted to write his own account of how the political and social issues of his time intersected with his life, but the several book projects he began fell by the wayside. He never found the time for the memoirs he had hoped to write, but he did produce something of an outline in the form of a massive inventory of letters, documents, oral histories, travelogues, court records, and draft essays. He was a notorious packrat, and the sum total of the collection he left at the Walter P. Reuther Library of Labor and Urban Affairs, located at Wayne State University (his alma mater) in Detroit, gives ample testimony to the interest he had in making sense of his long and productive life.

Goodman's compilation of this record was an obvious asset to the authors of this book. He was a good storyteller and he knew how to muster the evidence that would make his case. We have diligently mined the documentary lode that Goodman left behind, but we have also been mindful that he was, inevitably, selecting evidence that would advance his interpretation of events. We have been as prudent as we know how in checking his version against other accounts.

Goodman found many collaborators along the way who would help him tell this story, and two of these individuals deserve special mention. William Bryce, a labor educator and activist in Detroit, conceived of an oral history project in 1995 that would put Ernie's recollections on videotape. Goodman and Bryce planned the sequence of interviews with an eye for historical continuity, and Goodman carefully prepared for each session, attentive to the dates, circumstances, and people whose names might otherwise have eluded recall. The resulting seven hours of video, titled "Counsel for the Common People," is an unusually coherent and lively account of Goodman's life, made all the more engaging by the humanity and charm of Ernie's on-camera storytelling.

The interviews that Professor Edward Littlejohn conducted with Goodman in 1996 and 1997 cannot match the compelling immediacy of video, but they offer something just as valuable to anyone chronicling the life of a twentieth-century lawyer. A professor of law at Wayne State University, Littlejohn had hoped to write Goodman's biography. Although that project remained unrealized, the extended transcript of his conversations with Goodman provided us with many insights into the legal issues and trial strategies that defined Goodman's career as a defense attorney.

Both the Bryce and Littlejohn interviews are housed at the Walter P. Reuther Library of Labor and Urban Affairs. These oral histories, combined with the extensive collection of Goodman's papers (processed and unprocessed), would have been enough to make the Reuther archives our single most important resource. But as any labor or social historian who has used the Reuther archives can tell you, there is a massive amount of documentary material housed in this first-rate library. We relied on the Reuther's skilled and patient archivists to help us sift through the dozens of collections with material related to Goodman's professional and political life. We owe every member of the staff our gratitude.

Two other archival resources relevant to our work were the Bentley Historical Collection at the University of Michigan, Ann Arbor, and the Robert F. Wagner Labor Archives in the Tamiment Library at New York University. The Tamiment was especially important. The National Lawyers Guild collection, now expanded to three hundred boxes—including four hundred thousand pages of FBI documents is a deep reservoir of documentary material. Archivist Jan Hilley was our indispensable guide in plumbing this massive collection.

Any biography has to convey something of the social and political context that shaped the woman or man of interest. We have tried to do so with enough detail to make Goodman's life comprehensible. Above all, that background includes the social movements that his law firm grew out of and served, and the fellow lawyers who joined Goodman in the National Lawyers Guild.

First among these individuals was the late George Crockett Jr. From 1944 on, the friendship and collaboration between Goodman and Crockett was the defining aspect of their journey across Detroit's color line, and no recounting of either man's life can be rendered without including the other. Crockett's remarkable career—as labor and constitutional lawyer, Red Scare victim, elected judge, and U.S. congressman—deserves its own biography. In the meantime, there is, thankfully, an outstanding video documentary, *It's in the Constitution* (1993), that captures the breadth of Crockett's career. Tom Lonergan, who wrote and produced this tribute to Crockett's life, generously opened his files and provided us with, among other things, the transcripts of his extensive interviews with Crockett and Goodman.

Close behind Crockett as collaborators in Goodman's professional and personal life were four members of his law firm. Sons Dick and Bill Goodman knew Ernie as a father, a law partner, and a political ally. Their insights into all these varied aspects of Goodman's life were invaluable, and their willingness to make his personal correspondence available to us was enormously helpful. Dean Robb, a founding member of the Goodman firm, was likewise forthcoming with his recollections and understanding of Ernie, and his irrepressible sense of humor made him a particular pleasure to interview. Judge Claudia Morcom did not know Goodman for as long or as well as Robb, but her intensive work in the Mississippi campaigns of the 1960s and her understanding of Detroit's social and political dynamics in that tumultuous decade made her observations especially useful.

We interviewed dozens of others who knew Goodman or worked with him on particular cases or campaigns, and their names are logged in the endnotes. We could have interviewed many more people, and we should apologize now, before any one of those we overlooked has turned another page, for our oversight.

Many friends and associates helped us improve the manuscript before it went to the publisher, and chief among these are the individuals who read all or part of the manuscript: Nancy Brigham, Mike Hamlin, Jim Jacobs, David Radtke, Claudia Morcom, Julie Hurwitz, Alex Heard, Abdeen Jabara, and Nate Conyers. Any remaining errors are the responsibility of the authors. Tim Mantyla transcribed interview tapes, Maria Catalfio scanned photos, and Laura Dewey compiled the index.

There were many others whose published work helped us. Karen Sandlin, editor of the 2004 Detroit Lawyers Guild banquet book, *In Honor of the Legal Volunteers,* compiled a rich collection of personal histories from those who participated in the southern struggle of the 1960s. The producers, writers, and directors of *The Killing Yard* (2001), the Showtime Network movie of Goodman's role as defense attorney in the Attica trials, likewise deserve our thanks (Benita Garvin, Jim Korris, Robert Morris, and Euzhan Palcy). We also want to express our appreciation to Ron Aronson and Judith Montell, producers of the documentary *1st Amendment on Trial* (2005), a history of the Detroit Smith Act trials, who made available the transcript of their remarkable interview with prosecutor William Hundley.

We owe a debt of gratitude to the staff at Wayne State University Press for taking on the book and producing it with its usual professionalism. Special thanks go to Kathy Wildfong, acquisitions editor, who patiently guided us through the process, and Robin DuBlanc, copyeditor, who brought consistency to the manuscript.

The first in line when it comes to an accounting of the labor that went into this book is Dave Riddle, who began the work of researching and writing the manuscript a decade ago. He was later joined by David Elsila and Steve Babson, with Babson taking the role of lead writer in 2005. The three of us were friends long before the book project began, and our lives have since become all the more intertwined. To our families and friends who supported the work—and who almost always suppressed their understandable skepticism that we'd ever get it done—we owe our thanks.

Perhaps the most patient of all have been Dick and Bill Goodman, who enlisted Riddle to begin the work and who have supported the project throughout. They made it clear from the beginning that they did not want us to write a hagiography. We've done our best, though at times it was hard to shake the feeling that their father, in his work and in his being, was just a little bit larger than life.

1

In Dark Times

At 9:44 a.m. on 13 September 1971, a National Guard helicopter roared over the walls of Attica state prison in western New York and began dropping tear gas. The target was Cell Block D and its exercise yard, where twelve hundred rebellious inmates had seized control four days before. The rebels had captured thirty-eight prison guards at the start of the uprising and held them as hostages throughout, threatening to kill them all if the police attacked during negotiations over prison conditions and amnesty. Now, as clouds of tear gas spread across the prison, more than two hundred heavily armed state police and prison guards with gas masks poured into D yard and the surrounding catwalks, shooting nearly five hundred rounds of rifle and shotgun fire at the retreating rebels. By 9:50 a.m., six minutes after the attack had started, twenty-nine inmates and ten hostages were dead or dying.[1]

The small town of Attica was suddenly on the national stage, the site of one of the bloodiest single days of Americans killing Americans since the Civil War. Some blamed the inmates for refusing to compromise their demands and for threatening to kill the captured guards. Others attributed the uprising to the harsh conditions of prison life and condemned the police for the indiscriminate slaughter of prisoners and hostages. In either case, there was no mistaking how sharply the color line had been drawn at Attica: all of the hostages and police were white, and two-thirds of the rebel prisoners were African American.

When it later came to a settling of accounts, the state would indict sixty-two inmates for murder and kidnapping. None of them could afford legal representation and most of the attorneys in western New York would have refused to defend them in any case. Who would represent these men in court when the first pair of cases went to trial in 1975?

Ernie Goodman and William Kunstler were a study in contrasts. Kunstler, the lead lawyer in the first case to go to trial, was probably the

best-known attorney in the United States, drawing media attention well
beyond his home base in New York City. Raised in a prosperous family
and educated at Ivy League schools, he had been an estate lawyer and college professor until the early 1960s, when he joined the political Left as a
relative newcomer. Thereafter, his courtroom flamboyance and flair for
the dramatic had earned him a national reputation as he took up the defense of civil rights activists and antiwar demonstrators. He was tall and
striking in appearance, with a long face and heavy brows, glasses perched
on top of his head, a full mane of hair flecked gray at the temples. At age
fifty-five, Kunstler seemed to be comfortable in the role of the gadfly lawyer
and media-savvy personality, once more at the center of a controversial
case.[2]

Ernie Goodman, on the other hand, was a comparative unknown when
he became the lead lawyer in the second Attica case. In contrast to a headliner like Kunstler, he did not look or act the part. Twenty-five years later,
when Alan Alda played the role of Goodman in the movie *The Killing Yard*,
the image he conveyed was of a younger, urbane man—unmistakably
Alda. No amount of makeup could make him look as Goodman had in
1975, one year before he turned seventy. The product of Detroit's old Jewish ghetto, Goodman had earned his law degree in a nonaccredited night
school without attending a four-year college. Even in suit and tie, he often
looked rumpled and avuncular, his balding head fringed with unkempt
wisps of white hair. He had the look, indeed, of your favorite uncle: that
glint of interest in his watery eyes, the half smile on a face rounding with
age. To the same degree that Kunstler seemed tailor-made for the high-
profile role of a "new Left" lawyer, Goodman's presence begged the question: How did *he* get here?[3]

The personal journey that brought this aging, white, Jewish lawyer
to Attica is a compelling story in its own right. From the 1930s onward,
Goodman had fought the courtroom battles that helped advance labor
and civil rights in the United States. His name was in the headlines often
enough in Detroit, occasionally breaking into the national news when he
argued a case before the U.S. Supreme Court. He went seven times to the
high court and lost only once, but this is not what made him noteworthy.
Other lawyers went to the Supreme Court, some more often, but few could
match the stunning breadth of Goodman's life as a social activist and a
lawyer. Like colored yarn in the warp and weave of American history, his
career had wound its way from the sit-down strikes and labor militancy of
the 1930s to the early stirrings of the civil rights movement in the 1940s
to the Red Scare of the 1950s to, finally, the student mobilizations and
Black Power movements of the 1960s and 1970s. In all these varied set-

tings, two constants stood out in Goodman's work as an attorney: his clients were working class and poor, and more often than not they were African Americans.

Goodman had crossed the color line early in his career, long before racial integration won even a partial acceptance on Main Street or Wall Street. The working-class milieu of Detroit's Jewish ghetto had been whites-only during his formative years, but anti-Semitism was still common coin in American culture and Goodman learned the sting of prejudice at an early age. It was the Congress of Industrial Organizations (CIO), the militant and sometimes radical movement of workers in the 1930s, that tapped his latent sense of social justice and set him on his life course as counsel to the militant poor. As the first mainstream labor federation in the modern era to advocate racial integration, the CIO and its member unions served as seedbeds of civil rights activism. The movement that Goodman knew at its birth in the mid-twentieth century was nothing less than a merging of past reform efforts with the "union tactics" of direct action.

When that protest against racial segregation grew to sudden prominence in the early 1960s and thereafter broadened into a movement against the war in Vietnam and the status quo generally, many labeled it a "youth movement" with no ties to the past. Younger rebels in the new decade seemed to repudiate their elders on all points of the political compass, Left as well as Right. Underlying this generational breach, however, was something more complex. The "old Left," as it was called, was rooted in the working-class politics of the 1930s and the many Popular Front groups that united New Deal liberals with antifascists, socialists, and members of the Communist Party; the "new Left" of the 1960s, in contrast, drew its activists from students, antiwar protesters, young workers, and Black Power advocates who shared a general opposition to corporate culture and the status quo. There was no sharp break, however, between the old and new Left. The transition was so ill defined that, in the words of historian Maurice Isserman, it is "difficult to perceive exactly where the one ended and the other began." Goodman was the personal embodiment of that link between generations. The man who defended African Americans arrested in 1942, when a white mob attempted to forcibly prevent them from moving into the Sojourner Truth Homes in Detroit, was the same man who organized the defense of civil rights workers in 1964, when Mississippi police—under the color of law—arrested them for "blocking the sidewalk." He did not live to see the historic moment in 2009 when Barack Obama crossed the most extraordinary of color lines—a black man entering the White House. But Goodman's story is the story of the movement that made that moment possible.[4]

It is also a story that illuminates something about living in the dark times that have shadowed so much of the globe over the last century. Hannah Arendt, the German American political theorist, defined the dark times as the many occasions "when there was only wrong and no outrage." The 1950s was surely such a time for Goodman and thousands of others on the left, a period in which the very real prospect of nuclear war with the Soviet Union became, in the hands of an augmented national security state, the basis for a cynical mobilization of fear. In the hunt for "subversive activities" that began in the late 1940s, the Red Scare did more than destroy the Popular Front groups that Goodman and thousands of others had joined in the previous decade. The more profound impact was on the way people thought and spoke, the suffocating fearfulness that became endemic when contrary views made one liable to censure, to expulsion from job or profession, even to imprisonment for defending unpopular ideas in front of congressional inquisitors. "Even in the darkest of times," Arendt wrote, "we have the right to expect some illumination." In words that could easily apply to Goodman, she went on to speculate that "such illumination may well come less from theories and concepts than from the uncertain, flickering, and often weak light that some men and women, in their lives and their works, will kindle under almost all circumstances and shed over the time span that was given them on earth."[5]

Goodman's life and work shed such a light. In the 1950s, when many of his former companions on the labor-left had taken up safer pursuits, Goodman and a small but resilient cohort soldiered on. At a time when government inquisitors saw "racial integration" as synonymous with "Communist subversion," Goodman and George Crockett, his African American colleague, formed an integrated law partnership in 1951—the first in Michigan and perhaps the country. When the House Un-American Activities Committee came to Detroit the following year and subpoenaed black civil rights activists and left-wing union leaders for interrogation, Goodman and Crockett served as the principal cocounsels for the accused. When the government threatened thousands of foreign-born radicals with loss of citizenship and deportation because of their beliefs, it was Crockett who helped write the briefs and Goodman who argued the landmark case before the U.S. Supreme Court, *Nowak v. United States,* that won a reversal of policy and an affirmation of the Bill of Rights. In 1951, at a time when white supremacy was virtually unchallenged in the South and the legal lynching of African American men was still accepted practice, Goodman went to Mississippi to mount a last-minute defense of a black man railroaded to the electric chair. Joined by attorney (and future congresswoman) Bella Abzug, Goodman failed to stay the executioner's hand, but it was one of those moments—many lost to history—that prefigured the more successful movement to come.

Goodman was not born to this calling. Raised in the conservative faith of his immigrant parents, he had gone no further in his teenage years than a youthful skepticism toward received wisdom and organized religion. He was otherwise indistinguishable from his fellow second-generation ethnics in boomtown Detroit: an upwardly mobile striver eager to find his place in the land of opportunity. The prospects for success were widening in the 1920s, and Goodman found his way in the world of law, attending night school and pursuing a career as legal representative for small-business owners and corporations. It was the Great Depression that destroyed these prospects and forced Goodman, like millions of others, to reconsider his most basic values. Surrounded by the failure of capitalism and inspired by the popular protest against mass unemployment and starvation wages, he became a socialist and a labor lawyer. His new friends were Red and black, the Communists and African American organizers who taught him the lessons of interracial solidarity, the bedrock of the CIO's campaign to unite workers across the color line.

Goodman never abandoned his socialist faith, though in time he discarded his once vigorous admiration for the Soviet Union and settled on a more ecumenical and democratic vision of what an alternative world might look like. His understanding of the Bill of Rights also changed, though more subtly. In the 1930s and early 1940s, he saw the First Amendment and its protection of speech as a weapon in the class struggle, a legacy of the Revolutionary War against British imperialism that provided legal grounds for sweeping away the many local ordinances that muzzled union organizers. These rights were no less important in the 1950s—perhaps more so, when labor was on the defensive and the Left was in retreat. But it was now the Fifth Amendment and its prohibition against forcing people to testify against themselves that Goodman's clients invoked more often against government inquisitors trying to coerce their cooperation. In the following decade, with the rise of a rejuvenated civil rights movement, he would have more occasion to invoke the Fourteenth Amendment and its protection of due process for black as well as white Americans. This long-neglected amendment to the Constitution, a legacy of the Civil War and the struggle to impose a national standard of equal treatment on the defeated Confederacy, would have a special relevance to Goodman's career a century after its passage.

Along the way, Goodman acquired an insider's appreciation for the democratic foundations of American law, especially the prominent role of judicial review. As he summarized his perspective at the end of his career, "The judicial system in the United States stands alone among its counterparts in the world in one important respect. It is the repository of real state power. Those who have access to the system have access to power, and lawyers of course stand first in line." For a nominal filing fee, a lawyer with an idea, a client, and the required skill and tenacity could challenge bad law on constitutional grounds. "Something more is needed of course," he recognized, before the courts would overturn an ill-considered act of the legislature. "The time must be right [and] social pressure must exist or be generated to support the change." He had seen it himself during his career, and more than once. He had also seen that the time wasn't always right and that the required "social pressure" could be fleeting. Many of the most important court decisions upholding the freedoms protected in the Bill of Rights were concentrated between the late 1950s and the mid-1970s, when anti-McCarthyism, the civil rights movement, and public protest against the war in Vietnam combined to create an especially powerful current of social pressure. Immediately before and after this unique period in American history, the pressure for progressive social change was weaker, and so too was the scope of judicial review. The waxing and waning of this political dynamic is central to an understanding of the life and times of Ernie Goodman.[6]

This is especially so regarding the struggle for economic justice. Goodman recognized that the U.S. Constitution, which upholds the freedom of speech, association, and religion against government interference, remains silent on the social and economic rights protected in the constitutions (if not in the actual practice) of many other countries. The founders of our nation saw no need for articulating a constitutional right to shelter, employment, health care, or sustenance. As legal historian Michael Ignatieff aptly puts it, the U.S. Bill of Rights stands out in comparison with the similar documents of other nations as "a late eighteenth-century constitution surrounded by twenty-first century ones, a grandfather clock in a shop window full of digital timepieces." This ancient legal mechanism has nevertheless been reinterpreted at points in our history to permit statutory laws recognizing workplace rights and other kinds of social and economic liberties. Here especially, "the question of whether you get justice or don't get justice," as Goodman once observed, "depends in the final analysis on the political forces involved." In the 1930s, the Supreme Court upheld the National Labor Relations Act as an extension of freedom of speech into the workplace, protecting the worker's right to protest harsh working conditions and advocate union organization without fear of being fired. The growing power of the labor movement made this interpretation of the

Constitution compelling. With the decline of labor's power and the unraveling of the liberal coalition in the late 1960s, the judiciary's reading of those rights correspondingly narrowed.[7]

For Goodman, this direct link between political power and legal interpretation was always at the forefront of his thinking, not simply as a point of analysis but as a point of departure for the *actions* that would force the issue in the courts as well as the streets. "If you have any sense of relationship to the people who are most affected," he said near the end of his life, referring to the growing gap between rich and poor, "you have to do something about it. . . . Take a position, do something."[8]

Goodman had begun his career as a labor lawyer by *doing something* to advance the rights of workers in the 1930s, but it was not long before this became, more often, a matter of representing African American workers. When he looked back on his life, this seemed natural. "In Detroit particularly, but I'm sure it's pretty common all over the country where there is a black community within a white community, a lawyer could spend his whole life, day and night, month after month, year after year just handling nothing but cases arising out of racial conflicts and racial prejudice." There had certainly been no shortage of such cases in Detroit from the 1930s onward. "Affirmative action then was white," as historian Ira Katznelson has summarized the prevailing practice of white-skin privilege in the twentieth century, when good jobs, quality schools, and decent housing were explicitly reserved for whites. The law that upheld these racist norms had a whites-only hue, and justice was distributed accordingly— ample for the rich, constrained for white workers, prejudicial for blacks. Efforts to overcome the bigoted norms of mid-twentieth-century Detroit confronted not only the hate strikes and race riots provoked by the white majority but also the claims of national security imposed by the federal government. In the midst of a continual mobilization for wars hot and cold, all competing claims for social justice were devalued and deferred to some distant, more convenient time. National security called for national consensus, and dissenting voices were deemed to be, by definition, un-American.[9]

Even in those "dark times," as Arendt called them, Goodman would try to sustain the flickering and weak light that illuminated injustice. "Ernie was a voice for the hopeless, the voiceless and the downtrodden," as his friend U.S. federal judge Damon Keith eulogized him. "He was their lawyer and their spokesperson."[10]

In our own time, the twin specters of terrorist attack and illegal immigration have been used to justify imprisonment without trial and summary deportation of the undocumented. For all the differences of circumstance and time, Goodman would have recognized the same tension between the claims of the national security state and the liberties protected in the Bill of Rights. He would also recognize the same economic and social calamities we face in the new millennium, transposed again to a global arena—mass unemployment, poverty, hunger, the trampling of labor and civil rights. For all those confronting these multiple catastrophes, the prospects for economic revival and democratic renewal can appear slim. If the arc of history nevertheless "bends towards justice," as opponents of slavery once said in dark times, then the story of Goodman's life reminds us that it is only because people like him have soldiered on.[11]

2
Out of the Ghetto

On a hot day in the top-floor study room of Detroit's Central High School, fifteen-year-old Ernie Goodman heard shouting in the schoolyard below and went to the open window. It was 1921, and the gathering conflict between the school's white Anglo-Saxon Protestants and a growing minority of Jewish students had come to a boil. "There we see two gangs," Goodman recalled years later, "the Jewish and the WASPs—there must have been 15 or 20 on each side." The Jewish kids were the underdogs, the ones from the ghetto, poor and proletarian compared to their WASP opponents. But as Goodman watched from the windows over the schoolyard, the "whites," as he called the Protestants, were soon on the defensive. The Jewish toughs were the sons of Russian immigrants recently arrived in Detroit, and among them were kids Goodman linked with what later came to be known as the Purple Gang, the notorious Jewish mob that rose to prominence during Prohibition. They had been hustling newspapers on city streets where each hawker had to fight to defend his turf, and they were used to a cutthroat kind of combat that the Protestant kids couldn't match. As Goodman remembered it, the Jewish boys had "this cutting piece that you would put on your finger so that you could cut the strings around the newspaper quickly. A lot of them had that, some had brass knuckles." In the battle over who would wield power in the halls of Central High, the Jewish kids were drawing first blood.[1]

Ernie was not one of the "roughhouse Jewish guys" who fought the turf wars against WASP and Catholic gangs, but "we considered them our friends because they protected us." In the turbulent urban terrain of Detroit, where neighborhood boundaries were under constant pressure from newly arrived groups, protection mattered. Because many Polish Catholics attended parochial school, they were less prominent in the ethnic mix at Central High. Outside the schoolyard, however, it was Jew

9

versus Catholic. "They would call us 'Jews' and 'kikes,'" Goodman recalled, "and we would call them 'Polacks' and other names." The neighborhood boundaries between the two groups were hotly contested. "If
you walked past the borderline, you were likely to get beaten up. If they
came over, some of the guys on our side would reciprocate." Street-level
skirmishes were common, occasionally escalating into something bigger.
One such fight in 1920 involved two small armies, one of Polish Catholics
and one of Russian Jews, two hundred young men in all, marching grimly
toward each other on Hastings Street until they clashed between Farn-
sworth and Theodore streets, fighting to a bloody draw.[2]

At Central High, Goodman found that his religion made him a target
for bullies and bigots. "I would even have a problem," Goodman remembered, "bringing my lunch . . . during Passover, matzos, boiled eggs—
they made fun of me." This changed as the Jewish minority grew in size
and began to coalesce around an increasingly pugnacious core, the "ones
who thought they were as good as anyone else," Goodman remembered,
and would "put up their hands" to prove it in the schoolyard. Football remained a WASP stronghold, but when Jewish kids began to excel in basketball, the status quo shifted. In the schoolyard clash that Ernie witnessed in
1921, the "roughhouse" Jews had more than held their own before the police arrived, and Central High was different thereafter. "It had a real effect
upon the school itself," Goodman remembered. By his senior year, he did
not have to worry about eating matzos in front of his classmates. When he
later recalled the ethnic power struggles of his youth, he could see the
parallels with the racial conflicts of the 1960s and beyond. "It is very easy
to compare that struggle with [what] has been happening in Detroit in
recent years."[3]

Goodman's home during much of the 1910s and 1920s was Detroit's
Jewish ghetto, concentrated along Hastings Street on the city's east side.
In Goodman's youth, the neighborhood displayed a rich mixture of Jewish
culture: kosher food stores, synagogues (ten within a block of Hastings
Street north of Gratiot Avenue), Hebrew schools, and a variety of Jewish
newspapers. "You grew up as though you were in a Jewish city," Goodman
recalled. "You don't know the people of the dominant culture at all." This
would change as he came of age and entered the wider world of Detroit, a
city already pulsating with the rhythms of the auto age. Like millions of
second-generation ethnics in the opening decades of the twentieth century, Goodman would bear the unique traits that came from living in
these two worlds, the one steeped in the insular culture of the immigrant
ghetto, the other opening onto the expanding universe of the urban melting pot.[4]

From Shtetl to Ghetto

Goodman's parents had settled in Detroit in 1911, a decade before Ernie witnessed the schoolyard clash at Central High. Detroit was the end point of journeys that had taken his parents from villages in eastern Europe and the Ukraine through the small towns of rural Michigan before arriving in the state's leading urban center.

Harry Gutchman fled the Russian province of Estonia shortly before the turn of the century and, upon arrival at Ellis Island, was promptly rechristened "Goodman" by immigration officials. Little is known of his previous life in Russia. As a Jew, he had certainly been subjected to the anti-Semitic policies of the czarist state, which prohibited Jews from entering government service, set quotas on how many could be educated, excluded them from most professions, and placed increasingly severe restrictions on where they could live. The government's official anti-Semitism also produced spasms of deadly violence, the pogroms in which Christian mobs plundered Jewish settlements and attacked their inhabitants. There was ample reason, then, for Harry Gutchman to join the growing exodus from the shtetls, the small towns of eastern Europe and the Russian Empire where Jews predominated. He was one of 2.5 million Jewish immigrants who came to the United States between 1880 and 1924.[5]

"I remember him telling me how he—a greenhorn—landed in New York without money," Ernie wrote fifty years later to his family during a trip to Europe. "Later that day [he] ate a banana, a fruit he had never seen or heard of"—and which, in Harry's rendering of the tale, he ate *without* peeling. How he ended up in the Midwest is something of a mystery, but upon his arrival in Michigan he almost immediately turned to the vocation of itinerant peddler, a common occupation for the few Jewish immigrants who made their way to the rural hinterland. Ernie's description of his father's first year in the new world is pure Americana:

> When he came to Michigan he was provided with a stock of pictures and picture frames, a horse and a wagon, and away he went among the farmers in the "thumb" district, selling pictures of the sinking of the *Maine* [in 1898, at the start of the Spanish-American War]. However, he was at that time an orthodox Jew and could not eat anything "trefa" [nonkosher]. He slept in farmers' haylofts and ate eggs. He once told me that on one occasion, being inordinately hungry, he ate 13 hard-boiled eggs for a meal.[6]

Life as a Jewish peddler in rural Michigan could not have been easy, both because the farm economy was in a perpetual cycle of boom and

bust and because the isolation from fellow Jews must have felt uncanny
for a man accustomed to life in the shtetl. For Harry Goodman and the
few other Jewish merchants in Michigan's hinterland, establishing contact
with coreligionists was a perpetual challenge. To fill out their sales staff,
immigrant merchants would often pay the passage for family members
from Europe to come and work for almost nothing. That is how Ernie's
mother, Minnie Kostoff, arrived in Michigan. She and her two sisters left
their Ukrainian village in the early years of the new century and came to
work in their uncle Robert Kostoff's general store in Saginaw. It's unclear
how Harry came to know of Minnie's imminent arrival, but with no apparent opportunity for the kind of personal contact that might lead to
courtship, he turned to the traditional mechanism of the arranged marriage.
After contacting the Kostoff family, he initiated a correspondence with
Minnie. They exchanged photographs, but they did not meet until the
marriage ceremony in 1903. Minnie was all of seventeen years old on the
day of her wedding. This high-risk but hopeful beginning took on added
optimism as the newlyweds opened a general store in downtown Hem-
lock, just west of Saginaw. It was there that Ernie was born three years
later, on 21 April 1906.[7]

The store failed during the financial panic of 1907, but the young
couple, apparently able to salvage their inventory, opened another store
in Kawkawlin, a town six miles north of Bay City on the western shore of
Saginaw Bay. Ernie's mother worked full-time at the store while his wid-
owed grandmother looked after him and his baby sister, Rose. The grandmother spoke only Yiddish and Goodman did not learn English until the
family moved to Detroit when he was five years old.[8]

It is not clear what finally prompted the move south in 1911, though
it's likely that the hardship of maintaining a store in a farm economy buffeted by repeated financial crises finally persuaded the parents that Detroit's
booming economy was a better bet. The growing Jewish community in the
city also included Minnie's brother, a successful wholesaler of tobacco
products. In contrast to rural Michigan, there would be no shortage of
synagogues to choose from. Even so, for small-town folk accustomed to
the rural ways of Russia and northern Michigan, their arrival in Detroit
must have felt like a sudden, bewildering plunge into a fast-moving river,
a torrent of humanity and loud, clanging machinery. No major city in
North America could match Detroit's explosive growth in the early decades of the twentieth century, when the growing auto industry, the moving assembly line, and the Model T Ford powered the city's economy and
drew workers from around the world. Detroit was growing like a gold-
rush town, from a city of 466,000 in 1910 to a sprawling metropolis of

1.7 million people by 1930. Many of the new arrivals were midwestern farmhands and southern migrants, but the number of foreign-born and second-generation ethnics tripled in the same years, topping 1 million— Poles, Canadians, Germans, Italians, English, Russians, Irish, Scots, and Hungarians. Detroit's Jewish population more than tripled, to 35,000, between 1910 and 1920 as Russian and Polish immigrants poured into the city, overwhelming the long-assimilated German-Jewish families that had previously dominated community affairs.[9]

Years later, Ernie remembered these first years in Detroit as a struggle against cockroaches and bedbugs. "Rats were another enemy which you had to be constantly chasing, avoiding, and destroying." The family moved often, usually looking for better quarters within a Jewish ghetto that was self-contained even as it moved, steadily, as a migrating whole, northwest-ward. "Over the years, we moved north to Brady Street, to Garfield, to Palmer, to Euclid," Goodman recalled, the last address being a single frame dwelling and the "first time we ever lived in a house of our own." They didn't stay there long before moving again, across Woodward Avenue to Clairmount Street on the west side, then finally to a two-family home on Burlingame near Twelfth Street. The city's growing African American population followed in their footsteps, renting rooms from Jewish landlords in Detroit's peculiar southeast-to-northwest pattern of neighborhood succession.[10]

The outward appearance of the urban melting pot conveyed only one dimension of this life. Even as Detroit's hothouse growth brought dozens of nationalities into contact with one another, there was also a self-protective insularity that limited interaction with outsiders and slowed assimilation to the larger culture. Goodman's mother was devoted to her faith, and she made certain that Hebrew school, kosher food, and the synagogue were regular features of Ernie's upbringing. "I hardly knew any gentiles," Goodman later recalled. "We, like most families, didn't own a car. We traveled primarily by streetcar and lived, when we could, near where we worked and where our synagogue was located. Ours was an insular life for most of my childhood years."[11]

One study describes the Detroit Jewish population of 1920 as composed of those "who were generally not factory workers and who came from all horizons." Unlike New York City's Lower East Side, where a socialist political culture thrived among Jewish garment workers and union activists, Detroit's Jewish ghetto was more conservative and far less prominent. One-third of its inhabitants were classified as proprietors of stores or small manufacturing enterprises, and most of the rest were white-collar clerks, general laborers, and street peddlers. Poor as they were, Ernie's parents aspired to the respectable middle-class status that self-employment promised. This goal proved elusive, however, as his father's business ventures failed one after another, starting with the grocery and meat market he first opened on Hastings Street. Goodman later remarked that his father was "a kind, gentle person but a terrible businessman." By World War I, Harry Goodman had taken a job in his brother-in-law's wholesale tobacco company, delivering cigars, cigarettes, and candy to neighborhood stores by horse and wagon.[12]

Ernie was a healthy boy, by all accounts bright, curious, and affectionate. He was, in fact, a Boy Scout, joining the troop that met in the basement of Temple Beth El, Detroit's leading Reform congregation (now Wayne State University's Bonstelle Theater). At age twelve, joining the Boy Scouts marked an early step toward assimilation, but it was a contrasting moment in a life that was otherwise focused on religious education and, at age thirteen, the celebration of his bar mitzvah. Temple Beth El was certainly too liberal for Ernie's mother, who could tolerate young Ernie's participation in the Boy Scouts but was otherwise devoted—like many east European immigrants—to the observance of dietary and Sabbath laws. Temple Beth El did not follow these traditional practices, and this was probably what drew Minnie Goodman to Shaarey Zedek, Detroit's leading Conservative synagogue. Even this, however, was a partial concession to American practice, for unlike strictly Orthodox synagogues, the Conservative Shaarey Zedek permitted men and women to sit together. Minnie was known as a gregarious and generous soul who took seriously the commands of *tzedakah*, the Jewish philanthropic tradition that commands Jews to contribute to the amelioration of poverty and the eradication of injustice. She was not a political person, but she and her sister Hannah devoted considerable energy to organized charity and personal acts of kindness. Ernie absorbed much of this spirit and did not complain when, for instance, his parents invited newly arrived immigrants to share his bed, sometimes for weeks, before they were able to find a job and a place of their own.[13]

While Ernie's parents wanted him to become a doctor rather than a rabbi, they put a strong emphasis on his religious education, sending him to Hebrew school and paying a rabbi to tutor him at home for two years. This immersion in religious study shaped his earliest understanding of the world and his role in it. Goodman would later turn away from a belief in God, but he took with him something of the rebellious spirit of the Hebrew Bible, of the prophets who preached against oppression of the poor and the ill-gotten wealth of the rich. In his adult life, Goodman's protest against injustice would be voiced in the secular lexis of socialism and the

Bill of Rights, but in his unshakable faith in the righteousness of his cause there would always be a hint of the prophet Micah, denouncing the rich because they defraud the poor and "chop them up like meat for the pan." Isaiah prophesized a Messiah who would be the ideal judge, understanding of the poor and protective of their rights; Goodman would come to value exactly these qualities, shorn of religious vestments, in any occupant of the high bench.[14]

Out of the Ghetto

With his enrollment in Central High at the corner of Warren and Cass avenues (the clock-tower building now known as "Old Main" on the Wayne State University campus), Ernie had to come to grips with the jarring contrast between his life inside the ghetto and the competing claims of mainstream America.

Reconciling the two was no easy matter. Central High's secular curriculum and assimilationist ethos exposed Ernie to ideas that challenged the self-contained world of his immigrant parents. This was an era of profound anxiety among "old stock" Americans about the millions of immigrants crowding into the cities and the perceived threat this posed to social cohesion and traditional notions of morality and politics. Detroit's city fathers were already implementing "Americanization" programs in their factories, Henry Ford going so far as to require foreign-born workers to attend the Ford English School and open their homes to company inspectors— the better to guarantee that their wages were spent on what Ford regarded as a properly "American" standard of family life. Public schools were seen as a crucial agency in this campaign to Americanize the great unwashed, with a heavy emphasis placed on lessons in patriotism and citizenship. To stem the tide of new arrivals, the immigration acts of 1921 and 1924 also set strict quotas on the number of eastern and southern Europeans who could enter the country, virtually ending the mass migration that had brought Ernie's parents to Michigan. For immigrant families already in the United States, there was in all of this a clear message: their presence was unwelcome so long as they clung to their "foreign" language and heritage. The pressure to conform was positive as well: Detroit's economy was booming in most years, the city was expanding in all directions, and the emerging culture of mass consumption offered a dazzling display of new products that defined what an "American" lifestyle should look like. Even if the promise outstripped the reality, the mobility woven into the fabric of American life and its powerful, invasive culture in the era of the automobile and the radio acted as a solvent on immigrant cultures.[15]

Living in two worlds—the immigrant ghetto and the WASP-ruled metropolis—put Goodman in the middle of an intense culture war, with each side promoting alternative visions of community and self-fulfillment. The inward-looking universe of the ghetto was a confining but secure place, a tight network of religious and social groups that confirmed Jewish identity and reinforced community norms. The outer world was vibrant, multifaceted, and full of get-ahead opportunities, but it was also intolerant of outliers and could be coldhearted toward the poor. Could he aspire to commercial and professional success outside the ghetto and still observe the demanding rituals of his religious upbringing? Would the larger—that is, Christian—world let an outsider like him succeed? Should success be measured in private gain or public service? For a teenager also experiencing the psychological turmoil of puberty and young adulthood, these weighty questions could have a paralyzing effect. Although he had skipped a grade in elementary school and entered Central High at the age of twelve, Goodman later called himself only a "fair" student. Weighing the dominant rags-to-riches homily of self-improvement against the difficulties his father had experienced probably reinforced his skepticism about the get-ahead sermonizing of adults. On the other hand, the self-contained world of the ghetto was too limited for his growing aspirations. Unsure where to turn, he became lethargic and bored.

As high school graduation drew near, Goodman finally resolved to make his mark in the wider world. As the first available entry point, he chose organized sports and set himself the goal of "earning a letter" in the school's athletic programs. He approached this challenge in a typically analytical fashion. He concluded that he was too skinny to play football, and the high school team was dominated by Christian boys who did not welcome Jews. Basketball was where Jewish kids excelled, but the competition was fierce. Goodman decided to focus on tennis. "Not many people played tennis, and I thought . . . there wouldn't be that much competition," he recalled years later. He turned out to be right, but then showed his grit by practicing from morning to night until he became good at the game. Through excelling at tennis, Goodman learned that he could achieve success in the world outside the ghetto. "I wanted to be part of the world that I was beginning to see around me," he remembered. "I wanted to succeed in that way too, not in the traditional ways. So tennis became the goal through which I proved that I was as good as a white guy, a gentile." He was also becoming an avid bridge player—another portal to "white" culture, as he called it—and spent many hours in card games with his friends.[16]

After graduating from high school, Ernie still held back from making career decisions. He wanted to go to college, but his parents could not afford to send him to school outside of Detroit, and there were few options within the city beyond the University of Detroit—a Jesuit institution and, as Goodman described it, "an Irish school." Instead, and apparently with little complaint from his parents, he spent a year reading the poetry of Keats and Shelley, and writing his own verse. "I saw myself as going to Greenwich Village, a writer, a poet," he said. "That was what life looked like to me at the time." He continued to write poetry while he attended classes at a newly opened junior college at Central High School, where he also joined the Philomathic Debating Club as an outlet for his developing "philomathy" (love of learning). His literary tastes were making him, as he put it years later, "a product of nineteenth century English culture." Shorn of his youthful pretensions, the aptitude for writing that he developed in these years would serve him well as a politically active adult. But at the time, his neighbors knew him as a *luftmensch*—one who lives on air.[17]

He knew this bookish interlude could not go on for long, but he was at a loss where to turn. "I didn't want to go to work—it meant going into a factory, as far as I could tell. Or, I could go to work in my uncle's wholesale business. I just didn't want to; I was a poet in my heart." Goodman was open to any suggestion, even something as far-fetched as the plan one of his tennis partners floated in the summer of 1924: that they both enroll in the Detroit College of Law (DCL), where they could form a tennis team, recruit more players, and tour the state. That was enough to convince the eighteen-year-old Goodman that, even if he didn't particularly relish the prospect of becoming a lawyer, it wouldn't hurt to take some classes to learn more about the law. Compared to the chances of breaking into a career in medicine, which his parents favored, the legal profession seemed a better bet. Medical schools demanded higher standards for admission, were more expensive, more elitist, and more likely to reject Jewish and nonwhite applicants. The practice of law was by no means immune from these prejudices, but it was far more accessible. DCL was a bar-exam mill lodged in a converted downtown garage on the corner of John R Street and Elizabeth (today the outfield of Comerica Park). Despite its self-proclaimed status as a "college," there was no pretense that its curriculum had anything to do with a liberal arts education.[18]

In this respect, DCL was more of a white-collar trade school for the rapidly expanding legal profession. The number of law schools had grown dramatically after 1890, driven by the increasing scale and complexity of corporate enterprise, the demand for lawyers with specialized knowledge of commerce and contracts, and the massive immigration of eastern and southern Europeans. For the latter, law school was a mechanism of assimilation, preparing the first- or second-generation ethnic for participation in a

culture that placed a premium on individual rights and contractual relationships. DCL was Goodman's gateway to this world.[19]

It was not, however, what the Association of American Law Schools
(AALS) had in mind in its campaign to elevate the standards of the profession. The AALS at its founding in 1900 required member schools to
admit only those who had a high school diploma, and even this modest
criterion marked a significant upgrade from the traditional practice of
legal apprenticeship, in which aspiring lawyers with no more than a grade
school education could "read the law" and learn its intricacies while working for an attorney. Elite law schools generally regarded their night school
competitors with disdain for trying to turn "cart horses into trotters" (as
one Harvard professor put it), mixed with apprehension as the number of
night schools more than quadrupled between 1890 and 1910. Legal conservatives sought to stem the "great flood of foreign blood . . . sweeping
into the bar," as one contributor to the *Illinois Law Review* wrote in 1917,
particularly as these ethnics were alleged to have "little inherited sense of
fairness, justice and honor as we know them." Raising standards for admission to law school was a prime mechanism for achieving this end, and
in 1922, the American Bar Association (ABA) announced it would give
its stamp of approval only to schools that required "at least" two years of
college before admission. It would take years, however, for the ABA to
successfully impose the new criterion, and in the meantime Goodman
and thousands of others could still enter law school without the prerequisite years of college education.[20]

The curriculum could not have been very inspiring. Even in the elite
law schools, the prevailing standard of legal education was "the case
method," an approach that limited instruction to the minute examination
of seminal court cases and the fundamental principles they embodied. At
Harvard and elsewhere, there was little effort to examine the social context and the political conflicts that shaped the law. It was only in the
1920s that dissenting legal scholars were beginning to challenge this orthodoxy by calling for a kind of legal "realism" that would incorporate an
understanding of class, economics, and the many social determinants of
the law. But this was still a minority position within the profession, and
little of this could have made its way into the curriculum at DCL. For the
most part, Goodman just memorized case law.[21]

Goodman later recalled that he learned hardly anything from DCL's
part-time instructors, with one exception: Frank Murphy. Judge Murphy,
having won election the previous year to Recorder's Court (as the city's
criminal court was called), was just then embarking on an extraordinary
political career that would carry him to higher office as, in succession,

mayor of Detroit, governor-general of the Philippines, governor of Michigan, U.S. attorney general, and finally, justice of the U.S. Supreme Court. In 1925 Murphy was already building his political base, and the 120 immigrant and second-generation students crammed into the long narrow classrooms of the DCL's renovated garage were the perfect links to the ethnic votes he sought. Goodman remembered Murphy's lectures as the standout moment in his legal education. "He was a brilliant man and he was a liberal-minded person, a very humane guy. . . . All he would do is sit back in his chair—lean back with his hands behind his head—for a whole hour, just give a lecture. But not as a lecture: very down-to-earth. He was called the silver-tongued orator and with good reason. . . . [He] took criminal law beyond the law procedure into the area of philosophy."[22]

The students facing Murphy were often a tired lot, coming straight from their day jobs without a change of clothes, the "smell and sometimes stink" of their work filling the tight, unventilated quarters. Goodman was one of the few who actually got a job in the legal profession, working as a clerk in one of the nearby downtown law firms. Getting the job wasn't easy. Like the proverbial Horatio Alger, Goodman took the elevator to the top floor of the Majestic office building and worked his way down, knocking on every door and asking for work. He then walked across the street to the Hammond Building and did the same thing, eventually finding a lawyer who needed a typist. He faked his way through the typing test and got the job, clerking for $7.50 a week. A year later he moved to the office of his uncle's lawyer ("a hard, mean, tough guy"), who paid him $15 a week for the next two years as he learned the nitty-gritty of the lawyer's trade. Murphy's "philosophy" must have seemed beside the point. "The dominant method used in those days, you tried to find an error. . . . The error might consist of not having a comma in place, or having a word misspelled, or not having the paper filed in the right place perhaps—anything of this sort was an error on the basis of which you would move for judgment to dismiss. . . . Almost invariably, you'd win the case."[23]

The experience of clerking in a one-man law office turned out to be invaluable. The logic and procedure of the common law appealed to him, as did the competitive atmosphere of the courtroom, the arena where opposing lawyers matched wits and maneuvered for advantage. As he approached the end of his apprenticeship, Goodman knew that he could make it as a lawyer, but he wanted to excel in law, just as he had wanted to distinguish himself in tennis. The desire to achieve beyond the ethnic subculture and participate in mainstream society was the prime motivator, and it would carry him through the tedium of reading case law and clerking for an ill-tempered lawyer.[24]

At about this time, Goodman lost his religious faith. "I rejected the notion of a god," he recalled, "after going through all the experiences that one does at the ages of 17 and 18." He was able to cut loose from his religious moorings in part because two of his uncles were freethinkers, and a cousin, Fannie Zeif, was a "lefty" of sorts who scorned organized religion. Harry Goodman gave further (and probably inadvertent) support to his son's questioning. Years later Goodman described his shock the first time he saw his father and uncle eating nonkosher food at a restaurant. It was, he said, "like going to a whorehouse with your father. . . . Once these guys got away from the house and their wives, they'd eat anything." Confronted with this double standard, Goodman chose the tolerant camaraderie of his father and uncle over the confining orthodoxy of his mother. Still, "it was a difficult experience for me," as he later recalled, and it took him nearly four years to go through the whole process of losing his faith in God. He now faced the world without a consolidated belief system.[25]

This loss of faith accompanied a series of challenges to Ernie's youthful idealism as he moved into the mainstream culture. He began to realize that America's rhetorical commitment to equal opportunity and due process was contradicted by its continuing practice of social discrimination. Although offering more status mobility than Europe, American society reserved a sort of caste distinction for those whose history and culture set them apart. The immigration acts of the 1920s had redefined the meaning of citizenship by casting the new arrivals from eastern and southern Europe as "undesirables." Catholics and Jews were not regarded as the equals of Protestants, and black Americans were deemed inferior to them all.

It was this underlying racial divide that would come to define much of Goodman's adult life as a labor and civil rights lawyer. The city's racial boundaries had actually hardened during his youth as southern blacks fled Jim Crow lynch law and migrated northward in a widening stream, boosting Detroit's African American population from 6,000 in 1910 to 125,000 by 1930. The new arrivals crowded into the east side slums immediately south of Goodman's childhood home, joining the many immigrants who had entered the city through this long-established gateway. But as white ethnics moved out of the slums, only a handful of black professionals could follow, leaving most African Americans trapped inside the dilapidated tenements of Paradise Valley and nearby "Black Bottom." Outside was an unwelcoming world of whites-only housing enforced by white real estate brokers, white mortgage lenders, and, on occasion, the white mobs that violently evicted black home buyers in the 1920s. This determined defense of the color line sprang from multiple sources. The prevailing racism of the white majority, particularly the native-born Protestants on the city's west side, had long stigmatized African Americans as mentally inferior and sexually promiscuous, and these racial stereotypes were confirmed in the eyes of many city dwellers by the rural ways and idiomatic speech of southern migrants. Condescending white opinion gave way to angry opposition when white homeowners believed that a single black family moving into their neighborhood would provoke white flight and the collapse of housing values. Rock throwing and gunfire dissuaded all but the hardiest of black home buyers.[26]

Most of Detroit's workplaces were also divided along racial lines, with employers hiring on a whites-only basis to fill all but the most menial of jobs. Even Henry Ford, one of the few employers to hire a limited number of blacks for production jobs, said he did so because "dominance is an obligation" requiring the "superior" race to serve the weaker. Only a handful of unions had been able to recruit members in open-shop Detroit, and many of those affiliated with the American Federation of Labor (AFL) mimicked the prevailing racism by refusing to admit African Americans. White workers could thereby reduce the competition for jobs, but what they gained by this endorsement of racial solidarity with the boss they lost in the inevitable weakening of labor solidarity. The point was driven home in 1921, when the Machinists Union at Timken Axle and the Waiters Union at the Detroit Athletic Club both went on strike to improve wages and working conditions for their all-white membership. Managers whose primary loyalty was to the bottom line abruptly abandoned their racial solidarity with white workers and recruited black strikebreakers to defeat both unions. African Americans had few alternatives when it came to crossing the color line into better jobs, but the prevailing opinion among AFL members was that black workers could not be good trade unionists. Most black leaders, on the other hand, saw Ford's paternalistic racism as preferable to the exclusionary practices of most AFL unions.[27]

The result was a hardening line between two separate and unequal realms in the city: a white Detroit of assimilating ethnics and native-born Protestants moving outward in the 1920s to better homes in newly platted neighborhoods, and a rapidly growing but ghettoized black Detroit living in a diminished mirror-world. Whites-only churches, hotels, restaurants, clubs, and professional sports (including the fabled Tigers, led by avowed white supremacist Ty Cobb) all had their African American counterparts: Dunbar Memorial, formed in 1918 as the first hospital in the city that freely admitted blacks; Mack Field, east side home to the Negro League's Detroit Stars baseball team; the "colored" YWCA on St. Antoine Street;

and the black business and entertainment district along lower Hastings Street. There had been black families living near the Goodmans' east side apartment during Ernie's childhood, and the public schools and public transit had no official policy of racial segregation. But Ernie's social contacts with African Americans had otherwise been proscribed by the growing separation of the races. A white-owned dance hall might cater to black customers, but only at specified off-peak hours during the week; a movie theater might admit African Americans, but only to segregated seating in the balcony.[28]

Detroit was not Mississippi, but at times there seemed to be little difference between the two. In the years Goodman was making his way through law school, Michigan was roiled by the racial politics of the Ku Klux Klan. In Detroit alone, the Klan signed up thirty-five thousand native-born Protestants to the defense of the color line and the containment of Catholic and Jewish immigrants. Cross burnings and massive rallies of hooded Klansmen were frequent occurrences in 1924, when the Klan backed Chester Bowles as a write-in candidate for mayor. Bowles appeared to win the election by a narrow margin, but he lost the recount when election commissioners disqualified the many write-in ballots that misspelled his name. In the regular election the following year, ethnic and black voters on the east side combined to defeat Bowles outright. The Klan's Detroit membership soon after plummeted amid revelations that its leaders had bankrupted the organization and embezzled its funds. But it had been a close call.[29]

The white skin of European immigrants gave them the option of escaping the caste system by shedding their ethnic identities and internalizing the racial phobias of the white majority. But this path to assimilation was more difficult for Jewish families, whose religion and culture marked them as separate. Over time, elite suburban communities like the Grosse Pointes devised complex systems that ranked non–Anglo-Saxon home buyers according to complexion, accent, and religion. Even wealthy immigrants and ethnics found it difficult to buy a home in the Pointes, and Jews and blacks were excluded altogether. Help-wanted ads in Detroit's daily papers routinely specified that job applicants be "gentile" or "of good Christian character" during the 1920s. The University of Michigan's medical school was rumored to have a quota that limited the number of Jewish applicants accepted into the program, and the honorary medical societies and fraternities had no Jewish members. The Detroit Athletic Club was one of many elite institutions that "politely" excluded Jews, offering membership only to the famed architect, Albert Kahn, after he designed the club's building. (Kahn declined the invitation.) Henry Ford meanwhile gave anti-Semitism a patina of respectability in the early 1920s by filling his newspaper, the *Dearborn Independent*, with reprints of *The Protocols of Zion*, a forged document authored by the czarist secret police to justify the pogroms. Harry Goodman, who bought a Model T Ford in 1920, might not have done so a few years later when many in Detroit's Jewish community were boycotting the company.[30]

Goodman was stung by the underlying anti-Semitism he found even at the Detroit College of Law, where most fraternities excluded Jews. The sole exception was Alpha Theta Kappa, a recently organized alternative for Jewish students that had "all the rituals of a constitution and an oath of allegiance," Goodman remembered, but lacked a house of its own and had to meet in the clubroom of the Detroit Public Library. Most of the fraternity's energy went into organizing an annual tuxedo-and-gown dinner dance that brightened the otherwise "mundane kind of school life" that Goodman recalled. But there was also a mimeographed journal, the *Barrister of Alpha Theta Kappa*, which he helped organize as its first "editor in chief." He was probably the author, therefore, of the journal's inaugural editorial promising to pierce the "armor of empty words" and Latin terms that lawyers used to obscure the law. When it later came time for the bar exam and one of Alpha Theta Kappa's best-prepared members failed to pass, the whole fraternity rallied to the cause. "We knew a hell of a lot of people who passed the bar who were just absolutely ignorant. So we raised hell. We took it up to the bar association, which was where you had to go to appeal at that time." As he recalled the episode years later, everybody passed the next bar exam.[31]

DCL did admit women and even boasted one female among the sixty-nine graduates in the first class of 1892. But the occasional woman or African American student at DCL was the exception to the rule: the bar was largely the preserve of white men. In contrast to the nurturing roles that women might occupy in teaching, social work, or health care, the legal profession was too contentious, too entwined with politics and crime, and therefore too "mannish" to suit the stereotypical lady of that era. Elite law schools like Harvard and Columbia refused to admit any women, and the University of Michigan's law school didn't graduate a black woman until 1944. As late as the 1960s, women made up less than 4 percent of the legal profession. As a young law student, Goodman did not find this exclusion of blacks and women troubling. "At that time," as he remembered it, "I was really unaware of the issues." Alpha Theta Kappa was all male and the *Barrister*'s first issue included an article by Goodman's friend Isadore Berger arguing that "women should not practice in Courts, for trial work is unquestionably not within their province."[32]

As he approached the end of his formal legal studies, Goodman found it harder to tolerate the glaring deficiencies of DCL. The curriculum was limited and the school's unventilated classroom building was stifling in the summer and dirty and cold in the winter. There was no practical alternative, however, until 1927, when dissident faculty from DCL broke away to form a new law school in the College of the City of Detroit, forerunner of Wayne State University. A "great debate" followed among DCL students, Goodman recalled, over whether or not "you were going to be a rebel and go over to the new school"; he sided with the rebels—roughly half the DCL students—who followed their instructors to the top two floors of Goodman's alma mater, the old Central High building. Also a part-time evening program, the city-run law school aspired to a higher standard of instruction and an emphasis on public service that was lacking in the commercially oriented DCL; even so, it took until 1939 for the ABA to grant full accreditation. The new school caused a minor stir when it was announced that the inaugural class of 226 included 16 women. "There were some women in all of the classes," Goodman recalled, "but only a few of them graduated and practiced law successfully."[33]

As any upperclassman would hope, the last year of law school was the most enjoyable. Goodman turned his talent for writing to public use, serving as associate editor of the yearbook. When he finally took his degree in 1928 as a member of the school's first graduating class, his photo in the *Jurist* showed a serious young man of twenty-two wearing a black robe and a white bow tie, his handsome face shadowed by the same unsmiling expression that his classmates had affected. Even so, his deep brown eyes, his soft mouth, and the wavy black hair piled on his brow all hinted at something more flamboyant.

Hanging His Shingle

After passing the bar exam that fall, Goodman and two of his fraternity friends, Ed Stein and Fred Collier, established a law firm with downtown offices in the Detroit Savings Bank Building. They aspired to the more lucrative practice of commercial law, but as a practical matter took whatever paying work came their way. It probably never entered their heads to focus on labor law or civil rights as a vocation, for in the 1920s there was nothing "practical" about either of these callings.

Labor law, in fact, was a notorious dead end for lawyers when it came to earning an income and acquiring a reputable status. The majority of judges still held to the nineteenth-century belief that collective action by union members constituted a "conspiracy" of inferior workmen against the "able and ambitious" worker who strived to better himself through individual dealings with the employer. Defending unions in this legal climate was not a promising career. Even laws ostensibly passed to protect civil rights or discourage corporate monopolies were, with no sense of irony, turned into their opposite by a conservative judiciary. In 1890, after considerable debate about the growing concentration of corporate power and the mounting evidence of price-fixing and other practices that abused consumers, Congress had passed the Sherman Anti-Trust Act to prohibit any form of "combination . . . in restraint of trade." The law was supposed to address corporate abuse, but conservative judges used it to declare that strikes and picketing were a form of "combination in restraint of trade," to be suppressed by the nearly one thousand court injunctions issued against strikes during the 1920s. Judges even issued injunctions against unions that urged the public to boycott unfair employers. In such cases, civil rights and freedom of speech took a backseat to property rights, and by the end of the decade virtually every mass-production industry was nonunion, including Detroit's auto industry.[34]

Only a handful of lawyers challenged this orthodoxy on behalf of the legally marginalized. Goodman certainly knew something about the most famous of these legal gadflies, Clarence Darrow. In 1894, Darrow had abandoned his comfortable practice as a corporate lawyer to defend Eugene Debs, leader of the American Railway Union and future presidential candidate of the Socialist Party. Debs had been jailed during the union's nationwide rail strike for ignoring a federal court injunction brought under the Sherman Act. On appeal to the Supreme Court, Darrow had argued eloquently that depriving workers of the right to strike "would strip and bind them and leave them helpless as the prey of the great and strong." The judges were unmoved, however, and Debs lost. Darrow thereafter went from one high-profile case to the next, often losing before conservative judges but, by force of his eloquence and his dogged attacks on prejudice, always drawing public attention to the cause of his underdog clients. Detroit was the scene of one of his greatest triumphs when he was hired by the National Association for the Advancement of Colored People to defend Dr. Ossian Sweet, an African American physician charged with murder after he (or a member of his family) shot a white man during a mob attack on their recently purchased home. Darrow's successful defense of Sweet before Judge Frank Murphy on grounds of self-defense was front-page news in 1925 and 1926, the same years Goodman was studying at DCL.[35]

Goodman followed the case and may well have admired Darrow's principled commitment to social justice. But he had no interest in emulating it.

Four years of day work and night school had not only instilled an appreciation for the craft of lawyering, it had also suppressed much of his youthful idealism. Before entering law school he had "disliked the idea of making money, earning money, and having large sums of money as an ideal in life." But the old dreams of going to Greenwich Village to be a poet were now well behind him:

> I'd begun to accept the notion [about] making good as a lawyer and developing your social status in life and your economic status in life. Everyone else I knew was in law school for just that purpose and I began to assimilate that and accept it as a good way of life—especially since this was the 1920s, when the dominant attitude of the people in my society and all of American society was that everybody can get ahead and make it. The objective of all of that was to become bigger and better and wealthier and more prominent and more powerful than anybody else.[36]

Only the rare luminary like Darrow could afford to take cases at reduced fees that often ended in defeat, and Goodman and his partners had to make a living right away. It was slim pickings at first, with most of their work limited to the legal processing of bad debts and the occasional divorce case. Their formula was simple enough: devote the firm's energies to the acquisition of corporate accounts, do the work on retainer, and accept payment in stocks rather than cash. All this looked good on paper, so long as the economy continued to grow and the value of their stocks continued to rise.[37]

The work, Goodman discovered, was rather dull, although there was one case in his first year of practice that stood out in his memory. "It was a murder case . . . [and] in those days murder cases were most unusual. . . . When you had a murder case it was a really important thing. Everybody looked at you—'my God, you handled a murder case.'" Goodman's client had been robbed by a man who entered his house at night and took money from his trouser pockets; the client had awoken and followed the escaping thief, shooting and killing him when—he claimed—the man appeared to have a gun in his hand. Goodman argued self-defense, but there was the obvious possibility that it was premeditated revenge. It helped that his client was a young newlywed with a child and no previous criminal record. But it helped even more that Frank Murphy was the presiding judge. "It was wonderful to try a case before Frank Murphy. He was just a wonderful man on the bench, as he was in my classroom. He was very sympathetic with me . . . and he helped me over a couple of rough spots. He created an atmosphere in the courtroom in which a jury could feel that if they acquitted, the judge would feel OK about it." When the jury returned a verdict of not guilty, Goodman recalled being "up in high heaven for a few minutes." He had reason to be proud of his effort in a case where, unlike his commercial practice, life hung in the balance. But he had little doubt that he owed much of his success to Murphy's benign role.[38]

When he returned to his routine caseload and took stock of the yield on his invested labor, Goodman had to admit that the law had not been a good provider. He later estimated that during the first year of partnership with his law school friends, his income (not counting stock shares) barely covered expenses, leaving little more than $5 a week after the bills were paid. With these meager earnings he could not afford to leave his parents' home and would have to rely on the family's support until his legal practice took root. It was a frustrating time for the struggling lawyer, but not an altogether unhappy one for a bachelor in his early twenties. Already known for his "famous smile," as his sister described it, he enjoyed a varied social life that included late-night partying at Louie's, an after-hours "black and tan" on St. Antoine where the interracial clientele drank bootleg liquor. Excursions into Paradise Valley alternated with visits to the more refined world of the Detroit Symphony, where he developed a lifelong attachment to classical music. He took up golf, though not with much enthusiasm, and he began to smoke cigarettes. Together with these outward trappings of popular culture, he also pursued a deeper questioning of conventional thinking and received wisdom. He read Nietzsche's philosophical writings and was especially taken with Darwin's *On the Origin of Species*, a book he strongly recommended to his cousin for its "definite, useful, and interesting knowledge," more compelling "than many a novel I've read." A two-year romance with Florence Lathin (Flossie, as he called her) ended in 1929 when he confessed in a note to himself that he could not "return her love in the manner it was given." He was afraid of being "roped in." He was just twenty-three years old. "I am still immature— still learning life," he confided, "but I am content to remain in this changing state until I have found myself."[39]

The Great Crash

As Goodman finished law school and began his own practice, the economy was soaring and success still beckoned. The acquisitive culture that he now subscribed to offered a growing profusion of mass-produced products—radios, refrigerators, kitchen appliances, and ever-larger automobiles—all promoted by the relentless get-ahead propaganda of radio advertising. Unions were in retreat, business profits were soaring, and the number of millionaires rose accordingly. For people with money, the rising expectations that came with the dawn of a "New Era" fueled a speculative frenzy on the stock market, driving share values to new highs.

The bubble burst in 1929. Mass production had finally outrun the limited purchasing power of the working majority, and when sales flattened, employers cut their payrolls and panicked investors sold their overvalued stock. Across the auto industry, wages fell by as much as 50 percent as employers unilaterally cut the hourly pay of nonunion workers. Unemployment soared to an estimated 25 percent of the workforce across the nation and rose higher still in states like Michigan, where the avalanche of layoffs in the auto industry drove the unemployment rate to a staggering 46 percent by 1933.[40]

Detroit suffered worse still. More than half of the city's workers had no regular job in the winter of 1932, according to the Department of Public Welfare, and many of the remainder had only part-time work. There was no social safety net to cushion the fall, no federal- or state-funded programs to provide unemployment benefits, no old-age pension, no minimum wage laws, no deposit insurance to protect a family's savings. Private philanthropy was completely swamped, and the city's public programs were bankrupted by the unprecedented scale of the crisis. The banking system collapsed as hard-pressed depositors made panic withdrawals, and millions lost their life savings. Thousands of Detroiters who could not pay their mortgage or rent were evicted from their homes, their belongings stacked on the curb while the deputy sheriff escorted the humiliated family members out of the building. Winter cold and the lack of shelter took their nightly toll on the growing number of homeless families. A physician at the city's Receiving Hospital told the press in 1931 that four persons a day were brought to the hospital "too far gone from starvation for their lives to be saved." The story was denied by city officials, but few doubted that starvation was a contributing cause in many of these deaths. Begging was ubiquitous, only thinly concealed by the widespread practice of "selling" apples for a handout.[41]

Goodman was not among the early casualties of this catastrophe. Prospects certainly dimmed and customers who could pay in cash were harder to come by, but bankruptcy and foreclosure were growth industries in the Depression, and companies in stress needed lawyers. Catering to business clients cushioned the young lawyer from the initial shocks of the crisis. After paying office rent and other expenses, Goodman's net income actually rose in the first two years of the Depression, from $5 a week to $10 and then $15. Prices were generally low and falling (a pack of cigarettes cost 15¢ in 1932), but he was still barely clearing the equivalent of his weekly wage as a law clerk. Worse, the shares of stock that he and his partners had taken in payment were losing value as soon as they were issued. Even so, expert opinion counseled that the crisis was a temporary downturn, soon to be followed by renewed growth and prosperity. "Just grin, keep on working, [and] stop worrying about the future," advised Charles Schwab of Bethlehem Steel. "We always have a way of living through the hard times." President Herbert Hoover was equally cheery, claiming in one remarkable moment of denial that "many people [have] left their jobs for the more profitable one of selling apples." Goodman could see through the obvious deceit in Hoover's words, but he was slower to abandon Schwab's cheery counsel. He would weather the storm by postponing his departure from the parental home on Burlingame Street and by borrowing money from his uncle, whose cash-and-carry business selling cigarettes and penny candy did better than most.[42]

He could survive in this hunkered-down state, but he was already becoming impatient with what he called the "retroactive method of thinking" in the common law. In the spring of 1930 he vented his frustrations in the *Barrister*, which published a joint edition for Alpha Theta Kappa members from the Detroit College of Law and the Detroit City Law School. "The legal profession places a premium upon pedantry," he wrote in an article condemning the obsessive use of ancient court decisions to guide the judgment of current cases. "Instead of 'How should the law decide my client's case,' [the lawyer] asks himself 'Can I find a decision within which I can fit the facts of my case.'" Conformance with past precedent was the primary goal, while justice and fairness became "a secondary consideration." Goodman aligned himself with those calling for a new kind of legal realism based on the needs of society. "Can the new generation of lawyers build anew upon a more enlightened foundation of scientific knowledge and humanistic principles? . . . Will we continue to base our decisions upon the letter of the past, or upon the spirit of the present?" Reforming court procedures or passing new laws would not be enough to change attitudes inculcated in law school. "We need a new conception of the law and its purpose," he concluded. "We need schools of justice rather than schools of law." Goodman believed the legal profession's dogmatic adherence to ancient precedent and its disregard for social justice was an issue "full of dynamite" that would someday explode "in a fine display of fireworks." He was not yet prepared to throw the match, but "in the meantime we can at least light a few candles."[43]

While Goodman hoped to stir the "dormant conscience" of his fellow lawyers, Frank Murphy, his past professor, hoped to stir the conscience of the city. During his long-anticipated campaign for mayor in 1930, Murphy confidently promised Detroiters a "new deal" and the "dew and sunshine of a new morning." While his opponents promised to crack down on crime and uphold the Prohibition laws that made alcohol illegal, Murphy made the plight of the unemployed the focus of his campaign, promising to open shelters for the homeless and provide soup kitchens for the hungry. "I am for humanized government," he declared, "a government that will touch the citizens in all their activities, in all their distress." An Irish Catholic with extensive ties to the ethnic lawyers and politicians whom he knew from his teaching at DCL and the University of Detroit, Murphy also had the backing of the National Association for the Advancement of Colored People (NAACP) and of liberal leaders within the Detroit Federation of Labor. Black Detroiters who recalled his positive role as the presiding judge in the Ossian Sweet case were especially supportive. Union members and African Americans would vote for Murphy in the hope that a "new deal"—*any* deal—would spark the long-awaited turnaround in the economy. With huge majorities in the ethnic and black wards on the east side, Murphy won a citywide plurality in the five-man race and immediately launched programs to provide the unemployed with food, clothing, a Free Employment Bureau, shelters for the homeless (located in two empty auto factories), "thrift gardens" on vacant lots, and cash support for as long as the city's dwindling tax base allowed. He would win national recognition for these innovative programs and for his public support of federal funding of unemployment insurance and old-age pensions. When Franklin Roosevelt won the presidential election two years later on his own promise of a "New Deal," he would look to Detroit as one of the leading exemplars of liberal government.[44]

Goodman almost certainly voted for Murphy in the mayoral election that September, but he was not a politically active person. In the congressional elections later that fall, he found little to choose from. "Republican or Democrat?" he wrote a friend. "What difference does it make?" Neither party in Michigan had a program to address the economic crisis, and Goodman saw no reason to bother voting. "Thus," he added, "does the blood of our revolutionary heroes go for naught."[45]

In his social life, on the other hand, Goodman found grounds for optimism in the person of Freda Kesler, a beautiful eighteen-year-old South African he met within months of Murphy's election. Her family history had much in common with Goodman's. Fleeing the same anti-Semitism and poverty that bedeviled Ernie's parents, Freda's mother and father had emigrated from the western fringe of the Russian Empire in the late nineteenth century. They had turned south rather than west, drawn by the

South African gold rush of the 1880s and the encouragement of Freda's aunt, already settled near Capetown with her English husband. Freda was born in 1913 in the nearby town of Paarl, where her father had opened a general-goods store that catered to both the white colonizers and the black majority. Her parents were generally more open-minded on issues of race than their white customers, and Freda embraced their liberal views. She resolved to leave South Africa after her parents died, and came to Detroit early in 1931 to join her brother Saul, who had studied dentistry at the University of Michigan. Freda worked as a secretary in her brother's office in the Fisher Building and began to take classes at the College of the City of Detroit. As it happened, her brother lived next door to the Goodman family on Burlingame Street, and young Ernest had taken note of the lovely brunette in the neighboring house. Freda recalled their first meeting years later. "One day I was walking to the Fisher Building and a car was backing out of the neighbor's driveway. He asked me if I wanted a ride." Several days later Goodman invited her to go for a Sunday excursion outside the city. "We'd drive out into the country," she remembered, "and go to the apple orchards, and in those days you could still swipe an apple or two." In sharp contrast to the arranged marriage of Ernie's immigrant parents, he and Freda pursued a long courtship over the next year and a half. When they were married by Rabbi Hershman of Shaarey Zedek in August of 1932, it was for love.[46]

With his remaining money, Goodman bought a Chevrolet Cabriolet—a sporty two-seater complete with folding jump seat—and the two honeymooners took a five-week road trip to California and back. Rather than follow the better-known Route 66, traveled by destitute farmers and unemployed workers, the newlyweds took a northern route from Chicago to Denver to San Francisco. The diary they kept of the trip included a detailed list of expenses: 18¢ for a gallon of gas, as little as $1.25 for hotel rooms, and between 50¢ and $2 for meals which, in at least one roadhouse, had the look of "cat vomit" according to Freda. They took some pleasure in window-shopping the high-priced goods on Chicago's Michigan Avenue before retreating to the more affordable Woolworth's five and dime. Over the first half of the trip, with Freda sharing the driving, Ernie filled the diary with postcard descriptions of driving through Iowa's cornfields, of playing tennis and riding horseback in Colorado, of the gravel roads and sparse accommodations they found along the way. "If life could be any happier than it is now," Ernie wrote in one burst of exuberance, "I would be a god not a man."[47]

As the trip progressed, the diary entries talked less of the landscape and more of the people they met along the way. A forty-five-year-old hitchhiker they picked up in Utah, suitcase in hand, turned out to be a former skilled worker in the printing trades who had been driven from his job as a linotype operator by lead poisoning; he was now scavenging tires for their rubber and sleeping in barns, which accounted for the straw on his unkempt clothes. They picked up a callow young drifter from Detroit, a talkative eighteen-year-old well on his way, the diary noted, to being "a lazy tramp." They were much happier giving a ride to the old farmer who approached them in Nevada, asking for a lift. "He spoke of the many opportunities he had lost," Ernie wrote, "of his having settled in Nevada with high hopes, and how the hopes had been turned into disappointment." Goodman found him to be "a genial, gentlemanly, philosophical fellow" who ruminated on "the futility of ambition." On the return trip to Detroit, when conversation turned to President Hoover's campaign for reelection, "every person we talked to," Goodman wrote, "favored Roosevelt. From our observation he should be elected by a large majority." After a trip of more than four thousand miles over roads where forty miles per hour was considered "good time," they arrived in Detroit with only $5 left between them.[48]

Ernie was happy to begin his new life as husband to Freda and father of their first son, Richard, born in September of 1933. But there were problems as well, particularly as Freda and Minnie Goodman began to quarrel over the proper way to raise young Dickie. Freda was not a religious person, and while Ernie would sometimes go to synagogue for the sake of his mother, neither Freda nor her husband were concerned with religious observance beyond the celebration of Jewish holidays. This alone would have offended Minnie's religious sensibilities, and she was equally distressed by her daughter-in-law's "modern" and permissive notions of child rearing. In these and many other ways, she and Freda were a study in contrasts. Minnie was the heavy-set, round-faced mother devoted to "old world" ways that included arranged marriages and traditional family roles. She spoke English with a heavy east European accent and was, in Freda's opinion, a "coarse" and ignorant woman who "resents progress." Freda was altogether different—physically beautiful, culturally sophisticated, a secular Jew who carried herself in a regal manner and spoke with a British accent. For good reason, Ernie's friends would refer to her as "the Duchess." Except for her brother and Ernie, she had no family in Detroit to support her in the conflict with Minnie and the rest of the Goodman-Kostoff clan, and she soon retreated from what she saw as their disapproval and "ignorant criticism." For a time, she refused to join Ernie at Friday dinners with the family. "I feel utterly alone as I cannot take your family for mine," she wrote Ernie during a summer visit to the family cabin on Lake Michigan. "The differences are too great."[49]

The deterioration in Freda's relationship with Minnie must have weighed heavily on Goodman, who was already experiencing a profound discontent with his career. He was, in fact, losing interest in the law. It plainly didn't pay well, and by 1934 his law partnership was floundering. What remained of the available work put him in the uncomfortable role of defending private property in the midst of unprecedented poverty. "The work I was doing as a lawyer, all of it, was on behalf of small retail stores that sold furniture and jewelry on credit to working people. Our job was to try and collect these accounts or repossess if they couldn't pay, especially when they were laid off. The black community was particularly victimized by this practice. The more I did that kind of work, the more I felt that it was something I didn't want to spend my life on."[50]

In such situations, the ugly chore of collections and repossession fell to the sheriff and the lawyer. "I began to hate the law—a real hatred of it. I hated to come to the offices. I hated to do what I was doing. I hated to represent any more of these companies that were collecting debts from poor people, namely black people. And I hated the fact that I wasn't representing human beings." He couldn't have been further removed from the charitable tradition of *tzedakah*. After two years of this, Goodman would come into the office in the morning and spend a lot of time staring at the typewriter. He began to question the very foundations of his professional life. "I wanted to get out of law and do anything else except being a lawyer, but I didn't know how. It was the only knowledge I had of anything, I couldn't do anything mechanical. I didn't know how, wasn't good at it. I wasn't about to be a poet or a writer. . . . I had to make a living—now I had a family."[51]

He began to read liberal journals like the *Nation* and the *New Republic,* trying to make sense of what was going on around him. He also began to pick up the *New Masses,* a far more radical publication sold on the corner of Michigan Avenue and Griswold in the heart of downtown Detroit. Published by the Communist Party, it presented a thoroughly trenchant and explicitly Marxist critique of the crisis. He was still not sure what to make of it all. His reading of liberal and left wing periodicals not only introduced him to an alternative analysis of domestic issues, it also gave him a broader view of what was going on in the world: the purging of Jews from public office and government jobs in Germany, Italy's invasion of Ethiopia, the social tensions that would soon usher in the Spanish civil war. His own parents' experience in fleeing czarist repression led him to approach many of these issues with liberal concern, but he had no idea how to square this new sensibility with his faltering career as a commercial lawyer.[52]

Goodman was not alone in this gradual and confusing drift leftward, though for the time being "it was just an intellectual thing," he remembered, "nothing more, because my work was not related to that at all." In fact, his work put him directly at odds with the organized Left, for in these early Depression years the single most important focus of left-wing organizing was to prevent the very repossessions and evictions that Goodman was a party to.[53]

"Fight or Starve"

In Detroit and other cities, blocking evictions had become a new and prominent feature of working-class life by the early 1930s. As the most immediate form of resistance to the oppressive conditions of the time, it was also a natural recruiting ground for the Communist Party of the United States of America (CP-USA), which channeled these protests into the "Unemployed Councils" it organized in Detroit and elsewhere. Hard-pressed workers usually had no one else to turn to when the deputy sheriff arrived with an eviction notice. "The people responded to whatever leadership came along," remembered Shelton Tappes, a black autoworker who joined the Unemployed Council in his Detroit neighborhood. "In this case the vocal leadership were Communists, and I know nobody objected to it. People were glad to have somebody who would give them leadership." The Communists, for their part, generally focused their organizing efforts on immediate demands for expanded relief for the unemployed and an end to evictions. The councils' network of block captains and runners could quickly mobilize a crowd when the sheriff entered the neighborhood, and if they did not block the eviction at the start, they would return the furniture to the premises as soon as the bailiff left the scene.[54]

The grassroots militancy of these actions was new enough, but the racial equality evident in many of Detroit's Unemployed Councils was entirely unprecedented. Especially on the east side where Black Bottom bordered on Italian, Jewish, and east European neighborhoods, the Unemployed Council mobilized a multiracial following among the poor that would have seemed impossible in the previous decade. Many of the traumatized workers in these ethnic and racial neighborhoods recognized that they now had at least one thing in common: the experience of extreme underemployment, shading into joblessness and utter destitution. African Americans became council leaders in several cases, and one, Frank Sykes (a member of the CP-USA), served as citywide chairman.[55]

Those who went from the Unemployed Councils into the Communist Party often had little exposure to the theoretical writings on Communism. "I didn't worry through the thick books on Marx," one early recruit later remarked. "I joined the party when it moved a widow's furniture back into her home. I thought it was right. That's why I joined." The number of new recruits was modest, but it marked a turnaround from the organization's previous isolation. When the economy crashed in 1929, the CP-USA had been a small sect on the margins of U.S. politics, boasting fewer than seven thousand members; by 1934, membership had more than tripled to twenty-three thousand, with perhaps fifteen hundred members in Detroit. The Depression had dramatically changed the political terrain, particularly as most incumbent political leaders denied there was even a crisis. In this political vacuum, it was the Communists who stunned the political establishment on 6 March 1930, by the success of their worldwide demonstrations of the unemployed. In Detroit, to the astonishment of the local media, between fifty thousand and one hundred thousand demonstrators and onlookers had gathered downtown, the majority of them obviously not Communists. When demonstrators unveiled signs reading "Work and Wages" and "Fight or Starve," mounted police rode into the crowd, clubbing protesters and onlookers alike.[56]

Two years later, the Communist Party was again headline news when it led a demonstration of three thousand workers on a "Hunger March" to Henry Ford's River Rouge plant in suburban Dearborn. Ford had blamed the unemployed worker for not wanting to "really do a day's work unless he is caught and cannot get out of it." The young, spirited, and racially integrated demonstrators marching under the banner of the Unemployed Councils intended to call his bluff. They carried no weapons as they crossed from Detroit into Dearborn on 7 March 1932, determined to deliver a list of demands that called on Ford to contribute to the support of the unemployed. When they approached Gate 3 of the plant, Ford guards and the Dearborn police opened fire at point-blank range, killing five and wounding upward of fifty of the demonstrators. After the smoke had cleared, Wayne County prosecutor Harry Toy announced the formation of a grand jury to identify the "outside agitators" who had caused the disturbance. The prosecutor singled out no members of the police or the Ford security force for blame, but only Communist Party leaders and marchers, some of whom had already been handcuffed to their hospital beds.[57]

Goodman had little sympathy for Ford, whose anti-Semitism was well known, but he also had little sympathy for the marchers. Like many others, he read the early newspaper headlines that denounced the demonstrators as a "Howling Mob"; it was only later that more sober reporting established that the crowd was unarmed and its leaders were attempting to organize an orderly retreat when police gunfire tore through their ranks. "I shared many of the prejudices against people who were Communists or were called Communists at the time," Goodman later recalled. This sentiment was no doubt reinforced by the business clients and white-collar professionals he still worked with. "I didn't understand what was going on. So I heard about it, read about it, but it did not affect my life at the time." For a man still trying to square his get-ahead ambitions with the grim realities of the Depression era, fathoming the Hunger March could not have been easy. It must have been all the more difficult for the reluctant "repo" man who, on a daily basis, confronted the popular resistance to repossession that the Unemployed Councils represented.[58]

Turning Point

By 1935, Goodman could no longer sustain his commercial practice. He and his law partners "had lost everything. . . . We were just running big debts with no way of paying them. We decided to break up our partnership, which we did, and divided whatever little money was left." He continued to hang on by taking small cases and borrowing from his in-laws, but he was looking for a way out.

Fred Collier, one of his former partners, was the first to point the way. Collier had been working for the Labor Committee of the Michigan House of Representatives, which was drafting a revised workmen's compensation law. Needing help, he enlisted Goodman to do some of the work, and Goodman found the research both interesting and disturbing. The idea of compensating workers for job-related injuries was barely two decades old, and the first Michigan statute, passed in 1912, was now regarded by many as inadequate. Like other state laws passed in the Progressive Era, it had at least removed many injury cases from the courts, where hostile judges citing nineteenth-century principles usually held the victims at fault or blamed their "fellow servants." Public pressure had finally persuaded legislators to pass the "no-fault" statute of 1912, which ensured some kind of compensation to the injured worker while protecting employers from constant litigation and the occasional large settlement. But the process was slow moving, exempted many categories of labor, and didn't cover occupational illness. "I began to see that working people were being screwed out of their claims for injuries or disease caused by their work." Helping draft the revised statute gave Goodman something to do and think about. He no longer wanted to represent business clients, but representing working people was not a viable option when the poor and the unemployed could not afford to pay. Compensation cases offered an alternative, since the fee could be paid as a percentage of the amount recovered for the client. He began to see that it would be possible, if he had such cases, to make a living and also be "on the right side of the conflict."[59]

Often enough, he found that people with valid claims for disabling injuries had forfeited their rights by failing to report the injury in a timely way. "The United Auto Workers had just been organized in 1935, had just published a paper . . . and [I] saw that this would be a vehicle for conveying knowledge to working people of their rights under the workmen's compensation law." Goodman approached one of the editors and proposed a series of articles that would summarize the law and address common issues relevant to protecting workers' rights. He researched and published a half dozen such articles and then took the same idea to the Polish-language press and sold it on the idea of publishing these same stories in Polish. He got referrals from the articles, he got still more by word of mouth, and he was soon building a reputation for honesty and solid, effective representation.[60]

In 1935, Goodman also became involved in local politics when he agreed to speak on behalf of Fred Collier's campaign for circuit court judge. Collier had no compelling program that distinguished him from other candidates, but Goodman agreed to stump for his former law partner and longtime friend, perhaps as a payback for Collier's help getting him involved with the workers' compensation bill. Goodman spoke for Collier at several meetings, including a few gatherings sponsored by black ministers. Candidates running for a variety of offices would come to these small gatherings where, in return for a contribution to the event's organizer, they could speak to a handful of black residents and secure the sponsor's endorsement. The speeches were mostly paternalistic and embarrassing. "They told about how they liked black people and they thought that black people were fine people, and they had a maid that had been with them for 15 years and they just loved her—probably 'Mary.' And how they had given work cleaning up their lawns to a black person, and they had hired someone to fix their car."[61]

Goodman found these endorsement meetings dreary and pretentious, but on one occasion the agenda took an unexpected turn that would change his life. There were five speakers, including himself, and just ten neighbors sitting in the living room of the sponsor's house. The round of speeches began with little deviation from the usual insipid content, until it came to the turn of a newcomer, a self-described "labor lawyer" running as a candidate in the nonpartisan election for Detroit's Recorder's Court. Goodman marveled at the speaker's grasp of the issues. "This guy was speaking in a different way from any of the others I had ever heard." He declared that unemployment had ruined hundreds of thousands of people and that, rather than address the misery that the Depression had created in the city's neighborhoods, the state had tried to suppress the Unemployed Councils. He spoke of the relationship between law and society, arguing that the judiciary owed its authority to the community, that its legitimacy grew out of the community. But, he continued, this relationship had been corrupted by the concentration of wealth, which bent the law to the purposes of the ruling elite. He called for a reform of the judicial system, which, he said, no longer even tried to prohibit discrimination in society. "He spoke about the racial prejudice which is used to keep the working people divided and prevent the formation of unions. He told them his election as judge would enable him to bring into the system the concept of equality which the Constitution guaranteed to everyone." Goodman was familiar with some of these ideas through his wider reading, but this was the first time he had actually seen, heard, and conversed with a lawyer who articulated them in such a forceful way. He considered the speech "by far the most impressive, moving kind of political speech I had ever heard in my life—entirely different from anything else." In this moment of epiphany, he recognized that his growing alienation from the legal profession was not his fault. He had just been on the wrong side of a larger fight.[62]

The speaker's name was Sugar, Maurice Sugar. He didn't win the 1935 election for judge, but with heavy support in ethnic and African American neighborhoods, he garnered a respectable total of sixty-four thousand votes. It was a tribute to his hard work as a candidate, but it also attested to the trust he had won over the years as a champion of the city's poor and dispossessed. He was especially popular among left-wing union members who favored a broader-based movement that enlisted skilled and unskilled workers, blacks and whites. "While Maurice Sugar failed in the election," as the *Detroit Labor News* editorialized, the "votes cast for him by Detroiters, in spite of the silence campaign by the daily newspapers, was a splendid tribute to his outstanding qualities both as an attorney and as a man."[63]

Second only to Goodman's immediate family, Maurice Sugar would become the defining influence in the young lawyer's life, first as mentor and friend, and later, after Goodman joined Sugar's firm in 1939, as leader of one of the nation's foremost legal practices in labor and civil rights law. Sugar was fifteen years older than Goodman, but their lives displayed striking parallels. Both men were second-generation members of Jewish families from the western rim of the Russian Empire: Sugar's from Lithuania, Goodman's from Estonia and the Ukraine. Like many Russian Jews, both the Sugar and Goodman families were forced to emigrate by recurring economic crises and the threat of pogrom. Contrary to the stereotypic view of Jewish immigrants transported directly from traditional Russian village life to the cacophonous urban ghetto in America, both Sugar and Goodman were born in small farming and lumber mill towns in upstate Michigan. Until they moved to Detroit, both families lived in isolation from other Jews.[64]

Sugar's family had migrated from Baltimore in the late 1880s, but when they arrived in Detroit the city was in the midst of an economic depression. Like many internal migrants, they kept moving toward the frontier—in this case north rather than west. They ended up in the lumber mill town of Superior (later renamed Brimley) near the Soo locks in Michigan's Upper Peninsula. Maurice was born there in 1891. To ensure a better education for their children, the Sugars moved back to Detroit in 1900, ten years before the Goodmans. Maurice attended the same high school as Ernie, the prestigious Detroit Central High.

Although their personal histories had much in common, Sugar and Goodman also differed in several ways. For one thing, the Sugar family was relatively more prosperous, the father investing in a clothing business that kept the family solvent even after the store in Brimley failed. For another, religion was almost entirely absent from the Sugar household. Both men, however, strove to live outside the ghetto, seeking opportunities and responding to pressures that were common among second-generation Americans. The ideology of assimilation was in the foreground of their lives. Engaged as they were in the retail trade, the Goodman and Sugar families were especially receptive to the claims of this larger culture; indeed, to some degree, their fathers were the agents of it. Both families had owned dry-goods stores in rural immigrant settings. The small merchant furnished the items required for maintaining ethnic observances, but at the same time subverted tradition by promoting new products and new ways of thinking.

The year 1935 marked a common turning point for Sugar and Goodman, but they had arrived at this juncture from contrasting points on the political compass. Sugar's politics, unlike Goodman's, had been shaped from an early age in an explicitly socialist milieu, starting with his years in law school at the University of Michigan's Ann Arbor campus. Jane Mayer, his future wife, had grown up in a socialist family before enrolling at U. of M., and both she and Maurice became prominent leaders in Detroit's Socialist Party after moving to the city in 1913. There, Sugar emerged as a fearless and principled opponent of United States entry into World War I. Millions of Americans viewed the war as a European battle for empire and colonial booty when it began in 1914, and many Irish and German Americans were especially opposed to entering the conflict as Britain's ally. When the United States did so in April 1917, the Socialist Party led the opposition to forced conscription and won a sudden boost in popularity at the polls, winning between 20 and 35 percent of the vote in major cities from New York to Chicago. It was, however, only a momentary upturn in public support. Passage of the Espionage Act made advocacy of draft resistance a federal crime, and the U.S. government immediately launched a nationwide dragnet that swept up Sugar and an estimated ten thousand others, charging them with failure to register for the draft and "conspiracy to obstruct" its operation. Following his conviction on these charges, Sugar served a ten-month prison sentence in 1918–19.[65]

Even after the war ended, the hunt for foreign-born radicals had intensified, culminating in January 1920 with the Palmer Raids, named after U.S. attorney general A. Mitchell Palmer. In cities across the country, federal agents and local police swept up, by various estimates, between four thousand and ten thousand radicals—eight hundred of them arrested in Detroit and held for days without charges before deportation or release. The list of those to be arrested in the nationwide dragnet was drawn up by Palmer's assistant, J. Edgar Hoover, a young attorney who would become FBI director years later. It marked the birth pangs of the national security state.[66]

When Sugar emerged from prison at the age of twenty-seven, he was very different from Goodman at the same stage of life, professionally and politically. As a lawyer, Sugar had no doubts about where he stood: he was on the outside, engaged in a sharp and continuing conflict with the status quo. This had a literal meaning after conservative leaders of the Detroit Bar Association had him disbarred as a felon in 1918. He won reinstatement only in 1923, aided by an old colleague and fellow alumnus from the University of Michigan, Frank Murphy. Restored to the bar, Sugar was clear about who he wanted to serve in his practice, often without fees: the poor, the victims of racism, and Detroit's struggling unions. His effective defense of strikers and progressive union leaders won him little in the way of income but did earn him a long-lasting loyalty from a diverse spectrum of labor activists, including liberals and moderate socialists as well as

Communists. As one of the few white attorneys who would represent black clients, he also gained a substantial following in Detroit's African American community.[67]

Politically, Sugar was far more certain of his moorings at a young age than Goodman. He remained a Marxist throughout his life, though he no longer paid dues to a particular party. The Left had split into warring factions after the war, and Sugar, like many socialists, refused to make a public commitment to any of the splinter groups that emerged from the wartime repression. The Socialist Party could still draw nearly a million votes in 1920 for Eugene Debs, running for president from the federal penitentiary, but the party was wracked by factionalism and lost members throughout the decade. Its principal rival was the Communist Party of the United States, which modeled itself after the "Bolsheviks" who had seized power in Russia in 1917. Under Vladimir Lenin's leadership, the Russian Communists had repelled the European and U.S. armies sent to unseat them and, for or a time, Leninists enjoyed an almost unquestioned prestige among American leftists. Recent immigrants were especially inclined to see insurrectionary methods as the only answer to the brutality of the old regime, and this "revolutionary Left" scornfully attacked Socialist Party leaders for their devotion to the Bill of Rights and the lawful election of candidates. For foreign-born revolutionaries who focused primarily on the authoritarian regimes in their homelands, the "bourgeois democracy" they found in the United States was difficult to comprehend and easy to dismiss as a charade, particularly when government leaders in the United States resorted, as they often did, to extralegal violence against strikes and union organizers. In contrast to the Socialists, followers of Lenin believed that all capitalist governments were a "dictatorship of the bourgeoisie" that could only be vanquished by armed insurrection and the "dictatorship of the proletariat." With the defeat of revolutionary movements in Europe, however, hopes for a worldwide revolution faded and U.S. Communists found themselves preaching in the wilderness during the boom years of the 1920s.[68]

The doctrinaire purity of the Communist Party was repellent to Sugar, and joining such a sect would have been a risky proposition for a lawyer seeking broader contacts after his recent disbarment. Sugar would therefore define his politics on the same basis as his law practice: in both he demonstrated a strong commitment to working-class communities and the labor-Left (broadly conceived), combined with a pragmatic wariness about narrowing one's options. Sugar would serve as defense counsel for the non-Communists who dominated the Detroit Federation of Labor at

the same time as he contributed legal services to victims of the Hunger
March and to the International Labor Defense, sponsored by the Communist Party.

This did not mean that Sugar was hiding his politics: he was a Marxist, and said so publicly and without apology. He was equally unapologetic
about his admiration for the Soviet Union. When he and Jane Mayer returned from a visit in 1933, Sugar went on a nationwide speaking tour
and described what he had seen in glowing terms. The fact that the tour's
sponsor, the Friends of the Soviet Union, was generally regarded as a front
for the Communist Party did not seem to bother him. Like future United
Auto Workers president Walter Reuther and his brother Victor, who together visited the Soviet Union a year later, Sugar was impressed by the
visible evidence that people had jobs and were rebuilding the country, its
schools, and its economy. The standard of living inherited from czarist
Russia was still low and there were obvious difficulties, but public ownership of the economy's leading industries made a positive impression
when contrasted with the economic paralysis and widespread misery in
capitalist Detroit. The Sugars and the Reuthers were obviously not exposed to the grim reality of forced collectivization in Russia's countryside, nor did they focus on the leadership purges in the Soviet party that
were consolidating Stalin's dictatorial hold. The mobilization of the urban
working class was what they saw and admired.[69]

Admiration, however, didn't require membership in the Communist
Party, and only a fraction of the many thousands who joined the CP-
USA's street demonstrations and eviction blockings actually joined the
party. Membership did grow after 1929, but turnover was also high, as
many recruits quickly exited the ranks. Party membership put substantial
demands on a person's time and energy, and required an unquestioning
conformity to the official "line" that offended many radicals. The sectarian rhetoric of party leaders in the early 1930s was also off-putting. Communists dismissed their Socialist rivals as "Social Fascists." Mayor Frank
Murphy was an "agent of the bosses," President Franklin Roosevelt was a
"watchdog of the capitalists," and the New Deal was a clear example of
"the tendencies towards fascism." Millions of Americans fed up with the
status quo saw the New Deal in far more positive terms, thankful for its
emergency relief and public works programs. Victims of the Depression
often welcomed the "Reds" when it came to mobilizing for direct action
because Communist street leaders had a reputation for discipline, hard
work, and bravery. But the Communist idiom—exalting armed insurrection and the dictatorship of the proletariat—was foreign to a political
culture rooted in constitutional democracy and a strong sense of individ-

ual rights. While the CP-USA routinely denounced liberals and conservatives as capitalist twins, aligned (as one 1930 leaflet proclaimed) in the "Murphy-Ford Starvation Conspiracy," few workers found this convincing. Murphy won reelection in a landslide in 1931, garnering 64 percent of the vote in the final election. The Communist candidate, John Schmies, could do no better than 2 percent of the primary vote.[70]

Sugar had little reason to marginalize his legal practice and narrow his political options by joining the CP-USA. His chief biographer, Chris Johnson, aptly summarized Sugar's complex relationship to Detroit's Leninist organization in terms that would also apply to Goodman:

> Politically, he could agree neither with its hyperradicalism nor, especially, with its position on political involvement and on relationships with existing trade unionism. . . . Sugar thus became fixed in the political stance that he would retain for the rest of his life: an independent Marxist with a deep respect for the Soviet experience and an equally deep respect for the Debsian principles of broad unity of the Left, opposition to ideological nitpicking, full support for industrial unionism . . . and the building of a true workers' party in the United States.[71]

The year 1935 was crucial for both Sugar and Goodman because it was precisely at this moment that the Communist International called for a new strategy, the "Popular Front," in which Communists would abandon their revolutionary rhetoric and join coalitions with liberals and moderates to oppose fascism. Adolf Hitler's seizure of power in Germany was the primary cause of this strategic shift. Communists had previously insisted that Hitler's Nazi Party differed only by degree from the liberals and socialists who sought to reform capitalism. But Hitler's triumph and his subsequent extermination of the German Left finally persuaded the Communists that their revolutionary purity had blinded them to the murderous intentions of the Nazi Party. As a movement of the dispossessed middle classes and lumpen fringe, the Nazis not only attacked the labor movement and the Left but also mobilized small-property holders and the unemployed into violent crowds that attacked the bourgeois status quo. Many German industrialists found little to fear in an ideology of "National Socialism" that focused on the expropriation—and ultimately, the extermination—of the Jewish community. But over time, the Nazi state subordinated even the largest corporations to a program of conquest and genocide that now threatened all of Europe, especially the Soviet Union. In this context, the primary goal of the world Communist movement shifted from the revolutionary overthrow of the capitalist system to the defense of Russia, the "Socialist Motherland." Instead of attacking liberals and socialists, Communists were to join them in coalitions to defend democracy and promote progressive reform of capitalism.[72]

Many Michigan Communists active in grassroots organizing welcomed the new call to "unite all who could be united" against fascism. The Popular Front would include middle-class and even upper-class elements so long as their antifascist credentials were in order. The strategic shift entailed a renunciation of armed struggle (except in self-defense) and an about-face in the party's appraisal of Roosevelt. Whereas before, CP-USA leader William Z. Foster had treated the president and the New Deal as anathema, the new party leader, Earl Browder, supported both.[73]

Sugar had already shown the potential of the Popular Front in his 1935 election campaign for Recorder's Court, boosting the left-wing vote and drawing a wider following to progressive politics. It was this approach that now drew Goodman, the political novice, leftward. Sugar had long held, and Goodman would soon develop, a thoroughgoing critique of capitalism's many failures in the Depression era, but both would retain an abiding commitment to the defense of the legal rights enshrined in the U.S. Constitution and the Bill of Rights. Judges might subvert the Constitution and interpret it in ways that served the dominant class, but there was an underlying bedrock of equal rights and procedure that served the vital needs of an egalitarian protest movement. "Procedure is important, often vital," as Sugar put it years later. "Many of the provisions of the Bill of Rights are procedural in nature. The provisions relating to searches and seizures, to self-incrimination, to the right to trial by an impartial jury, to confrontation by witnesses, and to the requirement of due process are all procedural. The concept that one is presumed innocent until proven guilty beyond a reasonable doubt is a procedural concept. . . . Indeed, it is by procedural requirements that the substance of democracy is preserved."[74]

This was "bourgeois democracy," to be sure, but the American Revolution of 1776 and the Civil War amendments to the Constitution had nevertheless won the vital principle of universal rights and equality before the law. As second-generation ethnics whose immigrant parents knew firsthand what it meant to live without such protections, Sugar and Goodman shared a common conviction that the Constitution—even in capitalist Detroit—could serve the working class. This did not mean they believed that judges or juries were the arbiters of social reform. In a becoming spirit of humility, both Goodman and Sugar would hold that what went on in the courtroom merely registered victories or defeats that had already been decided in the streets, on the picket lines, and at the ballot box.[75]

Compared to Sugar, Goodman was a late arrival to this struggle. The year 1935 marked the beginning of a new life for him, and he was anxious to plunge into the possibilities that lay ahead. As he described it years later, "I just didn't have patience for anything except the work I felt I had to do to make up for all those years I had wasted."[76]

3

Taking a Stand

I f I worked for a wage," Frank Murphy announced to union supporters the night he became governor-elect of Michigan, "I'd join my union." Murphy had just been swept to victory in November 1936, on the same landslide that carried President Franklin D. Roosevelt to a second term. It was vindication for the New Deal and a strong mandate for the law FDR had signed the previous year protecting union organizing and collective action by workers. That law, the National Labor Relations Act, had since been blocked by court injunctions and ignored by police who broke up picket lines. Employers still fired union supporters and recruited strike-breakers to defeat the union. Most workers wanted something better.[1]

On the morning of 27 November, three weeks after Murphy's upset victory, six hundred first-shift workers at the Midland Steel Products Company stopped work and barricaded themselves inside the factory. They refused to leave or let management return until the company recognized their union, the United Auto Workers (UAW), and agreed to a uniform wage increase for the nineteen hundred men and women who made chassis frames for Chrysler and Ford. By remaining inside, they denied the plant to strikebreakers and discouraged the police assaults that so often dispersed outside picket lines in Detroit. They would remain barricaded inside their strike "fortress" for eight days, passing the time with pinochle, poker, even a daily game of football played in the plant yard. As Ford and Chrysler were gradually starved of frames, the pressure mounted on Midland's owners to find a compromise settlement.

On 4 December, management agreed to recognize the union and boost wages by 10¢ an hour, double its previous offer. The raise would bring the pay for most production workers to $1 an hour. It was the beginning of an unprecedented social revolution, one that would transform Goodman's life as well as the city's.

46

The Midland strike was the first sit-down in Michigan, and the novelty of the tactic wasn't the only remarkable feature of this confrontation. Midland Steel employed an unusually large number of African Americans, representing nearly one-third of the workforce, and a sizeable number of these black workers joined the occupation. In an unprecedented display of unity across the color line, the strike committee included Oscar Oden, a black assembler. The 150 women who worked in the plant did not join the occupation (a coed sit-down was deemed too controversial), but they picketed in support and established a strike kitchen in the nearby Slovak Hall on the Detroit-Hamtramck border. Detroit's labor movement had never seen anything so militant and broadly based, encompassing skilled and unskilled workers, blacks and whites, women and men. Thousands of workers would soon emulate their tactics.[2]

It was shortly before this moment that Ernie Goodman had entered the labor movement as a foot soldier in the struggle, serving his apprenticeship in political activism during the months leading up to the Midland sit-down. Maurice Sugar, already the UAW's lead lawyer, would introduce Goodman to the struggle as a legal associate and eager pupil. Goodman had only recently begun to ask how he could, in his words, "use my profession not simply to assist a client and secure an income, but also join with others to bring about significant social change." He was learning the answer now. "You didn't have to leave law," he realized, "to become a union organizer."[3]

It was a lesson he took to heart at a unique moment in American history. In the United States, the precarious growth of the UAW and the New Deal state confronted an entrenched status quo and a gathering reaction. Abroad, the rise of European fascism and Japanese militarism cast twin shadows across the globe, giving a special urgency to the defense of democracy and civil liberties in the United States and elsewhere. In Detroit, all these domestic and international conflicts would soon come to a head in the most polarized political arena in North America.

Goodman's personal loyalties and fundamental beliefs, the ideas that defined his adult life, were shaped by this confrontation as he joined the struggles of the day after 1935: the campaign to expose right-wing terror organizations and their links with local government, the mobilization to support the Spanish Republic against fascist intervention; and the defense of labor and free speech against the violent antiunionism of the Ford Motor Company. Within three years, Goodman's personal journey would take him onto the public stage in a high-profile confrontation with the emerging legal apparatus of the Red Scare. His leadership role in the series of cases surrounding the first Detroit appearance of the House Un-American Activities Committee in 1938 would mark the end of his apprenticeship and the start of a rapidly growing FBI file.

Labor and Civil Rights

Long before he became known to the FBI, Goodman found his "legs" as a labor and civil rights attorney in the Conference for the Protection of Civil Rights (CPCR), an organization that helped prepare the ground for the Midland sit-down strike and the union organization that followed.

Organized in 1935, the conference was an exemplar of the Popular Front in its membership and program. Union activists, Farmer-Laborites, ministers, lawyers, community leaders from Detroit's ethnic enclaves and racial ghettos, and a sizeable core of Communists and Socialists made for a diverse membership. This mixed gathering came together under the conference's banner of support for the Bill of Rights and extension of its protections to union supporters, racial-ethnic minorities, and the Left.[4]

Goodman joined the conference when the wife of one of his former law partners invited him to an early meeting. He liked the group and the variety of people it attracted. He was no longer "prejudiced" against Communists, as he had been just three years before at the time of the Hunger March, and he accepted their prominent role in the conference as a natural expression of the Popular Front. He was favorably impressed by the fact that the group was racially integrated and seemed to take political equality for African Americans seriously. "For the first time," as he later recalled, "I met black people . . . on a social level." In the near-apartheid conditions of Detroit in the 1920s, the social separation of the races had been commonplace, even for someone like Goodman who grew up within walking distance of Black Bottom.[5]

The initial encounters between blacks and whites could be awkward for newcomers, as Goodman learned when a black church invited him to speak at Sunday service on political matters facing the city:

> It was a store-front church on Hastings Street. I had never been in a store-front church. I walked in, in a shirt and trousers, without a jacket and without a tie. As I walked in, I saw all these people dressed up in their Sunday best. . . . I sheepishly sat down. . . . Finally, the pastor . . . introduced me by saying that Mr. Goodman doesn't understand the custom about Sunday church and has just come from home. I felt so embarrassed. . . . I wouldn't have gone to a white church the way I was dressed, but I did to a black church because I didn't understand.[6]

Goodman's belated recognition of this double standard was no doubt sharpened by his own experience as a ghettoized minority. As his circle of friends widened, he came to recognize the obvious discrimination that black attorneys were subject to. "In the first place, black lawyers could not rent offices in downtown office buildings. Many had their offices on Broadway just off Gratiot [a few blocks from Hastings Street]. They were treated differently in court. They were usually called by their first name. When blacks, in the criminal courts especially, were witnesses or defendants, they were always called by their first name. Nobody ever called them 'Mr. so-and-so.'" It would be another fifteen years before Goodman bridged this racial divide by forming Michigan's first integrated law partnership, but the process began in the mid-1930s when Maurice Sugar led an early challenge to the status quo. During his 1935 campaign for Recorder's Court, Sugar and other left-wing lawyers working with the International Labor Defense (ILD) took steps to desegregate the Hoffman Building, where the ILD rented offices. When the Hoffman's manager informed the ILD that its integrated office staff violated the building's covenant and that "we must ask you either to discharge your colored help or leave the building," the ILD refused to do either. After a two-month standoff, the building's owner relented and—amid considerable publicity in the black community favoring Sugar's candidacy—the covenant was abolished.[7]

Several of Sugar's African American supporters went on to become early leaders in the Conference for the Protection of Civil Rights. Among them was LeBron Simmons, a former garbage truck driver and Teamster member who worked his way through college, earning an undergraduate degree from the University of Michigan (which his brother and sister also attended) and a law degree from the University of Detroit. Admitted to the Michigan bar in 1935, he opened a law office on Gratiot Avenue and became active that same year in Sugar's follow-up campaign for city council (he narrowly missed election this time, with fifty-five thousand votes). Simmons was further distinguished by his close ties with the Communist Party and its Popular Front strategy of coalition building, running as a Farmer-Labor Party candidate for state senate in 1936 and serving as first president of the Detroit chapter of the National Negro Congress.[8]

This made Simmons part of a small but growing minority within the black community that had come to admire the Communist Party for its spirited defense of the Scottsboro Boys, the nine African American teenagers falsely accused in Alabama of raping two white women in 1931. The case had all the features of racist lynch law that Goodman would come to know personally in the 1950s, when he participated in the defense of another African American accused of rape in the Deep South: perjured testimony, white mobs threatening summary lynching, intimidation of local defense attorneys, and the almost inevitable death sentences. In contrast to the cautious approach of the National Association for the Advancement of Colored People, which hesitated before backing the Scottsboro Nine with quiet lobbying, the Communist Party organized interracial protest marches across the nation and sent thousands of supporters to petition the president and Congress. When these efforts stayed the executions and forced a series of retrials, many African Americans in the North, particularly young activists like Simmons, came to regard the CP-USA as a genuine ally in the black liberation struggle.[9]

Goodman would absorb much of this perspective as he settled into his role as an activist member of the conference. In addition to left-wingers like Simmons, his new colleagues also included the Reverend John Bollens, the white pastor of the Messiah Evangelical and Reformed Church and the first chairman of the organization. As secretary of the Detroit chapter of the American Civil Liberties Union (ACLU), Bollens was very likely the key influence in Goodman's decision to join the ACLU in 1935, the same year he became active in the conference. It was from this vantage point that Goodman would become a man of the Left.

Goodman was stepping into the political arena at the very moment it was polarizing along the most radical divide in the post–Civil War history of the nation. On one side was a gathering popular protest against the harsh conditions of poverty and insecurity that characterized the Depression era. For millions of workers, the corrosive effects of prolonged unemployment had leached away their faith in the good intentions of employers and government officials, leaving a volatile mix of exasperation and resentment toward the rich. Even when work was available, the downward spiral in wages and the intensified pace of work could spark a sudden explosion of protest. In the three years before the Midland sit-down, a massive strike wave had swept across the nation, led by dockworkers, truck drivers, coal miners, and garment workers. The rising militancy had culminated in 1934 with general strikes in San Francisco and Minneapolis and a massive walkout by four hundred thousand textile workers on the eastern seaboard, from Georgia to Maine. By year's end, National Guard troops had been called into strikebreaking service in fourteen states, from the Atlantic to the Pacific coasts. The estimated death toll from picket line clashes totaled between thirty and fifty workers killed—fifteen alone in the textile strike, where the violent countermeasures of the National Guard and local police defeated the effort to win union recognition and collective bargaining.[10]

In 1935, as Goodman became politically active, this upheaval was transforming the political and social landscape of the nation. Two milestone events of that year—the formation of the Congress of Industrial Organizations (CIO) and the passage of the National Labor Relations Act (NLRA)—would play an especially important role in Goodman's career and in the events leading to the Midland sit-down. At the national convention of the American Federation of Labor (AFL), a vocal minority urged fellow delegates to support all-grades industrial unions that would include both skilled and unskilled workers, tapping into the enthusiasm and broad-based militancy evident in the mass strikes of the previous year. Advocates of industry-wide organization further believed that the labor movement could succeed only by rejecting the whites-only policies of the AFL's dominant craft unions, inviting men and women of all races and ethnic backgrounds to join the movement. When conservative AFL leaders reasserted the primacy of skilled workers in whites-only craft unions, the dissenting delegates followed John L. Lewis, leader of the United Mine Workers, into forming the CIO.[11]

The rebels were buoyed, in turn, by the passage of the NLRA, whose section 7 promised to protect workers engaged in "concerted activities for the purpose of collective bargaining or other mutual aid or protection." The Wagner Act, as the NLRA was called, after its chief sponsor, Senator Robert Wagner of New York, was in effect a workplace civil rights law that protected workers' free speech in support of collective action. Wagner and other self-described realists believed that the extraordinary growth of corporate power destroyed the bargaining leverage of individual workers and made them easily subordinated. "What does it profit a man," Wagner had intoned during one Senate debate over the bill, "to have so-called 'political freedom' if he is made an economic slave?" To protect workers in their advocacy of collective action, the law established a National Labor Relations Board (NLRB) with the power to hold elections, certify majority support for the union, and seek court orders against employers whose "Unfair Labor Practices" denied workers their section 7 rights. Sponsors argued that the bill would help restore "the full flow of purchasing power" to workers and curb the massive protest strikes that had disrupted interstate commerce in 1934. Even a moderate like President Roosevelt, who preferred case-by-case mediation rather than a permanent board like the NLRB, reluctantly endorsed the legislation in 1935 as the only realistic alternative to renewed confrontations on the picket line.[12]

While these events signaled the emergence of a new labor movement, they also called forth a growing repression, marked not only by violent countermeasures to suppress strikes but also by vigilante attacks on union organizers and leftists. The Conference for the Protection of Civil Rights was organized with the expressed purpose of countering these attacks by exposing the links between right-wing terror groups and the local police departments that aided and abetted them. For Goodman, the mounting evidence of a vigilante campaign against labor and the Left was an eye-opener. "I was learning about the political struggle within our own community, which I'd never really been aware of, and something about the nature of the class struggle."[13]

In Detroit, that struggle left little room for moderation. Defenders of the status quo saw ranged against them a multifaceted protest movement dominated by radicals and socialists, and while conservatives typically exaggerated the movement's revolutionary potential, there was little doubt that left-wing leaders played a prominent role in the social upheavals of the era. The national AFL's failure, if not outright refusal, to organize mass-production workers had opened the door to left-wingers who braved the odds and attempted industrial organization—with little success before the 1936 sit-downs, but with considerable pluck. John L. Lewis and the CIO would turn to these left-wing organizers to reenergize the campaign in Detroit's auto industry, transforming the United Auto Workers into an industrial union that opened its ranks to all workers. Lewis, a onetime Republican and past supporter of Herbert Hoover, had little choice but to turn leftward: outside of his own mine workers' union and the Amalgamated Clothing Workers—both now the core of the CIO—the primary sources of experienced organizers were the Socialist Party, the Industrial Workers of the World, and the Communist Party.[14]

Until the sit-down strike at Midland Steel, Detroit's auto companies had fended off the UAW's organizing efforts by firing union supporters and hiring detective agencies to spy on workers. These repressive methods continued even after the National Labor Relations Act had declared them illegal. General Motors' court suit blocking implementation of the NLRA was one of many cases brought before sympathetic judges in 1935, leading to more than eighty injunctions nationwide that prevented the National Labor Relations Board from even meeting. No corporation, however, matched the Ford Motor Company in its determined and violent opposition to unions. Indeed, it was Henry Ford's extralegal campaign to repel unionization that gave Detroit its uniquely polarized politics. While other employers turned to outside detective agencies and uniformed police to counter union organizing, Ford relied on his own innocuously titled Service Department, a private army of three thousand armed plain-clothesmen recruited from Detroit's crime families, ex–police officers, and freelance thugs. Firings and physical assaults on union sympathizers were commonplace at Ford's sprawling River Rouge complex in Dearborn, where production was slowly reviving from the collapse of 1929–32. The Service Department's notorious boss, Harry Bennett, was able to exploit the declining mental health of the elder Ford, wielding a power that not only forced union organizers underground but also marginalized the saner counsel of Ford's son Edsel. Henry Ford was a well-known admirer of Adolf Hitler; Hitler, in turn, lavished frequent praise on Detroit's aging autocrat, honoring Ford in later years with the Nazi regime's highest civilian award, the Grand Cross of the German Eagle.[15]

Goodman and his fellow activists in the conference were convinced that Ford represented the cutting edge of an emerging fascist movement. They feared that Ford and others like him would tap the nativist resentments and Depression-era insecurities of whites, focusing their anxieties on the ethnic and racial minorities whose numbers (and competition for jobs) had grown so dramatically in Detroit. The recent rise to power of Hitler and Mussolini demonstrated the potential for such a reactionary movement, and the anti-Semitic rantings of both must have seemed especially ominous for Goodman, Sugar, and the many other Jewish members of the conference. Ford's affinity for Hitler undoubtedly encouraged local emulators in Detroit, and his company employed more than a few: among them, Fritz Kuhn, a chemical engineer at the Rouge plant and a veteran of Hitler's Free Corps who openly recruited members to the German American Bund, forerunner of the American Nazi Party. Ford's close friend Father Charles Coughlin, whose national radio program reached 30 million listeners, meanwhile railed against an imaginary "international Jewish conspiracy" in his weekly broadcasts from suburban Royal Oak. Coughlin, who had endorsed Roosevelt in 1932, would thereafter move rightward to an outright endorsement of Mussolini and support for "a Christian Front which is not afraid of the word 'fascist.'"[16]

Even more alarming were the revelations that a secret society, the Black Legion, was responsible for the murder of a dozen union organizers and New Deal supporters in the Detroit area, stretching back to 1933. Organized in Ohio in the 1920s as a breakaway from the Ku Klux Klan, the Legion's black-robed membership had spread northward in the early 1930s, enrolling Protestants and former Klansmen pledged to white supremacy and "the extermination of the anarchist, Communist, Roman hierarchy." Legion membership peaked in Michigan at over twenty thousand in 1935, with a core of some three hundred night riders organized into local death squads. Their first victim was George Marchuk, a Communist and a union organizer at Ford, murdered in the fall of 1933. Several months later, John Bielak, also a Communist and a union organizer at Hudson Motors in Detroit, was abducted and driven to rural Monroe County, where he was fatally shot. Silas Coleman, an African American construction laborer, was shot and killed the following year by Legion gunmen because, as one later testified, they wanted to know "what it felt like to kill a nigger." These and other murders had gone unsolved and barely noted by police until the spring of 1936, when sixteen Black Legion members were arrested for the murder of Charles Poole, an unemployed autoworker. With the highly publicized confessions and convictions of these and other gunmen (forty-eight were eventually sentenced to prison terms), a long list of previously isolated cases were linked to the Black Legion, including numerous floggings, bomb attacks, and fire bombings of union offices and left-wing meeting halls.[17]

The most spectacular revelation was the long list of public officials and police personnel who turned up on the membership rolls of the Black Legion. A front organization, the Wolverine Republican League, had allowed Black Legion members to publicly support conservative politicians like Republican governor Frank Fitzgerald—known, among other things, for appointing Harry Bennett to the Michigan Prison Commission and permitting the parole of ex-convicts directly to Ford's Service Department. The Black Legion had also recruited an impressive roster of members in city governments throughout southeastern Michigan, including especially large contingents employed in Detroit's Public Lighting Commission, Department of Street Railways, and police department.[18]

These revelations burst on the political scene at the very moment the Conference for the Protection of Civil Rights was focusing its efforts on ousting Detroit's police commissioner, Heinrich Pickert. Long a nemesis of labor and the Left, Pickert was widely suspected of membership in the Black Legion. The city's men in blue had a reputation for violent methods that long preceded Pickert's term, but his arrival in 1933 had coincided with the Depression-era strikes and unemployment demonstrations that provoked an escalation in strong-arm tactics. One timeworn method was called the "trip around the loop," a practice used to deny arrested union organizers and African Americans their constitutional right to habeas corpus (the obligation for the police to show cause for detaining a person). Goodman described the practice years later. "They would arrest a black person, hold him for about as long as they wanted—a week, two weeks, sometimes even longer. If a lawyer attempted to get him out because no charges had been brought against him, the police could transfer him from one precinct to another, and the judges would not acknowledge this common practice. Unless you served the subpoena at the precinct where the prisoner actually was at the time, the police could win this merry-go-round game." Armed with several hundred affidavits on police brutality, conference activists called on the Detroit City Council in May of 1936 to remove Pickert from office, citing a long list of unlawful arrests, beatings, persons killed on "suspicion," and unsolved cases of bombing attacks on workers' homes and union halls. When the council voted to take no action on these charges, the CPCR was not deterred. "We are not giving up the fight, and have written each councilman asking his reasons for so voting," Chairman Bollens wrote to Roger Baldwin, national leader of the ACLU. "We have heard, and suspect it is true, that police commissioner Pickert is involved and that thirty percent of the entire city police force is connected with the Black Legion."[19]

Goodman joined the conference as it mobilized for campaigns against police brutality, censorship of movies, and proposed municipal ordinances to ban leafleting in Detroit and Hamtramck. He was not yet a recognized leader or elected officer of the group, and in these first years of activism his name did not appear in the roster of weekly steering committee meetings held at the conference offices in the Hoffman Building. Goodman was more likely to be found in the monthly membership meetings at the nearby Electrical Workers Temple or in the volunteer activities that kept the conference going: serving as legal observer at demonstrations and picket lines, writing legislative reports, taking on pro bono legal work, speaking to groups affiliated with the conference, or contributing to the monthly newsletter, the *Civil Rights Bulletin*. In much of this activity, Goodman worked anonymously, seeking to "overcome a certain egotism that all lawyers develop, especially when your name appears in the [news] paper," as he explained years later. "I consciously tried to overcome it by not taking credit for things I should have, could have." His volunteer efforts were no doubt welcome. Only one officer, the secretary treasurer, received a salary, and office rent and other expenses had to be met by repeated rounds of fund-raising from affiliated unions, churches, and members.[20]

Inevitably, the high profile of conference activists in these demonstrations raised the possibility that they might themselves become targets of police commissioner Pickert's extralegal tactics. At a steering committee meeting in the Hoffman Building in the spring of 1936, Chairman Bollens reported to the fifteen leaders in attendance that "he had received information that the office used by the Conference may be raided at any time by the police and advised that all important documents and files be kept in another office." His apprehension was well advised, though belated: unknown to Bollens, the police had already gained entry to the organization's offices by planting a spy among the fifteen who listened to the chairman's warning. The unknown agent dutifully included his recollection of Bollens's words and those of every other speaker at the meeting in his report to the Special Investigation Squad (SIS) of the Detroit police.[21]

The Red Squad, as the SIS came to be known, had its roots in the Red Scare of 1917–20, when U.S. military intervention in World War I provoked a widespread antiwar movement and matching countermeasures by the government. In effect, spying on labor and left-wing groups had continued ever since, with employers taking the lead in the 1920s. In 1931, following the collapse of the economy and the massive demonstrations of the unemployed organized by the Communist Party, Mayor Frank Murphy had formed the Special Investigation Squad to put surveillance of these radicals on a regular basis. As a federal attorney during World War I, Murphy had participated in the antiradical raids of that era and expressed a strong desire to "fight the Bolshevists." His motivation for establishing the SIS was complex, since it combined his genuine opposition to revolutionary ideologies with a concern that the hunt for Bolsheviks should not trample on the Bill of Rights. Murphy hoped to professionalize intelligence gathering and place it in the hands of trained specialists, while also implementing a policy that granted parade permits and protected the free speech rights of any group that complied with the law. These concerns for civil liberties faded, however, after 1933, when Mayor Frank Murphy left office and Heinrich Pickert became police commissioner.[22]

By the mid-1930s, the SIS claimed to have forty undercover agents planted within the Communist Party and its allied organizations in Detroit. They were joined in the growing netherworld of political espionage by a corps of private-sector spies in Detroit's auto factories, planted there by employers to identify union organizers and target them for firing. That such activity was illegal under the National Labor Relations Act was of little concern to most employers, who regarded the NLRA as a temporary nuisance, something the conservative majority on the U.S. Supreme Court would surely nullify. General Motors executives would later admit in congressional hearings held by Senator LaFollette of Wisconsin that the company employed at least fourteen detective agencies in the mid-1930s, providing as many as two hundred spies at any one time—fifty agents alone from Pinkerton's, many of them winning election to local union leadership in the fledgling UAW as they secretly passed membership lists to the company.[23]

The Red Squad's surveillance of the conference was especially intense in light of the group's avowed purpose of ousting Pickert and dismantling the very spy apparatus that was infiltrating its ranks. The many reports that made their way to Pickert's desk were detailed accounts (at least one agent reportedly knew shorthand) that freely mixed fact and fantasy. As Goodman became more prominent in the organization's activities, agents began to introduce him in their reports as "a Jew," of "Jewish appearance," "of the Hebrew Race," and of "dark complexion." This last observation had less to do with Goodman's actual skin tone and more to do with the perceptual bias of informants who could only see Jews as Semitic "others," less than white in terms of race, and therefore suspect. An intense preoccupation with race mixing was equally evident in some reports. The agent who attended the "Liberty Ball" of another Popular Front organization, the Michigan Youth Congress, was apparently shocked to find "that a large percentage of those present were negroes and that these negroes were free to dance with white girls." This alone must have signaled to the offended agent a radical break with the status quo. Undoubtedly, agents also fabricated or embellished information to justify their assignment, which paid them for reports that validated the search for "subversive activities." On the assumption that lawyers who represented Popular Front organizations must be "imbedded" Communists, Sugar and Goodman were casually referred to as "communist lawyers."[24]

Even so, some of these police spies took their job seriously, submitting extensive reports on conference activities in 1936. At the 22 June membership meeting at the Electrical Workers Temple, one agent reported, the steering committee outlined "a plan to keep the question of the Black Legion before the public." The proposal "urged that Units be formed in neighborhoods by members of the Conference and that these Units work in churches, labor unions and etc., to spread the work of the Conference." Maurice Sugar, the report continued, stressed to the members "that the Black Legion is the rising tide of fascism in America and that a similar tide of murders and floggings preceded the rise of Hitler to power in Germany."[25]

Conference communications and leaflets also found their way into the Red Squad's files. In an open letter of 17 August, "To All Organizations and Individuals Who Wish to Maintain American Civil Liberties," Chairman Bollens informed the conference's allies that eleven men who had pled guilty to abducting and flogging members of the Pontiac Unemployed Council were released without punishment because the attackers were veterans and, according to Judge Milton Connoy, "their intent was good at the time." It was only a commendable "zeal for their flag," the judge claimed, that had prompted them to not only whip the Reds, but reportedly force them to drink castor oil and walk home without their

shoes. In response to the judge's tolerant ruling, Chairman Bollens reminded conference supporters that "service in the Armed Forces is not an
excuse for defiance of the law."[26]

It was an ominous world that Goodman was entering, one in which
advocates of progressive causes—union organizing, racial integration, the
defense of free speech—faced the prospect of being targeted by police
spies or, in extreme cases, a right-wing goon squad. Goodman threw himself into the midst of these dangers with a zeal that bewildered his family
and old friends. "I changed my life within a year," as he later recalled, and
"it was a real shock to my family." The compelling logic of his new commitments made perfect sense to him as he plunged into the gathering
struggle, but the sudden change was disturbing to those who had known
him until recently as the ambitious, though troubled, repo man. "The rules
and standards which I had to live by—which they were living by—were
suddenly not my standards any more." The transformation was especially
difficult for his mother to fathom, particularly when Goodman's name began to appear in newspaper accounts of picket line confrontations.

> I was always representing the CIO unions. My mother and her
> friends read or heard about it. I'll never forget, one day she came to
> me and said, very cautiously and quietly: "Ernie, friends say you're
> active in the CIO, that you represent the CIO. They tell me that the
> CIO is bad. Maybe you should think about it." She was hesitant to
> criticize me . . . [and] I realized that I couldn't give a dissertation
> on the nature of society. . . . So I said, "look mama, do you think I
> would do anything wrong?" She said, "Oh no, Ernie." So I said,
> "Then don't worry about it." That satisfied her.[27]

This gentle deflection may have satisfied a worried mother who
wanted to think the best of her son, but it did not satisfy many of his old
friends who were also alarmed by his new commitments. "I began to argue
about it. I had the right cause and anything that wasn't part of that, that
would be supportive of the wrong side, I had little tolerance for. I didn't
discuss. . . . I just took a strong position for what I believed was true and
I became very alienated from a lot of people. It was very difficult for my
family to reconcile themselves to what I was doing. . . . I had little
patience—very little patience."[28]

His exasperation with the status quo was a common trait in Depression-
era Detroit, where the sudden narrowing of future prospects pushed
thousands of people into some kind of conversion crisis. Goodman had
seen his hoped-for career in corporate law careen downward into the

tawdry business of debt collection. He had seen thousands ground into poverty through no fault of their own, mocking the get-ahead ideology of the previous decade, when hard work, it was claimed, would always be rewarded. Now there was no work, and Goodman was crossing over to the opposing side, joining the debtors, the unemployed, the workers who were finding their collective voice in a new labor movement. Detroit's Jewish community had little of the garment union culture that welcomed left-wing Jews in New York or Chicago, and Goodman's new friends on the proletarian left would therefore have seemed all the more alien to many of his previous friends and business partners.

His break with these past associates may have been facilitated, even accentuated, by his father's death in December 1935. Harry Goodman, the immigrant peddler and onetime grocer, had failed in business long before the Depression, ending as a drayman. He had nevertheless been a good provider and a loving father. He was gone now, and Goodman was on his own. He could mollify his mother with filial gestures, but his brother-in-law, a lumber merchant, was scandalized by Goodman's turn to the left. For his sister Rose, the breach between her husband and brother meant that even though she remained devoted to Ernie, she would see far less of him.

The abrupt transformations in Goodman's politics and professional life were especially disconcerting for Freda, who was already estranged from her husband's family and feeling abandoned. Years later, Goodman described his failure to communicate with his wife as a kind of "arrogance" that was all too common in an era when men were supposed to make the family decisions and the wife was expected to follow quietly. Goodman's failure to fully engage his wife in the new commitments he was forging meant that Freda "didn't understand it and didn't know why I was impatient with her. [It] created many, many problems." Freda had fallen in love with Ernie when he was an aspiring commercial lawyer struggling to establish a "normal" law practice; now he had suddenly become a political radical calling for the ouster of the police commissioner. That he justified this transformation with the prickly defensiveness of a recent convert could only estrange Freda all the more. She could not be expected to make the leap her husband insisted on without trepidation, and Ernie, by his own admission, failed to enlist her understanding. Try as she might, Freda would lag behind as her husband barreled forward into his new life with a cohort of friends who called him "brother" or—stranger still— "comrade."[29]

Among these new companions was a woman named Laicha Kravchik. Like so many people in the first years of Ernie's life, she traced her roots back to the shtetls of the Russian Empire, but she was otherwise like no other woman he had known. She was, first of all, not just a child of immigrants but an immigrant herself, having left the Soviet Union with her parents in 1926 at the age of fifteen. Her family arrived in the United States not as the get-ahead strivers of immigrant lore, but as already committed radicals with roots in the left-wing Zionist movement. Beyond the land of her birth, she had no inkling of the small-town life that Ernie, Freda, and Maurice Sugar had known in their childhoods; upon arrival in the United States, her family had lived in New York City on East Fourteenth Street, near the center of the unionized garment trades where her father worked. Ernie had been a Boy Scout in his youth; Kravchik had been a counselor at Kinderland, a summer camp in New York sponsored by the International Workers Order, a left-wing benefit society whose Detroit chapters Goodman now represented. She moved to Detroit around 1930 to live with her sister, and she met Goodman when he was still repossessing furniture. It's not clear when they began an affair, but many years later Goodman remembered Kravchik as a major influence in his political realignment from 1935 onward, second only to Maurice Sugar. She was probably a member of the CP-USA, but she was not a colorless hack parroting the party line; a lover of Yiddish songs and something of a romantic dreamer, she shared with Goodman a fondness for poetry, particularly that of Heinrich Heine, the nineteenth-century German romantic.[30]

Even after Kravchik left Detroit later in the decade, moving to Philadelphia and then New York City, Goodman would continue to see her on his many trips eastward. In the meantime, at least some of his ill-tempered impatience with Freda had to be a function of this deepening involvement with Kravchik. Where Freda was slow to comprehend a political culture with which she had little contact, Laicha was an insider who knew it better than Ernie. She was an ardent antifascist, impatient with those who couldn't see the danger or muster the courage to fight back. After reading of Austrian Jews committing suicide during the Nazi takeover, she wrote to Goodman that "men [would] rather kill themselves than face the cruelty of life which they helped bring to the world, by sitting quiet, by staying home, by having just good ideas but not doing anything to stop the terror." Her dedication to the struggle helped inspire Goodman's new commitment to the Popular Front. "Thank you Laicha," he wrote her, for "the paths you have led me over and the fertile fields I have seen from the mountain tops you taught me how to climb." She responded in kind. "It would be a real pleasure," she once wrote him from Philadelphia, "to rise higher and higher with you in the glorious fight against everything that's ugly." Freda could not possibly match this kind of passionate political discourse. She was a strong believer in civil rights and held to generally liberal views, but she was not a political person.[31]

She was still, however, the mother of Ernie's son. Ernie and Freda would stay together and Ernie would remain a devoted father. But the flame would flicker lower in their marriage.

Rise and Fall

It was an exhilarating time of protest and popular mobilization, and in this polarized context of progressive advance and conservative reaction, Detroit was about to be swept leftward by the most far-reaching and broad-based movement in the city's history. The sit-down strike at Midland Steel and a second plant occupation at Kelsey Wheel in Detroit had previewed the UAW's new tactic in the fall of 1936. It was the seizure of two General Motors factories in Flint, Michigan, however, that put the new approach to its most important test in December of that year. General Motors was the biggest manufacturing corporation in the world and had defeated all previous attempts to organize a union in its factories. The success or failure of the sit-downs at Fisher Body that started in the last days of 1936 would make or break the UAW.

Most of the fifteen hundred sit-downers in Flint viewed their militant tactics as a matter of expediency, not revolution. The occupation was, in effect, a "citizens' arrest" by workers who saw the reelection of President Roosevelt the previous month as vindication for their boldness: if GM refused to abide by the National Labor Relations Act and its prescriptions for resolving industrial disputes, then strikers would seize the factory and refuse to surrender the property until management obeyed the law and agreed to negotiate wages and working conditions. "You voted New Deal at the polls and defeated the Auto Barons," union organizers announced in Michigan after the November election. "Now get a New Deal in the shop." When the police attempted to evict the Flint sit-downers in early January with gunfire and tear gas, the unarmed strikers proved the effectiveness of their tactic when they repelled the attack from their barricaded positions inside the factory. Governor Murphy—inaugurated just days after the sit-down began—sent in the National Guard to prevent further violence, but not, as the company had demanded, to evict the sit-downers. With the police neutralized and production slowly strangled by plant occupations, GM finally agreed to negotiate with the union on 11 February 1937.[32]

This David vs. Goliath victory had an electrifying effect on union supporters in nearby Detroit, where the recovering economy gave further confidence to workers with a long list of grievances. Their anger over low wages, dictatorial managers, and precarious job security fueled what *Fortune* magazine described as "one of the greatest mass movements in our history." According to newspaper estimates (the *Detroit News* ran a daily box score in the month of March, "Plants Closed by Sit-downs") a total of thirty-five thousand workers in Detroit joined sit-down strikes in the two months after the UAW victory in Flint, closing nearly 130 factories, offices, and stores in what amounted to a "rolling" general strike. This flood tide of militancy did not escape the notice of the generally conservative justices of the U.S. Supreme Court, who came to the belated recognition that the National Labor Relations Act was preferable to the widening class war in Flint, Detroit, and elsewhere. In April they upheld the constitutionality of the NLRA by a narrow 5-4 margin, ruling that workers had as much right to choose their own representatives as business owners had to select their own managers. Since, in the court's words, a single worker confronting a massive corporation was "helpless in dealing with an employer," only collective organization could give workers the opportunity to "deal on an equality" with management.[33]

Goodman and his colleagues must have felt themselves rising on an irresistible tide of popular protest, a force all the more powerful because it was international in scope. In the very weeks that the sit-down strikes were rolling back the open shop, armed resistance by Spain's workers and peasants had finally put a halt to the spread of fascism in Europe. The previous summer, after a Popular Front of Spain's left-wing parties and unions had won a narrow election victory, General Francisco Franco had launched an uprising against the elected government with military support from Hitler and Mussolini. In March of 1937—just as the sit-down wave was cresting in Detroit—loyalist supporters of the Republic won their first outright victory, turning back the fascist troops sent to capture Guadalajara and encircle Madrid.[34]

The news was electrifying for Goodman and many others in Europe and the United States who saw the Spanish civil war as the pivotal showdown between fascism and democracy. Supporting the Republic's loyalist government "became a great, noble crusade," as Goodman recalled years later. "It felt like one at the time. I became involved in it fully myself, as fully as I could. And it was one of the great episodes in history from my individual viewpoint, which engaged your heart and mind and everything else you had." At a time when Stalin's show trials and suppression of dissent were raising doubts about the democratic credentials of the Soviet Union, the Spanish Republic was the far more compelling focus of socialist aspirations, particularly in the early months when peasants redistributed land and worker committees took control of factories, bakeries, theaters, and restaurants abandoned by their owners. "There you could see the struggle that we were thinking about in our own minds," Goodman remembered. "We didn't have to talk theoretically about the different ways in which the societies of the world would go."[35]

Spain also demonstrated the limits of liberal opposition to fascism. As the Spanish loyalists struggled against military rebels who promised to restore aristocratic privilege and state-supported religion, the capitalist democracies adopted a policy of neutrality and refused to ship arms to Spain's elected government. Many American liberals who opposed fascism also opposed the anticlerical violence of the Republic's early months, when angry crowds burned churches and attacked priests for their long collaboration with the old order. Hitler and Mussolini, on the other hand, had no qualms about the continuing atrocities carried out by Franco's followers. Italy supplied Franco with troops while Germany's Luftwaffe conducted the first large-scale bombardment of civilians in the attack on Guernica. Only the Soviet Union came to the Republic's defense, providing arms, airmen, and military advisors.[36]

Aiding the Republic in any way possible became an urgent priority for many Americans, particularly those on the left who believed that only an aroused popular movement could change the course of events. Several thousand Americans made the ultimate commitment by joining the Abraham Lincoln Brigade, an all-volunteer militia organized in the United States to go to Spain and fight for the loyalists. At least two-thirds of the twenty-six hundred men who volunteered were Communists and more than one-third were Jewish, motivated by their left-wing politics and their immediate identification with the victims of Nazism. There were also eighty African Americans in the brigade, several of whom rose to officer's rank and became the first black Americans to command white troops in the nation's history. In February of 1937—just as the Flint sit-down strike was ending in victory—the Lincoln Brigade's American volunteers had gone into their first battle in Spain, where they joined more than forty thousand volunteers from fifty-two other countries who had come to fight for the Republic.[37]

If Goodman ever contemplated joining them, he decided against it. The overwhelming majority of recruits for the Lincoln Brigade were blue-collar workers and single men with no family obligations (85 percent had never been married, by one count). With a wife and child to support, Goodman found that level of antifascist commitment more than he was honestly able to make. Instead, he threw himself into the support groups that raised funds, sent medical supplies to the Republic, and lobbied for a change in U.S. policy. Ultimately, these efforts would fail; Franco would defeat the loyalists in 1939 and Goodman would become defense attorney for persecuted veterans of the Lincoln Brigade. But in the spring of 1937, all things still seemed possible. Saul Wellman, a committed Communist and one of the thousands who went to Spain to fight fascism, had no doubt he was on the right side of history. "I don't really think in the two years I was in Spain," he recalled many years later, that "I ever thought we were going to lose."[38]

So it seemed in Detroit as well, where the Conference for the Protection of Civil Rights was growing by leaps and bounds in the first six months of 1937. By early summer, with the rapid growth in the number of affiliated unions (nearly seventy locals by midyear, evenly divided between the CIO and AFL), the steering committee resolved that the organization had outgrown its status as a mere "Conference" and was now a genuine "Federation" of unions, fraternal organizations, churches, and political parties. To mark this transformation, delegates to the June meeting voted to replace the organization's outmoded and cumbersome name with Civil Rights Federation (CRF). The newly minted CRF promptly took the lead in Detroit's labor-left movement when its long-time general counsel, former judge Patrick O'Brien, declared himself a candidate for mayor, joining a "Labor slate" of city council candidates led by Maurice Sugar. Sugar was now rising rapidly in UAW circles as he took on the union's major court cases during the sit-down wave, and his candidacy had serious potential in light of his 1935 showing. He was joined on the Labor slate by the young and rising leaders of the UAW, including Walter Reuther, president of West Side Local 174, and R. J. Thomas, president of Chrysler Local 7. Pledging to remove Pickert from power, to tax corporations rather than homeowners, and to distribute city jobs and relief benefits fairly and without racial preference, labor's political initiative promised to build on the substantial gains of the sit-down movement. "What a thrill it will be," said Chairman Bollens to candidate O'Brien in front of the CFR's June meeting, "to walk into the City Hall and say 'good morning, Judge,' the morning after the election."[39]

There would be no such "good morning," however, in the fall of 1937. The tide was turning against labor, and the signs were already evident in the spring. On 26 May, plainclothesmen from the Ford Service Department in Dearborn, Michigan, had clubbed and dispersed union organizers at the Gate 4 Overpass on Miller Road, where future UAW president Walter Reuther and others had attempted to peacefully distribute leaflets. The publicity surrounding Ford's violent attack on the leafleters had further damaged the company's reputation, but it had also highlighted the union's failure at Ford, where gangland methods drove union support underground and a sit-down strike was impossible. Five days after this "Battle of the Overpass," Chicago police had fired point-blank into a peaceful rally of steelworkers during their conventional walkout strike against Republic Steel. The ten unarmed strikers gunned down in this "Memorial Day Massacre" were added to a total that reached eighteen union supporters killed in Illinois and Ohio before the CIO called off the strike in defeat.[40]

The year 1937 also ended badly in economic and political terms. After recovering stride over 1935 and 1936, the economy suddenly slumped in the fall of 1937 and the city's unemployment rate soared to 41 percent in a matter of months. The recession, in turn, contributed to the defeat of the CIO's political aspirations in Detroit, with the Labor slate failing to win a single council seat and O'Brien losing the race for mayor by a lopsided margin of 261,000 to 154,000. In a context of growing job insecurity, the majority of Detroit's voters were anxious to avoid further disruption and uncertainty, and business leaders warned that a labor victory would provoke an exodus of jobs. "Labor" wasn't united in any case: the AFL, fearing that a CIO-backed mayor and city council would encourage raiding of its twenty thousand public sector members, endorsed the "reactionary slate," as the CIO dubbed it, led by Richard Reading. With Reading's victory, Pickert was assured a free hand in dealing with union militants, and Detroit's police spent much of the next year breaking picket lines and escorting strikebreakers into factories. The only positive feature of the new mayor's tenure was that it was brief. Revelations that he and his top police lieutenants were taking payoffs from the city's crime families contributed to his defeat in the next election, and he was soon after indicted and sent to prison.[41]

For Goodman and his colleagues in the Civil Rights Federation, the defeat of the Labor slate marked a dizzying conclusion to the roller-coaster events of the previous two years. For a brief moment in late 1936 and early 1937, the labor-Left in Detroit had seized the initiative and generated an apparently unstoppable momentum, promising a political and workplace revolution beyond the wildest dreams of the previous decade, when the city's employers boasted of the open shop and the KKK nearly captured city hall. The sit-down wave and the rise of the UAW-CIO had transformed not only the city but also the generation of activists, Goodman among them, who experienced firsthand the exhilarating triumphs of 1936–37. They had seen the power of a mass movement and joined its line of march. Along the way, Goodman acquired an abiding faith in the potential of popular protest that would stay with him long after the tide began to recede from the high-water mark of the spring of 1937. Thereafter, the movement's energy and unity began to dissipate, aggravated by factional fighting within the UAW and the growing rift between the CIO and the AFL. By the end of the year the Spanish Republic was in retreat, its Popular Front supporters riven by internal clashes between Communists, Socialists, and Anarchists. Further, bloody defeats loomed in 1938. There were still many gains to defend in Detroit and future battles to win, but there would never again be the same breathtaking sense that all things were possible. The conservative reaction, in fact, was about to intensify.

Red Scare

In the early morning of 24 August 1938, a squadron of officers led by Sergeants Harry Mikuliak and Leo Maciosek of the police "Red Squad" surrounded an apartment building on Brainard Street in central Detroit. The officers approached the apartment of one Robert Taylor with guns drawn and ordered him to open the door. When a sleepy young man still in pajamas warily unlocked the entrance, the officers immediately arrested him and two friends also sleeping in the apartment. Mikuliak and Maciosek (or "Mick and Mack," as they were derisively known in left-wing circles) had no arrest warrant and no authorization to search the apartment, which they nevertheless ransacked in their hunt for letters and personal belongings. When they finished their illegal search, they took Taylor and his two friends downtown to police headquarters where they were fingerprinted and grilled over the next thirty-two hours about their views on Communism, socialism, and Spain. At no time were the three men given the opportunity to call counsel or friends; when they were released the next day, the police brought no charges against them. The primary reason for their arrest and interrogation had been that Robert Taylor was a veteran of the Spanish civil war and the secretary of the Detroit office of the Friends of the Abraham Lincoln Brigade, a national organization created to repatriate surviving veterans of the war in Spain.[42]

So began the congressional inquisition of Detroit's labor and left-wing movements. As yet there was no inkling that the federal government had joined forces with the local Red Squad, but the link would become apparent five weeks later when the Civil Rights Federation sent a delegation to police headquarters to confront Commissioner Pickert over the blatant violation of Taylor's civil rights. The delegation included CRF chairman Bollens, Taylor, and—in his first public leadership role—Goodman. As the only member of the delegation who also served on the editorial board of the *Civil Rights News* (*CRN*), Goodman was probably the author of the unsigned article in the *CRN* describing this unique meeting. "The Brigadier-General was seated behind his large desk," the author reported, "flanked by Superintendent Frahm on the right and the Red Squad Mikuliak and Maciosek, appropriately on the left. . . . Upon the principal question of the attitude of the police department to the civil rights of citizens, toward which the delegation attempted constantly to direct the discussion, the position of the Commissioner may be thus summarized: 'The police department will continue to arrest people and search homes without warrants whenever, in the personal opinion of the Commissioner, such action should be taken. Until Federal, State and local laws are changed, this will continue to be our policy.'" As for the particulars of Taylor's arrest, Pickert refused to discuss the case. "He leaned his ample frame back in his chair, brushed his sandy hair off his forehead and with a severe expression upon his heavy features, announced that the subject matter . . . could not be discussed because the matter was in the hands of a higher body which was investigating the case. Upon being asked whether this higher body was the Dies Committee, [Superintendent] Frahm stated he would say neither yes or no."[43]

It was, in fact the Dies Committee, named for Texas congressman Martin Dies, chairman of the newly constituted House Committee on Un-American Activities (HCUA). The Texas Democrat and avowed enemy of the New Deal had multiple motives for enlisting the aid of Detroit's Red Squad in a wide-ranging investigation of the city's many radicals. For Dies and other southern Democrats, the same 1936 election results that had so electrified African American, ethnic, and union voters in the North had brought with it a troubling transformation in the party's social orientation. The price of electoral victory had been too high for conservative Democrats, who saw their predominant position in the party eroded as the proportion of House seats held by Democrats from urban areas jumped from 29 percent in 1931 to 46 percent in 1937. Many southern Democrats now viewed themselves as a beleaguered minority within their own party, and they saw the sit-down strikes, the growth of the CIO, and the New Deal's continuing reform agenda as harbingers of an unwelcome social revolution. "There is a racial question involved here," Dies had declared in opposition to establishing a federal minimum wage for all workers in 1937. "Under this measure what is prescribed for one race must be prescribed for the others, and you cannot prescribe the same wages for the black man as for the white." The blunt racism of Dies's comments in the House debate had summoned a chorus of rebel yells from his conservative compatriots, underlining a breach between the northern and southern

wings of the Democratic Party that would widen over the ensuing decades
and eventually destroy the party's hegemony in the once "Solid South." In
1938, southern Democrats were already looking across the aisle for support from conservative Republicans, and it was Dies who would mobilize
their energies to attack the leading symbol of the enemy within: Governor
Frank Murphy of Michigan, the man who had refused to evict the Flint
sit-downers and who must therefore be in league with the "Communist
instigators" of the strike.[44]

In October 1938, Dies opened public hearings of his House committee in Detroit to hear testimony on these matters. The timing was no
coincidence. Convened in the weeks immediately before the November
balloting in which Murphy sought reelection, the Dies Committee would
give center stage to a parade of witnesses testifying to Murphy's alleged
coddling of Communists. There would be no formal charges brought
against the governor or any others accused of the noncrime of being a
"Communist sympathizer"; mere exposure, as Dies put it, "[is] the most
effective weapon . . . we can trust public sentiment to do the rest."[45]

The newspaper headlines produced the hoped-for "exposure": "State
Hotbed of Reds, Dies Group Told" (Detroit Times, 13 October); "Dies to
Probe 1937 Sit-Downs" (Detroit Free Press, 13 October); "Link Reds to
Strikes in Detroit" (Detroit News, 19 October). Dies's goal was to cast the
turmoil of the sit-downs in the most sensational terms and to link the "lawlessness" with an alleged Communist conspiracy. In this regard he was
aided by two incontrovertible facts: first, left-wing radicals in general and
Communists in particular had, in fact, played leadership roles in some of
the earliest and largest sit-downs (along with non-Communist radicals,
liberals, and anti-Communists); and second, Communists who were active
in Popular Front organizations often concealed their affiliation to the
Communist Party. In many cases they did so because they risked dismissal
or harassment if their politics were known to employers and co-workers.
Whatever the motives, their secrecy gave some credence to the conspiracy
theories of Dies and others. It was an easy matter for Dies to imply that
anyone who had worked with, or had known, or had simply appeared on
the same stage with a suspected Communist was a deserving focus of suspicion. It was not actually illegal to be a Communist, secretly or openly,
but Dies made it seem so. For those accused of being a "Red," Dies offered
them "the privilege of coming in here and proving that they are not. The
doors are wide open." With this perverse logic, the Bill of Rights was
turned inside out: those accused of a noncrime were held guilty until they
came forward and proved themselves innocent.[46]

Goodman threw himself into the labor-left crusade to reelect the
governor, speaking on radio broadcasts sponsored by the International

Workers Order and writing campaign copy for the *Civil Rights News*. In the last issue before the election, the *CRN* featured the governor's defense of his administration. "Respect for authority induced by violent coercion is an ill-gotten thing," Murphy wrote under the front-page headline "Living Democracy." "True respect for government is not created by troops or by other instruments of force, but by cool, sympathetic and reasoned application of the elementary principle that government exists for the sole purpose of safeguarding and conserving the whole community and its civil rights." Working in the Detroit precincts where the governor's support was strongest, Goodman was confident of Murphy's chances. "Boy, what a wonderful thing it will be for all progressives if we are victorious," he wrote Laicha Kravchik on the eve of the election. Most urban and working-class voters felt the same when they went to the polls the next day, giving Murphy a 59 percent winning margin in Detroit. But in suburban and rural areas of the state, Murphy lost ground to the Red Scare and the statewide vote went to the Republican candidate, former governor Fitzgerald, by a margin of 53-47 percent. It was a crushing defeat for labor and the Left, which Goodman struggled to present as a "temporary setback" in his personal letter to Murphy. "I want to congratulate you on your splendid campaign," he wrote to his former law school instructor. "It was based upon progressive principles, as was your administration. You fought with courage and refused to compromise upon those principles." President Roosevelt held Murphy in equally high regard and promptly nominated him to become the next attorney general of the United States, an appointment widely applauded by the ACLU, the NAACP, and the CIO.[47]

This hardly ended matters, however, for the Civil Rights Federation and particularly for Goodman. The Dies Committee had left town, but not before passing the baton to the local Red Squad, providing it with a list of 115 homegrown "subversives" to hunt down. Walter Reynolds, chairman of the American Legion's Subcommittee on Subversive Activities, had testified that many professors belonged on this list because they supported "such causes as Spanish democracy," among them "the famous relativity wizard Albert Einstein" and nearly a dozen professors at the University of Michigan and Wayne University. "Many religious dignitaries are among the most fervent adherents of the Spanish cause," Reynolds had warned in rambling testimony that took most of an entire day. "Their clerical garb makes them especially desirable in the front of Communist meetings." Based on evidence gleaned from spy reports and the raid on Robert Taylor's apartment, Sergeants Mikuliak and Maciosek claimed that recruiting activities for the Abraham Lincoln Brigade had netted two hundred enlistees in Detroit, and that doctors working for the city's

Board of Health had used taxpayer funds to give many of these recruits medical exams before they left for Spain.[48]

It was this last case that brought Goodman into the fray. "As soon as the Committee left," he recalled years later, "the Mayor at the time, Reading, decided that he was going to do something about this 'Communist conspiracy.' So he directed his Board of Health to discharge all of these doctors from all their programs . . . without a hearing. That's when Sugar called me in to ask me if I would defend the doctors and get them reinstated, and expose this whole thing as far as one could." The doctors had sought Sugar's counsel because of his preeminent position as Detroit's labor and civil rights lawyer. But in his role as the UAW's lead attorney, Sugar was already occupied by the organizing drive at Ford and the intense battles within the union that pitted its conservative president, Homer Martin, against an executive board that included Sugar's fellow Labor candidates in the 1937 election, Walter Reuther and R. J. Thomas. Goodman had already helped Sugar on several civil rights cases "and we began to develop a relationship. He began to have some confidence in me, I guess. There were not many lawyers whom he could go to and work with, there were hardly any."[49]

The five doctors singled out for dismissal were practitioners of a new kind of preventive medicine that focused on the eradication—not just the treatment—of tuberculosis. In the mid-1930s, this potentially fatal bacterial inflammation of the lungs was still commonplace in urban slums and particularly among autoworkers exposed to workplace chemicals and fumes. Medical treatment had become more sophisticated, but the underlying problem required a public campaign that would screen the at-risk population and diagnose the disease in its early stages, when outward symptoms were barely visible but the bacteria was already transmittable. To break the cycle of transmission, the Board of Health compensated doctors who tested patients for the disease and identified those to be quarantined before they spread the bacteria. Launched in 1936, the program screened 118,000 people in its first eighteen months, and deaths from TB in Detroit fell by 20 percent in 1937.[50]

Sergeant Mikuliak had testified before the Dies Committee that Dr. Eugene Shafarman, one of the five doctors dismissed, had been paid more than $700 "for examining youths recruited by the Communists for the Spanish government army." The young doctor was a recent graduate of the University of Michigan's College of Medicine and had subsequently studied for a year at the Cancer Research Institute in Moscow. He was closely aligned with Communist and left-wing movements and made no apology for his fervent support of the Spanish cause. "Someone has discovered the amazing fact that I have had a Communist or two among my patients," he declared in a public statement that openly mocked the Dies Committee and the Red Squad. Among the twenty-two hundred patients he had tested for TB, "I am sure that my records will show far greater numbers of Democrats and Republicans." Shafarman then threw down the gauntlet, expressing his admiration for those who had died in Spain "fighting for democracy" while Dies was preparing the ground for an American Franco. "Since Mr. Dies is so determined to continue his publicity fiascos," Shafarman had continued, "I suggest he investigate next the American Red Cross which recently sent 250 cases of soap and 40,000 barrels of flour for Spanish needy."[51]

Soon after the departure of the Dies Committee, Mayor Reading ordered the Board of Health to remove Shafarman and his colleagues from the TB program. The specific claims against them, however, were no longer the politically charged accusations of the Dies Committee—that they had given medical exams to recruits for Spain. Instead, to give their dismissals a legal rather than political coloring, they were accused of improper billing and the dispensing of medical treatment outside of their private offices. Under obvious pressure from the mayor, health commissioner Dr. Harry Vaughan became the reluctant prosecutor. "These doctors have done highly effective work in detecting tuberculosis in its early and curable stages," he said of the accused. "Their bills were not as high as the bills of some of the others. The rules, however, must be observed."[52]

It was these very rules, however, that Goodman would cite in demonstrating the political implications of the case. If the rules were valid, he argued, then they should apply to all of the participating doctors, any one of whom had the right to a public hearing—before being judged—if charged with a violation. None of this, however, had occurred. In fact, seventy-five participating doctors had been charged in the spring of 1938 with billing improprieties similar to, or worse than, those brought against Goodman's clients. Yet "not one of the doctors who had committed these so-called irregularities was dismissed," as Goodman reminded the press and the Board of Health at every opportunity. The cause of this selective application of the rules was evident to Goodman: these doctors were all known for their support of the labor movement, several of them working in makeshift field clinics during strikes to treat those injured in picket line battles. "They were also working with the UAW," he recalled years later, "to promote a national health program, which was anathema, 'Communist' to the medical profession and everybody else."[53]

Under mounting public pressure from union members and sympathetic medical practitioners, the Board of Health finally agreed to hold formal hearings on the dismissals. Goodman was able to demonstrate that the city's investigation, as he put it, "had been conducted with such haste, and in so prejudicial a manner, that no real attempt had been made to obtain the truth." Many patients reported that they had actually refused to sign prepared statements that city investigators had pushed on them, yet these unsigned affidavits had been entered as evidence against the doctors. Other patients testified that they had been intimidated into signing affidavits out of fear that they, rather than the doctors, would be held in violation of the rules. The evidence against the doctors was clearly tainted, and after a prolonged investigation, the Board of Health voted on 8 December 1939 to reinstate all five doctors to the city's list of approved physicians. One board member publicly stated that the doctors should not have been removed without a hearing. Another said simply that his vote "was based on the idea of justice."[54]

Mayor Reading attempted to overturn this decision by firing the entire Board of Health and appointing a new one that would do his bidding. It was the last gesture of a corrupt regime. Reading had already lost the mayoralty election that fall to Edward Jeffries, the heir apparent to Frank Murphy's liberal mantle, who won labor's backing when he promised to reverse the union-busting policies of his opponent. Reading had only one week left in office when he appointed his puppet board, and he would soon after be indicted for his ties to the illegal gambling operations that flourished during his two-year reign. With Mayor Jeffries's inauguration, Pickert would depart from his long tenure as police commissioner, and the Red Squad would subsequently be disbanded (temporarily, as it turned out). By the fall of 1940, the doctors were exonerated and the city had agreed to a monetary settlement for the work they had done in the TB program.[55]

Before this final settling of accounts, however, there would be one final, brutish display of government power unrestrained by the Bill of Rights. It would begin again with Eugene Shafarman, Robert Taylor, and many others from the same cast who had figured so prominently in 1938. But this time, the role played by one leading figure, Frank Murphy, would be radically altered. And this time, it was not the Detroit police who would conduct the predawn raid.

Liberal Guilt

On 6 February 1940, Doctor Shafarman and his wife awoke at 4:20 in the morning to the sound of heavy pounding on the street entrance to their apartment building. A man yelled through the speaking tube that his injured companion needed medical attention, but when Blanche Shafarman opened the apartment door, two very healthy men told the doctor he was under arrest. Two more men joined the pair and the four, who claimed they were FBI agents, began to search the apartment as Shafarman dressed. Asked if he had a search warrant, the leader of the group said he didn't need one, Shafarman recalled. "He insisted that I stay exactly where I was, that I not move. . . . He refused to permit us to use a telephone to either identify him or to consult an attorney." Shafarman asked why he was being arrested and the same man would only give "some numbers of some code or section of the law." Knowing the history of the Black Legion, and having received two telephone threats since the Dies hearings ordering him to "leave town or else," Shafarman and his wife had the sinking feeling that these men might have come "to take me for a ride." Their apprehensions grew when the men refused to tell Blanche Shafarman where they were taking her husband, now in handcuffs. "They did permit me to kiss my wife goodbye. Some queer ideas ran through my head at that moment."[56]

When Goodman's phone rang at 5:30 that morning, he heard the voice of Ruth Clark, a frightened and angry woman. "The FBI just left our house. They handcuffed and arrested my husband, Joe. They ransacked the house. They refused to show a warrant or let me call my lawyer. What shall I do?" Her call was followed by others, Blanche Shafarman among them, and each caller described the same scene: husbands taken away in dawn raids by men who didn't always identify themselves, who broke down the door in at least two cases, who showed no arrest warrants and refused to say where they were taking their prisoners.[57]

Goodman told Clark, Shafarman, and the others to meet him at his office at 9:00 a.m. As he took more phone calls and talked with more people, the scale of what had happened began to emerge. In addition to Eugene Shafarman and Joe Clark, the FBI had arrested nine others that morning, including Dr. John Rosefeld (another of the city doctors Goodman had defended before the Board of Health), Robert Taylor (the Lincoln Brigade veteran, experiencing his second dawn arrest), and Mary Paige (a well-known union organizer). All attempts to reach the ten men and one woman under arrest had failed. Goodman knew only that they were being held somewhere in the Federal Building.

Hoping to learn more, he hurried across Detroit's downtown to the office of the federal district attorney, John Lehr. When he asked Lehr for a copy of the indictments against his clients, however, he was immediately rebuffed. "He told me they were secret," Goodman remembered, "and that I could not get a copy until the arraignment." This was frustrating enough, but when Goodman asked to see his clients, Lehr told him that the only person who could give permission to do so was John Bugas, head of the FBI's Detroit office. "I walked up to Bugas's office and asked for the right to talk to my clients. He first challenged my authority, stating that none of the prisoners had asked for me. This led to a bitter exchange." Bugas would permit Goodman to see the prisoners only five minutes before they were to be taken to court for their preliminary arraignment. Goodman considered this "a contemptuous insult to me as their attorney," but he had to comply with these extraordinary conditions. Waiting outside the courtroom, he finally saw the prisoners coming toward him in the hallway. To his utter surprise, they were manacled to a single long chain that bound them all together. "It was an eerie sight," something he had never seen in the dozen years he had practiced law. It was dawning on him that these Kafkaesque proceedings heralded something very unusual.[58]

Meeting with his clients in the only available space, a nearby jury room, Goodman learned that they had been strip-searched and interrogated for six straight hours, the questions tracking the same issues raised in the Dies hearings. Even at this point, no one knew what the charges were. Goodman told his clients that they should stand mute at the arraignment. "The corridor door of the jury room was open, so that not only was the 'interview' in the presence of the FBI, but observed by reporters and others crowding the doorway."[59]

It was only when the prisoners and their attorney were standing before the judge that they learned they had been charged with conspiracy to violate section 22, title 18 of the United States Code. This statute prohibited anyone from recruiting another person on U.S. soil to enter the armed forces of a foreign government—in this case, the Spanish Republic. The last overt act for which they were charged was in February 1938, two years before the arrests. Goodman entered a plea of not guilty for each defendant, but before they had time to ponder the meaning of these bizarre proceedings, they were dealt another surprise: bond for their release pending trial was set at $2,500 to $20,000 each, a prohibitive sum that ensured a prolonged imprisonment for most of the defendants even as they were technically presumed innocent. Mary Paige was taken to the Wayne County jail and placed in solitary confinement, and the eight men who could not post bond were taken forty miles west of Detroit to the federal penitentiary in Milan. Processed that night as if they were already convicted felons, they were denied visitation rights when they refused to fill out forms asking them to specify their "crime." By the next day, front-page reports of the dawn raids and news photos of prisoners in chains had aroused considerable protest, forcing the warden to reverse course and permit wives and family to visit the men.[60]

Goodman was not alone in concluding that all of this—the night raids and breaking of doors, the refusal to show search or arrest warrants, the denial of communication with attorneys or family, the chaining of prisoners, the prohibitive bail and swift imprisonment—"all this bore too close a resemblance to the tactics of the Nazis and their storm troopers." While public opinion was divided over the Spanish Republic and which country, Nazi Germany or Soviet Russia, posed the greater menace to the United States, the excessive force of the FBI raids and the harsh treatment of the prisoners had quickly won the defendants a considerable showing of public sympathy. The pressure was on the attorney general of the United States to account for the government's actions, but it was no longer Frank Murphy who served in this post. Following his nomination to the U.S. Supreme Court, Murphy had been replaced the previous January by Robert Jackson, the former solicitor general. He agreed to meet with a small delegation led by Goodman, and within days of the arrests they had traveled to Washington to present Jackson with the legal, moral, and political arguments for dismissing the indictments. The attorney general promised to seriously consider their views.[61]

Goodman did not expect immediate action, but on 16 February, just ten days after the arrests, Jackson announced that he would do exactly what Goodman and the committee had asked. The indictments were dismissed, he said, because "it would be manifestly unjust to single out these Detroit defendants . . . for activities so long known to the government," particularly when recruiting violations had also occurred on behalf of Franco, the Italo-Ethiopian, and Sino-Japanese wars.[62]

Jackson's sudden disavowal of the Detroit arrests came as a surprise, but Goodman and his fellow members of the defense committee had learned an even more shocking bit of news in their Washington meeting with the attorney general. Jackson had made it clear that he had not authorized the indictments in the first place. He had only been appointed to his post on 18 January, and had no knowledge of the orders sent the previous month by his predecessor—Frank Murphy—to the federal prosecutor in Detroit. "As I left," Goodman later wrote, "I thought, could it have been our old civil libertarian friend Murphy who had approved the prosecution?"[63]

Sadly, the answer was yes. When he arrived in Washington in early 1939 to take office as attorney general, Murphy was still dogged by accusations that he had "conspired with Communists" and failed to uphold the law during the Flint sit-down strike. Congressman J. Parnell Thomas of the Dies Committee had publicly criticized "our dynamic Attorney General" for being "strangely indifferent and listless" when it came to

prosecuting Communist Party leaders like Earl Browder, who had confessed to using a false passport. The constant drumbeat of accusation
clearly preoccupied Murphy, who began to tell his staff that the Justice
Department had to "take action" to steal the Dies Committee's thunder.
Interior secretary and fellow cabinet member Harold Ickes, for one, believed that Martin Dies had "buffaloed" the attorney general.[64]

Murphy's anxieties had slowly goaded him into the very actions he
had condemned the year before, when the Dies Committee used the Red
Scare to defeat his reelection campaign. The Archdiocese of Detroit was
calling on him in November of 1939 to prosecute Michigan Communists
who had recruited Americans to fight in Spain, publicly declaring that
failure to do so would expose government leaders "to ridicule or at least
the suspicion that they have been intimidated by some secret 'red' influ-
ences." For Murphy, a devout Catholic who had no doubt condemned the
anti-Catholic violence of the Republic's early months, this was apparently
the last straw. The recruitment of volunteers to fight in Spain was illegal,
but the Roosevelt administration had previously declined to prosecute for
political reasons: already under fire for refusing to aid the legally elected
government of Spain, the president did not want to further alienate liberal
opinion by blockading the efforts of private citizens. These concerns had
faded by late 1939, however, with the victory of Franco and the restoration of the Catholic Church to its privileged position as Spain's state-
supported religion. In December, when Murphy knew he would be nominated to the Supreme Court and questioned about his law-and-order
credentials, he gave the order to his Detroit district attorney to seek grand
jury indictments against the loyalist recruiters. Interior secretary Ickes
afterward confided in his diary that Murphy had approved "this rotten
thing" as the result of "Catholic Church influence." Goodman was especially disheartened. "It is sad to think," he wrote years later, that Murphy
"felt he had to approve a prosecution he must have personally abhorred.
Perhaps this is the price that those engaged in political life in our country
must sometimes pay for advancement."[65]

Murphy's actions during his short tenure as attorney general would
later haunt an entire generation of labor and left-wing activists. It was not
simply that he had demonstrated how easily a politician, including a liberal like himself, could subordinate the Bill of Rights to his personal
ambitions. Murphy had not specifically ordered the FBI to engage in the
brutish practices so evident in the Detroit arrests, but he had unleashed
the hounds and sent them on the hunt. This was troubling enough. The
attorney general had pledged himself, as historian Sidney Fine wrote in
his biography of Murphy, "to preserve civil liberties while seeking to

guard the national security, but civil liberties enthusiasts concluded that his actions during the closing weeks of his service were inconsistent with this pledge." There was also a deeper and more enduring legacy to his tenure, for it was in Murphy's twelve months as attorney general that FBI director J. Edgar Hoover consolidated his dominant position in the field of domestic intelligence and political investigation. Much of this was Murphy's doing, for he vigorously backed Hoover in the intradepartmental maneuvering between the State Department, Military Intelligence, and the Justice Department over who controlled domestic intelligence gathering in a time of war. Murphy urged the president to put the FBI in charge of investigations concerning foreign "espionage, counter-espionage, and sabotage." Roosevelt acted accordingly in June 1939 when he ruled that all investigations concerning such matters be concentrated under Hoover's command. While nothing was said of investigations into the alleged subversive activities of *domestic* radicals (as opposed to foreign spies), Hoover invoked the president's ruling as confirmation of his already extensive operations on this political front. Murphy not only acquiesced but persuaded the president to order all local police forces to transmit information on espionage and "subversive activities" to the FBI.[66]

In the following spring of 1940, the Detroit police announced the formation of an "espionage and sabotage squad" that would cooperate with the FBI's expanded powers to coordinate internal security investigations. The commanders of the unit would be officers Mikuliak and Maciosek, the same Mick and Mack who had ransacked Robert Taylor's home in 1938. After a hiatus of less than a year, the Red Squad was back in business.[67]

Hoover's overweening power was already drawing criticism from civil libertarians and many New Dealers, but Murphy continued to praise his bureau chief as "a great officer." He rejected the charge that the FBI was becoming an American version of the Soviet secret police, insisting that it could never become so as long as the Justice Department was committed to civil liberties. His remarks echoed the same faith he had expressed in 1931 when, as mayor of Detroit, his administration had established the Special Investigation Squad (the Red Squad) on the claim that "professional managers" would better regulate the police department's investigation of radical activities. As it happened, in the case of both the city and the federal government, the line between "illegal subversion" and "political opposition" was often ignored when politics intervened. Hoover's power grew thereafter, urged along by President Roosevelt, who welcomed the FBI's intelligence reports on his political opponents. The president might have been less welcoming if he had known that Hoover was also compiling secret dossiers on the personal lives and political activities of his attorneys general and other political leaders. Hoover's agents also kept an eye on anyone who publicly criticized the FBI's methods.[68]

Among those under surveillance was Goodman. In May of 1940, the FBI filed a background report from a "confidential Informant whose identity is known to the Bureau." It was a rather flattering entry. "He is reported to be of good moral character and temperate in personal habits," the informant said of Goodman. "He has a substantial income and appears to be living conservatively within his means." Other reports were less admiring and more focused on details that, in the eyes of these secret police, confirmed Goodman's outlier status. "Subject," the Detroit Red Squad reported to the FBI, "has a habit of shrugging his shoulders 'like Sugar does,' smokes a pipe 'like Sugar does,' and is just as active as Sugar is in all subversive organizations." Of special concern to Hoover, various "confidential informants" also indicated that Goodman was publicly critical of the FBI. The undercover agent who attended the rally celebrating the release of the "Spanish Loyalist Recruiters" reported that the Reverend Owen Knox (Bollens's successor as chairman of the Civil Rights Federation) introduced Goodman as the man "whose brilliant work" had won their freedom. Goodman, the agent continued, gave an account of the arrests that "stressed the violation of the Civil Rights of the defendants" and the fact that they had been given "the Third Degree by relays of FBI agents."[69]

The following June, Hoover leaked a confidential report to national columnist Walter Winchell claiming that a "Detroit attorney"—Goodman—was urging fellow members of the National Lawyers Guild to join the campaign to "weaken" and "hamper" the FBI. In response to Winchell's syndicated column repeating these claims, Goodman wrote Winchell confirming his criticism of the FBI's questionable methods but denying he had said anything about hampering its legal operations. The FBI, he stressed, was an "essential" department of government supported by "all people when it functions within its proper sphere," but rightly condemned when it "violates the law by disregarding the Bill of Rights."[70]

The public furor over the FBI's Detroit raids would quickly subside, aided in part by Hoover's effort to manipulate media coverage. A special investigation ordered by Attorney General Jackson also exonerated the bureau's agents, commending them (in Jackson's words) for conducting their investigation "with a fundamental purpose to observe the rights of defendants." Senator George Norris, the aging progressive Republican from Nebraska, was the lone congressional voice rejecting the attorney general's report. "I disagree with his whitewashing of what happened in Detroit," he declared on 7 May 1940 in his last major address on the floor of the Senate. "It is painful for me to discuss it and disagree with one in whom I have such great confidence." Goodman, who met with the senator beforehand and advised him at length about the details of the case, quoted Norris's bitter denunciation of the bureau in his own report on the Detroit arrests. "Mr. Hoover," said Norris,

> is doing more injury to honest law enforcement in this country by his publicity-seeking feats than is being done by any other one thing connected with his organization. . . . Unless we do something to stop this furor of adulation and praise as being omnipotent, we shall have an organization—the FBI—which, instead of protecting our people from the evil acts of criminals, will itself in the end direct government by tyrannical force, as the history of the world shows. . . . In my judgment unless this procedure is stopped, the time will soon arrive when there will be a spy behind every stump and a detective in every closet in our land.[71]

Born Again

Goodman was now nationally known—by the FBI, at least—as a lawyer for labor and the Left. As he rose in professional and civic prominence, he also took steps to consolidate the political and economic dimensions of his new practice, becoming a local officer of the National Lawyers Guild after its formation in 1937, and joining the Sugar law firm in September of 1939. It was a long way from his days as a repo man. He had reinvented himself as a recognized leader in the Popular Front.

The founding of the National Lawyers Guild (NLG) marked the emergence of a new generation of lawyers opposed to the staid conservatism of the American Bar Association. The ABA's well-heeled lawyers maintained a strict veneration for Supreme Court precedent, rejecting most New Deal programs as unconstitutional, if not protorevolutionary. As representatives of northern business and southern agriculture, they were predictably conservative on most matters of public interest, including their explicit policy of accepting only white lawyers as members. Goodman and his fellow attorneys in the Civil Rights Federation had little use for this Jim Crow conservatism, particularly as the ABA also ignored the dire economic straits that bedeviled most Depression-era lawyers: at a time when $2,500 was considered the poverty line for a family of four, almost half the 175,000 lawyers in the United States earned less than $2,000 a year. Most potential clients simply could not afford to pay. Efforts by unemployed lawyers in New York City to lobby the New Deal's Works Progress Administration for jobs merged with efforts by Maurice Sugar to organize a national network of lawyers ostracized for their "defense of those who otherwise would have been defenseless." In contrast to the ABA's status quo politics, the NLG promised to function, as the preamble to its constitution put it, "as an effective social force in the service of the people to the end that human rights shall be regarded as more sacred than property rights."[72]

A general commitment to progressive government and the use of the law as an instrument for social change made the NLG a natural home for a broad range of New Deal supporters. As a massive exercise in administrative law, the New Deal required attorneys at every turn, drafting new legislation and the accompanying regulations that would restructure the economy and society. Lawyers were the social engineers of this growing administrative state—60 attorneys in the Agricultural Adjustment Administration and no fewer than 250 lawyers working for the National Labor Relations Board. Many of these New Deal attorneys were among the 5,000 members who had joined the NLG in its first year, including NLRB chairman Warren Madden and chief counsel Charles Fahy. Other prominent New Dealers in the NLG included Robert Jackson (soon to become attorney general and later Supreme Court justice), Securities and Exchange commissioner Jerome Frank, and former assistant secretary of state Adolf Berle.[73]

"Through the Guild I became acquainted with lawyers across the country who held social and political views similar to my own," Goodman remembered years later. It wasn't always clear, however, which of those views would define the Guild's internal consensus. Bitter disputes wracked the organization over the issue of Communism. Some liberals and socialists believed that the dictatorial nature of the Soviet Union was proof enough that American Communists could never be reliable defenders of democracy; the Guild, they argued, should therefore denounce Communists as no less dangerous to the Bill of Rights than fascists. Some on the left rejected this as a form of red-baiting, and others argued that what people *thought* of the Soviet Union was much less important than what they *did* to support democracy in the United States. Guild president Ferdinand Pecora offered a compromise in which he denounced any "ism," Communism or fascism, "which seeks to supplant our democracy." This was not enough for many liberals, a growing number of whom resigned their membership. As secretary of the NLG's Detroit chapter, Goodman—whatever his qualms about Stalinism and the Soviet government's suppression of dissent—probably admonished these anti-Communists for being soft on Hitler and accepting of Franco.[74]

It was in the midst of this controversy that Goodman joined Sugar's law firm. He had actually declined an offer to join two years before, saying he wanted to get more experience before making such a commitment. "I decided," he remembered, that "I still hadn't proved to myself that I could do the work and do it well, that I could trust myself in the direction I was going. That's what I told him." He may also have been reluctant to work for a notoriously tight-fisted taskmaster like Sugar, who refused to consider turning his office into a partnership. Sugar preferred to work as the coordinator of a "labor exchange" for competent, pro-union lawyers on an overflow basis, enlisting allied attorneys to work on cases as they came in from the UAW and other unions. This arrangement—and Sugar's compulsive determination to charge unions rock-bottom prices for legal services—could not have been entirely to the liking of the lawyers who worked out of his office.[75]

By 1939, however, there were many more reasons for Goodman to cast his lot with Sugar. With the UAW's internal battles resolved in favor of Sugar's longtime allies in the Unity Caucus, there was, for one, the prospect of a growing caseload of work. R. J. Thomas, Sugar's fellow council candidate on the 1937 Labor slate, was now president of a revived UAW-CIO, and in the spring of 1939 he accepted Sugar's proposal for an expanded legal office with a full-time general counsel and three associates, all chosen by Sugar. "These attorneys should be men of experience," Sugar had written to Thomas. "All should have a knowledge of the labor movement. All should be devoted and loyal to the principles of the CIO. None should be of the type that might possibly desert, or betray, the CIO under any circumstances." To meet these special standards, Sugar chose three men who would serve as the core of his law firm for the next decade: Ernie Goodman, Jack Tucker, and Nedwin Smokler.[76]

Goodman would be known as the UAW's associate general counsel, but in fact he would work for Sugar, not the union. Despite his devotion to the UAW, Sugar refused to make himself entirely dependent on the union. "Although he had become general counsel to the UAW-CIO, he refused to move into the UAW offices," as Goodman recalled, "nor did he go on its payroll as a staff lawyer. He was determined to maintain his independence and his status as a lawyer in general practice." Sugar's motivation for this arm's-length relationship had several likely sources, not the least of which was his long established bond with many other unions, including AFL affiliates, and his still-recent ambitions as a labor-left political candidate. Becoming an employee of the UAW would jeopardize these links to the larger labor-left community and narrow his options, and he had good reason to avoid putting all of his eggs in one basket. The previous UAW president, Homer Martin, had secretly attempted to negotiate a sweetheart deal with Ford brokered by Father Coughlin; in the factional fighting that followed the exposure of this move, Martin had attempted to oust his opponents from the union and fire their allies, Sugar among them, before taking the UAW back into the AFL. The pendulum had since swung back in Sugar's direction with the victory of the Unity caucus and the UAW-CIO over the renegade "UAW-AFL," but the entire episode must have underlined the precariousness of a staff lawyer's position. With this experience in mind, Sugar preferred an arm's-length contractual agreement with the union, and the UAW Executive Board accepted his proposal in late April of 1939.[77]

For Goodman, a position in Sugar's expanding office would guarantee a steady income, however modest, and the opportunity to work on the cutting edge of social change and legal innovation. He must also have felt that his growing stature in the Civil Rights Federation and his high-profile role in the campaign to defend the victims of the Dies Committee now gave him enough leverage to deal with Sugar on something closer to an equal plane. He accepted Sugar's offer sometime that spring but delayed moving into his new office until the following September.

Sugar had a stoic demeanor, but when he and Goodman started working together they got along quite well and became personal friends. Goodman's energy and his high standards of research and preparation for trial mirrored Sugar's prodigious and methodical work habits. Although each handled his own case preparation, they discussed the cases together. Goodman was no rank amateur—he was eleven years out of law school when he joined Sugar's firm. Still, his relationship to Sugar was akin to that of a younger brother. It was Sugar, in any case, who ran the office. The UAW paid him a fixed fee of $1,500 a month to supervise the union's growing legal docket, from which Sugar took his salary after paying office rent, clerical workers, and supplies. Goodman, Tucker, and Smokler worked on UAW cases assigned by Sugar, but as independent "associates" rather than employees. They forwarded their billings to Sugar for his approval, and Sugar sent the bills to the UAW for payment to the attorney handling the case. The associates paid no share of these UAW fees to Sugar, but they did pay a percentage of net fees from non-UAW cases that he assigned. They also contributed their labor to allied labor-left organizations, with Goodman concentrating his volunteer work on the Civil Rights Federation. Sugar would retain additional lawyers across the country as needed on a case-by-case basis, but would drive a hard bargain with many of them when it came to fees. As Goodman later recalled, those who worked on UAW business for Sugar in these days were paid the same hourly rate as UAW skilled tradesmen in the auto plants.[78]

In managing the growing business of the firm, Goodman and Sugar each excelled in ways that complemented the other man. Over time,

Goodman became the more accomplished trial lawyer. This was partly because Sugar, convicted of draft resistance during World War I, had been reinstated to the bar only in Michigan's state courts. Excluded from other states and the federal courts, Sugar would hand off many cases to Goodman, including several that eventually went to the U.S. Supreme Court. In these settings, Goodman developed an engaging courtroom manner as well as high standards in the use of evidence and an intuitive sense of legal strategy. Sugar, on the other hand, was politically more astute. He brought to his legal practice his own rich life experience, his connections throughout the labor movement, and his understanding of the law and its history.

A compelling example of Sugar's grasp of legal history and its relation to present-day struggles involved the issue of picketing. By an 1898 ruling of the state Supreme Court, picketing was declared to be inherently coercive and therefore illegal in Michigan. Though this ruling was not always applied during strikes, it remained on the books until 1940, when the U.S. Supreme Court—in a decision written by Frank Murphy—declared that peaceful picketing was a form of free speech protected by the Bill of Rights. In the meantime, as the great campaigns to gain union recognition unfolded in the 1930s, the prohibition on picketing was frequently invoked by employers. The challenge for the union was to avoid or delay the company's recourse to a court injunction that would empower the police to clear the streets. Sugar knew of a useful precedent from English history. From the fourteenth century onward, England's landed gentry had fenced in the best land at an accelerating pace, evicting peasants from the ground they had tilled or shared by customary right. Wealthy landowners would seek approval for these "enclosures" in the courts of equity, and Sugar was struck by the *impatience* of the English gentry to secure an immediate ruling from the courts, before the poor could present their case. That impatience reminded him of Detroit's industrialists and their haste to secure an injunction against picketing. It also called to mind a unique feature of the law of equity. In the English case, the courts had adopted a custom that only men of good repute could petition for an injunction to uphold their claims; if it could be shown that a petitioner had engaged in nefarious activities—that he had "unclean hands"—then he could be denied injunctive relief.[79]

With so much of American law derived from English precedent, Sugar could invoke this ancient principle to postpone if not block an immediate injunction against picketing. When a company approached the court seeking enforcement of such an injunction, Sugar would file an "Answer to the Complaint" in which he argued it was first necessary to determine whether the company's "unclean hands" disqualified it from the court's protection. In 1936 and 1937 the Senate Sub-committee on Civil Liberties chaired by

Senator LaFollette had compiled reports of widespread illegal practices by employers, including physical assault, spying on pro-union workers, and illegal firings to punish pro-union speech. Using this record, Sugar would recite the company's violations of the National Labor Relations Act. The stage was set. Goodman later described the court proceedings he participated in:

> When the injunction hearing took place, the courtroom would be filled with workers, sometimes jamming the adjoining hallway and occasionally extending to a picket line encircling the courthouse. . . . Then Sugar would rise and, to the amusement of the workers, he would quote from decisions of the King's and Queen's Bench as far back as the 17th and 18th centuries, and from early decisions of U.S. state courts. As the audience observed the growing consternation of the judge, he would restate the old "unclean hands" rule which he asked the judge to apply in this case.

For as long as the judge permitted, Sugar would take the opportunity to argue all over again the injustice of the company's actions; and while that argument continued, so did the picketing.[80]

"As we went along we were making it up," Goodman later said of the unsettled nature of labor law in this period. "There was no class I could go to study, no books I could learn from at that time." In a context where the U.S. Supreme Court had only just ruled that the National Labor Relations Act was compatible with the Constitution, there remained an enormous range of issues to be resolved in 1938 and 1939. Many of these ended up in front of a judge as the NLRB sought court orders to enforce its decisions and establish the mechanisms for certifying unions and protecting workers' rights. As the militancy of the sit-down era receded, unions would become all the more dependent on these due process procedures, as enforced by the NLRB. "The time has passed," as CIO president John L. Lewis put it, "when the workers can be either clubbed, gassed, or shot down with impunity." The time had also passed when sit-down strikes and unvarnished militancy could bring employers to heal. In 1939 the U.S. Supreme Court ruled that sit-down strikes represented an illegal resort to forceful action and seizure of private property; most unions had already abandoned the tactic in any case after they gained recognition from the employer. Labor relations were now publicly regulated in a process that called for "good faith" bargaining, disrupted only by the occasional, and usually peaceful, strike with outside picketers.[81]

Government intervention was a giant step forward in the eyes of most trade unionists, though opinion would change in later years when government policy shifted to the right. For now, there was no plausible alternative for curbing the persistent antiunionism of corporate managers, the wealthy, and the many politicians who answered to them. A revolutionary assault on private property and corporate power was only a rhetorical project for a few Communist politicians and true believers. By the late 1930s, most socialists and independent progressives had renounced revolutionary goals in favor of a reformist agenda that sought to humanize and tame capitalism. Even in the Communist Party, the majority of members welcomed the intervention of the augmented and *reformed* capitalist state. Immigrant and second-generation radicals who had once embraced armed struggle against the Cossacks or the Coal Police now, in the late 1930s, were assimilating to a new reality. They *did* have something to lose other than their chains: the New Deal, with all its imperfections.

Sugar recognized what was happening and urged UAW president R. J. Thomas to take advantage of the unexplored potential of the Wagner Act. "The organization of workers into our Union," he wrote to Thomas, "and their retention, once organized, often depends upon action or lack of action under the Act." It was to help make good on this prescription for union growth under the law that Sugar hired Goodman in the fall of 1939.[82]

Taking a Stand

In all probability, Goodman was introduced to the fraternity of hunters by Sugar, a lifetime deer hunter famous for avoiding trial appearances in late November, when hunting season began. Goodman was an easy sell. A rationalist and a political realist when it mattered, he was also an optimist and a romantic, with the accompanying love of nature. When the stress of political combat, the crush of work, or the burdens of responsibility weighed on him, Goodman found renewal in Michigan's northland, rifle or fishing rod in hand.

When it came to the woodland arts, he soon developed his own opinion on everything, from his special way of threading a hook through a minnow, so that it lived for a time and attracted more fish, to the proper way to hunt whitetail deer. Above all, he deplored the "baiting" of deer with apples and carrots for weeks in advance of the season. He said that it corrupted the hunt by making the deer dependent on the hunter for food and therefore careless of him. For Goodman, baiting deer was an unethical and lazy practice, akin to fishing with dynamite.[83]

Instead, he argued that the hunt should be defined not by the hunter, but by the deer and its habits of feeding and mating. The whitetail deer was a "border animal," he said. It hung close to the margins of the landscape, to the tree line along the meadow, the cornfield, the upper slopes of the valley. The hunter's first task was to find a natural "stand," the fallen tree or the outcropping of woods (not an artificial structure) that gave cover. If there was a breeze, the stand should be downwind from where you found tracks in the snow or mud. Deer are nocturnal animals and, if you were on the stand early enough, you might catch them in the open before they retreated to the woods at daybreak. If not, you hunkered down in the brush and waited: two hours, three hours, with the occasional distant rifle report tailing off in the late morning. Your boots might be wet, the seat of your pants likewise, but in an approach aptly called "still hunting," you waited until the deer came to you. Another technique that Goodman favored was "the drive." With two hunters at the mouth of a draw, a third hunter would drive the deer toward them. Of course, you squeezed the trigger only when you knew for sure that the driver was not in your line of fire; he had to trust you on this score.

Goodman enjoyed the sociability of the hunt and the accompanying traditions that developed over time. These included everything from safety precautions (no loaded firearms inside the cabin and no alcohol on the stand) to, in later years, recorded folk songs of the Spanish civil war, played loud as a savage flamenco to waken fellow hunters. The oldest of these folkways was the ritual that followed one of the early hunts in 1929, when Maurice Sugar organized a venison feast for friends who contributed money to support the unemployed. As this "Buck Dinner" became an annual event, the guest list grew longer and the contributions more substantial, with proceeds directed to strike support and pending legal cases. During the buck hunt itself, there was also the settled pattern of evening debates in the hunters' cabin, ranging from good-humored speculation on how many deer had been alerted to Goodman's presence by the clouds of pipe smoke around his stand to the status of the labor movement and the drift of U.S. foreign policy. Argument on these and other issues went on into the night, with friends staring into the fire and sipping Scotch.[84]

Goodman the deer hunter was the same man most knew as Goodman the lawyer. In both realms he brought the same meticulous attention to detail, the same patience, the same geniality and loyalty to friends of long standing. As with any metaphor, there are limits to how much the parable of Goodman-as-hunter tells us about Goodman the defender of civil liberties; while in both he displayed a characteristic empathy and respect for the "other," in his law practice, as opposed to the deer hunt, the goal was to *defend* the hunted. What was irreducibly true about Goodman, however, was his commitment to principle and fair play. He rejected opportunism in both, whether it was the advantage gained by baiting deer, or the clients he might have gained by tacking with every shift in the political winds. As a labor and civil rights lawyer, Goodman had taken a stand with the downtrodden, the working class, "the masses." He would thereafter adjust his tactics as needed, but not his stance.

The principle that now guided his law practice was defined by his experience over the previous five years. He had seen how mass mobilization and popular protest could challenge the status quo and transform the law, but he had also learned how the law, and particularly the Bill of Rights, could serve as the indispensable shield for such a movement. This did not mean that Goodman venerated the amendments of 1791 as an unchanging liturgy. The Bill of Rights was a living document subject to reinterpretation and growth, expanding from the original ten amendments to twenty-one as slavery was abolished and voting rights were extended. In Goodman's adult life, the sphere of protected rights had widened still further, outstripping the confines of the Constitution and extending the law's safeguards into the private sector workplace. "In this industrial Twentieth Century," as he said in a prewar radio address sponsored by the Civil Rights Federation, "freedom of speech and press have come to mean also freedom to picket and to pass out leaflets." But these rights, new and old, did not mean the same thing to all people. "To those who control power and wealth, the Bill of Rights is not particularly important. The owners of huge industrial empires do not need trade unions; in fact, they can do very well without them. And their economic power frees them from danger of political persecution. It is the people who have no wealth and no privileges who find that democracy is a practical, day-by-day necessity."[85]

Many of Goodman's listeners on station WJBK could speak to this claim from their recent experience. They had voted for FDR in 1936 despite the nearly unanimous opposition of the corporate-owned media, and when management refused to abide by the law and the courts initially refused to implement it, the workers had upheld the National Labor Relations Act by their own exertions, through sit-down strikes and mass demonstrations. Democracy and the struggle for civil rights in the workplace had, indeed, become "a practical, day-by-day necessity" for Detroit's workers.

But as Goodman well knew, it was only a partial, unsettled truth that he spoke to. Ambiguities and hard questions abounded. Was hate speech also free speech, protected even when it inflamed public opinion and threatened violence? Did an employer's threat to retaliate against union organization qualify as free speech, or was it a form of coercive speech that denied workers their rights under the law? The Constitution protected democracy, but did it also protect the enemies of democracy? For that matter, did it protect dissenters on the right or left when they questioned the law itself? And who would decide when these dissenters presented such a "clear and present danger" to the Constitution that it should be suspended and the dissenters stripped of their rights?

These had been burning questions during the First World War, when the government brutally suppressed antiwar opinion. They would become urgent matters again as the United States now teetered on the brink of another world war. In September 1939, the same month that Goodman joined the Sugar law firm, this ultimate test of civil liberties was close at hand.

4

Home Front

Ernie Goodman had a lot to think about that morning as he crossed Cadillac Square and entered the Barlum office tower in downtown Detroit. It was September 1939, and this was the first day of his new job in Maurice Sugar's law firm. As he took the elevator to the thirty-second floor, he felt confident about his improving circumstances. Unfortunately, the world around him was spinning out of control.

As an associate in Sugar's law firm, Goodman knew he would be playing a key role in the legal battles that accompanied labor's forward march in Detroit. The city was still pulsating with the energy of that struggle, and the landmarks of battles won and lost were all around him. From the thirty-second floor Goodman could look out onto Cadillac Square, where just two years earlier more than a hundred thousand union members and their supporters had gathered to cheer the sit-down strikers and call for the resignation of police commissioner Pickert. It was a short lunchtime walk from there to the Woolworth's five and dime store on Woodward Avenue, where 250 saleswomen had occupied the store for eight days in 1937 to win union recognition and a 5¢ raise in hourly wages. The Woolworth's sit-downers had celebrated their victory at the Barlum Hotel in the shadow of Goodman's office building; two days later, the hotel's waitresses, elevator operators, cooks, and boiler tenders had started their own sit-down strike, winning 20 to 100 percent wage increases after a four-hour occupation. Taking the lead role in these strikes and a series of successful sit-downs in the city's hotels was the same AFL union that, sixteen years before, had lost the 1921 strike at the Detroit Athletic Club. It had been known then as the Waiters Union and had only recruited white men. It was known now as the Waiters and Waitresses Union and was led by younger activists who were opening its ranks to women and African Americans.[1]

The sit-down strikes had ended in Detroit's hotels and factories, but workers were still organizing and winning contracts at a rapid pace. As chief counsel for the UAW, Maurice Sugar would plot the legal strategies for consolidating the union's gains in the auto industry, and Goodman would be his right-hand man in this prolonged campaign. It was the ideal opportunity for Goodman, a job that would wed his professional skills and political values.

Yet, even as the new job marked the culmination of his efforts since 1935 to redefine himself as a lawyer, there was also in this moment reason for apprehension. Goodman had taken a stand with a movement that defined itself as antifascist and internationalist, a Popular Front against right-wing extremism at home and abroad. Now, at the very moment that the world was hurtling toward global war, the terms of that antifascist struggle had suddenly been turned upside down.

On 23 August 1939, the Soviet Union had signed a nonaggression pact with Hitler's Germany. The world leader of antifascist resistance and the sole country that had mustered international support for the Spanish Republic had, with a stroke of the pen, allied itself with the enemy. Days later, Nazi Germany's panzer divisions overran Poland and World War II had begun in Europe. While the Soviet Union remained officially neutral, the Red Army, acting under secret provisions of the Hitler-Stalin pact, quietly occupied eastern Poland.

Unpopular Front

Goodman, like many of his cohorts on labor's left wing, was stunned by the news of the Soviet Union's sudden rapprochement with Nazi Germany. His response, as he later described it, was one of "shock, very difficult to understand and to deal with." Russia, he believed, "was a socialist country moving in the right direction. . . . It shook many organizations and individuals."[2]

The complete turnabout in the official line of the Communist Party of the United States (CP-USA) was especially troubling. Parroting the Soviet government's official justification for the pact, CP-USA leaders insisted that the very survival of the Soviet Union was at stake in a context where the Western democracies had already abandoned republican Spain and were now waiting to see the Soviets annihilated in a stand-alone struggle with Hitler. Britain and France had already excluded the Soviets in 1938 from the Munich conference, where they acquiesced to Nazi Germany's seizure of land in Czechoslovakia. Forsaken at Munich, Stalin had no choice, the CP-USA argued, but to sign the nonaggression pact with Hitler and turn the tables on Britain and France, pitting them against Hitler's Blitzkrieg. Goodman recalled years later that he and Sugar could understand the logic, "but we were unhappy about the circumstances."[3]

The United States was not yet at war, but it was widely recognized that the Roosevelt administration sided with Britain and France and was exploring every opportunity to aid them against Nazi Germany. What the CP-USA would have welcomed before August of 1939 it now condemned in categorical terms, describing the European war as an imperialist struggle for colonial spoils that had nothing to do with opposing fascism. The same President Roosevelt the party had praised as "the most outstanding anti-fascist spokesman within the capitalist democracies" was now the reviled leader of the "War Party" and "a leading world sponsor of the imperialist puppets." Thousands of left-wingers who couldn't abide this parroting of the Soviet government's line resigned from the party.[4]

The long-term damage was far greater to the CP-USA's links with liberals and moderates in the many Popular Front groups the party had promoted since 1935. There were others besides the CP-USA who also opposed U.S. intervention in the widening war in Europe, from the Socialist Party to John L. Lewis to "America Firsters." But the CP-USA was a sudden convert to this antiwar position, and not a very convincing one. For liberals and antifascist New Dealers who favored supporting Britain's war effort, the Hitler-Stalin pact was a betrayal that left an indelibly bitter taste. Mass resignations led to the collapse of several Popular Front organizations, including the American Student Union and the American League for Peace and Democracy. Other Popular Front groups survived, but only after bitter disputes and the resignation of prominent non-Communists.[5]

Outside of the Popular Front, the CP-USA fared even worse. The ACLU banned Communists as well as fascists from its ranks and expelled Elizabeth Gurley Flynn, a prominent Communist leader, from its board of directors. While both the CIO and the UAW conventions in 1940 went on record opposing U.S. involvement in World War II, both also passed "Communazi" resolutions condemning in equal measure Nazi Germany and the Soviet Union. The following year, Vice President Walter Reuther led the campaign at the UAW's national convention to bar Communists and fascists from union office.[6]

The Civil Rights Federation made its way through this difficult period by focusing its energies on the domestic issues of labor and civil rights that had previously unified the Popular Front. As chairman of the CRF's editorial board, Goodman made sure that the *Civil Rights News* filled its pages with monthly reports on the same issues that had dominated its coverage before the Hitler-Stalin pact: strikebreaking, police attacks on unions and minorities, and the threats to civil liberties posed by local fascists, the Klan, and Father Coughlin. Foreign policy issues were only occasionally addressed in the monthly column of the CRF chairman, the Reverend Owen Knox, a committed pacifist who believed, as he stated in October 1939, that "it won't make a nickel's worth of difference in Europe who wins the war, so far as democracy is concerned." Otherwise, Goodman and his colleagues kept foreign policy issues out of the newspaper in the months following the Hitler-Stalin pact, except to note the *domestic* threat to civil rights that many war measures entailed. As a federation of organizations that included non-Communists from local unions and churches, many of them ardent supporters of President Roosevelt, the CRF's survival depended on this effort to avoid the foreign policy disputes rending the Popular Front.[7]

All the while, however, public anxiety about the approach of war was deepening with the dramatic news of France's defeat and the German Luftwaffe's savage bombardment of London. By the summer of 1940, even as polls indicated that the overwhelming majority of Americans still opposed U.S. entry into the war, two out of three believed it was inevitable and 80 percent wanted to boost material support for Britain. Alarmed by the stunning success of the Nazi Blitzkrieg, Congress voted a fivefold increase in military spending. FDR won election to his third term that year by a margin of 5 million votes, but it was national security, not New Deal reformism, that now dominated the legislative agenda. Fears that Germany would invade Britain and capture its navy, bringing Nazi battleships to the shores of Long Island, fueled a mounting hysteria about foreign agents and the loyalties of immigrant aliens, especially those associated with ideological groups on the left and right. In a move that underlined the nation's mounting fears of alien infiltration, Congress in 1940 moved the Immigration and Naturalization Service out of the Department of Labor, where immigration was treated as a social and economic issue, and placed it in the Department of Justice, where Hoover's FBI saw it as a security issue.[8]

In response to this rightward turn, the Civil Rights Federation sent Goodman and Milton Kemnitz, the CRF's executive secretary, to Washington to meet with other civil rights groups and explore the possibility of forming a national organization. Their efforts bore fruit in June of 1940 with the launching of the National Federation for Constitutional Liberties (NFCL), an umbrella group that united the national lobbying efforts of Popular Front groups. Goodman also took the lead in the CRF's campaign to oppose antialien legislation and to promote measures protecting civil rights for workers and minorities. He was now the chief legislative expert on the CRF's steering committee and his reports to the delegate body were a regular feature of the agenda during 1940. "Mr. Goodman pointed out that if any of the 'anti-alien' bills go through," as the minutes for May reported, "they will be the most un-American laws passed by a Congressional body since 1776."[9]

Most Americans thought otherwise. Despite heavy lobbying by the ACLU and the CRF, Congress did just as Goodman had feared, passing an omnibus bill in June 1940 that outlawed seditious speech—however defined—and required fingerprinting and annual registration by 4 million resident aliens. The Smith Act, as it was called after its sponsor, Democrat Howard Smith of Virginia, carried the House by a margin of 384-4 and the Senate by a unanimous voice vote. Title 1 of the bill made it a crime for individuals or political parties to advocate in speech or writing the use of force to overthrow the government, or to distribute literature that would impair the morale or discipline of the armed forces. As Goodman and other critics pointed out, the Smith Act was not aimed at actual acts or plans to use force against the government—these had long been illegal—but at the *advocacy* of such methods or even the *conspiracy* to advocate them. The latter was an especially murky realm, allowing government officials wide latitude in portraying a dissenting minority as dangerous simply because its members might be "conspiring" the *future* advocacy of sabotage. The CP-USA had already renounced armed insurrection and there was no credible evidence in the FBI's files that it was plotting to overthrow the government by force, or even to advocate such action. But the CP-USA's secretiveness, the concealment of party membership by some who rose in union or Popular Front organizations, and the party's obedient willingness to follow Stalin's lead in matters of war and peace— all this suggested a shadowy conspiracy of unknown dimensions. Merely joining a group labeled *subversive* by Martin Dies and J. Edgar Hoover made one suspect under the Smith Act, and Stalin's alliance with Hitler strengthened the conviction of most Americans that members of the CP-USA, in particular, were not protected by the Bill of Rights. It would take a small band of labor lawyers and civil libertarians the better part of twenty years to convince the Supreme Court otherwise.[10]

Goodman's long involvement with the doctors' case, beginning in 1938 and ending with the FBI's dawn arrest of his clients in 1940, meant he knew better than most how the politics of national security could be used to suspend the Bill of Rights. The role of former attorney general Frank Murphy in ordering the arrests had underlined the new political alignments following the Hitler-Stalin pact: now it was New Deal liberals who advanced the anti-Communist crusade. The Roosevelt administration had taken the lead the previous fall when the Justice Department indicted CP-USA chairman Earl Browder for passport violations the government had known about for years, but previously ignored. Browder was convicted and sentenced to a four-year prison term in 1940 as other Communists were swept up in a state and federal campaign that charged them with everything from falsifying voter applications to soliciting ballot signatures under false pretenses to violating old criminal syndicalist laws. In Detroit, a meeting convened at the Finnish Hall to protest Browder's indictment was attacked by fifteen hundred counterdemonstrators who assaulted the left-wingers as they fled the hall, sending four to the hospital while city police stood aside. The right-wing crowd burned effigies of Stalin, Hitler, Earl Browder, and Maurice Sugar.[11]

The same year, the Michigan state police formed a new division to "combat subversive activity," placing under surveillance more than nine thousand suspects. "The list is growing every day," police commissioner Oscar Olander announced in February of 1940. Among the names added that spring was Peter Malanchuk, a laborer for the State Highway Department fired for "un-American activities" after he signed a petition to place the Communist Party on the ballot. The CRF referred the case to Goodman, who wrote the highway commissioner, Murray Van Wagoner, reminding him that Malanchuk had been gathering signatures for *Van Wagoner's* gubernatorial campaign when he signed the Communist petition in a friendly swap with another campaigner. "I wonder who is really un-American," Goodman asked in his letter to Michigan's future governor. "Is it Peter Malanchuk, who signed a legal petition, legally distributed to place a legal party on the ballot? Or was it un-American of a state official . . . taking away his job, his only means of supporting a family, solely on the ground that he signed such a petition?" The distinction could not have mattered much to Van Wagoner, who was unlikely to restore Malancuk to the payroll before the election.[12]

J. Edgar Hoover had his own answer to the question of who was un-American and what should be done with them. Ten months after the announcement of the Hitler-Stalin pact, the FBI director began to compile a secret list of those who, in the event of war or national emergency, would be taken into "custodial detention" as security risks. There was no statutory basis for this draconian measure and Hoover did not inform Congress or the public of its existence. The list included United States citizens and alien residents who were, in the opinion of Hoover and the "Special Defense Unit" in the Department of Justice, aligned with the country's likely enemies in the coming war, Germany and Soviet Russia. Communists, radical labor leaders, journalists and others critical of the FBI or the administration figured prominently on the list of those to be swept up in the massive dragnet. On 29 March 1941, Hoover signed the memo to the Special Defense Unit recommending that Ernest Goodman "be considered for custodial detention in the event of a national emergency."[13]

Ford Falls

The political fallout from the Hitler-Stalin pact shadowed Goodman's first two years with the Sugar law firm, but it was the pressing demands of union organizing that dominated his day-to-day work. "Our responsibility was to labor and black people and to anti-fascist, anti-conservative forces," Goodman later recalled. "We had very little problem doing that kind of work. We were not involved in intellectual debates. We were involved in doing work for these organizations." To avoid the splits that could undermine the precarious coalition of political factions within the labor-Left, Sugar and Goodman "did everything we could not to raise, but to avoid ideological issues that divided," as Goodman put it years later. "Relatively few people we were working with raised the Nazi-Soviet pact as an issue."[14]

In Detroit, the dominant issue for progressives was the continuing effort to win union recognition at Ford, the last of the Big Three automakers to be unionized. The issue of free speech would take on a special prominence in this campaign, both within the factory and in the streets outside. Inside Ford's massive River Rouge complex, the company deployed more than three thousand plainclothesmen in its notorious Service Department, all answering to Ford's antiunion security chief, Harry Bennett. They were a tough bunch. Of fifty-three ex-cons on the Ford payroll listed by name in a detailed report by *Friday* magazine, eighteen had been convicted of armed robbery, seven of assault, and two each of murder, rape, and manslaughter. They were put to work suppressing any expression of union support among the eighty thousand workers employed at the Rouge. "Service men now patrol the aisles during all working hours watching for any signs of union activity," the National Labor Relations Board reported after extensive hearings. "Employees seen talking together are taken off the assembly lines by service men and discharged irrespective of the wishes of their foremen." Those fired included men who had done nothing more than wear a union button, go to a meeting, or talk with a fellow worker. In one case the NLRB found that a man was fired because his *son*, a GM worker, was a UAW member. Another was fired when he refused to name the men to whom he had given membership cards. "The use of the Service Department to intimidate employees and make them fearful of joining the UAW has quite evidently been successful," the NLRB said of Ford's illegal activity. "Discussion of the UAW, even during the lunch period, is carried on in hushed tones."[15]

In one celebrated case that Goodman handled before the Michigan Unemployment Compensation Commission, Ford worker and UAW activist John Gallo testified that his foreman had fired him for laughing while working on the line. Ford contended that Gallo, a former welterweight boxer who would later win union office as an avowed Communist, had quit and was therefore not entitled to unemployment benefits. But the hearing examiner found otherwise when the general foreman, called to testify, said that Gallo had been laid off after he was twice seen "talking and laughing with the other fellows." The foreman further testified that he could "tell when a man is talking about the job and when he isn't." An obviously exasperated hearing examiner ruled that "a shop rule against mirth would . . . make life in a modern plant a vale of tears," and declared Gallo eligible for unemployment benefits.[16]

Free speech was also in jeopardy outside the plant. Ford had served notice that the First Amendment did not apply to Dearborn in May of 1937, when Service Department men and supervisors attacked union leafleters at the plant gates. The NLRB characterized the beatings in this "Battle of the Overpass" as unprovoked and "unbelievably brutal," targeting not only union leafleters but also news photographers and reporters who were chased down on Miller Road, "their film and notebooks taken from them." This violent suppression of speech was ratified by the City of Dearborn, which already had an ordinance banning distribution of handbills not previously reviewed by the city clerk to "determine the truth" of their contents. There was little doubt that in the company town of Dearborn—its police chief, Carl Brooks, was a past plant detective for Ford and a subordinate of Harry Bennett—this law would be enforced with little regard to either the "truth" or the First Amendment.[17]

As an active member of the Civil Rights Federation, Goodman was well acquainted with Henry Ford's public flouting of the Bill of Rights and his stated refusal to abide by the National Labor Relations Act. The CRF had already blocked several proposed ordinances in Detroit that would have required a license to distribute literature, and the defeat of Mayor Richard Reading in 1939 gave hope for further gains on behalf of civil liberties and workers' rights. But there was now this crucial difference for Goodman as he turned his attention to Dearborn: instead of volunteering his spare time through the CRF for such campaigns, he was a full-time member of the Sugar firm and counsel for the CIO's most dynamic and militant union. He would be paid a regular income, however modest it was compared to the corporate fees he had once hoped to earn.[18]

This upward turn in his professional life had its domestic corollary in the home Goodman purchased that winter on the northern outskirts of the city, just south of Eight Mile Road and east of Livernois Avenue. Costing $8,000 (with a twenty-year mortgage), the brand-new four-bedroom brick house on Warrington Drive was a substantial step up from the housing Goodman had known in his youth. The neighbors were different as well: instead of the working-class families and ethnic retailers of the Jewish ghetto, the block on Warrington was entry-level middle class, home to building contractors, branch managers, sales reps, and foremen. They were all white and mostly Protestant, with only a handful of Catholics and even fewer Jewish families scattered along the tree-lined avenues. It was a long way from Hastings Street and a ten-mile commute to Goodman's downtown office. He took the bus, leaving the two-door Oldsmobile for Freda. For her, the new house was also a watershed. Since 1936, she had moved the family through a daunting series of relocations—two apartments and a rented home before the final move to Warrington Drive. She now had the chance to establish a permanent home for her family, including her second son, William, born in 1940. After the uncertainty and hard feelings brought on by her husband's change in career, the house on Warrington represented a welcome recompense for Freda.[19]

With the family settled into its new home, Goodman turned to the rapidly expanding caseload of the Ford campaign. Maurice Sugar had already done the spadework gathering evidence for the NLRB's first order calling on Ford to reinstate twenty-four workers fired illegally for union activity. With Goodman's arrival, the caseload would mushroom dramatically over the next two years as the Sugar firm initiated fourteen more NLRB complaints on behalf of four thousand workers fired from Ford plants in nine different states. Five of the NLRB's reinstatement orders would be contested in federal court, most of the rest appeared to be moving in that direction, and three different Michigan courts would rule on the Dearborn ordinance before the issue was resolved. As Sugar's top aide on the Ford campaign, Goodman had little time for anything but gathering evidence for NLRB hearings, building a network of allied lawyers across the country, and frequent trips to Washington. "I didn't learn labor law," as Goodman later said of the Sugar firm's role. "We helped *make* labor law, and I was part of the process of making it. And it was fascinating from the viewpoint of a lawyer, wondering how law is made, you see how it's made—through struggle, of people for their rights, for their freedom."[20]

It was a nonstop pace for all of Sugar's associates, notes historian Chris Johnson, "especially Goodman, who was rapidly becoming an expert on the intestines of the Ford Motor Company." It was difficult to find time for his continuing work with the CRF, even when it clearly overlapped with the broader interests of the UAW. Apologizing to Milton Kemnitz for failing to finish a pamphlet on pending antistrike legislation, Goodman confessed that he was "tied up with an important assignment on the Ford case which will keep me busy day and night, including Sundays, for about three weeks." In the meantime, he found it "absolutely impossible to get this pamphlet out." The occasional moments of free time were quickly consumed by the demands of work and home. Upon learning he would not have to attend a conference in Madison, Wisconsin, Goodman acknowledged to a colleague that he was relieved. "Freda and Billie are ill [and] I have a tremendous amount of work to do here."[21]

Of the many court cases keeping Sugar and Goodman busy, the first that came to fruition was the challenge to Dearborn's handbill ordinance. It was a classic demonstration of Sugar's approach. As he had long argued, only a mass movement could force a legal issue into the forefront of judicial consciousness and compel upholders of the status quo to reconsider bad law. At the same time, a mass movement for social change had to navigate existing law even as it sought to change it. The challenge for the lawyer, then, was to develop a legal strategy that was principled in its challenge to the status quo at the same time as it was pragmatic in its day-to-day defense of the movement. In the case of the Dearborn antileafleting ordinance, Sugar had noted that the law banned the unauthorized distribution only of "circulars and handbills." He therefore stipulated that when one thousand union members returned to Miller Road three months after the Battle of the Overpass, they would distribute only free copies of the UAW newspaper. The union was technically in compliance with the handbill ordinance, and the presence of state police and NLRB observers kept the Ford Service Department at bay.[22]

When the Michigan Supreme Court later declared the handbill ordinance unconstitutional, the Dearborn City Council—undeterred—replaced it with an ordinance prohibiting literature distribution in "congested zones" where leafleting created "traffic hazards." To give the suppression of free speech a legal coloring, the streets around the Ford plant were designated a "congested zone" and the police subsequently arrested nearly a thousand union leafleters. It was only with the UAW-CIO's revived organizing drive in 1940 that the campaign to overturn this "traffic" ordinance was effectively renewed. Sugar's efforts bore unexpected fruit that October when municipal judge Lila Neuenfelt, in defiance of the city fathers, declared the law an unconstitutional abridgement of freedom of speech and of the press. The police refused to accept her judgment and continued to arrest UAW leafleters, among them John Conyers Sr., father of Detroit's future congressman, and Stanley Nowak, the recently elected state senator for Dearborn and western Detroit. The following month, the Wayne County Circuit Court upheld Neuenfelt's courageous decision and issued a permanent injunction restraining the Dearborn police from arresting union leafleters.[23]

It had taken more than three years to bring the First Amendment to Dearborn's streets, and it would take another year to establish the rule of law inside Ford's plants. The NLRB's first cease-and-desist order against Ford had been a labored delivery when it arrived in 1939, the product of hearings, court challenges, and revisions stretching back more than two years. Citing the considerable evidence that Ford had fired union supporters and attacked union leafleters, the NLRB ordered the reinstatement with back pay of those illegally discharged for supporting the union. Few were surprised when Ford refused to take the men back, and few doubted that the U.S. Appeals Court for the Sixth Circuit, to which the NLRB petitioned for enforcement of its ruling, would uphold this part of the board's order. The evidence was too overwhelming, especially after the company's brutal attack on leafleters during the Battle of the Overpass.[24]

There was considerable disagreement, however, about the merits of the NLRB's additional order that the company "cease and desist" from distributing workplace publications featuring Henry Ford's antiunion opinions. The board deemed this to be coercive speech, unprotected by the First Amendment, because it sought to intimidate workers and nullify their right to self-organization under the National Labor Relations Act. "The publications must be considered in their context," the NLRB had ruled, and in a context where foremen personally put these materials in workers' hands and pressured them to sign a "vote of confidence," the publications had the "unmistakable purpose and effect" of coercion— particularly when those who refused to sign could expect a visit from the Service Department and summary firing. "Freedom of speech is a qualified, not an absolute right," the NLRB concluded, and in the conflicted terrain of the Rouge, where the boss still wielded dictatorial power, Ford's belligerent speech was coercive by nature, inextricably linked to the illegal bullying that awaited dissenters.

Critics of the NLRB were particularly aroused by this challenge to management prerogatives. Ford's lawyers condemned the board's alleged prejudice against business, invoked the Bill of Rights, and wrapped Henry Ford in the mantle of the First Amendment. Edward Bernard, a local power in the Republican Party, claimed to know the real source of the NLRB's animus. Every time the board's attorney, Harold Cranefield, rose to speak, "it's been exactly as though Mr. Sugar were on his feet." There was some truth to this, for Sugar's meticulous presentation of the evidence to NLRB investigators certainly played a role in shaping the case. Goodman now also lent his voice to the proceedings, particularly as he took on an unexpected adversary in the dispute over Ford's coercive speech: the American Civil Liberties Union.[25]

The ACLU's defense of Ford on First Amendment grounds shocked many in the labor movement who had come to know the organization for its vigorous defense of civil rights for workers. There had always been a palpable distrust of government, however, among the civil libertarians of the ACLU. The organization had been founded in opposition to the federal government's coercive power during the First World War, when the Espionage and Sedition acts effectively nullified the Bill of Rights and sent many dissidents to jail. A distrust of government born during the Palmer Raids was still evident in 1935, when ACLU director Roger Baldwin initially opposed the National Labor Relations Act on the grounds that the NLRB would inevitably be subordinated to business interests and shackle the labor movement. Others on the ACLU board forced Baldwin to rescind his public opposition and remain neutral, and he and other libertarians soon came to welcome the law's protection of free speech for workers. But the NLRB's order restraining Ford's speech roused their underlying distrust of government power—a power used here for good, perhaps, but with the potential for inviting future tyranny.[26]

This was hardly a unanimous opinion within the ACLU. "The idea of the Civil Liberties Union collaborating with labor's enemy," recalled ACLU secretary Lucille Milner, "was unthinkable to many on [its] Board." It was equally repellant to Goodman, who drafted a statement for the Civil Rights Federation opposing the ACLU's position before the federal appeals court. Goodman hoped, as he wrote to David Saposs in the NLRB's Washington headquarters, "to clarify the issue in the minds of the American people as one of industrial relations clearly within the province of the National Labor Relations Act," and therefore not a matter of First Amendment rights. The CRF recognized Ford's right to state his opinion on the public airwaves or in the press, as the Reverend Owen Knox stated while presenting Goodman's brief to the media. "We see no violation of the constitutional guarantee of free speech or press in prohibiting an employer from coercing and intimidating his employees, by obvious though indirect threats, so as to deprive them of their right to self organization." Goodman believed that the ACLU "will be put away [*sic*] out on the limb on this matter," as he wrote in March of 1940 to Carol King, a fellow Guild member in New York.[27]

When the appeals court finally rendered a decision the following October, it was a mixed result for the UAW. In a unanimous decision written by Judge Charles Simons, the court ordered Ford to reinstate twenty-three of the twenty-four workers named in this particular case, and to cease and desist from "threatening, assaulting, beating, or in any other manner interfering" with union leafleters in the vicinity of the Rouge plant. But in a victory for Ford and employers generally, the court also distinguished between *explicit* threats to punish union supporters, which were illegal, and the *implied* threats contained in Ford's antiunion propaganda. Ironically, the court cited the very existence of the NLRB as the principal reason for refusing to curtail Ford's speech. With passage of the Wagner Act, wrote Judge Simons, "the servant no longer has occasion to fear the master's frown of authority or threats of discrimination for union activities." Therefore, since "it is fundamental that the basic rights guaranteed by the Constitution belong equally to every person," Ford was free to express his opposition to the union in whatever extravagant tones he chose, and workers—protected now by the NLRB—were free to ignore him. It apparently did not occur to Judge Simons that a process requiring more than three years to adjudicate was not one that most workers would find reassuring, particularly when, as the court noted, "the orders of the Board are preventive and remedial and not in any sense punitive." The court here revealed the very weaknesses of the law that would compromise its protections for decades to come: if due process required years of hard litigation before the NLRB's orders were upheld, and if those orders were in no way punitive, then the servant might well have reason to "fear the master's frown of authority."[28]

When the Supreme Court refused to review this decision in February 1941, the notice of denial pointedly stated that Justice Frank Murphy "took no part" in its consideration. In his previous roles as Detroit's mayor and Michigan's governor, he had played a central part in the events at issue (declaring, for example, that the difference between Ford's guards and the Dearborn police was "a legalistic one"). He therefore withdrew from the case. In a decision he wrote later that year, however, Murphy indicated his support for the position argued by the NLRB and Goodman, ruling in *Virginia Electric* that when an employer blatantly and repeatedly suppressed the free speech of union supporters, then management's "language . . . merges with conduct" and should be restrained—just as the free speech of picketers could also be restrained in cases where picketing "substantially" endangered public safety. This decision hardly ended the debate, however, over management's latitude in disparaging the union in the workplace.[29]

In the Ford case, it was the court order reinstating fired workers—not the issue of free speech for management—that dominated public attention. The long delay in resolving this litigation would have deflated most organizing drives, but the Ford campaign was the rare case in which workers refused to be cowed, and the UAW was able to revive the struggle in the late summer of 1940. As Ford finally acquiesced to one reinstatement order after another, the return of tens, then hundreds of fired workers to their jobs demonstrated in the most dramatic way the limits of Henry Ford's power. The organizing drive was in full stride by February 1941, with over fifty organizers in the field and hundreds of volunteers from across Detroit's labor movement signing up Ford workers in neighborhood offices. Seven regular radio programs supporting the drive were carried on local stations, and volunteers distributed fifty thousand copies every week of the union's newspaper. Open recruitment was still difficult inside the plant, where only the most dedicated union activists dared to take on the Service Department's "gestapo," as Bennett's men were known. Many of these union stalwarts at the Rouge had long experience in the underground networks of support that stretched back to the 1920s and early 1930s, when only Communist organizers had effectively challenged Ford's dictatorial rule. Goodman came to know and respect these men as they took a leading role in the UAW's organizing drive. It was a diverse group that included immigrant and second-generation workers as well as a sizable number of African Americans. Among them were Art McPhaul and Dave Moore, two black workers who would be elected to union office in majority-white units of the Rouge complex. Years later, both would also be Goodman's clients during the Red Scare of the 1950s.[30]

At the Rouge, where Ford's sympathy for Hitler was well known and union organizers faced gangsters and ex-cops, being a Communist was not a handicap within the UAW. Victor Reuther, himself a factional opponent of the Communists within the union, nevertheless recalled years later that "the Communists at that stage, when we were organizing the union, had a damn good reputation of being a militant group—a group that would be up in the morning early to distribute leaflets, and would not shirk their responsibilities, would take any task." The Communist Party was especially prominent at the Rouge, with several hundred members "scattered throughout practically every section of that huge plant," recalled "Little" John Anderson, another factional opponent of the CP-USA. For years to come, local members would elect Communists as well as non-Communists to office, even after the political tide in the labor movement had turned against the Left. Goodman settled into this milieu as the local's trusted lawyer, forging lifelong friendships with leftists and fellow travelers. These included a young African American named Coleman Young. The future mayor of Detroit had just been fired from Ford and was now active in supporting the UAW drive through the National Negro Congress.[31]

The drive's gathering momentum came to a head the night of 1 April 1941, when Ford fired five more union supporters in the pressed steel building, provoking a strike that quickly spread throughout the dozens of factories in the complex. The next day, an estimated ten thousand strikers and supporters were massed at the gates and blockading the surrounding streets, confronting a smaller force of Service Department men and loyal workers who sortied out of the plant in violent attacks on the picket lines. The fact that most of the strikebreakers were recently hired African Americans and most of the picketers were white gave these confrontations the ominous hue of a race riot. The majority of the Rouge's twelve thousand black workers had left the plant at the start of the strike, but there was still considerable support in the black community for Henry Ford, whose policy of hiring African Americans into production jobs contrasted favorably with the whites-only practices of most employers and AFL unions. The overwhelming majority of black ministers supported Ford for these reasons, but younger African Americans were challenging the company's paternalistic conduct. They pointed to the concentration of most black workers in the foundry, where working conditions were harsh and the Service Department was equally brutish. While the majority of black workers held back from the union, a growing minority was gravitating toward the UAW-CIO and its promise of inclusive membership.[32]

The national NAACP weighed in on this debate by condemning a company strategy that seemed to hinge first on provoking a race riot, then calling for the National Guard to "restore order" and disperse the picket lines. Such a strategy seemed perilously close to success on 3 April when Ford's lawyers, appearing before federal judge Arthur Tuttle, blamed the violence on Communists and said the lawlessness was escalating to the point where "nothing short of an army" could restore order. The judge signed a temporary injunction against mass picketing that day, but set it aside until the following morning while Goodman and Jack Tucker gathered evidence that Ford had initiated the picket line attacks. The next day's edition of the *Detroit News* featured a photo of Goodman and Tucker, joined by UAW-CIO president R. J. Thomas, presenting subpoenas to the U.S. marshal for service on Harry Bennett and Henry Ford, ordering them to appear for questioning. Goodman's heated courtroom exchange with Ford's lawyer was front-page news, Goodman charging that "the Ford company itself comes into court with unclean hands." The subpoenas were never delivered but the court hearing dragged on for a week, postponing any intervention by the judge. As the days passed and the union cut the number of pickets, the violence abated and the issue lost its urgency.[33]

By the second week in April, the tide had turned in the union's favor as the local NAACP and a growing number of black community leaders, led by the Reverends Charles Hill and Horace White, endorsed the UAW-CIO on its promise to win equal pay for equal work regardless of race. When the strike finally ended with Ford's agreement to abide by an NLRB election, the outcome of the voting was a foregone conclusion: fewer than two thousand of the seventy-four thousand ballots from the Rouge plant favored "no union"—just 2.6 percent of the vote. The UAW-CIO was the landslide winner with 70 percent of the returns, the remainder going to the discredited UAW-AFL, now openly a company union endorsed by Bennett himself. "The UAW-CIO is ready to draw the curtain on the past," said a magnanimous R. J. Thomas after this stunning victory, and "we hope the Ford Motor Company will do likewise." With Ford's humiliating defeat in the NLRB balloting, Bennett was temporarily eclipsed by Edsel Ford, who negotiated a pattern-setting agreement with the UAW. In an accompanying settlement of the outstanding NLRB cases, Ford agreed to reinstate 1,836 fired workers with back pay and to arbitrate the remaining 2,184 individual claims not yet placed in formal board orders. The first check in this back-pay award amounted to $7 million, no small amount at a time when a production worker's wages rarely topped $1 an hour.[34]

At a subsequent celebration of the back-pay award to fired workers, the "photo op" included Sugar and Goodman standing among the beaming veterans of the Ford drive. "The nation's toughest and biggest anti-labor citadel," noted the *Daily Worker*, had "crumbled before the CIO."[35]

The Politics of War and Peace

When picketers and strikebreakers clashed on Miller Road that April, both sides linked the class war in Dearborn to the shooting wars in Europe and Asia. Each claimed that their adversary was the greater threat to national security. "This shows an extremely unpatriotic attitude on the part of the Communistic element to ruin our national-defense effort," Harry Bennett had claimed on the second day of the strike. The union responded in kind. "The Ford company has attempted to sabotage the national defense program," said Goodman, quoted in front-page coverage by the *Detroit News*, "because of its Nazi connection, including foreign investments."[36]

With changes only in name and place, the same scenario played itself out in hundreds of strikes and organizing drives during 1941. The looming prospect of war had triggered a massive increase in military spending, pumping billions of dollars into a reviving economy. Mass unemployment gave way to labor shortages as the consumer price index and corporate profits spiraled upward. Emboldened by the booming demand for their labor and goaded by speedup and the erosion of their purchasing power, workers joined unions and went on strike in numbers that surpassed all but the peak years of 1937 and 1919. The strikers marched under the American flag and questioned the patriotism of obstructionist employers. Company managers, on the other hand, were quick to invoke national security as justification for strikebreaking, and the U.S. War Department was just as quick to second their claims.

The federal government soon became a direct participant in collective bargaining. In most cases, federal officials served as mediators, cajoling labor and management into compromise settlements. "Whatever stands in the way of speed and efficiency in defense preparations must give way to the national need," said President Roosevelt, who enlisted business support by appointing corporate leaders and Republicans to administer his defense program. Their priorities were clear. "To prepare for war in a capitalist economy," wrote Henry Stimson, the lifelong Republican appointed by FDR as secretary of war, "you have to let business make money out of the process or business won't work." The government's sometimes heavy-handed intervention in local disputes met with resistance during 1941 as strikers in many cases defied government proposals to accept terms favoring the employer. As these picket line battles intensified, so did congressional support for laws to limit the right to strike, and worse. "I would not hesitate one split second," said Representative Hatton Summers of Texas, chairman of the House Judiciary Committee, "to enact legislation to send [strikers] to the electric chair."[37]

As a frequent spokesman for the CRF, Goodman took to the airwaves on station WJBK to condemn the invocation of national security as a pretext for attacking unions and workers. "We are told," Goodman said in a fifteen-minute talk on 8 June 1941, "that for the sake of national defense we must make sacrifices. . . . The common people of this country are accustomed to sacrifice. But people prominent in public life, newspapers, columnists and others are now telling us that for the sake of national defense, we should sacrifice our democratic rights." Goodman catalogued a lengthy list of victims in what he saw as a rightward drift toward a garrison state:

> Already, aliens have been registered and fingerprinted, mass arrests have already taken place, and a bill now before Congress threatens them with concentration camps. Already the Negro people are being victimized by a policy of segregation and discrimination in the army, navy, and air force. Already, anti-Semitism, the inevitable result of economic discontent, has begun to rise. Already, political and religious minorities are being suppressed and discriminated. Already, the threat is being made to take away the right to strike and many of labor's recent gains. In each case, it is the common man's rights that are in danger.[38]

Goodman was acutely aware of the dangers confronting America in the world and made it clear to his radio audience that he regarded fascism as the paramount threat. He spoke as a diehard partisan of the Popular Front, or what was left of it after the CP-USA's leap to the opposing corner. Goodman avoided the polemical slugfest over the European war and spoke as if nothing had changed since 1939. The CP-USA might publicly defend the terms of the Hitler-Stalin pact and denounce Roosevelt for supporting British and French imperialism, but Goodman said nothing about the pact or U.S. policy toward the European war. He took France to task only for its failure to mobilize a broad-based resistance to Hitler. The French, he explained to listeners, had succumbed to the Nazis because their rulers had destroyed trade unions and attacked democratic rights well before the German invasion, demoralizing its people and weakening their national unity. Goodman's gloss on a problematic history was open to question, but there was little to oppose in his call for a broad-based unity "against fascism and all its manifestations, abroad or at home." The current crop of antilabor and anti-alien bills clearly subverted that unity and jeopardized the "best defense against foreign enemies." Any group "denied the benefits of democracy," he continued, "cannot be expected to give democracy that full measure of devotion which a national emergency requires." Where the CP-USA sloganeered that the "Yanks are not coming" to the defense of the British Empire, Goodman focused solely on the antifascist struggle and assumed that war was unavoidable. "We must make our country a democracy in which all the people have a stake to defend," he told the listeners of WJBK. "The achievement of such a unity will present an impregnable defense against fascism."[39]

Rather than break with his coalition partners in the Civil Rights Federation, Goodman had spoken as if the Hitler-Stalin pact did not exist.

Two weeks later, it no longer did. On 22 June 1941, Hitler abandoned his détente with Stalin and launched a surprise attack on the Soviet Union. This sudden turn of events would dramatically alter the political landscape again, prompting yet another about-face by the CP-USA. It was now, once more, militantly antifascist and pledged to go "All Out for Victory." Goodman set aside whatever qualms he had about the party's zigzagging and welcomed the return to a united front against Hitler. "We breathed a sigh of relief," he recalled years later, "a remarkable release of tension."[40]

To reemphasize its Popular Front credentials, the CRF steering committee asked Goodman and John Zier, a fellow member of the editorial committee, to draft a statement of policy in the first week of November 1941. Previous civil rights organizations, wrote Goodman and Zier, had been narrowly based on "a small group of liberal minded persons." The CRF, in contrast, "placed the burden of the battle on the shoulders of those who have the greatest stake in it: the people themselves." Uniting CIO and AFL unions, churches, fraternal organizations, "all races, all nationalities, civic organizations, professional groups, women, [and] youth," the CRF had never advocated a specific foreign policy for America, nor did it intend to now. "We will continue, as we have in the past, to point out to our affiliates and our friends the dangers which confront our civil liberties, and the directions from which those dangers stem, whether it be from fascism abroad, or from fascists at home."[41]

Homegrown liberals and leftists might also threaten civil liberties, as the CRF acknowledged in a further statement marking the organization's distance from the opposing claims of the Roosevelt administration and the Communist Party. At the November delegate meeting, the CRF's steering committee issued a report condemning the prosecution of the Minneapolis Teamsters under the recently passed Smith Act. The case had gained national prominence in July when the Justice Department sought indictments against the leaders of Teamster Local 544, a left-wing union known for its leadership of the 1934 general strike in Minneapolis. The twenty-eight indicted were all members of the Socialist Workers Party (SWP), a Trotskyist group that had vigorously condemned FDR for his military support of Britain. Though there was no evidence of any actual effort or plan to overthrow the government, the defendants were charged with *conspiring* to advocate such a plan in the future. The Civil Rights Federation joined the ACLU and many other civil rights groups in condemning the transparent political calculation that actually motivated the government's action. "The indictments," the CRF's steering committee noted, "were handed down immediately following the switching of affiliations by the local from AFL to CIO, and a request by Dan Tobin, president of the AFL Teamsters International, that the Federal government take action against the local." Tobin, as president of the Democratic Party's National Labor Committee, had considerable influence in party circles, and the White House had acted accordingly, using the murky language of the Smith Act to punish the Teamster president's internal rivals.[42]

It was a dramatic confirmation of the dangers posed by a law designed to justify a witch hunt against the Left, but in a remarkable display of political myopia, the CP-USA actually *endorsed* the proceedings against the left-wing Teamsters. The international Communist movement regarded any group aligned with Leon Trotsky, Stalin's past opponent in the Soviet Communist Party, as a mortal enemy; since the SWP was Trotskyist, the CP-USA reflexively welcomed the indictments against its leaders. The Communist Party, in short, was prepared to endorse the prosecution of its rivals on the left even though the means for doing so—the Smith Act—was ultimately intended as a weapon against the CP-USA.[43]

The CRF's steering committee, in contrast, aligned itself on this occasion with the non-Communist Left, no doubt over the objections of its CP-USA members who were able to delay, but not block, the call for unity with the SWP defendants. As the organization's chief counsel, Goodman was likely the coauthor of the CRF resolution, which happened to dovetail with the position taken by his chief clients in the labor movement: "The Steering Committee, believing that the case is essentially one of political persecution and a threat to labor's freedom, has joined with the CIO, the UAW, and numerous other organizations in protest against the prosecution."[44]

Few noticed, however, when the eighteen individuals convicted under the Smith Act were sentenced to prison on 8 December 1941. The day before, Japanese bombers had attacked Pearl Harbor, killing twenty-four hundred servicemen and plunging the United States into a global war that would irrevocably change Detroit and the country.

With war declared on Japan and Germany, most Americans on the left and right rallied to the common cause, promising the kind of national unity that Goodman had envisioned the previous summer. The Soviet Union was now a wartime ally, and with this abrupt change in status many Americans agreed with British prime minister Winston Churchill that "any man or state who fights on against Nazidom will have our aid." Government surveillance of CP-USA members continued, but legal harassment abated and, to signal the new détente, President Roosevelt commuted the prison sentence of CP-USA leader Earl Browder. In light of the new alignment of global war, the government also secretly revised Goodman's status as a potential security threat. Ten weeks after Pearl Harbor, FBI director Hoover sent a memo to the bureau's Detroit office concerning "the classification, as to dangerousness, of the individuals under consideration for custodial detention." With left-wingers now officially considered less of a security threat, Goodman was assigned to Group C, meaning he would be "subjected to general surveillance" but would not be "interned in the event of war," as would those in Group A.[45]

Within weeks of the attack on Pearl Harbor, the president also convened a national conference of labor and management and asked the two sides to reach a common accord. CIO and AFL leaders responded with a voluntary pledge to forgo strikes and to submit workplace disputes to binding arbitration before the newly established War Labor Board (WLB). The Civil Rights Federation's steering committee welcomed these initiatives in its January report to the delegate conference, noting that in the face of "this grave national crisis, requiring the maximum of national unity," Congress had dropped the antilabor bills heading toward passage before Pearl Harbor. "This voluntary, democratic solution was seen by the entire nation as infinitely preferable to the hysterical, repressive measures proposed by the labor-baiters in Congress."[46]

The spirit of wartime unity, however, would be sorely tested over the next four years by the tectonic shifts in population and policy that total war set in motion. Drawn by the promise of war work, some 440,000 whites and 60,000 blacks would flock to Detroit between 1940 and 1943, more than matching the outward flow of men mustered into the armed forces. The city ballooned into the surrounding countryside in a sudden burst of suburbanization, north into Warren and west to Ypsilanti, as corporations turned farmland into sprawling defense complexes building everything from tanks to bombers to antiaircraft guns. It was a boon for Depression-era workers who could not remember having a steady job before Pearl Harbor, and an especially heady time for women and African Americans hired into factory jobs previously closed to them. Support for the war effort was broad and deep, marked by the thousands who planted victory gardens to supplement food supplies, the local unions that used strike funds to purchase war bonds, and the general public's patient compliance with wartime rationing.[47]

The expanding warfare state was rapidly eclipsing the New Deal's welfare state. The field of administrative law grew with breathtaking speed as the federal government took charge of America's economy and workforce, issuing binding orders through the War Labor Board, the War Production Board, and a galaxy of federal agencies tooled for total war. Negotiating the arcane legal practices of these administrative agencies

was enough to swamp Sugar's modest staff, but there were also the demands of a rapidly growing UAW membership, now topping 1 million as
war work swelled the union's ranks. During the chaotic conversion to
military production, much of Goodman's time was taken up with hearings before Michigan's Unemployment Compensation Commission, where
he argued the case for paying benefits to workers on short-term layoffs
as their plants were retooled. "Additional lawyers were needed," Goodman later wrote, "to represent the international officers of the UAW, the
new UAW locals springing up in all directions in Detroit, and also to represent individual workers when they were injured on the job, or when
they wanted to write a will or get a divorce or defend a criminal case."
The ranks of Sugar's associates grew accordingly in 1942 as Mort Eden
and Harry Anbender joined Goodman, Tucker, and Smokler in the firm's
General Division. Attorney Ben Marcus meanwhile took the leading role
in a separate Workmen's Compensation Division.[48]

Mobilization for war also had a personal dimension for Goodman and
his associates, since it was unclear for many months what their final status
would be regarding military conscription. With two young boys at home,
Goodman was initially exempted by the widespread sentiment against
drafting fathers, but this would change. Less than two years after Pearl
Harbor, it was clear that global war demanded higher levels of recruitment, and in October of 1943 Goodman lost his 3-A status and became
1-A, eligible for induction to the military at the age of thirty-seven. Like
much else in his personal and professional life, this too was secretly
monitored by the Detroit FBI, which had the assurance of the local draft
board that the bureau "would be notified in the event the Subject is in-
ducted into the armed forces." The FBI also knew from one of its informants that the UAW had requested a deferment for its associate counsel,
whose role in arbitration and representation of Detroit's workers made
him a contributor to uninterrupted production in the war plants. Like
thousands of other Michigan workers—from bus drivers to farmers to
toolmakers—whose work made an economic contribution to the home
front, Goodman would eventually be classified as "a necessary man" and
exempted from the draft.[49]

The role he and others played in the wartime regulation of the labor
market would be sorely tested. The initial unity of purpose that followed
Pearl Harbor had inevitably faded with the endless slog of overtime,
speedup, and rising prices. Workers, in particular, harbored a mounting
frustration with employers who reaped the easy profits of cost-plus contracts, even as they demanded sacrifice from hard-pressed workers. The
War Labor Board was swamped by thousands of workplace disputes over

discipline and workload, leading to bureaucratic delays that typically ended with a decision favoring the company—the union representatives on the WLB outvoted by business and "public" members (the latter consisting of academics and corporate lawyers). Wildcat strikes over unresolved grievances flared throughout the war despite the opposition of top union leaders. Most walkouts ended within one or two shifts, but the sheer number—with Detroit leading all other cities—surpassed the peak years of the 1930s.[50]

There was a shadowy underside to this factory unrest. Many white men nursed a smoldering resentment toward the newly hired African Americans and women working in factories where the new arrivals had once been excluded. This sudden and massive breach of the workplace color line was especially threatening to those who saw black workers as competitors for jobs and housing, or worse, as dangerous interlopers in a white world. "Here we have the feeling," the WLB's regional director said of Detroit, "of sitting on top of a smoldering volcano, which may explode at any time."[51]

The fallout from these rapid changes in the factory and community would dominate Goodman's life during the war, first in matters of union organizing, and second in matters of race and civil rights. One would take him to the Supreme Court by way of Texas, the other to citywide prominence when the volcano, in fact, erupted.

From River Rouge to Goose Creek

The small town of Goose Creek on the Gulf coast of Texas was more than fifteen hundred miles from Detroit, but it was closely related to the fate of labor in Michigan and every northern state. "As long as the south remains unorganized," the CIO had declared as early as 1939, "it constitutes the nation's Number One economic problem and is also a menace to our organized movement in the north." With the dramatic expansion of war industry into the South, the CIO resolved in 1941 to make union organizing in Texas and elsewhere "the No. 1 task before the CIO." Goodman would soon be enlisted to play a key role in that struggle.[52]

To develop a legal strategy for labor's southern organizing drive, the CIO's general counsel, Lee Pressman, convened a meeting of labor lawyers in the summer of 1943. Chief among their concerns was the growing number of laws passed by southern legislatures that curtailed or suppressed the rights of unions and union organizers. Texas was a prime example. In 1943, the state legislature passed the Manford Act requiring union organizers to register and get a license from the Texas secretary of state before they could speak to workers and urge them to join the union. Similar bills in other southern states posed the same threat to free speech as the Dearborn handbill ordinance: in all such cases, government officials who opposed unions could give the color of law to practices that would hamper, if not prevent, communication between organizers and potential members. The CIO's attorneys debated how they should go about challenging these legal obstacles.[53]

"There were two proposals on the floor for final decision," Goodman later recalled of the lawyers' meeting in New York City. "One was that the unions ask for an injunction to prevent [or] prohibit the state from enforcing these laws on the grounds they were unconstitutional, which would mean you'd get before a judge—no jury—and the judge would examine the law and make a decision as to whether [it] was constitutional or not." Pressman and most of the others at the meeting favored this approach. Goodman and Sugar argued for a different strategy. "We decided it would be much more effective," Goodman remembered years later, "if we made it a more human thing."

> Our proposal was that we test it [by getting] the most important person we could—in this case, we suggested Phil Murray, who was the president of the CIO—to be that person and to go to Texas and find a good meeting . . . and have him get up at that meeting . . . and ask someone to join the union, and as a result of this speech, have him arrested. That would get national and international attention not only to Phil Murray and that particular law, but to all similar laws in the South. Well, there was a long discussion, and [the majority] finally voted against that.[54]

While others wanted a judge to declare the law invalid on its face, Goodman and Sugar were arguing for the same combination of legal action and civil disobedience that had overturned the Dearborn ordinance and secured public support for the union. Returning to Detroit, they resolved to implement their strategy without the CIO. They asked UAW president R. J. Thomas if he would go to Texas to give an organizing speech, inviting arrest and providing a high-profile opportunity to test the law. Thomas, not known for shying away from confrontations—he had, after all, been arrested outside Ford's River Rouge plant for challenging Dearborn's leafleting ban—readily agreed. "I was assigned the job of going to Texas and developing this whole test case from the ground up," Goodman recalled. "From the start, this was a wonderful opportunity [because] I knew this was the kind of case that would go before the U.S. Supreme Court. I was about to be able to build that case up from scratch in a way I thought would be most effective." The test would take place at a rally of Humble Oil refinery workers sponsored by the Oil Workers International Union at the city hall near Goose Creek.[55]

On Tuesday, 22 September, Thomas flew from Detroit to Texas. Goodman had arrived earlier and hired Herman Wright, a local lawyer and a vice president of the National Lawyers Guild, to help. They soon learned that Thomas would face arrest not only for violating the Manford Act but also for violating the state's newly issued court injunction that prohibited Thomas from giving any speech at all. "Every radio station was carrying stories [about] this union-organizer Yankee from up North coming down to Texas to flout our laws," Goodman remembered. There were "screaming headlines: 'Carpetbaggers of the 20th Century!'" At the airport, Goodman broke the news to Thomas that he might have to go to jail for violating the injunction. He later recalled the ensuing exchange with the UAW's gruff and amiable president. "'What's the biggest rap I can get out of this?' [Thomas] asked. 'Well,' I said, . . . 'all you can do is three days in jail and a hundred-dollar fine.' 'Oh, shit,' he said, 'I can do that standing on my head.'"[56]

The *Houston Chronicle* began its story on the coming event with Thomas's defiant words: "I'm going to violate the law." So heavy was the turnout of oil workers the next evening that the rally was moved from inside city hall to a nearby bean field. As dusk approached, organizers lit large torches. "It was a dark night and a fascinating scene," Goodman remembered. A thousand or more workers filled the field, sitting on folding chairs that had been brought out of city hall, with the overflow standing along the sides. All around were Texas Rangers with their white hats, badges, and guns. Mayor C. L. Olive welcomed the crowd, and the local leader of the oil workers introduced R. J. Thomas. It took the UAW president forty-five minutes to read his speech, which ran to twenty-six typewritten pages—written out, Goodman emphasized, so that when the case got to the Supreme Court, there would be no doubt what Thomas had said. Knowing that the Manford Act specifically proscribed "soliciting" union membership without a license, Thomas ended his speech by asking people to come up and sign union membership cards.[57]

Surprisingly, Thomas's solicitation wasn't sufficient to warrant arrest. "The Assistant Attorney General came over to me and Herman Wright and said, 'It's not good enough. He has to solicit a particular person; otherwise, it may not be a violation.'" Sheriff's deputies had been ordered, in fact, not to arrest any speaker unless he asked someone *by name* to join the union. "Well, we weren't about to do all this for nothing," Goodman recalled. Union organizers quickly corralled a willing listener and sent his name on a note to Thomas. "You must say this before you stop speaking," Goodman wrote on it. With that, Thomas told the crowd, "I'm going to ask one person in this crowd to come up and join the union." When the crowd saw who was coming forward to fill out a membership application, "there were loud laughs," Goodman remembered, because the man being solicited happened to be a foreman. That direct solicitation was enough, however, for the authorities to move into action. They arrested Thomas and two other union leaders, taking them off to be booked before Goose Creek's justice of the peace. Thomas paid the $400 bail that allowed him to leave Goose Creek, pending his return the following month to face charges for violating the court injunction.[58]

The arrest of Thomas was applauded by most of the Texas media, but it drew a scathing condemnation by J. Frank Dobie, a newspaper columnist and University of Texas professor. Dobie minced no words in denouncing the Manford Act in the pages of the *Houston Post*. "A man can stand up anywhere in Texas . . . and without interference invite people, either publicly or privately, to join the Republican Party, the Holy Rollers, the Liars Club, the Association for Anointing Herbert Hoover as a Prophet, the Texas Folklore Society—almost any kind of organization. . . . But it is against the law in Texas for a man, unless he pays a license and signs papers of one kind or another, to invite any person or persons to join a labor union."[59]

When Thomas returned for his trial on the injunction charges, the courtroom atmosphere was unlike anything Goodman had seen back home in Michigan. "It was an old courtroom," he recalled, where "the judge sat way up on a high bench and there were lawyers and onlookers and other people around there, and you could smoke—cigars, cigarettes, whatever you wanted. That was part of the frontier tradition yet in Texas." When Thomas—who chewed tobacco—came before Judge J. Harris Gardner, "he started sort of looking around, and the judge said, 'Mr. Thomas, you got chewing tobacco? Go ahead and chew. Bailiff, come up here and bring up that spittoon there for Mr. Thomas.'" After this show of courtesy, Gardner still found Thomas guilty and sentenced him to the penalty that Goodman had predicted, a $100 fine and three days behind bars. But after spending a few hours in the jail office and kitchen, Thomas was released on $1,000 bond, while Goodman prepared an appeal to the state supreme court.[60]

On 19 October, Goodman and Assistant Attorney General Fagan Dickinson squared off before the court in Austin, Goodman arguing that licensing provisions like those under the Manford Act were unconstitutional because they infringed on free speech, and Dickinson maintaining that the act was no more than "a very mild, gentle attempt of the legislature to regulate unions, and this particular [registration] section is for their benefit." Not so, responded Goodman. Even though the license might be cheap and easy to get, free speech must really be free, and not merely cheap. "If an organizer is not able to obtain a permit card at an opportune moment, he loses the opportunity to solicit a membership, or if he does not obtain one and asks a person to join a union he is subject to $500 fine and 60 days in jail." Free speech—in this case, of a worker asking a fellow worker to join a union—is not a commercial enterprise subject to regulation, Goodman argued, but an essential right granted by the Constitution and extended to the states by the Fourteenth Amendment. The judges thought otherwise, ruling against Thomas on the basis of precedents involving the licensing of insurance agents and real estate brokers. Their ruling paved the way for taking the case to the U.S. Supreme Court.[61]

On 1 May 1944, as the Allies prepared for D-Day and as workers from Moscow to New York celebrated May Day, Goodman, not yet forty years old, found himself for the first time before the U.S. Supreme Court defending the freedom of unions to organize without prior approval from the state. Goodman knew it would be a tough case, even with a liberal majority on the nine-member court. Justices Frank Murphy and Wiley Rutledge were generally inclined to protect individual freedoms against intrusive legislation, but others in the liberal majority, including Justices Robert Jackson and especially Felix Frankfurter, held to a theory of "judicial restraint" that made them reluctant to overrule laws passed by elected state legislatures. Plunging into a debate that still echoes in today's courts, Goodman pressed his arguments with the help of CIO attorney Lee Pressman, who now supported the UAW's strategy for challenging the Texas law. Goodman welcomed Pressman's role. "Of course I wanted him in because I had never appeared in the United States Supreme Court," he acknowledged years later. Pressman, a graduate of Harvard Law and a former student of Frankfurter, had little patience for the kind of careful research that Goodman and Sugar invested in the writing of legal briefs, but the CIO's general counsel was well versed in the internal debates that divided the court and knew what arguments would be most effective with individual members.[62]

This was important because the union attorneys wanted the Court to rule not only that the Texas law was an unconstitutional denial of Thomas's free speech but also that unions differed from other organizations, particularly profit-driven commercial enterprises. Unions are democratic organizations of the people, Pressman and Goodman argued in their presentation to the Court, and should enjoy constitutional protections against state regulation. They were not operated for profit. As the *collective* voice of workers, they served as instruments through which workers exercised their civil liberties of free speech, press, and assembly. In this respect, a union organizer could be compared to a minister of a church, they insisted. When a labor organizer—or any worker, for that matter—asked another worker to join a union, he should be entitled to the same protection afforded by the Bill of Rights to a minister who asks someone to join his church. To deny unions this protection paved the way for denying it to churches and other membership organizations.[63]

The Court, paralyzed by philosophical divisions over whether state licensing would subvert free speech, asked the lawyers to return and reargue the case that October. Finally, in January 1945, some eighteen months after Thomas had given his speech in the Texas bean field, the justices ruled in the union's favor by the narrowest of margins, 5-4. Thomas's constitutional right of free expression had been violated by the Manford Act, the majority held, and no clear and present danger had been shown to justify these curbs on union organizing. "The threat of the restraining order, backed by the power of contempt, and of arrest for crime, [had] hung over every word" as Thomas spoke, wrote Justice Rutledge in the majority opinion. The Texas law had imposed only mild restrictions, but "it is from petty tyrannies that large ones take root and grow." Rutledge decisively rebuffed the Texas attorney general's contention that it was fine for Thomas to speak in favor of unions without a license so long as he didn't actively solicit membership. Obeying the strictures of the Manford Act, Rutledge wrote, "compels the speaker to hedge and trim. He must take care in every word to create no impression that he means . . . [to] ask those present to take action" and join the union.[64]

The Court's ruling in *Thomas v. Collins*, although greeted by Goodman as a ringing endorsement of free speech, was also a disappointment because the justices did not accept the premise that unions have a special role as the collective voice of workers, distinct from commercial enterprises. "We put aside the broader contentions both parties have made," Rutledge stated, "and confine ourselves to the narrow question" of Thomas's individual right to free speech. As noted by historian Gilbert Gall, "the CIO had found the most liberal Supreme Court of the twentieth century unable to reconceptualize labor liberty beyond an individual, rights-based nexus."[65]

Voting with Rutledge were Justices Murphy, Jackson, Hugo Black, and William Douglas. The dissenting justices included Felix Frankfurter, whom the UAW's *United Automobile Worker* castigated as "a one-time outstanding liberal" who was "veering in the direction of reaction in recent years." The "swing person on the court was Jackson," said Goodman, "who wrote a separate, concurring opinion in which he said Thomas had the absolute right to ask someone to join the union and the employer has the same right to tell employees they don't have to join." Goodman conjectured that Jackson's concurrence came only after some of the other justices had privately assured him that they would, in future cases, agree with him on this understanding of employers' rights.[66]

"It was a great ruling," said Goodman years later, justifiably proud of his work. The high court's decision made similar laws in other states invalid, and Goodman and Pressman moved quickly to win a decision in the Colorado Supreme Court overturning such a statute. It was the kind of outcome Goodman had always dreamed of. For him, the Texas case was "a fascinating tale of how a lawyer using a legal tool in connection with the workers' right to organize and to oppose oppressive law, could do a useful, educational, and important political job in the process."[67]

Under the Volcano

Reports of a coming race war had been mounting for many months. Migrating workers were crowding into the city in 1941, competing for scarce housing and scrambling to find a place on overcrowded buses and trolleys. As rents and tempers began to rise, so did reports of racial clashes. In August, whites on Detroit's east side attacked a black family living in a predominantly white area and "disfigured their 13 year old daughter with acid," according to Jack Raskin's report to the steering committee of the Civil Rights Federation. A crowd then "stoned their house, ruined its appearance with acid and tar," and attacked family members. The CRF and NAACP protested the lack of police protection and sent observers to stay with the family, but the racial divide was widening at an alarming rate, outpacing these case-by-case responses. The CRF report that August concluded that racial tensions on Detroit's north side were rooted in "the KKK and Black Legion background of the neighborhood," now marked by "the recent erection of an eight-foot concrete wall dividing the white and Negro neighborhoods."[68]

The war would put a match to this bone-dry kindling of racial antagonism, and not just in Detroit. One of the federal government's first acts in the months following Pearl Harbor was to arrest over nine thousand immigrant aliens, mostly Japanese and German, who the FBI had targeted for custodial detention. If Japan had attacked the United States six months earlier, before Hitler invaded Russia, it would have been Goodman and his colleagues on labor's left who would have been arrested and jailed for months or years. As it was, Pearl Harbor came after the Soviets had become U.S. allies and Japanese Americans were now the despised people. Anti-Japanese sentiment soon came to a boil on the West Coast, and military leaders decided that the FBI's custodial detention had been too selective. Two months after Pearl Harbor, they persuaded President Roosevelt to sign an executive order authorizing the forcible evacuation of 120,000 Japanese Americans from the West Coast to a dozen concentration camps in the interior. Japanese Americans were held to be uniformly dangerous as a *race*, and collectively stripped of their rights in February of 1942— the very month Goodman was reclassified as no longer deserving custodial detention.[69]

That same month, a virulent race consciousness fueled Detroit's first large-scale violence of the war. The focal point was the federal government's plan to open a segregated housing project on the north side of Detroit, to be either all black or all white, as the prevailing policy required. When the government finally decided that it would be an all-black housing project named after Sojourner Truth, the escaped slave of the pre–Civil War era, white property owners and realtors objected violently. On 28 February, more than one thousand white picketers blocked the road and attacked furniture trucks when the first black families tried to move in. A smaller crowd of African Americans fought back in an escalating street brawl that spread through the neighborhood, seriously injuring more than thirty people. After clearing the area with baton charges and repeated volleys of tear gas, the police arrested 217 African Americans and only three of the white instigators. Goodman joined with two African American colleagues, Lebron Simmons and Elvin Davenport, to argue that the arrest of African American protesters had violated their constitutional rights. All but nineteen were released, and only two would serve jail sentences. When African American families made a second attempt to enter the Sojourner Truth Homes, they did so under the protection of a thousand National Guardsmen, bayonets fixed.[70]

There was racial discord elsewhere in America, but nothing would match the looming explosion in Detroit, where the wartime labor shortage was redrawing the color line inside the city's factories. Pressured by A. Philip Randolph's highly publicized threat to march on Washington with ten thousand black workers unless defense jobs were desegregated, President Roosevelt had issued an executive order in 1941 ordering employers to open their factories to African Americans on an equal basis. As the pace of integration accelerated in Detroit, so did a white backlash, leading to dozens of "hate strikes" by whites refusing to work next to blacks. The growing conflict threatened to unravel the hard-won unity of the industrial union movement, prompting the Civil Rights Federation, the NAACP, and the Inter-Racial Committee of the UAW to organize an "Emergency Conference on the Fifth Column." The conference title referred to the Spanish civil war and the claim by one of Franco's generals in 1936 that the four columns of fascist troops attacking Madrid would be aided by an underground "fifth column" within the city. Conference organizers saw the hate strikes and the Sojourner Truth riot as evidence of a similar conspiracy in Detroit to aid fascist Germany.[71]

Goodman chaired the public meeting of the Emergency Conference in June of 1942, in which he and Jack Raskin described the evidence of KKK involvement in the hate strike of ten thousand white workers at the Hudson Naval Armory. "If these incidents are the result of concerted conspiracy," Goodman told the delegates, "they cannot be handled individually." The CRF had already published a thirty-six-page pamphlet, *Smash Detroit's Fifth Column*, that outlined such a conspiracy and focused special attention on the National Workers League (NWL), a Nazi front group that recruited some five hundred extremists in Detroit from the declining ranks of the Black Legion and the America First Committee. NWL leaders had helped organize the white picket lines at Sojourner Truth and they continued their agitation against black occupancy afterward. In nearby Highland Park, a reporter infiltrated an NWL meeting and reported that leaders Parker Sage and Garland Alderman "harangued against President Roosevelt and international Jewry" before introducing a man named Virgil Chandler as "the big fella" fighting "to keep dirty niggers out of the Sojourner Truth Homes." In a front-page article in the *Michigan Chronicle*, Goodman reminded readers that "the Klan and the National Workers League were spreading filthy anti-Semitic literature in Detroit factories . . . at the very same time they were brewing their cauldron of race hatred at Sojourner Truth." These "twin problems" of racism and anti-Semitism "will either be solved together or not at all."[72]

A federal grand jury eventually indicted Sage, Alderman, and Chandler on charges of conspiring to incite the riot at the Sojourner Truth homes, but the Justice Department said it could not find enough evidence to support the CRF's assertion that the Klan had also mobilized its far larger membership against the federal government. The delegates to the Emergency Conference, many of them veterans of previous clashes with the Black Legion, had little reason to doubt that a fifth column of pro-Hitler white supremacists was now conspiring to spread the violence to the plants. At the conference's close, they resolved to send the Emergency Committee to Washington and seek a federal grand jury to investigate the KKK. "We cannot wait for a long process of education," said the Reverend Charles

Hill, expressing the urgent concern of the black community. "We must use the forces of the law to enforce the President's order."[73]

Goodman's role as cocounsel for the Sojourner Truth defendants and chairman of the Emergency Conference did not escape the FBI's attention. Reflexively, the bureau's operatives were apprehensive about any mobilization led by African Americans and left-wingers, and they had reason to believe that it was Goodman who was leading the Civil Rights Federation in this direction. Confidential informant "T-12" reported to the Detroit FBI "on numerous occasions" that it was Goodman, "outwardly the legal counsel for the Federation," who was "in reality one of the leading figures" in the organization. John Bugas, head of the Detroit Bureau, sent a summary report to Washington that paraphrased T-12's observations:

> She has stated that Goodman takes a part in all Steering Committee and other meetings of the Federation, usually in the capacity of Chairman or speaker. She stated that [Executive Secretary] Raskin seldom proceeds with any plan for a program or conference without consulting Goodman for his opinion and advice. She also advised that many press releases, action letters and other literature distributed by the Federation are drawn up by Ernest Goodman and that if the work is done by Raskin, it is usually submitted to Goodman for his final approval.[74]

Goodman's intensive involvement in the Civil Rights Federation was welcomed by the UAW's top leaders because the union saw the value of a multiracial movement outside the factories preaching the same interracial unity that the union was promoting inside the workplace. But it meant something different to the Justice Department, which noted the prominent role of Communists in the CRF as well as "racial agitators" like the Reverend Hill. In their eyes, Goodman was advancing the same goals of racial integration as the CP-USA, and was therefore indistinguishable from it. The FBI's phone taps, informants, mail intercepts, and document analysis (including the inspection of office wastepaper) all indicated that Goodman was associating with known leaders of the CP-USA. If he wasn't a dues-paying member he was, in the bureau's estimate, a "key figure" in advancing the party's goals, and it was on this basis that the government began yet another reevaluation of Goodman's security classification. On the last day of June 1942, the War Division of the Department of Justice informed the FBI director that "in light of additional information received from the Bureau," Goodman's "tentative dangerousness classification" was being raised from the "general surveillance" of Group C to the somewhat more threatening status of Group B, whose members' activities were to be "restricted" in the case of a national emergency. In March 1943, Detroit Bureau chief John Bugas notified Hoover that Goodman's reclassification for custodial detention was again under consideration. Goodman, of course, knew nothing of these secret deliberations over his fate.[75]

All the while, as overcrowding and overwork eroded the tolerance of Detroit's workers, many were turning to racial stereotyping as an explanation for the frustrations of wartime life. Black servicemen on leave were especially loath to accept the second-class status that segregation demanded, and newly arrived blacks from the South, naively expecting to find racial equality, sometimes reacted with loud indignation to the many slights of a whites-only world. As the Detroit area's black population grew in size and assertiveness, many whites succumbed to an intense "Negrophobia," marked by widespread rumors that physical contact with blacks—touching the same machine, using the same toilet, sitting in the same streetcar—would transmit disease. The visceral nature of these beliefs was captured by historian Alan Clive: "In the minds of many angry, frightened whites, accidental contact with or occasional rudeness from individual blacks was magnified into a vast concealed conspiracy, the best-known manifestation of which was the rumor of a 'bump club.' This mythical organization purportedly enrolled blacks to jostle whites deliberately."[76]

Right-wing organizations inside the factories stoked these prejudices as they recruited whites newly hired to wartime industry and hostile to the UAW's call for racial equality. The National Workers League, the Dixie Voters, the Southern Society, and other shadowy groups added their voice to a resurgent Ku Klux Klan, which was challenging the UAW for control of several local unions. The Klan's efforts came closest to success in Local 190 at the Packard Motor Car plant, aided by managers who publicly argued that production work was "a white man's job." When twenty-five thousand whites struck Packard in June of 1943 to protest the government-mandated upgrading of black workers, UAW president R. J. Thomas vigorously denounced the "KKK and the rest of the nightshirt boys," promising that the union was "ready and willing to take them on." The Klan lost its bid to take over Local 190 and the UAW publicly supported the firing of the hate strike's leaders, but white supremacists continued their agitation. Chief among them was Gerald L. K. Smith, the former preacher and advisor to Louisiana senator Huey Long who moved to Detroit in 1939 and quickly gained a following among discontented whites. Smith saw himself as the heir to Father Coughlin, now silenced by the Catholic hierarchy, and broadcast his weekly tirades against desegregation over the same radio network that had carried the right-wing priest.[77]

For Goodman, the parallels between Smith and Europe's fascist leaders were obvious. Like Hitler, Smith enjoyed the financial support of wealthy industrialists, including Horace Dodge, Henry Ford, and Lewis Brown, president of Johns-Manville. Like Mussolini, Smith had specialized in aiding his corporate benefactors with strikebreaking and relentless attacks on left-wing labor leaders, routinely referring to Sidney Hillman of the CIO, for example, as an "atheistic, Communist Jew." Smith even called President Roosevelt a "secret" Jew and warned that Great Britain and Russia were greater dangers to the United States than Germany, with which he favored a negotiated peace. Time, Inc. produced a newsreel on Smith that compared him to Hitler and Mussolini, the narrator wondering at its close whether he was "a man of destiny or merely a political windbag." Many believed he might follow the same upward arc as Hitler, also once dismissed as a troublesome lunatic. Smith's political operation in Detroit was formidable, occupying an entire floor of the Industrial Bank Building and employing twenty-five to fifty clericals to conduct his direct-mail campaigns. Michigan's Senator Arthur Vandenberg and Representative Clare Hoffman read his speeches into the Congressional Record and called him a friend. His monthly magazine, *The Cross and the Flag*, railed against Jews, Communists, and the "promiscuous mixing" of races in factories and streetcars. Many whites found something to agree with in these jeremiads, including the 110,000 Republicans who voted Smith second in the three-man Senate primary of 1942, trailing Judge Homer Ferguson's 195,000 votes.[78]

Contemplating the toxic brew of racial antagonism that buoyed the likes of Smith, *Life* magazine concluded that "Detroit can either blow up Hitler or it can blow up the U.S."[79]

Detroit Explodes

The blast came on 20 June 1943, two weeks after the Packard hate strike. Beginning with racial skirmishes on the bridge to Belle Isle Park, the fighting spread downtown, fueled by rumors in both black and white neighborhoods that hoodlums of the opposing race had thrown a woman and her baby off the Belle Isle bridge. Black crowds along Hastings Street attacked white pedestrians in retaliation, and white crowds on Woodward Avenue assaulted any African American they found outside the ghetto. Police were quick to open fire on Hastings Street, shooting rioters and onlookers alike, but slow to respond at all on lower Woodward, where a white crowd of ten thousand gathered in Cadillac Square on the twenty-first, preparing to march on Hastings Street. The fighting ended only with the arrival of five thousand federal troops, but not before nine whites and twenty-five blacks had been killed.[80]

The neighborhoods of Goodman's youth had been the epicenter of disaster, now littered with broken glass and patrolled by military police. The white crowds in Cadillac Square on the riot's second day had mustered directly beneath the windows of the Sugar law firm, a painful spectacle for someone like Goodman who could remember CIO marchers arriving in the same square in 1937. It was now a different working class. Many of the militants from the sit-down era had been dispersed to the armed forces or to new plants outside the city. The recent arrivals were younger workers, women, and southern migrants, many with no union experience. The children of European immigrants were joining the armed forces and assimilating in varying degrees to a uniform status as "white," their families moving outward with the defense work to new subdivisions along the same outlying border of Eight Mile Road where Goodman had moved his family. He voted that fall for the CIO-endorsed candidate for mayor, but most of his neighbors cast their ballots for the incumbent, Edward Jeffries. In a campaign marked by the most overt race-baiting since the 1920s, Jeffries abandoned the liberal rhetoric of his recent past to defend the police department's indiscriminate shooting of blacks. He blamed "Negro hoodlums" for starting the riot and pledged to defend white neighborhoods against an "invasion" of black home buyers.[81]

When Jeffries won reelection with 56 percent of the vote, Goodman and his colleagues in the CRF had to confront the hard truth that in Detroit, a labor stronghold, the politics of race had trumped the politics of class. Understanding how this happened would occupy nearly as much of Goodman's time over the next year as the demands of his continuing work for the UAW and the Goose Creek case before the Supreme Court. Goodman and others focused on the media as the most immediate factor in Jeffries's victory, since all three daily papers and virtually every radio station had backed the mayor. But underlying this contributing cause was the deep reservoir of racial prejudice that had fueled the hate strikes over the previous two years, and it was Goodman who now took the lead in a series of public meetings and reports that plumbed the wellsprings of those violent events. In August, two months after the riot, he was the presiding chair at the CRF's "United We Stand" conference at the Masonic Temple, where four hundred delegates from across the state rejected the mayor's race-baiting and called for policies that would "remove the causes of discrimination and segregation of the Negro people in housing, recreation, education, employment, the armed forces and other places."[82]

As secretary of the Civil Rights Committee of the National Lawyers Guild, Goodman was also a coauthor of the Guild's post-riot report identifying the "one basic, continuing cause" of racial violence: "the persistent, irrational prejudice of the white against the Negro." In this detailed assessment of the violence, Goodman and his fellow committee members did not deny the contributing role of so-called black hoodlums, but noted that they were "the exact counterpart of the many white mobsters . . . growing up in city slums in ignorance, poverty, neglect, superstition and uncorrected delinquency." The black-on-white violence along Hastings Street was "a manifestation of hysterical defensiveness . . . which we believe [is] bitterly regretted by the vast majority of the negro community." It was, in any case, more than matched by the white-on-black violence on Woodward Avenue, where crowds attacked African Americans in full view of the police. Dismissing the widely held theories of white superiority, the report drew attention to the countless ways that "the white population condones or participates in daily discriminations designed to keep the Negro on a level of inferiority. And thus, by denial of opportunity to the Negro on a theory of utter falsity, a condition is created which gives apparent support to the theory." The committee pressed this point beyond the usual focus on street violence. "Let this also be clearly stated: That the sadistic cruelty of white mobs that dragged unoffending Negroes from street cars and automobiles and beat them to unconsciousness is merely the expression . . . of the same contemptuous prejudice that inspires more respectable whites to speak habitually of 'niggers.' "[83]

When Goodman sent this report to U.S. attorney general Francis Biddle in late July, he noted the additional evidence the Guild had gathered that "the riot was not spontaneous but was instigated by subversive individuals and organizations." He gave particular weight to the role of one Tony Lamarito, a recent employee of Gerald Smith who worked out of the offices of the National Workers League. Lamarito was pictured in the *Detroit Free Press* as an active participant in the rioting, leading Goodman to conclude that this "and considerable additional evidence of a similar character" warranted a thorough FBI investigation and a federal grand jury to evaluate the evidence. Biddle's assistant attorney general, Wendell Berge, promised in August to investigate, but nothing came of it.[84]

With no federal action against the Klan and no concerted government effort to address the underlying issues, there was good reason to expect further racial conflict. "The situation is still explosive," Goodman wrote in 1944. "The presence of thousands of troops . . . is quite an important item in preventing any major disturbance, although it doesn't solve any of the basic problems." To address these issues and develop a shared understanding of what was a stake, Goodman and the Civil Rights Federation organized an "Institute on Race Relations" to sponsor a remarkable series of seminars at Cass Technical High School in February through March of 1944. The more than five hundred participants represented the same constituency as the CRF's affiliated groups—unions, churches, civil rights organizations, and mutual-aid societies. While the "Six Week Course of Study for Community Action" placed a heavy emphasis on political mobilization, the institute's presentations and group discussions also explored a deeper analysis that in many ways anticipated the "revisionist history" of the 1960s and 1970s. In the opening session Dr. Max Yergan, president of the National Negro Congress, presented an overview of African civilization, a history of slavery and slave rebellions, and closed with a summary (following the seminal work of W. E. B. DuBois) of the positive contributions of the Reconstruction Era. Subsequent speakers presented scientific evidence that there were no significant genetic differences between the races and that race prejudice was a learned rather than innate feature of human psychology. "The brotherhood of man is a scientific fact," as Goodman summarized the evidence in his keynote speech.[85]

There was, however, a tension between these compelling claims of the social sciences and the less nuanced polemic of the campaign to "Smash the Fifth Column." Where the Lawyers Guild report of the previous year had focused on the white population's "daily discriminations" against blacks and the ways in which denial of opportunity gave "apparent support" to claims of racial inferiority, the institute's program emphasized that race hatred, as Goodman put it in his keynote address, was "the result of an attempt to obtain economic domination by a small powerful group against the mass of the people, utilizing prejudice . . . to keep [them] divided." The two claims—one emphasizing the broad and self-perpetuating basis of racism, the other the manipulative role of powerful elites—were not necessarily incompatible, but it was the latter claim that Goodman now highlighted in his call to suppress the fifth column.[86]

The evidence for a right-wing conspiracy had also changed, following the lead of Albert Kahn, the speaker at the institute's fifth session and the coauthor of Sabotage! The Secret War against America. "He pointed out that those of us who are concerned in dealing with the Fifth Column have completely mistaken the period in which we live," Goodman confessed in his wrap-up speech to the institute. "The enemy doesn't depend on physical sabotage but rather on psychological sabotage, making use of the prejudices that have existed among the American people." Race hatred strengthened the hand of those like Gerald Smith who favored a negotiated peace with the Nazis. They did Hitler's work, "consciously or unconsciously."

Goodman drew the harshest of conclusions: "We must put in jail those people openly and notoriously dividing the American people, creating race hatreds and prejudices and stimulating an atmosphere in which riots and other incidents of that kind are bound to occur."[87]

Without saying so, Goodman was drawing on the well-known axiom of Supreme Court Justice Oliver Wendell Holmes Jr., who held in 1919 that "the most stringent protection of free speech would not protect a man from falsely shouting fire in a theater and causing panic." Particularly in wartime, Holmes had ruled, the government could suspend the Bill of Rights in cases where dissident speech posed a "clear and present danger" to the state. Ironically, Holmes had articulated this principle to uphold the imprisonment of wartime opponents of conscription, including Maurice Sugar. Goodman would not have endorsed the imprisonment of those peaceful opponents of the wartime draft in 1917, but the hate speech of Gerald Smith and the Klan was another matter, no more deserving of protection than Ford's when such speech was specifically intended to deny the rights of others. Besides imprisonment of fifth columnists, Goodman also called for government action to shut down Gerald Smith's newspaper and deny him rental of space for meetings in the public schools. There was too much at stake, Goodman believed, not to take action. The war was now turning against the Axis powers, but the memory of the Blitzkrieg was barely two years old, and the toll of Nazi aggression had a personal dimension for Goodman and other Jewish Americans. The Wehrmacht, after all, had rolled across the same Russian provinces his parents had called home, sweeping up family members and millions of other victims for the death camps. Germany's defeat and unconditional surrender was still an urgent priority, and there was no telling what political calculus or new weapon—V2 rockets, jet fighters, a mega-bomb—might divert the Allies from this goal and produce a negotiated détente with Hitler. The Führer's allies in Detroit hoped for just such an outcome, and promoted the same anti-Semitic and racist ideas.[88]

President Roosevelt was equally concerned with these threats to the war effort and had, from Pearl Harbor onward, urged Attorney General Biddle to bring charges against pro-Nazi leaders. Under intense pressure from the White House, Biddle had reluctantly announced indictments in mid-1942 against a group of twenty-five antiwar fascists, charging them with conspiring to undermine the morale of the troops. Biddle, however, had little stomach for the case. A Philadelphia-born aristocrat and graduate of Harvard Law, he was also a committed civil libertarian and member of the ACLU who opposed the kind of government repression so evident during World War I. Biddle had argued against the military's decision to intern Japanese Americans and he had come to regret the Smith Act indictments that the president had pressured him to bring against the Socialist Workers Party. The SWP leaders had been guilty of nothing more than rhetorical excess, he concluded, and he now saw the prosecution of fascists as another "dreary and degrading experience" that had little to do with national security. The rancid hate speech that the defendants directed at Jews, blacks, and the president was reprehensible, but Biddle could find little evidence that these "wild-eyed . . . lunatic fringe characters" (as one press report described them) were conspirators acting in concert with the enemy. When the judge in the trial of antiwar fascists suddenly died during the proceedings, the prosecution ended in a mistrial and the government eventually dismissed the indictments at the end of the war.[89]

Goodman was much closer than Biddle to the repeated rounds of violence that swept Detroit, and he felt greater urgency about combating it. He also believed that the federal government was dragging its feet because of the FBI's links to the Ford Service Department, and he found confirming evidence for this thesis in the recent transfer of John Bugas, Detroit Bureau chief, to Ford's labor relations staff. Reluctance to dig too deeply into right-wing activity in Detroit and its links with managers at Ford, Packard, and other companies may have been a contributing factor in Biddle's caution, but his genuine distaste for government suppression of free speech was probably the more compelling motive. In July of 1943, he went so far as to notify the FBI director that the entire classification system for defining degrees of "dangerousness" was a "mistake" that could not serve as a reliable "determination of fact." In Biddle's estimate, the evidence the FBI was using to classify people "was inadequate."[90]

He might well have had Goodman's case in mind. The files on the CRF leader in the Detroit office of the FBI were full of disconnected bits of information, a jumble of fact, hearsay, idle speculation and, in some cases, blatant error. Interpreting the sometimes contradictory details was not easy. One FBI informant reported that Goodman was "very critical" of a particular CRF publication that was mailed out because he thought "it was *Daily Worker* [the CP-USA paper] style and would not reach all types of people." According to another informant, Goodman believed that Communist support for a news handlers' strike in New York "puts the Party in a foolish position" when it was simultaneously opposing strikes in Detroit.[91]

These reports of mild criticism of the CP-USA alternated with others describing Goodman as a Communist lawyer who met with CP-USA officials on a regular basis, usually linked to court cases involving the party or individual members (including one arrested for "indecent exposure" and another for street fighting). Goodman, the FBI reported, was not only "well acquainted with" his Communist clients, but "appeared to be on very friendly terms." There is little reason to doubt this particular assessment: Goodman knew many party members and he clearly supported the CP-USA's wartime policies. But whether or not he was a fellow traveler or even a secret member of the Communist Party should have been irrelevant to an investigation of whether he represented such a "clear and present danger" to national security that he should be targeted for custodial detention. There were no grounds for such a finding in Goodman's files, but there was ample evidence that he was a prominent critic of the FBI, and this alone would make him dangerous in the eyes of J. Edgar Hoover. In the widening search for evidence that would justify the FBI's surveillance, agents often abandoned professional norms and passed along information that was inaccurate or speculative. One FBI informant who described a party at the Goodman home ("attended by negroes and whites," he stressed) indicated that it was sponsored by Freda Goodman, "daughter of Ernest Goodman." Another agent mistakenly reported that Goodman had attended high school in Port Huron, and yet another speculated that Goodman must still be working for the UAW because he had read an article in the *Detroit Free Press* that said so. This was not high-level police work.[92]

Biddle may or may not have been familiar with the particular contents of Goodman's file, but he knew enough about J. Edgar Hoover's operation to be skeptical about a secret list that ranked citizens according to their perceived "dangerousness." The notion that it was possible "to make a valid determination as to how dangerous a person is in the abstract," he wrote the FBI director, "and without reference to time, environment, and other relevant circumstances, is impractical, unwise, and dangerous." Unfortunately, Hoover ignored Biddle's order and simply renamed his list a "Security Index."[93]

Within a few short years, the FBI would be hounding Communists, fellow travelers, and former partisans of the Popular Front, and Goodman would be gaining a well-deserved reputation for defending their civil liberties. But in 1943 it was the U.S. attorney general, not Goodman, who made the stronger defense of free speech. In this one case, it was Goodman who spoke from the standpoint of national security. He had reason for doing so. Unlike the 1950s, when there was no actual threat of a domestic uprising, in 1943 the indisputable fact of insurrection was measured in death tolls, troops deployed, factories closed. Undoubtedly, the hate strikes and violence came from the Right, urged on by the likes of Tony Lamarito and his racist followers in the National Workers League.

Where Goodman and Biddle differed was their assessment of the dangers this posed. Goodman may have been *too* close to the ground: he lived in the city where the U.S. Army had to patrol the streets and where Gerald L. K. Smith, as Goodman reported to Biddle, was calling for both the mass deportation of Jews and the use of sterilization as a "solution" for minority problems. Understandably, Goodman saw this as a clear and present danger, one that he urged Biddle to address with preemptive arrest and suppression of Smith's newspaper. The attorney general, on the other hand, had reason to pause. Smith was a homegrown fascist, repugnant to Biddle and deserving of scorn. But Biddle held to the view that the best way to counter un-American speech, however defined, was counter-speech, not suppression. It was a view Goodman would later come to appreciate in the 1950s, long after Biddle had retired.[94]

A New World

"We are through talking," Goodman said in his closing speech to the CRF institute. "Now is the time to translate our thoughts into actions." He outlined a comprehensive program that encompassed education, political action, open housing, workplace integration, desegregation of the military, and a code of conduct for unions and churches.[95]

He was relentlessly optimistic. The riots, the hate strikes, the political setbacks of the mayor's race were all significant in the short term, but he still put the long-term struggle in a hopeful perspective. "A person must be absolutely blind to the facts of life," he told the CRF's partisans, "if he has failed to see the tremendous and significant developments in the past few years." First among these was "the political maturity of the Negro people," who had in less than a decade gone from being supplicants to the Republican Party and strikebreakers for the Ford Motor Company to allies of the UAW and block-voting opponents of racist politicians. Equally heartening was the new calculus of labor solidarity. Negro Americans had been struggling "for centuries almost alone," but now the industrial unions of a revived labor movement were "fighting side by side with them," especially the CIO and the UAW. The power of this progressive movement was all the greater, Goodman continued, because it was international in scope. "In China, Yugoslavia, Norway, Russia, Africa, Asia, in the South Pacific, all over the world people are struggling, the same kind of fight against the same kind of enemies that we here in this room are concerned with, and for the same goal." This was not a struggle for socialism but "a people's war for the liberation of subjugated people all over the world." Americans had an obligation to win this battle for social justice on the home front as well as overseas. "People all over the world . . . will look upon our motives and our ideals by the way we deal with the problem of the Negro people here."[96]

Goodman was celebrating nothing less than the growth of the modern civil rights movement. Its power was centered in the consolidation of an urban black community in the North and its alliance with a labor movement committed to racial equality in principle and—to a lesser but still unprecedented degree—in practice. The evidence of this new movement was seated in front of Goodman, measured by the hundreds of participants in the institute's deliberations, blacks and whites. Among them were the many African American union members who had joined the NAACP's Detroit chapter and broadened its social base beyond the previous narrow circle of businessmen and professionals. The Detroit branch had grown from fewer than three thousand members in 1938 to twenty-one thousand by the end of 1945, making it the largest NAACP chapter in the country. The organization's tactics had broadened as well, moving beyond fundraising for legal challenges to segregation to a more activist approach that borrowed much from the repertoire of the CIO—picket lines, boycotts, and political mobilization. The new recruits also took inspiration from liberation and anticolonial movements around the globe, and they understood the links between the domestic and international dimensions of the struggle.[97]

As Goodman had stressed, the whole world actually *was* watching. When Detroit had exploded in racial violence in the summer of 1943, Nazi Germany's propaganda machine had been quick to exploit the obvious contradiction between the idealistic rhetoric of Allied war aims and the seamy underside of American apartheid. "So for international, as well as national unity," Goodman concluded, "we must openly and vigorously fight for Negro equality in America." In this regard, the logic of a national security state had unexpected outcomes with respect to civil rights: the call for national unity during global war could justify the suppression of dissenting opinion on the left and the right, but it could also strengthen the call for implementing the war aims of the Allied powers—for freedom and democracy—at home as well as abroad.[98]

The compelling question was whether the unity of purpose among the Allies would continue after the war. Goodman, as always, was hopeful. Like many, he placed great store in the results of the recent summit meeting in Tehran, the capital of Iran, where President Roosevelt met with Stalin and Winston Churchill to plan military strategy and the postwar occupation of Germany. Much was left unsaid at Tehran about the final disposition of power in Eastern Europe, where the Red Army would soon establish de facto control. But the meeting itself—the first wartime gathering of the three Allied leaders—raised hopes for future collaboration. Preliminary agreements at Tehran anticipated the organization of an international body, the United Nations, that would maintain global peace and encourage cooperation in solving economic and social problems. "We have already welded and forged an instrument which has committed the peoples of the world through their three most important governments to a course of conduct by which oppression and tyranny will be eliminated from the world," Goodman enthused. The Tehran agreement, he acknowledged, was only words, and the enemies of cooperation with the Soviets were already minimizing its significance. "But we, the people, can use [Tehran] as the banner under which we can rally and fight."[99]

In 1944 it was hard for Goodman to imagine a cold war with the country's Soviet allies. After nearly three years of common struggle, it was clear to many in the United States that it was the Soviet Union that had borne the brunt of the war against Nazi Germany at an unimaginable cost in human life. Soviet losses over the entire war would total 26 million people; in the single battle of Stalingrad, the Red Army lost 490,000 men and women—more than the U.S. death toll for the *entire* war. The new image of Russia was dominated by "Ivan," the Red Army's equivalent of GI Joe, fighting on heroically against the Nazi juggernaut. The Hitler-Stalin pact was a fading recollection, and Stalin effectively erased it by linking Soviet resistance to the memory of the struggle in Spain. In 1941 he paraded his troops through Moscow directly to the battle lines outside the city in a deliberate harkening to the march of the International Brigades through Madrid in 1936. The symbolism could not have been lost on Goodman and others of his generation for whom the Spanish struggle was the crucible of their socialist faith.[100]

For Goodman, the Soviet Union's mobilization for the "people's war against fascism" was an inspiration and a model for the long-term struggle to eliminate racism. "Prior to its revolution," he told the final session of the CRF's institute in April of 1944, Russia "was a land in which there were more pogroms and more organized hatred and prejudice against minority groups than possibly anywhere else in the world." He spoke from the experience of his own family. Things were different now, he believed. "From 1917 until today . . . that prejudice has been completely eradicated and wiped out in the Soviet Union and our singer here tonight, Celeste Cole, will tell you of that from her own experiences, as will Paul Robeson in very moving fashion tell you that in all his travels throughout the Soviet Union the one thing clear to him was that—there he was a free man among free men."[101]

This mistaken tribute to Soviet liberty would later become impossible to defend. Goodman might have known better, and probably should have. But Soviet intolerance for internal dissent was not a message that Robeson or other partisans wanted to report from their escorted trips to Russia, and Goodman didn't want to hear such a dissonant message. Neither did most Americans. Spurred by the blood guilt that Russia's death toll inspired, U.S. public opinion concerning the Soviet Union changed dramatically during the war, with close to half those polled in 1944 expressing trust in the country's Russian ally and only a third dissenting from this favorable assessment. The heroism and patriotism of the Russian people was real enough, and the warm glow of wartime propaganda emphasized these positive features of Soviet resistance. It turned many heads. "The most common portrayal," historian Melvin Small found in his study of the wartime media, "was one of a system which was opening up and which was slowly moving toward the West in terms of freedom." Even the conservative media frequently expressed approval of the Soviets, and centrist and liberal publications were all the more positive. *Life* magazine published a special edition on Russia in 1943 that portrayed the Soviet Union as progressive and economically innovative, a fit partner for the United States. *Time* magazine featured Stalin as its "Man of the Year."[102]

For both liberals and conservatives, attitudes may also have softened toward the Soviets as the CP-USA adopted a militantly pro-war stance that included not only endorsement of the no-strike pledge but public calls for speedup in defense industries. In 1944, the CP-USA actually dropped its party structure and redefined itself as the Communist Political Association, the better to lobby within the two-party system and become, as former Communist Joseph Starobin later wrote, "a more coherent influence in the real world where revolution was not the order of the day." In this atmosphere, the list of sponsors for the Detroit Council of American-Soviet Friendship included not only partisans of the Popular Front like Goodman but also middle-of-the-road Democrats like Judge Frank A. Picard—the same anti-Communist crusader Goodman would face ten years later in the Smith Act trials of the 1950s. In 1943, both Goodman and Picard could agree with the editors of the *Detroit News,* who editorialized that "we are happy in having so effective and loyal an ally in the war on Nazi Germany." President Roosevelt's declaration of American-Soviet Friendship Week had been "turned into something of a grass roots celebration," the *News* noted with approval. "We are complimenting our own good sense and our loyalty to the highest interests of mankind when we compliment those same qualities in the Russians." It was one of the rare *News* editorials Goodman would agree with.[103]

The world was at a crossroads. Would it return to the recent past of economic depression, colonial empire, and white supremacy? Or would the postwar reconstruction build something new, a world of economic justice, mutual security, and interracial collaboration? Goodman's closing words to the institute conveyed the hopes of his generation. "I believe we have reached the point in the history of this nation, of this world, where discrimination and prejudice can be eliminated and can be eliminated now."[104]

5

Hard Landing

He was getting used to flying. He had to during the war and especially now afterward as his work took him across the continent, from New York City to San Francisco and, on this October day in 1946, Milwaukee. The DC-3 taxied along the edge of the Willow Run Airport and turned at the head of the runway, revving its prop engines in a sudden burst of noise and blue smoke before the plane lurched forward, gaining speed, pressing the twenty passengers back in their seats. The tail rose from the runway. Then came the giddy moment when the aircraft drifted upward, detached from the earth, climbing nose up, and Goodman could see the world below as no human had seen it before his lifetime.[1]

It was a world transformed by the war. The very airport had been farmland six years before, when the government bulldozed the fields and Ford built the gigantic Willow Run bomber plant, stretching westward from the airport for three quarters of a mile beneath Goodman's plane as it circled over the huge complex. More than forty thousand UAW members had built B-24 bombers at a rate of one every hour during peak production, sending eighty-six hundred skyward and across the Atlantic to bomb Hitler's Germany into rubble. He could see the ganglia of arterial roads that looped the plant, feeding traffic onto the four-lane superhighway stretching eastward to Detroit, fifteen miles distant on a hazy horizon. The government built the Detroit Industrial Highway (later I-94) to carry war workers to the Willow Run plant, marking the start of the nation's first interregional expressway, now continuing westward toward Chicago. It would soon become an exit ramp from Detroit, accelerating the suburbanization of the region as it also carried UAW members to the new occupant of the bomber plant, the Kaiser-Fraser Corporation, building cars for a booming peacetime economy. Even the government-built housing for war workers north and west of the plant was taking on new life, the dorms and single-story apartment projects now home to returning veterans and

134

their families. Goodman could see the neat rows of prefab housing beneath his plane, obscured by the haze of gray smoke from coal-fired cooking stoves—installed during the wartime shortage of oil. Many of the vets had found work at the Kaiser-Fraser plant and were taking classes at the University of Michigan or Michigan State Normal College (now Eastern Michigan University) in neighboring Ypsilanti, supported by the generous benefits of the GI Bill.[2]

The panorama captured the recent past and emerging future of Detroit's social landscape, and with it, the parameters of Goodman's professional life. His legal docket was filled with the dislocations and disputes of an economy in transition, of laid-off war workers and returning veterans, UAW members past and future. Two cases were already taking him back to the U.S. Supreme Court, and both would end in clear-cut decisions favoring the union. A third case involving the son of a UAW member, an innocent veteran condemned to death, would lead to a landmark decision in front of a military tribunal. Goodman would also take on a widening range of cases in the expanding fields of administrative law and private arbitration as the UAW fought to reestablish collective bargaining and broaden its social and political reach.

It was a heady time for the forty-year-old lawyer. Maurice Sugar and the UAW now trusted Goodman with some of the most sensitive cases confronting the union, including the one that took him to Milwaukee on this autumn day in 1946. The UAW's militant local at the Allis Chalmers plant in West Allis was taking on one of the country's more reactionary owners in a confrontation characterized by strikebreaking and a government-orchestrated witch hunt against the local's left-wing leaders. As soon as the plane touched down, Goodman was off to strategy meetings that night with the union's local lawyers; then to court the next morning to answer contempt charges related to the union's mass picketing; then to more meetings that afternoon to prepare the filing of charges with the National Labor Relations Board; then back to the airport that evening for the return flight to Willow Run. There was no time for the train connecting through Chicago, and the $29.34 round-trip airfare was worth the price. Goodman's time was more valuable to the union than the money saved on train tickets. He was at the zenith of his career as a union lawyer.[3]

It would not last. A rapidly escalating cold war with the Soviet Union was already dashing the high hopes for a postwar détente that Goodman and others had embraced. The brewing Red Scare that corporate and government leaders were directing at the UAW's Milwaukee local was likewise infecting the entire labor movement, igniting bitter factional wars between the CIO's right- and left-wing caucuses. Within little more than a year from Goodman's flight to Milwaukee, Sugar's left-wing allies within the UAW would be routed and Sugar's contract terminated. The fall from national prominence to persecuted outcast would effectively end Maurice Sugar's career. It would be a hard landing from the heights of 1946.

Headwinds

Postwar confrontation with the Soviet Union was not inevitable, and neither was the Red Scare that accompanied it. But both became far more likely after 21 July 1944, the third day of the Democratic Party's national convention in Chicago. That evening, southern "Dixiecrats" united with big-city machine politicians to drastically alter the party's ticket for the upcoming presidential election. Within a year, their success would put U.S. foreign policy on a collision course with the Soviets and accelerate the rightward turn in domestic politics.

The day before this turning point, Franklin Roosevelt had easily won his party's nomination for a fourth term as president. Party leaders, however, wanted to block the renomination of Henry Wallace, the incumbent vice president who many saw as Roosevelt's likely successor. He was just too liberal in their eyes. His speech seconding Roosevelt's nomination was a case in point, Wallace calling for something most party leaders considered wild-eyed and revolutionary: "equal wages for equal work regardless of sex or race." Wallace, as one southern senator complained, "is the leader of the most radical group in America," that being "the extreme elements of the CIO." Roosevelt's worsening health would almost certainly put the next vice president in the White House, and southern Democrats did not want it to be a liberal who promoted racial equality. Roosevelt personally favored Wallace, the third-generation editor of an Iowa farm newspaper who had served in his cabinet since 1933. But FDR, fearing that southern Democrats would bolt the party if Wallace became president, acquiesced to the pressure of party leaders by withholding his endorsement. Wallace led the voting in the first convention ballot on 21 July but fell short of a majority, and when southern delegations switched their votes to Missouri senator Harry Truman, the nomination was his. To soften the blow for Wallace, Roosevelt later appointed him secretary of commerce. The president won reelection that November but died within six months, elevating Truman to the presidency.[4]

Like many others on labor's left wing, Goodman's life would soon be buffeted by the growing headwinds coming from Washington. Truman immediately began to replace Roosevelt's brain trust with allies from Missouri and conservatives from the business world who favored a rollback of New Deal labor policy and a confrontational turn toward the Soviets. "The New Dealers are out and the Wall Streeters are in," as the *Chicago Tribune* later put it. This rightward drift did not go uncontested. Many Americans held high hopes for the same kind of peaceful coexistence with the Soviet Union that Goodman had articulated in his Detroit speech, and many in the UAW likewise believed it was time to settle accounts with employers who had gouged consumers and weakened unions during the war. A clash was inevitable.[5]

The first skirmish came on the domestic front in 1945 when UAW members at General Motors, freed from the wartime no-strike pledge after Japan's surrender, downed tools in a nationwide walkout to win a 30 percent wage increase. The 113-day strike, which began in November, would keep Goodman fully occupied with Labor Board complaints (focusing on GM's refusal to open its books), unemployment benefits (many of the strikers were already on layoff during changeover to car production), and government price controls (lobbying the Office of Price Administration to hold the line on auto prices). These issues took on a special urgency given the target—GM was the world's most profitable manufacturing company—and the ambitions of Walter Reuther, the UAW vice president in charge of GM bargaining. It was widely understood that Reuther aspired to the UAW presidency, and mobilizing his followers to do battle with GM was a step toward this goal. Autoworkers were eager to join the crusade, voting 6-1 in favor of a strike that promised to win "purchasing power for prosperity." Company profits had more than doubled during the war, while inflation had dramatically eroded the buying power of hourly wages. Without a pay increase to expand consumer purchasing power, the economy would be "hell bent for depression," Reuther warned. To avoid being paid in the "wooden nickels of inflation," Reuther demanded that GM hold the line on prices, making the wage demand truly redistributive and— equally important—popular with much of the public.[6]

GM executives, on the other hand, saw Reuther's bargaining agenda as a genuine threat, a form of "co-determination" over pricing and other decisions that corporations traditionally made with little or no public scrutiny. George Romney of the Automobile Manufacturers Association vented management's collective spleen with his famous complaint that the UAW vice president was "the most dangerous man in Detroit" precisely because he promoted "revolution without seeming to disturb the existing forms of society." Reuther's brand of liberal reformism hardly qualified as revolutionary, but it did represent a potent challenge to corporate power.

The UAW's social unionism dramatically widened the union's base of support by advocating measures that benefited not only UAW members but all workers and consumers. This crusading agenda would keep Goodman on the go in 1946 with efforts to curb inflation, establish health care for all, expand nonprofit radio broadcasting, and promote consumer co-ops.[7]

The dwindling number of New Dealers still in the government, led by Secretary of Commerce Henry Wallace, saw much to support in this reform agenda. According to a Commerce Department report, the auto industry could afford a 25 percent wage increase without raising prices and still remain profitable. President Truman's fact-finding committee, however, concluded that GM could afford only a 17.5 percent wage increase without raising prices, and when the company rejected even this diminished amount, the president did nothing. Reuther reluctantly accepted the recommendation of the president's committee, but even this gesture brought no agreement. GM stonewalled the union, the government, and the public, finally forcing the union to accept a 16.5 percent increase in March 1946, with no mention of prices. Within weeks, GM began hiking the price of its new models.[8]

Two months after the strike settlement, Reuther sent Goodman to Washington, DC (by train this time), to prepare a formal protest of GM's price increases. Goodman submitted the complaint to the federal government's Office of Price Administration (OPA), charging that GM had violated the wartime Price Control Act. The OPA, however, denied all of the UAW's protests, following a pattern already established during the national strike wave that began in January of 1946. As in auto, workers in a wide range of industries had walked off the job to protest the declining purchasing power of their wages, the number of strikers topping 4.6 million during the course of the year, the highest strike total in U.S. history. Unlike past eras of labor conflict, there was little strikebreaking and no fatal violence on the picket lines, a telling measure of how far the labor movement had come in winning recognition as the legitimate representative of workers' interests. But business leaders were demanding an end to wartime regulations, and the Truman administration would dutifully comply, allowing companies to raise prices and force the cost of wage increases onto consumers. When it appeared that these price increases ran counter to the spirit of the law, the law was ignored, then gutted. "I undertook preparations to appeal the [OPA] decision to the court," Goodman noted in his bill to the union, "but the emasculation of the Price Control Act prevented further action along this line." In the eight months following the end of the GM strike, the consumer price index soared by more than 14 percent, nullifying most of the gains won on the picket lines. Wooden nickels, indeed.[9]

Goodman spent much of the month of May in Washington working not only on the OPA protest but on two issues—public broadcasting and national health insurance—that typified the wide reach of the UAW's social unionism. The first of these was the union's campaign to counter the concentrated power of the commercial media. During both the GM strike and the Detroit mayoral election of 1945, the UAW had been victimized by the slanted coverage of media companies that denied the union airtime, misrepresented its goals, and promoted antilabor candidates. To secure pro-union radio coverage in the future, the UAW decided to seek its own license in 1946 to operate noncommercial FM broadcasting stations in Detroit and Cleveland. Goodman prepared the engineering reports, drafted the supporting documents for the license applications, and presented the union's case to the Federal Communications Commission (FCC) in Washington during the same week he was developing the OPA complaint. The union eventually won its licenses, but its foray into FM broadcasting proved to be ill-timed, particularly when so few autoworkers owned FM receivers. Lacking advertising revenue, WDET in Detroit turned out to be an expensive proposition, and the UAW later donated the station to the city-owned Wayne University.[10]

Goodman returned to Washington in late May to take up another priority on the UAW's social agenda, national health insurance. From the late 1930s onward, CIO and AFL unions had pressed for group health care plans that would pool the risks and costs of sickness, making medical care more affordable and, equally important, more accessible through community-based clinics, outpatient services, education, screening, and prevention. By the mid-1940s there was also widespread support in the labor movement for a program of national health insurance that would fund these services through the same kind of payroll tax that financed Social Security. President Truman supported legislation along these lines in 1946, and Goodman became one of the UAW's key lobbyists for such an initiative. He prepared a brief in support of the National Health Bill and returned to the capital in May with UAW secretary treasurer George Addes to present the material to the Senate Committee on Labor and Education. In response to these labor initiatives, the American Medical Association, Aetna Insurance, Equitable, and other insurance companies lobbied aggressively against "socialized medicine," as they called it, even though the measure left medical services in private hands and was no more socialistic than old-age pensions. The National Association of Manufacturers (NAM) was no happier with the UAW's fallback proposal that companies contribute the equivalent of 3 percent of payroll to a health plan administered by the union. "Not only do these plans represent a heavy payroll burden," the NAM charged, they also drive "a wedge which tends to make the employee feel that his bargaining agent is more sympathetically concerned with his well-being than the employer."[11]

None of labor's health care initiatives would survive the vigorous counter-lobbying of the medical establishment and business. Conservative leaders in the House refused to even hold hearings on national health insurance, and most employers refused to bargain over health and pension benefits until the Supreme Court finally forced them to in 1949. By then, the terms of the debate had shifted as many employers refused to consider anything but employer-defined plans, leaving unions to negotiate only the proportion of the premium paid by workers. Instead of a public system of near-universal coverage, the result was a private system of welfare capitalism centered on the employer. It marked a retreat from Reuther's social unionism during the GM strike, when he denounced price increases as "a conspiracy against the public" and promised that the union would "make progress with the community and not at the expense of the community." In the end, when it was clear the union lacked the bargaining leverage and political power to make good on that kind of promise, the UAW reluctantly settled for the employer-based health care system that soon became commonplace in unionized industries.[12]

The sea change in the union's strategy was evident by 1948, when the UAW and GM agreed that inflationary price increases would be compensated by a cost-of-living adjustment to wages—an important gain for UAW members, but as GM passed along the added cost to consumers, it literally came "at the expense of the community." The payoff for accepting this private, company-based welfare system was substantial: autoworker wages would nearly double between 1947 and 1960, allowing UAW members to buy into something like a middle-class lifestyle. There may have been no better alternative in the political and social climate of the postwar era, when a resurgent business class had the upper hand in defining the limits of collective bargaining. But the gulf between union and non-union workers would widen thereafter, making UAW members less of a working-class vanguard and more of a labor aristocracy.[13]

In this emerging environment, it was the Sugar firm that won many of the legal precedents that confirmed the union's role under the new collective bargaining model. Four Supreme Court cases in 1945–46 marked the firm's preeminence, with Goodman's victory in the Goose Creek decision the most celebrated. Mort Eden won a second case the same year that established the union's right to communicate with its members during nonwork time on company property (in this case, Republic Aviation). Goodman argued the remaining two cases. In *Trailmobile Co. v. Whirls,* he successfully defended the principle that returning veterans should be credited with seniority rights for the time they spent in the armed services (as called for by the law and UAW policy), but that zealous Selective Service officials could not unilaterally impose an additional "super-seniority" that preempted the rights of nonveterans and nullified the collective bargaining agreement. In *Social Security v. Nierotko,* he won a decision stipulating that the back-pay award for workers illegally fired by Ford in 1937 should be counted toward future Social Security benefits. Justifiably proud of his work, Goodman noted in his bill to the union that three thousand Ford workers and thousands of others in similar cases could now look forward to higher Social Security retirement benefits. His fee for this work came to $475.[14]

At the standard $5 an hour that Sugar's attorneys billed the union, this was hardly an extravagant fee. "It didn't make any difference," Goodman recalled years later, "whether I was going into the lowest court in the community for a traffic case, or whether I was arguing a case before the United States Supreme Court, my time was $5 an hour, and that's what I was paid. It's rather unique I think, but Sugar wanted to get the lowest price he could for the [union]." Goodman and his colleagues nevertheless made a substantial income by the sheer volume of work they turned out. Maurice Sugar was known for his fanatical work habits and fourteen- to sixteen-hour days, and his allied attorneys were expected to keep pace as the firm plowed new ground in union governance, private arbitration, unemployment compensation (still a major part of Goodman's work), workers' compensation, and injunction proceedings. With the union also pressing for fair employment practices to desegregate the workplace and for consumer cooperatives to distribute affordable food, Goodman and his colleagues had all the work they could handle.[15]

For Freda, the most reliable way to find time with her husband and get away from the house were the occasions when, child care permitting, she could join Ernie on his work trips to New York City, San Francisco, or (for the 1946 UAW convention) Atlantic City. During the day she often joined the proceedings as a court spectator or convention guest, and she and Ernie found time for recreation at the end of the day. "Would it be possible for you to obtain two tickets for the evening of April 27th," Ernie wrote to the secretary of the National Federation for Constitutional Liberties before he and Freda traveled to a 1944 board meeting in New York

City. He had an eclectic mix of theater options in mind, asking for tickets to any "of the following in the order indicated: 'Oklahoma,' 'Othello,' 'Jacobowsky and the Colonel.' "[16]

Time away from work was in short supply, but Goodman's income provided a comfortable standard of living in the house on Warrington Drive. By 1945 his frenetic work schedule (which also included a substantial docket of volunteer work) was netting $7,800 a year in fees, a sum that put him well ahead of the $6,900 average for nonsalaried lawyers in the United States. In the mid-1940s Sugar was supervising forty-five to fifty lawyers across the country—Goodman and seven other associates in Detroit, plus local attorneys hired on a case-by-case basis. While the rising cost of everything from rent to clerical labor was eating into Sugar's gross earnings from UAW work, he still netted a substantial income from the non-UAW cases he assigned to his allied lawyers. Sugar's combined income made him a prosperous lawyer by the standards of the day, though his lifestyle remained frugal, even parsimonious. While Ernie and Freda were buying their house in a leafy middle-class neighborhood, Maurice and Jane Sugar still lived in an apartment near Woodward Avenue, preferring to invest their earnings (hers as a teacher) in their house on Black Lake at the northern tip of Michigan's Lower Peninsula.[17]

Sugar remained the hard-driving taskmaster, straightforward and honest, but also aloof. "Sugar was an independent guy when it came to his own life and his own finances as well," Goodman later observed. "He played everything in his life as a loner, at least during the time I knew him. Well, that was all right. It worked out very well, with some difficulties." Goodman rarely elaborated on what these difficulties amounted to, but his collected papers include office memos from Sugar that give some insight into his mentor's prickly nature. In lighter moments, Sugar's memos offered playfully sardonic advice, but the sarcasm became more biting and the advice more nitpicking when associates left windows open ("wind and rain blows in . . . paper blows out!") or left his office unkempt ("it does make me sore as hell") or ignored protocol ("letters sent out on [office] cases [should] be on my stationery and signed by me"). The Sugar firm was not a partnership or band of brothers. The associates were independent attorneys, but they were bound to Sugar by a signed agreement that promised "as far as practicable" to assign cases on an equitable rotation, while reserving to Sugar the right to impose "deviations from the rule of rotation" for reasons of union policy "or considerations of a nature personal to Sugar." The associates accepted these rules because of Sugar's prestige and the obvious fact that his name drew more than enough work to the office, keeping everybody busy. Once you gained his confidence,

Sugar was also a loyal and concerned mentor, particularly if you joined—
as Goodman had—his close circle of deer hunters. "Mr. Goodman came
back without a buck," Sugar's secretary wrote to her boss during one deer
season. Sugar, naturally, had shot his buck early on the first morning of
the hunt. "When I return," his handwritten reply promised, "I'll explain
to Goodman just how it is done."[18]

Working in the Sugar firm also allowed—in a real sense, required—
a commitment to political and professional work outside the office caseload. Ben Marcus was nationally known for his efforts in 1946 as cofounder
and first president of the National Association of Claimants Compensation Attorneys. NACCA (better known years later as the Trial Lawyers
of America) would grow in five years from its original nine members to
fifteen hundred as it took the lead in setting standards for affordable fees
and effective strategies for representing injured workers. Ned Smokler
served as executive secretary of the Detroit chapter of the National Lawyers Guild, which Sugar helped subsidize with office space, financial
contributions, and travel expenses to national executive board meetings.
Goodman was active in the Guild as well, but was better known for his
leadership in the Civil Rights Federation, providing legal services without
compensation and contributing considerable time to the CRF's programs
and publications. When the federation merged into the Civil Rights Congress (CRC) in April 1946, Goodman transferred his allegiance as well,
becoming a member of its executive board. As a national membership organization devoted to civil rights for minorities and workers, the CRC
pursued goals that were compatible with the official objectives of the UAW
and the CIO, particularly in the realm of desegregating the workplace and
establishing fair employment practices.[19]

It was in this intersection between civil rights activism and UAW
policy that Goodman met his future law partner and friend George
Crockett Jr. The grandson of a freed slave and son of a railroad carpenter,
Crockett was a self-described member of the "talented tenth," the professional elite of the black community who saw themselves as the vanguard
of Negro advancement. Raised in Jacksonville, Florida, by parents who passionately held to the transforming power of education, Crockett became a
diligent student and worked with a special urgency to hone his skills as a
high school orator. His efforts paid off when a speech he gave on the U.S.
Constitution won him a scholarship to Morehouse College, the all-black
Christian school in Atlanta. There he learned his first lessons in the liberating potential of the labor movement from an economics professor who
had worked his way through school as a Pullman porter on the railroads.
As Crockett recalled years later, "that's where I first heard of A. Philip

Randolph," founding leader of the AFL's only all-black union, the Brother-hood of Sleeping Car Porters. Crockett's summer jobs on merchant ships to South America furthered his early understanding of labor issues.[20]

Graduating from Morehouse with honors, he enrolled at the University of Michigan Law School as one of two blacks in a class of three hundred. "At this time, I literally couldn't tell one white person from another," he remembered, "and I was scared stiff every time the professor called on me. I had the feeling that . . . I carried the whole weight of the race every time a question was put." He graduated in 1934 in the upper third of his class and, finding there were no law firms in Michigan that would hire a black lawyer, he chose the border state of West Virginia to open his law practice. Like many aspiring black professionals of the previous generation, he joined the local Republican Party—still the "party of Lincoln" in the eyes of many blacks—but he soon recognized that the New Deal offered wider alternatives. "At heart, I was a New Deal Democrat anyway, so I switched over." In recognition of his singular skills as a lawyer and orator, he won a coveted appointment in 1938 to the U.S. Department of Labor. From there, he won promotion in 1943 to the position of hearing examiner for the Fair Employment Practices Commission, the agency responsible for desegregating war-related industry.

Crockett came to Detroit in 1944 after a chance encounter with UAW president R. J. Thomas on the now-desegregated Pullman cars of the "Red Arrow" train to Washington. The UAW's top officers were searching for ways to confront the workplace segregation that bedeviled Detroit's factories and divided their membership, and Thomas, not long after the meeting on the Red Arrow, invited Crockett to take charge of what eventually became the union's committee on Fair Employment Practices (FEP). It was in this capacity that he first met Goodman and Sugar, both actively involved in the FEP's mission.

"I was deeply impressed by his fluency as a speaker," Goodman remembered of these early encounters, "the clarity with which he expressed his views, his avoidance of typical cliches and superficialities, and the compelling logic of his theme—that racial discrimination and segregation must be eradicated from our society." Crockett's work demanded all of these qualities as he came to grips with the racial conflicts, large and small, that plagued the union. His tactics alternated between frontal assault and subtle compromise. When black workers from Dodge Local 3 in Hamtramck complained in 1945 that their dues supported an annual dance that played only polka music for the Polish American majority, Crockett proposed to the local leadership that they hire a second band and alternate the music. "Well, they did, and had the best dance they ever had." The refusal of a local GM union in Atlanta to admit black workers to membership required a more blunt approach. After interviewing the local officers in 1946, Crockett called Walter Reuther and urged him to come to Atlanta and address the membership. "Well, he did," Crockett recalled years later. "He called a special meeting of the local and he read the riot act to them. I'll always give him credit for that. He said, 'You take them in or there's going to be an administrator appointed.' They said, 'Let's take a vote.' He said, 'You can take a vote if you want to, but regardless of how the vote turns out, you're taking them in.' "[21]

It was Crockett who broached the subject of working for the Sugar firm. The first conversation he could recall with the union's general counsel was regarding legal challenges to the segregated bowling allies that were excluding the UAW's integrated teams. Crockett commented that Sugar's reputation for championing racial integration was hard to square with the fact that none of his allied lawyers were black. "Well, maybe it's because I haven't found the right one," Sugar answered. "Well, that shouldn't handicap you," Crockett remembered saying. "You're looking at the right one now." As it turned out, Sugar had already expressed an interest in hiring Crockett away from the UAW, but R. J. Thomas had warned him off. For the time being, George Crockett would remain on the staff of the UAW president.

Martial Law

Goodman's already diverse caseload expanded yet again in 1946 when the UAW agreed to take on the case of a black GI accused of murder and condemned to death by a military court-martial. The case came at an opportune moment for the UAW and Goodman. Opponents of desegregating the armed forces could no longer invoke the crisis atmosphere that followed Pearl Harbor, when "social experiments" like racial integration were deemed too risky. With the end of the war, the renewed call for integrating the armed forces now converged with mounting criticism of the archaic rules of military justice. The case of Private Lemas Woods would highlight both of these issues. It would also be a defining moment for Goodman, the first in which he took on a high-profile case of an African American facing the gallows.

Lemas Woods had grown up in a Detroit boardinghouse with his father, a factory worker and member of the UAW. Drafted in 1942, the younger Woods had been placed in a segregated combat unit assigned to the postwar occupation of the Philippines. In March of 1946, Woods was brought before a court-martial on charges of shooting and killing a fellow black soldier, Private Robert Patterson. Woods claimed that his gun had fired accidentally, but the army prosecutor had produced a signed confession and an alleged eyewitness. The confession, Woods maintained, had been coerced and he had signed it only after being beaten and threatened by two army interrogators. The military had provided him with no trained counsel, and after a trial lasting little more than three hours he was found guilty and sentenced to hang.[22]

It was his distraught father who brought the case to the UAW and the Civil Rights Congress. "I was working with the CRC on a number of things," Goodman remembered, "and they asked me if I would investigate. I immediately wrote to the Army and asked for a copy of the trial record." It took three months to get the transcript, and after Goodman read the short twenty-nine-page document, he found it "simply incredible that Lemas Woods had been convicted on the kind of evidence presented and in the mechanical, almost indifferent courtroom atmosphere indicated by the record." It was, he said later, nothing more than a "kangaroo trial." When Goodman learned that the judge advocate at the tribunal had reported substantial irregularities in the prosecution's case, and that this report had never been sent to the military's Board of Review, he felt a deliberate effort had been made to suppress material evidence. Rather than a case where no one cared one way or the other, it was, he believed, "a concerted effort on the part of the Army to consolidate around this decision and prevent any disclosure of unfairness. . . . [I]t seemed unlikely that the Army would have dealt with a white soldier in the way it had with Lemas Woods." Goodman was genuinely moved by the young man's story, but he also saw an opportunity to focus public attention on racial discrimination in the army and the need for change in the notoriously undemocratic court-martial system of military justice.[23]

The military was a focal point of liberal concern after the war because the government's practice of racial segregation in the armed forces was a matter of deliberate rule making. Unlike the private prejudice that prevailed in daily life, these public policies could be changed by a single executive order from the White House. President Roosevelt had issued such an order to desegregate jobs in war industry, but he had allowed the armed forces to relegate eight hundred thousand African American soldiers and sailors to second-class status. Not only was the army totally segregated into separate black and white regiments, but many black recruits were excluded from combat units altogether, sent instead to dig ditches, cook, or serve meals. For those who did see action, the army maintained segregated blood banks for wounded African Americans. The few blacks trained to become officers were not promoted to the higher ranks and were never assigned to the command of white troops.[24]

A second issue, which transcended race, was the inherent injustice of the military court-martial system. "Particularly during and after World War II," as one scholar in *Army Lawyer* magazine has written, "there were widespread perceptions of unfairness, and of unlawful command influence, in the court-martial process." Defendants had no right to competent counsel and no choice in selecting a lawyer. Only officers could serve as jurors. Even in a murder trial, there was no way a defendant could have full discovery of the evidence. In civilian courts, in contrast, the prosecution was expected (if not always compelled) to bring forward all evidence, even when it was favorable to the defense. "These basic rights were just not there," Goodman observed, "and there was a developing effort to try to change these rules." With the support of UAW secretary treasurer Addes, who agreed to cochair the Lemas Woods Defense Committee, Goodman decided to pursue an appeal and to waive his fee, with an understanding that the UAW would cover expenses.[25]

As Goodman read the court-martial transcript, he saw that the prosecutor had presented what appeared to be a straightforward case: Lemas Woods had confessed to quarreling with his tent mate over a woman and had arisen on the morning of 16 March, gone to the man's bunk, pulled aside the mosquito netting, yanked the victim's head off the pillow, and shot him in the arm; the bullet had passed through the arm and pierced the victim's torso and heart. When a commander came to investigate, he found the revolver under Woods's pillow. John Hicks, a soldier bunking three tents away, testified that he had seen Woods grab the victim and tell him to "wake up" before shooting him. Woods's army-appointed counsel—a soldier with no legal training who would become a Coca-Cola salesman after his discharge—had offered practically no defense during the trial. Although Woods had repudiated his "confession" as having been beaten out of him, it was nonetheless entered into the record.[26]

Goodman needed to make a firsthand investigation of these charges, but this appeared to be impossible given the thousands of miles separating Detroit and Manila. He found the access he needed, however, through the Philippine Lawyers Guild, a kindred organization of the National Lawyers Guild. Through this fraternity of like-minded liberal and radical lawyers, Goodman found a valuable ally, Carlos Ramos, the executive secretary of the Manila Guild chapter. Ramos, a former lieutenant in the U.S. Army and veteran of the Philippine resistance to the Japanese, responded enthusiastically to Goodman's request for help. His interview with Woods in Bilibid prison revealed a very different story. Woods said he and Patterson were close friends and had often talked about working together in Virginia when the two were discharged. He said he had taken his revolver to a movie the night before as protection against an increasing number of attacks by local residents against U.S. soldiers. Instead of returning it to the supply room when he came back late that night, as regulations called for, he brought it to his tent. Preparing for an inspection in the morning, he said he asked another soldier to store the gun in his footlocker, which would not be inspected. While walking past Patterson's bunk, he noticed a piece of lint stuck to the oil on the hammer and brushed it off, forgetting the gun was loaded. The revolver discharged, he heard Patterson moan, and reaching into the victim's bunk realized he was dead. After hiding the gun in panic, he soon admitted he had shot his friend by mistake.[27]

As Goodman compared this account to the court-martial testimony, several issues bothered him. There was, first of all, the prosecution's "improbable" claim, as he described it in the petition to President Truman for a new trial, that Woods would deliberately shoot Patterson in broad daylight, surrounded by other soldiers, and aim for his arm rather than his head or chest. There was also the recurring image that kept fluttering across Goodman's imagination as he pondered the case: the mosquito netting. If the prosecution were correct—that Woods had pulled the netting aside before shooting Patterson—then there would be no hole in the netting. If Woods, on the other hand, were telling the truth—that the gun had discharged by accident while Patterson was asleep behind the net—then there would be a hole. According to Ramos, Woods reported that he had been told in the presence of the judge advocate that the army's Criminal Investigation Division had examined Patterson's mosquito net and found a hole and powder burns. But the netting had never been introduced in the trial, and Woods had wondered why his defense counsel advised him not to bring up the matter during the proceedings. Ramos had gone on to interview John Hicks, the prosecutor's sole eyewitness, who admitted that from one hundred yards away he could have been mistaken about the several things he saw, and was willing to make a sworn statement to this effect.[28]

Swayed by Goodman's brief and the mounting public pressure building around the case, President Truman agreed that Woods should have a new trial. Goodman was elated and began making plans for traveling to San Francisco, where the army had scheduled a new hearing for July of 1947. Woods was transferred to the military base at the Presidio, held in solitary confinement and handcuffed to a guard during his meals and a daily thirty-minute exercise period. It was in this setting that Goodman met his client for the first time, just two months before the trial. "He was a wonderful person, with a warm smile," Goodman recalled.

> I remember shaking his hand and looking in his eyes, his face. He was the kind of person you'd say, "This is a nice young guy," but a simple person—no evidence of duplicity or that he was a person who could think in that direction at all. You knew that what he was saying was true. He couldn't be telling complicated lies. Just by looking at him. He responded with a smile and we embraced each other. . . . He captured you just by his smile himself. He was everything you would want in a client.[29]

Reassured as he was by this initial meeting, Goodman was still nervous about trying his first case before a military tribunal. When he met Major Evans Bunker, whom the army had appointed as co-defense counsel, Goodman told him, "I need you, I want you to be here so that I know what has to be done." Evans had his own reason to be nervous. An experienced attorney, he knew that if an army lawyer fought too hard for a client in a way that the commander didn't like, he would feel repercussions. He welcomed having a civilian lawyer take the lead. "I'd be a shield for him," Goodman said, "and he could do what he wanted to through me." As the two lawyers prepared their defense, Carlos Ramos arrived from the Philippines with the crucial bit of evidence: the missing mosquito netting, found in a broom closet on an army base near Manila.[30]

Goodman, meanwhile, continued to work the media, talking frequently to reporters in an effort to build public support. "Hub" George of the *Detroit Free Press* wrote a memo to his colleagues after one such session with Goodman. "He says the case has all the elements of a 'Thin Man' radio mystery thriller and that he is ready to unfold to us the one clinching fact that proves Woods couldn't have been guilty. He thinks, and I have respect for his news judgment, that he has some excellent material for a Sunday feature." There was national interest as well, much of it generated by the series of articles written by Albert Deutsch for Marshall Field's daily newspaper *PM* in New York City. "I didn't get a fair trial in Manila," Woods told Deutsch in a prison interview. "I think it's because I'm a colored man. I know a white boy who killed another soldier in the Philippines. When they asked him why he did it, he said he just didn't like that man's looks. They gave that fellow life. Me, I killed my friend by accident. They gave me death." Goodman showed his media savvy by persuading authorities at the Presidio to let Woods don his military uniform for a photo and interview session with a *San Francisco Chronicle* reporter, knowing the uniform would strike a more positive chord than prison garb.[31]

Back in Michigan, Sherwin Wine, a reporter for Detroit's *Jewish News,* captured Goodman's feelings as the trial approached.

> The treatment of Lemas Woods seems to Goodman to reveal the general indifference of the Army to the civil rights of Negroes. "When Lemas Woods goes on trial this July 21, the whole system of Army justice likewise will be tried. The innocence of the defendant questions the legality of the entire proceedings," the attorney declared. . . . As to the gradual solution of this problem, Goodman showed much apprehension. "I feel that very notable steps in reducing discrimination lie in two legislative acts which are before Congress—the FEP [Fair Employment Practices] Bill and the Anti-Lynching Law. Factors which tend to encourage their passage include the continued [union] organization of whites and Negroes in the South . . . which is slowly revising traditional prejudice."[32]

The second court-martial of Lemas Woods opened on 21 July in an austere, one-story wooden building in the Presidio built especially for the trial. Woods's family, newspaper reporters, and spectators took seats on benches in a long, narrow room with tables set at one end for members of the court. Freda was among the spectators, having traveled to San Francisco to stay with her husband at the fashionable Bellevue Hotel, less than four miles away near the downtown theater district. At the front of the room, a brigadier general and five colonels were gathering to hear testimony. Perhaps worried by the media interest in the racial dimensions of the case, the army had also named one black lieutenant to the tribunal, a fact that raised hopes in the Detroit offices of the Lemas Woods Defense Committee.[33]

Goodman entered the trial confident of victory, assuming that the army would simply repeat the claims made in the first trial and that the hole in the mosquito net would effectively refute the charges. But when Captain Eger, the prosecutor, began to present his case, Goodman soon realized he had made a potentially fatal error. Eger said he would not only introduce Woods's "confession," he would also prove that the angle of the bullet's entry showed that Patterson, the victim, could not have been in a natural sleeping position when he was shot, implying that, as one witness had testified, Woods had awakened him before the shooting. Further, said Eger, he would demonstrate that the skin around the entrance wound was burned, meaning that the weapon was only two inches from the body when the trigger was pulled—evidence, if true, that would contradict Woods's claim that he was several yards away when his gun accidentally discharged. "We had overlooked the possibility of another piece of evidence," Goodman said later, referring to the entrance-wound burn. "And we were not in a position to refute it by our evidence. . . . Suddenly all was revised, and we were in trouble."[34]

Almost immediately, however, Goodman had the opportunity to enter the mosquito net into evidence. In the usual trial procedure, the defense would call its witnesses after the prosecution had finished making its case, but an exception was made for Jack Waddy, a defense witness and a fellow soldier in Woods's unit, who had to return to a gravely ill wife in Texas. With the whole court watching, Goodman and his fellow counsel unpacked the net and showed it to Waddy, who quickly identified it as the one he'd found right after the shooting. The court refused to allow the net as physical evidence, claiming there was no record covering the chain of handling from the scene of the shooting to the Manila laboratory where Ramos had had the net examined; it therefore could not be accepted as proof, even though it was the army that had mishandled it. But Waddy was able to testify that when he had arrived at the scene of the shooting, he had pointed out the bullet hole in the mosquito net to the other soldiers present.[35]

The prosecution countered with the testimony of Dr. Bray O. Hawk, who had performed the autopsy on Patterson. Hawk testified that the angle of the bullet as it cut through the victim's right arm and chest precluded the possibility that Patterson was sleeping—it was too "unnatural" a position, and therefore (as the "eyewitness" had claimed) Woods must have roused Patterson before he shot him. Having been alerted to this testimony by the prosecutor's opening statement, Goodman was prepared to counter these claims. It was here that he demonstrated his penchant for dramatic confrontation. Cross-examining Hawk, Goodman stripped to the waist in front of the court and had Hawk use ink to mark his arm and chest where the bullet had entered Patterson's body. He then tied one end of a piece of string around his arm at the point of entry. Goodman assumed Patterson's position in a cot brought into the courtroom and gave the other end of the string to his cocounsel, Major Bunker, who stood by with an unloaded gun.

> In this way, I demonstrated the various positions Patterson might have been in consistent with the angle of the bullet's path through his body. In the process, Hawk admitted that the angle of the bullet's passage could not be established precisely, . . . [and] Patterson could very well have been sleeping with his arm in a natural position at the time he was shot. . . . The hours Major Bunker and I had spent rehearsing a dramatic reconstruction of the shooting using the cot and the gun had paid off well.[36]

Goodman had considerably more difficulty, however, countering the testimony of Major Edmund Winslett, an army photographic interpreter. He was a "guy with a big belly and chest filled with medals, who sat up there like King Canute himself," Goodman recalled. Winslett, whose specialty was interpreting aerial reconnaissance photos, testified that the photographs of the victim's wound showed evidence of a gunpowder blast at close range and that the discoloration at the entrance point was caused by gunpowder, not hair. "There seemed to be no way to shake his simple yet telling testimony," Goodman said later, "and with a sinking feeling I allowed him to leave the stand without cross-examination."[37]

While Winslett was giving this potentially damaging testimony, Freda Goodman was sitting in the courtroom next to one of the prosecution's earlier witnesses, ballistics expert Thomas Baty. They shared a common colonial heritage—Freda in South Africa, Baty in Australia—and during breaks in the testimony, the two traded stories about life in the British Commonwealth. Before court adjourned for the day, Baty gave Freda his telephone number and suggested that she have her husband call him. "When I did," Ernie recalled, "he said, 'I'd like to talk to you about the testimony of this fellow Winslett. You may be interested in what I have to tell you.'" Over dinner that evening, Baty explained that he had been assigned by General Douglas MacArthur to investigate the theft of valuable artworks by U.S. occupation forces in Japan. His work had led him to a palatial home used as a U.S. command center, where he was ushered into the office of the commander—Winslett. Baty immediately noticed that the office walls were lined with several of the missing artworks. As he told Winslett of his mission, the commander's pomposity soon gave way to fear. An interesting story, Goodman thought, but how could this possibly affect the potentially damaging testimony Winslett had given earlier that day?[38]

Baty had asked Goodman to bring along the court photos of the wounds on Patterson's arm and, after dinner, he examined them with a magnifying instrument. "Just as I thought," he told the Goodmans. "There are no powder burns indicated here." For many years, Baty explained, one of his jobs had been checking photographic evidence of gunshot wounds. "Look," he told Goodman, "these fine black lines extending right up to the opening of the wound are hairs," not gunpowder. Baty's expert opinion would directly challenge Winslett's testimony and corroborate Woods's statement that the gun was fired from across the room. Baty volunteered to testify if Goodman called him. After mulling over the possibility that Baty, who still worked for the army's Criminal Investigation Division (CID), might be setting him up, Goodman decided he had no choice but to accept the offer. If Winslett's testimony went unchallenged, it would give the court what it wanted to convict Woods.[39]

On the witness stand, Baty repeated to the court what he had told the Goodmans over dinner. The blackened area around the wound was probably congealed blood, evidenced by its glistening appearance, rather than charred tissue, and there were several fine hairs reaching down to the area of the wound that showed no sign of being burned. "With this testimony of the prosecution's own expert specifically and effectively refuting its theory of powder burns, the prosecution's case of murder collapsed," Goodman recalled.[40]

That left only two issues for Goodman's defense team to clear up: the eyewitness testimony of John Hicks, and Woods's alleged confession. Hicks was the easiest of the two. Unlike in the first trial, he now said he could not recall any of the particulars of the shooting and didn't recall even seeing the gun fired—testimony so "vague, confused, and contradictory," Goodman remembered, that the prosecution twice moved to impeach its own witness. As to the alleged confession, Woods testified that CID agents John Walls and Omer S. Bowen had beaten and threatened him behind the walls of Bilibid prison, and only after Walls had repeatedly struck him in the back and stomach and bent his left hand back while Bowen punched him in the kidney did he sign the confession that Walls had prepared. On the stand, Walls and Bowen had given contradictory and vague accounts of the interrogation, which Goodman now demolished under cross-examination. Walls admitted that he couldn't remember if Woods had used the word "murder," and Bowen acknowledged that "the biggest part of the statement was paraphrased by Walls" before Woods signed it.[41]

The trial ended after two weeks of testimony, a telling contrast with the three *hours* devoted to the first court-martial. While Woods and Goodman waited outside the courtroom, the panel of judges conferred in secret. "It took quite a long time," Goodman remembered. "All afternoon we were pacing and walking and talking." Then, in a ritual strangely reminiscent of the vote in choosing a pope, the judges individually wrote their verdicts on pieces of paper and, after they were tabulated, burned them in a container near the window, the smoke drifting outside and signaling that a verdict had been reached.[42]

Woods had been acquitted of the murder charge. He no longer faced the hangman's noose, but this good news was tempered by the panel's ruling that Woods was guilty of "involuntary manslaughter" and would serve three years at hard labor. Goodman eventually won a reduction in the sentence to include time served, and in October 1948, Woods returned to

Detroit. "It's great to be home again," he told reporters as he paid tribute to Goodman and the Civil Rights Congress. "I certainly have them to thank for my life and freedom."[43]

Within weeks of the verdict, the army publicly acknowledged the pattern of abuses highlighted in the Woods case and implemented needed reforms. Three years later, Congress gave these changes the force of law when it ratified the Uniform Code of Military Justice. Under the new regulations, enlisted men could serve on court-martial juries, rules of evidence would be brought into closer alignment with civilian courts, and defendants would have the right to competent lawyers of their own choosing. GIs would no longer have to place their lives in the hands of a future Coca-Cola salesman. In 1948, the year following Woods's acquittal, President Truman would finally issue the long-awaited order desegregating the military.[44]

In the meantime, the case had won universal acclaim for Goodman in the black community, elevating him to the same status of respect and trust that Sugar had won in the 1930s. "One of the most popular heroes of the day in Detroit is hardworking attorney Ernest Goodman," the *Pittsburgh Courier* reported to the predominantly black readers of its Detroit edition. Beneath a headline heralding "Detroiters of Goodwill," the *Courier*'s editors featured a portrait photo of Goodman, his eyes fixed on the camera, pipe turned to one side in a clenched mouth, his head tilted to the same side. Here was something rare: a white lawyer who waived his fee to save an innocent black man from the gallows.[45]

Goodman would come to appreciate the support of his black friends in the years ahead. Even before Woods had come to trial, it was clear that the political winds were shifting, filling the sails of a revived Red Scare that would dwarf the prewar persecution of the Left. And this time, Sugar and his colleagues were to be among the first casualties.

Cold War

Signs of potential discord with the Soviet Union had been evident before 1945, but the flashpoints of conflict were multiplying dramatically after the war ended. The immediate issue was control of Eastern Europe: Russia had been repeatedly invaded and laid waste by European armies, the last two coming from Germany in the space of twenty-five years, and Soviet leader Joseph Stalin would insist on a postwar settlement that ended that threat. After the Red Army had fought its way to Berlin, Stalin expected that Soviet influence would prevail in Eastern Europe, much as the United States expected to predominate in the Caribbean and Latin America.

President Truman, however, was far less inclined than Franklin Roosevelt to compromise on these issues. He saw Stalin as Hitler's equal, seeking control of Eastern Europe as a first step toward global domination. Soviet power could be countered, he believed, only by the United States' continuing monopoly of the nuclear weapons it had used to destroy Hiroshima and Nagasaki, forcing Japan's surrender. To signal this hard line, the Truman administration immediately cancelled aid shipments to the Soviet Union, repudiated Roosevelt's willingness to discuss loans, and cut off the payment of war reparations from West Germany to Russia. When Truman later announced generous subsidies for European reconstruction under the Marshall Plan, the Soviets were excluded—*unless* they opened their zone to U.S. corporations and accepted U.S. control of how aid monies were spent. To no one's surprise, the Soviets rejected these humiliating terms. Denied alternative sources of capital to rebuild his ravaged country, Stalin stripped Eastern Europe of its movable assets and brutally repressed the dissent these policies produced.[46]

There was ample support in Congress for this get-tough policy, particularly after the 1946 elections produced something unseen since 1928: Republican majorities in both the House and Senate. Low voter turnout and public anxiety over strikes, inflation, and Soviet expansion accounted for this sea change in national politics, with devastating consequences for labor's left wing. Of 318 CIO-endorsed candidates, only one in four survived the conservative flood tide that brought to Congress newcomers like Richard Nixon and Joseph McCarthy. The Eightieth Congress was all the more receptive, therefore, to Truman's articulation of a new international crusade. While just three years before, Goodman had celebrated the approaching victory of "a people's war for the liberation of subjugated people all over the world," Truman now redefined the global struggle as one that pitted a free world of Western democracies against a Communist bloc of tyrannical dictatorships. The "Truman Doctrine," as it came to be known, called for U.S. military and economic intervention in local conflicts around the globe to defeat Communist insurgencies and uphold America's unique vision of political freedom. There was an altruistic appeal to this crusade, which promised to oppose the old colonial empires of Britain and France no less than the expanding dominion of the Soviets. Most Americans also believed in what historian William A. Williams called the "virtuous omnipotence" of American policy: the United States had, after all, just defeated Hitler and humbled the Japanese emperor, and wartime hatred of these two personifications of evil was now transferred to Stalin and his dictatorial methods.[47]

From the very beginning of the Truman Doctrine, however, critics—Goodman among them—would note an underlying hypocrisy in a policy that so often supported kings, shahs, generalissimos and other local tyrants whose dedication to "freedom" was limited to free entry for U.S. corporations. There was also widespread war weariness and matching apprehension about the horrors of atomic war that weakened popular support for aggressive military action. To win unquestioning support for the Truman Doctrine it would be necessary, as Michigan's Senator Arthur Vandenberg put it, "to scare the hell out of the American people."[48]

A revived Red Scare was the tool at hand, and conservatives were eager to put it to use. Goodman was already well acquainted with Martin Dies and the prewar version of congressional inquisition. He had been happy to see it fade (and Dies retire) during the war. But with the approach of victory, congressional conservatives had moved to revive the House Un-American Activities Committee (HUAC) as a permanent body devoted to the investigation of "the diffusion within the United States of subversive and un-American propaganda." The expanding military power of the Soviet Union, previously celebrated when the Russians were U.S. allies during the war, now inspired a growing concern that the battle-hardened Red Army would continue marching westward into Europe and south into the Middle East. The potency of this challenge to U.S. power rekindled the fears of many Americans about foreign enemies, and the ideological ties between the CP-USA and the Soviet regime linked this collective apprehension to a revived fear of domestic radicals. The merging of these two anxious states would give the postwar Red Scare its special staying power, linking the New Deal, the CIO, and domestic radicalism to a hydra-headed conspiracy allegedly centered in Moscow. By the spring of 1947, the Gallup Poll reported that 61 percent of those surveyed agreed that membership in the Communist Party should be forbidden by law.[49]

Buoyed by this popular sentiment, HUAC targeted Communists and their "fellow travelers" in the government, labor movement, and Hollywood. People like Goodman and Sugar who had celebrated the wartime alliance with the Soviets too vigorously, who had admired Soviet society too uncritically, and who now opposed the Truman Doctrine too publicly—they and others would be targeted as "un-American." HUAC's grounds for suspicion steadily widened to accommodate the personal politics of the committee's inquisitors. John Rankin, the Mississippi Democrat who sponsored the bill creating HUAC, was a public defender of the Ku Klux

Klan. According to him, race mixing was a Communist plot and President Roosevelt's Fair Employment Practices Commission was "the beginning of a Communist dictatorship."[50]

To match the zealous Red hunters of HUAC and establish his credentials as a determined anti-Communist, President Truman launched his own "Loyalty Program" in March of 1947. Under its provisions, millions of civil servants in the federal government and workers in defense industries were subject to investigation and dismissal if they were found to be members of—or even in "sympathetic association" with—organizations designated by the attorney general as "totalitarian, Fascist, Communist, or subversive." Like the roster of HUAC suspects, the attorney general's list grew as the Red Scare broadened and as the president and Congress vied to outdo each other in the hunt for subversives. The list could have served as a registry of Goodman's life over the previous decade. Among the ninety-three groups the attorney general first singled out for their unacceptable views were the Veterans of the Abraham Lincoln Brigade, the Civil Rights Congress, the International Workers Order, the Michigan Civil Rights Federation, the National Federation for Constitutional Liberties, the National Negro Congress, and the North American Committee to Aid Spanish Democracy. He had worked for all of them.[51]

The Fall

Goodman and Sugar must have known they would soon be in the crosshairs of a revived Red Scare. But when the moment came, it was not HUAC or the Truman administration that delivered the blow. It was their new boss, UAW president Walter Reuther.

Reuther had won the union's presidency in 1946 on the heels of his militant leadership of the GM strike. His narrow victory over R. J. Thomas—124 convention votes out of 8,765—was a measure of the precarious balance of power between the union's two major factions. Reuther, a former socialist and toolmaker who once traveled to the Soviet Union and worked in its auto industry, had gravitated since the late 1930s to an anti-Communist position that put him on the so-called right wing of the union's internal politics. To the larger public, however, he was a prominent left-wing critic of corporate capitalism, a vigorous advocate of "economic democracy" who would borrow ideas from the Social Democratic parties of Europe. Within the union, his eclectic brand of reformism drew a diverse following of socialists, Trotskyists, liberal Catholics, southern whites, and conservative business unionists. The unifying pole for most of them was Reuther's relentless attack on his former allies in the

Communist Party, men he condemned for their frequent zigzags in policy and their support of speedup during the war.[52]

Reuther's opponents in the so-called left wing of the union still held the majority of the UAW's executive board seats in 1946. Following Thomas's defeat, they pinned their hopes for a comeback on George Addes, who had won reelection as secretary treasurer without opposition. There was little that separated Addes and Reuther when it came to bargaining priorities or support for the New Deal. Reuther would even try to enlist the secretary treasurer to his cause, but only if he abandoned his Communist allies. Addes refused. He was a devout Catholic who had an uneasy relationship with party members, but he still felt a personal loyalty to the center-left coalition that had built the union and defined so much of his adult life. He counted Goodman and Sugar among his allies, with Sugar playing an especially important role in Addes's inner circle of advisors. They were joined by others who faulted Reuther for his ambition and his collaboration with conservative anti-Communists.[53]

The result was a no-holds-barred confrontation that dominated the internal life of the union in 1946–47. Clancy Sigal, a member of the UAW staff during these years, later described a regional union meeting in his novel *Going Away*. It was, he recalled, "a revelation."

> A mixture of old soldiers' get together, a primitive soviet, clubhouse whingding, the French Assembly in a financial crisis, and a World Series baseball game; it was in almost constant uproar from the opening gavel as delegates argued, shouted, shoved for the "mike" and occasionally settled it in the corridor. . . . It was not subtle but it was democracy.[54]

Reuther fired a warning salvo in this uncivil war immediately after his election, pledging to unite 90 percent of the union against the 10 percent with "outside loyalties." One of his first targets was George Crockett. Contrary to subsequent accounts that he was simply fired, the actual process that separated Crockett from the union began with parliamentary maneuvering at the union's 1946 convention. In response to Crockett's intensive lobbying, the delegates agreed to elevate the Fair Employment Practices *Committee* to the more permanent status of the Fair Employment Practices *Department*; the Reuther caucus supported this initiative but added an amendment specifying that only UAW members who had come up through the ranks could serve as the department's director. Crockett, the hired lawyer, was therefore disqualified and replaced by Bill Oliver from Ford Local 400, one of the few African Americans to support

Reuther. Crockett, as it happened, had only just declared himself an Addes supporter, following Reuther's failure to win at GM the kind of nondiscrimination clause already included in the Ford and Chrysler contracts. "Up until that time or a maybe a few months before," as he remembered it, "I was still trying to ride the fence between these two factions. But more and more, I was finding that the people willing to do something about discrimination by and large were in the Addes faction, and they included all your so-called Reds, besides many of your old-line socialists."[55]

Ousted from the Fair Employment Practices Department, Crockett became Addes's administrative assistant and continued to do for Addes the same work that Oliver now did for Reuther. This intraorganizational feuding continued until the winter of 1947, when Sugar invited Crockett to take a leave of absence and work in his firm. With Addes's consent, Crockett left the UAW payroll, but both he and Sugar still hoped that the union's upcoming convention in November would return the Left to the presidency and Crockett to leadership of the Fair Employment Practices Department. To make the latter possible, Crockett had to become a dues-paying member of the UAW. "So it was arranged that I would work in a garage over here on Canfield [Street]. I would go there every Saturday, work as a janitor, clean up grease on the floor, put in rear-view mirrors on new Fords, etc. until I had the requisite number of hours to become a member . . . of the UAW Garage and Mechanics Local."[56]

It would be hard to imagine what his fellow mechanics thought of the moonlighting lawyer who arrived each Saturday to perform janitorial tasks traditionally assigned to unskilled African Americans. Come Monday, however, when the newly arrived lawyer ventured downtown, the response was predictably hostile. "There wasn't a single black lawyer who had an office in downtown Detroit," as Goodman recalled years later. "The only black people who were in the building were the janitorial staff and black clients." Even black clients, when they came to visit Sugar's offices in the Barlum Tower, were not allowed to ride the passenger elevators. "I remember quite a protest that we had," recalled Ford worker and Local 600 officer Art McPhaul, "because blacks had to ride the freight elevator." In this whites-only environment, even the simple act of going to lunch was fraught with racial tension. Goodman and Crockett could eat together only in the greasy spoon on the first floor of the Barlum Tower or in the most expensive hotels. Otherwise, their arrival in a downtown restaurant provoked what Goodman remembered as a sudden shortage of food. "'Well, we don't have that,' or some other excuse, and we would just have to wait and ultimately it was very rare that we'd actually get served food. So the upshot was that you couldn't eat around here and sometimes we'd get mad. George would get mad. I'd get mad. We'd make a civil rights issue out of it. We'd threaten to file a complaint and we'd call up the police."[57]

It was only possible to "file a complaint" because Governor Murphy had signed into law the Equal Accommodations Act of 1938, making Michigan one of the first states in the country to outlaw segregation in public places. Sponsored by Detroit's Charles Diggs Sr., the first African American elected to the state senate, the "Diggs Act" made it a misdemeanor for restaurants, hotels, theaters, and other public places to deny service for reasons of "race, creed, or color." As such, it was a little-known milestone in the civil rights struggle and a testament to the power of the political coalition that had swept both Murphy and Diggs into office in 1936. But local officials ignored the law, and the low fines ($25) and lengthy proceedings usually discouraged litigation. Nevertheless, the threat to bring charges could occasionally produce a reluctant, if temporary, compliance. More often, Goodman and Crockett found it easier to leave the downtown altogether and eat at the Lucy Thurman YWCA, where Goodman was sometimes the solitary white customer in the cafeteria. "You can't live by continuing everyday to have a civil rights fight on your hands," Goodman recalled of these more tranquil (if out-of-the-way) meals. "You wouldn't have time to represent people who really needed it."[58]

Among those in need were the many people in UAW local unions across the country who were under attack by employers and Congress. Undoubtedly, the most beleaguered among them were the eleven thousand members of UAW Local 248, still on strike at the Allis Chalmers plant near Milwaukee—the same local Goodman had represented the year before in contempt hearings related to mass picketing. Since his October plane ride from Willow Run Airport, Goodman had watched with what must have been a sinking heart as things went from bad to worse. By early 1947, Local 248 had become the high-profile target of congressional red-baiting and the focal point of the UAW's factional wars.

Reuther had initially joined with his left-wing opponents to support the strike and the militant local union that called it in April of 1946. There were ample grounds for the walkout at Wisconsin's largest corporation and leading manufacturer of agricultural equipment. The notoriously antiunion management at Allis Chalmers refused to comply with orders of the War Labor Board, refused to accept grievance decisions of the neutral arbitrator, refused to renew the union security clause or deduct dues from paychecks, and refused the union's offer to arbitrate wages and other strike issues. As the strike wore on month after month and thousands of discouraged workers returned to work, the local's left-wing leaders and shop stewards had grown desperate. These were the same kind of men Goodman had come to know at Ford Local 600: hard-nosed working-class radicals, some of them Communists, more of them independent socialists or New Deal liberals, all of them devoted to a now-fading vision of rank-and-file militancy. Six months into the strike, they had launched a last-ditch campaign to physically block access to the plant gates. Goodman had defended their old-style combativeness in court, but as escalating picket line violence pitted police and strikebreakers against thousands of strikers, public apprehension grew.[59]

The national media was now focused on the strike, and HUAC and other congressional committees soon followed in the winter of 1947. The company's attorney and lead strategist, Harold Story, testified before the House Education and Labor Committee that Local 248's leaders were Communists—certainly true of some—and that strike strategy was authored in Moscow—certainly a fabrication, for which Story offered no evidence. Strike orders, he continued without corroboration, were "transmitted to Communist Party headquarters, which in turn transmits it to its members who are heads of labor unions, who then transmit Communist doctrine to members in union meetings." Thus, he concluded, "the attempt is going on to radicalize and poison the minds of American workers."[60]

Committee chairman Fred Hartley later cited these claims and the lengthy testimony of Allis Chalmers officials as justification for the Taft-Hartley Act. Passed just a few months after these hearings, Taft-Hartley amended the National Labor Relations Act in ways that would dramatically alter the internal factional fighting in the UAW. Employers won the statutory right to speak against the union during organizing drives, permitting wider use of the kind of implied threats Goodman had opposed in the Ford campaign. Workers could no longer conduct sympathy strikes, promote boycotts of stores or businesses carrying goods made by strikebreakers, or conduct mass picketing during walkouts. The capstone that linked these antilabor measures with the Red Scare was the additional requirement—inspired by the hysteria surrounding the Allis Chalmers strike—that all union officers sign an oath that they were not members of the Communist Party. If they failed to do so, their union would lose all of the remaining protections of federal labor law, including the right to even appear on the ballot when the National Labor Relations Board conducted elections to certify the union's majority status. There was no matching obligation, as critics pointed out, that Henry Ford and other employers declare their loyalty to the United States and their opposition to fascism.[61]

As the Red Scare conjured into the public eye these phantoms of foreign interference and Soviet mind control, Reuther concluded that the

Allis Chalmers strike was a political liability the union could not afford. The UAW president did not endorse the paranoiac claim that the strike was "called by Moscow," and he publicly supported the right of UAW members to join whatever party they chose. But, echoing management's claims, he blamed the Communists for prolonging an unwinnable strike and accused them of using "our union and its members for the prosecution of their alien ideology." Goodman knew that these charges of conspiracy and manipulation were unfounded. The members of Local 248 had voted their leaders into office many times over the years, well aware that they supported the Popular Front and such radical causes as racial integration. Confronted by the company's concession demands and intransigence, the members had voted to go on strike by the lopsided margin of 8,091 to 251. Local 248's leaders had not always used the best judgment: allowing Communist Party election petitions to circulate on the picket lines was probably unwise (but hard to prohibit), and the fact that many local leaders signed them was certainly bad publicity. But there was nothing illegal in any of these activities.[62]

There was another dimension to Reuther's attack, however, that was not so easily dismissed. What was happening in Milwaukee, Reuther warned the union's executive board, was "just a small, a little dress rehearsal compared to what is going to happen in this country." He said he was "prepared and will take my place to fight against the witch hunt, but I say it is nothing short of criminal negligence for a union not to recognize these basic facts and get its house in order," the better "to resist the full impact of that attack." This was an argument based not so much on principle—*the Red Scare is wrong or right*—as on the practical needs of survival—*the Red Scare is too powerful to resist and will destroy us if we don't jettison the Communists*. It was, however, no more practical than the position taken by the Left. Both sides were demanding the impossible of their opponent. Reuther expected his factional rivals to discard their comrades like excess baggage off a storm-tossed boat, when for many on the left, Goodman included, such a parting would have seemed more like self-mutilation. Whatever the faults of the Communist Party, its grassroots activists had been early and key leaders in the struggle to build the union, and Goodman counted many of them as friends and clients. The Left, on the other hand, insisted on a principled rejection of red-baiting that too often opposed *any* criticism of Communist practice, meanwhile turning a blind eye to the approaching juggernaut of the cold war–infused Red Scare.[63]

It was the Addes caucus that blinked first at Allis Chalmers. With HUAC holding hearings in Milwaukee and grilling Local 248's leaders in a high-profile investigation of their ties to the Communist Party, the left-wing majority on the executive board finally threw in the towel and agreed with Reuther's proposal to send the remaining strikers back to work. In June, Congress passed the Taft-Hartley Act over Truman's veto, and the union's leaders had to confront the issue of whether they would sign the non-Communist "loyalty" affidavits called for by the law. Sugar coauthored the pamphlet with Crockett and Goodman that initially instructed the UAW's local leaders not to comply; signing the affidavits "would appear to be unnecessary," the pamphlet bravely asserted, "in view of the stated policy of the International Union not to use the facilities of the Labor Board." The union had lived without the NLRB before 1937, said the leaders of the Addes caucus, and it could do so again. It was a call to working-class independence and freedom from government thought-control that even the crusty old coal miner and part-time Republican John L. Lewis could endorse. Lewis could afford to, since no other union would dare challenge his United Mine Workers in the coalfields. For the UAW, however, it was another matter. As Reuther pointed out, there were AFL unions competing for members in dozens of metal-working industries that were eager to sign the Taft-Hartley oath, giving them an open field in NLRB elections where the UAW's refusal to comply would keep them off the ballot. Rawboned militancy could not easily overcome these odds even when supported by the members, and there was little prospect in 1947 that workers were willing to return to the combative tactics of the 1930s. The very integration into the economic mainstream that union members now aspired to, along with a patriotic self-identity encouraged by wars hot and cold, made such a return to extralegal militancy improbable. By late October, Reuther was able to persuade most of the left-wing members of the executive board to either abstain or vote in favor of compliance with the Taft-Hartley non-Communist oath. Addes was left in the minority, abandoned by his own supporters.[64]

The left-wing caucus was by then in headlong retreat as the advancing Red Scare turned its alliance with the Communist minority into a dangerous liability. When the delegates arrived in Atlantic City for the union's November convention, the Addes caucus failed to hold its own on the executive board and didn't even try to seriously contest the reelection of Reuther. Emil Mazey, still a member of the Socialist Party and famous for his militant leadership of Briggs Local 212, defeated Addes in the balloting for secretary treasurer. The Reuther caucus took eighteen of the twenty-two seats on the executive board, and convention delegates voted their approval of the decision to comply with the Taft-Hartley Act by a 3-1 margin.[65]

It was no surprise to anyone on the thirty-second floor of the Barlum Tower that the first order of business when the new executive board convened was Reuther's proposal to terminate Maurice Sugar's contract as general counsel. Sugar, despite his public posture as a neutral servant of the union, was widely known for his behind-the-scenes role as a strategist for Addes. It was only logical that Reuther would replace him with counsel he could trust. There was considerable shock, however, at the vindictiveness of the president's attack. Goodman recalled the separation years later with evident anger. "It was not a pleasant sort of . . . 'look, you think differently than I do, and so goodbye, thanks for what you've done.' It wasn't that. It was bitter, and he tried to do a job on Sugar every way he could."[66]

For the first time in many years, Sugar was not present as the UAW Executive Board gathered at Detroit's Fort Shelby Hotel in late November for its first meeting since the convention. Reuther had told Sugar the day before that his contract would be terminated and he would be expected to finish his pending cases. It was a foregone conclusion that the UAW president had the votes to oust Sugar, and Reuther's argument for doing so included at least one point that was difficult to deny: that Sugar and Crockett had allied themselves with his factional opponents. This was certainly true, though Reuther and the board majority, when challenged by the left-wing minority, were hard pressed to identify a concrete case where this had made any difference to the counsel Sugar had provided. It was, nevertheless, hard to argue with Reuther's insistence that "the attorney for this Union has to be someone with whom the President . . . can go with the most inward secrets of this union on a purely confidential basis."[67]

Rather than limit himself to these legitimate grounds for terminating Sugar's contract, Reuther went on to make additional charges that provoked considerable rancor. Reuther went off record to cite evidence from the late 1930s that Sugar was either a Communist or so closely allied with the party that the distinction was moot. The few remaining left-wingers on the board would have none of it, and went on record to ridicule the president's claims. Paul Miley, a regional director from Ohio, objected to the selective use of "ancient history," and then offered some of his own, recalling a speech in 1937 in which Reuther had recounted his work in Russia and stressed the need to learn from the Soviet Union. Miley continued: "I remember something of those days. . . . And I was firmly convinced then that the Reuther brothers were members of the Communist Party. I think I was wrong, now, but at that time. . . . [Walter] was a lot closer to the Communist Party in those days than we were." Dick Reisinger, the other left-wing regional director from Ohio, added that he also knew "a lot of people that were meeting with those people [Communists] at that time,

including the president of this union, the now president of this union. . . .
I assume people have a right to change their opinion." Even one of Reuther's board allies, Norm Matthews, agreed with Reisinger that Sugar's
past associations were not important. In response, Reuther vented his exasperation. "When people say I am a member of the Communist Party,
that is redbaiting. When you call a Communist a Communist, that isn't
redbaiting."[68]

The debate was no less heated when the board turned to the final
accusation, delivered by Emil Mazey, that Sugar and his associates "had
built up a very lucrative practice" by overcharging the union. None of his
claims could have been sustained if Sugar and George Addes had been
at the meeting, but in their absence Mazey was free to misrepresent the
complex details of Sugar's contract. Throughout, the newly elected secretary treasurer misconstrued Sugar's retainer—$2,100 a month, or $25,200
a year in 1946—as the principal payment the union was expected to make
for legal services. There were many lawyers, Mazey claimed, who could
handle all of the union's legal work for $15,000 a year or less, and only
"occasionally" would they need to hire local attorneys to pursue cases
around the country. Instead, he continued, Sugar's associates—Goodman
included—were billing for particular jobs that Sugar should have been
handling by himself. "We paid for the same service twice," he insisted.[69]

Mazey's charges would not only define the circumstances of Sugar's
severance, they would soon serve as justification for mobilizing a general
boycott of the Sugar firm by virtually every union in Detroit. With so
much at stake, Mazey could have been expected to know the details. But
when Paul Miley noted that Sugar's net income was probably only a third
of the total retainer, and then asked if expenses like rent, clerical labor,
and other costs didn't account for the rest of the payment, Mazey said he
didn't know and had not been able to find a copy of the contract to con-
firm its details. Reuther also claimed that he had been trying to get a copy
of the contract "for many, many months to this date and I have not seen a
copy of it."[70]

They were almost certainly lying on this score: a copy of the contract
had been delivered to them six months before, as they well knew. Mazey
had asked Reuther to send him a copy of Sugar's contract in May 1947,
and after Reuther had passed this request along to Addes, the secretary
treasurer had sent copies to both Mazey and the president's office in early
June along with a memo explaining its myriad details. Signed in 1939
and annually renewed thereafter, the contract specified in detail that the
retainer would cover office expenses and leave roughly $500 a month to
compensate Sugar for his full-time attention to advising the executive

board and the "co-ordination and supervision" of the many attorneys hired on a case-by-case basis to handle the union's growing legal agenda. "The attorneys associated with the general counsel," the contract specified, "should be paid for their services *in addition*" to the monthly retainer that went to Sugar (emphasis added). The same procedure would be followed for the many local attorneys hired across the country. With this information only recently placed in their hands, Mazey and Reuther would have known exactly what was in the contract. They would have understood, as Miley pointed out, that it was "a little naive" to believe that one man in the Barlum Tower would handle the *hundreds* of legal matters that came before the national union each year, with only the "occasional" need, as Mazey had claimed, to hire additional counsel.[71]

Little of this could be known at the board meeting given the absence of Addes and Sugar, and Reuther flatly refused to call them to the next day's meeting or any future gathering of the board. It would not have changed the outcome even if he had. "Go ahead boys," Miley exclaimed at one point. "I will talk for the record. I know it doesn't make any difference. The die is cast." With the board's lopsided vote to terminate the contract, Sugar's long tenure as general counsel came to a close. Both he and Goodman would now face some difficult times.[72]

The next months would mark the agonizing transition as Sugar and his associates finished their pending cases and turned their files over to the union's new lawyers. Irving Levy, former head of the U.S. Department of Labor's legal division, would serve as the UAW's temporary general counsel with offices in Washington, while a new firm in Detroit led by Abe Zwerdling, Reuther's assistant since 1944, would carry most of the caseload. For all the acrimony that had accompanied Sugar's dismissal, there was a surprising degree of camaraderie between the departing attorneys and their replacements. Labor law was still a new and controversial specialty, and the small coterie of lawyers aligned with the CIO had often worked collaboratively, sharing legal strategies as well as membership in the National Lawyers Guild. Two months after his termination, Sugar wrote to Reuther that he was "pleased at the prospect" of meeting with the new general counsel. "Levy is far from a stranger to me," Sugar noted, "and I have a high regard for him." Goodman had equally high praise for Harold Cranefield, the man who eventually replaced Levy. As a fellow member of the Lawyers Guild and the former regional attorney of the National Labor Relations Board in Detroit, he had become Goodman's ally in the late 1930s and early 1940s during the organizing drives at Ford and elsewhere.[73]

Cranefield took the job as a salaried "in-house" attorney for the UAW with some trepidation, noting in his correspondence with Levy the same concerns over job security and professional integrity that Sugar had faced ten years before. "A professional person who accepts a salaried position without definite tenure is in a very difficult position," Cranefield wrote Levy before taking the job of associate general counsel. "The mere possibility of abrupt termination"—Sugar's recent experience no doubt in mind—"requires him to be attentive to other . . . possibilities of employment." To avoid this "distracting" consideration, Cranefield demanded a two-year contract and an understanding that he would not have to engage in "political activity" within the union, or submit to scrutiny of his "strictly private and personal relationships." These personal links included Goodman and others on labor's left wing with whom Cranefield continued a discreet but unapologetic friendship after his promotion to general counsel. In Goodman's eyes he remained "a good friend, a wonderful man." Years later, Goodman's son Dick recalled that Cranefield—"a funny man with a dry sense of humor"—and his wife, Eleanor, were frequent visitors to the house on Warrington Drive.[74]

The union's legal matters would be competently handled, but the changeover was difficult nevertheless, particularly as Mazey delayed full payment of Sugar's promised severance check by four months. ("Am I still on probation?" Sugar wrote to Reuther after two months.) Sugar's periodic visits to the UAW headquarters on Milwaukee Avenue, in the shadow of the GM Building, were another painful reminder of his lost status. The executive board had complained that Sugar's outside offices and practice had made him too independent; Zwerdling therefore maintained offices within the union's headquarters, where he and Sugar would meet to arrange the handoff of cases and the billing for work done before and after the termination. Goodman's docket in April 1948 was an impressive catalogue of unfinished business for the union: six current court cases (four of them out of state); twelve separate cases involving denial of unemployment benefits (one appealed to the Michigan Supreme Court, where Goodman won benefits for a woman returning to the workforce after childbirth); drafting public statements for three of the union's top officers; review of two state laws; administrative details before the FCC, Labor Department, and Social Security Board; one NLRB case; work on Taft-Hartley compliance; and finally, perhaps the largest single demand on his time, the injunction hearings, conspiracy cases, and criminal proceedings related to the prolonged and violent strike of UAW garage mechanics in Detroit—Crockett's recent workmates.[75]

In the months following the 1947 convention, the triumphant Reuther caucus dismissed nearly one hundred UAW staff members, one-third of the total working at the Milwaukee Avenue headquarters. Some found jobs elsewhere in the labor movement; others left the movement altogether. Among the left wing's defeated officers, R. J. Thomas took a job with the CIO and George Addes became a tavern owner. For Goodman and Sugar, however, there was no alternative employment to the law practice they had built up over the years. Reuther's vendetta would hound them relentlessly, as Goodman well remembered. "When Reuther cleaned house, he cleaned our house pretty thoroughly. Nobody who he supported or supported him thereafter sent any legal work to us, as a matter of fact they made sure that none came to us as far as they could. So things changed very quickly. A large number of the lawyers in the office just left because they knew there was no work for them, and they had to make a living."[76]

It was a slow death for the once-proud firm, and an especially difficult one for Sugar. His stature had once generated a kind of gravity that attracted clients and associates to the firm, but now, as his reputation diminished, so did his ability to hold together what had always been a confederation of potential competitors. Sugar could not reverse a process that made him an actual liability to anyone associated with him. The pain of it would drive him away from the office, to long trips north, away from the city and into the country. As early as March of 1948, when he was invited to give a speech in Detroit on the Red Scare, he opened his remarks by acknowledging that he had been "asked to come out of what had been a long period of hibernation." In fact, he never really did. Slowly, he was withdrawing from the firm and from his lifelong involvement with the labor movement.[77]

"There were only a few of us left at the end," Goodman recalled. He was now their de facto leader. If they could not practice law in the current environment as they once had, they would have to change the environment. As it happened, at that very moment the prospects for such a transformation seemed especially good. A new political movement was emerging that promised to overturn the two-party system and remake America. Goodman would join it and run for public office, a candidate of the Progressive Party.[78]

Left Out

"The time is long overdue for taking concrete action in the building of an independent labor party of workers and working farmers." This was no voice in the wilderness that called on Detroit's UAW locals in 1947 to break with the two-party system and launch a new movement to remake America's politics. The author was UAW leader Emil Mazey, Sugar's adversary in the factional wars that ended with the dismissal of Sugar and Goodman. The left and right wings of the labor movement could agree on little else, but they were in accord on this critical issue: President Truman and the Democratic Party no longer represented the needs and aspirations of the working-class majority.[79]

Radicals and liberal New Dealers cited a litany of missteps that damned the president in their eyes. During the 1946 strike wave, Truman had temporarily nationalized the coal mines to force union members back to work, but during the GM strike he did nothing to punish the company's open defiance of federal mediation. He had called on Congress to give him the power to draft striking workers into the armed forces, power even some Republicans were loath to grant him. He had caved to business lobbyists calling for the lifting of price controls, while surrounding himself with cronies from his Missouri political machine. Congressional Democrats had little more to offer, split as they were between southern conservatives and northern liberals, the latter demoralized and numerically diminished after the 1946 elections. Mazey's frustration with Truman and the Democrats was echoed across the labor movement: in a survey conducted by sociologist C. Wright Mills, 23 percent of the CIO's union officers said they favored the immediate formation of a labor party and over half saw the long-term need for such a regrouping. In April of 1946, the UAW's executive board had already resolved to "work towards the eventual formation of a broad third party based on the thinking and interests of millions of the labor, farmer, professional and other progressive people of our nation."[80]

Goodman and Sugar also looked forward to the formation of a new party, but in addition to their concerns over the president's drift to the right on domestic issues, they saw his warlike belligerence toward the Soviet Union as a prime motivator for independent action. The president's "increasing concern over the spread of Communism," Goodman told reporter Sherwin Wine of Detroit's *Jewish News*, "has transferred our [nation's] interest from a constructive policy to one entirely negative, and if we continue to expend all our energies to oppose the doctrine, we are going to be diverted permanently from those actions which will truly insure democracy." Where Reuther and others in the UAW wanted to postpone the formation of a new party until after Truman's anticipated defeat in the 1948 elections, Goodman and others on the left favored immediate action. By the end of 1947 they had their candidate: former vice president Henry Wallace.[81]

While serving as secretary of commerce in the Truman administration, Wallace had pushed for a continuation of FDR's policy of constructive negotiation with the Soviets. He favored what he called a "progressive capitalism" that would promote global free trade and foreign markets for U.S. exports, providing loans and investments to rebuild Russia as well as Europe, while also guaranteeing that Germany and East Europe would never again be mobilized against the Soviets. "On our part," as he had argued in a major policy speech in September of 1946, "we should recognize that we have no more business in the political affairs of Eastern Europe than Russia has in the political affairs of Latin America." Speaking on that September day in New York City's Madison Square Garden, Wallace had outlined a set of principles that would soon define his third-party run for the presidency. "I believe that we can get cooperation," Wallace announced, "once Russia understands that our primary objective is neither saving the British Empire nor purchasing oil [in the Middle East] with the lives of American soldiers." Anticipating the arguments raised decades later by Richard Nixon for constructive engagement with Communist China, Wallace was confident that "peaceful competition" between Russia and the United States would gradually eliminate the sources of conflict. "The Russians will be forced to grant more and more of the personal freedoms, and we shall become more and more absorbed with the problems of social-economic justice." In the meantime, the two systems could coexist "in a profitable and productive peace."[82]

President Truman regarded Wallace's call for coexistence with the Soviets as a naive and unwelcome relic of the wartime alliance with Stalin, and dismissed him from his cabinet after the speech at Madison Square Garden. But the former vice president's message resonated with many of those who had supported the Popular Front in the 1930s: left-liberal Democrats, left-of-center trade unionists, civil rights advocates, idealists and peace activists. After barnstorming across the nation and speaking to sold-out crowds, Wallace announced to a national radio audience in December 1947 that he would run for president as an independent. "The people are on the march," he declared. "We have assembled a Gideon's Army, small in number, powerful in conviction, ready for action."[83]

When Wallace and his army of supporters swept into Detroit four months later, Goodman was the opening speaker at a packed-to-the-rafters rally at Detroit's Olympia Stadium, where Wallace spoke to repeated standing ovations by the twelve thousand in attendance. It was "very emotional, very messianic," recalled Goodman's son Dick, who attended the event as a fifteen-year-old boy. "There was a feeling as if the fate of the world was depending on this new party." Goodman certainly knew that Wallace had no realistic chance of winning the presidency, but he and his fellow Progressives believed this first campaign could draw 10 percent of the vote or more, planting the seeds for future victories, perhaps in 1952. When the Michigan Progressive Party gathered that September for its nominating convention at Detroit's Music Hall, the preamble to the platform raised just that possibility by referring to an earlier event in Michigan history: the 1854 gathering in Jackson where thousands of delegates had organized a third party—the Republican Party—that won the presidency six years later. The platform went on to call for "full equality for the Negro people, the Jewish people, and all other nationality and minority groups in the state," as well as repeal of the Taft-Hartley Act. The convention nominated forty-nine candidates to run on this program, including Goodman for Michigan attorney general, Dean Robb (his future law partner) for Wayne County commissioner, and Ned Smokler, the Reverend Charles Hill, and Coleman Young (executive director of the Wayne County CIO) for state senate.[84]

From the moment Wallace announced his candidacy, however, his campaign was under attack for accepting the support of the Communist Party. "If I fail to cry out that I am anti-Communist," Wallace had explained during his national tour in 1947, "it is not because I am friendly to communism but because at this time of growing intolerance I refuse to join . . . that band of men who stir the steaming cauldron of hatred and fear." He didn't doubt, as he said after announcing his candidacy, that Communists supported his call for peaceful coexistence with the Soviet Union, but pointed out that this was "the same way that I believe I'll get considerable support from Quakers and Methodists who want peace also." Most political pundits rejected these homilies on tolerance and drew, instead, the sinister conclusion that Wallace had become a tool of the Communists. "Moscow's American agents and those who follow their line," wrote Blair Moody in the *Detroit News*, "are doing their best to split the American liberal movement and elect a reactionary president next November," the better to "wreck the country and bring a violent overturn via depression."[85]

As evidence of the Communist Party's subordination to foreign control, many cited the abrupt shift in strategy after the Soviets signaled their disapproval in 1945 of Earl Browder's leadership. Browder had dissolved the CP-USA during World War II and reconstituted it as the Communist Political Association, a first step, as he saw it, toward a cross-class alliance with progressive capitalists to peacefully rebuild the postwar world. When Soviet leaders indicated their displeasure with this conciliatory strategy, American Communists dutifully replaced Browder with Eugene Dennis and reestablished the CP-USA as a top-down Leninist party, though with explicit language in its constitution repudiating the use of force and violence. Even with this disclaimer, conservatives and many liberals saw the CP-USA as little more than a Trojan horse for Soviet Russia. Whatever the CP-USA endorsed, anti-Communists opposed.[86]

In fact, the CP-USA had been slow to endorse Wallace's candidacy, in part because his calls for peace were often coupled with criticism of particular Soviet policies, and in part because his movement was decidedly middle class compared to the labor-based party that Communists favored. But with Wallace's formal announcement of his candidacy, the CP-USA swung behind the campaign and sent organizers into the field to help collect ballot signatures. Wallace's top advisors were former New Deal liberals like himself, but there were also former and present Communists working in his campaign, including Lee Pressman, Goodman's colleague in the Goose Creek case, who resigned his position as the CIO's chief counsel to serve as secretary of the Progressive Party's platform committee. Much was made of the fact that, unlike past elections in which the Communists ran their own nominee (usually winning a token one hundred thousand votes), in 1948 they fielded no candidate and concentrated all their efforts on supporting Wallace—leaving the impression that he was, in fact, "their" candidate. Responding to the drumbeat of criticism for tolerating this support, Wallace tried to distance himself from the CP-USA. "If the Communists would run a ticket of their own this year," he told a New Hampshire audience, "we might lose 100,000 votes but we would gain 3 million."[87]

In the meantime, Wallace had already lost the support of the CIO's national executive board, which voted 33-11 against endorsing his third-party campaign. Affiliated unions and central labor councils were expected to fall in line with this policy and make no endorsement of the Progressive Party. In August the CIO went a step further and gave its belated endorsement of Harry Truman. Labor leaders had applauded Truman's veto of the Taft-Hartley Act in 1947, but were disappointed by the president's failure to rally support for his position among congressmen of his own party (when the Eightieth Congress overrode his veto, half the Democrats in both houses voted against their president). Even so, the Democrats now seemed less odious after they adopted a platform calling for civil rights legislation and repeal of the Taft-Hartley Act. Adopted in part because of Wallace's challenge from the left, the civil rights plank finally drove the most reactionary southern Democrats out of the party and into the camp of South Carolina governor Strom Thurmond, the presidential candidate of the States Rights (or Dixiecrat) Party. With this *fourth* party now on the ballot as the undiluted expression of white supremacy, many African Americans who might have voted for Wallace's principled but impractical crusade now turned to Truman as the realistic alternative. Even the president's critics in the labor movement gave him their grudging support, Reuther included. Calling the Progressive Party candidate "a lost soul," the UAW leader said it was "tragic" that the Communists were using Wallace to draw votes from Truman and ensure the election of Thomas Dewey, the Republican candidate. Emil Mazey now warned workers against "the third party rantings" of Wallace. "His movement does not represent a genuine party of the workers, but is in fact a third capitalist party whose sole aim seems to be to sell the foreign policy of Soviet Russia."[88]

Red-baiting was not the only problem that Progressive Party candidates had to face in Michigan, for it was here that Reuther's strategy of "realignment" within the Democratic Party had produced tangible results. The state Democratic Party had long been dominated by a handful of urban bosses who shunned the likes of Frank Murphy and relied on FDR's coattails to deliver votes and patronage. In 1948, however, the gubernatorial candidacy of G. Mennen Williams had transformed the party. Heir to the Mennen family's shaving-cream fortune, "Soapy" Williams had graduated from the University of Michigan Law School in 1936 as a New Deal liberal and gone to work for Governor Murphy, serving first in the state attorney general's office and later moving to Washington when Murphy became U.S. attorney general. After the 1946 election fiasco, Williams enlisted fellow reform Democrats and union leaders in an effort to oust the state party's conservative and generally corrupt leaders, many of them aligned with Jimmy Hoffa's Teamsters. "We are not accepting the Democratic Party as it now is," explained the *CIO News*, which encouraged shop stewards to run for precinct office in the party's district conventions. "Our purpose in going into it is to line up with its liberal elements and remold the party into a progressive force." With the support of Reuther and state CIO leader August Scholle, Williams defeated the Hoffa slate in the 1948 primary and became the party's nominee for governor. The new Democrats promptly endorsed a platform committed to taxing corporate profits, improving workers' compensation, protecting civil rights, and expanding public housing.[89]

The Progressive Party now had to address the classic dilemma of an insurgent third party: should it run a separate candidate for governor in a race in which Williams had a good chance of defeating Kim Sigler, the Republican incumbent? Sigler was an arch red-baiter who, in testimony before HUAC, had denounced even the NAACP as a "Communist front" (a charge he later withdrew with the embarrassed explanation that the initials were the same as another group). In contrast to the race for president, in which Progressives saw little difference between Truman and Dewey, here there was a significant difference between the Republican and Democratic candidates. In this context, Goodman and the rest of Michigan's Progressives left the top of their slate empty—in effect endorsing Williams. They did so despite the fact that the lack of a "headliner" candidate would undoubtedly diminish their campaigns for lesser office.[90]

They made the best of it even so, spending long hours on a campaign trail that took them from one end of Michigan to the other. When Goodman took to the hustings in his campaign for state attorney general, he was accompanied by folksinger Bernie Asbel, who entertained the crowds at campaign meetings, and by Roberta Barrow, the party's candidate for secretary of state. Barrow, an African American and former Republican who served as secretary of Detroit's Calvary Baptist Church, was something of a curiosity in rural and outlying districts. "For the first time in the history of the state," as Goodman told the *Iron Mountain News* in the Upper Peninsula, "candidates of a major political party—Negro and white—will 'stump' the state together for their common program." Goodman's brave words collided with reality, however, in the town of Ironwood, where neither the St. James Hotel nor the Commercial Hotel would book rooms for "colored people." Hotel bias notwithstanding, the candidates drew enthusiastic crowds in the Upper Peninsula. "A lot of the old-time radical Finlanders came out to meetings and were very responsive," recalled Goodman's son Bill, referring to Finnish immigrants and their descendants who had helped organize the Western Federation of Miners and left-wing co-operatives. Speaking to one such crowd at the Kingsford Heights Community Hall in Iron Mountain, Goodman fired up the audience with a stump speech calling for "unemployment compensation of $35 a week, workmen's compensation equal to the worker's wages for as long as disability lasts, and 100-dollar-a month old-age pensions at the age of 60." All this, he declared, could be had for only a small part of the billions spent every year for "armaments for unnecessary war preparation."[91]

Little of this message was audible, however, in a campaign dominated by the noisy fearmongering of red-baiters in the government and media. In July, less than four months before the election, newspaper headlines across the country broadcast the sensational news that federal agents had arrested Eugene Dennis and eleven other national leaders of the Communist Party for "conspiring to advocate" the violent overthrow of the government. Goodman and Crockett would later become personally involved in this and other Smith Act prosecutions, but the immediate impact of the arrests was to heighten an already palpable hysteria about "Communist subversion." The *Detroit News* had fueled such fears with a series of front-page articles titled "Communist Plot Exposed." "As Petrograd Fell, So Detroit Can Fall," headlined one such story; "Blueprints Disclosed for Seizure of Detroit," warned another. The "blueprint," it turned out, was nothing more than "what-if" speculation about "foreign-born spies and . . . American-born traitor dupes" all working in an "iron-ruled Fifth Column disguised as the Communist Party of the United States." When members of the United Public Workers, a left-wing union representing city employees, organized an informational picket line to support higher wages, Detroit's leading newspaper put another hallucinatory spin on events, reporting that the picketing was actually a "Commie 'rehearsal' . . . aimed at familiarizing Commies themselves and their dupes with parts they will play on 'Take Over Day.' "[92]

Harry Toy, the former prosecutor of the Ford Hunger Marchers of 1932 and now Detroit's rabidly anti-Communist police commissioner, embellished these tall tales with his own hysterical warnings about Soviet agents "coming into the U.S. disguised as Jewish rabbis." When challenged on these remarks, Toy announced that members of the Progressive Party were "un-Americans" who "ought to be shot, thrown out of the country, or put in jail." Days later, Toy sent squad cars and dozens of plainclothesmen to disrupt a meeting of two hundred people calling for his ouster. The intimidating police presence apparently persuaded the manager of the Danish Hall to cut the auditorium lights. The April issue of the *Wallace Campaigner* described what followed: "Calm assurance by the Chairman, Detroit lawyer Ernest Goodman, and magnificent cooperation by the audience prevented the kind of incidents which the police were obviously trying to provoke. . . . By matches and flashlight, resolutions were read demanding Toy's removal . . . and an end to growing police brutality against Negroes." The accompanying flash photo over the caption "Not Afraid of the Dark" showed Goodman standing on the stage and reading from a sheet of paper as Dean Robb, head of Students for Wallace, held a flashlight over Goodman's shoulder.[93]

The harassment continued throughout the campaign. When Henry Wallace came to Detroit with the world-famous singer and actor Paul Robeson for a rally the month before the election, the Book-Cadillac

Hotel refused to give them lodging. Both were welcome at the Goodman home on Warrington Drive, but it must have felt like they were under siege.[94]

On Election Day, Progressive Party slate passers in Wayne County and out-state reported that "voters were friendly, took slates, indicated that Wallace was their favorite candidate, but that they would vote for Truman because they couldn't see Dewey in the White House." Across the country, this sentiment carried Truman to a surprise victory with 49 percent of the vote, well ahead of Dewey's 45 percent. Wallace and Thurmond finished in a virtual dead heat, each with only 2.4 percent of the vote. Thurmond's Dixiecrats actually won four states in the Deep South, while Wallace took only thirty precincts across the entire country. In Michigan, he got just 46,500 votes, or 2.2 percent of the total. The Progressive Party's statewide candidates fared even worse, Goodman topping the list with just 19,400 votes, most of them concentrated in Detroit. Mennen Williams, on the other hand, handily defeated Sigler and took office as Michigan's liberal governor for the first of his six terms.[95]

Four months after the election, Goodman put a brave face on the results in a letter to Progressive Party members in the Thirteenth Congressional District. "We devoted our time and energy because we felt that only through the Progressive Party and its leader, Henry Wallace, could the American people express themselves for peace, equality, and security," he wrote. "Although many thousands of people who were sympathetic with our program voted for Truman because they believed he might redeem his election promise, it is rapidly becoming apparent to them that we were right." To prove the point, Goodman called attention to the fact that "the bi-partisans have refused to pass civil-rights legislation, they are scuttling rent control, and they are only lukewarm toward a social security program. But they act fast when it comes to an armaments program and for ending the cold war by making it a hot one."[96]

These were partisan claims, to be sure, but worthy of debate. In his disappointment over the failure of the Wallace campaign, however, Goodman was probably reluctant to address the deeper question of whether a third party was the best vehicle for transforming American politics. In contrast to European parliamentary systems in which a minor party could join a larger coalition and participate in the choice of prime minister, the winner-take-all vote for president in the United States meant that third parties had little prospect for immediate success—except, as with the Republicans in 1860, when the country verged on civil war. In contrast, the Popular Front of the 1930s had pushed the New Deal to the left from within the Democratic Party, and the example of the Mennen Williams campaign in Michigan suggested that this approach had a better chance of success.

Blair Moody had succumbed to the prevailing hysteria when he accused the Progressives of being "agents of Moscow," but he was correct that the Wallace campaign would irrevocably split the liberal movement in America. The minority of CIO unions that had supported Wallace would soon be drummed out of the labor movement for their apostasy, and Goodman and other Progressive Party members would be driven to the margins of political life. Even the Communist Party, in hindsight, would come to regret the entire third-party enterprise for "the great harm it did in splitting the most advanced forces away from the main stream of political action." Saul Wellman, a Communist leader in Michigan (and soon to be a client of Goodman), later recalled that "the thing that tipped us over and produced the massive isolation . . . was the 1948 Wallace campaign." Coleman Young, who was expelled from his leadership position in the Wayne County CIO for his role in supporting Wallace, concluded that his venture into third-party politics was "the biggest political mistake of my life."[97]

Goodman made no such apology for his role in the Progressive Party. For a time, he even held out hope for future success. Mort Eden, his colleague in the Sugar firm, tallied ninety thousand votes in 1949 in a losing bid for the state supreme court, doubling the turnout for Wallace the year before. Ever the optimist, Goodman pointed to Eden's campaign and the relatively high votes for slates in Ann Arbor and Willow Run as "real evidence that our party is beginning to move ahead." There was considerably more evidence, however, of an escalating crusade against the Left. In the same year that Eden campaigned for statewide office, Detroit's voters passed a charter amendment by the lopsided margin of 264,000 to 78,000 to create a municipal Loyalty Commission; Detroit's inquisitors thereafter made it clear that any city employee who supported the Progressive Party was under suspicion and subject to discharge or suspension. In this climate, few would step forward to support the party's candidates, and the hoped-for revival of 1949 proved to be stillborn.[98]

Goodman himself would never run for public office again. In this, he differed significantly from Sugar, who had campaigned repeatedly in the mid-1930s, never winning but running up respectable totals that foreshadowed a growing movement. That movement was now in decline, and defeat only highlighted the changed circumstances. Even so, Goodman stubbornly clung to the cause, one of the last to abandon a strategy that, because he had urged it on others, he almost certainly felt obligated to see through to the finish. The end came with the next presidential election, when the Progressive Party could muster little more than seven thousand votes in Michigan. With this final thrashing, "Gideon's Army" was driven from the field.

6
Winter Soldier

A January day in 1950 and the offices seemed deserted. Goodman had just returned from his first trip overseas, to Germany, where he had defended another black GI accused of murder. He had flown back to Detroit invigorated by the wider world he had seen for the first time, but now the darkened offices on the thirty-second floor of the Barlum Tower mocked his enthusiasm. It was painfully obvious: the Sugar firm was dying, starved of customers by the ebbing fortunes of labor's left wing. "When I came back to my office, I had no clients, no money, and nowhere to look for any."[1]

Sugar himself was gone, semiretired to northern Michigan and only passing through on the way to somewhere else. He had spent much of the last year in New York City, advising Crockett and other members of the defense team in the first Smith Act trial of Communist Party leaders. Crockett had been charged with contempt of court at the conclusion of the trial and was headed for prison along with three other defense attorneys. The judge had deemed their persistent and sometimes noisy protest of his rulings out of order. Sugar's office overlooking Cadillac Square now had the still air of a neglected storeroom; Crockett's office was also deserted, a mounting pile of unopened mail spilling across his desk. Neighboring offices were empty or little used. Their occupants were drifting away, foraging for clients further and further from the barren ground left by the Red Scare and the widening boycott of Sugar's firm.

Winter was in the air, and many on the left were abandoning the field. Defending the rights of workers and joining the struggle for social justice had once had considerable appeal for young lawyers, those who came of age in the 1930s. There was a romance to it, the call to popular struggle and common cause with "the people." Goodman and other like-minded professionals had joined the crusade, aligning their careers with a

179

working-class majority fighting for its rights against a small but powerful aristocracy of wealth.

This had changed during the 1940s with wars hot and cold, with escalating racial conflicts, and with strategic errors on the left. At the end of the decade, the labor movement was split and its progressive wing ostracized. Unionized workers had fought their way onto a beachhead of modest prosperity and a tenuous claim to middle-class citizenship. The prewar status quo had been overturned, but it was reformulating into something unanticipated, a resurgent capitalism with a broadened base of blue-collar consumers, prompted and cued by the new mass media, television. Respectability was on sale, conformity was a virtue. The suburbs beckoned.

It was now the prejudice of the majority that confronted the dwindling number of radicals in the working and middle classes. Majority rule was the abiding principle of democratic government and was heartily defended, at least rhetorically, by most Americans; yet that same majority could also be mobilized to support—or at least tolerate—the witch hunt and racial segregation. Militant blacks and unrepentant Reds were the new demons, the twin targets, of the national security state and its war on subversion. Politicians who exploited the majority's prejudice and fear by attacking these beleaguered minorities could always find an audience. Lawyers who defended them, on the other hand, were at risk, for there was little to be gained and much to lose when the many found reason to turn on the few.

"The summer soldier and the sunshine patriot," as Tom Paine described the faint-of-heart in another, long-ago winter, would soon desert the field. Not Goodman. While many rebels of his generation had turned a blind eye to Stalin's dictatorial rule, and some had also trimmed their sails to every tack in Soviet policy, the Bill of Rights protected them even so—or it protected no one at all, since it was only the dissenting minority that had need of it in the first place.[2]

A winter soldier still had to pay his bills, however. In the lengthening shadow of the Red Scare, Goodman would have to find a way to earn a living while he defended clients who rarely had the means to pay. He would have to form a new firm on a new economic basis. He would have to take the leadership role that Sugar, his mentor and friend, had filled for so long.

Brothers in Law

Goodman knew it would have to be a different kind of firm. He could replace Sugar but he could not replicate the man who had become the father figure to an entire generation of left-wing attorneys. Sugar's prestige and thirty-five years as a labor lawyer had given him an almost unquestioned authority within his field. He had structured his firm as a makeshift confederation of associates, but it stayed tightly wound so long as Sugar was at its center.

Now Sugar was withdrawing from active leadership, and the firm's internal discipline had unraveled. "Office clients" who came to the thirty-second floor asking for "Mr. Sugar" were supposed to be assigned to particular attorneys according to an agreed-upon set of rules: workers' compensation cases—the most dependable income stream—went to the department headed by Ben Marcus; other cases went to lawyers specializing in particular areas or unions; most of the rest were distributed by rotation to available attorneys, with Sugar occasionally intervening to reassign cases. In practice, these rules had always been muddied by the fact that each lawyer also pursued his own business on the side. The boundary between "office" and "personal" cases had always been hard to define, and the resulting ambiguity had produced an ongoing tension. The hoops were now coming off the barrel as the once-allied attorneys became competitors, vying for whatever business came off the elevators on the thirty-second floor. It could not go on forever, and in September of 1949 Ben Marcus had blown the lid off the whole affair when he distributed an angry memo announcing that he, Jerome Kelman, and Don Loria—the firm's compensation attorneys—were leaving. "All of you have been free to develop your 'own' practices," Marcus told the other attorneys, whom he accused of poaching the compensation cases that should have been referred to him. "I will not walk out minus everything, including my own clients, whom I have surrendered to the pool. This is not only unfair but ridiculous."[3]

By December, the new firm of Marcus, Kelman, and Loria was installed in offices on the twenty-fourth floor of the Barlum Tower. It was the final straw for the Sugar firm. Mort Eden took over the few workers' compensation cases that remained after the split, and Dean Robb, a recent graduate of Wayne University's law school, was brought on to help Eden develop the practice. But clients were hard to come by. At the same time that the "comp" lawyers were quitting the firm, the national CIO was expelling left wing unions whose leaders had broken ranks by supporting the Wallace campaign and refusing the non-Communist oath. The CIO's purge began in November of 1949 with the United Electrical Workers (UE) and continued the following year with the expulsion of the Fur and Leather Workers, the United Public Workers (UPW), and seven other organizations. The 1 million members in these banished unions represented nearly 25 percent of the CIO's total. UE, Fur and Leather, and the UPW had a modest membership in Michigan and northern Ohio and their locals had continued sending business to the Sugar firm, but they were now being slowly decimated as CIO and AFL unions raided their membership.[4]

With the firm no longer able to afford the monthly rent of nearly $900 for the entire suite of offices on the thirty-second floor, the remaining lawyers agreed to surrender roughly one-third of the space and sign separate leases for their individual offices. Goodman's office had the same view from the thirty-second floor of the Cadillac Tower (the new name for the Barlum), but he was formally severed from the larger collaboration that had once been the Sugar firm. Personal ties, however, still linked him with his former colleagues, even as they moved into new areas of law. Jack Tucker kept his office on the thirty-second floor but began to shift into a practice centered on real estate. Harry Anbender remained for several years before moving to the Guardian Building. Ned Smokler began to work with his brother, who had a successful construction business, and moved to the David Stott Building in 1951. Goodman remained close friends with many of these colleagues and would, over the years, recall their departure without bitterness ("they had to make a living"). Smokler remained active in the National Lawyers Guild and, as a longtime participant in the deer hunt, he and Goodman continued a durable friendship. Don Loria also remained politically active through the Guild and the civil rights struggle; decades later, he and Coleman Young would give the keynote speeches at Goodman's testimonial dinner.[5]

But in 1950, Goodman was on his own, and it was not a comfortable feeling. Without the income stream generated by Sugar's firm, it appeared he would have to abandon the political and civil rights cases that had become his defining practice. There was, he well knew, little money to be earned in these areas of law. An obvious alternative was the kind of commercial practice—repossessions, bankruptcy, real estate, corporate law—that he had fled in the 1930s. He had no stomach for returning to it now, particularly after his recent trip to Germany. At age forty-three, he had traveled abroad for the first time to practice law in a foreign country, and he had found the experience exhilarating, "every bit as fascinating as I had hoped it would be."[6]

It had been just the kind of case he wanted to continue taking. At its center was Andrew Cockrell, a corporal in the U.S. Army stationed near Stuttgart who had been accused of stabbing a young German man to death in a dispute over a woman. Cockrell was an African American from Texas on his second tour of duty, recently recommended for promotion to sergeant; the eigteen-year-old German was a former member of the Hitler Youth, steeped in the racism of the Nazi movement. The U.S. government, for its part, was caught between two conflicting goals: on the one hand, to avoid the racial bias evident in the Lemas Woods case, and on the other, to conciliate German outrage that a black soldier had killed one of their own while consorting with a white woman. The Civil Rights Congress had referred the high-profile case to Goodman, who agreed to take it pro bono, reimbursed for little more than his travel and expenses. Boarding the four-engined Boeing Stratoliner in early December of 1949 for the flight to Germany, he had "tried to look like an oldtimer," he wrote Freda and the boys, "but felt like a kid." The arrival in Frankfurt and train ride to Stuttgart had been an emotional experience, taking him past bombed-out houses at night, the "moonlight shining through the windowless walls," as he wrote home the next morning, the "streets narrow, dark, and gloomy." The silent passengers in his railcar loomed large in his thoughts. "As I sit I can't help but thinking to myself that these are the people who lived in a society which slaughtered six million Jews—perhaps some of my companions participated or stood by, approving. I silently accuse them and I seem to feel their silent hatred."[7]

Speaking a passable German that borrowed heavily from his childhood Yiddish, he had plunged headlong into this alien world, reading the documentary evidence and interviewing dozens of witnesses during his first week. He wrote home describing his anger that Germans expressed so little remorse for the crimes of the Nazi regime, that their anti-Semitism remained open and causal, that even the friendliest among them claimed "the Jews hated the Germans more than vice versa." ("I hope so," Goodman noted.) His impatience on this score drove him through long days of preparation, and no doubt sharpened his political understanding of a case that centered on interracial sex. His intervention proved to be vital. Where the army-appointed counsel had urged Cockrell to plea-bargain a claim of drunkeness and diminished capacity, Goodman urged Cockrell to return to his original plea of innocent on grounds of self-defense.[8]

It had to be an emotional moment on the opening day of the trial when Goodman, acutely aware of his Jewish heritage, rose to defend an African American accused of murdering a former member of the Hitler Youth. Goodman focused on this underlying dimension of the case. The German, "believing that Hitler was the greatest of all, and his country was the strongest of all, and that the whites were better than the blacks," had assaulted Cockrell as he approached the woman's house; Cockrell, backing away, had inflicted only a shallow chest wound with his knife. "It just

touched [the] heart, the autopsy showed, enough to kill him shortly after-
wards." The defendant, Goodman noted, had been in uniform, had not
previously known the assailant, and had no idea the man was in jealous
pursuit of his girlfriend.[9]

Goodman's arguments persuaded the panel members to drop the
murder charges, but the jury still convicted Cockrell of manslaughter.
In a civilian court, Goodman believed, "he would have been acquitted,
I'm sure."[10]

After a month in Germany, Goodman took the train to Paris and spent
a week walking the narrow streets, visiting the museums and marveling
at the abundance of "Bookstores!" as he wrote home in one of several
long and exuberant letters. "Sometimes two or three in a block. Do all the
people in Paris buy books and paintings the way we buy groceries?" Frustrated by his inability to speak French, his cheerful rummaging still turned
up a book he had "wanted to get for some time," an English edition of
Dostoevsky's *The Brothers Karamazov.* Between these solitary explora-
tions, Goodman visited American friends living in Paris or passing
through. His letters to his wife and children described a convivial group
that spent Christmas Eve together in a prolonged round of drinking, eating, and dancing that lasted into the following morning. It's hard to know
what Freda and the kids would have made of the news that Daddy had
spent the night before Christmas on the town, but the story was sent in
apparent confidence that it would be well received.[11]

Goodman also recounted long conversations with friends who worked
for the World Federation of Trade Unions (WFTU), the global labor alliance born at the end of the war in a spirit of cross-border solidarity, but
now split by the departure of non-Communist labor movements. The
WFTU would come to be dominated by Soviet-bloc unions aligned with
their ruling parties, but in 1949 his friends were still full of news about
the global struggle to organize unions. It was a revelation for Goodman,
who confessed in one letter that he realized now he was "an unconscious
victim" of the "national egotism" that plagued the American labor movement, "all confident of its own wealth and power and proudly ignorant of
the traditions and struggles of other peoples." He flew home with high
hopes that these emerging labor movements around the globe "were the
early forms of development of a world trade union movement which would
eventually sweep across all national boundaries."[12]

The return to Detroit brought him back to earth. Considering the
state of things in the winter and spring of 1950, there was no avoiding the
fact that his professional prospects were narrowing. He could not earn a
living as a solitary civil rights lawyer and he could not imagine returning

to a commercial practice in which he would be, as he put it years later, chained to his desk "every day, every week, every month of the year and not able to leave it for reasons that I thought were important, such as traveling." At the same time, there was no going back to the loose confederation of lawyers that had once been the Sugar firm. He felt temperamentally unsuited for the role Sugar had played as austere taskmaster to allied, but subordinated, associates, and the former associates had little incentive to reenlist in a secondhand version of the Sugar firm. "So," Goodman resolved in 1950, "I wanted to have a partnership." It was the only plausible alternative. A partnership that united its members in a defined structure of co-governance and shared liability would suit his more collaborative nature. Goodman would be the first among equals, but there would be no sidebar practice for the partnership's members or competition for clients. All income would be pooled and shared according to the agreed-upon split.[13]

There would still be much of Maurice Sugar, however, in the partnership that Goodman now contemplated. Its members, first of all, would be drawn from the surviving core of associates that Sugar had recruited: George Crockett, Mort Eden, and Dean Robb. With Crockett's participation, it would also be the first integrated law partnership in Michigan and perhaps the country, building on Sugar's initiative in 1947 when he first brought Crockett into the firm. In 1950, he was still the only African American lawyer with offices in Detroit's downtown. To work now as an equal partner with white lawyers was an unprecedented breach of the city's color line, particularly when the partners raised Crockett's visibility another notch by listing him second to Goodman, ahead of the more senior Mort Eden. "Although Eden had more experience than Crockett," as Goodman later explained, "I felt the importance of our firm was largely this interracial relation."[14]

In this environment, Goodman and his prospective partners had every reason to assume they would pay a price for their unique experiment. Goodman later recalled their apprehension when Goodman, Crockett, Eden, and Robb went public in January of 1951, still housed on the thirty-second floor of the Cadillac Tower:

> We wondered, "well, how are clients going to react to having a black person in a white partnership?" . . . The secretary was told that "if somebody wanted a lawyer, if Crockett was in, you just send him into Crockett, just like anybody else." And there were some cases when the person said, "no I want to see Mr. Goodman," and they'd come to see me and say, "Look, I don't want to go to Mr. Crockett, I don't know him, I don't like to talk to a black man."

And some of the time they would say, "what chance have I got in court if he's representing me? I don't have a chance in hell." And you know, I couldn't say that wasn't entirely true, because there was a good deal of prejudice in the court. . . . But we worked at it.[15]

There were, in fact, fewer client problems than would have been the case in a typical law practice, since many of the firm's remaining customers were left-wingers who supported racial integration. But no segment of political opinion was exempt from the multifaceted prejudice of the day. In later years, Goodman would often recall one episode that had an especially "paradoxical twist," a case involving a white client who came to the office and, after a long consultation with Crockett, confided to the black attorney that he was "glad they didn't send me in to one of those Jewish lawyers."[16]

For a law firm that was so far ahead of its time when it came to racial integration and defense of civil liberties, the Goodman firm was otherwise conventional in many of its internal practices. Its members were well schooled in the protocols of legal discourse, meticulous in their preparation of briefs (another of Sugar's legacies), and articulate in their presentation of the law. As Dean Robb would later describe it, the courtroom appearance of his fellow partners was decidedly traditional—"they would look like button-down Oxford-suit reactionaries if you looked at their style." They were equally conservative when it came to gender: all of the firm's lawyers were men; all of the secretaries were women. In this regard, Goodman and his partners were hardly distinguishable from their mainstream counterparts, who generally regarded women as unfit for the contentious combat of the legal profession. The larger society was actually moving backward in the postwar era when it came to women's rights, with government, media, and "expert" opinion mobilized against women who refused to accept their "natural" role as homemakers. Goodman and his partners did not endorse this reactionary variant of the "wife-at-home" ideology, in part because they couldn't afford to economically, and primarily because they had married strong-willed women who refused a one-dimensional role. At the same time, however, it was assumed that the deer hunt was for men only, and so were the other personal and political networks that made the legal profession, in particular, a distinctly masculine club.[17]

Given the bleak prospects for employment, only a few women braved this gauntlet of social censure to seek a law degree. Among them was Ann Fagan Ginger, a daughter of socialist parents who applied for a job with

Sugar in 1947 after graduating from the University of Michigan Law School. "I wrote seven letters in all asking, in various ways, if he would hire me," Ginger recalled. "He would not. But he had to do something, given his past history and friendship with my father." Sugar would hire her only as an office manager for the National Lawyers Guild, paying her $25 a week to collect delinquent dues and work, she remembered, "in an office on the way to the men's room." There may have been personality clashes or other considerations for the refusal by Sugar, and later Goodman, to hire her as an attorney, but as she saw it, there was "no other reason . . . but that I was a woman. I was a fool to think I could get a job as a lawyer." The obstacles were undoubtedly daunting. A woman lawyer might, in fact, have had less chance of winning the respect of male clients and judges than an African American man. But the same partners who "worked at" overcoming the prejudice against a black lawyer were not yet prepared for this second challenge. Ginger soon quit her Guild post and moved to Cleveland. Sugar and Goodman, she recalled decades later, "could take on an African American lawyer of great dignity and ability, but they would not hire a woman."[18]

At the same time, however, Goodman and his new partners had to depend on the economic contributions of women who were anything but homebound traditionalists—namely, their wives. Ethelene Crockett was a mother of three when she graduated from Howard University's medical school in 1944; after a difficult residency in New York separated from her family, she returned to Michigan and established a successful practice as the first black woman in the state to become a board-certified obstetrician-gynecologist. Her professional success provided a crucial income stream at a time when her husband was still contesting the contempt charges and prison sentence resulting from the Smith Act trial in New York. Barbara Robb made a similar contribution to her family's survival, earning a modest income as a speech therapist. "She was not making much, neither was I," Dean recalled, "but making ten or eleven thousand [combined] in the early 50s, that wasn't bad." Freda Goodman's economic contribution was also critical. With an eye for style and a nose for marketing, Freda had discovered a rare business opportunity in the late 1940s while visiting her brother, Louis Kesler, in London. Kesler was the owner of a small clothing factory and lived near Portobello Road, site of vast open-air markets selling (among other things) cutlery, silverware, and other estate-sale offerings. "Somehow they came up with this idea of selling antiques," her son Dick recalled, "buying them in England and selling them in Detroit, and she got really involved in that and was doing pretty well." Selling from the home on Warrington Drive, Freda cultivated a growing business with decorators in the city and suburbs who learned word-of-mouth that—as her son put it—"she had good taste."[19]

This second income helped sustain Freda's husband as he struggled to develop a long-term strategy for supporting the new law practice. Slowly, the division of labor within the partnership was settled. Goodman and Crockett would practice the "political law" (as Goodman called it) that defined the firm's core values. Their primary responsibility would be cases concerning the civil rights of workers, African Americans, and radicals, the latter including Communists and others on labor's left accused of being Communists. While Goodman and Crockett focused on this expanding docket, Mort Eden would quietly handle the remaining workers' compensation cases that came to the firm. In effect, Eden's caseload would support the far less remunerative work of Goodman and Crockett. It was a telling measure of Eden's unassuming nature and his commitment to the firm's political agenda that he was willing not only to subsidize the two headliners but also to take a lower listing on the firm's roster, behind the less-senior Crockett. Eden and Crockett would take equal shares in the division of net income, both of them second to Goodman's split. The junior member of the firm, Dean Robb, would work with Eden on comp cases and take the smallest share of the proceeds.[20]

Robb's responsibilities, however, also included the development of the single most important—and speculative—strategy that would make or break the firm's long-term viability. "Dean Robb would study medicine," as Goodman described his mandate years later. "He would study how to appeal to a jury in a case where a person was injured or killed under circumstances where somebody was responsible for negligence." Negligence cases were at that time a far smaller part of tort law. *Tort* is a medieval term for an act that is wrong, but not *criminally* wrong; that is, the guilty parties have not violated a particular law, but their negligent behavior ("tort") has injured another party and made them liable for damages recovered through a civil suit. Such cases had grown in importance after 1860 for reasons rooted in the changing economy. "The explosion of tort law," as legal historian Lawrence Friedman notes, "and of negligence in particular, has to be laid at the door of the industrial revolution—the age of engines and machines." Railroads, mechanized factories, and later the automobile cut a wide swath through society, boosting productivity and generating wealth, but also producing a bloody mayhem in the mounting toll of workers and passengers killed and injured. Mass production had separated people from local producers and made them dependent on products manufactured by distant corporations. Even health care, as it became more high-tech and effective, was losing the personal touch as the midwife and the doctor on house-call gave way to the central hospital and the crosstown clinic.[21]

In the early 1950s, it was no easy matter for individuals to find recompense in the courts for the harm done by errant corporations, culpable doctors, and negligent drivers. Conservative judges often sympathized with the institutions being sued and they would frequently dismiss the case as groundless rather than bring it before a jury. It took considerable effort to overcome their reluctance to hold companies or hospitals liable for negligence, as Goodman discovered in a case concerning two girls killed in a collision with a truck. In Goodman's recollection of the case, the truck driver was clearly at fault for crashing into a taxi carrying the girls from Ann Arbor to Detroit, throwing both out of the vehicle and onto the highway median. The company's lawyers claimed that because the girls died instantly (with no doctor bills) and because they were students (with no lost wages), their client's liability was limited to the cost of the funerals. In other words, if the company's negligent actions *killed*, rather than *injured*, the victim, its liability was actually reduced; if the truck had collided with a cattle carrier, it would have paid more for the value of the dead livestock. Goodman, however, had found a witness who testified that one of the girls groaned heavily before she died, allowing a claim for pain and suffering. "What is the sigh worth just before you die in the mud, a young girl with a life ahead?" Goodman remembered asking the judge and the jury. "How much is that last second worth to a person if you have to put a value on it?" The jurors sided with Goodman, but when the judge threatened to cut down a more generous verdict, they had to limit the award to $28,000.[22]

"The cost and time and money of going through this whole process made it unprofitable to handle most of these cases," Goodman recalled. "Only a couple of lawyers did it, really. So we were going to change all that, and that's [what] Dean Robb's part of the partnership was." Robb would find allies in the National Association of Claimants Compensation Attorneys (NACCA), the organization of workers' comp lawyers founded by Ben Marcus in 1946. Slowly, NACCA would widen its mandate to include attorneys active in personal injury cases. But decades before the organization dropped its original name (always a mouthful) and became the Association of Trial Lawyers of America, it was Robb and a few Guild members from the Detroit chapter who began to develop many of the early concepts of personal injury law. Robb had no background in medicine; just twenty-five years old when he joined the Sugar firm straight out of Wayne University, he had been raised in the farmlands of southern Illinois by schoolteacher parents who urged a career in social work. To gain the needed medical knowledge, he hosted a series of workshops in the basement of his Allen Park home in which sympathetic doctors helped a roomful of lawyers translate medical argot into terms a jury could understand. "We must've had about seven or eight doctors total, that we'd met along the way," Robb recalled. "Some of them were liberals, and some of them were just good doctors that were willing to do it." By offering practical assistance for attorneys trying to build a tort practice, the classes drew many young lawyers into the Guild, despite the Red Scare. Among them was a young African American named John Conyers Jr., Detroit's future congressman.[23]

Goodman and Robb were plowing new terrain at the very moment when conditions in the surrounding society were making tort law a more fertile ground for litigation. During his six terms in office, Governor G. Mennen Williams would appoint a new generation of judges more sympathetic to the plight of injured workers and consumers. Among them were Charles Jones, Wade McCree and Elvin Davenport, the first African Americans to serve as judges on the Wayne County and Recorder's courts. Goodman must have found Davenport's appointment especially heartening: as an officer in the Guild's Detroit chapter and a lawyer for the Civil Rights Congress, Davenport was an old colleague who had joined Goodman on several cases, including the Sojourner Truth trial during World War II. At the same time that he and other new judges were donning their robes, liability insurance was reducing the economic burden of damage awards on business, and the courts were removing the charity exemption from hospitals that were "nonprofit" in name only. Bringing a court suit was still an expensive proposition, but "contingent fees" made it possible for the poor to sue the rich. The lawyer earned nothing if the case was lost, but if there was a settlement of the claim, the attorney won a healthy cut of the award. Robb and his partners took 30 percent or less, depending on circumstances. "If you take a case that's a real long-shot, it's a gamble," as Robb described it. "Can you [afford to] put a year's work into a case and maybe lose it?"[24]

Contingent fees democratized personal injury law, but elite opinion derided "P.I." lawyers as "ambulance chasers." There was a whiff of this even in the Goodman firm. According to George Crockett III, his father "did not like the notion of earning a living due to the suffering of others. . . . 'How much is an arm worth? How much is a leg worth?' . . . That didn't sit well with him." Goodman did not share these sentiments, though he certainly preferred to have Robb take on the bulk of the firm's personal injury docket. He was well aware that tort law was the only way to subsidize the political cases that he and Crockett wanted to take on.

And with the Red Scare in full stride, they both knew there would be no shortage of such work.[25]

The Great Fear

The firm's first political case couldn't have struck any closer to home. In 1950, with two rulings over the course of the year, the U.S. Court of Appeals upheld the convictions and contempt citations of the first Smith Act trial. Before the new partnership could even hang out its shingle, George Crockett faced imprisonment and possible disbarment for his role in defending the national leaders of the Communist Party.

It had been an impossible case from the start. The original indictment in the summer of 1948 had charged Communist Party chairman Eugene Dennis and eleven other national leaders with "conspiring to advocate" the violent overthrow of the U.S. government. Under the tortured logic of the Smith Act, this meant that Dennis and his cohorts were not charged with seditious *acts*, such as insurrection, riot, or sabotage. It was generally acknowledged that they had not even *advocated* such conduct. Nor had they *conspired* to commit such acts. The charge, instead, was that they were *presently* conspiring the *future* advocacy of violent revolution.

In normal times, this convoluted reasoning would have confounded most any jury. But these were not normal times. In the months preceding the 1948 indictment, the Soviets helped organize a Communist takeover in Czechoslovakia and a blockade of Berlin. In 1949, during the trial in New York's Foley Square Courthouse, the Soviets tested their first atomic bomb and the Chinese Communist Party fought its way to power after decades of civil war. In 1950, the Communist regime in North Korea invaded South Korea, igniting a brutal war in which Chinese troops with Soviet weapons fought American and allied soldiers for control of the Korean peninsula. Weeks after the start of the war, the U.S. Court of Appeals upheld the conviction of Dennis and his fellow CP-USA leaders. It appeared to the court and the general public that the balance of world power was shifting relentlessly toward the Communists, and there was a mounting fear that this turn of events was being advanced by Soviet spies in America.

The first spy scare in 1948 had produced little reliable evidence to support such charges, but by the time the Foley Square convictions had come before the court of appeals, there was ample proof that some Communists had, in fact, been spying on the United States for years. Any doubts on this score were eliminated in 1950 by the public confession of Klaus Fuchs, a German physicist and Communist who fled Hitler's regime in the 1930s to become, during World War II, a member of the scientific team that designed the first atomic bomb. While working at the Pentagon's Los Alamos center in New Mexico, Fuchs had transmitted vital information about the bomb to Soviet agents, aided by two American Communists, David Greenglass and Harry Gold. Their confessions led to the arrest and conviction of Julius and Ethel Rosenberg, who both went to the electric chair denying any role in the Soviet spy ring. Many on the left believed a brutal witch hunt had victimized the Rosenbergs, but subsequent evidence (including decoded Soviet diplomatic cables made public in the 1990s) strongly indicated that Julius, at least, was one of nearly two hundred American Communists who gathered intelligence for the Soviet government during World War II. After Pearl Harbor, many of these individuals no doubt believed that, rather than betraying their country, they were aiding a beleaguered ally in the struggle against fascism. But the more zealous partisans of the Soviet cause had crossed from intelligence gathering into the illegal realm of espionage, stealing classified secrets that the U.S. military had no intention of sharing with Russia during the war or after.[26]

The Foley Square defendants were never charged with aiding or abetting atomic spying or any other acts of espionage. But by the time the Foley Square case reached the U.S. Supreme Court in 1951, American casualties in Korea were climbing rapidly toward the final total of 157,000 dead and wounded, and in this emotionally charged context, there was little prospect of a sympathetic hearing for anyone allied with the Communist foe. The government argued that the CP-USA's national leaders represented "a clear and present danger" because of their ideas: they espoused Marxism-Leninism, they were apologists for the Soviets, they were *Communists*. In reply, Crockett asked the courts to uphold the First Amendment's protection of free speech, even if the justices found such speech distasteful. The liberal Supreme Court of the 1940s might have accepted such an argument, but with the death of Justices Frank Murphy and Wiley Rutledge in 1949, the defendants faced a court dominated by President Truman's appointees. On 4 June, they rejected the appeal by a 6-2 margin. It was enough, said Chief Justice Fred Vinson, to note "the inflammable nature of world conditions" and the fact that Communists had led "uprisings in other countries." Despite the lack of evidence of illegal actions in the United States, Vinson held that the Communist Party was a clear and present danger because it was preparing its members to strike in the future, "when the leaders feel the circumstances permit."[27]

Justices Hugo Black and William Douglas dissented, Douglas noting that the puny size and unpopular ideas of the Communist Party made it "the least thriving of any fifth column in history," while Black rejected Vinson's "ghost conjuring" of future uprisings. "Public opinion being what it is now," Black admitted, "few will protest the conviction of these [Communists]." One could only hope, he added in words that would have a special significance for Goodman, "that in calmer times . . . this or some later Court will restore the First Amendment liberties to the . . . place where they belong in a free society."[28]

In the meantime, Chief Justice Vinson and the conservative majority would have their way. In March of the following year, they reviewed the contempt citations and prison sentences issued against Crockett and his fellow attorneys in the original Foley Square trial, with the same unfavorable outcome. Justice Robert Jackson wrote the majority opinion that upheld the actions of Judge Harold Medina, who had cited all five defense attorneys for contempt at the end of the 1949 trial. Long before he issued summary judgment against the lawyers, Medina had displayed a personal animosity toward the defendants that bordered on the pathological; he stated years later, for example, that he avoided eye contact with spectators during the trial for fear that the Communists had placed a hypnotist among them. Jackson nevertheless rejected the argument that Medina's erratic behavior had compromised the proceedings and ruled instead that the defense lawyers' repeated and sometimes raucous objections to Medina's bias had "prejudiced the expeditious, orderly, and dispassionate conduct of the trial." Douglas and Black again dissented, joined this time by Justice Felix Frankfurter, who scolded Medina for his provocative behavior and concluded that "the conduct of the lawyers had its reflex in the judge."[29]

Though he now faced a four-month sentence in federal prison, Crockett expressed no regrets about defending the Communist Party's national leaders through three years of fruitless litigation. There had been difficulties. Personality clashes between fellow lawyers Harry Sacher and Richard Gladstein, each seeing himself as putative chief counsel for the defense, had created what Crockett later described as a "two-ring circus," with each of his more political colleagues "trying to outdo the other." The defendants had been equally difficult to work with, refusing Crockett's advice on admissibility of evidence and insisting, instead, on an obscure and dogmatic rhetoric that he—a "naive radical," as he put it—"didn't know from nothin'." The result, as described by historian Ellen Schrecker, was that the defendants came across "as wooden, doctrinaire ideologues instead of the victims of government repression that they also were."[30]

Even so, Crockett regarded the Foley Square trial as "the highlight in my life," the culmination of a journey that began decades before with his high school oration on the U.S. Constitution. Years later, he still regarded himself as an "absolutist" on the protections of the First Amendment, a defender of the principle that "liberty is indivisible. You can't have it for one group and deny it to another." His courtroom response to Medina's contempt citation had expressed the same measured pride in his role:

> I regard it as a badge of honor to be adjudicated in contempt for vigorously prosecuting what I believe to be the proper conception of the American Constitution. . . . For the first time in the 15 years that I have been practicing law I have found the opportunity to practice as an American lawyer and not as a Negro lawyer. I have enjoyed that brief trip into the realm of freedom, as far as the practice of law in America is concerned. I have enjoyed it so much that I intend to continue that way.[31]

Three years later, however, he was reporting to the minimum security penitentiary in Ashland, Kentucky. His four-month sentence at the segregated facility would pass slowly, marked by long hours in the prison carpentry shop. There was also the occasional visit by family and friends, including Goodman. "He seemed to accept it," Goodman recalled of his visit. "He was not bitter about it while he was there and he had some amusing tales to tell about how people were seeking him out because he was a well-known lawyer and they wanted his advice, and he'd come out as the most sought after jail lawyer in that whole institution." The small favors that Crockett's jailhouse "clients" lavished on him hardly compensated for the fact that he was unable to earn a living for his family. But Goodman and his fellow law partners were proud of the role he had played—the first black lawyer, in their estimate, to take the national stage in a major political trial before the Supreme Court—and they continued to pay him his share of the firm's earnings.[32]

Following his release, he still had to defend himself against charges of "unprofessional conduct" before the Michigan state bar. With the support of the National Lawyers Guild and the Wolverine Bar Association, Crockett successfully fended off disbarment and accepted, in the end, the lesser punishment of a public reprimand. The two-year battle was a humiliating experience, marked by several extraordinary encounters with his old nemesis, Judge Medina. The first of these was a meeting imposed on Crockett by the state bar, which required him to go to New York and apologize to the judge before the court—a "galling" experience for Crockett that took no more than five minutes, ending with Medina's wordless nod of assent. The second encounter was one sought by Crockett and Goodman, who traveled together to Lansing to attend a convention of the state bar at which Medina was scheduled to speak. "We decided we were going to go there together and confront this directly," Goodman recalled, "to show to . . . the lawyers of Michigan that George was ready to stand up and at least attend a Bar convention." Their arrival had the desired effect, as Goodman recalled it years later. "Everybody was looking at us from the moment we came in. . . . I think they were more conscious of George than they were of anything else that was going on." When the crowd rose to applaud Medina, Crockett and Goodman stood with their hands at their sides, silent and unmoved. "George handled himself with great dignity. . . . He couldn't do any better if he had been an actor."[33]

He could not undo the damage, however, to his reputation, his family life, and his state of mind. He believed (with good reason) that his phones had been tapped and that government agents shadowed his every move. He believed that his wife was denied a position at Women's Hospital in Detroit not only because she was a black woman in a profession still dominated by white males, but also because her husband was an ex-convict and a "Red." He knew that his children were taunted at school. By his son's recollection, the neighbors at one point even circulated a petition to remove the family from their home on American Street, a name that must have seemed highly ironic to the besieged family. There were individuals in the black community who supported Crockett and resented the abuse he took from the government and the media, "but not that many" came to his defense, according to Goodman. Crockett was still a relative newcomer in Detroit and he had worked primarily with white attorneys, making him something of an outsider. He was now suddenly front-page news as a "Red lawyer," and many former colleagues worried about associating with the notorious "Counsel for the Communists." "There were times when I would be walking down Woodward Avenue," as Crockett later said of these dark days, "and I'd see approaching me someone that I'd known for some time. But for some strange reason that person wouldn't see me or they would . . . go off to the right or to the left, that kind of thing."[34]

Most people assumed that as attorney for the Communists, Crockett must have been one himself. It hardly mattered that in his summation to the Foley Square jury he had stated, with considerable emphasis, that defending the rights of Communists "to make known their beliefs" did not mean that he endorsed them. Few believed him. In an age of conformity and fear, allegiance to the Bill of Rights was not considered sufficient grounds for risking livelihood and reputation in defense of a reviled minority; Crockett therefore "had to be" a secret Communist. He had, in fact, been invited to join the party by Benjamin Davis, editor of the *Daily Worker* and Harlem's representative on the New York City Council in the

1940s. Crockett respected Davis, a fellow alumnus of Morehouse, a graduate of Harvard Law School, and one of his clients in the Foley Square trial. But he declined the invitation. In his eyes, black members of the CP-USA were, as he wrote in his 1946 column for the *Michigan Chronicle*, "the present-day 'shock troops' in the Negro's march to complete freedom, just as the Abolitionists were in the pre–Civil War days." But Crockett himself was no Marxist, and however much he admired the CP-USA's commitment to civil rights, he was also aware that "the pole-star of Communist action is a foreign country," as he wrote in 1946. "A dyed-in-the-wool Communist has one loyalty which overshadows all others and that loyalty is Russia." The stigma of being a member of such a party, added to the disabilities he already suffered, was a prospect that "just didn't make sense to me." Crockett would describe himself years later as a nonaligned and democratic socialist. In the 1950s, however, such a distinction would have been lost on most Americans.[35]

It certainly made little difference to FBI director J. Edgar Hoover how those on the left classified themselves. In his eyes, "every American Communist was, and is, potentially an espionage agent of the Soviet Union," with a host of fellow travelers "ten times" more numerous. The fact that some Communists had, indeed, spied for the Russians during the 1940s gave this blanket indictment a gloss of credibility. The danger, however, had already passed: the same intercepted diplomatic cables that confirmed the secret Soviet espionage campaign of the 1940s also showed that by 1950 "it was all but over with," as historian Ted Morgan summarized the evidence. Arrests, defections, and disillusionment had destroyed the spy networks recruited from the CP-USA, and the wartime alliance of 1941–45 between the United States and Russia—once a prime motivator for American Communists to aid the Soviet cause—was long gone. Henceforth, Soviet spy recruitment among Americans would avoid the CP-USA and rely on the traditional nonideological inducements of the spy trade: money, sex, and blackmail. Federal intelligence agencies nevertheless continued to feed the flames of a national spy scare focused on the roughly 1 million Americans who had joined the CP-USA at some time in their lives and the millions more allied with the Popular Front. It was good business. The FBI had grown from nine hundred special agents in 1940 to nearly five thousand by the end of World War II, and the Red Scare justified increased spending on internal security. Fighting an exaggerated Communist threat was certainly easier than taking on the real and growing threat of the Mafia, which Hoover refused to even acknowledge until the late 1950s. The FBI director knew the CP-USA "didn't amount to a damn," according to William Sullivan, a former assistant, but Hoover used it as "an instrument to get appropriations from Congress."[36]

The result was a witch hunt. As Thomas Powers has noted in his comprehensive study *Intelligence Wars*, the few hundred informants and outright spies the Soviets recruited in the 1940s came "from a sea of tens of thousands, and it was the ordeal suffered by this larger group that explains why the purge was called a witch hunt." As Powers summarizes it, "thousands of Americans of vaguely leftist bent paid the price for the convenience the Moscow spymasters found in tapping party activists for secret work."[37]

Among the many victims Goodman would represent was Charles Hill Jr., the son of one of Detroit's most prominent African American ministers, the Reverend Charles Hill Sr., pastor of the Hartford Avenue Church. The elder Hill was a stalwart of the Popular Front, active in support of labor and civil rights, an officer of the Progressive Party, and a candidate for city council in 1949. The Reverend Hill failed to win office but did well in black and immigrant wards, garnering 117,000 votes. The younger Hill was by any reasonable standard a model patriot, both as an officer in the army air force reserves and as a decorated combat veteran of the Second World War. When the Korean War began, Captain Hill stepped forward and volunteered for active service. But instead of welcoming this patriotic gesture, the military informed him in December of 1950 that, on investigation, he had been found to be "disloyal to the government of the United States" and was to be *discharged* from the army if he did not voluntarily resign. As evidence, the army provided a "Statement of Reasons" that focused primarily on the fact that his father was on the board of directors of the Civil Rights Congress and other Popular Front groups. The father's links to these groups was enough for the army to conclude that Captain Hill must be "a member, close affiliate, or sympathetic associate of the Communist Party."[38]

Goodman, a close friend of the Reverend Hill and a fellow activist in the Progressive Party, was happy to represent Captain Hill in a case that quickly gained the attention of the *New York Times* and the *National Guardian*, both of which editorialized on Hill's behalf. This was not a case, however, that followed normal legal procedures: as in all loyalty investigations, Hill could not even know, much less confront, his accusers, and Goodman would not be allowed to cross-examine them. To protect its paid informants, the government simply refused to divulge its sources. Hill had no idea who had told the FBI or Military Intelligence that his sister showed "an active and sympathetic interest" in the Communist Party, or who it was that reported he was seen "on numerous occasions to read the *Daily Worker.*" In a courageous letter to the army rebutting these claims, Hill said he had never read the Communist Party's newspaper, but that now, his curiosity aroused, he intended to exercise his constitutional right to "read the paper . . . just to see what is so damnable about it." His sister's husband, he pointed out, was already fighting in Korea and had been awarded the Silver Star. As for his father, "what would you have me do? Give my father a loyalty test and if he failed to conform to Army standards of loyalty—to disown him?" Goodman noted in a letter to the *National Guardian* that the army was demanding a kind of "first loyalty" to the government that was reminiscent of the Hitler regime, which also required young citizens to report "disloyal" parents to the Nazi state.[39]

The army soon withdrew its charges and apologized to Hill, but this happy ending eluded thousands of others who were caught up in the government's indiscriminant hunt for Reds and fellow travelers. The FBI conducted nearly 5 million file checks on civilian employees of the federal government under Truman's loyalty and security programs, followed by forty thousand field investigations of those deemed suspect. None of those investigated were subsequently charged with sedition or sabotage, but the federal government nevertheless fired twenty-seven hundred people between 1947 and 1956 because of the anonymous testimony of snitches and paid informants. Another twelve thousand federal employees who lacked the courage or public support that fortified Captain Hill quietly resigned to avoid the nightmarish proceedings that a field investigation and public hearing entailed. If they were actually members of the CP-USA, a hearing was futile in any case: even though membership in the Communist Party was not illegal, it was now widely regarded as automatic grounds for dismissal. The majority accused of disloyalty, however, were not party members but fellow travelers like Captain Hill. They had supported Henry Wallace or "prematurely" opposed fascism in Spain or listened to the records of Paul Robeson or joined a group on the attorney general's list of subversive organizations.[40]

Near the top of that list was the Civil Rights Congress, the organization that Goodman served as both counsel and member of the executive committee. The attorney general was under no obligation to hold hearings before adding the CRC or any other group to the "subversive" list when it was first issued in 1947, and there was no provision for appeal or judicial review that would allow a group to challenge such a listing. The official criteria for "subversive" was not stated in President Truman's executive order, but loyalty investigators generally believed that any group advocating racial equality was automatically suspect. "Of course the fact that a person believes in racial equality doesn't *prove* that he's a communist," as one inquisitor in Washington state put it, "but it certainly makes you look twice, doesn't it."[41]

In this context, government investigators were bound to turn their attention to the CRC. Founded in Detroit in 1946 through the merger of the Detroit Civil Rights Federation, the International Labor Defense, the National Negro Congress, and other Popular Front organizations from across the country, the CRC had initially drawn a mixed group of leftists and liberals to its national office in New York and its local chapters in a dozen major cities. Early supporters included Arthur Schlesinger of Harvard University, screen actor Edward G. Robinson, poet Langston Hughes, and educator Mary McLeod Bethune. This liberal roster was salted with Communist luminaries as well, including Councilman Ben Davis from New York, Elizabeth Gurley Flynn, novelist Dashiell Hammett, and Congressman Vito Marcantonio, the only member of the American Labor Party to serve in Congress (representing East Harlem), and a close ally if not member of the CP-USA. Communists were also prominently represented in staff positions, with William Patterson, an African American lawyer, serving as national executive secretary after 1948, and Art McPhaul, the former committeeman at UAW Local 600, replacing Jack Raskin in 1950 as leader of the Detroit chapter.[42]

Many of the CRC's left-wing leaders would end up in jail, and Goodman would represent one of them, McPhaul, in an eight-year legal battle that would eventually bring the case before the U.S. Supreme Court. The government's relentless harassment would finally destroy the organization, but from the start of its ten-year life span the congress established a compelling record of civil rights activism. One of its first campaigns in Michigan was a petition drive to put a proposal on the ballot for a state Fair Employment Practices Commission, Goodman drafting the antidiscrimination measure and CRC canvassers collecting 180,000 signatures before the Michigan Supreme Court disqualified the petition on a technicality. In a subsequent campaign, which foreshadowed the tactics of the 1960s, the CRC's interracial followers invaded segregated restaurants in Detroit to demand service and push for compliance with the Michigan Equal Accommodations Act. Absent this kind of direct action, the Diggs Act, as it was called, was slow moving and ineffective. But when dozens of blacks and whites crowded into the Cream of Michigan restaurant on Twelfth Street in December of 1948, the owner immediately complied with their demand for service. The CRC was not alone in mobilizing this kind of direct-action campaign: UAW members who had formed Fair Employment Practices committees in their local unions or had joined the Detroit chapter of the NAACP were also crowding into restaurants and hotels across the city in the late 1940s and demanding service for their interracial members. "We were," as activist Ernie Dillard put it, "ahead of [Martin Luther] King." But it was the CRC that was often in the lead, organizing public demonstrations to protest lynch law and summary justice in the South, and raising funds in support of Lemas Woods and Andrew Cockrell, the two African American servicemen that Goodman defended.[43]

Detroit's CRC also focused on employment, picketing Neisner's five and dime stores in 1948 to protest their failure to hire African American sales staff. The police followed these campaigns closely, sending Red Squad detectives in mid-December, for example, to shadow fifteen pickets at the company's Twelfth Street store, where the CRC called on Neisner's to "hire a colored clerk for full time employment." (The store's thirty-three current employees, the Red Squad noted, included "a colored porter and 26 Jewish clerks.")[44]

In the summer of 1948, the CRC led mass demonstrations against Detroit's police for the fatal shooting of an unarmed African American boy, fifteen-year-old Leon Mosley. Eyewitness accounts varied, but much of the testimony indicated that four white police officers, having arrested Mosley for stealing a car, severely beat him for several minutes before shooting him in the back as he tried to stagger away. Goodman, Crockett, and Elvin Davenport represented the family (as usual, without fees) before the coroner's jury, which unanimously ruled the shooting "unjustifiable under the evidence of the law," forcing the county prosecutor to take the extraordinary step of issuing a warrant against one of the officers involved. Under the law at that time, the defendant could waive a jury trial (today, the prosecutor would have to agree), and "the police then made sure," Goodman recalled, "that the case was assigned to a judge who would be understanding of their point of view." As expected, the judge acquitted the officer after a short trial. Still, the "fact that any kind of warrant was issued against a police officer," as the Reverend Hill observed, was unprecedented, the "direct result of organized protest and demonstration [by] an aroused community." When the judge publicly dismissed the CRC's lawyers as "pink devotees of agitation," Goodman replied in an open letter. "I assume that you use the word 'agitation' as a form of epithet. I do not consider it so. . . . From the American revolutionists (many of whom were lawyers) who agitated for freedom from England, to the Abolitionists who agitated for the emancipation from slavery of the American Negroes, to the union organizers of the 1930's who agitated for economic freedom and security for American workers, the 'agitator' has advanced the cause of freedom."[45]

Grand pronouncements like these were enough to bring Goodman and the CRC to the attention of the attorney general, but it was the street demonstrations, petition drives, picket lines and boycotts that made the CRC especially dangerous in conservative eyes. Liberals were also becoming apprehensive. The CRC often worked in alliance with the NAACP's Detroit branch, which was especially supportive during the Reverend Hill's tenure as president. But when the U.S. attorney general placed the CRC on its list of subversive organizations, any "sympathetic association" with the CRC could now serve as evidence of disloyalty, and the taint of subversion was all the stronger after the government arrested two founders, Elizabeth Gurley Flynn and Benjamin Davis, under the Smith Act indictments of 1948. Over time, most liberals would sever their ties with the congress. Even the Detroit NAACP, which was generally to the left of its parent organization, began to disavow many of the CRC's street demonstrations.[46]

As lead lawyer for the Civil Rights Congress, Goodman found himself in the unhappy position of recommending defensive actions that would almost certainly send someone to jail. The CRC's national chairman, George Marshall, was a case in point. When HUAC demanded he turn over the membership lists and donor information of the National Federation for Constitutional Liberties (NFCL), the group Marshall had led into the CRC at its founding, the intent was clear. The committee's stated interest in determining "whether the organization is engaged in subversive activities" was a thinly disguised effort to scare away CRC members and donors. Goodman urged Marshall to resist. "Such [a] request should be refused and the authority of the Committee challenged," he wrote. "The Committee will undoubtedly extend its investigation to many other organizations who would be in a less favorable position to test [its] power and authority." Marshall refused HUAC's demands and thereafter served a three-month prison sentence for contempt of Congress. He was followed to jail in 1951 by Dashiell Hammett, Frederick Field, and two other trustees of the CRC's bail fund, all of them cited for contempt of court when they refused to answer questions about Communists who had jumped bail.[47]

These actions of Congress and the federal government gave further impetus to the local Red Scare. The Jewish Community Council of Detroit warned its affiliates in 1950 not to be "duped" by the local chapter of the CRC, which "is one of the organizations appearing on the U.S. Attorney General's 'subversive list' as a conveyor belt and a fellow-traveler organization of the Communist Party." The City of Detroit's Loyalty Commission, which had failed to find a single case of espionage or sabotage since its creation in 1949, nevertheless warned in 1951 that the CRC was planning a deliberate attack on the police department by "stirring up antagonism" among Negroes. This drumbeat of denunciation had the desired effect on membership. In his 1953 report to the national office, Art McPhaul noted that with "the unprecedented wave of hysteria" sweeping Detroit over the previous years, "we saw trade union leader after trade union leader move from left and center to right, because of fear and opportunism." Leadership turnover further eroded the CRC's support as local officers in left-wing unions lost their reelection bids. With the withdrawal of these unions from CRC affiliation, the organization gradually became more and more akin to what the red-baiters, as a self-fulfilling prophecy, had called it from the start: an arm of the Communist Party.[48]

That it continued to operate at all is testimony to the resourcefulness and commitment of its beleaguered staff. As liberal donors and supporting unions fell away, there was little money to support the work of the Detroit chapter. "Right now we're in very tough shape," wrote Anne Shore, administrative secretary, in a letter to the national office. "No pay for four weeks for anyone and a million creditors breathing down our necks. Not unusual and you're probably in worse shape." Apparently unable to keep the landlord at bay, the CRC moved its offices from one downtown location to another, four different buildings in the six years after 1947—an inconvenience, no doubt, for the FBI and the Detroit Red Squad, which had to move their wiretaps and surveillance sites as well. Even the chapter's executive secretary had to volunteer much of his labor when the lack of funds forced McPhaul to turn to the plastering trade for a subsistence income. Unable to pay its staff on a regular basis, the CRC was dependent on volunteer labor, which ranged from the women who would "come down a couple of hours a day," as Jack Raskin recalled, "and sit around clipping newspapers" for the files to lawyers like Goodman and Crockett who would forgo legal fees to represent CRC clients.[49]

Lynch Law

Among Goodman's CRC clients in the late 1940s and early 1950s, two in particular were casualties of the most atavistic of prejudices—the toxic mix of fear and rage that interracial sex inspired in the white majority. There had long been an unseemly contradiction in white thinking on this score. In the slave South and for generations thereafter, white men raped African American women with relative impunity; consensual sex between the races, however, was strictly forbidden by moral convention and the law. No "decent" white woman, it was argued, could find a black man attractive, and any case of "miscegenation" was therefore assumed to be rape. Only in urban centers of the North was interracial sex becoming acceptable, and even there it was limited primarily to left-wing circles. The prevailing sexual taboos were otherwise intensifying: when the attorneys general of eleven southern states filed an amicus brief against school desegregation in the early 1950s, they warned the justices that whites did not "want their women folk in intimate social contact with Negro men."[50]

It was in this context that Goodman would defend two African Americans, James Henderson in Michigan and Willie McGee in Mississippi, convicted of rape for what they insisted were consensual relations with white women. There were substantial irregularities in both trials, and it was this blatant violation of due process that made the two cases emblematic of the larger constitutional issues at stake. Henderson was tried in a hastily convened night court in suburban Mount Clemens within hours of his arrest, with no lawyer, and with only police and prosecutors in attendance. Following his hurried conviction, he was transported that same night to jail in the neighboring county, and the next day to the state penitentiary in Jackson. "Regardless of the innocence or guilt of the defendant," Goodman would argue after taking the case on appeal in 1951, "the defendant is entitled . . . to an open trial so that not only the court . . . but the general public could have access to the proceedings." Goodman would return to this argument in a series of court hearings stretching over the next seven years.[51]

In the McGee case, the denial of due process by Mississippi's courts was even more blatant, and the stakes higher. McGee had been severely beaten by his jailors to extract a confession, then carried into a courthouse surrounded by an angry mob. His court-appointed attorneys declined to cross-examine the alleged victim, who claimed that McGee entered her house and raped her while a sick child slept at her side and her husband and children slumbered in adjoining rooms. Many observers believed that, in fact, McGee's three-year affair with the woman had been discovered by her husband, and the charge of rape concocted after the fact. It was never established that a rape had actually occurred, and no defense witnesses were called during the one-day trial. The all-white jury reportedly took three minutes to convict and the judge immediately sentenced McGee to death. It would have ended there but for the CRC's six-year campaign to win McGee a series of new trials based on venue (the mob menacing the courtroom had intimidated the defense) and the exclusion of African Americans from the jury. In the second and third retrials, however, the juries were still all white: even without overt exclusion, the same end was achieved by drawing names from voter rolls that had long been purged of most blacks. Because of archaic Mississippi rules, McGee also had to continue relying on local lawyers in the retrials, and in each case these attorneys were intimidated by the palpable threat of violence. At one point, the husband carried a pistol into court and promised to use it on anyone who questioned his wife's denial of the affair.[52]

Recognizing the limits of a strategy that relied solely on litigation, the CRC augmented its legal challenge with a campaign of public demonstrations and political education that anticipated the wider movement of the 1960s. CRC chapters across the North portrayed the campaign to save McGee as part of the struggle to overturn segregation and white supremacy in the South, and many unions, churches, and civil rights groups that remained wary of supporting the CRC were nevertheless willing to support McGee. Unions were especially receptive in Detroit, where many saw lynch law as part of the same terror campaign that menaced union organizers across the region. Anne Shore could report in the fall of 1950 that "our steady stream of little leaflets into the auto plants" had "reopened some long-shut doors to us here."[53]

Spurred to action by the CRC, UAW-Ford Local 600 and fifteen other unions raised money for legal expenses, circulated petitions calling for clemency, and sent delegations to lawmakers in Lansing and Washington. When interracial teams of CRC volunteers took petitions into Detroit's downtown shopping district, the police temporarily blocked their efforts by taking five of the canvassers into custody. "But quick action by our lawyers, Crockett and Goodman," Art McPhaul wrote to the national office, "resulted in their release in short order." A mass meeting at Detroit's Music Hall drew "close to 1,000 people," Shore reported, "a real demonstration of Negro and white unity." The UAW's Walter Reuther and the NAACP, despite their wariness of the CRC's Communist ties, joined the campaign by calling on Mississippi's governor to grant clemency (the national NAACP pointedly adding that it was "acting independently and had no affiliation with the Civil Rights Congress"). Across the North, the CRC worked to keep McGee's case before the public eye with rallies, prayer vigils, letter-writing campaigns, and picketing of the White House. Delegations also traveled south to Mississippi, including a car caravan from ten states that converged on Jackson in the summer of 1950.[54]

By the spring of 1951, however, there was little more the CRC could do after the U.S. Supreme Court refused to review the evidence that only blacks convicted of rape—never whites—were sentenced to death in Mississippi. With only a few weeks to go before the scheduled execution on

8 May, Goodman joined the defense team in a final gambit: they would go to Mississippi and seek an injunction against the execution in federal court as a *civil* (rather than *criminal*) proceeding on the grounds that state officials had harmed McGee by denying him his rights. It was a long shot, as Goodman recalled: "That [civil] process had been very rarely, if ever, tried before, certainly not in this context. But a group of us in different cities by long distance or by letters discussed it, corresponded on it. Finally, we agreed to try it. And Bella Abzug, who was then a lawyer in New York, and I agreed to develop the complaint with the assistance of others and to go down and file a suit, to see what we could do."[55]

On his arrival in Jackson with Abzug and John Coe, a CRC attorney from Florida who had worked on previous appeals, Goodman was immediately aware that "everybody's eyes were turned towards us. They knew all about us coming." According to the local press, "we were a [bunch] of Yankees coming down to stop justice from being done . . . and the looks we got were filled with contempt and hatred." The potential for violence had been demonstrated the previous summer when the CRC car caravan from Detroit and other cities had arrived in Jackson. "Why the hell go to Korea to shoot Communists," the *Jackson Daily News* had editorialized, "when the hunting is good on home grounds?" On cue, crowds had attacked CRC demonstrators, leaving several battered and bloody. In this context, Goodman was happy to have Abzug at his side. In addition to being an accomplished lawyer, the future congresswoman was fearless, outgoing, and—of special import—attractive. Wearing her signature broad-brimmed hat, "she looked like a southern belle," Goodman recalled years later, "out of the movies, you know." People who despised the CRC from afar became, in Abzug's immediate presence, polite and gracious. "I would push Bella in front of me every time," Goodman remembered with a laugh.[56]

Abzug's charm, however, could not alter the outcome of the court proceedings, scheduled for a Monday afternoon hours before McGee's midnight execution. Anticipating the district court's denial of their request for an injunction, Goodman and Abzug had arranged for an immediate appeal to the federal court in New Orleans and, if that failed, to the U.S. Supreme Court the same evening. In the meantime, the electric chair had been installed in the state courthouse in Laurel, eighty-five miles away, where McGee had first been convicted and where a crowd had gathered to await the killing. Goodman found reports of the holiday atmosphere unsettling. "They brought their lunches with them," he remembered, "and they sat around with their families, kids, waiting for the 12 o'clock execution." It was a jarring contrast with the CRC demonstrations in Jackson the previous weekend, when black and white protesters had rallied on Mc-Gee's behalf and the police had jailed fifty of the demonstrators.[57]

With word from Washington that the Supreme Court had denied their injunction request, Goodman and Abzug played their last card, an eleventh-hour request to Governor Fielding Wright for clemency. The two CRC attorneys were welcomed into the governor's white-columned mansion by an African American butler and ushered into the living room, where Wright and the state attorney general invited the CRC attorneys to make their case. "We looked at them and realized how hopeless it was," Goodman remembered. The "charade," as Goodman called it, ended with the expected refusal, and the governor rose from his chair.

> "Thank you for coming," and he escorted us out of the front door. I'll never forget this scene. It was almost 12 o'clock. As we got out on the porch, a great portico with these huge white wooden pillars, a May night, the smell of magnolias was in the air, just beautiful, sweet and lovely. And . . . there was a full moon, the perfect scene of the beautiful South. . . . We ran to the nearest telephone booth . . . to call a newspaper reporter [on the scene in Laurel] . . . and just as we got him on the phone, we heard the rebel yell [over the phone], the rebel yell of victory, just so loud, we couldn't hear him talking. They had just turned on the switch.[58]

"No case is lost if you make the fight right," Goodman would later say, and the campaign to win justice for Willie McGee, though unsuccessful, had at least thrown a bright and persistent light on the state-supported terror that subjugated African Americans in the South. But Willie McGee was dead, and it would be a long ride back to Detroit.[59]

Un-American Activities

When the House Committee on Un-American Activities announced it would hold hearings in Detroit in the early months of 1952, Goodman must have felt a stomach-turning dread. Fourteen years after the Dies Committee had come to Michigan to attack Governor Murphy for his conciliatory role in the Flint sit-down, the Un-American Committee would return to visit the same punishment on the Civil Rights Congress and UAW-Ford Local 600.

Since its elevation to a permanent status in 1945, the committee had changed its style and personnel, but not its mission. Gone was its first chairman, John Rankin, the Mississippi Democrat who once called slavery "the greatest blessing the Negro people ever had," and who later denounced one of his critics, the Jewish radio commentator Walter Winchell, as "a slime-mongering kike." His successor, New Jersey Republican J. Parnell Thomas, had also departed—to federal prison in his case, after conviction for staff kickbacks and expense padding. By 1952, "HUAC," as critics called it (reordering the title to identify the *committee* as "Un-American") had settled into a prosecutorial style that was less rabid than Rankin's overt racism and anti-Semitism, but just as overblown. HUAC's two primary goals remained the same: to attack the wider Left, and to attract the widest possible publicity to the committee's super-patriots (none of them more than two years away from the next election).[60]

It was no coincidence that HUAC planned to target Detroit's CRC and Local 600. As the two most prominent remnants of the labor-Left in the city, they shared a common history rooted in the Popular Front. The Detroit CRC and its predecessor organizations had always found their most reliable labor support in Local 600, still the world's biggest local union with more members in the late 1940s than all but eleven of the thirty-six national unions in the CIO. Art McPhaul, the CRC's executive director, had been a volunteer organizer and a Local 600 committeeman at the Ford Rouge complex before being fired in 1950, and he now joined his former union allies on the strategy committee that planned their common defense against HUAC. They shared the same lawyers as well: Goodman and Crockett, who between them would represent twenty-six of the thirty-five left-wing leaders subpoenaed by HUAC to the Detroit hearings. Crockett would represent McPhaul, the Reverend Charles Hill, Coleman Young, Stanley Nowak, and three other community leaders. Five Guild lawyers (Ben Probe, Chester Smith, Harold Norris, LeBron Simmons, and Ty Maki) would represent ten others. Goodman would represent the largest single group, the nineteen elected officers of Local 600 targeted for HUAC's special brand of scrutiny.[61]

There was no other union like Local 600 and no other worksite like the Ford Rouge complex, the square mile of densely packed factories, blast furnaces, steel mills, and foundries that employed sixty-one thousand hourly workers in 1950. A thriving left-wing political culture had taken root during the brutal struggle against Harry Bennett's gangsters and brass-knuckle "Service Men," and despite the general turn to the right in the rest of the UAW, the left-wing's "Progressive Caucus" still retained a loyal following at the Rouge. It was "a rank-and-file kind of a local," Goodman would fondly recall years later. "None like it anywhere in the country I don't think. And I worked for them for many years and it was a pleasure, a wonderful pleasure just working with them. Not that I always agreed with everything that they did or wanted me to do. Everybody disagreed with almost everybody else in many ways. It was pretty anarchic in their thinking at least. But every idea was out there and everybody could take it or leave it. It was wonderful democracy-in-action in a local union."[62]

Goodman would represent Local 600 in two overlapping roles that winter: as counsel for the leaders soon to be called before HUAC, and as point man in the legal challenge to Ford's decentralization of production away from the Rouge. In the first case, HUAC threatened the veteran leaders who had pioneered union organization at Ford; in the second case, the company threatened to dismantle their base of support as thousands of jobs were moved to distant locations. All of this figured prominently in the internal politics of the UAW, since Local 600 president Carl Stellato had become the rallying point within the larger union for those opposing the five-year contracts that Walter Reuther had signed with GM and Ford. Stellato, a former supporter of Reuther, now denounced the five-year agreements as an "entrapment" that handcuffed the union and demobilized its members. He called for an alternative program of "30 hours work for 40 hours pay" to avoid layoffs during the transition to military production for Korea, and for a concerted campaign to block the dismemberment of the UAW's biggest local. At the very moment that HUAC was subpoenaing many of the local's left-wing leaders, Stellato was calling on Reuther to support the local's court suit against the decentralization of production.[63]

As it happened, not only would the two cases come to a head at the same time in the winter of 1952, but both would be played out in adjoining courtrooms in the same federal courthouse in downtown Detroit. Local 600's newspaper, *Ford Facts,* saw nothing coincidental in the common time and place of the two proceedings. In one courtroom, HUAC would "seek to do to Ford Local 600 and its membership the same thing the Ford Motor Company seeks to do in [the] other courtroom just down the hall."[64]

Only one of these two proceedings, however, would be governed by legal norms. In the courtroom where Judge Thomas Thornton presided over Local 600's suit for an injunction to block the dismantling of the Rouge, Goodman could count on a reasonable adherence to due process. He would file a written complaint, the company would submit a written reply, and the proceedings would be governed by rules of evidence and lawyerly conduct. Goodman's brief was a fact-laden submission that hinged on section 301 of the National Labor Relations Act, which permitted either party to a collective bargaining agreement to sue in federal court for breach of contract. Citing the company's assurances during negotiations that it would at least maintain, if not expand, the workforce at the Rouge, Goodman argued that the subsequent dispersal of jobs to other plants and outside contractors constituted a deliberate fraud, with unemployment and lost wages the result. "Unless restrained by the timely intervention of this court," his written complaint continued, the Rouge would be reduced "to a mere shell of its former capacity." UAW general counsel Harold Cranefield praised the work of his friend in a memo to Reuther, calling Goodman's brief "novel in its conception" and "very well thought out." If the court moved "even an inch in the direction of the theory of this complaint it would be a great gain for labor."[65]

There would be none of this consideration for law and due process in the HUAC hearings down the hall. The fact that the hearings even took place in a courtroom was something of a fraud, a conscious effort by the committee to give the proceedings the appearance of due process. In fact, there were few rules regarding how the hearings were to be conducted except those set by the committee itself. Under the color of law, due process would become its opposite: Goodman's clients were deemed guilty until they proved their innocence; accusers remained anonymous; hearsay became hard evidence; cross-examination of informants was prohibited; defense attorneys were not to speak above a whisper; there was no appeal process; there weren't even criminal or civil charges brought—just exposure of one's "un-American" beliefs and associations to the community, to employers, and to local police.

Even the Bill of Rights was distorted in this hall of mirrors. In one of HUAC's first major hearings in 1947, Hollywood directors and writers questioned about their left-wing ties had refused to answer on constitutional grounds, claiming that the First Amendment protected their political speech against government inquisition. In response, HUAC had cited the "Hollywood Ten" for contempt of Congress, and the Supreme Court had upheld their prison sentences. (Justice Robert Jackson explained that it would be an "act of judicial usurpation to strip Congress of its investigatory power.") HUAC was thereafter free to subpoena people for their political beliefs and demand that they name their associates in the Popular Front or the Communist Party. Flat refusal to name names would invite a contempt citation, and there was little doubt that HUAC would act on this threat: during its first twelve years, the committee cited 135 "hostile" witnesses for contempt, sending most to prison for terms lasting from three months to a year.[66]

The Fifth Amendment was the only constitutional protection the Supreme Court would recognize for refusing to inform. The amendment's stipulation that no person "shall be compelled in any criminal case to be a witness against himself" was a legacy of the seventeenth-century struggle in England against the king's Star Chamber courts and their use of torture to force "confessions" from Protestant nonconformists. Parliament had prohibited such practices in 1641, and the former colonists who inherited England's common law took care to include this protection against forced self-incrimination in the Constitution. As historian Leonard Levy writes, to the framers of the Fifth Amendment it was "not so much a protection of the guilty, or even the innocent, but a protection of freedom of expression, of political liberty, and the right to worship as one pleased," free of government inquisitors.[67]

But you could not be selective, Goodman warned his clients: if they testified freely about their *own* politics, as many wished to, they would thereby waive their Fifth Amendment rights and would have to *continue* testifying when the committee demanded—as it always did—that they "name names." In most cases the committee already knew the names, but pursued this ritualized interrogation to test whether the witness was a "true" patriot willing to expose former associates. A witness who "took the Fifth" to avoid this could not easily respond to any of the committee's speculations about "what you are hiding" without jeopardizing the legal grounds for refusing to rat on friends. From there it was easy to portray all such witnesses as, in Senator Joseph McCarthy's words, "Fifth Amendment Communists."[68]

It made a great deal of difference whether the UAW would join the opposition to these Star Chamber tactics. As the dominant union in the state and a major ally of Governor Williams, the UAW could potentially mobilize a sizable resistance to HUAC's methods, already condemned by Reuther and the CIO in formal resolutions. But Reuther could also recall the damage that the Dies Committee had done to Governor Murphy in 1938, and the HUAC of 1952 was a far stronger adversary, fortified by cold war anxieties and outrage over the Korean War's mounting casualties. At the same time, HUAC was equally wary of taking on the entire UAW. Public pronouncements before its arrival in Detroit focused primarily on the "Red Tinged" local at the Rouge, saying little about the rest of the union. Most of the labor movement, said committee member Charles Potter, the Republican congressman from Cheboygan, "has become conscious of Communist activities and taken every possible step to combat them." In effect, Potter was offering the larger UAW a truce in return for its cooperation in the assault on Local 600; Potter, in turn, would have an uncluttered stage for launching his U.S. Senate campaign.[69]

Defending the leftists at the Rouge would not only jeopardize this truce but would also commit Reuther to defending his only remaining opposition in the union. The first hint of where this kind of thinking would take him had come the previous fall, when Reuther declined to join Local 600's court suit against Ford's decentralization of production. Notwithstanding Cranefield's high regard for the case Goodman was arguing, political expediency was the more compelling factor: decentralization away from Local 600 would undermine Stellato's base and move the jobs to locals where Reuther was stronger. The same logic could apply to HUAC, but it was anyone's guess how far this would take the UAW in collaborating with the witch hunt.[70]

There was, in contrast, no mistaking where the Civil Rights Congress stood with regard to the committee's Detroit investigation. After distributing a reported fifty thousand anti-HUAC leaflets at plant gates, the CRC greeted the opening day of hearings with a spirited picket line in front of the federal building's Lafayette Street entrance. The picketers drew special attention to HUAC chairman John Wood, the Georgia Democrat whose repeated election to the House depended, in part, on the systematic disenfranchisement of black voters. "Everybody in Local 600 can vote," as one favored sign read, "How about Georgia?" Other signs called on HUAC to investigate lynchings in Florida or to simply "Get Out of Detroit."[71]

On the courthouse's seventh floor, Goodman and Crockett had meanwhile taken their seats in the courtroom gallery with clients scheduled for the first day of testimony. Crockett sat in the front row with the Reverend Hill, Goodman in the row behind with Dave Miller, the Scottish-born left-winger and former Ford worker who had gone on to win the presidency of the UAW's Cadillac local. They had to first sit through the testimony of informants who established the basis for the hearings: that Communists had targeted Detroit's factories, and particularly the Rouge, for membership drives in plants that were vital to defense production. It hardly mattered to committee members that other groups—from the Association of Catholic Trade Unionists to the Socialist Workers Party—also recruited members at Ford. The lack of any evidence that Communists had sabotaged production was likewise irrelevant. In the eyes of committee member Donald Jackson (R-CA), the mere act of joining the CP-USA was deserving of censure. "When our men are dying by the thousands," he announced with unflinching certainty, only turncoats would "commit the treason of membership in the Communist Party."[72]

The committee's hostility was evident when Local 600's accused leaders tried to make opening statements that condemned HUAC for its un-American attack on dissident minorities. "Friendly" witnesses who collaborated with the committee were routinely allowed to make personal statements, but "Unfriendly" witnesses were just as routinely denied this courtesy. The committee likewise tried to muzzle their lawyers. The early exchanges between Crockett and committee chairman John Wood were especially sharp on this score:

MR. CROCKETT: I would like to make a statement for the record.

MR. WOOD: Statements by Counsel are not permitted in this committee.

MR. CROCKETT: Counsel may not note anything on the record on behalf of his client . . . ?

MR. WOOD: Nothing at all.

MR. CROCKETT: May I inquire Mr. Chairman—

MR. WOOD: Let us get this clear right now. You are at liberty to confer with your client . . . and that is as far as counsel is permitted to go in this committee.

MR. CROCKETT: My advice to you— [addressing his client, the Reverend Hill]

MR. WOOD: Counsel, give him your advice in private, please.

MR. CROCKETT: He has no objection to my stating them out loud.

MR. WOOD: We do.[73]

Crockett and Goodman nevertheless persisted in challenging the committee's bullying tactics, particularly its repeated efforts to construe the Fifth Amendment as an admission of guilt. The issue came to a head during HUAC's interrogation of Pat Rice, the Irish-born vice president of Local 600. Rice was not a Communist and was never questioned on this score, but he was a leader of the left-wing Progressive caucus and therefore, as a "fellow traveler," he was targeted for rough treatment. The committee grilled him relentlessly and denounced his reliance on the Fifth Amendment. Goodman came to his client's defense:

MR. GOODMAN: Mr. Rice's effort to avoid this, which obviously appears to be a frame-up for him, is not to be considered under the Fifth Amendment as any evidence of guilt. . . .

MR. WOOD: I am going to take issue with you on that proposition. When a man takes advantage of the Fifth Amendment to refuse to answer a question, he is testifying falsely or the question, if answered, would be exactly what he says—

MR. GOODMAN: Would you allow me to say this: I have read a number of decisions of the United States Supreme Court . . . and one thing they have all said, Representative Wood, is this: That the Fifth Amendment protection being derived from the English law following the Inquisition is such that it is considered a protection for the innocent primarily. . . .

MR. JACKSON: I make no charge of guilt against Mr. Rice. I say the cognizant agency of Government should proceed immediately in my opinion to determine the facts in this case.

MR. GOODMAN: Will you agree with me that no person is deemed to be guilty because he refuses to answer under the Fifth Amendment? Won't you agree with that?

MR. JACKSON: I will agree with you to that extent, but what the American people think and what assumption they draw is an entirely different thing.[74]

Goodman prevailed in this particular skirmish, but he was no doubt aware that, as Jackson said, the American public would draw different conclusions, particularly as HUAC and the media coached them to do so. The *Detroit News* contributed to this willful distortion by attributing to Goodman the word "cloak" to describe the protections of the Fifth Amendment, implying that Rice, like other witnesses who refused to name names, was "hiding" (another word the *News* favored) some nefarious wrong. Supported by the media's distorted coverage, the committee pressed on day after day: one accusation followed another, forcing witnesses into a monotonous mantra of Fifth Amendment refusals. Did Stanley Nowak speak at a meeting in Pittsburgh where he called for the withdrawal of U.S. troops from Korea? Nowak said he would speak on Korea if the committee liked (it refused his offer), but he would not speak about that particular occasion because "I would have to proceed then and tell you all about the meeting in Pittsburgh," including the people who were there. Was Ford worker and Local 600 officer Dave Moore a member of the Communist Party? Moore, counseled by Goodman, also refused to answer, but not before denouncing the proceedings as an "inquisition" designed to frame him for perjury or set him up for prosecution under the Smith Act. "I am damned if I do and I am damned if I don't."[75]

When the Reverend Hill was asked if he had sponsored a banquet for the incoming and outgoing leaders of the Michigan Communist Party, he likewise invoked the Fifth Amendment and refused to say anything about the meeting—to do so would have forced him to answer the inevitable follow-up question about who was there. He was free, however, to speak his mind outside the hearing room, and his barbed remarks found wide support in the black community. Interviewed by the *Pittsburgh Courier* for its Detroit edition, he reminded readers that the government had previously tried to slander his son, "and now they tackle me." Hill speculated that he was being punished for his fight against "discrimination, segregation, police brutality and injustice," but that he would carry on with whatever allies cared to join the struggle. "It is laughable," he added in a remark aimed at the HUAC's chairman, "that I polled more votes in seeking to be elected to the Common Council of the city of Detroit than Congressman Wood polled to be elected in Georgia because of Georgia's disenfranchisement of the Negro."[76]

Art McPhaul brought this same audacity into the hearing room by refusing to surrender to HUAC the local records of the Civil Rights Congress, as his subpoena had ordered him. The *Detroit News* captured the heated exchange between the CRC's executive secretary and the committee chairman. "I wonder," McPhaul said to the Georgia congressman, "whether the Ku Kluxers ever have been asked to produce their records in Georgia." Chairman Wood took the bait, announcing that he had been the first official in Georgia to prosecute a Klan official and send him to prison. "For lynching?" asked McPhaul, temporarily assuming the role of inquisitor. "For a brutal flogging," replied Wood, who abruptly cut off McPhaul's rejoinder before the discomforting role reversal continued any further. Despite the fact that failure to turn over the CRC's records would certainly lead to prosecution for contempt of Congress, McPhaul held his ground. Many of the organization's past members had gone on to higher office in government or the labor movement, and he knew that HUAC would use the records to harass and red-bait them. His refusal to comply would bring the anticipated contempt charges and an eight-year case that Goodman would take all the way to the U.S. Supreme Court.[77]

Whereas McPhaul had turned the tables on HUAC temporarily, the following day's witness, Coleman Young, stayed on the offensive from start to finish. Young had a well-documented record of "subversion" in the eyes of HUAC dating back to World War II, when he and other African American pilots in the Army Air Corps crashed the whites-only officers club at Freeman Field in Indiana, leading to his arrest with one hundred other black officers. He brought this same penchant for direct action to the National Negro Labor Council (NNLC) as its executive secretary. "We were a hell-raising outfit," as he later described it, "operating on the premise that the struggle for jobs had to be carried forward with the tactics of mass protest, such as picketing, boycotts, and national campaigns. It was a matter of introducing union methods to the pursuit of social equality." These tactics, which anticipated the broader movement of the 1960s, differed significantly from the legalistic approach of the national NAACP, an organization Young and other militants regarded as "a little too genteel for our designs." The NAACP, in turn, regarded Young's organization as too closely aligned with Communists and other leftists whose militant tactics threatened to bring the Red Scare down on their heads. The NAACP steered a safer course by excluding the Left and focusing, instead, on court suits and lobbying to pass a Fair Employment Practices bill and end school segregation. These contrasting strategies of the liberal center and far Left would both bear fruit in the future, but in the early 1950s they were a study in contrasts, one relying primarily on elite lawyers and lobbyists, the other on street demonstrations and economic pressure.[78]

It was the brassy defiance of the streets that Young brought to the HUAC hearings, with Crockett seated next to him at the witness table. When the committee's chief counsel, Frank Tavenner, opened with the pro forma question, "Are you now a member of the Communist Party?" Young shot back that he would not answer "since I have no purpose of being here as a stool pigeon." Tavenner, a Virginia man accustomed to deferential behavior from African Americans, proceeded to engage Young in a heated exchange that became legendary in Detroit's black community. "You told us," he began in his southern accent, that "you were the executive secretary of the National Negro Congress—" Before he could finish the question, Young was on the attack.

MR. YOUNG: That word is "Negro," not "Niggra."

MR. TAVENNER: I said, "Negro." I think you are mistaken.

MR. YOUNG: I hope I am. Speak more clearly.

MR. WOOD: I will appreciate it if you will not argue with counsel.

MR. YOUNG: It isn't my purpose to argue. As a Negro, I resent the slurring of the name of my race . . .

MR. TAVENNER: I am sorry. I did not mean to slur it.[79]

Tavenner never recovered the initiative, and the committee's chairman fared no better when he took Young on, challenging him in a heavy Georgia accent. Again, the word "Negro" was mispronounced.

MR. YOUNG: I would inform you, also, the word is Negro.

MR. WOOD: I am sorry. If I made a different pronouncement of it, it is due to my inability to use the language any better than I do. I am trying to use it properly.

MR. YOUNG: It may be due to your southern background.

MR. WOOD: I am not ashamed of my southern background. For your information, out of the 112 Negro votes cast in the last election in the little village from which I come, I got 112 of them. That ought to be a complete answer of that. . . .

MR. YOUNG: I happen to know, in Georgia Negro people are prevented from voting by virtue of terror, intimidation, and lynchings. It is my contention you would not be in Congress today if it were not for the legal restrictions on voting on the part of my people.[80]

And so it went, the committee pressing Young on his relationship to the Civil Rights Congress and his work for the National Negro Labor Council, and Young finding every opportunity to attack his adversaries, reminding Congressman Jackson, for example, that there was widespread discrimination in California and that it was only the NNLC that had forced the Sears stores in his state to finally hire black saleswomen. The NNLC, he continued, had likewise fought in Tavenner's home state against the denial of voting rights for African Americans. Throughout, he repeated his contention that the committee should investigate the real "un-American activities" occurring across the country in the daily attacks on black civil rights.[81]

"Coleman Young did the most magnificent job I've ever heard before the investigating committee," remembered Goodman, who watched with Crockett as their client defied HUAC's inquisitors. "He had them hamstrung, moving backward in their tracks." Black Detroit was no less impressed. A phonograph record of his testimony became a popular item on Detroit's lower east side, and Young was widely acclaimed on the street and in the black press. "It was a vicarious thing," he later wrote. "I had said words that the people of Black Bottom had dreamed all their lives of saying to a southern white man. . . . I had spoken for all of them." Esther Shapiro, a CRC volunteer, recalled that when she was walking with Young that summer in Black Bottom, they could hardly make their way for the admiring crowds. "I wanted to get going, and finally I said 'Oh, for heaven's sake, Coleman, are you running for office?' Prophetic last words!"[82]

HUAC, however, would have the last word in 1952. Goodman had already suspected the worst when he saw Reuther's publicity director sitting with HUAC's invited guests. "All doubts vanished," he remembered, when the committee now called two of Reuther's staff to testify about Communist influence in Local 600. "They would never have done it, could never have done that, if he hadn't given his consent," Goodman observed years later. "And [he] probably worked out some kind of deal with the committee in advance to lay off him and anybody else except Local 600, and he would give them [in return] two people who were willing to become informers against their former brothers and sisters." Both men were past members of the Progressive caucus at Local 600: Shelton Tappes, the local's first recording secretary, and Lee Romano, a former local vice president. Romano had quit the Communist Party years before; Tappes, a respected African American leader at the Rouge, had been pushed aside by party members in the Progressive caucus when (according to his friend Art McPhaul) he refused to join the CP-USA. "He felt that he had been let down by the Left," recalled McPhaul, who disapproved of Tappes's agreement to testify, but still believed he was "a good trade unionist."[83]

Tappes admitted to another motivation years later. "I was divorcing my first wife . . . and I wanted custody of the children. I was really—I was really frightened on that." The climate of fear was such that Tappes believed he would lose his children if he failed to testify. But others faced similar threats without collaborating, and many of Tappes's former allies would shun him for decades to come. It was, Goodman recalled, "a despicable performance. It was sickening to so many of us."[84]

Tappes and Romano named names, Romano speculating that the Communists at the Rouge, with four hundred party members and another two thousand fellow travelers, had "never been more powerful." Their testimony merged with that of other informers who added names to a lengthening list of alleged Communist sympathizers scattered throughout Detroit's auto plants. Daily radio commentary and newspaper headlines blared the news of "Communist Infiltration" and "Red Subversion," preparing the ground for a community-wide assault on the remnants of Detroit's labor-Left. Representative Jackson announced that it was time "to take some of these Communists by the seat of the pants and throw them out of the unions," regardless of their rights under the UAW's "bylaws and constitutions." Even Romano, the "friendly witness," meekly objected that this approach would "use the same methods they do in Russia." Jackson was unrepentant. When Paul Boatin, one of Goodman's clients, took the congressman to task for his endorsement of vigilante tactics, Jackson repeated his call for ejecting Communists from the plants, adding that "loyal Americans in the union should see that it is done." Detroit's self-proclaimed patriots took the cue, led by white workers in a dozen factories who launched sit-down strikes and violent "runouts" against the "Red Leaders" listed in the media's daily accounts. The UAW Executive Board condemned the vigilante attacks in a single public statement, but unlike the aggressive countermeasures taken during World War II, when top UAW leaders went into the streets to personally oppose the hate strikes, there was no such effort in 1952.[85]

Employers tolerated the lawlessness and ratified its outcome by summarily firing seven of the named leftists. Labor journalist B. J. Widick captured the ugly consequences of HUAC's incitement. "An effigy of one Negro was hung up. In other plants, workers came in with ropes, just as in the deep South. In another plant, where the local union president is Jewish, vulgar anti-Semitic signs were posted or scrawled on bulletin boards. It was a week of hate and fear and violent anger. Many a committeeman or steward was threatened for defending the union position [against the runouts]." When the violence finally abated, eighteen workers had been physically driven from the auto plants or fired. Others named by HUAC were evicted from their apartments in Detroit's public housing projects, fired from teaching positions in Detroit's public schools, or expelled from Wayne University. None of these victims of the witch hunt had been charged with a single criminal act. They were driven from their homes or workplaces because of their political beliefs.[86]

Reuther now moved to finish the work that HUAC had begun. As the hearings ended their second week, he ordered Carl Stellato and Local 600's officers to appear before the UAW Executive Board and account for their failure to enforce the union's constitutional ban on Communists in office. This decision to join the witch hunt had not gone unopposed, with board member Leonard Woodcock arguing against taking any action that would dignify HUAC's "neo-fascists," as he called them. Reuther, however, was more concerned that HUAC would "try to put the union in a position where we were . . . covering up for the Communists." After a daylong hearing, the executive board voted to strip Stellato and his fellow officers of power and place the local under an administrative board headed by Reuther and Secretary Treasurer Emil Mazey. The purge was not entirely successful, however: when Reuther finally relinquished control of Local 600 (as the union constitution required), sentiment among the members had turned so completely against him that his remaining supporters didn't even bother to field a candidate against Stellato, who ran unopposed.[87]

The more telling damage to Local 600 would follow the defeat of its court suit against the dismemberment of the Rouge. In a letter to Stellato during the HUAC hearings, Goodman had predicted that "the judge will undoubtedly render a decision within a few weeks," but the proceedings dragged on for many months. By August, Goodman was conceding to a colleague that the chances of winning the case were "very doubtful." This had something to do with management's sophisticated reply to Goodman's brief. Gone was the paranoiac anti-Communism and brute force associated with Harry Bennett and the senior Henry Ford. Bennett had retired in 1945 and the company's patriarch had died two years later, leaving his grandson, Henry II, as the company's undisputed leader. With him came a new generation of professional managers and an accompanying discourse of "scientific" management. "Decentralization means breaking down a large business into a number of smaller businesses," as a company pamphlet explained, making each "an independently managed 'profit center.'" There was, undoubtedly, an interest in moving production to regions where, as one company memo acknowledged, "the CIO has not been able to establish a dominating position." Decentralization would serve this agenda well, but it was also a strategic response to an economy expanding westward and south, and few judges would question Ford's claim that it was simply following the market. The UAW, in any case, had already conceded Ford's right to manage the nonlabor aspects of the business, and the local's contention of fraud was "rendered doubtful," according to the court, by the refusal of Reuther and other top officers—all of them signatories to the contract—to join the suit.[88]

With the judge's dismissal of the case in July of 1953, Ford was free to continue moving production to the suburbs, to the South, and beyond. Combined with the labor-saving consequences of automation, the impact on Local 600 was a steady decline in membership, from over sixty thousand in 1950 to forty-two thousand by the end of the decade. Similar declines across Detroit's industrial landscape would leave growing pockets of long-term unemployment, particularly in inner-city neighborhoods where the oldest plants—Packard and Hudson especially—fell victim in the mid-1950s to the competition of the Big Three. African Americans trapped in Detroit's expanding ghetto would take the brunt of the structural unemployment that followed this first wave of plant closings.[89]

Last Stand

Local 600's rebellion had come to an end, and with it, the curtain came down on a chapter in Detroit's history and in Goodman's career. The Left was already in retreat when HUAC launched its assault on Local 600, but it was now completely routed from the UAW. Reuther no longer faced organized opposition, and while he still championed many liberal causes and social democratic reforms, he henceforth eschewed any claim that he or the UAW had once represented a more militant, if not radical, challenge to the status quo. "Certainly I am not a socialist," he told the Detroit Economic Club in 1953. In a retroactive airbrushing of his youthful radicalism, he added that he had joined the Socialist Party only for "about a year" at the nadir of the Depression. It was no longer politically wise to acknowledge that he had actually grown up in the party of Eugene Debs and that he had worked for more than a year in Soviet factories. His contrived amnesia was emblematic of the larger process at work, as the Red Scare made liberals out of former socialists, and liberals into collaborators with HUAC.[90]

The HUAC hearings marked a different kind of watershed for Goodman. As in the Dies Committee hearings of 1938, congressional investigators had again used their powers of subpoena and investigation to hound political dissidents and impose a species of thought control on American opinion. The experience would strengthen Goodman's appreciation for the Bill of Rights and the importance of an unfettered arena for contending views. Thirteen years later, when HUAC announced it would investigate the Ku Klux Klan and other right-wing organizations, Goodman would urge the Lawyers Guild to oppose the proceedings with the same vigor it had directed at the 1952 hearings. "Merely because the Committee investigates one group rather than another," he would write a colleague at Yale University Law School, "does not eliminate my basic opposition to the functioning of any such Committee within a democratic society." In response to Goodman's prodding, the Guild executive board would issue a statement condemning "any general investigation of the membership or activities of the Klan . . . conducted for the purpose of exposure" because such an inquisition "cannot fail to undermine and destroy fundamental rights of opinion, expression, and association." Rather than persecute the group for its unsavory *beliefs,* the need was to prosecute the illegal *activities* that subverted black civil rights.[91]

As Goodman's commitment to the Bill of Rights was deepening, his admiration for the Soviet Union—once expressed so freely during the "great anti-fascist struggle" of World War II—was now fading. In 1950 the National Lawyers Guild had already repudiated Stalin's efforts to isolate Joseph Tito, the Yugoslavian Communist leader who defied Soviet orthodoxy, and the following year the Guild condemned North Korea's Communist regime for invading South Korea. Goodman would later voice his opposition to the suppression of dissent in Soviet-bloc countries, but for now he focused on the issues he found directly in front of him, in Detroit: police brutality, racial segregation, congressional inquisition, and the growing list of friends, colleagues, and clients threatened with jail and the blacklist for their political beliefs. As for the Soviet gulag or the Red Army's grip on Eastern Europe, these were troubling but distant matters compared to the state-supported terror in Mississippi. For Goodman, the largely hallucinated threat of Communist subversion in the United States deserved no serious consideration.[92]

In this respect, he was clearly out of step with the majority of Americans, a fact underlined in the fall of 1952 when Michigan voters elected Charles Potter, the star of HUAC's Detroit hearings, to the U.S. Senate. Yet even as this confirmed Goodman's outlier status with respect to the white majority, the events of that year just as clearly reinforced his alignment with black Detroit and the early civil rights movement. This is not to say that the African American community was immune to the Red Scare; George Crockett could attest to that. But at the time of the Foley Square trial, Crockett had lived in Detroit for only four years, and his early legal battles had taken him to New York and points east, where he defended the little-known leaders of the Communist Party. The HUAC hearings of 1952 were something altogether different: an attack on the Reverend Hill, Coleman Young, Art McPhaul, and other local leaders, galvanizing a widespread resentment in the black community against the targeting of African Americans. The result was by no means a unanimous condemnation of the Red Scare, but there was certainly far more opposition to HUAC among black Detroiters than white. They had, after all, seen it before: bogus courtroom proceedings, violent runouts, the brandishing of a hangman's noose.

HUAC's arrival in the city was another chapter in the same long struggle. At the very moment that the historically whites-only American Bar Association threatened to expel Communists and those who defended them, the Wolverine Bar Association, representing Michigan's black lawyers, issued a stinging denunciation of HUAC. The committee's primary goal, it charged, was "to defame, malign and endeavor to destroy the good reputation of any witness whose associations, beliefs and opinions on controversial issues of the day do not conform with the committee's notion of what is or is not Americanism." Black informers, Tappes included, were little different from the whites who also named names, but among the "unfriendly" witnesses, McPhaul, Moore, Hill, and especially Young were noticeably more defiant than their white counterparts. Likewise at the plant level: there were white union officers who spoke out against the runouts, but it was only black workers who physically resisted them in significant numbers—in one case, a group of one hundred African Americans at the Chrysler Jefferson plant reportedly holding a larger mob of whites at bay.[93]

The reasons for this were articulated by Young in his courageous testimony. When HUAC's chief counsel asked him if he would denounce Communists running for office, Young patiently explained that the "Negro people would be more interested in what a given candidate's program might happen to be, and what he was going to do to improve the condition of the Negro people, than any label tagged on him by such a committee as yourselves." Young and many other African Americans of his generation knew that the Communist Party, for all its faults, was the first majority-white organization that had actively championed black liberation. "The reality of the day," as Young wrote in his autobiography, "was that anyone who took an active interest in the plight of black people was naturally drawn toward the Communist Party—not as a member, necessarily, but at least as a friend and ally." Young was overstating the case, for there were certainly many liberals in the NAACP and elsewhere who did not regard the CP-USA as a friend or ally. But it is equally certain that blacks and whites viewed the link between Communism and the militant espousal of civil rights from different vantage points. In the midst of the HUAC hearings, even the Baptist Ministers Alliance of Detroit pledged its unanimous support for the positions taken by the Reverend Hill.[94]

The emblematic tactics of the civil rights movement in the 1960s were already there, in embryo, in the 1940s and early 1950s: the picket lines, restaurant sit-ins, boycotts, protest marches, petition drives, and rallies of the CRC, the NNLC, and local NAACP chapters in Detroit and elsewhere. The tactical continuity was evident in the same application of "union methods," as Coleman Young put it, to the pursuit of social equality. It is worth recalling that the inaugural "Freedom Ride" was not in 1961 but in 1947, when Bayard Rustin and the Congress of Racial Equality (CORE) first challenged segregated seating in interstate bus travel. The "Mississippi Summer" of 1964 had its precursor as well, in 1950, when CRC militants from Detroit and elsewhere converged on Jackson, the state capital, in support of Willie McGee. The CORE and CRC campaigns both failed, and the significance of these efforts faded thereafter. But for Goodman and Crockett and the many other refugees of the Popular Front who survived the witch hunt, the two movements—civil

rights for blacks and workers, civil liberties for leftists and Communists—
were inextricably linked.[95]

It would be a long journey back from the winter of 1952, when Young,
Crockett, and Goodman traded verbal barbs with HUAC. For all his faith
in the future, even Goodman might have found it hard to believe that he
was in the same foxhole with Detroit's future mayor and U.S. congressman.

7

Getting By

"It was a constant, ambivalent feeling," Goodman remembered of the early 1950s. "Year after year, case after case came along. The stress, not only on myself, but other lawyers in the same predicament, it was enormous." Goodman believed that history was "ultimately" on his side. "Yet you knew that the public at large was hostile," that it believed

> you were wrong and what you were doing was wrong. And it affected not only yourself . . . but it affected your family as well, your relations with other people whom you knew, your friends. . . . So there wasn't the feeling, you know, of the martyr going to the stake and "I'm going to die for a cause and history will absolve me," sort of thing. It was "what am I going to do tomorrow, the next day? What about the kids?"[1]

There were the occasional moments when it was hard to ignore the physical risks involved. He must have felt like a targeted man in Mississippi when the *Jackson Daily News* editorialized that it was too bad the courts could not "send some lawyers to the electric chair along with their clients." When the crosstown paper published a large photo of Goodman and Abzug on the day of McGee's execution, he must have felt like the target was on his back. Closer to home, the hate mail arriving in the CRC's Detroit offices included one petition to "Save Willie McGee" that had been scornfully filled with mock names ("Stealin Stalin," "Freddie Fascist"), all fictitious but one: "No good Goodman, Lawyer's Guilt [*sic*]," with "DROP DEAD" scrawled across the page in heavy red crayon. The most frequent reminder of his pariah status, however, came from the kind of spontaneous shunning that Crockett experienced after the Foley Square trial. No matter where Goodman turned, "you're walking down the street downtown and you see people that you know . . . for many years [and] . . . they would walk across the street [so] they wouldn't have to say hello. . . . You're constantly being made aware of that, that you were isolated and on the outside, sort of quarantined, a leper in your thinking and what you are doing." You had to "sort of get accustomed to it," as he later said of the quiet spurning. "You do develop some armor against it so it doesn't hurt you so much." It was harder to protect two sons who had to deal with the fact that "everybody," as his oldest boy Dick recalled, knew their father "was lawyer for the Reds and so you got a certain amount of static from that." Son Bill, at age thirteen, wondered why his father was so different. "Gee Dad," he remembered asking after people on the street had turned away, "doesn't *anybody* like you?" Goodman knew it was tough for his kids, "but they withstood it pretty well. . . . We always had to keep explaining, keep telling them what we were doing and why we were doing it."[2]

The two boys found their father's explanation convincing enough to emulate his career in the 1950s and join his law firm in the 1960s. Dick, who graduated from Central High School the same spring that Willie McGee was executed, got his bachelor's degree from the University of Michigan in 1955 and his law degree from the University of Chicago three years later. Bill went to a different high school (Mumford) but the same law school, graduating in 1964 and immediately entering his father's firm, four years after his brother.

For all the political turmoil surrounding their father's career over the preceding twenty years, they had grown up in a relatively peaceful setting in the home on Warrington Drive. The neighborhood's remaining lots filled up with new houses, some bought by Jewish families moving north from the Dexter-Davison area, where Ernie's mother still lived. Central High at the corner of Linwood and Tuxedo streets (his father's alma mater by name, but moved to a new building four miles northwest of its old site) was by Dick's recollection 75 percent Jewish when he graduated, with a small but growing number of black students. (There were "some white—uh, Gentile kids, too," he recalled on one occasion, slipping into the same vernacular merging of ethnicity and race that his father had learned in the old ghetto.) On Dick's way home from school he would sometimes stop at his grandmother's apartment, where he could always count on a piece of cake and, no doubt, the occasional piece of Minnie's mind regarding the lack of religious observance in the Goodman household. Ernie and Freda would accompany Minnie to temple on high holidays, but neither Dick nor Bill would be bar mitzvahed, and Minnie must have known that her son's family put nonkosher food on the dinner table (bacon was a particular favorite of Ernie's). She might not have known, however, that during at least one Hanukah season the boys pressured their parents to put up a Christmas tree—secreted in the basement to avoid Grandmother's disapproval.[3]

A small but welcome compensation for Ernie's loss of UAW work was that he traveled out of town less often, and his comings and goings from the office became a little more predictable. Goodman still took the bus downtown so he could leave the car (now a four-door Hudson "swept-back") for Freda. Dick would often intercept his father after he got off the Livernois bus at Chippewa in the early evening. "I can remember seeing many, many times, [him] coming around that corner with a briefcase and a newspaper."[4]

Crossing the Color Line

Goodman's youngest son recalled a world balanced between the conventional hallmarks of middle-class family life, which Freda insisted on and Ernie largely supported, and the unconventional ideas and associations attached to his father's politics. "I think my parents made a conscious decision to shield me from some of what was going on during the Red Scare period," Bill recalled. It was a porous defense, however, and intentionally so. His father, in fact, wanted him to know about the labor and civil rights movements firsthand. "I went to meeting after meeting with my dad, so I was exposed to politics. I would go to all these political meetings, including a Paul Robeson concert at Hartford Avenue Baptist Church. My dad was a friend of Reverend Charles Hill, and Hill's kids and Crockett's kids were friends of mine. The families would come visit us, and when the black kids would sleep over, it exposed an incredible amount of racism and talk in my neighborhood of 'nigger lovers.'"[5]

The local gossips had a lot to whisper about. Coleman Young and the Reverend Hill were visitors to Warrington Drive, particularly during Progressive Party campaigns when Young and Goodman were leaders of the state party. Paul Robeson was a rare guest on occasions when the renowned actor-singer-lawyer was in Detroit for a union rally or Progressive Party gathering. George Crockett and his family were also visitors, with the Goodmans making return visits to the Crockett home on American Street. Every year the two families took an excursion to Stratford, Ontario, for the Shakespeare Festival, and a trip north to Maurice Sugar's home on Black Lake was an annual tradition for all of the families in the partnership. "He had three structures," recalled Crockett's son, George III, of Sugar's lakeside estate, "his home, a structure he called 'The Shack,' and another that was called 'Aunt Nettie's.'" Despite their father's prodding, neither Dick nor Bill took to hunting or fishing, but they loved the week or two spent at the Sugar lodge every summer: the swimming, hiking, reading, and (in Dick's recollection) the lakeside barbecues. "There would be all this steak and the corn and the vegetables from the garden and big piles of ice cream, and Michigan blueberries and all this stuff, and we'd sit around and talk, and Maurice was probably as good a storyteller as I've ever heard. He would love to do it, he would sit around and tell the stories about his courtroom battles . . . and some of the early labor stuff." In the darkest of times, these moments sustained the firm's partners and their families. Maurice Sugar's stories were a portal to the heroic past, his home on Black Lake a refuge from the FBI. "It was a good, warm, dedicated law firm," George Crockett III recalled years later, "that believed as much in earning money to survive and feed their families as it did in defending the rights of persons who were unable to afford lawyers."[6]

Returning to Detroit, it was in the day-to-day business of running the firm and representing clients that Goodman and Crockett grew into something that is uncommon enough today, and was a rarity in the 1950s: an interracial friendship that was also a professional collaboration. With adjoining offices, they worked together on a wide range of cases in which strategy was decided jointly and roles—who wrote a brief, who presented a case—were assigned interchangeably. Goodman later recalled how this partnership changed his understanding of the world:

> An integrated partnership was a very great thing for us, and for me personally, to be on that kind of a level with a black person, where we were equal partners, living together, working together, doing everything that anybody else would do together, to the point where you became accustomed to it, it became a part of our life which we didn't even think anything about, speaking for myself now. You can't do that just by reading or by intellectualizing it. The necessity for working with people on an equal basis is absolutely crucial to living in an integrated society. I learned that. It was a wonderful lesson.[7]

Crockett also saw his friendship with Goodman as a unique thing in a largely bigoted world. Talk of brotherly love was cheap in this color-conscious society; the real question always came down to what your friend—black or white—would actually do when careers or reputations were at stake. Crockett saw himself as "typical of most blacks":

> Until that white [person] has, how shall I put it, "proven himself," if you want to use that term, you have some reservations. From the very beginning, I never had such reservations with Sugar. Same

thing is true of Ernie. Those two people. But now everybody else? White person? I have to be around him awhile before I finally decide, "yeah, he's for real."[8]

"For real" trust could be elusive, even among the like-minded leaders of the Civil Rights Congress. The conflicted work relations between Art McPhaul and Anne Shore were a case in point, with Goodman serving as go-between. In McPhaul's estimate, Anne Shore was one of "the best white people that had been developed up to that time," handling the many details of the Michigan chapter as administrative secretary. But speaking of her years later, McPhaul described Shore as a "white chauvinist" who "just could not accept leadership from a black person." These contrasting judgments were not necessarily incompatible, though their apparent opposition speaks to the complexity of race relations in the early civil rights movement. Shore and her husband, Jerry, were frequent visitors to Warrington Drive, and Goodman was among the many activists who regarded Anne as indispensable to the CRC's hard-pressed Detroit chapter. Yet even friends understood that her intelligence, single-mindedness, and blunt manner could come across as imperious, and conflict on this score was aggravated when the CRC's national leaders directed their communications to Shore rather than the Michigan chapter's executive secretary, McPhaul.[9]

At the same time, McPhaul's charges undoubtedly had something to do with the internal politics of the CP-USA, for it was in these years (1949–53) that the Communist Party launched a crusade to purge its ranks of "white chauvinism." This ritual of self-purification quickly moved from criticism of language (questioning the use of phrases like "black sheep" or "whitewash") into a small-scale witch hunt, with party rivals attacking their opponents for racial slights real and imagined. "Both whites and blacks," recalled Joseph Starobin, a former Communist and editor of the *Daily Worker*, "began to take advantage of the enormous weapon which the charge of 'white chauvinism' gave them to settle scores, to climb organizational ladders, to fight for jobs" within the party. The result was a mirror universe: while the U.S. government, alarmed by the armed might of Russia and the tide of anticolonial revolutions around the world, responded with a paranoiac campaign to destroy the disloyal "enemies among us," the target of this government-sponsored hunt for subversion responded with its own internal inquisition against the "virus" of white chauvinism.[10]

There was undoubtedly much to question in the behavior of whites newly won to the cause of racial equality. With no model and little experience of egalitarian race relations, some whites inevitably reverted to a patronizing manner, and most were prone to the kind of unwitting insensitivity that Goodman, in 1935, had demonstrated in his first visit to a black church. But how far should such a campaign go? Jack Raskin, for one, believed that the decision in 1950 to replace him with McPhaul as local director of the CRC had less to do with competence than with a doctrinal campaign to promote black leadership. Whatever the merits of this early case of affirmative action, McPhaul thereafter managed to work with Shore over six years of tumultuous but effective effort, notwithstanding Shore's alleged resistance to black leadership. Indeed, the rhetoric of self-purification was so malleable that even Shore, the purported white chauvinist, could accuse the national office of the same when she complained that important communications were being sent to her but not to McPhaul. "This too often repeated error smacks of white chauvinism," she accused the national staff. "Pat is guilty too," she added in an final assessment that underlines the complex overlay of race relations and party politics: William "Pat" Patterson, the national executive secretary of the CRC, was black.[11]

The Hunt

Sectarian infighting would drive scores of activists out of politics altogether, but there was also a deep reservoir of camaraderie that helped sustain the besieged survivors of the Popular Front. Nothing tapped these wells of fellow feeling quite like the annual "Buck Dinner," a gathering of the clan that combined a venison feast with ribald skits, group singing of political songs, fund-raising, a few speeches, and dancing.

By 1950, this midwinter tradition had evolved into something qualitatively different from the ceremony that Sugar had inaugurated during the Great Depression, when the buck hunt in Michigan's north woods was the primary focal point and the subsequent dinner in Detroit was only a modest gathering of a few dozen souls. The monetary "bucks" raised in these early dinners were a welcome contribution to the causes that Sugar and his cohorts favored, but the amounts had been modest: just $275 in 1939. Over the next decade, the fund-raising took on greater importance and the scale of the Detroit dinner grew accordingly. By 1949, the printed invitation made no bones about the primary goal of the event:

> We've got a buck and you're in luck—To eat it is your pleasure.
> Come eat your fill, come dressed for the kill,
> Then we'll collect the treasure.[12]

By 1950, the Buck Dinner's 326 guests were contributing a sizable treasure: $3,243 in that year, a twelve-fold increase over 1939 (and the equivalent of $29,000 in the purchasing power of the dollar sixty years later). All of the net proceeds went to the dinner's sole beneficiary since 1946, the hard-pressed Civil Rights Congress. "The money, as usual, saved all of us from starvation," Anne Shore wrote in thanks to the dinner committee the following year, "and the CRC staff from the imminent threat of debtors prison." There was no doubting the financial importance of the Buck Dinner's contribution at a time when the CRC's staff was paid a weekly salary of $30, and when the chapter's plant-gate newspaper, the *Labor Defender*, cost $400 for the monthly press run of fifty thousand. Equally important was the boost to morale. "I think we can all feel very proud of the dinner this year, particularly in view of the times," Shore wrote to the dinner committee in 1951. "The response in enthusiasm and in money should make us all feel better about the response of the people to fine causes."[13]

Ernie and Freda were key organizers of this event in the late 1940s and early 1950s, though their roles were sharply distinguished by gender. The actual deer hunt remained a decidedly male affair, restricted to Goodman and a handful of hunters who drove north every fall to link up with Sugar. This annual trek was not for everyone. Crockett crossed many color lines in his career with the Goodman firm, but joining the buck hunt was not one of them. Dean Robb confessed to killing one deer in his life—"and I felt guilty ever since." The only woman known to have actually killed a deer was the one who didn't have to travel north to do it: Sugar's wife, Jane Mayer. Ben Probe, Goodman's friend and fellow member of the Lawyers Guild, was a regular hunter, and others included Harold Cranefield, Leonard Grossman, Dr. Mike Bicknell, and (before 1947) UAW leader George Addes. Mort Furay, state director of the United Public Workers and a past UAW organizer from Local 174, was another regular. He was also one of Goodman's close friends, and certainly one of the most demonstrative. A hefty Irishman of radical bent, he had started in politics in the 1930s as a follower of the right-wing radio priest Father Coughlin, and moved leftward as he joined the labor movement's Depression-era battles. "Organizing was not a pink-tea affair," as Goodman recalled years later of Furay's career. "To him, the enemy was the boss, and it didn't take much for the fists to fly when he and Jimmy Scanlon and Jack White tangled with scabs." He was known for his equally combative expression of opinion, sometimes laced with enough profanity to drive Freda upstairs when Furay visited Warrington Drive. He was at the same time capable of a sensitivity to others, as Goodman described it, "which seemed completely at variance with his outer toughness." A self-taught student of history, poetry, and music, it was Furay who encouraged Goodman's love of opera. "Each night our hunting cabin would turn into a concert hall for operas, concertos, and symphonies," Goodman recalled. "Tosca meant for him the musical expression of the eternal struggle between political oppression and love of man."[14]

Over time, killing the bucks was less important than collecting them at the actual dinner in Detroit. For this, a larger cadre of "headhunters"—also all male—recruited tablemates who would be able to afford a contribution at the end of the meal. In addition to the deer slayers, the headhunters in the early 1950s included a sizable number of lawyers who had worked at one time or another on the thirty-second floor of the Cadillac Tower: George Crockett, Mort Eden, Dean Robb, Harry Anbender, Ned Smokler, and Jack Tucker among them. Other headhunters included journalist Carl Haessler, editor of the left-wing *Federated Press,* and Goodman's past client Dr. Eugene Shafarman, whose continuing work on public health and respiratory disease had made him an early critic of cigarette smoking. The Reverend Hill had a table one year, as did Irving Richter, the former Washington lobbyist for the UAW and one of the first union staffers fired by Reuther in 1947. Two of Goodman's closest friends were also headhunters: Sid Rosen, owner of Hayes Jewelry on the east side, and Morrie Gleicher, a former local-union president in the United Public Workers who now ran a printing business.[15]

Coleman Young was a guest of Harry Anbender in 1950, joining a table of twelve that included Erma Henderson, a clerical worker and labor activist who went from the CIO (working for the National Maritime Union) to the Progressive Party and, decades later, the Detroit City Council as its first African American woman. Young nearly became a headhunter in 1952 but apparently had to decline the honor—and the financial obligation—at the last minute, probably due to his difficulties finding a job. Confronted by a well-maintained blacklist that barred entry to most employment, he and Jack Raskin had opened a dry-cleaning business in 1950 that catered primarily to left-wing customers. "I was a hell of a spotter," he later claimed, "it's just that there wasn't much call for politically enlightened spotters in those days." Teaching in night school and washing walls during the day were no more remunerative. "I was in low cotton," as he put it, and he knew he wasn't alone. "I saw a dear man like Sid Rosen driven out of his jewelry business . . . by damning newspaper and FBI persecution." Rosen, a past activist in the Progressive Party, had scandalized many of his Grosse Pointe neighbors by inviting Paul Robeson to his home for a benefit.[16]

The actual meal and much of the preparation for the Buck Dinner was handled by a committee of women led by Jane Mayer until the early 1950s. Freda Goodman was usually the chief provisioner, buying the groceries for more than three hundred people and serving as one of three head cooks in the kitchen of the Jewish Cultural Center, the left-wing hall on the city's northwest side where the Buck Dinner was housed in the late 1940s and early 1950s. The banquet moved to the Parkside Hall in 1953 and to UAW Local 51 at the end of the decade, but the annual program was roughly the same. Each year, in a ritualistic reversal of gender roles, the headhunters were expected to bring the food to the tables and clear them of plates at the end of the meal. There was also a considerable investment of time and energy, particularly by Sugar and Goodman, in composing and producing song sheets and comic "operettas" for entertainment.[17]

For the harried souls who joined these sing-alongs, the Buck Dinner was a festival of renewal and hope, a welcome sanctuary from the hostile world outside. Reminders of the proximate danger were literally at the door. "Everyone attending the Buck Dinner was aware of the two carloads of FBI agents very conspicuously parked in front of the hall," recalled historian Ed Pintzuk, a participant. "Everyone knew that they were recording the license plate numbers of all the cars in the parking lot and on adjacent streets." Some people entering the hall would taunt the agents, and the spirit of defiance was fortified during the evening by various rites of affirmation, including group singing of original ditties lampooning Joe McCarthy, the right-wing senator from Wisconsin:

> *McCarthy was a Senator, he got him a committee*
> *The way he tried to run the show, it really was a pity.*
> *Some democrats got mad at him: "Dictatorship" they said.*
> *So they walked out, but they came back, because he hollered "Red!"*

At a time when the CRC and other left-wing groups were all under intense scrutiny by the Department of Justice and HUAC, keeping the FBI *outside* of the hall was no small matter. Fear of informers was endemic on the left, and rightly so given the lengthening list of former colleagues who had named names before HUAC (among them Lee Pressman, Goodman's colleague in the Goose Creek case). Goodman's table guests, like those of every headhunter, were admitted only if they could produce the printed invitation signed by Goodman. "Admission by Invitation Only," it read in large type across the bottom. "Invitation must be filled out. WE MEAN IT!!"[18]

Shadow of Doubt

The police never crashed the Buck Dinner, but they were known on other occasions to arrive without invitation. Even the most innocent of gatherings could be targeted for a raid, as on the evening of 25 July 1953, when CRC staff and supporters gathered at Art McPhaul's house for a garden party in the backyard.

"Japanese lanterns decorated the garden," as one CRC flyer later described the scene. "Hot dogs were on a charcoal fire. A victrola played softly on the porch, and beer was in a cooler." The several dozen guests who had paid $1 to cover the cost of food and beer were talking in small groups. This tranquil scene was suddenly interrupted shortly after 10:00 p.m. when a squad of police converged on the backyard from all sides and announced that the party was in violation of the state's liquor control law—selling beer without a license. However, instead of ticketing McPhaul and Anne Shore, who both took responsibility for this minor offense (a common one in Detroit), the police arrested all twenty-six people on the premises, took them to the station house, fingerprinted everybody, strip-searched the men, and jailed everyone until the next morning. When the case later went to trial, the judge made it clear that more was at stake than a minor liquor law. "These people," he publicly declared, "were meeting as an American front of our enemies when our sons were fighting and dying in Korea."[19]

CRC activists put the arrests in a different light. "Police and many top government officials don't want to see people of all colors and nationalities together in friendship and equality," one flyer declared. "Police are particularly vindictive to interracial gatherings and to the Negro people." The police were not alone in this regard. Except near the factories or on the lower east side, most restaurants and bars were whites-only, and the arrival of an interracial group like the one at the garden party would have roused considerable hostility. For that reason, blacks and whites who wanted to socialize in a public place often gravitated toward the jazz clubs and bars in "The Bottoms," as Black Bottom was known. "That was one of the few places where we could all go out together," recalled Esther Shapiro, a CRC volunteer and friend of Ernie and Freda. "That and Chinatown, we had no problem."[20]

Otherwise, it was difficult to feel at ease, even at a private garden party. Esther's husband, Hal Shapiro, knew this better than most. As a union representative for the Fur and Leather Workers, another of the left-wing unions expelled from the CIO for supporting the Progressive Party, Shapiro had become an activist in the Henry Wallace campaign and a close friend of Goodman, whose firm represented the Fur and Leather Workers in dealings with upstate tanneries and Detroit furriers. Shapiro's close ties with the CP-USA also drew the attention of the House Un-American Activities Committee, which called him to appear in a second round of hearings held in Lansing. The FBI thereafter tapped his phones and put his house under drive-by surveillance. "I lost some good friends," Esther remembered. "They stopped, they just stopped calling. They . . . knew our phone was tapped, they were afraid to be seen with me. I thought they were my good friends."[21]

Under these circumstances, it was hard not to be constantly looking over your shoulder, particularly when it was revealed months later that two of those arrested at the garden party, Harold Mikkelsen and Milton Santwire, were paid FBI informers posing as CRC activists. Who could you trust? What could you safely say in front of people you were not sure of? Was your own family at risk? Goodman and Crockett were defending more than fifty people in deportation proceedings where the government would go to any length to strip these foreign-born leftists of their citizenship—because they allegedly had been Communists before they arrived, because they allegedly had misrepresented some detail in their past when they applied for citizenship, because they were now, undoubtedly, leftists. For these political reasons, they were threatened with expulsion from the country and separation from their family and children. Together with the many court cases in which Goodman's clients faced imprisonment for their political beliefs, all of this must have weighed on his imagination and contributed to his chronic insomnia.[22]

Among those he considered most vulnerable, one case gave special cause for worry. His sporadic affair with Laicha Kravchik had ended by the mid-1940s when she married and started her own family. She was now potentially at risk of being targeted for investigation as a foreign-born Communist, subject to FBI scrutiny and perhaps even arrest and deportation. If a case was brought, the FBI would seize every available piece of evidence that might give proof of her subversive potential, including the letters Goodman had sent her over the years. There was nothing in what he had written that would give credence to a charge of subversion, but his political commentary could be misconstrued and bent to that purpose, putting her at risk; his expressions of affection, if made public during an investigation, would put *him* at risk. Driven by his anxious speculation on these matters, Goodman went to the extraordinary length of contacting Laicha through a mutual friend and asking her to burn the letters.[23]

It was too late, however, to escape the government's invasive scrutiny, even after Laicha reluctantly destroyed the correspondence. Years later, when Goodman obtained his voluminous FBI file, he learned that the bureau had already gained access to the letters he sent Kravchik between 1938 and 1944. "Some of these letters were of a personal nature," the FBI reported in its summary file on Goodman, "and others dealt with UAW-CIO matters and unrest in America." Some of this commentary must have excited the bureau's interest, especially Goodman's blunt assertion in a letter of July 1938: "We are heading for the upheaval—even in America." This was not the bullish claim of a confident revolutionary, however. Writing at a time when the Left was facing defeat in Spain and the UAW was retreating in the face of Ford's violent countermeasures, Goodman had clearly viewed the coming cataclysm with a sense of dread. "Surely we cannot avoid it and if we can't, we must prepare ourselves. We must not be caught in the trap of our own contentment, humanity and deep desire for peace—as in Spain." It's not clear how the FBI interpreted Goodman's readiness to counter this challenge from the Right, or how the bureau planned to exploit his expressions of affection for Laicha. For the time being, the bureau's agents filed these letters away. They may have been intercepting Kravchik's mail all along, or they may have searched her apartment. In addition to these surreptitious (and probably illegal) methods, another key source had been "Confidential Informant T-1," a friend who reported to the FBI on the letters Kravchik had shown her.[24]

Besides her affection for Ernie, Laicha had something else in common with Freda: both were foreign-born citizens at a time when this alone made one suspect. For Laicha, this danger was heightened by her lifelong association with the Left in general and the Communist Party in particular. For Freda, on the other hand, there was no credible way that immigration authorities could accuse her of Communist sympathies at the time she came to the United States. The government's goal was harassment, however, not credibility, and Freda's travel to London on buying trips for her antique business made her vulnerable. The Eisenhower administration was not above exploiting this to ratchet up the pressure on Freda's high-profile husband. On 18 June 1953, the U.S. Department of State informed her that her application for a new passport was denied because of her "consistent and prolonged adherence to the Communist Party line" and because she was "closely associated with known Communists" and subversive organizations like the Civil Rights Congress.[25]

The harassing nature of the government's action was evident in the fact that her husband was publicly defending Communists and other radicals before HUAC and the courts, yet he did not lose his passport—only the far less political Freda. If this was meant to create added tension in the Goodman household, it probably succeeded. In appealing the government's groundless lifting of her passport, Freda wanted none of the publicity that Ernie would otherwise have favored in so political a proceeding. "Freda does not want to raise a public controversy because of the effect on her business," Ernie wrote to fellow Guild member Leonard Boudin, who handled the legal dimensions of Freda's appeal. "I hope you won't feel offended by this approach." Ernie respected his wife's wishes, but he must have winced at the affidavit Freda submitted in support of her case. She not only had never been a Communist, she wrote in her notarized statement, but she had "only occasionally taken what might be considered a position on political issues," and these were "almost entirely confined to matters of civil rights." She was no longer a member of the Civil Rights Congress and her past involvement had been "largely confined to helping on social affairs by way of the preparation and serving of food." Her closest associates, she insisted, were either apolitical or were supporters of the Democratic or Republican parties.[26]

Freda's submission was a truthful and somewhat pained inventory of the differences between herself and Ernie. She was an interior decorator and seller of antique English silver to the rich; he was a labor and left-wing attorney publicly identified with the "Reds" he defended. It must have been difficult for the FBI to untangle these very different realms when they converged at the house on Warrington Drive. Freda sold her antiques from the home; Ernie invited clients and political allies to social gatherings, including an "open house" for Steve Nelson, a national leader of the CP-USA who had recently been convicted under the Smith Act. The FBI stakeout of the home noted these comings and goings, recording the license plates of the guests. "My husband's position as an attorney for labor unions . . . and his legal representation of communists," as Freda put it in her sworn statement, made it "impossible" for her not to know something about the "issues regarding communism." But, she continued, "I trust that this is not the test for denying me a passport."[27]

It was a pointed statement, but it was not a rousing endorsement of her husband's work. Freda may well have exaggerated the distance between Ernie's political associations and her own with an eye to strengthening her appeal, but there had been an undeniable distance between the two from the moment Ernie made his abrupt shift to the left in 1935. He had failed, by his own admission, to bring Freda along. She had since embraced his causes and his work up to a point, but her antique business represented an alternative life outside of politics. The denial of her passport now threatened that economic and social independence, making her another casualty of the national obsession with foreign-born intruders. "She was self-conscious about her accent," Esther Shapiro recalled, "and she began to withdraw from the public events where Ernie was involved." Ernie and Freda would continue to have many friends in common, but they would also cultivate their separate circles of acquaintances and intimates.[28]

It would take more than two years before the State Department would reverse itself and grant Freda a passport. Ernie wrote former senator Burton K. Wheeler, the Montana Democrat who had personally lobbied the State Department on Freda's behalf, to thank him and convey his wife's happiness with the outcome. "Freedom—any degree of it—is certainly exhilarating," he noted on her behalf. Responding to a preceding letter in which Wheeler had described his own experience with red-baiting during the 1920s, Goodman agreed that those not-so-long-ago events seemed "as fresh to me as yesterday's loyalty hearings." It was, he added, an unending cycle. "There is certainly a continuity between the past and present and, I believe, the future in this reoccurring job of remaining free."[29]

8

Conspiracy of Belief

Goodman had been the subject of media attention during the HUAC hearings of 1952, but this would intensify dramatically as he moved from one trial to the next over the following eight years. As defense counsel for local Communists threatened with deportation or charged with contempt of Congress or indicted under the Smith Act, he would try four major cases that made their way toward the U.S. Supreme Court. The media would follow him every step of the way, attentive to the smallest detail.

Even the contents of his briefcase would draw their attention. During the trial of local Communists under the Smith Act, the *Detroit Free Press* reported that federal court aides "have daily seen Ernest Goodman, attorney for the six accused Michigan Communists, come into court toting a briefcase with a mysterious bulge in it." Even after Goodman unloaded his trial documents, the ominous bulge remained. "There was Ernest Goodman," the *Detroit News* reported on the trial's second day, "a man known by every judge in Detroit for his knowledge of the law and feared by some for the ease with which he can use that knowledge to force the bench into legal error." Two weeks later, a *News* headline would announce, "Goodman's Glasses Play Major Role in Courtroom Drama He Enacts for Reds." The story focused on Goodman's cross-examination of John Lautner, an FBI informer:

> Waving his glasses in the general direction of the witness, Goodman asks a question. He chews on one bow meditatively as Lautner answers.
>
> This procedure is repeated until Goodman asks the question with which he expects to knock the witness for a legal loop.
>
> At this point Goodman takes firm grip on his glasses with both hands and holds them out in front of him. Then he explodes the question. If the witness can't understand, Goodman whirls his glasses around in the air for emphasis during the explanation.

As he was speaking, at least one of the jurors (eleven of whom, it was noted, wore glasses) was seen unconsciously miming Goodman's gestures with his own spectacles.[1]

So it would go through the months and years of courtroom struggle that followed, Goodman often holding center stage. "The trial was adjourned until Tuesday," the *News* would report in mid-November during the Smith Act trial, "Goodman saying he had made commitments to go deer hunting." Surprisingly, much of the attention would be good-humored. Even the mysterious "Case of the Bulge in the Briefcase" had an innocent ending, as the *Free Press* reported in the winter of 1954. "Goodman likes to ice skate. He hurries out of court at the noon hour, sprints to the ice rink at the Veterans Memorial Building, removes the 'bulge' and swings into action." The "bulge," the paper was happy to report, had been nothing more than a pair of ice skates. The paper's press photo showed Goodman, age forty-eight, hairline receding, V-neck sweater and tie under his suit coat, skating with his fists clenched against the cold.[2]

There would be no such good cheer, however, in media coverage of his clients, the "weasel communists," as the *Detroit Times* called them, who "bring the Red Plague to the United States." Police officials and federal prosecutors knew they had no more evidence of sabotage, sedition, or espionage against the CP-USA's Michigan leaders than they had against Goodman's fellow skaters at the Veterans Memorial rink. But for being *Communists,* and only for being Communists, they would be barred from running for office, fired from public employment, threatened with deportation, tailed day and night, arrested for their beliefs, jailed pending bail, fined thousands of dollars, and imprisoned for contempt of court. It was their conspiracy of belief, not action, that would bring this punishment upon them.[3]

Ultimately, their freedom would depend on whether the U.S. Supreme Court would uphold the Bill of Rights. Goodman believed there was a chance the high court would rally to a defense of the Constitution. The Court, after all, had upheld the rights of other controversial groups, including (in Goodman's own experience) the CIO's right to advocate union organization in the hostile environment of Texas. The Constitution had even protected sectarian groups that challenged mainstream religion. The Jehovah's Witnesses, an evangelical sect whose door to-door proselytizing offended Baptist and Catholic opinion across the country, would take forty-five cases to the Supreme Court between 1938 and 1955, winning thirty-six rulings that overturned restrictions on their right to canvass and sell literature.[4]

But as Goodman well knew, the Supreme Court's resolve in defending civil liberties often faltered when issues of national security came to the fore. The children of Jehovah's Witnesses could be forced to salute the flag because, as Justice Felix Frankfurter had ruled on the eve of World War II, "national unity is the basis of national security." (Frankfurter did not welcome the subsequent comparison with Hitler, who banned the Jehovah's Witnesses for much the same reason.) After Pearl Harbor, the Court had also sanctioned the forcible evacuation of Japanese Americans to concentration camps despite the lack of any evidence they had engaged in sabotage. Fear had likewise usurped the Bill of Rights in 1951 when the Supreme Court upheld the first Smith Act convictions.[5]

To overcome the high court's credulity concerning internal subversion, Goodman would have to counter not only the prosecution's conjuring of phantom conspiracies but also the dogmatism of his own clients, who placed a greater priority on making the courtroom a forum for their political ideas than they did on mounting a defense based on the Bill of Rights. To both he would insist, as he had a decade before in his radio address for the Civil Rights Federation, that "the Bill of Rights is the very cornerstone of our form of government. . . . Those who ask us to sacrifice these civil liberties in the name of national defense are therefore asking that we give up the very thing which makes our form of government a democracy, and worth defending."[6]

Horns of a Dilemma

Long before the local trial of Michigan's Smith Act defendants, the state's political leaders knew they confronted a troubling dilemma. On the one hand, a rising chorus of public opinion and media criticism called for prosecution of Communist leaders. HUAC's Detroit hearings had dramatically escalated the level of fearmongering in state politics, and the *Detroit News* kept the pot boiling with "exposes" of the "communist insurrectional techniques" that could be used to takeover the city. Citing a former "Soviet insurrection expert," this daily diet of make-believe scenarios (a rehash of the 1948 series) included the dynamiting of highway bridges and the planting of trained "confusionists" to stampede crowds during the insurrection's "C&B stage" ("confusion and bewilderment"). The *News* spared no dramatic device in conjuring this imaginary takeover, including the possible seizure of radio stations and the broadcast of surrender from the captured mayor—a revolver "within a few inches of his head."[7]

There wasn't a shred of evidence, however, that Communists in Michigan were even talking about such scenarios, much less acting on them. State police commissioner Donald Leonard, goaded by newspaper editorials calling for prosecution of local Communists, reluctantly acknowledged as much in the weeks following the HUAC hearings:

> So far, we have never been able to prove that any person, even an admitted Communist, taught or advocated overthrow of the government by that means [force and violence]. . . . We have no proof that they committed subversion. Even our undercover agents who attended Communist meetings could get no such proof. When the Communists talked about what they wanted to do, they spoke of "reforms" to be sought without violence. Any citizen can talk about changing the system by peaceable means.[8]

Federal prosecutors could sidestep this problem by invoking the Smith Act, which required only quotation from ancient texts like the 1848 *Communist Manifesto* to infer that Communists *must* be plotting future insurrections. In the spring of 1952, Michigan's lawmakers devised their own solution to the lack of evidence. Shortly before federal officials got around to issuing their Smith Act indictments against six Detroit Communists, the state legislature enacted the Michigan Communist Control Act with only one dissenting vote. Signed into law barely a month after the conclusion of HUAC's Detroit hearings, the so-called Trucks Act (named for its Republican sponsor, Kenneth Trucks) was even more draconian than the federal McCarran Act upon which it was loosely modeled. The bill defined "Communist" to mean not only dues-paying members of the CP-USA but also nonmembers whose words or deeds were "calculated to further the overthrow of the government." All persons so defined by the state attorney general were obligated to report to the nearest state police post every year, register as a member of a "world communist movement" controlled by the Soviet Union, and submit to fingerprinting and interrogation concerning the "names of persons known by the registrant to be communists or members of any communist front organization." Failure to comply was a felony punishable by imprisonment for up to ten years and a fine of $10,000. For good measure, the Trucks Act also banned all Communists and their sympathizers from state employment or running for office.[9]

Michigan had now decreed—by law rather than evidence—that all Communists were *automatically* guilty of advocating "force and violence" and would be jailed if they failed to register every year. State police commissioner Leonard welcomed this tidy solution to his dilemma. "In future trials or arrests," he told the *Detroit Free Press* on the day the Trucks Act was signed, "if a proven Communist is picked up he can be tried under the new Michigan law instead of requiring the state to *prove* that he is a subversive" (emphasis added). Anticipating that members of the CP-USA would refuse to register, Leonard announced that his officers were preparing to apprehend five hundred "known Communists" in the initial round of arrests.[10]

It was now the members of the CP-USA who were, in Goodman's words, "on the horns of a dilemma." If they refused to register under the terms of a law that defined them as already guilty of advocating "force and violence," they would go to jail; but if they *did* register to avoid prosecution under the Trucks Act, they would invite prosecution under the Smith Act, which made advocacy of force and violence illegal. They would go to jail no matter what they did. The law, as Goodman would argue in court, violated the Constitution on numerous grounds, including Article I (prohibiting "Bills of Attainder" that impose punishments without trial), the First Amendment (protecting freedom of speech and association), the Fifth Amendment (prohibiting forced testimony against oneself), and the Fourteenth Amendment (protecting the right to due process).

Goodman would become the lead attorney in the court challenge to the Trucks Act, but he became so by default rather than choice. Already swamped with litigation that followed on the heels of the HUAC hearings, and anticipating the long-awaited Smith Act indictments against local Communist leaders, he had initially urged the CP-USA to ask Detroit's leading law firms to take the case on a fair-fee basis. "There's no reason they shouldn't," Goodman recalled arguing at the time: the First Amendment issues were obvious and these mainstream firms wouldn't be "tarred with the Communist brush because of their own status in the community." Nevertheless, every downtown firm refused to take the case. "They gave different excuses, but in the end, it was the same." The only lawyer who would join him in bringing suit for an injunction blocking the Trucks Act was Joe Brown, one of Michigan's first African American state senators, and now (since leaving office in 1949) a practicing attorney. He would stay with the case all the way to the U.S. Supreme Court despite the smear campaign launched by Donald Leonard, now a candidate for governor in the Republican primary. Leonard announced on television that because Brown received favorable coverage in the *Daily Worker,* he must have ties to the Communist Party. While many of Brown's former colleagues in Lansing (including several Republicans) publicly refuted Leonard's charges, it was precisely this kind of negative publicity that drove most lawyers away from the case.[11]

From the start, Goodman and Brown resolved to bring suit against the Trucks Act in federal rather than state court. Neither court offered much hope at the district or state circuit level, but the prospects for appeal were better in the federal system, where Supreme Court judges were further removed from (though hardly immune to) the local politics that produced bad law. There was a risk, however, that the U.S. Supreme Court might refuse to accept a case that had not first been tested in the state courts; unless the law in question was especially outrageous, most high court justices were reluctant to take cases on appeal that might first be overturned at the local level. Goodman and Brown regarded the Trucks Act as sufficiently outrageous to warrant such federal intervention, but another consideration may have been the prospect that the state courts were not only more likely to uphold the Trucks Act, they were also more likely to permit its immediate implementation during the appeal process.[12]

In this respect, Goodman was dealing with a very different set of circumstances from those that had prevailed ten years before in the Goose Creek case. There, implementation of the Texas law imposed only a minor inconvenience on the sole plaintiff, R. J. Thomas, while Goodman appealed the case through the Texas courts first, and then to the U.S. Supreme Court. In Michigan, however, even the briefest implementation of the Trucks Act would have a devastating effect on hundreds of people who would lose, as Goodman put it years later, "their jobs, their families, their liberty." The political context had also changed dramatically. In the 1930s and early 1940s, the labor movement had mobilized its members for civil disobedience to challenge bad law, whether it was restrictive handbill ordinances in Dearborn or restrictive licensing laws in Texas; in 1952, with the political focus now shifted to national security, there was no such popular support for mass actions that confronted bad law at the local level. In this setting, the federal courts appeared to offer the best hope for blocking the Trucks Act.[13]

The strategy seemed vindicated when the U.S. District Court, within days of the law's passage, granted a temporary injunction against its implementation. The case immediately went to a three-judge panel made up of Chief Judge Charles Simons of the U.S. Court of Appeals in Cincinnati, and two district court judges, Theodore Levin and Frank Picard. Three months later, their 2-1 ruling upholding the Trucks Act was a disappointment for Goodman and Brown, but it came with a strong dissent by Judge Levin that would strengthen the anticipated appeal to the Supreme Court. Levin agreed with Goodman's argument that the law placed individuals on the "horns of a dilemma," obligating those forced to register as "subversives" to, thereby, provide testimony against themselves. "The Trucks Act," said Levin, "delegates to State . . . authorities power [to] arbitrarily . . . label individuals and organizations as Communists"; once labeled, "such possibly innocent individuals" could contest the state's actions only by refusing to register, thus inviting "the shame and ignominy of a criminal trial if they would defend themselves."[14]

While this condemned the law in Levin's eyes, Simons and Picard focused on the claims of national security. "We might frankly concede," Judge Simons wrote, "that in another climate of world conditions, some of the contentions of invalidity might wear a different aspect." But when the United States was threatened by a totalitarian movement "seeking world expansion," as Simons put it, "the experience of East European peoples may not be ignored." Judge Picard was equally adamant. Communists, he declared, "seek the shield of our constitution long enough so that they may prepare and equip themselves to destroy the very constitution and government that gives them that protection." Implementation of the Trucks Act was, he concluded, "a matter of survival." Even so, he and Simons were willing to join with Levin in continuing the injunction against the law's implementation until the U.S. Supreme Court reviewed the case.[15]

Liberal opinion on the matter was as divided as that of the court. Governor Williams, for one, had signed the law despite its obvious flaws. "While the Trucks bill is not as I would have written it," Williams explained in his weak apology for endorsing the Red Scare, "it is not an unreasonable answer to the dangers of communism." Williams was well aware that the near-unanimous majority that voted for the Trucks Act would easily override his veto. Rather than expend his political capital on a futile defense of civil rights, he chose the easy way out. "I will not only sign the bill, but I will ask the legislature to . . . allow employment of more State Police officers to increase the anti-subversive squad." Goodman recalled his chagrin at Williams's craven behavior. "It took me some time to understand the liberals," he later said of Williams's action. "I considered myself a liberal."[16]

He was heartened nevertheless by the opposition that others voiced to the Trucks Act. In the fall of 1952, the American Civil Liberties Union announced that it would join the appeal of the case to the U.S. Supreme Court, filing an amicus brief in support of Goodman's contention that "the rights of all citizens are tied up in the same bundle with the rights of the Communists." The truth of this claim had already been demonstrated by state attorney general Frank Millard, who announced on the very day the governor signed the Trucks Act that he intended to remove not only the Communist Party from the ballot but also the Socialist Workers Party (SWP). As a left-wing rival to the CP-USA and a bitter enemy of Stalinism, the SWP hardly qualified as an organization that was "directed, dominated, or controlled" by the Soviet Union, as the Trucks Act specified. Millard's broad interpretation of the law highlighted the potential for targeting any dissident group that government leaders (current or future) chose to define as a "communist front." Many in the labor movement could recall the not-so-distant past when employers and conservatives had so labeled the CIO, and it was this potential for abuse that alarmed many liberals and socialists. "The real danger of the Trucks law," as the Association of Catholic Trade Unionists editorialized in its newspaper, the *Wage Earner*, "is that it is so vague, so all encompassing, so patently open to abuse that it could, if strictly enforced, permit half of the population of the state to put the other half in jail."[17]

Goodman had little time to appreciate this slow but growing resistance to the Trucks Act. Even with the gradual mustering of liberal opposition, he knew the Red Scare was still outrunning its opponents. The pace had already accelerated in September of 1952 when FBI agents, as expected, arrested the top six leaders of the Michigan Communist Party under Smith Act indictments that charged them with "conspiring to advocate" the violent overthrow of the government. The arrests in Detroit were part of the government's nationwide campaign to complete the "decapitation" of the CP-USA by bringing Smith Act indictments against 126 local leaders in more than a dozen states between 1951 and 1956. Detroit's Communist leaders had known they were marked men and women, but they had no idea when the ax would fall. They learned on 17 September when, as the *Detroit Times* reported, "the FBI men nabbed the Communists at bus stops and street corners near their homes." The accused leaders immediately called Goodman from jail and asked him to represent them. He agreed.[18]

At the same time, the persecution of foreign-born leftists was bringing dozens of clients to the Cadillac Tower's thirty-second floor, many of them threatened with revocation of their citizenship and deportation to their birth lands. Goodman and Crockett were already staggering under this growing caseload when the district court served notice on former state senator Stanley Nowak of the government's intention to revoke his citizenship. Nowak was a longtime colleague of Goodman, going back to the days of UAW organizing at Ford and the campaign to overturn Dearborn's antileafleting law. Naturally, Nowak sought legal representation from his old friend Ernie Goodman. Naturally, Goodman agreed.

His workload of major cases had now tripled. With both the Nowak and the Michigan Smith Act cases starting their long trek toward the U.S. Supreme Court, Goodman was buried in a sudden blizzard of legal paper—bail proceedings, preliminary hearings, pretrial motions—all in the very weeks he was preparing to argue the Trucks Act appeal. There was hardly time at all for the lesser cases coming his way from the Civil Rights Congress and a steadily growing docket of personal injury suits. In what amounted to a continuous round of overlapping cases, one on top of the other, Goodman rushed from deadline to deadline, his concentration on any single case broken, as he recalled years later, into fragments of "two hours one day, a half-hour another day, six hours next week."[19]

Nevertheless, on 2 February 1953, when he walked down the Great Hall of the U.S. Supreme Court building in the nation's capital, he felt fully prepared to argue the case against the Trucks Act. At least four of the nine justices had agreed to hear the appeal, an indication that they, too, saw the importance of reviewing a law that violated the Bill of Rights on so many counts. Goodman stepped to the podium with his notes and written brief in hand, the justices seated before him at the high bench in their black robes. Behind them were the massive Ionic columns and red velvet curtain that gave the high-ceilinged room the feel of a Greek temple. He began his oral argument with some confidence. Then, suddenly, it all fell apart.

> I didn't get very far in my argument before Judge Frankfurter . . . began to ask me "why does this case come here? Why didn't you bring it up in the state court? . . . They should interpret their own law before you ask us to decide whether it's constitutional." On the left, Justice Douglas was arguing through me, just asking questions of me, but really arguing with Frankfurter—I'm just a sounding board I felt after a while. His argument was, "this court has a primary duty to make sure that an unconstitutional law, particularly one involving the First Amendment, is not put into operation." And this argument went on, it drove me nuts, I couldn't hardly ever get to the basic argument I was prepared to make.[20]

Justice Frankfurter pressed on with his questioning of why the case had not gone to state court before coming before the U.S. Supreme Court. In response, Goodman reminded the justices that in some cases the court had ruled on a law's constitutionality without a prior decision at the state level, and on other occasions it had sent the case back to the state courts. His impromptu response did little, however, to clarify these conflicting precedents. As he bluntly acknowledged years later, "I was not prepared." It was an exasperating and humiliating moment. "Finally I said . . . 'Judge Frankfurter, I cannot answer your question. . . . All I can do is tell you why I think it should come here and why it is here. And you granted the appeal, now that you have it here, I'm prepared to argue its merits.'" But even as he proceeded with his prepared remarks, he knew he had failed to parry Frankfurter's challenge. "They allowed me then to finish it and I went to bed for three days with the flu. That was a disastrous experience."[21]

It was not a total loss. While the justices voted to send the case back to the Michigan courts (Douglas and Black dissenting), the comments and questions of even those who voted in the majority gave a clear indication that they held the Trucks Act in low regard and expected Michigan's solicitor general to postpone enforcement of the law until the case came before the state supreme court. Within weeks, an amended version of the Trucks Act was making its way through the Michigan legislature with new provisions that narrowed the definition of "Communist," provided a hearing for groups contesting their status under the law, and allowed individuals to refuse questioning. Governor Williams signed the amended Trucks Act saying the changes would "furnish added safeguards against abuse." Goodman was less sanguine. "The fundamental constitutional objections have not been met," he told the *Federated Press*, including the fact that the act still barred otherwise legal parties from the ballot and treated their members like criminals. Even so, he acknowledged that the amendments had at least eliminated "some of the cruder language in the original version."[22]

Above all, with the revised statute held in abeyance as the case slowly wound its way through the state courts, Goodman could turn his attention for the time being to the avalanche of new work that awaited him.

Conjured Evidence

William G. Hundley had the same problem that had troubled Donald Leonard when he was commander of the state police. As the prosecuting attorney for the U.S. Department of Justice, Hundley had to prove that the leaders of Michigan's Communist Party were guilty of violating the Smith Act—that they were, in fact, "conspiring to advocate" the forceful overthrow of the government. The problem he faced was simple and vexing: he could find no evidence to support the charge.

Hundley had fully expected to find that the six people arrested in September of 1952 represented a clear and present danger to the country. He was only a year out of Fordham Law School, devoutly Catholic, a lean and tight lipped young man with little reason to question the prevailing prejudice about Communists and their deviant beliefs. But as Hundley went through the FBI files, he found a glaring mismatch between the stereotypical image of "traitor-dupes" conjured by Senator Joseph McCarthy and the actual people he now had to prosecute. There was no doubting that Saul Wellman, chairman of the Michigan party and clearly the lead

defendant among the six, was a tough customer: a veteran of the Abraham
Lincoln Brigade in the Spanish civil war and a decorated member of the
101st Airborne in World War II, Wellman at age forty still projected the
same hard-guy swagger he had cultivated as a Brooklyn teenager, modeled
after screen actor James Cagney. ("He was the only Communist," novelist
Clancy Sigal later wrote of a character based on Wellman, "of whom I was
always, in his presence, afraid.") But Hundley, to his surprise, recognized
a common bond with Wellman. "I knew he was in the Airborne Infantry,"
Hundley recalled years later, "and he had been wounded in the Battle of
the Bulge. I was in the Battle of the Bulge in the 87th Infantry. You know,
I remember what it was like, and I guess even then I felt that anybody who
had done that couldn't be all bad."[23]

Hundley would have also found it hard to think ill of Thomas Dennis,
the thirty-five-year-old organizational secretary of the Michigan Communist Party and the highest-ranking African American on its state committee. A Ford worker and Local 600 member before Pearl Harbor, Dennis
had also joined the U.S. Army during World War II, serving ten months
in the Pacific. He had gone to work at the Kaiser-Fraser plant in Ypsilanti
on his return home, rising rapidly through the party's leadership ranks
while also serving as president of the NAACP's Ypsilanti Youth Council
and senior vice commander of Ypsilanti's American Legion Post. Was
he less patriotic than Hundley? For that matter, what was lacking in the
patriotism of Scottish-born Billy Allan, the Detroit bureau chief for the
Daily Worker? After becoming a U.S. citizen, Allan had joined the
army in 1942 and won five battle stars before his honorable discharge in
1945.[24]

The remaining three defendants had not served in the military, but
Hundley would find it difficult to portray them as unpatriotic subversives.
Phil Schatz was declared 4-F during the war for poor eyesight; Helen
Winter was exempt as a woman and a mother; and Nat Ganley was a
thirty-eight-year-old father at the start of the war and a "necessary man"
during it, serving as the elected business agent for skilled UAW toolmakers in Detroit's war plants. All three were born to immigrant parents—
Schatz and Ganley (like Wellman) to east European Jews in New York
City, Winter to a German-born father in Seattle. Schatz had gone to the
City College of New York on a Boys' Club scholarship and later worked as
a teacher in one of the New Deal's job programs. Winter had organized
office workers in Cleveland and had run for election to the Library Board
in Minneapolis (drawing thirty-five thousand votes). Ganley had worked as
a punch-press operator under an assumed name to avoid the employers'
blacklist of union organizers.[25]

All six defendants were avowed Communists who served on the party's payroll as full- or part-time functionaries. This alone was enough to put Hundley at odds with Wellman and his comrades, but he well knew that however objectionable he found the defendants' Communist politics and their support of the Soviet Union, none of this was illegal. To make a stronger case, he had to find evidence that they were secretly conspiring to advocate the violent overthrow of the government and that they had reorganized the CP-USA in 1945 to achieve that purpose. Given the hundreds of informants, infiltrators, detectives, and police investigators probing every detail of Communist activity, there should have been some credible evidence to that effect. The CP-USA was, in fact, riddled with government spies. "I began to find out that in each cell of three [Communists], there would be two FBI informants," Hundley observed years later with only a touch of exaggeration. Their written reports detailed the party's internal debates concerning civil rights, union politics, the poor, the unemployed, and the appropriate tactics—all legal and nonviolent—for addressing these issues. Nowhere did the government agents find seditious conspiracy or advocacy of force and violence.[26]

Only once did Hundley think he had found the smoking gun. An informant's report described a routine meeting in which one of the participants suddenly stood up and called on his comrades to "cut out all of this nonsense, when are we going to start a revolution?" "So I'm a young lawyer," Hundley later recalled. "I get all excited, that's the kind of evidence I want to use at the trial and what not, so I go to the FBI and I said 'I want that.' And they all huddled and they came back and they say, 'Listen Bill, you can't have that, because that guy that jumped up at the meeting was one of our informants.'" In the end, Hundley could find no credible witness to support the charges. "I realized," he recalled, "that they were about as much as a clear and present danger as my late grandmother." He would prosecute the case nevertheless because his boss, J. Edgar Hoover, had "invented the threat, and he was determined to keep it alive."[27]

Hundley would have to rely on circumstantial evidence, much of it taken from the public library: Marx and Engel's *The Communist Manifesto*, Lenin's *State and Revolution*, and other Marxist-Leninist classics that did, indeed, espouse violent revolution against Europe's old order. Juries animated by the genuine fear of thermonuclear war and the hysterical fear of Communist subversion would pay scant attention to the fact that Marx was writing in the previous century and Lenin was preaching against despotic regimes on the far side of the world. In the United States it was perfectly legal to read these books; in the hands of Communist teachers, however, they somehow became blueprints for revolution.

It would help Hundley immensely that Frank A. Picard, the white-haired district court judge who would preside in the Michigan Smith Act trial, was already convinced that the six defendants were guilty. His previous ruling to uphold the Trucks Act was based on the straightforward assumption that membership in the Communist Party, *and that alone,* was reason enough to treat Communists as subversives. "Admittedly," he would later write, "rarely has it been established by worthwhile proof that any Communist will openly come right out and teach and advocate overthrow of this government by force and violence." Picard believed there was a simple reason for this lack of evidence: "No man stands on the corner and shouts that he intends to commit a crime." Picard was not troubled by the fact that the government, for all of its spies and informants, could find no *secret* cabal or meeting—much less a street corner—where such ideas were advocated. The only proof he needed against American Communists was that "anything the United States does . . . and Russia opposes, they are against it." This, in fact, was usually true, and there were ample grounds for criticizing the CP-USA's defense of all things Soviet, including its unconvincing claim that any report of Stalinist tyranny was to be dismissed as capitalist propaganda. Picard, however, went well beyond criticism. "I am of the opinion," he wrote, "that we can pass a law that once having shown the defendant to be a member of the Communist Party by proof or admission, the burden should be upon him to prove that he is not a believer in the Marxist-Leninist brand of communism or ever taught or advocated it." Communists, in short, should be held guilty until they proved themselves innocent.[28]

Goodman would come to know more than he cared to about Picard's prejudicial brand of justice. He had already sampled it during the Trucks Act case, and he would now confront it in two back-to-back trials, the Smith Act case followed by the Stanley Nowak trial. In each, Picard would find a stage for his lifelong aspirations as a politician and entertainer. As a teenager, he had dreamed of joining his older brothers in their high-wire circus act as the Flying Picards, but his father (a Saginaw hotelkeeper) had steered him instead to the University of Michigan, where young Frank received his law degree in 1912. After seeing combat in the U.S. Army during World War I, he returned to his private law practice and (ever the entertainer) later became known for his monologue "The Trial of Christ from a Legal Standpoint" ("the very highest type of entertainment," according to the *Cass City Chronicle* in 1931). In 1932 he had joined the New Deal bandwagon and reaped the spoils of FDR's victory with appointments to the State Liquor Commission and the Michigan Unemployment Compensation Fund. In 1934 he narrowly lost the election for U.S. Senate to incumbent Arthur Vandenburg, and five years later President Roosevelt rewarded him for his efforts with an appointment to the federal bench.[29]

Goodman had known something of Picard during the Second World War when the judge agreed to cosponsor, of all things, the Detroit Council of American-Soviet Friendship. This was almost certainly a matter of political expediency at a time when the Soviets were still highly regarded as wartime allies and when the Detroit Council's sponsors included union leaders from both the CIO and AFL. During the cold war, however, past affiliations such as this had potentially dangerous implications, and Picard, in particular, might have had reason to worry about his collaboration with an organization whose list of sponsors included Stanley Nowak and Nat Ganley—the very people he would now try as subversives. Their lawyer, Ernie Goodman, had also been a sponsor, but the judge could at least count on Goodman to forgo the endemic red-baiting that so poisoned American politics during the cold war.[30]

The Red Scare would, of course, make it all the more difficult for Goodman to win acquittal for his clients. "The minds of the jurors," as he wrote in an early memo to the defendants, will "have been so conditioned . . . as to make it impossible, within the confines of a courtroom trial, to overcome their prejudices" against Communists, particularly when the media had already sensationalized the case by reporting that the defendants were charged with nothing less than "conspiring to overthrow the government." Goodman had to remind the WJBK-TV news manager (among others) that the actual charge was conspiracy to *advocate* the overthrow of the government. "The difference is of the greatest importance," he explained. "No one questions the authority of the government to act where there is a conspiracy to overthrow the government." Advocacy, on the other hand, was an entirely different matter, raising issues of First Amendment rights that were still to be decided in the upcoming trial. Goodman expected the media to sensationalize the case, but even Judge Picard, in pretrial correspondence, was misstating the charge as "conspiracy to overthrow the government." Goodman had to write the judge to correct him on this fundamental point of law and remind him that "if the government were to introduce evidence of a conspiracy to overthrow, no issue of free speech would be involved." Picard wrote back to acknowledge his "inadvertent" mistake, but Goodman must have known that the judge's public statement, two weeks later, that "espousal of communism is not the reason [the defendants] are in court" was insincere.[31]

Nevertheless, Goodman believed there was a small chance of acquittal given the altered circumstances of 1953 compared to 1951, when the

Supreme Court had upheld the first Smith Act convictions. For one thing, the Korean War had ended in a truce during the long pretrial proceedings, and with this de-escalation of the "clear and present danger," Goodman had filed a motion to dismiss the case altogether. Predictably, Picard denied the motion with the petulant claim—widely reported in the press—that the truce "was no gesture of good will on the part of the other side. It was the hydrogen bomb, which we have more of than they do." Goodman nonetheless hoped that the jurors, if not the judge, might be less swayed by the government's charges if the daily press was no longer reporting U.S. combat casualties.[32]

Goodman was determined to present his defense of the "Michigan Six" in a way that would maximize the slender possibilities of acquittal at the district court level and improve the prospects of success on appeal. To do so meant rejecting the strategy that the Communist Party had imposed on the first Smith Act trial of 1949. Crockett, who played a key role in developing strategy and writing briefs for the Detroit trial, was intimately familiar with the disastrous consequences of the party's "political defense" in the Foley Square proceedings. In that trial, the Communist Party's national leaders, rather than focus their defense on the First Amendment, had instead "taken the offensive" by putting capitalism on trial in long-winded polemics from the witness stand. This approach had invited continual objections from the prosecution, with Judge Medina upholding virtually all of them. To evade these restrictions on testimony, party chairman Eugene Dennis had served as his own attorney, delivering orations on Communist virtue that succeeded only in further alienating the jury. In the meantime, as a matter of policy imposed by the Communist Party, the defense lawyers had declined to cross-examine any of the prosecution witnesses, most of them paid informants and spies. Courtroom outbursts by the defendants and boisterous picketing on the streets outside had also been used by the government to justify a massive police presence in the courthouse, sending a clear message to jurors about the dangerous nature of the defendants. Crockett, whose courtroom demeanor had been far more restrained than that of his fellow defense lawyers, later noted "the sheer impossibility of trying to fit a political trial into the framework of common-law procedure."[33]

Goodman and Crockett emphasized this point in their memos outlining defense strategy to the Michigan Six. An effective strategy had to mean "something more than making speeches from the witness box as though one were on a lecture platform," as one memo (apparently by Crockett) argued. A political defense was feasible only in continental Europe, where a long history of political trials had produced "certain rules and

procedures . . . which are not permissible in common-law courts." The
so-called free defense in European trials permitted the defense "to put in
evidence almost anything that it thinks is relevant—any speech, any writing, any opinion which the defendant believes will aid his cause." The
judge (not a jury) would then sort out which evidence was relevant and
render a decision. In contrast, the tradition of trial by jury inherited from
England did not recognize "political trials" and prescribed, instead, narrow rules of evidence based on time-honored precedent. In criminal cases,
these rules often protected the defendant by prohibiting certain kinds of
evidence (hearsay, for example) from going before a jury. But in a Smith
Act trial these rules more often worked to the advantage of the prosecution: even though the defendants were, in fact, being tried for their political beliefs, under common-law rules they would be tried for a specific
"crime" (like failing to register under the Trucks Act), and only evidence
related to that offense would be admissible in court. A political defense
was therefore likely to be ruled "out of order" by judges schooled in
common-law precedent.[34]

Goodman also argued against the tactic of self-representation used by
Eugene Dennis in the Foley Square trial. The supposed advantage of this
approach—that it allowed the defendant, as counsel, to make a "political
defense" in opening and closing statements to the jury—was, in Goodman's
words, "an illusion." It was a highly unusual practice in common-law trials and would serve to "create in the mind of the jurors the opinion that
the particular defendant . . . [has] something to hide and, for that reason,
prefers to make a speech rather than subject himself to cross-examination
under oath." In a biting repudiation of the CP-USA's strategy in the Foley
Square trial, the memo insisted that "our strategy must be based on legal
principles; the gimmicks and the unusual will not do. They only tend to
create in the minds of the jurors the idea that 'this is another Communist
stunt.' "[35]

Instead, Goodman recommended that he, representing all six defendants, make a "positive defense" that would include not only vigorous
cross-examination of prosecution witnesses but also a direct appeal to
the jury's faith in the Bill of Rights. Arguing the details of whether or not
Marxism-Leninism was inherently wedded to force and violence would
"almost automatically" produce a guilty verdict. The jury, however, might
be able to grasp an alternative proposition—that the framers of the Bill of
Rights had believed that if any "group of ideas were suppressed, or the
persons who held or advocated them persecuted," then it was this "suppression and persecution which, in the end, bred force and violence,
and not beliefs and advocacy." Goodman proposed to offer the jury three

historical examples: first, that the murderous suppression of antislavery opinion in the South had foreclosed the potential for peaceful change and made the Civil War inevitable; second, that the relatively more accommodating response to the advocacy of women's suffrage had permitted peaceful change; and third, that the suppression of union organization—not as deadly as the persecution of abolitionists, but far more brutal than the harassment of suffragettes—produced more violence than would have been the case if the First Amendment had been applied to the advocacy of labor rights.[36]

This thumbnail survey of U.S. history was not intended for historians, and certainly not for Marxist-Leninists, who would argue that class conflict and violence were the *inevitable* handmaidens of capitalist imperialism. Goodman's history lesson was intended solely for the jury. "The defendants must be acquitted," he would argue, "not because of the jurors' concern for communism or communists, but because of the jurors' belief in the Bill of Rights." This case had to be made by Goodman and Goodman alone. His firm could afford to put only a single attorney in the trial; Crockett was already busy with deportation cases, and adding his physical presence to Picard's courtroom would have had the wrong effect, reminding the court not only of the Foley Square shouting match, but of its outcome. The defendants, in turn, could make an effective case only from the witness stand, not from the counselor's table. It was the only strategy, Goodman and Crockett insisted, that had a chance of winning acquittal from the jury.[37]

Goodman, however, would not be able to test this claim in court. The sharp break with Communist practice that he and Crockett proposed might have had a slim chance with a Detroit jury in 1953, but it was too much of a departure from CP-USA orthodoxy for the defendants to swallow. The first indication of their discomfort came in the form of a "Memo on the Memos," probably authored by Wellman, that proposed amendments to Goodman's conception of American history: "Of course Counsel['s] views and our views on this subject are not the same. Hence even with my amendments, [the] Goodman theses still remain a bourgeois liberal rather than a Communist concept of American history." For the time being, the defendants otherwise agreed with most of the strategy outlined by Goodman and Crockett. They seemed to recognize that the Bill of Rights was their best hope for acquittal, and they understood the importance of the Communist Party's 1945 constitution, which repudiated violent revolution and called for a peaceful transition to socialism. The CP-USA, in fact, had argued from the mid-1930s that the likely source of "force and violence" would be a refusal by right-wing forces to permit the seating of a democratically elected left-wing majority, as had happened in Spain.[38]

Underlying these points of agreement, however, were fundamental questions about the current course of American politics and the advisability of the defendants representing themselves in front of the jury. It is not clear why the defendants waited until the last minute to bring these issues to the fore, but for whatever reason—party orders or cold feet—they suddenly demanded a meeting with Goodman just one week before the trial's scheduled beginning. As Goodman recalled it years later, the six defendants came to his office and announced that, contrary to their previous agreement, they were now convinced that the political situation had so deteriorated that a fair trial was impossible and only a "political defense" was warranted. Fascism, they insisted, had already come to America and they believed it was their job to expose that fact in the courtroom. "As I listened to it," Goodman remembered, "I couldn't believe what I was hearing."

> I said, "In the first place, I do not agree with that. I don't believe that fascism has come to America. . . . We're on the road there, we may well get there, I don't know. Sometimes I think we will, but I don't know, I don't give up. And one of the ways which I agreed to defend this case was to try to show in that court room that what's on trial in here is the First Amendment. Not fascism. . . . That was our strategy. Now you want me to reverse this strategy.

Feeling, no doubt, betrayed, Goodman flatly refused to accept their late-hour demand. Crockett seconded his decision. The defendants would have to find another lawyer if they insisted on this change in course. They agreed to talk it over and return the next day with their decision.[39]

There is no record of their discussion, but it likely followed the prevailing line within the Communist Party. For some time, party leaders had concluded that war between the United States and the Soviet Union was inevitable, that fascism was imminent, and that it was only "five minutes to midnight" before the CP-USA was declared illegal. In support of this apocalyptic vision, they had drawn selectively from the undeniable evidence of a rightward drift in U.S. society: the conviction of the party's national leaders at Foley Square; the rumors that the federal government had drawn up lists of those to be taken into "custodial detention" during a national emergency; the mob violence at places like Peekskill, New York, where police stood by as American Legionnaires attacked a Paul Robeson concert sponsored by the Civil Rights Congress. Party leaders had interpreted these events as harbingers of fascism, and they responded with a hypermilitancy that was at odds with reality. Like a millennial sect preparing for Judgment Day, the party had launched a disastrous campaign to purify its ranks by expelling proponents of psychoanalysis along with anyone who supported the "anti-Soviet" independence of Yugoslavian Communist leader Joseph Tito.[40]

The final act of self-destruction had followed the Supreme Court's upholding of the Foley Square convictions in 1951. Persuaded that Armageddon had arrived, four of the convicted CP-USA leaders had jumped bail and—joined by Wellman and others—gone into hiding in an "underground" organization modeled after the wartime resistance of the French and Italian Communists. In a catastrophic misreading of history, the CP-USA's leaders had failed to recognize that, unlike the wartime undergrounds, their party had little public support and was still nominally legal. By going underground, they had simply branded themselves as outliers.

Goodman could not have found them an easy group to defend, however much he believed in the Bill of Rights. The Detroit defendants made it all the harder when they returned to his office the next day and proposed a radical restructuring of strategy: three of the six (Schatz, Winter, and Allan) would continue to be his clients and proceed with the First Amendment defense previously agreed to; the other three (Wellman, Dennis, and Ganley) would represent themselves and conduct a political defense based on the political program of the Communist Party. "I think that's a foolhardy thing to do," Goodman remembered telling them. The mixed messages of the two approaches would confuse the jury, and the three defendants representing themselves would be helpless amateurs in front of Judge Picard. "You know where he stands," Goodman reminded them. "He's a pretty clever guy up there, and he'll know how to turn you and twist you around his finger. . . . You won't know how to defend yourself."[41]

Goodman nevertheless agreed to this compromise approach. After a year of preparation, he may have felt it was too late to withdraw. To an uncomprehending network of supporters, it might appear that he was cutting bait at the last minute and abandoning his clients. As a matter of personal pride, he no doubt wanted to make the case that he and Crockett had labored to prepare, and by proceeding with the trial in district court they could at least establish a record for appealing the now apparently inevitable conviction. As a matter of personal loyalty, he felt an obligation to clients like Billy Allan, a man he had known and respected through years of union organizing at Ford and elsewhere. Even a newcomer like

Wellman, a veteran of the Abraham Lincoln Brigade, evoked for Goodman one of the defining moments in his personal conversion to socialism. The Bill of Rights protected these nonviolent radicals (no matter how disoriented) just as much as it protected the Jehovah's Witnesses—who at this point might have seemed like more reasonable clients.

The court issued a withdrawal notice for Goodman as attorney to Wellman, Dennis, and Ganley on 19 October 1953, and issued notices of appearance to the three defendants the same day to serve as their own *pro se* counsel. The trial opened eight days later.[42]

"We have a cliche," Wellman acknowledged years later, "[that] 'a man who defends himself has a fool for a client.' I think it's true." He in particular made "a lot of stupid mistakes." Some occurred right away during jury selection. Goodman wanted jurors who could grasp the importance of civil rights issues and have enough self-confidence to hold out for acquittal, probably against a majority favoring conviction. The pool from which the two sides could accept or veto potential jurors included a Grosse Pointe woman with a university education who read widely and was interested in politics. Goodman favored putting her on the jury, arguing that the First Amendment was a difficult abstraction for many people to grasp, particularly when it had to compete with the prosecution's emotionally charged exhortation to fight the foreign foe. "I said, 'look, she's . . . an intellectually minded person, strong will[ed], and with . . . enough money and prestige so that she can afford to take some risks, without worrying too much about it—a chance, at least.'" There might be working-class jurors who would also consider acquittal, but the prosecutors could be counted on to use their preemptory vetoes to keep them off the jury. The "Grosse Pointe lady" might slip though this filter, and if she refused to convict and produced a "hung jury," the government would have to start all over again—or drop the charges. The defendants, however, wanted only working-class jurors. "I said, 'Don't you realize there's more prejudice among the working people on the issue of communism than in almost any other circle? You saw that when all these plants were kicking out people who were identified as Communists before the House committee.'" It didn't matter. Hewing to the CP-USA's proletarian line, the defendants vetoed the Grosse Pointe lady.[43]

The twelve who eventually took their seats in the jury box (two of them African American) could not have known of the ongoing conflict between Goodman and the defendants, but they could certainly hear the difference between Goodman's opening statement and that of Nat Ganley, speaking for the *pro se* attorneys. Goodman highlighted the tortured logic of the government's indictment against his clients. They were *not* charged, he reminded the jury, with attempting to overthrow, or conspiring to overthrow, or even advocating the overthrow of the government by force and violence. If any of those charges had been brought, Goodman stressed, "it would make it much easier to try this case, because then the prosecution would bring in witnesses [to testify] that on a certain day at a certain time the defendants, or one of them, [did] . . . something concrete, something you could put your finger on." Instead, the charge was "conspiracy to advocate," meaning the defendants had allegedly reorganized the CP-USA in 1945 for the secret purpose of conducting *future* advocacy of force and violence. The defendants were, indeed, Communists, Goodman emphasized. They had always publicly proclaimed so, and yes, they advocated Marxism-Leninism. "But . . . Marxism-Leninism is a political doctrine, a body of ideas, not something for which these defendants ought to be convicted." The jury need not agree with the ideology, only that the defendants had the right to teach it and to ask others to join with them. "They have that right as Americans," he concluded.[44]

Ganley followed with a rambling discourse on "what we Marxists believe," read from a script nearly twice as long as Goodman's. Predictably, the prosecution made frequent objections that Ganley was introducing unrelated political issues, and the judge, predictably, gave frequent instructions to the jury to ignore the defendant's remarks. Ganley, a thin man with large round eyeglasses that gave him an owlish look, tumbled into deeper waters when he blurted out that the FBI had illegally planted Dictaphones in private buildings. Hundley jumped to his feet and announced that if Ganley's statement were true, the indictments would be dismissed. "If you have that proof," Picard instructed Ganley, "we will let the jury go and you can bring it in now." Ganley, admitting he had no such proof, sheepishly withdrew his statement.[45]

The jury could not have been impressed with this introduction to "counselor" Ganley. There would be other moments in the days that followed when the *pro se* defendants stumbled unwittingly off the straight and narrow path of courtroom procedure. As Goodman had predicted, they would find themselves at the mercy of Judge Picard, who in one moment of exasperation told Dennis that "I can't keep allowing you to ask the court for advice." Chastened perhaps by these early encounters, the defendant-lawyers generally deferred to Goodman as the lead attorney. They addressed the judge with the customary "Your Honor" throughout the proceedings, and there were few of the angry outbursts that had characterized the Foley Square trial. Goodman had insisted that there be no picketing outside the courthouse, since this would inevitably attract a reinforced police presence and potentially alarm the members of the jury.

Judge Picard reciprocated with a generally respectful treatment of the defendants. As a result, the trial proceeded "in an atmosphere entirely different from that of similar previous trials in other cities," the *Detroit News* reported. "The courtroom was calm and quiet." In this regard, Frank Picard was an improvement over Harold Medina, the Foley Square judge.[46]

In matters of substance, however, Picard was transparently biased in favor of the government's contrived evidence. The prosecution witnesses, all of them paid informants for the FBI and other security organizations, were "rather unsavory," as prosecutor Hundley acknowledged years later. By now, many years into the Red Scare's continuing round of trials and legislative hearings, several of them had become veteran performers, appearing repeatedly as "expert witnesses" to testify on Communist affairs. John Lautner, a twenty-year functionary in the CP-USA, was one of the newer faces on the government roster and probably the most appealing to jurors. He had, in fact, been expelled from the party in 1950 on hearsay evidence (later proved false) that he was a government spy. The party's rough interrogation and hasty purging of Lautner gave this leadoff witness on party organization a plausibly human motivation for his testimony—revenge. It was not so clear what motivated the likes of William Nowell. An African American party member at the Rouge, he went to Moscow in 1929 to receive (he now claimed) training at the Lenin School in street fighting and weapons handling. Picard denied Goodman's objection that this testimony was not only unverifiable (the Lenin School having closed in 1937), but also had nothing to do with the six defendants. It was testimony patently designed to prejudice the jury against *all* Communists. Goodman had better luck in cross-examination, forcing Nowell to recount his bizarre wanderings after quitting the CP-USA in 1936—first to the side of white supremacist Gerald L. K. Smith, followed by a stint working for Ford as a labor spy, then to his current position as a paid witness for the federal government in deportation proceedings. Goodman also established that in return for a comfortable income of $5,400 a year, Nowell had repeated his testimony verbatim from trial to trial, claiming to remember small talk from twenty-five years before with word-for-word exactitude.[47]

Bereniece Baldwin's vita was closer to the norm for paid employment by the FBI. Never a Communist by belief, the "50-year-old gray-haired practical nurse," as the *Detroit News* described her, had joined the CP-USA at the government's urging. As she rose within the Michigan party's administrative structure, so had her stipend from the FBI. It was her membership tally of 1948, introduced into evidence, that reported 1,332

dues-paying Communists in Michigan, nearly 500 of them in the state's
auto and aircraft industries. Membership had since declined from these
modest totals, but the party continued to operate its Michigan School
of Social Science for the remaining stalwarts. Picard overruled Goodman's objections that Baldwin knew nothing of what the defendants had
actually taught in the school, and he likewise rejected Goodman's contention that her pilfering of desks in the party offices was an illegal
search and seizure, prohibited by the Fourth Amendment. Goodman had
more success, again, with cross-examination, revealing contradictions
in Baldwin's testimony and fault lines in her character. She confessed to
liking those she was spying on and thinking they were "nice people";
she had even helped make arrangements for a member's wedding ceremony at Wellman's home. The *Detroit Free Press* reported the subsequent
exchange:

"Did you kiss the bride?" Goodman asked.
"Yes," Mrs. Baldwin replied.

"And then did you turn her name in to the FBI?" Goodman continued.
"Yes I did," she said.

Laughter rippled across the courtroom. Mrs. Baldwin smiled slightly.[48]

Goodman would later stress to the jury that it was not normal human
behavior to continue liking people while you secretly reported their names
to the police, knowing they would henceforth be marked for firing and
legal harassment. "This informer system," he concluded, "is doing something to the ordinary decent human instincts of American people which is
wrong, which is very wrong." If they were motivated by patriotism, as
they claimed, then "patriotism pays off pretty well," as Goodman com-
puted it: a total of $170,000 paid to the eight informants who testified
during the trial. Goodman asked the jury to compare the defendants with
the informants. "Every single defendant . . . is married to the same person
they first married; never divorced; they live with their families, those who
have children live with their children, and they have done so through this
whole period of time. And contrast that with the record of the Government
witnesses who total eleven divorces and one present separation among
them."[49]

Goodman's charge that the informers were unreliable opportunists
willing to give whatever testimony suited their paymaster was confirmed
in his aggressive cross-examination of Milton Santwire and Steve Schemanske. The two operatives had joined the CP-USA at Ford's Rouge
plant, Santwire as a paid FBI informant who was also active in the union,

Schemanske as an investigator for the company as well as the FBI. The government introduced the two witnesses as unknown to each other, but Goodman's "devastating" cross-examination (as the *Detroit Times* called it) caught them in a lie: Santwire, it turned out, had been paid by Schemanske with company funds to spy on left-wing members of the union. To prevent disclosure of this potential violation of labor law (which prohibited employer espionage), the two men had lied to both the prosecutors and the jury about their relationship to Ford. "Am I hearing this right?" Judge Picard had asked in astonishment. "Is he saying he was paid by Schemanske all this time?" Picard was clearly "roiled," as the press reported, and said he would consider contempt charges against the two men. But in the end he did nothing, much to Hundley's relief. "In a normal case," as the federal attorney later observed, "that probably would have killed the prosecution. But not in 1953 when you were trying a bunch of admitted Communists."[50]

Picard held the defendants to a harsher standard. When Wellman and Schatz went to the witness stand and refused to name fellow party members, the judge immediately cited them for contempt and sent both men to jail. Thereafter, they appeared in court every morning in handcuffs; in the meantime, the government's paid informers were happy to lie on the stand, admit it under cross-examination—and then walk out of the courthouse as free men. Picard could not recognize the bias in this contrasting treatment, and the defendants, despite Goodman's best efforts, were also unmoved by the prosecution's perjured testimony. "Unfortunately," Goodman wrote a fellow attorney in New York, "I cannot prevail upon the defendants to take advantage of these disclosures and make this the primary issue in the case. They are more concerned with proving what they cannot prove, a conspiracy by the government to get this country into war and to establish fascism."[51]

So it went, through four months of wearying testimony, Goodman fighting a solitary battle against the judge, the prosecution, and, at times, the addled judgment of his own clients. During it all, he had to continue coaching the *pro se* defendants as best he could on the rules of evidence and orderly procedure that so often eluded them. Occasionally, the strain of it all was obvious to the sizable crowd of spectators and reporters that packed the courtroom every day. At one point Wellman snapped at Ganley in front of the court over the latter's failure to keep the defense files in order and provide Goodman with the documents he needed. Reporters could subsequently hear Goodman tell Picard that "I think your files are probably in better order than ours" as he asked the judge for a copy of a document. ("I know," the judge replied, "but I'd like to keep them that way.") It must have been galling to the usually meticulous Goodman that so much of the defense was beyond his control, making a difficult case all the more frustrating. As was often true in these years, he was having trouble sleeping. "I had to work in the courtroom all day, at night I had to work half the night in order to prepare for the next day's testimony. There was no surcease of this. And it was difficult, and I was getting ill, and I knew it." He was, in fact, coming down with his usual winter cold. It was finally Hundley who took sympathy on his adversary and asked the judge to call a recess. Picard did so and called the defense attorney into his office. Goodman remembered the next few moments as a hallucinatory blur. "I went into the office . . . and he said, 'Something wrong Ernie?' (He still called me Ernie.) I looked at him, and suddenly everything that was in me just swelled up, and I was looking down on myself and I saw tears just flowing like a stream down my cheeks. I felt humiliated, frustrated, angry, I felt all of this piling up on me. And I just turned and I ran out of the room, and I ran out of the courthouse, and I just drove home."[52]

A startled Picard recessed court until the next morning. He had always worried that the defendants would try to physically wear him down with delaying tactics, but he must have worried now that it was their defense attorney who was more likely to succumb to the strain of the trial. Goodman's doctor would have agreed. He prescribed bed rest, which was out of the question, and sleeping pills, which Goodman gladly took. Decades later, the recurrence of these symptoms would cause him to finally scale back his law practice, but for now he put the entire episode down to the combined effects of his cold and the mounting stress of the trial. "The next morning," Goodman recalled years later, with a laugh, "as I came through the [courtroom] door, the entire jury all applauded." It was now Goodman's turn to be startled. "I was thinking to myself, 'if I was on trial here they would probably acquit me.'"[53]

Unfortunately, they would do no such thing for his clients, despite Goodman's eloquent closing statement. In his summary to the jury, he recalled the unconvincing statements of the paid informants, the memorized and rehearsed testimony that rarely even mentioned the defendants, and the prosecution's extensive quoting from old books and distant lands. He reminded the jury of what he thought to be the trial's most dramatic point, the moment when the FBI informants from Ford had given perjured testimony. Ultimately, all the government could say was that the defendants had supported an underground organization and had espoused Marxism-Leninism; the defendants denied neither, insisting both were legal. Going underground in the context of the government's repressive measures was, Goodman offered, akin to the instinctual behavior of Michigan's deer, which also abandoned their usual haunts every fall when

Goodman and others stalked the woods. The dozens of Marxist-Leninist books introduced into evidence were subject to interpretation, "like the Bible," as Goodman had argued during the trial. His concluding words anticipated the First Amendment case that he and Crockett would make on appeal of the expected conviction. "The whole essence of our democracy . . . is lost without the right to express these ideas and freely sell and teach these books and documents without fear that your intent in doing so is going to result in your conviction as a criminal. Such a result would be so inconsistent with basic concepts of democracy that it seems to me that one cannot exist along with the other." He asked jurors to acquit the defendants "not to vindicate their innocence, but to uphold . . . a philosophy so deep-rooted in all of us that we would not want to see it taken away."[54]

There is no record of how the jurors debated these matters in the two half-days it took to reach a verdict. During their deliberations, however, Picard apparently came to the conclusion that Goodman's call to civic pride and constitutional duty might have made an impact on some of them. Finding Goodman in the otherwise empty courtroom during the wait for the jury to return, Picard could not contain himself. Years later, Goodman recalled the strange encounter.

> [H]e walks over [and] he looks up to me in my face and he says, "Ernie, you know, I think, I think they may acquit them. . . . You think that they might?" He was asking me, [after] trying the goddamn case, to give him some solace and comfort! . . . I put my arm around his shoulder, . . . and I said, "Judge, don't worry, they'll all be convicted." He looks up and he said, "Do you think so?" I said, "yes, they'll all be convicted." He said, "oh," and he turned around and walked back to his chambers.

An hour later the jurors returned to the courtroom and announced their unanimous guilty verdict for all six defendants. The convicted Communists showed little emotion. Goodman, in contrast, was "visibly moved," according to newspaper reports. "I expected it," he later told reporters, "but it doesn't make it easier to take."[55]

When it came time for sentencing three days later, Picard had regained his confident bluster. He noted "with great emphasis and emotion," according to the *Detroit Times,* that the defendants' crimes were "akin to treason." Mocking their claims of independence from Russian influence, he dwelled at length on the flip-flops in CP-USA policy following the Hitler-Stalin pact of 1939. The military record of the defendants who had served during World War II was misleading, he argued, since they had only joined the fight once the Soviets were allied with the United States.

"You're not going to jail for your beliefs," he lectured them, but "because you want to force those beliefs on others"—condemning the defendants for the very thing the government had not been able to prove. He then threw the book at them: prison sentences of four to five years, $10,000 fines for each, and revocation of bail bond for all but Winter, who was bedridden with phlebitis. The harsh sentences were headline news in the local media, and Picard's ill-tempered denunciation of the defendants soon appeared in *U.S. News and World Report* under the headline "What Makes a Communist Tick."[56]

William Hundley, in contrast, took little pleasure in the outcome of the case. He had come to admire several of the defendants during the trial, even as he and Fred Kaess, his cocounsel, made every effort to convict them. He had especially come to admire Goodman, even to the point of seeking his counsel. Goodman became "in a sense a mentor of mine and I respected him," Hundley said years later. During the trial, the young prosecutor had become so disillusioned with the government's handling of the informants and their dubious testimony that he questioned his career as a trial lawyer. He met with Goodman "in out-of-the-way places because the FBI didn't like me meeting with a communist lawyer." In these clandestine settings, Goodman had told him to "keep trying cases because I was good at it," recalled Hundley. After the trial, he followed Goodman's advice by immediately transferring into the Justice Department's organized crime section, where he rose to director and later served as special assistant to Attorney General Robert Kennedy. "I chased racketeers," as he put it, a career he deemed "a little more worthwhile." Winning the Detroit trial was no point of pride for Hundley, who later said he did not list it on his résumé. It had been "a stacked deck," as he put it, and "no matter how good Ernie Goodman was, there was no way that he was going to win that case." He was sorry for the defendants, sorry that "any of these people ever had to go through this."[57]

Hundley and Picard could at least agree on Goodman's role. The judge went out of his way to compliment Goodman at the trial's close, noting that the while the defendants at times had been "a little bit unruly," Goodman, in contrast, had conducted himself as a gentleman. "Sometimes it puts a lawyer in a bad light to defend people in a situation like this," the judge continued. "I am certain that Mr. Goodman has conducted himself properly throughout." The *Detroit News* added its own compliment. "Goodman's defense, marked by thoroughness and restraint, had won the praise of judge, government attorneys, and lawyers who frequently appeared among the spectators."[58]

But he had lost just the same. The five men were handcuffed together and led to the county jail pending final determination of bail; Winter was sent home to convalesce. For Goodman, there was little solace in the fact that all previous and subsequent Smith Act trials ended in convictions. Whether it could have ended differently if the defendants had agreed to a unified defense focused on the First Amendment was conjecture. There was no time to contemplate the matter in any case: bail proceedings demanded immediate attention, followed by preparation of the appeal brief for the Sixth Circuit Court in Cincinnati. This time, at least, the defendants would defer to Goodman and Crockett as their sole counsel, with Crockett the principal author of the brief.

Goodman, however, could hardly take a deep breath before he had to return to the same courthouse to confront the same demands of the national security state—this time brought not against a political party, but against one man and one entire category of people.

Alien Rights

It had been unseasonably warm that Christmas Eve in 1952. Former state senator Stanley Nowak, his wife, Margaret, and their thirteen-year-old daughter, Elissa, were decorating the Christmas tree in their west side home when there was a knock on the door. Expecting family visitors or the late arrival of a Christmas package, Elissa ran to the door and found, instead, a man in a dark suit asking for her father. Margaret recalled the scene years later in her memoir. "I'm sorry," the man had apologized with some emotion as he handed her husband an envelope of legal papers. "This is only my job, you know. I don't issue these, I just deliver them. I'm sorry."[59]

The papers notified Nowak that the federal government had filed suit in federal court to cancel his naturalization as a U.S. citizen. Nowak was to be stripped of his rights and deported to Poland, the land he had left forty years before as a ten-year-old child. According to the government, he had lied in his 1938 application for U.S. citizenship when he told the hearing examiner that he was not a member of the Communist Party. For this alleged fraud, Nowak and his family were to be expelled from the country as aliens and undesirables.

Nowak had made many enemies over the fifteen years since 1938, but his friends were usually more numerous at the ballot box. As a UAW organizer in the 1930s, he had applied for citizenship and run for the state senate in 1938 as way to communicate with Ford workers in Dearborn; since free speech for union organizers was impossible inside Ford's company town, Nowak would have a better chance speaking in public as a candidate for office. Surprisingly, he defeated the conservative incumbent in the Democratic primary and went on to win the general election against Republican Orville Hubbard, a former member of the *Wall Street Journal*'s Detroit bureau (and in later years, Dearborn's segregationist mayor). In the decade that followed, Nowak had run for reelection four times as a Democrat and won handily, supported by voters who appreciated his vocal support of New Deal legislation and the rights of workers. For the same reason, many employers and conservatives had come to regard Nowak, the state senate's only radical, as a bothersome anomaly, a man who was close to, if not secretly a member of, the Communist Party. Nowak denied membership, but it was widely understood that the CP-USA had few more loyal "fellow travelers" during the Popular Front era. Conservative Democrats had tried to exploit this charge before, in 1942, when the federal government first accused him of lying on his application for citizenship. Goodman had represented Nowak in that brief encounter with the national security state, which ended when public protest persuaded Attorney General Francis Biddle to drop the case in 1943 as an "error of judgment."[60]

Ten years later, there was no mistaking the government's new resolve to target foreign-born radicals for rough treatment. The legal grounds for this campaign had widened dramatically in 1952 with passage of the Walter-McCarran Act. Named for its sponsors, Democrats Francis Walter and Pat McCarran, the Immigration and Nationality Act had for the first time brought all the government's separate immigration laws under a single code that further tightened the screws on the foreign-born. Resident aliens would have to register with the government every year, as they had since 1940, and could be arrested at any moment without warrant, held without bail, and expelled without a hearing if the attorney general ruled their activities "prejudicial to the public interest." Aliens who became naturalized Americans could be stripped of their citizenship and deported if they had joined any "subversive" group (as defined by the government) within five years of becoming citizens. Conservatives believed that many partisans of the New Deal were vulnerable on this score. Among the 13 million foreign-born residents in the United States (10 million of them citizens like Nowak), a disproportionate number of these immigrants and their American-born offspring had joined the Popular Front and voted for the New Deal, tipping the balance of power in the Democratic Party away from the South and toward the urban political machines of the North. Nowak was the visible representation of this constituency, rooted in Detroit's west side Polonia and the surrounding factories where Poles, Italians, and their American-born progeny had flocked to the CIO.[61]

The Red Scare would now single out these naturalized citizens and legal aliens in unions and local governments across the country. In March of 1953, U.S. Attorney General Herbert Brownell announced to a gathering of the Friendly Sons of Saint Patrick that as many as ten thousand naturalized citizens were under investigation for their subversive affiliations. "It's a job worthy of a modern-day St. Patrick to drive these snakes from our shores," he told the dinner guests. More than fifty of those vilified by the nation's top law enforcement officer would eventually become clients of the Goodman firm, with George Crockett handling the largest number of cases. Besides Nowak, they included Peggy Wellman (the wife of Goodman's client Saul Wellman), who had been brought from Canada to Detroit as a child and who now worked for the Michigan Committee for the Protection of the Foreign Born. Billy Allan, the Scottish-born reporter for the *Daily Worker* and another of Goodman's Smith Act clients, was also threatened with denaturalization. Henry Podolski, a journalist for the leftist Polish-language newspaper *Glos ludowy*, had already left for Poland with his American-born wife after a long stretch of jail time; Greek American activist James Papandreau had also been jailed and forced into exile.[62]

The government was well aware that most of those singled out for denaturalization could not be deported even if the government successfully revoked their citizenship. Deportation required the cooperation of the country of origin, and while this was forthcoming from U.S. allies like Greece and Britain, pro-Soviet regimes in Eastern Europe refused to accept the forcible return of those who wanted to remain in the United States. The law specified that in such cases, these "stateless" immigrants could be jailed for months without bail and then released to a "supervisory parole" that required them to make regular reports on their daily movements. The aim was to harass the individual to the point where he or she would voluntarily emigrate, as some did, or retreat to a quiet despair, as their predicament surely invited.[63]

It didn't always work that way, as Goodman happily recalled years later. On one occasion, the government arrested an especially large number of people in Detroit on immigration charges and held them overnight until Goodman arrived to represent them. The Immigration and Naturalization Service had its offices in an ancient brick structure near the Detroit River, and as Goodman walked toward the building in the early morning, he could see his forty clients crowded onto the heavily screened porches on the upper stories, the men on one floor, the women above.

Most were sixty years and older, "and as they saw me, they began singing union songs with gusto," he remembered. "And they were singing with a verve. . . . It was not with a feeling of defeat at all." Their pride in still being a part of the struggle was infectious. "It was a wonderful feeling. It was like getting an elixir of life, to breathe that air and to listen to them, and get the feeling that they possessed at that moment. None of them could be deported. They knew it, [the] government knew it. This was just a scare tactic, an effort to try and hit in a way that might stop this resistance. It didn't work."[64]

Scare tactics worked often enough, however, when those caught up in the dragnet were alone or nearly so, without the steadying effect of friends and colleagues. As the hunt for foreign-born radicals intensified, the Civil Rights Congress published a pocket guide advising immigrants that if they were visited by a government agent, they should give only their name and no other information, "neither the fact that you are foreign born, the date you landed, the name of your ship, etc." By 1954, many Americans no longer needed prompting on the dangers that came with an immigrant heritage: in one survey that year, 20 percent of the white people questioned refused to say where their ancestors came from. It was safer to be simply white, and American.[65]

Nowak, however, was a secret Red, according to the government, an immediate and compelling danger to the Republic. This had been difficult to prove in 1943, when the Lansing correspondent for the *Detroit Free Press* wrote that Nowak, as "Labor's Senator," had become the "voice of the consumer, the employee, the welfare client, the pedestrian." In fact, the writer continued, "Nowak never has preached revolution or anything approaching revolution in the state senate. . . . He *has* preached a gospel of giving the victim a better break." Ten years later, after Nowak had lost his bid for election to Congress, the *Free Press* reversed field and joined the cold war chorus that charged him with falsifying his application for citizenship. Under the 1906 law that had regulated naturalization when Nowak applied, the would-be citizen had to answer question 28 on the application: "Are you a believer in anarchy? . . . Do you belong to or are you associated in any organization which teaches anarchy or the overthrow of the existing government in this country?" The questions reflected the concerns of 1906, five years after a self-proclaimed anarchist had assassinated President William McKinley—and more than ten years before the CP-USA was even founded. Nowak had truthfully responded "No": he was not an anarchist, and neither he nor the people he associated with advocated the violent overthrow of the government. In 1943 the Supreme Court had ruled in *Schneiderman v. U.S.* that immigrant radicals could not be denaturalized for their beliefs, a decision that, in Goodman's view, should have protected Nowak from further harassment. The author of that opinion, Justice Frank Murphy, had emphasized that citizens were free to believe in any ideology so long as it was not accompanied by "exhortation calling for present action" against the rule of law.[66]

Much had changed, however, since the *Schneiderman* decision. Subversive thoughts were now considered culpable, not just actions, and thoughts could easily be attributed to a defendant by the same hostile witnesses Goodman had come to know in the Smith Act trial. This time, however, they would direct their testimony to Judge Frank Picard alone, presiding without a jury: because the government was bringing a suit to revoke citizenship rather than prosecute a crime, the trial would be governed by federal rules of civil procedure as a "bench trial," argued solely in front of the judge.

On 13 July 1954, some eighteen months after his arrest, Stanley Nowak was finally brought to trial. Prosecutor Dwight Hamborsky immediately set out to show that Nowak, in his *verbal* response to question 28, had lied to immigration examiner Stanton Smiley, among the first witnesses to be called. Smiley insisted he had supplemented the written questionnaire by asking Nowak directly in 1938 whether he was a member of the CP-USA, Nowak responding that he was not. Smiley's confident rendering of the word-for-word interview became less convincing, however, under cross-examination. When Goodman asked when the government had first approached him about the case, Smiley admitted he could not remember whether it had been three years ago or more recently. "Yet," Goodman responded, "you want the court to believe [that] your recollection is good enough to independently remember your examination in the Nowak case 16 years ago?"[67]

The moment was wasted on Judge Picard. The case had made the television news and the judge was again warming to his central role in the public drama, particularly when the government put its professional witnesses on the stand. "All of the famous ones were there," said Goodman, "and Picard just loved that. Whenever a famous expert witness came on the stand, he would take over the examination, a good part by himself, ask all kinds of questions." He was especially excited by the appearance of Louis Budenz, a former editor of the CP-USA newspaper who had quit the party and now enjoyed a comfortable government stipend (totaling $70,000 by the time he arrived in Detroit) for testifying as an "expert" on Communism in thirty different courtrooms. In addition to earning a reputation as a pathological liar, Budenz was also known to make extravagant and very public displays of his Catholic faith. In anticipation of his testimony in Detroit placing Nowak in closed party meetings, priests and nuns crowded into the visitors' section to watch his dramatic entrance from the door directly behind Picard. Goodman made every effort to expose the inconsistencies in Budenz's testimony, but the judge was undoubtedly swayed by the performance of his star witness.[68]

Picard had to be less pleased with the performance of other prosecution witnesses who, like Smiley, recited word-for-word conversations from long ago, but under Goodman's cross-examination could not remember events from the recent past. Thaddeus Zygmunt, a former Communist who identified Nowak as a fellow party member, turned out to be an especially poor choice for the prosecution. Zygmunt testified at length that the CP-USA was devoted to the forcible overthrow of the government, and that Nowak had followed the party line. Under cross-examination, Goodman produced a Polish-language pamphlet that Zygmunt had authored in 1938. Goodman reminded Zygmunt that the pamphlet actually accused the CP-USA of *abandoning* the revolution, Zygmunt arguing that its support for the New Deal meant it "was opposed to the revolutionary movement . . . and was in collaboration with capitalism." Zygmunt tried to argue that he hadn't meant those words at the time, but it turned out that he had, in fact, resigned from the CP-USA to join a rival party. Even Judge Picard acknowledged that Zygmunt's testimony was unconvincing.[69]

Picard was clearly impressed, however, with William Hewitt, a well-groomed and well-spoken professor who testified that he had paid his party dues to Nowak during the 1930s when he was teaching at Michigan State University. This was enough for the judge, who stated in court that the CP-USA's goal was "the overthrow of this government by force and violence" and that collecting dues for such an organization made Nowak an accomplice. Picard also made it clear that if Nowak wished to rebut the evidence brought against him, he should take the witness stand. Nowak was eager to do so, but Goodman and Crockett would not allow it. It was, in fact, a trap. Because his testimony would be voluntary, he would not be protected by the Fifth Amendment, which prohibited only *forced* testimony against oneself. Once Nowak took the stand, he could not decline to give the names of everyone he had seen at the meetings referenced in the testimony, exposing all of them to the same harassment he now suffered. If he refused to name names, he would be cited for contempt of court and jailed, as Wellman and Schatz had been during the Smith Act trial.[70]

Goodman therefore rested his case without calling Nowak or any other defense witnesses to the stand. The contradictory and patently rehearsed testimony of the prosecution witnesses had failed, he argued, to meet the law's standard of "clear, convincing, and unequivocal" evidence. As Goodman expected, Picard rejected this argument and stripped Nowak of his citizenship on 15 July 1955. The U.S. Court of Appeals upheld the decision the following year, but the Supreme Court, as Goodman had hoped, agreed to review the case. "The fact that the Supreme Court has decided to accept the appeal," he stated in a press release from his office, "indicates that the court believes that the events of the 14 years since it decided the *Schneiderman* case makes it necessary to re-examine the legal basis upon which so many hundreds have already lost their citizenship." The court's decision, he predicted, "is likely to affect the rights of naturalized citizens for years to come."[71]

He had good reason to hope that it would, for it was a far more sympathetic court than the one he had addressed five years before, when he argued the Trucks Act case. Felix Frankfurter was still there, but Chief Justice Fred Vinson and Justice Robert Jackson, both upholders of the first Smith Act verdicts in 1951, had died. To fill their seats, President Eisenhower had chosen men who would dramatically change the tenor of the court. The first, California governor Earl Warren, had been a wartime supporter of Japanese internment, but had since gone on to win a liberal following and the endorsement of both major parties in his state. Warren replaced Vinson as chief justice in 1953 and immediately set to work crafting the decision in *Brown v. Board of Education* that would make segregated schools unconstitutional. He was joined in 1955 by John Marshall Harlan II, a corporate lawyer and judicial conservative who supported fundamental civil liberties, and by William Brennan, a New Jersey Supreme Court judge who replaced the retiring Sherman Minton in 1956. Eisenhower had already nominated Brennan before learning that he was a public critic of Joe McCarthy and the Red Scare. The president later quipped that he had made two mistakes in office and both—Earl Warren and William Brennan—were sitting on the Supreme Court. Goodman, on the other hand, was happy to see these new faces on the high bench in front of him, along with William Douglas and Hugo Black, the two most consistent defenders of civil liberties on the Supreme Court.[72]

Goodman's brief for the appeal, coauthored with Crockett, drew attention to the long delay in the proceedings against Nowak and the contrived testimony of the paid informants. The unfairness of the proceedings, he emphasized, was underscored by the fact that the government had indicted Nowak in 1942 on the same charge and then voluntarily dismissed the indictment. In effect, the government had simply waited ten years "until the political atmosphere . . . had become hostile to [Nowak's] alleged earlier Communist associations and ideas." In the cold war environment of the early 1950s, "the witnesses would be most susceptible to direct and indirect social and political pressures," their recollections likely "to conform to the Government's theories and their own current fears or prejudices." Even so, none of these well-coached informers had been able to provide credible evidence, as called for in *Schneiderman*, that Nowak had advocated deliberate *actions* to undermine the rule of law.[73]

Goodman actually argued two cases that day, the second, *Maisenberg v. United States*, an appeal of the decision to revoke the citizenship of another left-winger, Rebecca Maisenberg. The briefs in both cases were strong and Goodman thought his presentation had been effective, at least as far as he could tell. Walking down the front stairs of the Supreme Court building that afternoon, he certainly had more bounce to his step than five years before, when Justice Frankfurter had questioned his very presence in the building.[74]

Deliverance

Goodman had every reason to be optimistic. The legal apparatus of the witch hunt was still in place in 1958, but it was slowly losing its capacity to command an unquestioning allegiance.

The shift in judicial thinking had already become evident in 1956, when the courts overturned Michigan's Trucks Act. In April of that year, the U.S. Supreme Court ruled in *Pennsylvania v. Nelson* that because the national government had sole responsibility for the conduct of foreign policy, only Congress, not state legislatures, could enact laws against *foreign* subversion. In light of this decision, the Michigan Supreme Court had ruled the following May that the Trucks Act—targeted as it was on groups "directed, dominated, or controlled" by the Soviet Union—was likewise in violation of the federal government's exclusive jurisdiction. Goodman probably found this ruling narrow and uninspiring, based on technicalities rather than the Bill of Rights, but he was no doubt relieved to see the law struck down.[75]

He had to be more pleased with the Supreme Court's change of heart on the Smith Act. The original Supreme Court decision of 1951 had made it all but inevitable that federal appeals courts would continue to uphold Smith Act convictions, as the Sixth Circuit had in 1955, rejecting Goodman and Crockett's argument that there was insufficient evidence to convict the Michigan Six. Two years later, however, the high court signaled a fundamental change in perspective. Ruling in June of 1957 on the conviction of local CP-USA leaders in California, the court majority held in *Yates v. U.S.* that advocacy could only be regarded as criminal when, in the words of Justice John Harlan, "those to whom the advocacy is addressed . . . [are] urged to *do* something, now or in the future, rather than merely to *believe* in something." Joining a "conspiracy of belief" no longer made one a criminal, and in light of *Yates*, the Court of Appeals for the Sixth Circuit ruled in March 1958 that the Smith Act convictions of the Michigan Six had to be thrown out and the case retried.[76]

Two months later, the judicial dismantling of the Red Scare gained additional momentum with the Supreme Court's decision in the Nowak case. In a decision written, again, by Justice Harlan, the court overturned the rulings against both Nowak and Maisenberg by a 6-3 margin. Question 28 on the naturalization form was ambiguous, Harlan wrote, and Nowak could reasonably have assumed that it related solely to "anarchy." The government had proven, in Harlan's estimate, that Nowak was a member of the Communist Party, but Harlan otherwise questioned the reliability of the prosecution witnesses. "At no point," he emphasized, "does the record show that Nowak himself ever advocated action for violent overthrow." The statements attributed to Nowak were "equivocal" and could be "taken as merely the expression of opinions or predictions about future events, rather than as advocacy." The testimony on these matters "was itself quite uncertain, given as it was from 17 to 19 years after the event" and, in some cases, "elicited only after persistent prodding by counsel for the government."[77]

With this unambiguous statement upholding *Schneiderman* and the rights of citizenship, the government was forced—as Goodman had predicted—to abandon its campaign against foreign-born American citizens whose beliefs deviated from the norm. Goodman and Crockett had much to be proud of.

The good tidings continued into the fall. In the retrial of the Smith Act indictments that the *Yates* decision called for, prosecutors could no longer rely on ancient texts and dated evidence. They now had to prove there was explicit incitement to illegal action, and the government could not match this stricter standard. "Of significance," wrote District Attorney John Kaess to his superiors, "is the fact that [after *Yates*] we have nothing left to squeeze on." Further prosecution, he suggested, was "a lost cause." The Justice Department agreed. "With the presently available evidence," wrote the head of the Internal Security Division, "retrial . . . is not feasible." In September of 1958, all charges against the Michigan Six were dropped. That same month, as it happened, the attorney general also abandoned the government's five-year campaign to declare the National Lawyers Guild a subversive organization.[78]

The Red Scare was finally losing some of its potency, but it was hardly a spent force. The Supreme Court had raised the standard of evidence for convicting radicals of subversion or revoking their citizenship, but the Smith Act and the Walter-McCarran Act were still on the books. Michigan's Trucks Act had been overturned, but the Internal Security Act (the federal statute that inspired the Michigan law) still called for the registration of "subversives" and remained on the books until 1965. In the end, the National Lawyers Guild had thwarted the government's prolonged effort to label it subversive and force it to register, but it had suffered enormous losses during the struggle. From its formative years in the late 1930s, when the NLG boasted 5,000 members and thirty-five chapters nationwide, dues-paying membership had fallen by 1957 to just 489 attorneys willing to brave the gale-force winds of the Red Scare. "The only chapters that were functioning at that time were New York, San Francisco, Los Angeles, and Detroit," Goodman later recalled. "The others were pretty well shot to pieces." Many prominent liberals had resigned in the early years of the cold war, including Thurgood Marshall, director of the NACCP Legal Defense Fund and future Supreme Court justice. Others fled in the early 1950s when the American Bar Association recommended disciplinary action for attorneys with "communist affiliations." Nearly 700 members resigned in one fell swoop following Attorney General Brownell's initial charge in 1953 that the NLG was a subversive organization.[79]

The government's crusade against the Civil Rights Congress had been even more devastating. The FBI flooded the organization with informants, burglarized its offices, tapped its phones, tailed its members, and pressured employers to fire CRC activists. With its leaders in and out of prison for refusing to surrender membership and donor lists, the organization finally collapsed in 1956.[80]

The Communist Party was likewise destroyed as a viable political movement. Its organizational structure survived in skeletal form only, stripped of flesh-and-blood members by external force and internal collapse. Membership had plummeted from the near-record high of eighty thousand at the end of World War II to little more than five thousand by the end of the 1950s—and as many as fifteen hundred of these were thought to be FBI agents. Many members quit the party to escape the unrelenting pressure of government persecution and social opprobrium. Many also came to reject the CP-USA's internal practices, including its unthinking defense of the Soviet Union. Those who had previously doubted reports of Stalinist tyranny were particularly moved by the revelations of Nikita Khrushchev, the Soviet leader who came to power after Stalin's death in 1953. Reporting to the Soviet Communist Party's Twentieth Congress in 1956, Khrushchev confirmed the sorry tale of totalitarian rule and bloody purges that had characterized Stalin's regime. His frank disclosures had inspired hopes for democratic renewal, but Khrushchev had crushed those expectations eight months later when he sent Soviet tanks to suppress the Hungarian uprising.[81]

Goodman's wartime admiration for the Soviets would dim all the more after visiting Eastern Europe, where he found much to admire in Czechoslovakia but less to celebrate in Poland and Romania. Goodman was impressed by the reconstruction and rising standard of living he saw in Prague. A concern for the "common welfare," he wrote in the detailed diary he kept during his 1961 visit, "cannot be produced by force and must arise, if it is to arise at all, out of the new economic relationships which underlie a socialist society." He believed that in Prague "they are in the process of building this kind of society." He was less enthusiastic, however, about Poland, where the bureaucracy seemed especially "cold . . . hard and impersonal," and where his hosts generally refused to acknowledge the recent history of the Holocaust. Contemplating the Warsaw ghetto and the wartime uprising of its Jewish inhabitants, he wondered how anyone could "fail to shed tears for these hopeless, surrounded people whose bodies are now part of the rubble and dirt on which a new city is being built—one to which they and their agony appear to be alien." He was further troubled by the evident censorship of the press in Romania and the use of military courts to try dissidents for "insulting the order of the state." His objection that such measures would "discourage creative thought within the socialist society" did not find a receptive hearing among the Romanian lawyers he talked with. "Our views could not, of course, be reconciled."[82]

Soviet Communism was no longer the compelling alternative it had represented in the 1930s, and the CP-USA was no longer the focal point of radical thought. Yet even with the virtual disappearance of the U.S. party, the FBI would continue its obsessive hunt for Communist subversion. William Hundley immediately recognized the skewed priorities of the bureau after he transferred to the organized crime section in the Department of Justice. Before, when he worked on internal security cases, the FBI "would assign any number of agents I requested to investigate communists," he remembered years later. For an investigation of organized crime, however, "they wouldn't lift a finger," even though the Mafia controlled hundreds of armed men in a secret organization devoted—literally—to the use of "force and violence." Thurgood Marshall was equally impatient with the distorted priorities of FBI director J. Edgar

Hoover. While Marshall was ideologically opposed to the CP-USA and the Civil Rights Congress (and cooperated with the FBI's campaign against both), he frequently complained of the bureau's failure to investigate the "force and violence" that terrorized African Americans in the South. "I have no faith in either Mr. Hoover or his investigators," Marshall confided to Walter White of the NAACP, "and there is no use in my saying so."[83]

In the "haunted fifties," as writer I. F. Stone labeled that anxious decade, national security took precedence over all competing claims. The congressional majority (particularly its southern wing) was more than willing to turn a blind eye to the organized violence of mobsters and white racists to invoke, instead, the phantom of Communist subversion. "The Negro situation," Hoover reassured Congress in 1958, was in the news only because it was "being exploited" by Communists who "take advantage of all controversial issues on the racial question." The FBI's role as arbiter of national security had grown dramatically, along with a payroll that topped fourteen thousand people by 1958. Throughout the decade, Hoover assigned many of these employees to work with HUAC and other congressional committees, all the while feeding them (and the media) with selective evidence to condemn anyone who dared challenge his methods. Despite the past misgivings of Attorney General Biddle, Hoover continued to maintain a "Security Index" with the names of those to be picked up by the police and held without charges during a national emergency. The list had grown to twenty-six thousand names by mid-decade.[84]

Goodman's name, however, was no longer on it. Sifting through the evidence gleaned from informant reports and general surveillance, the FBI concluded that Goodman's close association with his clients apparently didn't make him a "key figure" in the CP-USA. There were "informants of known reliability" who reported that he was still attending and speaking "at numerous communist and related front group activities." But there was at least one informant familiar with the details of Goodman's law practice who put a different interpretation on his role as counsel for the defense. "In his opinion," the Detroit office said of this informant, "Goodman did an outstanding job in the defense of the Smith Act defendants. He stated that he had never discussed communism with Goodman and did not know whether he was a CP member, but assumed that he was not." Goodman was still suspect, but not so dangerous that he required custodial detention. "Remove from Security Index," the Detroit office recommended in a terse memo to FBI director Hoover in June of 1955. "No information developed placing Subject in a basic revolutionary group within the last five years or activities in a leadership capacity in front group in the past three years." His name would go into a "Reserve Index," one of several FBI lists that flagged more than two hundred thousand Americans for continued surveillance. Ostensibly, they were investigated for reasons of national security; more often, they were targeted because they fell outside the director's personal criteria of acceptable political belief.[85]

Goodman's fate was being deliberated in secret, of course, based on intelligence that was often gathered on spurious legal grounds. Nat Ganley had not been able to prove FBI malfeasance during the Detroit Smith Act trial, but his allegations were correct nonetheless. Unauthorized wiretaps and bugs, illicit opening of mail, unlawful break-ins, forging of documents, unwarranted search and seizure—all these illegal measures would be revealed, years later, as FBI tactics during the cold war. It was, in fact, a point of continuity between the haunted fifties and the turbulent sixties, with protagonists like Goodman and Crockett straddling both decades.[86]

There was, in this respect, no single point where the Red Scare was repudiated. It was a transition measured by degrees, a gradual improvement in the political climate that could still bring a wintry blast of disappointment. One such moment for Goodman turned on the Supreme Court's refusal to overturn the contempt conviction of Art McPhaul, the former executive secretary of the Detroit Civil Rights Congress. The case stretched all the way back to the HUAC hearings of 1952, when McPhaul had defied the subpoena ordering him to surrender the CRC's membership lists. For his refusal to expose members to HUAC's unfriendly scrutiny, McPhaul had been convicted for contempt of Congress, his prison sentence postponed pending appeal. In McPhaul's defense, Goodman would make the same First Amendment argument that Thurgood Marshall had raised when Alabama demanded the NAACP's membership lists: that the attempt by a hostile government agency to identify the members of a legal (if unpopular) group would discourage future membership and effectively silence the organization. The U.S. Supreme Court had ruled in 1958 that Alabama's actions, by exposing NAACP members to retaliatory firings and physical assault, would discourage free association and subvert constitutional rights protected by the Fourteenth Amendment.[87]

The Supreme Court refused, however, to apply the same standard in the CRC case. As Justice Charles Whittaker argued in the majority opinion, there was "reason to believe that the Civil Rights Congress was being used for subversive purposes." With this constitutional protection foreclosed, Goodman had to narrow his defense to a technicality: the fact that HUAC's original subpoena had failed to properly identify McPhaul as someone who was actually in possession of the documents. Goodman lost the debate on this fine point as well, the Court upholding McPhaul's conviction by a narrow 5-4 majority in November 1960. More than eight years after the HUAC hearings and four years after the collapse of the CRC, Art McPhaul would be forced to serve a nine-month prison sentence.[88]

Goodman also lost his appeal on behalf of James Henderson, the African American man who had already spent nearly two decades in prison following his 1942 conviction for raping a white woman. The CRC had taken up the case in 1951, and Goodman had since been working without fee on a series of appeals. Henderson had been sentenced to life in prison in a hastily convened circuit court on the night of his arrest, based solely on the typed confession that the police had pressured him to sign. At no point was Henderson provided an opportunity to speak with a lawyer, and the next morning he was in Jackson State Prison. He later recanted his confession, but Goodman made no claim that Henderson was innocent. His appeal through the state courts was based on Henderson's right to a jury trial and to representation by an attorney. Though he lost on both counts and the U.S. Supreme Court refused to review the case in 1958, the tide of judicial thinking was clearly moving in Goodman's direction. His defense of the constitutional right to a fair trial would be vindicated five years later when a majority of the justices on the high court came around to the line of reasoning that Goodman and others had argued in the 1950s. In the celebrated case of *Gideon v. Wainwright,* the U.S. Supreme Court finally ruled in 1963 that the Sixth Amendment established the defendant's right to counsel in all felony cases, not just those that called for the death penalty. "The right of one charged with crime to counsel may not be deemed fundamental and essential to fair trials in some countries," the justices unanimously ruled, "but it is in ours." If the decision in *Gideon* had been in place when Henderson was arrested, Goodman later argued before the Michigan parole board, he would have had a trial in front of a jury rather than an overnight trip to Jackson prison. Henderson, who had an excellent prison record, was finally paroled.[89]

Goodman might have won his client's freedom sooner but for the confession that Henderson had signed. Here again, the Supreme Court would rule several years later that when the police failed to inform a suspect of the right to remain silent and the right to consult a lawyer, any confession extracted would too often be compromised by the psychological (if not physical) force that produced it. Long before the Supreme Court established this principle in its *Miranda v. Arizona* decision of 1966, Goodman and a growing number of defense lawyers had already developed a healthy skepticism of "voluntary" confessions. "Police find it easier and quicker to 'solve' a crime by obtaining a confession," Goodman had written in 1957 to Carey McWilliams, editor of the *Nation*, "than by a thorough investigation." This only reinforced "the natural sloppy habits of city police which, together with inadequate staff and poor training, make good investigations the exception rather than the rule." After alerting McWilliams in a friendly aside that "you may yet regret having solicited comments from me," Goodman proceeded to detail his other concerns: confessions under duress "tend to reflect the theory of the police rather than the recollection of the prisoner," and therefore could be contradicted in court by the available facts. When the suspect, as "in most cases," was guilty, a coerced confession could jeopardize conviction and obscure the real causes of the crime. When the suspect was guiltless, an innocent person would go to jail and the real criminal would remain free. Abusive interrogation, Goodman argued, also undermined respect for the police, "especially among the Negro and other minority groups who are the usual victims of this treatment."[90]

There was an additional factor, Goodman added, one which "opened the possibility of a fresh approach" when it came to the rights of suspects. It had less to do with criminal justice and more to do with the changing international situation. Referring to Khrushchev's revelations of Stalinist injustice, Goodman reminded McWilliams of "the recent admission by the leaders of the Soviet Union and other Communist countries that many innocent people were unjustly convicted on the basis of confessions improperly obtained." The resulting "widespread criticism in those countries of the use of confessions" was matched, in this country, by the U.S. Supreme Court's growing condemnation of coerced confessions "in Northern as well as Southern states." Perhaps, Goodman suggested, there was a "confluence of circumstances" in these trends.[91]

Such a potential would have been unthinkable in the opening years of the decade, when HUAC and Senator Joseph McCarthy were virtually unopposed in their mobilization of fear. But by the late 1950s, the "confluence of circumstances" that Goodman referred to included not only Khrushchev's partial rollback of Stalinist terror, but a matching thaw in the cold war confrontation between the Soviet Union and the United States. Following the end of the Korean War, Khrushchev had signaled the new turn by announcing a strategy of "peaceful coexistence" with the West. There would be future conflicts in the years ahead, but the possibility of "détente" between the two superpowers had at least become plausible.

In the United States, a backlash against McCarthyism was also gaining traction at the same time that the Supreme Court was curbing the worst excesses of the government's war on the Left. One of the earliest moments in this turnaround centered on the case of Lieutenant Milo Radulovich, an air force reservist who worked in Ann Arbor, Michigan, as a meteorologist. In a case that paralleled that of Captain Charles Hill, the air force's Loyalty Board had recommended the dismissal of Radulovich in 1953 because of the alleged Communist "associations" of his father and sister. As in Captain Hill's case, Goodman became involved in Radulovich's effort to win reinstatement. But unlike 1950, when most of the mainstream bar had sided with the Red Scare, this time the Detroit Bar Association had appointed Goodman to a special committee to investigate the military's handling of the case. Goodman and fellow attorney Thomas Roumell had written the committee report condemning the air force's use of anonymous testimony and guilt-by-association procedures, but it was the subsequent coverage of the case by Edward R. Murrow on his nationally televised program, *See It Now*, that galvanized a wider protest. Murrow's unprecedented attack on the Red Scare finally compelled the air force to reinstate the lieutenant, and from there Murrow went on to challenge Senator McCarthy, the national leader of the witch hunt. "We cannot defend freedom abroad by deserting it at home," Murrow had said of McCarthy's use of fabricated evidence and character assassination. Unrepentant, McCarthy had widened his attacks to include the U.S. Army and fellow Republicans, questioning their loyalty in televised proceedings that exposed his ruthless demagoguery. The U.S. Senate finally mustered the courage to officially condemn McCarthy's methods in 1954, and his popularity immediately plummeted.[92]

It was the stirring of a new civil rights movement, however, that really signaled the beginning of the end of the Red Scare. In effect, the movement's two contending strategies—the legalistic approach of the national NAACP, and the militant direct action of local organizations—both turned a corner at mid-decade. Thurgood Marshall and the NAACP Legal Defense and Education Fund had conducted a fifteen-year campaign of litigation that finally produced the Supreme Court's 1954 decision in *Brown v. Board of Education*. Citing the equal protection provisions of the Fourteenth Amendment, Chief Justice Warren declared that segregated schools, being inherently unequal, placed a badge of inferiority on black students that affected "their hearts and their minds in a way unlikely ever to be undone." A prolonged struggle lay ahead, but the court had delivered a seismic blow to the legal foundations of segregation.[93]

It would take direct action to widen this breach and claim new ground, a point driven home in the most dramatic fashion by the grassroots movement to desegregate the bus system in Montgomery, Alabama. The leader of that movement, E. D. Nixon, had been cut from much the same cloth as Detroit's Coleman Young and the Reverend Charles Hill. Like his Detroit counterparts, Nixon had been highly critical of the national NAACP's cautious legalism, drawing on his experience as a union organizer in the Brotherhood of Sleeping Car Porters to espouse a more militant program emphasizing mass mobilization and direct action. When Rosa Parks was arrested in December 1955 for sitting in a "whites-only" seat on the bus, Nixon (after paying Parks's bail) immediately launched a boycott and promoted a little-known minister, the Reverend Martin Luther King Jr., to the leadership of the movement. Eleven months later, the Supreme Court ruled that segregation on Montgomery's buses was unconstitutional.[94]

No one doubted the importance of the victory in Montgomery, but it could no more produce a sudden reversal of racial discrimination than the Supreme Court could produce an immediate desegregation of American schools. It would take years before these seeds of change would germinate into a movement that could challenge the still-dominant claims of white supremacy. When that movement finally burst onto the national scene in the following decade, it was a new generation of younger activists who would take center stage in the struggle. But it was not just a youth movement. The survivors of the Red Scare would also play a vital, if less celebrated, role in the uprising, and Goodman and Crockett would be among the first to cast their lot with the young rebels.

Fathers and Sons

For Goodman, this intergenerational partnership would soon take on a personal as well as a political dimension. In July of 1959, he received a letter from his son Dick, then living in California, raising the possibility that he might return to Detroit and join his father's firm. Dick's letter and Ernie's response would plumb the problems and prospects of the Goodman firm at the very moment it was emerging from the shadow of the Red Scare.[95]

Dick was not altogether sure he could find a place in his father's law practice, and he raised his doubts on this score with an honesty that spoke to the trust and high regard he felt for his father. "The position of the firm after the collapse of labor law work has not been clear," he began, referring to the consequences of the UAW-led boycott. "Almost of necessity, negligence [cases have] more and more occupied the firm's attentions, to the joy of some and the apathy of others." He understood the economic necessity for the growing financial dependence on personal injury work, "but I know that at least George [Crockett] and possibly you do not get out of negligence practice what at one time you derived from labor practice." Dick was certain, in any case, that he personally could not "with any enthusiasm devote the rest of my legal life" to negligence law. This had nothing to do, he emphasized, with the social worth or intellectual challenge of such work. "In my opinion negligence lawyers do a hell of a lot more to help the ordinary slob than labor lawyers today." It just didn't happen to suit his needs, and he worried that the firm and some of its partners had fallen into a rut. "It is sort of demoralizing to me," he offered by way of example, "to know that Mort Eden doesn't really care if he or the firm never does anything but Workmen's Compensation and Negligence." George Crockett, on the other hand, seemed "immobilized" by the politics of the Red Scare and needed to "pull himself out of his tremendous intellectual rut and start thinking again." Dean Robb, in contrast to Eden, was doing political work as well as negligence law, and Dick underlined his affection for Robb's "unlimited tolerance and openness of mind. . . . We need about 10 more like him."

If he were to join the firm, Dick concluded, he would want the freedom to explore new possibilities in antitrust law and international claims, or work with credit unions. He made it clear that he wanted more than his father's passive endorsement of these efforts. "It is not enough for you to say to me, 'you go ahead and do it, I'm too old' or some goddam crap like that—you may be too intellectually lazy but you are not too old; your ability, furthermore, is obvious." It was time, Dick insisted, for Ernie and his partners to break out of their "present ruts" and rethink the firm's future course.

Ernie could not have been more pleased, as he emphasized in his reply, with "the serious thought" his son had given "to the problem of a thinking, socially concerned lawyer in our society today. It's good to know that you care deeply about where you and the rest of us are going." He acknowledged much of what his son had said, including the disappointment of losing his labor law practice at the start of the cold war. "As you know," he added in an aside that spoke to that turning point in his life, "I had the choice of maintaining and even expanding my role as a labor lawyer providing I went along with the cold war. Many, perhaps most, labor lawyers did. But we didn't—a decision I have never regretted." He had learned the painful lesson that labor unions "could become the vehicle for obtaining mass acceptance and support for a government policy leading to war and repression." This did not mean that unions could not again become instruments for social progress, but the sense of fulfillment he had found in the labor movement of the 1930s was gone. In its place, workers' compensation and negligence cases were all that had kept the firm solvent. "We didn't know whether or not we would survive as lawyers or as individuals—but our common resolve hardened in the conflict. Never did I have such an inner conviction of the justness of my cause. And the Firm not only survived but gave courage and leadership and help to others. . . . Gradually, our outlaw status disappeared and we even began to appear to some as legal heroes in a gallant fight." What Dick saw as "present ruts," Ernie described as the hunkered-down legacy of that time. "The battles had toughened us and we were better, more able lawyers than the soft ones we encountered."

Dick was right, however, to note the dangers in relying on what was now a surprisingly successful negligence practice. "I have the same concern," he acknowledged, particularly regarding "the insidious corruption that comes with the acquisition of money," the "sense of apartness" it creates from "the people with whom I am most concerned." He still believed that "the social ownership of the basic production processes and their planned use" was a prerequisite for human progress, and he believed that underdeveloped nations as well the United States would eventually adopt such a system. But for now, Ernie had to acknowledge to his son that he could not find "a way of identifying my work as a lawyer with any important political movement leading to necessary changes in society." Without such a movement, "lawyers will be able to accomplish little."

Ernie also wanted to avoid being "swallowed up in a negligence practice" (a "business," as he termed it). He therefore kept as active as he could working on criminal cases and on the Civil Rights Committee of the Detroit bar. He welcomed Dick's interest in exploring new realms for an expanded practice, though he wasn't entirely persuaded that antitrust work, for example, didn't amount to "tilting against the windmills of monopoly capitalism." Dick would also have to address what his father saw as "one of your weaknesses," which Ernie described as Dick's tendency to go his own way and withdraw from open debate. "If you work with others you must be prepared to consult and convince," he counseled. "In the end, if you learn to reach objectives by bringing others along with you, you have acquired a quality useful in a democratic society."

He closed on a happy and hopeful note. "There is a place for you here if you want it," he assured his son, and "if I have given the impression that I feel too old to embark on new projects or entertain new ideas—perish the thought. I am thinking, examining, and seeking." He was still optimistic. "One of these days, the new opportunity will come, I believe. And when it does, I'll be back in the thick of the fight. You see, I already think of the 'new' in terms of 'fight.' I guess that's because I am happiest then."

The chance for a "new opportunity," a social movement that would give meaning to their work as lawyers, would come sooner than either father or son could have imagined.

Harry Goodman with young Ernie and sister Rose in front of his meat and grocery market on Detroit's Hastings Street, circa 1912. (Courtesy of the Goodman family)

Ernie's yearbook photo, 1928, as a member of the first graduating class from the new law school in the College of the City of Detroit, forerunner of Wayne State University. (Courtesy of the Goodman family)

Ernie and Freda at the Buckingham Fountain in Chicago's Grant Park during their honeymoon drive across the country, 1932. (Courtesy of the Goodman family)

Spring of 1934 in Detroit: Harry Goodman standing on the left, with daughter Rose and son Ernie between him and Minnie, holding her new grandson, Richard. A distracted Freda is sitting on the grass. (Courtesy of the Goodman family)

Members of the Unemployed Council, Pontiac, Michigan, 1931. To an unprecedented degree, the Unemployed Councils of the early 1930s united workers across the color line. (Courtesy of Walter P. Reuther Library of Labor and Urban Affairs, Wayne State University, Detroit)

Sit-down strikers inside the plant fence at Midland Steel and supporters outside, November 1936. This first sit-down strike in Detroit heralded the rise of the Congress of Industrial Organizations, with membership open to black and white workers, women and men. (Courtesy of Walter P. Reuther Library of Labor and Urban Affairs, Wayne State University, Detroit)

Judge Patrick O'Brien led the Labor slate in the Detroit municipal elections of 1937, along with council candidates Maurice Sugar and two future UAW presidents, R. J. Thomas and Walter Reuther. (Courtesy of Walter P. Reuther Library of Labor and Urban Affairs, Wayne State University, Detroit)

Goodman and Laicha Kravchik in Washington, DC, where they attended the 1938 Conference of the American Committee against War and Fascism. (Courtesy of the Goodman family)

The annual deer hunt, northern Michigan, 1940. From left to right: Ben Probe, fellow lawyer and Guild member; Goodman; Mort Furay, an organizer for the United Public Workers; Bob Blamer, a local resident and guide. (Courtesy of the Goodman family)

UAW strikers parading on Miller Road in front of the Ford Dearborn plant, April 1941. Union organizers often drew attention to Henry Ford's links with Nazi Germany. (Courtesy of Walter P. Reuther Library of Labor and Urban Affairs, Wayne State University, Detroit)

The Sojourner Truth riot, February 1942. When white crowds attacked black families moving into a newly built public housing project, the police arrested African Americans who tried to defend themselves. (Courtesy of Walter P. Reuther Library of Labor and Urban Affairs, Wayne State University, Detroit)

Freda and Ernie Goodman with Maurice Sugar at the 1946 UAW convention in Atlantic City. (Courtesy of Walter P. Reuther Library of Labor and Urban Affairs, Wayne State University, Detroit)

Pete Seeger performing in the Goodman home, 1946, at a fund-raising party for the Civil Rights Congress. (Courtesy of the Goodman family)

The coroner's inquest into the police shooting of fifteen-year-old Leon Mosley, June 1948. Goodman is seated center left (marked #1), with George Crockett behind him (#4) and Elvin Davenport to the right of Goodman. Billy Allan, reporter for the *Daily Worker* and a future client of Goodman, is seated at the press table (marked #2). The Mosley family and supporters are crowded into the gallery. (Courtesy of the Goodman family)

Progressive Party rally at Olympia Stadium, 1948. Presidential candidate Henry Wallace spoke to twelve thousand supporters, with Goodman (seated beneath the Wallace poster) the master of ceremonies. Seated to the left of Goodman is actor and former boxer Canada Lee, and next to him is state senator Stanley Nowak. Goodman's law partner, Mort Eden, is standing behind Nowak. The singer is Bernie Asbel. (Courtesy of the Goodman family)

On the campaign trail, 1948. Denied accommodations in several hotels because they were members of a mixed-race group, Roberta Barrow, Bernie Asbel, and Goodman relax after a day of campaigning in Michigan's Upper Peninsula. (Courtesy of the Goodman family)

Progressive Party candidates and activists in the home of the Reverend Charles Hill, Detroit, 1948. Singer, actor, and political activist Paul Robeson is standing at the center with state senator Joe Brown to the right. Goodman is seated on the right, with Roberta Barrow standing behind him. Coleman Young is seated on the left, and standing behind him are, left to right, Sid Rosen, Dean Robb, and Alan Sayler, chairman of the Michigan party. (Courtesy of the Goodman family)

Detroit hearings of the House Committee on Un-American Activities, 1952. Goodman, seated, waits as one of his clients, Celia Edwards, an office worker for UAW Local 600, is sworn in. (Courtesy of the Goodman family)

Coleman Young and his attorney, George Crockett, at the 1952 Detroit hearings of the House Committee on Un-American Activities. (Courtesy of Walter P. Reuther Library of Labor and Urban Affairs, Wayne State University, Detroit)

The Detroit Smith Act trial, 1954. Following their conviction, the five male defendants leave the court in handcuffs. In the first row, starting second from left: Saul Wellman, Nat Ganley, and Thomas Dennis. In the second row is Billy Allan, second from left, and next to him is Phil Schatz, third from left. (Courtesy of Walter P. Reuther Library of Labor and Urban Affairs, Wayne State University, Detroit)

Brothers Dick (on the left) and Bill Goodman with Ernie and Freda, 1961. (Courtesy of the Goodman family)

Claudia Shropshire and Anna Diggs pictured in Goodman's law office shortly before they traveled south for Freedom Summer in 1964. Two decades later, both had become judges, Claudia Morcom in Wayne County Circuit Court and Anna Diggs Taylor in U.S. District Court. (*Jet,* 9 July 1964)

Goodman, George Crockett, and Benjamin Dreyfus at the Lawyers Guild conference in New Orleans, October 1963, shortly before the police arrived. The Airport Hilton Inn was one of the few desegregated hotels in Louisiana, but the swimming pool was still whites-only and the Confederate Room, where the conference was held, typified the hostile environment. (National Lawyers Guild)

One of twenty-nine people arrested in 1965 for a sit-in at the Ann Arbor draft board, an early protest of the war in Vietnam. Goodman defended the protesters by invoking the Nuremburg judgment as justification for civil disobedience. (Courtesy of Walter P. Reuther Library of Labor and Urban Affairs, Wayne State University, Detroit)

The aftermath of the Detroit rebellion/riot of July 1967, Linwood Avenue west of Twelfth Street. (Courtesy of Walter P. Reuther Library of Labor and Urban Affairs, Wayne State University, Detroit)

Goodman plays the harmonica and dances for the children of the Dong Fow farm co-op in North Vietnam during the first anniversary celebration of the Paris Peace Accords, 1974. (Courtesy of the Goodman family)

Members of the Attica defense team visit D yard, site of the prison rebellion of 1971 and the massacre that ended it. From left to right: Haywood Burns, Goodman, Shango, and Linda Borus. (Courtesy of the Goodman family)

Rounding third, circa 1976. At the age of seventy, Goodman had a vitality that was an inspiration to younger attorneys. *Guild Notes* ran this photo with the caption "The Guild is good for you!" (Courtesy of the Goodman family)

The last arrest, 1996. At the age of eighty-nine, Goodman was taken into custody during the Detroit newspaper strike after participating in a peaceful sit-down in front of the doors of the *Detroit News.* (Courtesy of the Goodman family)

9

Southern Exposure

oodman looked out over the audience. It was a big crowd, over-whelmingly black. Speaking to large assemblies still made him nervous, the tension knotting his stomach. The planners of the event had predicted that two thousand people would crowd into the First Baptist Church in Petersburg, Virginia. Now, as forecasted, an overflow audience spilled out the doors and into the basement hall, where folding chairs and a portable sound system awaited latecomers.

It was 28 March 1962, and a resurgent civil rights movement was entering its third year of whirlwind growth, marked by sit-ins, boycotts, and militant protest across the South. From Jackson, Mississippi, to Petersburg, Virginia, young African Americans had given the movement a new urgency, infusing their nonviolent demonstrations against racial discrimination with a moral fervor the nation could not ignore. To support this growing rebellion, Goodman had come to Virginia to announce a bold initiative by the National Lawyers Guild, itself undergoing something of a renaissance. The "old Left" was reaching out to the new.[1]

He was one of only three white people onstage, including two young lawyers from Washington, DC, Richard Scupi and Hal Witt. They were well aware that the crowd had not come to hear what they had to say; it was Martin Luther King who drew this throng. The national leader of the Southern Christian Leadership Conference (SCLC) had come to Virginia to rally the movement and defend its leaders from persecution by the state government. Seated with King at the front of the stage was the principal focus of that attack, the Reverend Curtis Harris.[2]

Harris was a part-time preacher and a full-time janitor at the Allied Chemical plant in the nearby town of Hopewell. At age thirty-eight, he was five years older than the Reverend King and noticeably taller. His heavy, dark-rimmed glasses and measured speech conveyed something of the steady courage that Hopewell's worker-preacher was known for. He and dozens of others had already gone to jail for sit-ins at segregated lunch counters and pray-ins at everything from segregated cemeteries to the whites-only public library. By Harris's count, he would eventually go to jail thirteen times for these nonviolent protests of racial segregation. His home would be firebombed in a blatant act of retaliation. As if to invite such violence, the Virginia legislature's Committee on Offenses against the Administration of Justice had subpoenaed Harris for questioning the previous fall and cited him for contempt when he refused to answer its questions. The state circuit court would hear his case the morning after the Petersburg rally.[3]

Harris and thousands like him needed lawyers. Across the South, defenders of white supremacy were defying the Constitution and handcuffing a growing civil rights movement with contempt citations, injunctions, excessive bail, and municipal ordinances that made even leafleting illegal. Goodman had seen this kind of state-sanctioned harassment before, in Detroit and Dearborn after 1935, when local governments and police violated the Bill of Rights and federal law to resist the CIO. He had seen something of it in the 1950s, when Mississippi's courts approved the legal lynching of Willie McGee and Michigan's Trucks Act threatened left-wing activists. Now, thousands of new activists were confronting state-supported segregation in the South, but few southern lawyers were willing to take on the risk of defending them in court. Among those exceptional few was Len Holt, a key organizer of the Petersburg rally and one of a handful of African American attorneys in the South who took civil rights cases. A navy veteran and a graduate of Howard University's law school, Holt was the movement's tireless legal counsel in Virginia, representing Harris and scores of others. He had gone to Detroit just weeks before to ask for help from the National Lawyers Guild, and Goodman had come to Petersburg to announce the Guild's response: the Committee to Assist Southern Lawyers (CASL).[4]

Holt's letter of invitation allowed Goodman just ten minutes to announce CASL's new program. "Guild concern and participation in aid to southern lawyers is nothing new," Holt had reminded him. "It just happens that it has been one well kept secret." That would change with King's presence on the stage. "There will be ample press coverage," Holt predicted. As Goodman stepped to the podium, however, he was more aware of the densely packed crowd immediately in front of him.[5]

"Looking, as a lawyer, at the South," he began, "it is clear to me—as it should be to any lawyer—that the Constitution guarantees equality to all, Negro and white alike." The audience nodded its approval as he described his recent visit to South Africa, where he had observed the trial of

Nelson Mandela, charged with treason for his opposition to white supremacy. He had met and talked with Mandela as well as the judges, who acquitted the future president of South Africa on the same grounds that the U.S Supreme Court had overturned the Smith Act convictions. In response, the government had passed new and more punitive laws, and would later send Mandela to prison on Robben Island. In South Africa, Goodman noted, racial segregation—apartheid—was the law of the land, and the government, in the course of enforcing that law, "acts cruelly and remorselessly to suppress, prosecute and imprison Africans who even advocate equality." In the southern United States, on the other hand, racial segregation was enforced *contrary* to the Constitution, which called for equal treatment under the law. Was this not, he asked the crowd, a criminal conspiracy to subvert the Constitution? Were not the state and local officials who carried out this conspiracy more deserving of censure than the demonstrators who called attention to their unconstitutional acts? "Those who possess constitutional rights," Goodman continued, bringing the crowd along in noisy agreement, "must resist—must defend themselves—must fight back as best they can."[6]

But they needed lawyers in that struggle, and the southern bar had failed them. "Under our law, under the law of practically every nation on earth, even South Africa, they are entitled to lawyers." The National Lawyers Guild would step into the breach, Goodman promised. "Every Guild member from New York to Hawaii—from Florida to Texas—is being canvassed and asked to commit himself to give voluntary, unpaid assistance to any lawyer in the South who requests such assistance in any case involving the system of segregation. More than forty lawyers in ten states have already agreed. More such commitment forms are coming in every day."[7]

Scupi and Witt, he said, nodding in their direction, were the first to arrive under the program that Len Holt had done so much to inspire in his recent visit to the Guild's national convention in Detroit. At the close of that gathering, Holt had led the Guild delegates in a spirited rendition of the movement hymn, "We Shall Overcome." Goodman confessed at the close of his speech in Petersburg that he could not sing as Holt had in Detroit. "I can't sing at all," he admitted. "But, with all my heart, may I say 'We shall *help you* overcome.'"[8]

"The response from the audience," Goodman later reported, "was tremendous." Forty lawyers could meet only a fraction of the movement's needs, but any outside help was a psychological boost for local activists. For years, they had felt isolated and forgotten in their confrontation with state-supported white supremacy. The white men in dark suits had almost always been on the other side of the bar, justifying segregation and the violent suppression of black protest. Now, *these* men in suits promised to help them bring a higher law to bear, the law of the Constitution and the federal courts. Goodman and his colleagues stayed with their SCLC hosts on the black side of town and slept as guests in their homes—a rare act of solidarity in the South, where such race mixing was always taboo, and often illegal. When the three Guild lawyers appeared in court the following day to assist Holt at the Reverend Harris's hearing, the break with precedent was evident again. "Seldom have I seen or heard," as Holt later wrote to Reverend King, "of a white attorney serving as a defense counsel for a Negro in a racially controversial case who gave the appearance of being [an] assistant to the Negro lawyer." Goodman and his colleagues, he added with a note of disbelief, "only got travel expenses."[9]

When Goodman left the next day for Richmond's airport and the return flight to Detroit, he passed through the historic capital of the Confederacy, only a short drive from the Appomattox courthouse, ninety miles further west, where General Lee surrendered in 1865. Almost a century later, the nation was turning back to the unfinished business of the Civil War. The federal government had long exempted the South from enforcement of the Fourteenth and Fifteenth amendments to the Constitution, turning a blind eye to Jim Crow segregation. Now, as this new movement in the South forced the nation to come to grips with its history of racism, the FBI took note. One month after the meeting in Petersburg, the bureau placed Len Holt on the same "Reserve Index" of potential subversives where Goodman's name had been listed since 1955.[10]

Marching Feet

The new civil rights movement had much in common with its predecessor of the 1930s and 1940s. As a participant in both movements, Goodman would come to know just how much they were alike, and how much they differed.

Like the CIO's Depression-era crusade for workplace rights, the civil rights movement faced an entrenched status quo that controlled local government, including the police. Local elites in both eras often tolerated, even promoted, extremist violence against protesters. In the 1930s, the Black Legion, the Ford Service Department, and the Ku Klux Klan had terrorized union organizers in the North and South; twenty-five years later, the Klan was still in business. A growing minority of southern whites was joining its hooded ranks, with cross burnings, bombings, and murder to follow. There were federal laws and court decisions in the 1930s and 1960s that nominally protected the civil rights of workers and African

Americans; in both decades, state and local governments defied federal law and declared themselves beyond the reach of the Bill of Rights. In 1936, frustration with the federal government's failure to enforce the Wagner Act led to direct action in the form of sit-down strikes; in the winter of 1960, the same frustration with endless rounds of litigation fueled the sit-ins that began that February, when four black college students in Greensboro, North Carolina, peacefully demanded service at Woolworths's whites-only lunch counter. These young radicals looked to international events for inspiration, much as Goodman and his generation had focused on Spain and the global struggle against fascism. One of the Greensboro sit-downers of 1960 later recalled that he and his fellow activists took their lead from Mahatma Gandhi, India's leader in the long struggle against British colonialism. As the legendary proponent of nonviolent civil disobedience, Gandhi had played the central role in winning India's independence in 1947. Ghana's emergence ten years later as the first independent state in sub-Saharan Africa had deepened the exuberant feeling among movement activists that a new age was at hand. In 1960, eleven new nations in Africa emerged from colonial subjugation to full independence.[11]

While there was nothing like the organizational schism that had once divided the AFL and CIO into warring camps, there was considerable tension between old guard and new in the civil rights movement of the early 1960s. The NAACP's venerable campaign of courtroom litigation against Jim Crow still had many admirers, but it also had many more competitors. Younger activists impatient with prolonged court proceedings were turning to the SCLC, organized in 1957, or the Student Nonviolent Coordinating Committee (SNCC), organized in 1960 as the lunch counter sit-ins spread across the South. The Congress of Racial Equality (CORE), whose roots in the movement stretched back to the Freedom Rides of 1947, revived its old tactic in 1961, eventually sending hundreds of activists south on interstate buses to face arrest and mob violence for their defiance of segregated seating. Publicly, the NAACP, SCLC, CORE, and SNCC (the latter known by the sound of its spoken name: "Snick") could still find common ground in these struggles, but there were already underlying tensions. As in the 1930s, much of the discord had a generational hue, with younger activists advocating militant tactics in local campaigns that pushed the movement forward, while older leaders in the movement's national organizations tried to rein in these initiatives and harness them to achievable goals.

There was one difference between the social movements of the 1930s and the 1960s that would have been obvious to Goodman as he looked out over the audience in Petersburg. In the 1930s and 1940s, he had often spoken at the Civil Rights Federation to a working-class crowd that was predominantly white and overwhelmingly union. Many of the people before him in 1962 were also workers, but they were predominantly African Americans and—because they were excluded from whites-only jobs and labor organizations—there were fewer union members among them. The Depression-era rebellion that Goodman had joined was a majoritarian movement that claimed to represent "the common man" (if not always women). The new civil rights movement also claimed to represent universal aspirations, defined in global terms, but *in the United States* it was a movement for minority rights. Its primary orientation was race rather than class, and its organizational strength in the South—in the absence of a secular and racially inclusive labor movement, such as Detroit's—came from the black church.

Labor, in fact, was now on both sides of the barricades. When the AFL and CIO finally ended their twenty-year feud and merged in 1955, the movement's national leaders had joined with the NAACP to lobby Congress for civil rights legislation. State AFL-CIO leaders and industrial unions with black membership—the UAW and the Packinghouse Workers among them—generally supported these efforts, contributing money and personnel to the movement. The construction trades and many local unions, however, withheld support or opposed integration altogether. As Goodman well knew, efforts to enlist white workers in a multiracial movement had a mixed history. Thousands of white workers in Detroit had repudiated their union and joined hate strikes in the 1940s against racial integration of the factories; in these same years, many white workers in the South had opposed union organization on the same grounds, eyeing the labor movement and its integrationist rhetoric as foreign to the "southern way of life." On this bedrock of white support, southern Democrats in Congress still allied themselves with conservative Republicans to blockade labor's legislative agenda.

This was reason enough for many AFL-CIO leaders to support the civil rights movement: setting aside matters of principle, it was also a means of breaking the political monopoly of southern white racists. The CIO had once hoped that organizing drives like the one Goodman had defended in Texas in 1943 would bring enough union voters to the polls to defeat Jim Crow candidates and transform the Democratic Party. With the failure of that strategy, union leaders now hoped that voter registration and civil rights campaigns would eventually bring newly enfranchised blacks to the voting booth.

In the meantime, however, the AFL-CIO's public support for black civil rights marginalized the labor movement all the more in a region where the white majority was mobilizing to defend racial segregation. The White Citizens Councils, which first appeared in Mississippi in 1954 and quickly spread across the South, were part of a cross-class alliance of white business leaders and white workers, joined in a campaign of "massive resistance" that threatened to close public schools rather than submit to court-ordered desegregation. Blacks who signed local petitions for school desegregation, as well as their white allies, found themselves targeted for retaliation—fired from their jobs if they were workers, denied credit if they were farmers, boycotted if they were business owners. Things grew worse for southern labor after the national AFL-CIO contributed $5,000 to CORE, sponsor of the Freedom Rides. White outrage at the multiracial Freedom Riders had spiraled into the firebombing of buses and the beating of passengers in the Deep South, often with the assistance of local police. In Mississippi, where the AFL-CIO's white leader, Claude Ramsay, supported the NAACP and racial integration, over one-third of the state's local unions dropped their affiliation in the early 1960s and stopped paying dues to the state body. Mississippi's labor federation, already one of the smallest in the country, survived only because the national AFL-CIO heavily subsidized its diminished operations.[12]

The idiom of class solidarity and civil rights that Goodman had long espoused in Detroit was a foreign tongue to southerners who joined the Klan or supported its upscale variant, the Citizens Council. For many white workers, there was more to gain—psychologically as well as economically— from defending the racial hierarchy of the South and the caste privileges it promised. Even at its margins, the status quo assured poor whites that they would always have better jobs, better social services, better schools, and better public facilities than blacks. Desegregation, on the other hand, was seen as the program of northern courts and northern civil rights organizations, threatening a replay of the region's humiliating subjugation after the Civil War. Yankee "race mixers" represented something so foreign and subversive to southern segregationists that they could only be *Communists*. "The racial revolution seeking to wreck America's entire social system," warned the newspaper of the White Citizens Councils, "is the offshoot of a diabolical plot first hatched in Soviet Russia." In much of the former Confederacy and particularly in the Deep South, it was axiomatic that civil rights activists were "part of the communist movement in the U.S.," as Senator James Eastland of Mississippi declared in 1961. Their goal, according to Eastland, was to subvert "the mutual love and affection" between the races that he claimed to see. As historian George Lewis has noted, in the South's campaign of massive resistance to racial integration, "anticommunism outlived McCarthy."[13]

Goodman was certainly familiar with *that* idiom. Red-baiting had nearly destroyed the National Lawyers Guild in the 1950s, and among the five hundred surviving members there were many who believed the damage was irreparable. "Guild members had been so knocked about during this McCarthy period," Goodman later wrote, "that for many, just being left alone was a condition they relished." Others, he recalled, felt it was hopeless to continue at all. "The Guild had been so ostracized, condemned, and stigmatized, they believed, that it could not hope to function any longer as a viable organization. Many wanted to dissolve the Guild and form a new liberal bar association without the Guild taint, which could recapture old members and recruit new ones."[14]

At the start of the new decade, only one of the surviving chapters seemed to have any spark left. Detroit, according to Victor Rabinowitz, a Guild leader in New York, was "then the most active—and certainly the most optimistic—chapter in the Guild." The turnaround from the mid-1950s was striking. Detroit's dues-paying membership had fallen to just twenty stalwarts at the organization's nadir in the fall of 1957, but membership had crept upward thereafter. The American Bar Association inadvertently gave the Guild a boost in 1959 when its House of Delegates called on Congress to limit the power of the Supreme Court and affirm the right of state governments to suppress "sedition" in any form. The ABA's pronouncements against the high court were so harsh that Chief Justice Warren felt compelled to resign his membership. "The role of the ABA is clarified," Ann Fagan Ginger had noted in her report to the Guild's executive board, and "this clarifies further the role of the Guild."[15]

Dean Robb, president of the Detroit chapter, exploited the opening with a concerted effort to reach out to younger lawyers alienated by the ABA's attacks on the Warren court. By the fall of 1960, membership had topped 110 and the Guild's national newsletter was heralding the Detroit chapter as a leader in enrolling new members. The Guild's executive secretary, David Scribner, was confident he knew why Detroit had excelled: other chapters organized "many worthwhile meetings on a variety of subjects," he reported, but the emphasis was on "self-education without any outlet for Guild *activity.*" The Detroit chapter was the contrasting case. Its Civil Liberties Committee (chaired by Goodman) not only held forums on such things as the common practice of police arresting people "for investigation" without warrants or probable cause, it then turned these discussions into action by bringing the issue before the state's bar associations. In this case, the Guild's initiative led to the formation of a special subcommittee of the Detroit bar (also chaired by Goodman) that generated publicity and at least one television appearance (Goodman again). All of this *activity* finally culminated in discussions with the Detroit police commissioner (Goodman the chief negotiator) and implementation of at least some of the Guild's proposals for informing arrestees of their rights. The Detroit chapter was also one of the first to focus attention on the emerging struggle in the South, bringing Robert Williams, the embattled leader of the NAACP in Union County, North Carolina, to a Guild luncheon chaired by Goodman in 1959. Williams spoke on the infamous "Kissing Case," in which two Negro boys, aged seven and nine, had been arrested and sent to the state reformatory for the "crime" of kissing a seven-year-old white girl on the cheek. James Walker, a civil rights lawyer from the same state, came to Detroit two years later and spoke at the annual dinner on "The Role of the Negro Lawyer in the South."[16]

According to Harry Philo, chairman of the chapter's expanded membership committee, these diverse activities drew another sixty members to the local Guild between 1960 and 1962. Among them was the highest proportion of African Americans in any Guild chapter, with a leadership roster that included Chester Smith (national executive board member and former chapter president), John Conyers (vice president), Nate Conyers (financial secretary), Anna Diggs (executive board), Myzell Sowell (executive board), Myron Wahls (executive board), and an advisory board of past officers that included George Crockett, Judge Elvin Davenport, and Edward Turner, president of the Detroit NAACP. When the national Guild's executive secretary visited Detroit, he was struck by "the stable enthusiasm and confidence in the Guild's future" expressed by these and other Guild activists. He had come to promote membership recruitment, but "there was little for me to say to the members and leaders of the chapter. This was Newcastle! I put my warmed-over coals back into my suitcase for use elsewhere."[17]

Goodman "never seemed to lose his vigor," Rabinowitz later recalled of Detroit's most prominent member, and it was Goodman, in 1962, who linked the Guild's fate to the civil rights struggle in the South. He was not alone in this effort. Guild members Ben Smith and Bruce Waltzer of New Orleans were already deeply involved in the southern struggle and had been urging the executive board to take supportive action for months. George Crockett had also reported on the growing activism of fellow black attorneys in the National Bar Association, and he, too, was urging the Guild to follow suit. They were joined by Ann Fagan Ginger, a long-standing advocate for "concentration" of the organization's resources on selected struggles. As editor of the Guild's *Civil Liberties Docket,* Ginger had been reporting on civil rights cases since 1955, with a growing list of contacts that included Len Holt and his law partner in Virginia, E. A. Dawley. Goodman had resolved to learn more, and as so often in his life, this meant learning it firsthand. The Guild's developing links with Holt and Dawley gave him his first opportunity in 1961 when, at Crockett's suggestion, he went to Virginia "to get the feel of it." Living in Holt's home in the black section of Norfolk, he met many of the local activists he would join the following year on the stage in Petersburg. "It was a wonderful experience," he recalled years later. "I learned a good deal about what was happening."[18]

The Guild's 1962 national convention, held in Detroit, was his chance to bring that experience to the attention of his northern colleagues. "Ernie had set up the convention program with skill," recalled Rabinowitz. Delegates from other chapters had to be impressed with the vitality of the Detroit chapter, able to enlist the participation of federal judges, a Michigan Supreme Court justice, and even the state's liberal governor, John Swainson—all of them speakers on the program. It was the focus on the South, however, that moved the convention to action, and here it was the dramatic presentations from the floor by Holt and Dawley that had galvanized the delegates and sent Goodman, weeks later, on his mission to Petersburg.[19]

The picture that Holt and Dawley had painted for the Guild's convention delegates was both inspiring and grim. The arrest of thousands of African Americans and sympathetic whites protesting racial segregation had become national news, highlighted by media coverage of police brutality and crowd violence against the demonstrators. Decades of uneven but slowly accumulating progress in challenging Jim Crow was suddenly accelerating at an unimaginable pace, driven by the mass civil disobedience and collective bravery of the young activists. The resistance of southern whites, however, had proven to be far more stubborn than Thurgood Marshall and the NAACP's lawyers had anticipated at the time of *Brown v. Board of Education.* Marshall had hoped that white resistance would give way to the "decency of men" in just a few years. It had been a naive hope. Massive resistance had not only persisted, it had escalated into a brutal counteroffensive by state and local officials.[20]

In some cases, as Holt and Dawley reported, defenders of the racial status quo had revived ancient laws from the pre–Civil War era, including one in Virginia they were personally familiar with, the "John Brown statute." John Brown had been executed under its provisions in 1859 for "conspiring to incite the colored population to insurrection"; the law had since been revised to make this loosely defined "incitement" punishable by five to ten years in prison. While movement leaders were singled out for prosecution under this "antisubversion" statute, the police arrested rank-and-file demonstrators under the pretense of "public safety" ordinances that prohibited trespass, loitering, parading without a permit, disorderly conduct (however defined), or just plain traffic violations. Any of these misdemeanors gave the color of law to violent arrest, steep fines, or jail time for the most peaceful of demonstrators, and high bail often kept them behind bars for days or weeks. Local courts were also issuing injunctions that further restrained the right to demonstrate, and state legislatures were retooling the weapons of the Red Scare to hamstring the movement before it even took to the streets. Mississippi's State Sovereignty Commission and Louisiana's Joint Legislative Committee on Un-American Activities borrowed directly from HUAC's playbook, lending their investigatory powers to the local police as they tapped phones, raided movement offices, and seized files. "In almost every state in the South," as historian Jeff Woods has summarized it, the "little HUACs" and "little FBIs" would "use the national anti-Communist consensus to promote state sovereignty and the regional racial cause."[21]

As Ann Fagan Ginger later commented in a note to Guild leaders, Goodman and others of his generation were in a unique position to put these countermeasures in perspective. After all, she reminded Goodman, he was a veteran of Red Scares that went back to the 1930s, "when union organizers got treatment not unlike what is happening in the South today, including the police threats, murders, licensing laws, etc."[22]

In 1962, as Holt reminded the convention delegates in Detroit, there was the same pressing need to protect demonstrators from the extralegal attacks of local government. The federal government, he also stressed, could not be counted on in this regard. President John F. Kennedy had hinted at support of black civil rights during the 1960 election, but JFK's first priority following his narrow victory was to appease the southern Democrats who could derail his legislative agenda. Holt could recall innumerable cases "where either the Justice Department or the FBI had taken affidavits or made investigations of violations of civil rights of Negroes and done nothing, even though the violations of Negro rights were absolutely clear." Even when FBI agents had known in advance of the KKK's plans to savagely assault Freedom Riders in May of 1961, the bureau had done nothing to prevent it. Months later, the Kennedy administration nominated Thurgood Marshall, director of the NAACP Legal Defense fund, to the federal court of appeals; but in a move calculated to win favor with white segregationists, the president also filled a vacancy on the federal district court in Mississippi with Harold Cox, an unapologetic racist who addressed black plaintiffs from the bench as "niggers" and "chimpanzees."[23]

The southern bar was even more opposed to court-mandated desegregation. To begin with, there were only a few African American attorneys in the South: just twenty-two black lawyers in all of South Carolina, according to the Guild's informal survey, seventeen in Alabama, and only four in all of Mississippi. Few among them had experience with constitutional and civil rights law, and there were some who believed, with good reason, that white judges and white prosecutors would destroy their practice if they defended protesters too vigorously. Among the far more numerous white lawyers in the South, all but a handful refused civil rights cases either "because of their views on segregation," as Goodman later noted, or because they were "unwilling to accept the social and economic consequences of defending 'integrationists.' " Some sidestepped the issue altogether by demanding outrageous fees that made their services, by design, prohibitively expensive.[24]

What this meant for SNCC organizers in the Deep South was underlined by the case of Robert Zellner, the Alabama son of poor whites arrested during a 1961 demonstration in Mississippi. To represent Zellner in court, SNCC could have approached one of the three black attorneys in the state—Jack Young, R. Jess Brown, and Carsie Hall—who took such cases. But these men were already staggering under an impossible workload and SNCC wanted to test the availability of white attorneys. The results were sobering: Zellner had to contact over forty white lawyers before he found one—William Higgs—who would represent him in court.[25]

Just weeks before the Guild's Detroit convention, Eugene Rostow, dean of Yale's law school, had published a series of articles—often cited by Goodman and fellow Guild leaders—that chastised the southern bar for precisely this failure to represent unpopular clients. Noting that "barristers" in England were required, much like cab drivers at the airport, to take any client who sought their services, Rostow called on the ABA to amend its Canon of Ethics and to establish (as some state bars had in the 1950s) a program that would assign counsel to cases in which the accused could not find representation. This proposal never had a chance of serious consideration, however, from the American Bar Association's president, John Satterfield of Yazoo, Mississippi. Satterfield was, as *Time* magazine later observed, "the most prominent segregationist lawyer in the country," a distinction he earned by drafting legislation for the White Citizens Councils and representing the state's governor, Ross Barnett, in his failed attempt to block integration at Ole Miss. After winning the ABA presidency in 1960, Satterfield had met with FBI director Hoover and secured his support for a campaign to drive Guild members out of the bar association. His successor as ABA president, Sylvester Smith Jr., would at least acknowledge that the courts had declared segregation illegal. But Smith was a corporate lawyer, an officer of the Prudential Insurance Company and treasurer of the New Jersey Highway Authority, and he would be slow to defend protesters who challenged the status quo.[26]

The Guild could remake itself, Holt and Goodman argued, by filling the void that the ABA's inaction had created. Holt's stirring oratory had brought the convention delegates to their feet and, at the close of the banquet, he had brought them together in song, as Goodman reported weeks later from the stage in Virginia. The words to "We Shall Overcome" were still new to the delegates gathered in Detroit's Sheraton-Cadillac Hotel, and so was the political terrain they now ventured into with the formation of the Committee to Assist Southern Lawyers. The Goodman firm's central role in the undertaking was underlined by the choice of Goodman and Crockett as CASL's cochairmen, their offices in the Cadillac Tower serving as the committee's official address. The commitment to black-white leadership was underlined by the choice of two co-secretaries from the South, Len Holt of Virginia and Ben Smith of New Orleans, Louisiana. "The Bar has generally defaulted," read the convention resolution forming CASL, "on what Ernest Angell has correctly called 'the responsibility to make effective in practice the fundamental right of all persons, regardless of color or economic status, to competent, fearless legal representation.'" In addition to compiling a roster of lawyers prepared to contribute their time, CASL would launch a public campaign urging other bar associations to take similar action.[27]

To give leadership to these efforts, there was a quiet movement at the convention to make Goodman the Guild's national president as well as CASL's cochair. Delegates from Texas and Louisiana, in particular, had urged him to run, but Goodman declined. The incumbent, Benjamin Dreyfus of San Francisco, was a man he respected. Goodman also had every reason to believe that CASL alone would keep him busy enough in the months ahead. Events would prove him right. In little more than a year, CASL and the National Lawyers Guild would shame the American Bar Association and help move the president of the United States to action.[28]

Raising the Bar

When Goodman announced CASL's formation the following month from the stage in Petersburg, Virginia, the National Lawyers Guild became the first—and for many long months, the only—bar association in the country to give legal support to protesters in the South. For Goodman, it was a rare opportunity to assist the struggle with which he had identified and worked for twenty-five years. It was also, he well knew, the best and perhaps last hope to revive the National Lawyers Guild.

The response from SNCC's Atlanta office was unequivocally positive. "We really need about 300 Len Holts," wrote SNCC leader (and future congressman) Julian Bond in a long letter to Goodman and Crockett. "Lacking this, we deeply appreciate your aid and assistance." SNCC field secretary Dion Diamond learned of CASL during a fifty-eight-day stint in a Louisiana jail, charged with "criminal anarchy" for encouraging a student boycott at Southern University. "I was quite gratified to hear of it," he wrote the CASL chairmen. "The psychological state and the morale level of the person who is imprisoned is dependent to a great extent on the attitude of his attorney. When this attitude borders on obsequiousness [toward authority], as I considered that of my most recent counsel, the morale level sinks to great depths." He expected better of CASL and gave his thanks to the Guild for establishing the committee. Guild members, in turn, were thankful for the opportunity to assist the southern struggle. "I find it virtually impossible to indicate my positive feeling about the minuscule role I played," Michael Standard wrote to Goodman and Crockett after returning to New York from Virginia, where he represented the Reverend Harris and four others subpoenaed to appear (again) before the state's investigating committee. "Such activity seems to me the tithe every Northern lawyer in this country must pay if he is to retain a sense of himself as a human being." Within six months of Goodman's speech at Petersburg, the number of Guild volunteers prepared to give forty hours of their time in the courtroom or in legal research had nearly doubled, from forty to seventy-five.[29]

The response of southern lawyers, however, was mixed. "I believe that the climate here is good for interesting Negro lawyers in North and South Carolina in the Lawyers Guild Program," Samuel Mitchell wrote to Holt in July of 1962. "I personally believe that is particularly true in view of the aid and inspiration which the Guild and its members have given me in my moments of crisis." But this was not a unanimous opinion among civil rights lawyers, and finding work for Guild volunteers was initially difficult. This had something to do with the very premise of CASL's mandate, which limited the Guild's program to one of assisting overworked civil rights lawyers: since there were only a few such lawyers in the South, there were only a few who would seek the Guild's assistance in the first place. There was, in addition, the continuing stigma of the Red Scare, which discouraged many from associating with the Guild. From the start, Ben Smith had assumed that Jack Greenberg, Thurgood Marshall's replacement as director of the NAACP Legal Defense Fund, "would probably have a fit" if the southern lawyers he worked with contacted the Guild. Even among those lawyers who welcomed the Guild's assistance, some were still wary of making it public. "Every white lawyer in the State of Alabama some day expects to be either Governor or Attorney General," Victor Rabinowitz reported to Goodman and Crockett after assisting Charles Morgan Jr., a young white lawyer, in an injunction case. Morgan was "very good on the integration issue," but for fear of jeopardizing his political career he was reluctant to join the Guild or publicize its assistance.[30]

Frustrated by the reluctance of southern lawyers to call upon the Guild for help, Len Holt proposed that CASL provide "legal aid directly to victims of southern injustice." CASL's convention mandate had ruled out such direct representation, primarily to avoid conflict with the NAACP Legal Defense Fund and other civil rights organizations. Goodman and Crockett continued to defend this approach despite the frustrations they shared with Holt. Competition with preexisting civil rights groups would be counterproductive, they argued, and courts in states like Mississippi often required that local attorneys sign all the necessary court papers, making it a practical necessity for out-of-state attorneys to collaborate with southern lawyers. In any case, as Goodman explained in a letter to Carl and Anne Braden of the Southern Conference Educational Fund, "direct legal aid would require a very large budget and an administrative set-up which we are in no position to undertake at this time." Time, in fact, would gradually bring more requests for assistance as local lawyers became familiar with the practical and professional dimensions of CASL's program. Carl Braden would later call Goodman's attention to one such recruit, Edward Lynch of Maryville, Tennessee, who had just "got beat up by a segregationist and is now almost a zealot on our side." Goodman immediately made contact with Lynch on Braden's recommendation that the young lawyer "is just beginning to get his preliminary lumps as a worker for freedom, so he needs moral support and information."[31]

In the meantime, Guild lawyers were especially active in Virginia, where they helped Holt argue two "omnibus" court suits launched in 1962 against the cities of Lynchburg and Danville. Rather than file suit in federal court for separate injunctions against each aspect of racial segregation—in schools, in public housing, in hospitals, and so on—the omnibus suit bundled all of these together and focused on the local government's *systematic* violation of the Constitution. Jack Greenberg of the NAACP

Legal Defense Fund opposed the strategy as unworkable, arguing that the omnibus suit was "so big and complex it could not be litigated." Greenberg dismissed the tactic as "a publicity stunt that got nowhere," and thought that Holt "wasn't a very good lawyer." Holt, however, knew what he was doing. A student of James Nabrit Jr., the highly regarded dean of Howard University's law school, he knew that the judge would probably divide the suit into separate cases. He also understood the potent political message of the omnibus complaint. To Holt, it was an organizing tool that exposed the all-encompassing nature of segregation, generating a kind of publicity that had "tremendous[ly] favorable psychological and sociological advantages for the Negroes in the community." In this regard, "the omnibus suit is not strictly a legal instrument," as he explained to the Chicago Guild members Goodman had recommended for the case. His words conveyed the same underlying approach to the law that Goodman had inherited from Maurice Sugar. "If it does nothing else," Holt said of the tactic, "it does formalize the urgency and the scope of the demand shouted so long: All and Now." The mere filing of the suits boosted the movement's visibility and brought political pressure on city officials to take the first small steps toward desegregation.[32]

With the gathering momentum of these and other court challenges, CASL could count a total of twenty-three cases by the fall of the year in which Guild volunteers were active. Many lawyers and activists were also learning about the Guild's program through the widening distribution of Ginger's *Civil Rights Docket* and the drafting of a fourteen-page *Manual for Laymen* by Guild members in Los Angeles, led by Ben Margolis, former attorney for the Hollywood Ten. Written as a guide for demonstrators on the front lines of the struggle, the *Manual* included such sections as "Arrests, Searches, and Seizures," "Between Arrest and Appearance in Court," and "In Court—From Arraignment to Commencement of Trial." By the end of the year, SNCC was committed to distributing the *Manual* as widely as possible under its own logo.[33]

CASL also took the first tentative steps to enlist law students in its southern campaign. The Guild had organized several law school chapters in the 1940s, but these had disappeared during the Red Scare when membership in the Guild became a liability for young lawyers. A yawning "generation gap" had grown in the 1950s as the dwindling survivors of the Red Scare grew older and younger lawyers steered clear of the "pinkish" Guild. Goodman and Crockett now proposed a summer project that would send law students south to serve as clerks for black civil rights lawyers. The first two students named to the program for 1962 were hardly random choices: Bill Goodman and George Crockett III, the sons of

CASL's cochairmen. "My classmates . . . were headed off to Wall Street and other similar summer jobs," Bill recalled of his fellow students at the University of Chicago Law School. "[They] thought I was both crazy and suicidal to undertake this project." Bill's own account of working with Len Holt and Ed Dawley would probably have confirmed such a prognosis in the minds of his classmates:

> We went to one small community after another throughout Virginia and North Carolina—Danville, Lynchburg, Hopewell, Monroe and so on. Len would talk to the community at local churches. He would sing "Oh Freedom," and then he would sign up plaintiffs for the omnibus integration lawsuit. . . . After each meeting, we would find a typewriter and a mimeograph machine. We would stay up all night [preparing to] sue every public official within a 50 mile radius, make dozens of copies and rush off to federal court for summonses and stamped copies. Then we would take our lives in our hands and run off to serve [the court summons on] . . . dozens of racist officials.[34]

Holt and his allies in the SCLC were building the movement along two parallel fronts: one in the courtroom, where the omnibus suit attacked local government policy across the board, and one in the streets, where the sit-ins, picketing, and boycotts led by the Reverend Harris and others dramatized the persistence of Jim Crow. It was the effectiveness of this approach that led Virginia's legislature to subpoena Harris and to charge Holt and the Guild, by name, with "conspiracy to boycott," "aiding and abetting the commission of misdemeanors," and solicitation of litigation. Holt and Guild members Shirley Fingerhood and Sanford Katz of New York had countered by asking the federal courts to enjoin Virginia "from taking further unlawful action to harass and intimidate" movement leaders, arguing successfully before the U.S. Court of Appeals that the state legislature was attempting to deny them First Amendment rights and to "discourage and impede the use of the courts as a means for ending unconstitutional racial practices."[35]

In this case and many others, however, even successful litigation generated no income for Holt and Ed Dawley. However loudly the state accused them of soliciting litigation, in truth there was little money to be made from the often penniless clients and "improvement associations" they represented. The hostility of the local judiciary made matters all the worse. "I couldn't even get a continuance so that I wouldn't have cases going on in two places at the same time," Dawley later wrote. "I had to give up any idea of making money." Holt's letter to Goodman and other members of CASL in September of 1962 underlined the problem. "We have nothing from a net worth point of view and have excellent records in proof of the income we didn't make. But it's the fight. Ed's ulcers are active again. . . . The doctor thinks I have them too. Now all everybody needs is the money that is supposed to go along with the rich man's disease, ulcers." "Sorry Len," Goodman had written in reply. "I can't help you acquire the money to go with your ulcers—all I can do is to help you acquire more ulcers I am afraid."[36]

Actually, Goodman and his law partners were already working on a remedy. They had faced the same problem in the 1950s, and they now proposed the same solution. "We began," as Robb remembered it, "by sharing our experience in personal injury and workers compensation law in an effort to help black lawyers make a better living." The Goodman firm was well placed to provide such counseling. From his days convening Guild seminars on medical malpractice in the basement of his home, Robb had gone on to become a lecturer for the National Association of Claimants Compensation Attorneys and the president of its Michigan chapter. The Goodman firm had also significantly expanded its roster of attorneys who could handle negligence and workers' compensation cases, as well as political and civil rights work. Harry Philo, who came from a left-wing background in New York, had been a Ford worker in Detroit and activist in UAW Local 600 before entering the Detroit College of Law in his thirties. He joined the firm in 1960, the same year Dick Goodman accepted his father's invitation to also join the firm. Robert Millender, Mississippi-born but raised in Detroit, had followed his father into a job at Ford before joining the army during World War II and becoming a fellow officer with Coleman Young; after graduating from the Detroit College of Law, he went to work for the Michigan Compensation Commission and rose to deputy director before signing on with the Goodman firm in 1962. He joined Mort Eden on workers' compensation cases while Philo and the younger Goodman (now warming to negligence law) worked with Robb on personal injury suits. With Millender's arrival, there were two black attorneys in a partnership already known for its commitment to affirmative action.[37]

Crockett, Robb, and Philo were soon riding circuit across the South. Crockett focused on civil rights law in meetings that took him from Atlanta to Jacksonville to New Orleans, while Robb and Philo traveled through Alabama, Virginia, and North Carolina talking with black civil rights lawyers about expanding their practice into negligence law. Whatever Crockett's private reservations about personal injury cases, he could recognize the urgent need to merge Robb and Philo's work with his own. By the fall of 1962, therefore, he and his law partners had resolved to elevate the "Goodman model" to a special prominence by organizing a landmark meeting for southern lawyers.[38]

The "Workshop Seminar for Lawyers on Civil Rights and Negligence Law," held in Atlanta on 30 November and 1 December, would prove to be a breakthrough for the Guild's southern campaign. There were moments in the preceding months, however, when Crockett and Goodman must have wondered if they could find the funding, facilities, or even participants to make it happen. CASL's acute shortage of money was alleviated by a modest contribution from the family foundation of Victor Rabinowitz, but finding an Atlanta location that would accommodate a multiracial gathering proved more difficult. Robb recalled years later that all the major hotels turned them away and even Morehouse College, Crockett's alma mater, declined to host the event. The only site that would accommodate them was the black-owned Waluhaje Hotel apartment building in northwest Atlanta, a meeting place for black organizations that featured, in addition to its distinctive name (a composite of family names of the owner), the city's first integrated jazz club. Don Hollowell, Martin Luther King's attorney and Atlanta's leading civil rights lawyer, agreed to serve as conference chairman, with the SCLC and the National Bar Association cosponsoring the event.[39]

Jack Greenberg, however, declined the invitation in a terse two-line note to Crockett that conveyed, by its very brevity, the wariness of the Legal Defense Fund toward the Guild. This could only have amplified Crockett's worries that southern lawyers aligned with the NAACP would also stay away, and this seemed confirmed when, with just two weeks to go, only thirteen black lawyers had registered for the event. "Our big concern now," Crockett wrote Hollowell, "is to forestall the possibility of having a conference made up predominantly of white attorneys from the north who have indicated a desire to attend." To avoid this, Crockett was limiting their participation and sending another round of invitations to black attorneys through the National Bar Association. Ann Fagan Ginger meanwhile urged Crockett and Goodman to scale back their "grandiose" plans. "I think 25 lawyers attending this conference will be a great victory," she wrote CASL's worried cochairmen. "Fifty would be spectacular. But it is quality and not quantity that counts."[40]

When the conference opened on the last day of November 1962, there were nearly sixty lawyers in attendance representing every state in the South as well as California and a half dozen states in the East and Midwest. Even if many participants were drawn at the last minute by Martin Luther King's featured role as luncheon speaker, the seminar rooms were

nonetheless filled to capacity and the first-day panels on negligence law
continued long after the formal sessions. "Dean Robb and Harry Philo,"
the *Guild Lawyer* reported, "were busy until 3 a.m. Sunday morning
working in their rooms with numerous lawyers on legal problems." It was
not just the information that these participants found compelling, though
the workshops and informal meetings all rated highly. There was, in addition, the unprecedented interaction between black and white attorneys
in a public gathering—something rarely seen in the South. Crockett commented on this unique feature of the conference in a subsequent letter to
one of the panelists, Herman Wright of Houston (the same lawyer who
had collaborated with Goodman on the 1943 Goose Creek case). "To me
the most significant thing was the fact that several of the Negro attorneys
expressed to me their 'astonishment' that we had in you and Ben Smith
two 'identifiable' southerners who spoke with a pronounced southern
drawl and yet exhibited in their speech, comments, and their warm and
sincere geniality none of the attributes which these Negro attorneys had
come to expect in their white southern members of the bar."[41]

"Whites and Negroes stayed together at the same hotel," another
black delegate commented, "mixed socially and encountered hardly any
raised eyebrows." The Guild's executive secretary, Aryay Lenske, after
talking with black attorneys from North Carolina who had attended the
conference, reported that they, too, were impressed by the fact that blacks
and whites stayed at the same hotel and socialized after hours. Several
said they had come to the conference only to attend the panels on negligence law but had been so impressed with these that they stayed for the
following day's program on civil rights, chaired by Goodman.[42]

Here again, discussion continued well into the evening on a wide
range of issues, including two important debates focusing on injunctions.
The first of these, led by Victor Rabinowitz, proposed a tactic that har-
kened back to Goodman's formative years in the Sugar firm: the use of
the old "unclean hands" doctrine to block or delay court injunctions
against the movement by showing that southern officials, having flouted
federal law and the Constitution, were unworthy of the court's protection.
The second debate focused on the use of omnibus suits as an offensive
weapon, with panelist Ann Fagan Ginger advocating key amendments to
the strategy favored by Len Holt. "The omnibus technique is valuable,"
Ginger had argued in a letter to Goodman and Crockett before the convention, "but it may be valuable to file 3 suits rather than 1." The primary
suit against segregated libraries, museums, parks, and other services still
made sense in her judgment, but segregated hospitals and whites-only employment were better addressed in separate suits: hospitals because the

federal funding they received made them especially vulnerable to suit in federal court, and employment because the courts generally ruled that plaintiffs who brought suit could not be (as with city services) anyone potentially damaged by discriminatory practices, but had to be people who had, in fact, applied for jobs and were denied because of race. This put Ginger somewhere between the polarized views of Holt, who favored the economy and political focus of a single suit, and Greenberg, who favored a legalistic approach based on multiple and narrowly targeted suits. Goodman endorsed Ginger's views before the conference and urged her to express them; if there was some division of opinion on the matter, "so much the better," he counseled.[43]

However divided opinion may have been on this issue, conference participants could rise as one in standing ovation of Martin Luther King's luncheon address. "Rights on paper are given lifeblood when people begin to act," he emphasized in words that defined the conference's unifying agenda. The two keys to achieving integration, King stressed, were litigation and powerful, nonviolent, direct action. Goodman delivered the same message in his report on CASL's efforts to defend in court what the movement demanded in the streets. That record was impressive enough when compared to the inaction of the American Bar Association, but CASL would now have something else to recommend it: the word-of-mouth testimony of southern lawyers returning to their homes after the conference. Conference participants had met black lawyers, Crockett and Holt among them, who were leaders of a multiracial organization. They had also seen something at the conference's final banquet that was unknown in the South since the defeat of Reconstruction: a black member of Congress, Charles Diggs Jr., and a black judge, Wade McCree Jr. (both Detroiters) sitting on the speaker's dais with Goodman and Crockett. By the end of the banquet, the 150 delegates and guests dining in the ballroom of the Butler Street YMCA (Atlanta's unofficial "black city hall") were already asking about the next conference. Goodman and Crockett were planning for one in New Orleans as they checked out of the Waluhaje Hotel.[44]

Media attention had already shifted toward the Guild in late September, when Attorney General Robert Kennedy criticized the ABA for failing to urge compliance with the court-ordered desegregation of the University of Mississippi. Two days later, after crowds of armed whites had rioted on the university's Jackson campus, wounding twenty-eight federal marshals and killing two bystanders, ABA president Sylvester Smith responded to Kennedy with a petulant scolding that belittled the younger man for his age and gave only a perfunctory nod toward the duty to obey court orders.

In contrast, Guild president Ben Dreyfus had immediately telegrammed the attorney general in support of his remarks, announcing that two of the Guild's "experienced constitutional lawyers," Herman Wright and Ben Smith, would appear as friends of the court in the NAACP's suit against Ole Miss. Some in the media took note. "The National Lawyers Guild was quick to respond to Attorney General Kennedy's appeal," the *St. Louis Post-Dispatch* editorialized in early October of 1962. "The American Bar Association should have been as quick, for the bar is deeply concerned with a government of law, and law has been defied in Mississippi." Press accounts of the barbed exchange between the attorney general and the ABA president now mentioned the Guild without the dismissive tag line that it was an alleged "front for the Communist Party." It was a remarkable turn of events considering how recently the group had been a candidate for the attorney general's list of subversive organizations.[45]

The Guild was meanwhile mustering support in state and local bar associations in the North. In the early spring of 1963, Goodman convened a particularly successful one-day conference in Chicago's Pick-Congress Hotel, "Southern Civil Rights Litigation and the Northern Lawyer." Co-sponsored by the Cook County Bar Association, the meeting was designed to acquaint lawyers outside of the Guild's tiny ranks with the struggle in the South and the need for help. The main panel featured Goodman, Donald Hollowell of Atlanta, William Higgs of Mississippi, and George Leighton of Chicago. Noting that the ABA was at that moment participating in a conference in Greece entitled "Peace through Law," Goodman pointedly observed that "it would be nice if the ABA were asked, before the bar associations of the world, what they are doing to promote peace in Mississippi." The *Chicago Maroon*, student newspaper for the University of Chicago, reported that "the Detroit lawyer has recently returned from a tour of Europe and Africa, where he observed the operation of legal systems differing greatly from our own." Goodman felt that few of these were as alien to the U.S. Constitution as the system in the old Confederacy. "Each of you," he told the lawyers in Chicago, "should go down South and see how the legal system works there."[46]

President Kennedy and his attorney general might well have endorsed such a tour for the ABA's obstinate leaders. The spiraling lawlessness of massive resistance was embarrassing the United States in the global arena, and the ABA had only made matters worse in 1961 when its invited guest, Ghana's ambassador, had been turned away by the segregated hotel in Houston where the ABA was meeting. To galvanize support in the profession for the civil rights legislation he had just submitted to Congress, the president therefore invited leading members of the bar to the East Room of the White House for a face-to-face conference on 21 June 1963. Kennedy welcomed 244 lawyers to the event, which included the ABA's Sylvester Smith and John Satterfield as well as Detroit Guild leaders George Crockett and John Conyers. The two Detroiters were initially heartened by the president's call for biracial committees of lawyers who would volunteer their services in support of civil rights. The president also urged the formation of a national committee to coordinate such efforts and to make sure, as the attorney general later emphasized in a letter to Crockett and other participants, "that legal aid is available to all who need it on a non-discriminatory basis." Immediately after the White House conference, Bernard Segal of Philadelphia and Harrison Tweed of New York became cochairs of this Lawyers Committee for Civil Rights under Law, also known as the President's Committee.[47]

Crockett and Conyers applauded Kennedy for convening the White House conference, but they were disappointed with its results. The president, as they stated in a subsequent press release, failed "to fully comprehend either the magnitude or the intensity of the mass action presently sweeping the nation." In their view, Kennedy was more concerned "with the reduction of tensions than with the elimination of their causes," a priority driven by the mistaken belief that passage of civil rights legislation would be "enhanced by a cessation of precisely those mass protests which account for the filing of these bills in the first place." They noted that despite the president's call for biracial committees, the cochairs of his national committee were both white "and without conspicuous concern in their careers, to date, with civil rights." The president, they argued, had to take urgent action that included the dispatch of Justice Department lawyers to the South "to defend the thousands of beleaguered Negro citizens jailed or facing trial." The ABA, they added, should be asked to do likewise.[48]

The ABA was no more welcoming of such a request than it had been before the White House conference. In response to the president's call for lawyers to "speak out publicly to urge respect for the judiciary," the ABA's House of Delegates could do no better than to condemn, in *equal* measure, publicity-seeking demonstrators and obstructionist officials. To placate southern members, the ABA also withheld endorsement of the president's civil rights legislation, and would only support biracial committees in places "where local conditions permit"—effectively excluding the South. In contrast, the newly established President's Committee was at least willing to recruit volunteers to provide legal services in support of civil rights. Even so, this would be a very different kind of mobilization from the one the Guild had embarked on more than a year before. As described by historian Ann Connell, membership in the President's Committee "was chosen not on the basis of demonstrated commitment to civil rights but by virtue of professional stature and reputation." It was a self-consciously elitist gathering whose primary goal, as Connell puts it, was "specifically to help move the civil rights crisis out of the streets and into the courts." Its executive board refused to work directly with civil rights organizations, preferring to focus on lobbying the southern bar to provide legal representation. In the meantime, the President's Committee would limit itself to a behind-the-scenes role as legal advisor to the National Council of Churches and ministers active in the South.[49]

The Guild placed no such limits on its support for protest organizations that asserted their right to speak freely, to assemble peaceably, and, in the words of the First Amendment, "to petition the government for redress of grievances." Unlike President Kennedy, the ABA, or the President's Committee, the Guild would enthusiastically endorse the massive protest marches that summer for jobs and justice. The first of these unprecedented gatherings brought more than one hundred thousand marchers to Detroit's "Walk for Freedom," led by the Reverend King; the second drew a quarter of a million people to the nation's capital, where they heard King utter the famous words, "I have a dream"—words he had first spoken at the Detroit march. CASL's campaign on behalf of that dream had already taken the Guild to the far corners of the South and to a degree of national prominence that few members could have imagined at the start of the decade. "Yep," Goodman wrote in reply to Ann Fagan Ginger during the first year of tumultuous activity, "life is more interesting and exciting since CASL. I am happy that there is enough interest and excitement to spill over from coast to coast." It would become all the more exciting in the summer of 1963 as the Guild sent a growing stream of volunteers south. But it would also become more frustrating, at times intimidating, as these legal activists confronted the blunt racism of southern courts.[50]

The Color of Law

Eugene McCain, chief of police for Danville, Virginia, could not easily stand aside as his officers clubbed the defenseless women kneeling in prayer beside the courthouse. *He had to join them.* According to nineteen-year-old Mary Thomas, he did. It was McCain himself, she would later testify, who swung his nightstick into her face, crushing her nose and sending her to the pavement, screaming in shock and pain.[51]

Danville was known in south-central Virginia as the "Last Capital of the Confederacy," the place just ten miles from North Carolina where

Jefferson Davis and his cabinet had fled in the last days before Lee's surrender at Appomattox. A century later, Danville was another battlefield in
the summer-long campaign of the civil rights movement. On this day, 10
June 1963, waves of demonstrators had marched on city hall to protest
the local government's stubborn defense of whites-only jobs, segregated
schools, and denial of service to blacks in downtown theaters and restaurants. Over the preceding two weeks, repeated demonstrations had raised
these demands in peaceful protest, escalating occasionally to temporary
blocking of traffic and, on one occasion, a brief and nonviolent sit-down
in the city manager's office. The evening of 10 June, Mary Thomas had
joined the last contingent of sixty demonstrators, men and women, who
marched from Bible Way Church to protest the previous arrest of picketers.
Their prayer vigil had barely begun when firemen turned on their high-
pressure hoses and police and deputized sanitation workers waded into
the group of kneeling women, swinging their clubs. Of the sixty who had
marched, at least forty were taken to the hospital—not the 315-bed Memorial Hospital for whites only, but the "colored" Winslow Hospital with
just 35 beds, little bigger than a clinic. Three doctors worked through the
night on broken wrists, lacerations, and contusions.[52]

Chief McCain later testified that there were no reports in his files indicating that Danville's police had injured anyone that night. He claimed
to have seen nothing, though he admitted to a reporter for the *Greensboro Daily News* that his men "were tired and their nerves were on edge.
They were not acting in their best capacities." City officials had reason to
regret the national publicity generated by the brutal assault, but they re-
pented only the violent methods and held fast to the same goal: the segregation and subordination of Danville's 11,500 black residents, one-fourth
of the city's population. They would do so under the color of law, violating the protesters' civil rights by invoking local ordinances that gave their
actions the appearance of legality. Their point man in this ostensibly legal
suppression of dissent would be Judge Archibald Aiken of Danville's municipal court. Aiken, in his early seventies, was a pistol-toting segregationist who had already issued an injunction against "unauthorized gatherings
and loud, boisterous and concerted demonstrations." To make this prohibition of *noisy* dissent permanent, the city council followed with an ordinance requiring application to the police for a parade permit thirty days
in advance of any demonstration, and a second ordinance limiting marches
to single-file processions "unattended by noise" and with "no shouting,
clapping or singing." Most of the seven hundred people arrested that summer for violating these restrictions were taken to jail without the violent
methods—or media coverage—that had attracted national attention on

10 June. To quietly decapitate the movement, a special grand jury convened in Aiken's court also issued indictments against fourteen leaders of SNCC and the Virginia SCLC, all charged under the state's "John Brown statute" for conspiring to incite "acts of violence and war against the white population." To justify these draconian measures, Danville's city officials and local newspapers denounced the movement as "communist inspired."[53]

Here were hundreds of people who needed the federal protection that Guild leaders were calling for. Federal support was forthcoming, but it was still equivocal and uneven. On 11 June, after sending troops to enforce the court-ordered desegregation of the University of Alabama, President Kennedy went on nationwide television to call for legislative action and a moral crusade to ensure civil rights. Coming just one day after the violence in Virginia, the president's words bolstered the morale of Danville's protesters, who were further heartened when the Department of Justice sent staff and FBI agents to monitor the demonstrations against Aiken's court injunction. When Attorney General Robert Kennedy called Danville's SCLC leaders in mid-June, however, it was not to support the demonstrations but to urge their cancellation—something the SCLC's local leaders refused to do.[54]

With hundreds of court cases pending, Len Holt and the small band of black attorneys who defended Danville's movement were in desperate need of assistance. The caseload was far beyond their means and the black community was already tapped out for funds, having pledged their homes as security to cover bail that eventually totaled $300,000. Movement leaders turned to the NAACP Legal Defense Fund (LDF) for help, and in mid-June it appeared the LDF would come to the SCLC's aid. A complicated political history, however, had to be addressed first. For years, the NAACP's Danville chapter had been poorly organized and poorly led, compiling a record of cautious conservatism that appealed to its middle-class base, but not to activist ministers who broke away in 1960 and formed the SCLC's local affiliate. Joined by organizers from SNCC, it was these ministers who led Danville's civil rights movement and supported the omnibus desegregation suit Holt had filed in 1962. The LDF was now willing to support their protest of Aiken's injunction, but its legal assistance did not come without strings. "We needed control," as LDF director Greenberg later wrote, "over how demonstration law developed. We didn't want conflicting theories and unattractive facts before the courts."[55]

In the case of Danville, where Samuel Tucker delivered this message for the LDF on 11 June, that meant the SCLC's local leaders would have to amend their protest strategy to suit the LDF's legal strategy. It was not an unreasonable demand; as a national organization already stretched very thinly across the South, the LDF had to be concerned with how its finite resources were deployed. Danville's local leaders might have accepted these constraints, but for one thing: when they asked if Len Holt would still be welcome as one of their attorneys, the answer was no. "NAACP money can only go to NAACP lawyers," Tucker responded, "and Holt isn't in that category." Holt and Dawley, in fact, had publicly condemned the state NAACP for its lack of militancy, and even though Tucker himself had reason to find the state organization wanting, he knew of the LDF's wariness toward Holt and the Lawyers Guild. The SCLC's local leaders, loyal to Holt and suspicious of the NAACP, rejected Tucker's terms.[56]

Where, then, would they find legal assistance? Holt made two phone calls immediately after the meeting with Tucker: one to Goodman and Crockett, the other to Arthur Kinoy and William Kunstler, two New York lawyers who had recently collaborated with Holt on an unrelated criminal case. Kunstler was destined to become a nationally known figure for his flamboyant courtroom defense of antiwar leaders, but in 1963 he was a relative newcomer to radical causes. Kinoy, in contrast, had been a lawyer for the left-wing United Electrical Workers in the 1940s and 1950s and had represented clients before HUAC. Otherwise, the two men had much in common. Both had been born to Jewish parents and raised in New York City; both were combat veterans of World War II and postwar graduates of Columbia University's law school; and both would soon become partners in the same law firm. They differed primarily in physical appearance; where Kunstler was tall and athletic looking, Kinoy was short, full of nervous energy, and—as a recent survivor of spinal meningitis— somewhat pallid. For much of the next two years, both men, Kinoy in particular, would work closely with Goodman and Crockett.

Their arrival in Danville was a relief for Holt and the overworked group of local attorneys facing an avalanche of court cases. SCLC leaders were also thankful, especially after they learned that CASL's lawyers came without charge. "They'll merely take part of their vacation in Danville rather than Bermuda or Bar Harbor," Holt glibly explained. When the first volunteers arrived from Detroit less than a week later, however, they did not give the impression of happy-go-lucky vacationers. They were "frightened and anxious," as Holt recalled, "because it was their first trip to a racial protest center." Nate Conyers, younger brother to Detroit's future congressman, had reason to be nervous. "I was told to book a plane into the airport only during the daylight and to look for a particular black-owned cab," he remembered. "I was to wait for it and take no other vehicle." Dean Robb arrived the same weekend on a night that was "dark and scary like an English movie, landing in a strange place where I didn't know anyone." They were followed over the balance of the summer by rotating teams of Guild attorneys, each spending a week or two in Danville: Harry Lore, Erwin Miller, and William Akers of Philadelphia; Michael Standard of New York; and Dick Goodman, George Downing, and Fred Findling of Detroit. All the while, Ernie Goodman and George Crockett were coordinating the effort from Detroit, including the work of local Guild members who drafted briefs and petitions for use in Danville. CASL's formal meetings and continuing bull sessions in the Cadillac Tower developed strategy and offered advice to the volunteers on the ground, ringing up a substantial phone tab in long-distance calls to Virginia. "Crockett called every day and talked with Holt and others," Conyers recalled. "He was more of the lifeline. Goodman was more engaged in the macro picture dealing with other organizations."[57]

Guild volunteers arriving in Danville stepped into a world that was equal parts alien and inspiring. It was a city dominated by the Dan River Mills, a massive textile manufacturer employing twelve thousand workers, including fourteen hundred African Americans crowded into lower-wage jobs in the bleaching plant and cleaning crews. "I received a rude awakening," recalled the German-born Findling, whose parents had both died in the Holocaust. "The African Americans were living in the poorest section of the city. . . . There were no sidewalks, no street lights, and no other city services." While walking the streets, Findling became aware "that I was surrounded by African Americans so as not to present myself as a target." Dick Goodman, on his arrival in downtown Danville, heard "a huge swelling sound in the background—people noises and people singing." Accompanied by Holt, "we walked down the street to the courthouse; the jail was next door. Everyone inside the jail was singing 'We Shall Overcome.' There was no one in sight, but the sound enveloped the whole neighborhood!"[58]

Defending these prisoners in the adjacent courthouse would be a new experience for lawyers accustomed to the comparatively standard procedures of northern courts. In the first trials of those arrested in Danville, Judge Aiken made it clear that he would not be hindered by due process. One of his first acts was to deny requests for a bill of particulars so that defendants could know, before appearing in court, what specific violations they were charged with. Aiken also refused to grant continuances allowing lawyers to prepare for a case, and pronounced defendants guilty from a pretyped script; he would then refuse to set bail or stay the sentence to permit appeal. All the while, the judge barred the public from the courtroom and packed it with twenty to forty heavily armed policemen.

Black attorneys were searched before they entered the courtroom, but not whites. The sham proceedings for each defendant often took less than five minutes. "This was not the law I was taught at Wayne State," as Conyers wryly observed.[59]

Appealing these cases through the Virginia system before they could be taken to federal court would take three or more years, a demoralizing prospect that would certainly bankrupt the movement and cause irreparable harm to those arrested. In the meantime, the prohibitions on demonstrating would effectively discourage dissent. The alternative to this slow death was to take the offensive, to go immediately to federal court and challenge the constitutional validity of the laws and court orders being used to arrest the protesters. Goodman had done the same a decade before when Michigan passed the Trucks Act; even though the U.S. Supreme Court eventually sent the case back to the state, the move had helped postpone its implementation until subsequent federal action nullified the act. The case for federal intervention seemed even stronger in Danville, where the local government was using bad law to suppress lawful dissent. In short order, therefore, Guild lawyers filed suits in federal court against Aiken's injunction and the city's ordinances, arguing that they were being used to stifle free speech and assembly "under color of authority derived from the Constitution and laws of the United States."[60]

For those already arrested, Kunstler had an additional proposal: the use of an obscure feature of the 1866 Civil Rights Act that permitted the immediate removal of civil rights cases from state to federal court. Passed during Reconstruction, this little-known statute had been designed to protect the recently emancipated slaves in the South from state courts that used bogus criminal proceedings to nullify the freedmen's newly won rights. Anyone threatened with such court action could file a simple petition with both the state and federal courts and the case was automatically removed from the former to the latter, where the federal judge was obligated to hold hearings on the validity of the petition. There was no right to appeal if the judge decided to "remand" the case back to the state courts, but in the immediate aftermath of the Civil War, federal officials were expected to enforce the civil rights laws of the Reconstruction Congress. Unfortunately, the political will to do so had waned, and in the 1870s and 1880s the statute had been compromised and forgotten—but not repealed. William Higgs, the lone white attorney in Mississippi who would defend civil rights protesters, had rediscovered the ancient statute in the U.S. Code and brought it to Kunstler's attention. It had not yet been used with much success, but Kunstler now argued that the Danville movement had few alternatives.[61]

There was no consensus among civil rights lawyers concerning the use of this Reconstruction statute. Goodman and Crockett favored any device that gave the movement a chance to fight its way out of the strait-jacket fashioned by the state courts, and Dean Robb and Nathan Conyers supported its use as well. ("Three little ol' pages," Robb said of the petition's simplicity, speaking in a southern Illinois drawl that made him sound to Holt like "a popular cowboy actor.") The local lawyers allied with the NAACP, however, were uncertain of Kunstler's proposed maneuver, and a phone call to LDF director Jack Greenberg reinforced their skepticism. Greenberg had little use for the obscure tactic of removal petitions, arguing it verged on "playing with the courts." The racial attitudes of federal judges in the South, he argued, were indistinguishable from their state counterparts and they would remand the cases anyway. Even Holt was skeptical. "For once in our lives, Jack Greenberg and I are in agreement," he told Kunstler at one point. But he was at a loss for an alternative and he finally concluded that the removal petition could at least buy time for a movement that desperately needed to take positive action. Citing the same reasons, Conyers and Robb eventually persuaded the local NAACP lawyers (Sam Tucker among them) to file removal petitions for their clients. In the Danville court, Judge Aiken flatly refused to recognize the validity of a statute he'd never heard of, but federal district court Judge Thomas Jefferson Michie, a wealthy Virginia aristocrat no less bewildered by the novel tactic, felt compelled to schedule hearings on the matter.[62]

Critics and advocates of the movement's legal strategy both had reason to feel vindicated by subsequent events. In early July, Judge Michie confirmed Greenberg's assessment of federal judges in the South when he sent the cases back to Aiken's court, claiming he had no jurisdiction to intervene. He likewise refused to overturn either the city's antipicketing ordinances or Aiken's injunction, and, to boot, issued his own *federal* injunction against the demonstrations. It was hardly the end, however, of the summer's roller-coaster legal battles, for the case now went to the federal court of appeals in Baltimore, where the justices of the Fourth Circuit ordered Judge Michie to dissolve his injunction. On the suggestion of George Crockett, the Guild's lawyers also filed an emergency motion in federal court to block the state from trying the Danville cases in courtrooms scattered across Virginia. Chief Justice Simon Sobeloff did so in early August, preventing further prosecution until the federal appeals court held hearings on the constitutionality of Aiken's injunction and the city's antipicketing ordinances. Justice Sobeloff hoped the intervening weeks would allow "persons of goodwill of both races to establish communications and to seek . . . acceptable solutions." The weeks stretched into months when the appeals court later called for additional hearings the next year. "We had won!" Kinoy later exulted. "All the prosecutions were halted. The movement was free to breathe and fight."[63]

This was as far as the lawyers could go, however. The strategy of seeking removal of the cases to federal court and the parallel effort to challenge the constitutionality of the city's actions had given the SCLC and SNCC time to regroup, but legal action could not substitute for a unified movement. The demonstrations, boycotts, and picketing would continue, but so would the city's repressive actions, including mass arrests and a police raid on the movement's offices. In this war of attrition, white segregationists would become more unified and the civil rights movement less so. In city council elections the following year, the white majority voted out all five moderates who had agreed to talk with movement leaders. The local SCLC and NAACP, on the other hand, lapsed into periodic feuding, and Martin Luther King's on-again, off-again commitments to the Danville struggle would slowly demoralize the local movement. Organizers and lawyers were at risk of burnout, especially Holt after his indictment under the John Brown statute. With arrest imminent and his nerves frayed, Holt left town at the urging of Conyers and Robb, who recommended he "go somewhere and get drunk." When he returned, it was only the presence of CASL's out-of-town volunteers who prevented his arrest. So long as Holt was accompanied by Harry Lore and Bill Akers, the police trailed at a discreet distance, including the night Holt drove the two Philadelphia attorneys to the train station for their return home. "Twenty minutes after we left him," Lore reported in a letter to Goodman, "he was in the custody of police." He remained in jail for two days before another CASL lawyer, Michael Standard, could muster the $5,000 from Guild members in New York to bail him out.[64]

When Robb and Conyers finished their stint in Danville, Holt noticed that these "workhorses" for the movement returned to Detroit with darkened rings around their eyes from the sleepless grind of preparing removal petitions, writing briefs, and appearing in courts from Danville to Baltimore. Their haggard appearance "gave the impression they had lost a fight," Holt observed. In the end, they had. Danville's white power structure had united around a strategy that, except for the violence of 10 June, gave a lawlike veneer to its suppression of dissent. National media attention had flickered off as a result and the movement's national leaders had moved on to other struggles. As the demonstrations slowly petered out, the "Danville method" became a model for white resistance to desegregation. "Officials of other Virginia cities have traveled here to observe and learn," the *New York Times* reported in August 1963, "an unspoken compliment to a defense strategy that is the most unyielding, ingenious, legalistic, and effective of any city in the South."[65]

When the federal appeals court finally issued its decision the following year, it served as an epitaph for the Danville movement. Acknowledging that police "excesses" and the state's attempt to move the trials to distant locations had previously threatened irreparable harm to the protesters, the judges, by a narrow 3-2 majority, concluded in 1964 that "the quieter atmosphere of the present" in which "things have simmered down" allowed them to lift their injunction against the prosecution of protesters. The law, they ruled, permitted no appeal of Judge Michie's decision to send the cases back to Danville, and the protesters could now receive a fair trial given the more tranquil setting they claimed to find. In dissent, Chief Justice Sobeloff took the majority to task for its facile conclusion that the situation had changed for the better when, as the majority acknowledged, there were no findings of fact before the court to substantiate such a claim. The diminished level of protest "could mean that the plaintiffs have been so cowed that they no longer care to express themselves," and until the district court had the opportunity to review this very question, there were no grounds to lift the injunction against further prosecutions.[66]

It was as an eloquent dissent, but it was one vote short of making a difference. "In 1963 Negroes tried to move Danville, and failed," Holt later concluded in his bittersweet memoir of the summer's campaign. Whether this was the failure of a fragmented movement, a hesitant president, or a long-shot gamble against white supremacy, the *legal* strategy of challenging state actions in federal court had at least been vindicated. The white power structure's hand had been stayed for more than a year, and the lawyers who engineered this delaying action had reason to be proud. "Your Brief in the Danville case is a magnificent job," Goodman wrote Kinoy in September of 1963, shortly before the first appeals court hearing. CASL was already promoting the case as a model, featuring Kunstler at a successful fund-raiser in Detroit that same month. There would be additional opportunities to publicize the strategy at the Guild's upcoming "Second Workshop on Civil Rights and Negligence Law"—the sequel to the Atlanta conference—scheduled for New Orleans in early October. "Let's talk this and many other things over at New Orleans," Goodman wrote Kinoy. Kinoy, in turn, thanked Goodman for his notes and input on the removal briefs, and likewise anticipated that the gathering in New Orleans would be a chance to talk "with you and George at some length" about the "acute problems" and complicated relationships already evident in the Danville movement.[67]

New Orleans

The CASL meeting in New Orleans would take on a special urgency in light of events. On 15 September 1963, the Klan signaled its continuing contempt for the movement's nonviolent strategy by dynamiting the Sixteenth Street Baptist Church in Birmingham, Alabama, killing four young girls attending Sunday school.

When Goodman and Crockett opened the New Orleans conference little more than two weeks later, this barbaric act cast a worrying gloom over the landmark proceedings—the first open gathering of black and white attorneys in the city's history. Cosponsored by the ACLU and the Louis A. Martinet Society (the local organization of black lawyers), the program followed on the Atlanta conference with an opening day focused on developing personal injury cases to support civil rights work. Dean Robb was scheduled to address problems of medical evidence, John Conyers to speak of his experience as a referee for the Michigan Workmen's Compensation Department, and Don Loria (Goodman's old colleague from the Sugar firm) to cover the use of psychiatry in personal injury cases. A panel of southern attorneys including Oscar Adams of Birmingham and Charles Conley of Montgomery, Alabama, would also share their thoughts on the particular problems black lawyers faced in developing a personal injury practice. On the second and third day of the conference, the agenda called for a shift in focus to civil rights, with a program that emphasized "How a lawyer in Danville, Va., or Birmingham, Ala., or Albany, Ga., meets the legal problems where all branches of government are arrayed against him." Panelists and presenters included Donald Hollowell and C. B. King of Atlanta, Kunstler and Kinoy of New York, Ruth Harvey of Danville, Peter A. Hall of Birmingham, and Leo Pfeffer, general counsel of the American Jewish Congress.[68]

The FBI and Louisiana state police were especially interested in the participation of past Communists like John McTernan, a Los Angles Guild member who had represented Smith Act defendants in the 1950s, and Anne Shore, the former administrative secretary of Detroit's Civil Rights Congress. Goodman and Crockett were also on the list of "subversives" who arrived on 3 October at the Airport Hilton Inn, one of the few deseg regated hotels in the state. Conference participants were not intimidated by the police presence or the reminders of Jim Crow, including, as Dean Robb recalled, the still-segregated swimming pool. "I remember integrating the pool at the hotel with a black woman, the wife of Oscar Adams. The state Red Squad was openly watching us from the upper balconies around the pool, with cameras, and they made no attempt to hide. We held hands on the diving board, looked up at them and jumped in the pool. We were ready to be arrested."[69]

When the conference convened the next day in the hotel's eerily named Confederate Room, the agenda included a presentation of special interest by Robert Collins of New Orleans. As part of the civil rights panel chaired by Kunstler, Collins was scheduled to speak on "Reprisals against lawyers . . . arising out of direct action." Conference participants had no idea how relevant this issue was about to become.[70]

Shortly before 3:00 p.m. on the meeting's opening day, more than a hundred state and local police cordoned off the streets in front of the homes and law offices of local Guild activists Ben Smith and Bruce Waltzer. With guns drawn, they began a three-hour search of the two lawyers' files, bookshelves, and personal belongings. The offices of the Southern Conference Educational Fund (SCEF) were simultaneously ransacked and its membership records seized. At around 4:30, the police arrived at the Hilton Inn and, in front of the stunned delegates, arrested Smith and Waltzer and took them from the building in handcuffs. In a subsequent report to Guild members, Goodman described coming out of the building "just in time to see Ben, in the back seat of a sheriff's patrol car, under arrest and about to be driven to prison. The few of us who were there called to Ben to cheer up—we would get him out of jail." They did late that night, when a local judge released Smith, Waltzer, and James Dombrowski, executive secretary of the SCEF. All three were under investigation by the Louisiana legislature's Committee on Un-American Activities for failing to comply with the Subversive Activities and Communist Control Act, which required members of the SCEF and Guild to register as supporters of "subversive" organizations. Any doubt as to the meaning of "subversive" was eliminated by James Pfister, chairman of the state committee, who announced to the press that the raids and the arrests resulted from the "racial agitation" of the three men.[71]

"They're going back to the weapons of the 1950s," Dombrowski observed on his release. He would know: as director of the SCEF in the 1950s, he had witnessed the repeated (and previously unsuccessful) efforts of Senator James Eastland of Mississippi to seize the organization's membership and donor lists. Goodman could also recognize the cold war pedigree of the state's actions, which so clearly mirrored the intent of Michigan's Trucks Act. "We know," he wrote of the indictment later brought against Smith and Waltzer, "and the southern power structure knows, that the real reason for the indictment is the work of Ben, Bruce and the Guild's Committee for Legal Assistance in the South," as CASL had been renamed. With only seven or eight white lawyers in the Deep

South willing to take civil rights cases, "the jailing of Smith and Waltzer would eliminate 25 percent of this handful," as he emphasized in a letter to Ben Dreyfus. Concern on this score was not limited to the Guild's small band of partisans. "Breaking into offices with sledge hammers . . . and arresting citizens without evidence," said the Reverend Fred Shuttlesworth, national secretary of the SCLC and president of the SCEF, "are the methods of a totalitarian state and betoken the breakdown of all law." Jack Greenberg, for all his caution regarding leftist groups like the Lawyers Guild and the SCEF, filed a supporting brief for the suit that Dombrowski, Smith, and Waltzer brought in federal court against Louisiana's witch hunt. "While we have no connections with Smith and Waltzer," the LDF stressed, "if the files of our legal staff . . . may be subjected to the same lawless invasion . . . the cause of civil rights will be most severely prejudiced."[72]

For this moment, at least, the historic distinction between "civil rights" and "civil liberties" was irrelevant. Few in the civil rights movement could disagree with Ben Smith's comments during the press conference held the day after the arrests. "By these prosecutions," said Smith, speaking in the ballroom of the Hilton Inn, "the wider aspect of our efforts becomes clearer to us all. We cannot desegregate a witch-hunting society. We cannot integrate a silent and fearful nation. We cannot provide equal rights that have any meaning to citizens of a police state."[73]

Federal judge John Minor Wisdom of the Fifth Circuit Court in New Orleans was likewise convinced that Louisiana, "under the guise of combating subversion," was "in fact using and abusing its laws to punish the plaintiffs for their advocacy of civil rights for Negroes." He granted the request for a temporary injunction against further state action, but it was too late to recover the files and membership lists the police had seized: unknown to the courts until after the fact, a truckload of materials had already been spirited across the border to Woodville, Mississippi, where it came under the control of Senator Eastland. The Mississippi senator had finally gotten the list of SCEF members and contributors he had not been able to legally obtain in the 1950s. Facing the combined power of Eastland's Senate Internal Security Committee and the state of Louisiana, Smith, Waltzer, and Dombrowski had to rely on the federal courts for protection. Judge Wisdom's temporary injunction was in effect until a three-judge panel heard the case in December, after which the two additional judges overruled Wisdom and voted to allow Louisiana, under its right of "self preservation," to prosecute the three. Judge Wisdom delivered a stinging dissent. "The crowning glory of American federalism," he wrote, "is not states' rights. It is the protection the United States Constitution gives to the private citizen against *all* wrongful governmental invasion of fundamental rights and freedoms."[74]

For now, Smith and his fellow plaintiffs were on the short end of the 2-1 decision. Goodman wrote to his friend and thanked him for helping to organize a conference that had produced such a momentous confrontation between the Bill of Rights and states' rights. "In addition," he continued, tongue in cheek, "the contribution made by you and Bruce in becoming guinea pigs for the working seminar represented a single act of gratitude beyond the call of duty." For many of the delegates, the drama of the arrests had underlined the importance of the issues debated in the conference workshops. "I was impressed, enriched, and enormously stimulated by the meeting," John McTernan wrote Goodman and Crockett in a heartfelt report on the conference. "The Guild and progressive lawyers generally are greatly in your debt." Arthur Kinoy was equally moved. "We rarely take out time to say certain things to one another which ought to be said," he wrote to Goodman and Crockett. "From a very personal point of view I would like to say that the weekend conference was one of the most important and exciting experiences I have recently had." Over the next year he would devote the largest share of his time to the court proceedings that followed on the conference's dramatic events.[75]

Kinoy would eventually take the case of *Dombrowski et al. v. Pfister* to the U.S. Supreme Court and one of the most important decisions on civil liberties in the court's history. Goodman, in the meantime, would take the Guild to Mississippi, where history also waited.

10
Mississippi

In the late winter of 1963, somewhere inside Detroit's massive, granite-faced Federal Building, Special Agent Wayland Archer sifted through a thick file of reports on Ernest Goodman. The file had grown along with the civil rights movement and the FBI had decided to take a closer look at Goodman's role in the protests spreading across the South, from Virginia to Louisiana to Mississippi.

Special Agent Archer skimmed the newspaper clippings and read the informant reports on Goodman's activities—who he saw, who phoned him, who he ate dinner with, where he traveled. His work as counsel to Detroit's Communists and other left-wingers in the 1950s had already put his name on the "Reserve Index" for monitoring as a security risk. Archer now had to decide if Goodman's recent activism warranted reclassification to the "Security Index," the list of individuals subject to detention during a declared emergency. It was a firm belief within the FBI that Communists were fomenting the civil rights agitation, and Goodman, Archer noted, had long been associated with Communist front groups. "Subject," he concluded in a memo to Director J. Edgar Hoover, "is in a position to influence individuals against the national interest in a time of national emergency. It is, therefore, recommended that the Subject be placed on the Security Index." Two weeks later, the director's office signaled its agreement.[1]

Once again, the federal government had declared Goodman an urgent threat to national security. Of course, Agent Archer's investigation had been a secret procedure, held without hearings or notification to the accused. In the eyes of the FBI, Goodman was a suspected agent of the Soviet Union and only covert surveillance could avoid tipping him off to the ongoing investigation. The FBI had already learned from a cooperating clerk at British Overseas Airways that Goodman had booked a flight that winter to London and from there to Paris; ten days after his arrival in

Western Europe, he would board a Soviet Aeroflot plane, flight 050, to Moscow. After a week's stay in the Soviet Union, Goodman's itinerary would take him to Vienna, to Rome, and finally to Ghana, returning to Detroit in late February. The following month, a Mr. "B. N. Agapov," accompanying a group of Soviet tourists in Detroit, had placed several phone calls from the Henrose Hotel to Goodman's office. An FBI informant soon after reported that Goodman was to speak at the Communist Party's Global Forum at the Central Congregational Church on Linwood Avenue. His speech would be "Personal Freedom: USSR and Ghana." The bureau was also well aware that two of Goodman's associates in the National Lawyers Guild, Victor Rabinowitz and Leonard Boudin, served as legal representatives in the United States of the Castro government, and that Goodman's oldest son had not only visited Cuba in 1960, but had fallen in love with and married a woman who worked for Castro. For Agent Archer's superiors, these were ample grounds for putting Ernest Goodman on the Security Index.[2]

There were, however, contrary facts. The victory of the Cuban revolution over the U.S.-backed dictatorship of General Batista was still a widely celebrated event in 1960, and many people believed it was the U.S. government that had subsequently promoted sedition by supporting a counter-revolutionary invasion of the island and repeated attempts to assassinate Castro. Goodman's travels also had a benign interpretation. If asked, he would have described his trips to Europe, the USSR, and Africa as part of his research for a proposed book on comparative legal systems; he would, in due course, submit a manuscript to the Lawyers Cooperative Publishing Company in the same week that Special Agent Archer was reviewing his file. (Goodman received the rejection letter two weeks later.) The FBI report on phone calls from the Soviet tourist group gave no information on who the caller was or what was said; it could well have been a return of the hospitality his Russian hosts had shown him in Moscow.[3]

The bureau reported, in any case, that its investigation had "failed to develop Communist Party membership by Goodman," and there was no indication in any of these reports that Goodman's actions were remotely illegal or seditious. Even his reported comments about the Soviet Union at the Global Forum had been ambiguous. According to the FBI informant at the event, Goodman "stated that religious freedom was available to everyone in the USSR but not the right to propagandize religion." He had also expressed his belief that there could be no "freedom of the press in the USSR when difficulties between China and the USSR were kept out of the Russian papers." This was not the fulsome denunciation of all things Soviet demanded by the cold war Right, but neither was it the uncritical praise expected of Soviet apologists.[4]

These anomalies mattered little to FBI director Hoover. In his view, two incontrovertible facts about Goodman justified his placement on the Security Index: first, he was publicly critical of the FBI, and second, he was a civil rights agitator who was now urging the Lawyers Guild to concentrate its resources on Mississippi. Hoover could not easily abide any of this. The FBI director was, after all, a central figure in the edifice of white supremacy that Goodman and his fellow activists hoped to bring down. A product of Washington, DC's segregated school system, he had internalized all of the derogatory stereotypes concerning blacks. "The colored people are quite ignorant," he once blurted out to a conference of newspaper editors, "and I doubt if they would seek an education if they had the opportunity." The FBI employed more than seven thousand agents, but Hoover recruited only a handful of African Americans—and they served as drivers and personal stewards. The fact that the Klan in Mississippi was reorganizing into clandestine cells with at least five thousand armed members violently opposed to federal law made little impression on Hoover. Senator Eastland of Mississippi was a loyal ally of the FBI director, supporting his budget requests and applauding his relentless pursuit of Communists. In return, Hoover made no effort to defend civil rights workers in Mississippi, and refused to even open an FBI office in the state until the president ordered him to do so.[5]

Hoover's fixation remained first and foremost the specter of domestic Communism. Goodman and thousands of others on the Security Index were the small fish to be scooped up in the event of a national emergency; the big catch, Hoover's primary target, was always Martin Luther King. By 1963 and 1964, as the civil rights campaign moved toward a fateful and bloody showdown in Mississippi, Hoover had become obsessed with bringing the movement's leader to heel. He believed he could do so by exposing King's long-term association with Stanley Levison, the New York businessman who advised King and financed his early efforts to build the Southern Christian Leadership Conference. Levison was everything Hoover distrusted: Jewish, left-wing, and close to, if not a member of, the Communist Party during the 1950s. Hoover relentlessly pressed these facts upon the president and the attorney general, and when they weren't sufficiently alarmed, he selectively leaked the information to reporters. At no time did Hoover present evidence that Levison's had somehow "maneuvered" King into actions that threatened the national interest. Indeed, when the FBI's files were opened to scrutiny years later, it was revealed that Hoover had suppressed evidence of Levison's break with the CP-USA and his subsequent advice that King denounce anti-Semitism in the Soviet Union.[6]

It was a measure of Hoover's animus toward the civil rights movement that the FBI would turn to blatantly illegal efforts to undermine King and (in countless smaller ways) the likes of Goodman. Having won Attorney General Robert Kennedy's grudging consent to place wiretaps on King's phones, Hoover exploited this opening to launch a secret campaign of surveillance and harassment. When the wiretaps, the unauthorized break-ins, and the microphones planted in King's hotel rooms and home revealed adultery and marital discord, Hoover's lieutenants leaked the tapes to cooperating journalists and hounded King with forgeries, blackmail, and anonymous letters urging him to suicide—actions commonly associated with the very police states Hoover so frequently denounced in public.[7]

It was in this context that Goodman now urged the Lawyers Guild to concentrate its efforts on Mississippi. He had every reason to believe that he was already under government surveillance, and he must have known that the Guild's augmented role in Mississippi would only intensify the scrutiny. It was of little concern to him. There was nothing in his professional or political life that he had to hide from the FBI.

Line of Fire

Mississippi was different. Other states in the South harassed and jailed civil rights leaders. In Mississippi, Byron de la Beckwith dispensed with such halfway measures in June of 1963 and murdered Medgar Evers with a single bullet in his back as the field secretary of the state NAACP stood in his driveway. Even Beckwith's fellow members of the White Citizens Council regarded him as an extremist, but two all-white juries refused to convict him. Beckwith subsequently boasted of his act at Klan rallies.[8]

Other states in the South discouraged African Americans from registering to vote and arrested or clubbed many of those who protested their disenfranchisement. In Mississippi, Herbert Lee attempted to register in McComb and was shot dead in the street by a member of the state legislature. The local coroner's jury ruled it was self-defense and the killer was never charged. When another African American, Louis Allen, testified that he saw Lee murdered in cold blood, he was shot and killed in front of his home by two shotgun blasts to the head.[9]

In the ten other states of the old Confederacy, an average of only one in four African Americans was registered to vote in 1960. In Mississippi, where blacks represented 43 percent of the population, only one in twenty was registered to vote that year. Apologists for the "southern way of life" claimed the other 95 percent simply didn't want to bother. In fact, they had been excluded by a well-organized counterrevolution stretching back to 1890. In that year, a special state convention had repealed the lingering effects of Reconstruction by enacting, first, a tax on would-be voters (discouraging poor whites as well), and second, a requirement that voters be able to read and interpret the arcane language of the state constitution (a rule selectively waived for whites). Within two years, the number of registered blacks had fallen from 190,000 to fewer than 9,000. The state thereafter kept African Americans off the rolls with additional requirements that they be of "good moral character" in the estimate of white registrars, who found only a handful of cooperating black professionals and business leaders worthy of the vote. Those who tried to overcome these obstacles were fired from their job or evicted from their tenant farm. A rock through the window or a warning shot through the car door often followed. When they persisted nevertheless, Herbert Lee, Louis Adams, and Medgar Evers paid the ultimate price for their peaceful efforts to breach the color line.[10]

It was the gathering campaign to overturn this political bulwark of white supremacy that drew Goodman and others to Mississippi. By 1963 many activists had come to the conclusion that African Americans could not win equal access to jobs, public facilities, and social services unless they first won the right to vote for the local sheriff, the municipal judge, and the state and federal legislators who controlled public policy. The footing for such a campaign had already been established by the courageous work of Robert Moses, the lead organizer in Mississippi for the Student Nonviolent Coordinating Committee. Moses had spent most of his twenty-eight years in New York, a product of Stuyvesant High School and Harlem's public housing projects before earning a master's degree from Harvard and coming to Mississippi in 1961. Moses soon recognized that years of state-sanctioned terrorism made blacks understandably fearful about registering to vote or demanding entry to the Democratic Party's whites-only meetings. To demonstrate that African Americans wanted to vote, Moses and Allard Lowenstein, a white organizer from New York, came up with a symbolic alternative: a "Freedom Vote." Conducted at the same time as the official 1963 election, this unofficial canvass would register blacks in their own communities and tally their votes from a list that included Freedom candidates favoring racial integration and voting rights for all. An overwhelming majority of the eighty thousand African Americans who participated in the simulated election that fall voted for the Freedom slate's candidate for governor, Aaron Henry, state president of the NAACP and a longtime associate of the recently slain Medgar Evers.[11]

Thousands of blacks had proven they wanted the right to vote, and many among them were emboldened by the experience to demand the real thing. In 1964, they would join a bigger, more sustained campaign that Moses and Lowenstein called Freedom Summer. It would be a far more dangerous undertaking. To register for the vote, African Americans would have to leave the relative safety of their own communities and march to the center of town, where the police and the Klan would be waiting. White leaders were bound to retaliate against the movement, particularly when the Council of Federated Organizations (COFO)—the umbrella group in the state uniting SNCC, the Congress of Racial Equality, the Southern Christian Leadership Conference, and the NAACP—announced a separate slate of congressional candidates for the Democratic nomination. Organized as the Freedom Democratic Party (FDP), the ticket would offer blacks and sympathetic whites an alternative to the politics of white supremacy.

Moses and Lowenstein recognized that to stem the expected Klan violence, four groups were needed from outside the state: college students, the federal government, religious leaders, and sympathetic lawyers. Moses was frank about the role of college students, particularly whites from northern schools, in creating the kind of publicity that black victims of the Klan rarely generated. "These students bring the rest of the country with them," he observed. "They're from good schools and their parents are influential. The interest of the country is awakened, and when that happens, the government responds to that interest." The role of the national government was crucial, for only the federal courts and the Department of Justice could bring the rule of law—*constitutional* law—to Mississippi. Religious leaders, by their mere presence, might discourage retaliatory violence against the movement. And with the prospect of mass arrests and police harassment of COFO organizers, there would also be an acute need for lawyers who were on the scene and prepared to give immediate representation.[12]

Here, of course, was the rub. As Goodman and Crockett reported to the Guild's national executive board in November of 1963, their efforts over the past twenty months had made little progress in moving the legal profession toward active support of civil rights. "The conscience of some bars, including the ABA, may have been stirred, but the results have been meager." With so few lawyers available in Mississippi, the need for direct representation by northern attorneys could no longer be ignored.[13]

Two early meetings in New York City developed parallel—and initially compatible—responses to this growing need for legal representation. Both occurred on 10 November, just days after the symbolic Freedom Vote in Mississippi. At the first gathering on that autumn Sunday, Goodman and others active in the southern struggle met in the Manhattan offices of the American Civil Liberties Union to plan strategy for the coming year. Among the dozen lawyers in attendance were fellow Guild members Ben Smith and Bruce Waltzer, both fresh from their recent arrest at the Guild conference in New Orleans, as well as Arthur Kinoy and Michael Standard of New York. William Kunstler was also on hand along with Mel Wulf, legal director of the ACLU, and a collection of allied attorneys working with SNCC, CORE, and the NAACP. The focus of the gathering was a proposal for a new lawyers' organization to provide legal support for the expanding civil rights movement. There was general agreement that none of the participants wanted to compete with or take away from the existing work of the NAACP Legal Defense Fund. But several of those present were also convinced that "for historical or other reasons," as the minutes of the meeting reported, the LDF was "more disposed towards taking purely defensive action" than it was to the kind of "offensive action" favored by the Guild. Danville was frequently invoked as the appropriate model for legal strategy, including the use of rotating teams of volunteer lawyers working, wherever possible, with local counsel.[14]

The Guild's established record in developing this approach meant that it would play a pivotal role in the proposed organization, but with the added membership and resources of the ACLU and other liberal organizations, this augmented effort could take on the direct representation of protesters that had previously been beyond the Guild's reach. After a long discussion regarding the funding and feasibility of the proposal, the ACLU's lawyers indicated that, before assisting in the sponsorship of the new organization, they would consult with the NAACP Legal Defense Fund and the recently organized President's Committee regarding "the advisability of the entire project."[15]

The ACLU's minutes of the 10 November meeting gave no inkling of conflict or rancor in these discussions. In contrast, the meeting that same afternoon of the Guild's national executive board proved to be, by all accounts, an especially vituperative confrontation. This did not surprise Goodman. As he rode the uptown subway to the Summit Hotel on Lexington Avenue and Fifty-first Street, where the Guild executive board was to meet, he was acutely aware that this second gathering would be something of a brawl. A bitter debate had flared up between the Guild's two

biggest chapters, Detroit and New York, and the focal point of the controversy was Goodman's proposal to restructure the Guild and focus its
energies exclusively on the civil rights revolution in the South.

At stake were two distinctly different visions of what kind of bar association the Guild should be. The New York chapter, with its nearly three
hundred members, had long promoted a smorgasbord of committees and
round-table discussions on labor law, international law, immigration law,
criminal law, and finally, civil rights, but with no particular urgency or
activity attached to any one of these concerns. Many New York members
were active in the civil rights movement, but it was not an organizational
priority. The New York Guild was, in fact, overwhelmingly white, and
there was a perceived air of complacency in the national office, located in
lower Manhattan, about this and other matters. While Detroit and the
Committee for Legal Assistance in the South made the Guild relevant on
a previously unimaginable scale, the national office quietly consumed
more than two-thirds of the organization's income, with little to show for
it but position papers and publications. Resentment on this score had
flared when the New York office announced that the upcoming national
convention would be held at the Pierre Hotel, a luxurious facility on Fifth
Avenue overlooking Central Park. At a time when the Detroit chapter had
emptied its pockets to support the southern campaign, the Bourbon excess and apparent smugness of the New York chapter was more than
Goodman and his allies could accept. Their reaction, as he acknowledged
years later, tapped a streak of provincial exasperation with the long dominance of the New York Guild. "We felt that many very able New York chapter members looked down on us and we were not about to accept the view
that New York . . . had all the answers to the problems of society and the
Guild."[16]

Goodman and his fellow midwesterners arrived at the Summit Hotel
determined to take control of the national organization. The meeting was
well attended, with at least eighteen board members and officers from
New York and seven from Detroit, including Goodman, George Crockett,
Dean Robb, Harry Philo, Nate Conyers, and George Bedrosian. After preliminary reports and formalities, Goodman got down to brass tacks: the
Guild, he proposed, after finishing his report on current aid to the southern struggle, should trim the bloated budget of the national office and
direct the bulk of its dues and fund-raising to the support of a Guild office
in the South. Such an office could help address the growing needs of the
movement and could be supported with the joint cooperation of other
civil rights organizations. "The issue was one of priorities," as Goodman
later summarized the debate. "Since there weren't a hell of a lot of mem-

bers left and our financial position was highly precarious, there wasn't much left for other activities. All the Guild resources were necessary if we were to make an impact in the South."[17]

Goodman's presentation was typically evenhanded and careful to avoid inflaming the already polarized debate. His supporters were not so inclined. "They raised hell, the younger guys," he remembered years later, "and the language wasn't very nice either." Philo led off with a frontal attack on the national office, proposing not only a drastic cut in its budget, but its complete elimination for the next two to three years. New York members objected vigorously, led by their chapter president, Victor Rabinowitz. A Marxist and a past member of the CP-USA, Rabinowitz believed (as he later wrote to Goodman) that "all issues are interrelated," and it was therefore wrong to decouple civil rights from concerns with unemployment, imperialism, and disarmament. He was personally active in the civil rights movement, but in response to Philo's confrontational attack on the national office, Rabinowitz countered with the equally provocative claim that "civil rights organizations will have to learn to take care of their own problems."[18]

The Detroit delegation would have none of it. If the Guild could not aid the southern struggle, several Detroiters made clear, it was not worth sustaining. "The Guild does not have to continue," Nate Conyers bluntly put it, "if it is not dedicated to the needs of today. What programs are we planning that makes it necessary for the Guild to continue?" Why, in particular, he asked, did New York recruit so few African Americans? "Young lawyers and Negroes are demanding that we act in a situation that is vital to their existence." Crockett was not so inclined to question the very existence of the Guild, and he opposed Philo's demand that the national office simply be abolished. But like Conyers, he questioned the New York chapter's commitment to integrating its own ranks. "The Detroit chapter is growing because of activity," he pointed out, and there needed to be a comparable effort in the Guild's flagship chapter. "If we don't have a growing New York chapter, the Guild is simply a paper organization. We must have a revitalized New York chapter."

Goodman later regretted "some of the language" used by his younger colleagues, but the Detroit delegation was otherwise united behind the motion that the Guild make a strategic commitment to the civil rights movement that would continue "from now," as Goodman put it, "until we decide that some other emphasis should be made." New York had the votes to turn back this proposal, but it had no comparable unity of purpose. Several New Yorkers actually agreed with the provincial rebels. "As young lawyers we resent the top-heavy structure of the New York Guild," observed Betty Olenick Elder, one of only two women in the meeting. John Silverberg likewise sided with Goodman and the insurgents. "It is self-evident that there is today a social revolution and very obvious that the New York Guild has not become a part of it. We are," he added, "useless because we do not participate."[19]

After several hours of debate, Goodman's motion to make the civil rights struggle the "primary emphasis" of Guild activity won by a narrow 8-6 margin, the abstention of many New Yorkers eroding the potential majority that could have defeated the proposal. Philo's provocative motion to abolish the national office lost, 14-6. In addition, the New York convention was canceled, to be replaced by a no-frills "working conference" without banquet or keynote speaker. Given that Goodman's motion had won only a plurality on the total board, the executive board subsequently decided that the conference, scheduled for February of 1964, would give delegates the opportunity to decide the future direction of the Guild. The hosting chapter, appropriately enough, would be Detroit.

In the meantime, the gravity of the proposed undertaking in the South was underlined by the news from Dallas, Texas. On 22 November, less than two weeks after the meetings in New York, the assassination of President Kennedy revealed all of the fault lines that were widening so rapidly in the social upheaval of the early 1960s. Many initially assumed that Castro's Cuba was behind the killing, retaliating for the Kennedy administration's blockade of the island and its secret campaign, revealed later, to kill Cuba's leader. Others suspected organized crime or anti-Castro Cubans who condemned Kennedy for his temporizing role in the failed Bay of Pigs invasion. There were others, however, who believed that southern segregationists, infuriated by even the halfway measures of the Kennedy administration, had killed the president. These competing theories found advocates across the political spectrum, but there was little doubting that the reaction to the killing in the South differed from that in the rest of the country. "In schools across Mississippi," historian John Dittmer notes, "children cheered when they heard the news, reflecting the prejudices of their parents."[20]

Three months later, the Guild conference in Detroit debated Goodman's proposal to focus the organization's efforts on this very environment. The Detroit meeting was, of course, a different kind of gathering from the chandelier-and-crystal event New York had planned. Detroit's Henrose Hotel, in the shadow of Goodman's offices in the Cadillac Tower, was another of Detroit's faded testaments to the building boom of the 1920s. With the auto industry's collapse in 1929, the twenty-one-story Henrose had fallen on hard times and never really recovered, going through a sit-down strike in 1937 (when it was still the Barlum Hotel), a tax foreclosure, and five owners before the Teamsters' pension fund took over in 1963. The Guild certainly got better rates here than at the Pierre Hotel. There was less for delegates and spouses to do in Detroit's undersized downtown, but sightseeing wasn't on the agenda when the conference opened on 21 February, 1964.[21]

"The first (and almost the only) subject of discussion," Rabinowitz remembered, "was Guild work in the South." Goodman had to reassure his opponents that the Guild would remain a bar association and not become a civil rights group, and that concentration on the South was a strategic decision subject to reassessment, not a permanent redeployment. Above all, he stressed the importance of the work. The month before the conference, SNCC had publicly announced its plans for the voter registration drive in Mississippi. Hundreds of student volunteers would head south to join the campaign, and Goodman had learned from Dave Rynin, the Guild's executive secretary, that movement leaders "expect that a number of them will not come out alive"—a sobering and prophetic assessment. Organizers of the Mississippi campaign were calling upon the Guild for assistance, and with this direct appeal for help, the delegates swung behind Goodman's plan to provide legal representation for the campaign. "Ernie led the debate for the Detroit chapter," Rabinowitz recalled, "which seemed to be united in defending his views, and I presented the views of the New York chapter, which was not so united." In the end, "the debate was never a close one." The delegates not only endorsed Goodman's program but gave equally strong support to the proposal that the national office be moved from New York to Detroit.[22]

It was obvious by then who should be president. "I have been urged to become a candidate," Goodman wrote to a supporter before the convention. "My partners insist that if I really feel strongly about the future of the Guild I should be willing to undertake the responsibility of the office. . . . I can't in good conscience just say no." Benjamin Dreyfus had already signaled his willingness to step aside, despite his opposition to the Detroit program. "As you know," he had written Goodman in January, "there is one office at least that can have new personnel without any quarrel from the incumbent." Goodman immediately sent Dreyfus a note of apology. "Your letter," he wrote, "reminded me that we sometimes forget human beings in our concern about humanity. That is not one of your faults—but it is one of mine." Goodman reassured "Barney" that the Detroit chapter's criticism of the New York office did not reflect on Dreyfus, who lived in San Francisco and faced "insurmountable" problems of geography and finances in changing the status quo. For any unwitting suggestion to the contrary, Goodman hoped Dreyfus would "forgive my insensitivity." It was Goodman's attention to this kind of fence-mending and consideration for long-term friendships, as well as his keenness for meaningful action, that made him the consensus choice for president. The pivotal role of Detroit as instigator and host of the proceedings was further ratified in the choice of local members James Lafferty as executive secretary and Bernard Fieger as treasurer.[23]

Little of this escaped the attention of the FBI, which had placed an informant in the midst of the proceedings. Whether this mole was an agent playing the role of committed lawyer or a once-loyal member "turned" against the organization, the infiltrator attended every session of the conference and provided the FBI with an almost verbatim report on the proceedings, including Goodman's role. "The subject," the government spy reported, told the delegates "that he thought the NLG should advance 'the liberal human view'" and that he "wanted it done in the atmosphere of a bar association and not as a civil rights group." The FBI report went on to summarize Goodman's plans to open a southern office and to spend "the entire budget furthering the civil rights work in the South." Reading the informant's report years later, Goodman remarked that it "was not really a bad summarization." Unfortunately, it was made on behalf of a campaign to isolate and oppose the Guild's efforts.[24]

The bureau focused particular attention on the NLG's emerging alliance with SNCC and the dispute this ignited between the Guild and its liberal counterparts. Goodman had already gotten wind of the coming rift with his liberal allies the previous November, little more than a week after the meeting hosted by Melvin Wulf in the ACLU's Manhattan offices. "I received a disquieting phone call from New York yesterday," he wrote Ben Smith, "indicating that Mel Wulf is playing around with the idea of involving the President's Committee instead of [us] in the Southern law office project." At the conclusion of the New York meeting, Wulf and his ACLU colleagues had indicated they would explore the "advisability" of such a southern project with the President's Committee and the Legal Defense Fund, but it now appeared that they had explored instead the advisability of excluding the Guild altogether. If the Guild was to be shunted aside," Goodman had confided to Smith, "we should know as quickly as possible so that we can move ahead with our own project which," he now believed, "we can finance from our own sources." Liberals who already feared that SNCC was too closely aligned with the Guild's left-wingers would become all the more alarmed that winter when Victor Rabinowitz, president of his family's foundation, approved a grant of over $40,000 to finance SNCC's voter registration drive. Not long after,

Goodman met with SNCC leader Robert Moses to plan the details of their collaboration.[25]

Cold war condemnation of the Guild had been muted during the spring and early summer of 1963, when no other bar association challenged the ABA's indifference to the southern struggle. But the underlying distrust of radical organizations had been only temporarily hushed. Claudia Morcom (then Shropshire) had discovered just how deep these feelings of apprehension ran in her own hometown of Detroit when the Goodman firm offered her a job in 1960. The offer came more than three years after her graduation from Wayne State's law school and the start of her long search for any firm, black or white, willing to hire an African American woman. That Goodman and Crockett were the only ones willing to do so had been enough for Morcom, who otherwise knew little about the partnership except for the unusual fact that it was already integrated. She quickly learned more. "When it became known that I was going to join the firm, people would come up to my father and ask 'are you going to let her join that Communist firm?'" Her father, owner of a patent-medicine drugstore on Hastings Street, was Mississippi born. He was also an admirer of Marcus Garvey and Paul Robeson, and had taken his daughter to rallies in support of Willie McGee. "Well my father, bless his heart, he was my advocate for civil rights," and he strongly approved of the Goodman firm. But for this, the social opprobrium attached to Detroit's leading left-wing law firm might have dissuaded Morcom from becoming its first female associate.[26]

Allard Lowenstein, on the other hand, came to the unflinching conviction that SNCC's association with Goodman and the Guild, along with SNCC's stated admiration for the Cuban revolution, were further signs of Communist infiltration. When SNCC refused to disavow the Guild's support, Lowenstein urged students at Stanford (where he had been a dean) to withdraw as Freedom Summer volunteers; in one ill-tempered outburst, he reportedly told them that Bob Moses was "being run by Peking." Jack Greenberg of the NAACP Legal Defense Fund did not comment publicly on this fanciful claim that Moses and Goodman were agents of the Chinese Communists, but he opposed the Guild's participation in Freedom Summer out of fear that it would further inflame southern anti Communists. When SNCC turned to the Guild for help, Greenberg warned that the LDF would withdraw its support altogether. SNCC was unmoved by the threat, and Greenberg backed down. The LDF would continue to assist the umbrella group, the Council of Federated Organizations, but it would not represent SNCC organizers or work with Guild attorneys.[27]

To gain further distance from the Guild, Greenberg joined with Melvin Wulf and the American Civil Liberties Union in the winter of 1964 to form an alternative organization, the Lawyers Constitutional Defense Committee (LCDC). The LCDC's announced goal—to send volunteer lawyers to the South in rotating teams to provide representation for civil rights organizers—was precisely the mission contemplated at the meeting attended by Goodman the previous fall in New York. Joining the ACLU and the LDF in this truncated alliance was the Congress of Racial Equality, the American Jewish Congress, and the American Jewish Committee. Organizers in Mississippi welcomed their support, but credit for the sizable number of lawyers the LCDC would send south "must be given to the Guild," as Len Holt observed in his memoir of the summer campaign. It was clear to Goodman, at least, where Melvin Wulf got much of his inspiration.[28]

Although the Lawyers Constitutional Defense Committee was organized in part as a reaction to the Guild, its volunteers in Mississippi generally welcomed the Guild's participation. "As individuals down there, we got along fine," Goodman recalled. "These young lawyers, or law students, they weren't going to get into this kind of ideological struggle." Conditions on the ground wouldn't allow it. "When you got down there, you knew who the enemy was. It wasn't the Guild." Many of the LCDC's national leaders, on the other hand, were less sure of this, and some went to considerable lengths to dissociate themselves from the left-wing group. Much of this became evident only years later when FBI documents on the matter became public. One report described a meeting in Washington in the spring of 1964, shortly before Freedom Summer, at which several representatives of the LCDC's constituent organizations met with the FBI to express their concern with "the plans of the National Lawyers Guild to supply attorneys for civil rights demonstrators in the summer." Carl Rachlin, counsel for the Congress of Racial Equality, was particularly "perturbed," the report indicated, with Guild attorneys who "were trying to encroach on the role of CORE lawyers in defending civil rights demonstrators." Rachlin worried that many younger lawyers did not have sufficient experience in "opposing the Communists."[29]

As the lead organization in Mississippi, SNCC never wavered from an ecumenical policy that welcomed support from radicals as well as liberals. In this regard it was quite unlike the national office of the NAACP, led by Executive Director Roy Wilkins. Wilkins privately distrusted the militant leaders of Freedom Summer and quietly withheld staff and funds from the campaign. The NAACP's conservative middle-class base was isolated in Mississippi's urban enclaves and county seats, worlds away from the state's rural counties, especially in the Delta, where sharecroppers and workers predominated. SNCC organizers put down roots in many of these agricultural communities, where people like Fannie Lou Hamer found her light in the movement's rollicking mass meetings and group singing of civil rights songs. After she made the dangerous trek to the Sunflower County seat in 1962 to register to vote, her landlord had evicted her sharecropper family from the land they had cultivated for eighteen years. Hamer gladly accepted the help of any lawyer who came south to support the cause, and couldn't care less what group he or she came from. Neither did James Foreman, the Mississippi-born and Chicago-raised organizer who, with Moses, welcomed the alliance with the Guild. There was, he later recalled, "almost no one either willing or able to do the kind of aggressive legal work that needed to be done—except members of the Lawyers Guild."[30]

It was this "aggressive" legal work that would finally spur liberal lawyers to greater activity. That spring, Victor Rabinowitz relayed to Goodman the comments of a mutual friend, Hal Witt, that captured the Guild's galvanizing role. "I sat at a table with certain people from the President's Committee," Witt had written after attending a conference on civil liberties, "and was amused at how anxious they seemed to prevent the Guild from working in the South this summer. It almost looks as though you were supplying them with their principal motivation." Goaded into action by the Guild and by the dire circumstances on the ground, the President's Committee would provide legal representation that summer for the National Council of Churches, whose allied ministers and rabbis were an integral part of Freedom Summer. But the President's Committee was still reluctant to provide direct representation for civil rights workers and continued to focus primarily on behind-the-scenes lobbying of the southern bar. The Lawyers Constitutional Defense Committee was more forthcoming with direct support, sending a large contingent of lawyers south to provide legal representation.[31]

It was the Guild, however, that would send the first and the largest number of attorneys to Mississippi.

Gathering Forces

Mississippi was preparing to repel the "invasion." Government officials added two huundred men to the state police, acquired hundreds of new shotguns, and purchased an armored "battle wagon" to patrol the capital. The legislature enacted laws making it illegal to picket a public building or distribute flyers advocating a boycott. Another bill allowed public officials to transfer prisoners to the state penitentiary in Parchman in the event of "crowded and inadequate" facilities. A bill to "reform" the penitentiary permitted guards to whip troublesome prisoners.[32]

The Klan, meanwhile, escalated its terrorist activity, burning crosses in sixty-four counties on a single night in May. The Imperial Wizard of the Mississippi Klan, Sam Bowers, issued orders that "weapons and ammunition must be accumulated and stored; . . . maps, plans and information must be studied and learned; radios and communication must be established." This was precisely the sort of conspiracy the *Detroit News* and other media had attributed to the Communist Party fifteen years before. It had been a phantasm then; it was a deadly reality now, coming from the radical Right. State officials publicly distanced themselves from Klan violence and the adverse publicity it would bring, but they did nothing to prevent it. It was understood that the Klan, like the Black Legion in Goodman's younger days, had recruited a sizable following in state and local police forces. Even when the local sheriff was not a Klansman, he was usually in sympathy with the men who stalked civil rights activists across the state. To no one's surprise, there were no arrests in the winter and spring of 1964 for the escalating assaults that left at least five dead before Freedom Summer had even begun.[33]

Business leaders in the more upscale White Citizens Council favored economic coercion rather than overt violence, and their efforts had a particular bearing on Guild members. Mississippi placed special burdens on out-of-state lawyers, prohibiting their admission to state courts if any two local lawyers questioned their qualifications. Federal district courts in Mississippi could be even stricter, in some cases prohibiting out-of-state lawyers unless they were accompanied at all times by a local attorney. Any white lawyer who so assisted the movement could expect the Citizens Council to shun his services thereafter, and it was just this kind of boycott that contributed to the departure from the state of William Higgs, the first and for many months the only white lawyer in Mississippi who would represent protesters. Most Mississippi judges applied the law according to their personal prejudices; federal district judge Harold Cox, for one, waived the rules for *commercial* lawyers from out of state with the explanation that only "Jews and niggers from New York" had to comply.[34]

The federal appeals court in New Orleans would eventually put some constraints on Cox's discriminatory practices, but in state court it was the local members of the bar, not the judge, who had the power to move against out-of-state lawyers. Goodman wrote the Mississippi bar urging white lawyers to "begin to undertake their professional responsibilities" and provide representation to civil rights workers. "Perhaps the reality behind the system of justice in Mississippi," he wrote later that summer, "may best be understood by the fact that only one [white] lawyer . . . has responded to our direct written request to hundreds of lawyers in Mississippi." These entreaties may nevertheless have persuaded local attorneys to at least refrain from challenging the credentials of Guild attorneys. The lobbying of the President's Committee might have had more influence in this regard, but the end result, as Crockett later observed, was that "the Mississippi bar was in effect shamed into permitting us to come in and practice in Mississippi." Self-interest may also have played a role: local attorneys who challenged an out-of-state-lawyer's admission to state court might be expected to take the case. "We'd made it abundantly clear," Crockett remembered, that "if we don't do it, who is going to do it?"[35]

To do it effectively, the Guild opened a southern regional office in Jackson, Mississippi. For the job of running the new office, there were only two serious candidates, Len Holt and George Crockett. It could not have been an easy choice for Goodman. He had stayed in Holt's Virginia home, collaborated with him in the Guild's turn south, and clearly respected his friend's abilities. Holt had a unique talent for capturing the imagination of a crowd and moving it toward action. His humor and idiomatic style, no less than his singing and guitar playing, contributed to his reputation as the consummate charmer—the "Snake Doctor," as his friends knew him. It was hard not to return his affection. In their frequent correspondence, Holt occasionally closed his letters to Goodman with a heartfelt "God bless you!" and Goodman, in response, with a playful "Yours in Darrow." Goodman's sons had also come to know him. "Holt was the most charismatic lawyer and leader I've ever met," recalled Dick. In later years, he and his wife opened their Lafayette Park apartment to Holt when he stayed in Detroit. "As an orator, I would rank him nearly as high as Martin Luther King." Bill knew him at least as well after working with Holt in 1962 and living in his Virginia home. "People who were behind him would follow him over a cliff. I certainly was in that category."[36]

Some worried, however, that Holt was too prone to cliff jumping. While he drank and liked to party, these were not uncommon traits among his supporters (nor unknown to the Goodmans). More troubling was the perception, as Victor Rabinowitz put it, that Holt was "too quick to hop on any passing bandwagon that gave him an opportunity to exercise his considerable skills as a speaker." In Dick Goodman's recollection, Holt always dealt "very effectively and humanely" with whites, but he was also increasingly frustrated with liberals of any color, particularly those in the NAACP and the Kennedy-Johnson administration who were, in his view, slow moving and temporizing. Nearly twenty years younger than Crockett, Holt was also struggling to justify his continued commitment to nonviolence in the face of murderous—and usually unpunished—attacks on civil rights activists. In this frame of mind, the very spontaneity and emotive style that made him so appealing to a mass audience also made him a potential loose cannon in the political minefield of Mississippi, where an ill-considered word could trigger internal discord as well as external attack. There had already been occasions when Goodman and Crockett had taken him to task for his propensity to substitute his own judgment for agreed-upon procedures. "We are concerned about your issuance of public statements," Goodman had written Holt in 1962, "without some mutual discussion or agreement."[37]

The contrast between Holt and Crockett foreshadowed the generational conflicts to come. Unlike his younger colleague, Crockett had a personal demeanor that was measured and cautious, belying his radical credentials. He was in many ways a social conservative, Christian and nondoctrinaire in his political thinking. While Holt had left Norfolk, Virginia, and no longer had a base, Crockett had settled into Detroit and was developing ties with local labor and civil rights leaders. His lawyerly manner and steadier hand made him more effective with the black middle class, an attribute Holt was quick to recognize. "I shall never cease to be amazed," he wrote Goodman in 1962, "at the power that George can wield among the no-account, sterile Black Bourgeois. For him they do things. In humility ask I forgiveness for grossly underestimating the powers of the co-chairman." For Goodman, despite his fondness for Holt, the choice was obvious. In a job that would demand considerable courage, Crockett and Holt were equals. But when it came to the diplomatic skills that would be no less important, it was his law partner and longtime friend who clearly had the edge.[38]

The office Crockett opened in the late spring of 1964 was located on North Farish Street in Jackson's black business district, four blocks west of the state capitol. Housed on the second floor of a ramshackle building owned by a black physician, the Guild office shared the premises with the Medical Committee for Human Rights, another support group bringing volunteers south to aid the movement and its expected casualties. Three staff members soon arrived to work with Crockett: law students Michael Starr of Georgetown University and Cornelia McDougald of Harvard, joined by attorney Lawrence Warren, a law clerk for the Michigan Supreme Court. After a week's work building office cubicles and repainting the premises (supervised by master carpenter Crockett), the office opened for business on 9 June, less than two weeks before the arrival of the first student volunteers from the North.[39]

Segregationists and anti-Communists were united in their belief that the Guild's arrival in Jackson heralded subversive and revolutionary intent. In a sense they were correct. "They all got frightened," as Goodman commented years later. "'The Guild is going down there, they're going to overthrow the government.' Which of course we wanted to do, the kind of government they had down there, but not by violent means—by law, by applying the Constitution." The distinction in methods was lost on white supremacists.[40]

"I would be lying if I said I wasn't afraid when I first went down there," Crockett admitted years later. Called upon almost immediately to secure the release of a local civil rights worker arrested in Hattiesburg, Crockett asked himself ("trembling like I don't know what") how the arrival of a black attorney from Detroit would be received in the Piney Woods of Mississippi. It was his client's dire condition after only one night in jail that snapped Crockett out of this nervous state. "[He] took off his shirt to show me the welts across his back, how he'd been beaten." Crockett immediately filed a writ of habeas corpus to compel the government to show cause why the man was being held; the hearing judge, however, would not allow the prisoner to take off his shirt and submit evidence of his beating. The judge's explanation was a common subterfuge in the South: it was not the guards who had beaten the man, who was white, but other inmates who had taken offense at his "outrageous" ideas. "After that," Crockett remembered, "I wasn't afraid. Just angry."[41]

"I was terrified," recalled Don Loria, the first Guild volunteer to arrive at the Jackson office, just five days after its opening. Following a quick briefing with Crockett and Warren the night of his arrival, Loria and Charles Markels, vice president of the Chicago chapter, drove the next morning to the town of Meridian, eighty miles east, where thirty-five demonstrators had just been arrested for picketing the segregated business district. On their way to the Meridian courthouse, they met with the lead organizer in the area, Michael Schwerner, a twenty-four-year-old Cornell graduate from New York. Schwerner, who was Jewish, was teamed with his friend and fellow organizer James Chaney, a twenty one year-old African American born and raised in Meridian. Both were organizers for CORE, the lead organization in the Fourth Congressional District (SNCC took the lead in the four other districts). Both were about to leave for Ohio to help train student volunteers, but before departing, Schwerner gave Loria a brief recap of what had happened two days before, when Schwerner (with Larry Warren from the Guild office) had sent pickets downtown to protest whites-only lunch counters and discriminatory hiring. As the protesters had gotten out of their cars, the police had arrested the entire group for "obstructing the sidewalk."[42]

At the pretrial conference in the courthouse, Loria knew he was in a different world when the city attorney bluntly told him he could expect a "kangaroo" court. "It was a novel experience," Loria wrote in his journal, "to try a case and to be certain of the [negative] result beforehand." He soon discovered, however, that there was a compensating feature of this preordained outcome. In an "ordinary" setting, defense counsel might not want to antagonize the court by openly ridiculing a police officer on the witness stand, but here, with the verdict determined in advance, "we were completely free." For the African American audience packed into the courtroom, it was a rare and inspiring display as Loria and Markels— their courage growing—ignored the customary deference to white authority and openly challenged the court's sham proceedings. Loria's journal account focused particular attention on their cross-examination of the arresting officer, who had made the absurd claim that peaceful demonstrators smaller than himself were somehow blocking the sidewalk. "The officer, a tough, huge, 300 pound ex-marine," as Loria described him, "was asked if he obstructed the sidewalk by merely walking thereon. The Negro audience responded spontaneously and erupted with laughter." The judge, obviously not amused, convicted the twenty-five adults in the group. Even if they hadn't been a physical obstruction, he explained, they had violated "the spirit" of the ordinance.[43]

In the kind of mutual appreciation that lawyers and their clients would inspire in each other during the months that followed, Loria and Markels were deeply moved by the courage of the young African American protesters they represented. As the defendants were lined up in single file to leave the court at the end of the day, they began to sing "We Shall Overcome." It was a moment that more than compensated for the fact that, minutes later, when Loria and Markels left the courthouse, they found all the tires on their car deflated. Until they left Meridian the next day, an unmarked car followed them wherever they went.

"These lawyers," Goodman later wrote of the Guild's volunteers, "went, learned, experienced the terror that existed there, the difficulties of obtaining the most elementary justice, and came back as converts. They became fighters for the cause and wanted to do more." Loria may not have needed additional motivation, for as president of the Detroit Guild he was already immersed in the fund-raising and recruitment of volunteers that preceded the campaign. On "Law Day" (the usually staid observance created in the 1950s, at the ABA's urging, to preempt left-wing celebrations on May Day) the Detroit Guild had made a special effort to focus attention on the upcoming Freedom Summer. "Many lawyers," Goodman wrote Father Robert Drinan, dean of the Boston College Law School, "collected money through canisters at building entrances." It was a novel undertaking for attorneys who did not customarily collect money with a coin can. Aided by a mail solicitation endorsed by Harold Cranefield, Damon Keith, former governor John Swainson, and other leaders of the Michigan bar, the take on Law Day topped $2,000. Detroit's Cotillion Club, an organization of black professionals organized in 1949 to advance the civil rights struggle, pitched in another $1,000. With expenses for the Farish Street office fluctuating between $1,400 and $2,000 a month, this start-up money was enough to keep the Guild's Mississippi operation in business through the first half of the summer, with Crockett and his small staff coordinating the work of 125 volunteer lawyers. Half of this number were pledged to forty hours of pro bono labor writing briefs and pleadings, the other half to one-week stints in Mississippi (starting with Loria and Markels) providing direct representation.[44]

Goodman's FBI file was growing all the while, the bureau's Detroit office paying particular attention to media accounts of his role in Freedom Summer. A *Detroit News* story (23 April), "Peace Corps of Lawyers for Dixie," quoted Goodman's observation that Guild members were "professionally and personally united to the defense of civil rights and liberties for all people"; a *Michigan Chronicle* photo (20 June) showed Dr. Alegro Godley, a black physician (and, the FBI noted, a member of "Wallace Progressives" in 1948), presenting Goodman with a check for $250 to support the Mississippi project; a report from Los Angeles alerted the Detroit FBI that Goodman was the featured guest on radio station KPFK speaking on "Lawyers for Mississippi." These and other clippings were embellished by reports of a bizarre death threat. "The Bolshevik Brigade of the Communist Party" had issued a broadside in May that denounced Goodman and fifteen other Detroiters as "revolutionary traitors" slated for execution within the next eighteen months. Fellow Guild leaders Crockett, Robb, and Bernie Fieger were on the death list, along with Guy Nunn, the UAW radio host. The FBI's Detroit bureau reported that the police had interviewed Goodman on the matter and that he dismissed the flyer as the work of a right-wing group. There was, in fact, no record of any so-called Bolshevik Brigade. "Goodman," the report concluded, "did not desire police protection."[45]

Freedom Summer

Late on Saturday afternoon, 20 June, George Crockett received a phone call from Michael Schwerner, just returned to Meridian from the training program in Ohio. Schwerner and fellow organizer James Chaney had made the sixteen-hour drive back to Mississippi in haste, accompanied by one of the first student volunteers, twenty-year-old Andrew Goodman from New York. While they had been in Ohio, Klansmen had burned the Mount Zion Methodist Church near the town of Philadelphia, Mississippi, and assaulted members of the congregation, punishing them for their anticipated participation in Freedom Summer. Schwerner had met with church leaders the month before and won their commitment to host a Freedom School. Feeling an urgent need to "do something" on their behalf, he now called Crockett in Jackson for advice.

> He wanted to know was there any legal recourse for that type of situation. And I explained to him that it might be possible to get some sort of federal proceeding going but we'd have to have more information, and we'd have to have witnesses when we go into court. He said, "Well, we will go over to Philadelphia tomorrow morning, Sunday, and see some of the people who've been at the Freedom Schools and who attended these churches." I said, "All right, you do that and we will come over to Meridian and talk with you on Monday morning."[46]

The rest of the story is history, the sad tale of the murder of Schwerner, Chaney, and Andrew Goodman by the Ku Klux Klan. As one of the iconic events of the southern struggle, it is a story that has been told often enough, but rarely with attention to the role of the Lawyers Guild. Schwerner, Chaney, and Goodman would have gone to Philadelphia that Sunday even if Schwerner had not talked with George Crockett. But it was Crockett who helped give that trip a mission, a goal that would link it to the possibility of fighting back, of bringing a civil rights suit against the arsonists who had burned the church.[47]

When the three did not return from Philadelphia that Sunday, Crockett was among the first to organize a search. After assigning Guild volunteers to investigate at several points between Meridian and the charred remains of the Mount Zion Church, he led a small team to the heart of Neshoba County on Monday, 22 June, for a meeting with Sheriff Lawrence Rainey. Accompanying him was Anna Diggs, another of the Guild volunteers, who had arrived earlier that day from Detroit with Claudia Morcom. The two African American women (and future judges) were immediately thrown into the deep end of the struggle, Morcom going to Parchmon penitentiary to seek the release of a prisoner, Diggs leaving for Philadelphia with Crockett and two others. Organizers from the Council of Federated Organizations had already learned from calls to the jailer's wife that the three men had been arrested the day before and released Sunday night. In addition to Sheriff Rainey, among those now confronting Crockett and Diggs in the sheriff's office was Deputy Cecil Price, the man who, it was later confirmed, had conspired with Rainey to rearrest the three on a highway south of Philadelphia and turn them over to the Klan. "Rainey and his men denied any knowledge of anything," Diggs recalled. "Their denials were given loud support by a crowd which came to the jail and pressed close around us." Crockett told Rainey that they wanted to investigate the ruins of the burned church. "He proceeded to give us detailed instructions on how to go," Crockett remembered, "where to turn and so forth and so forth." He thanked the sheriff and led his small group back to the car, jeered by the crowd that followed. "Crockett whispered that whatever Rainey had told us," Diggs remembered, "we had to do the opposite." Crockett immediately turned the car back to Meridian, ignoring Rainey's instructions. "The sheriff wasn't talking to me, he wasn't talking to any of us. He was talking to that crowd behind him, telling them exactly which route we were going to take."[48]

Crockett's worst fears regarding the missing activists were confirmed the next day when the FBI found the burned-out remains of Schwerner's station wagon. President Johnson immediately ordered federal officials to mount an intensive search for the bodies. "We all know," said Rita Schwerner in a public statement, "that this search . . . is because Andrew Goodman and my husband are white. If only Chaney was involved, nothing would've been done." This bleak assessment was borne out in the weeks that followed as the massive search recovered three bodies from Mississippi's bayous and rivers. All three were African American males, one wearing a CORE T-shirt. All of them had gone missing that spring; all of them had been bound and beaten to death; none of them had been known to the outside world until the events in Neshoba County.[49]

Ernie Goodman was one among many who called again on the federal government to protect civil rights workers in Mississippi. Noting that the attorney general had reiterated his opinion that the federal government had no power to take preventive police action, Goodman wrote to President Johnson in mid-July to argue that existing law already provided for government intervention "to overcome systematic resistance to the execution of federal law or the exercise of federally protected rights." To avoid the extreme measures that might become necessary if the situation deteriorated further—that is, Goodman said, "the use of federal troops to take over the administration of the State of Mississippi"—he urged Johnson to send additional federal judges to the state. "The present complement of *three* district judges is obviously inadequate," he argued, without belaboring the fact that obstructionist rulings by Judges Cox and Sidney Mize left only Judge Claude Clayton as a sometime protector of the Constitution.[50]

The president and Congress would eventually add two judgeships in Mississippi, but this action was taken on the recommendations of the Judicial Conference of the United States, not the Guild. Goodman's recommendations carried little weight with the Johnson administration, which was still making every effort to separate the Guild from the Freedom Summer campaign. "We find it unpardonable that you would work with them," Arthur Schlesinger told SNCC leaders Bob Moses and James Foreman in a midsummer meeting arranged by Burke Marshall, the assistant attorney general. "Bob Moses and Burke Marshall had a hot exchange" on this point, recalled Foreman, especially when Moses contrasted the Guild's work with "the unwillingness of the Justice Department and the NAACP Legal Defense Fund to take aggressive legal action in Mississippi."[51]

With an eye to his reelection, President Johnson declined to send federal marshals to Mississippi and tried, instead, to placate southern white Democrats who were threatening to bolt the party. As a less obtrusive form of intervention, he had already ordered Hoover to establish a massive FBI presence in the state. When Hoover objected, Johnson made it clear that "we want to avoid the marshals thing and the troops thing. . . . Maybe we can prevent more acts of terror by the very presence of your people." By the end of the summer Hoover had finally established an FBI office in Jackson, had assigned more than 150 agents to the state, and had given the governor a list of known Klansmen serving on the state police force. Under intense scrutiny from the national (and now international) media, the governor ordered them fired. Hoover, however, still insisted that the FBI was solely an investigative agency. "We most certainly do not and will not give protection to civil rights workers."[52]

The students, ministers, rabbis, and lawyers who had pledged to go south could not have found Hoover's words very reassuring. Nor could they have been comforted by the public statements of Senator Eastland, Governor Paul Johnson, or the editorial writers of the *Jackson Clarion-Ledger*, all of whom speculated that the disappearance of Schwerner, Chaney, and Goodman was a hoax organized by the Communist Party to embarrass the state. The FBI's subsequent discovery of the bodies of the three men buried in an earthen dam had no discernible effect on East-land's penchant for red-baiting. He would subsequently read long reports into the *Congressional Record* denouncing Ernie Goodman, George Crockett, Ben Dreyfus, and the other "legal carpetbaggers" in the Guild for "capitalizing on racial unrest to create violence and bloodshed." Eastland singled out Goodman for being "reportedly" active in Communist-related activities from 1940 to 1964, for being "reportedly" held in the high es-teem of Communist Party leaders, and for being a well-known defense attorney in the Smith Act trials. The senator scorned the "Mississippi invaders," seventy in all, that Goodman and the Guild had recruited for Freedom Summer. He listed them by name and quoted from the Guild's own report on the group, which quantified the number of African Ameri-cans (fourteen), women (eight), non-Guild members (twelve), and the dis-proportionate number from Michigan (twenty-three) and Detroit (fifteen) compared to California (twelve), Chicago (twelve), and New York City (nine). "This is not a complete list of the Mississippi invaders recruited by the National Lawyers Guild," Eastland noted, "but it helps build the re-cord." What the Guild reported as a point of pride, the senator presented as an indictment.[53]

The story of the campaign these attorneys joined is a well-chronicled tale of heroism and perseverance. The summer's achievements were im-pressive enough: more than sixty thousand people recruited into the Free-dom Democratic Party (FDP); scores of precinct and district meetings held for the FDP across the state; fifty Freedom Schools organized for over twenty-five hundred students; and seventeen thousand African American adults mobilized to go to the local courthouse and attempt to register. The violent backlash from white supremacists was breathtaking: thirty-five shooting incidents, eighty activists beaten, thirty homes and other buildings bombed, thirty-five churches burned to the ground, and roughly one thousand movement people arrested. Estimates of the number killed over the spring and summer ranged from six to fifteen, depending on how closely the victims were linked to Freedom Summer.[54]

The daily tally of Klan violence and police harassment that the Coun-cil of Federated Organizations kept from mid-June through August was a chilling inventory of lawless aggression conducted under the color of law. On the single day of 26 June, for example, fifteen voter registration work-ers were detained by the police in four counties for "leafleting without a permit," illegal parking, or "disturbing the peace"; a church in Clinton County was also firebombed, tires were slashed in Marshall County, and an organizer was beaten in his jail cell in Hinds County. On 4 August, sixty-two were arrested in Jackson County during a voter registration meeting for "breach of the peace"; an LCDC lawyer was beaten by a city marshal in Marks; thirteen were arrested in Bolivar County for leafleting in violation of an "antilittering" ordinance; and a volunteer was shot at in Jackson. On 15 August, a volunteer in Jackson was hospitalized after being beaten over the head with a baseball bat, and four crosses were burned in the city, one of them in front of the Sun 'n' Sand Motel, where project lawyers, ministers, and correspondents stayed; that same day, gunshots were fired at volunteers in their cars in Jackson and Meridian, an activist was shot in the face in Greenwood, and four volunteers were beaten with baseball bats in Laurel when they entered a department store cafeteria. The presence of FBI agents may have discouraged violence in some locations, but local activists discounted the deterrent effect. "The relative paucity of violence in some communities," historian Clayborne Carson wrote, "was attributed by SNCC workers not to the federal presence but to the willingness of blacks to arm themselves."[55]

Goodman and Crockett urged Guild volunteers heading to Mississippi to remember that if they wanted to work effectively as lawyers in this brutal environment, they were far more valuable to the movement as disciplined members of the bar than they were as protesters in the streets or hell-raisers in the courtroom. They were to monitor police actions and provide a spirited—but professional—defense for those arrested. "We had to tell the people that went down south," as Goodman recalled, "that their job was not to come down there to go to prison, [but] to get people out of prison." Much of this involved the kind of nickel-and-dime legal work that normally would seem routine and dull—defending people charged with traffic violations or petty misdemeanors. But Sheriff Rainey had used such minor charges to detain Schwerner, Chaney, and Goodman until a lynch mob could be assembled, and in this context, even the simple filing of a removal petition to transfer a case from state to federal courts was an urgent matter.[56]

Like soldiers on guard duty, Guild volunteers alternated between moments of tense confrontation and periods of relative calm, the whole of it bracketed by an underlying anxiety. "We were required to call into the Guild office every half hour while we were in the field," recalled Myzell Sowell of the measures taken to ensure a quick response to another abduction. This was not the only reminder of the dangers a black lawyer from Detroit might face in Meridian, Mississippi. "I remember being particularly conscious of the fact," Sowell remembered, "that I was, most often, traveling by car with white female students in the deep South at a time when racial conventions were being violently changed." Robert Stein, a white lawyer from Detroit, described his stint in Greenwood as

"5 days scared out of my wits." His fear gave way to a puckish anger, however, when confronted by the blatant disregard for due process in Mississippi's courts. Defending SNCC organizers arrested for trumped-up traffic violations, Stein was immediately challenged by the judge's belligerent inquiry whether he was a Communist. "I said to the judge, 'Your honor, I am not now, nor have I ever been, nor will I ever be a Communist.' I paused, then asked the judge, 'Are you a member of the Ku Klux Klan?' You could have heard a pin drop." Stein probably found little comfort in the judge's response that, no, he was a member of the White Citizens Council.[57]

Concern for the safety of the Guild's volunteers grew in late July when the Mississippi legislature appointed a committee to investigate the role of Communists in the civil rights movement. Lawyers in particular were being singled out, with subpoenas anticipated against likely prospects. "Under these circumstances," Goodman wrote to John Caughlan, a Seattle attorney who had joined the CP-USA in the 1930s, "we feel that you should reconsider your planned trip." The Guild had already recruited enough volunteers, and given Caughlan's long history of defending victims of the Red Scare in the 1940s and 1950s, Goodman cautioned, "they might let the boom down on you." Caughlan went to Mississippi anyway and this particular danger passed, but the fear of violent assault remained. Allen Zemmol and Roger Craig, two Detroit attorneys assigned to Greenwood, relied on a frequently used technique for dissuading potential attackers. Confronted on the courthouse steps by six men with blackjacks shortly before the arrival of SNCC organizer Stokely Carmichael and a group attempting to register, Zemmol and Craig folded their arms and, with their short haircuts and dark suits and ties, tried to intimidate the intimidators. "I told Roger," Zemmol recalled, "to pull up his tie, act like he owned the town and tell them he was under orders not to reveal his name. . . . We looked tough enough, just long enough, to have left the impression that we might be FBI agents."[58]

These moments of high anxiety were often followed by stretches of relative inactivity, as Oscar Baker, a black attorney from Bay City, Michigan, reported on his return from Hattiesburg. "The area was quiet so far as police activity or trouble involving the students," he wrote in late July. Acknowledging that he had violated the recommendations of Goodman and Crockett concerning his role as a lawyer, Baker joined the student canvassers on their home visits to recruit African Americans to register to vote. "It was satisfying to see the appreciation of the people for the interest and help. . . . As one lady put it, 'I never thought to see the day when things like this would happen in Mississippi.'" He was happy to find students at the Freedom School who were "intelligent and militant about not following the old practices of having faith in the Lord and letting things go as they will." Many adults were also becoming more assertive in defending their rights. When black attorney Carsie Hall invited Baker to return to Mississippi in the future and go hunting, Baker responded that he'd never stalked game before. "Well," Hall responded, "you will feel a lot better with a gun in your hands around here, won't you."[59]

As Baker's experience suggests, legal work and courtroom representation did not always fill the time of Guild volunteers in Mississippi. Having heard that others who had gone south "had not had their services fully utilized," Fay Stender of San Francisco wrote Goodman and Crockett in late July wondering if it was worthwhile for her to go. In reply, Goodman acknowledged that "not all of the lawyers who have gone to Mississippi have been busy every moment of every day," but their presence was still valuable to the movement. "They have all been able to do useful, sometimes important work. Their presence in key centers around the state has been a big morale booster for the COFO workers and the local people, as well as a deterrent for the authorities." There was, in fact, a lot of work to keep Stender busy when she arrived in Jackson that August, including the drafting of briefs in opposition to the state's motion to send twenty-five cases from federal court back to state court. With passage of the Civil Rights Act that summer, the law had been changed to permit appeal of a federal judge's order sending a case back to the state court, and Crockett wrote Goodman that Stender "has done a fine job in preparing a basic reply memorandum and motion for hearing."[60]

It was still Goodman's hope that local attorneys could take on some of this work, and he was encouraged by the apparent change of heart in the Mississippi bar when its Board of Commissioners passed a resolution in July favoring legal representation for all persons, "popular or unpopular, respected or despised, and regardless of race." Goodman wrote the state bar to express his view that, if the resolution were acted on, such a change in course "may enable us to withdraw our commitment" and leave the field to Mississippi lawyers. By August, however, it was obvious that the state bar had no intention of acting on the July resolution, which was intended for media consumption only. After the departure of William Higgs, the only white lawyer from Mississippi who would defend civil rights workers was Len Rosenthal—and his landlord promptly ordered him to vacate his Jackson office. Goodman vented his disappointment with mainstream attorneys in a letter to the American Bar Association:

If the bar of our country is to give more than lip service to the concept of "equal justice under law"; if it is to take seriously the belief that social change can occur without violence only where aggrieved people have available a ready and friendly forum for the judicial enforcement of their legal rights; then American lawyers must undertake to act now and effectively make justice available to every person in Mississippi and other areas in the South where justice is not "equal" and where the judicial system, with rare exceptions, cannot or will not vindicate the rights of the Negro people.[61]

Digging In

The rights of African Americans, denied for three centuries, could not be vindicated in a single summer. The movement would have to dig in for a prolonged campaign.

The summer's efforts had made a difference, setting in motion an irreversible process of social change. But this unprecedented challenge to white supremacy in the Deep South had also inspired white resistance. Some seventeen thousand African Americans had braved the odds and marched to the courthouse to fill out voter registration forms, but in the end, local officials allowed only sixteen hundred names—fewer than one in ten—to actually go on Mississippi's voter rolls. The federal government sent FBI agents south and Congress passed a Civil Rights Act that dramatically widened the avenues for legal action against discrimination. But in the meantime, the Department of Justice limited itself to a piecemeal strategy focused on correcting "patterns" of voter discrimination while avoiding the prosecution of local officials who used intimidation and violence to discourage would-be voters. For the Kennedy-Johnson administration, the problem with such an aggressive strategy, as historian Taylor Branch notes, was that it might succeed in sending those officials to jail, "causing a vacuum of public order that the U.S. government might be obliged to fill with soldiers and bureaucrats in numbers not seen since Reconstruction."[62]

To avoid such revolutionary measures, the Johnson administration chose to placate Mississippi's Democrats. The state's "Regular" Democratic Party had forcibly excluded blacks and refused to even endorse the national party's civil rights platform, yet President Johnson went to extraordinary lengths to seat the Regulars that August at the Democratic Party convention in Atlantic City. The Freedom Democratic Party sent its own delegation to Atlantic City, led by Fannie Lou Hamer and Aaron Henry, to claim its place on the convention floor as the only organization in Mississippi pledged to support the national party's candidates and platform. A compromise proposal allowing two FDP representatives to serve as "at-large" delegates was rejected by both sides. Even when the Regulars refused to pledge their loyalty to the party and withdrew from the convention, the FDP delegates were physically barred from taking their place.

In hindsight, it is hard to imagine how President Johnson could have believed there was the remotest chance of winning a majority of white votes in the Deep South in 1964, short of his renouncing the Emancipation Proclamation. Even running against the overmatched Barry Goldwater, the far-right nominee of the Republican Party, Johnson had difficulty shaking the long-held belief that Democratic Party success depended on the precarious unity of the Solid South's white segregationists with the industrial North's urban-based ethnics and liberals. He was well aware that his personal commitment to pushing civil rights legislation was a major contributor to the dissolution of this improbable coalition, and he probably hoped that stiff-arming the FDP as well as the Regulars would avoid a breach with white Democrats in the upper South and border states. Goldwater, in fact, would win majorities that November in Mississippi, Louisiana, Alabama, Georgia, South Carolina—and nowhere else except his home state of Arizona. Johnson's victory was the most lopsided (61 percent of the popular vote) in American history to that moment, yet he had fretted about the outcome from Atlantic City to the general election. So had many of his liberal supporters, some of them convinced that the black vote for Johnson might have been jeopardized by the public spectacle of Fannie Lou Hamer being turned away at the convention. For this they blamed SNCC and its left-wing ally, the National Lawyers Guild.

Liberal anger on this score was evident at a high-level meeting in September hosted by the National Council of Churches in New York, where representatives of the NAACP and prominent white liberals served notice that the tenuous coalition of civil rights groups in Mississippi was nearing its end. Moses and Foreman were not present—they and other SNCC leaders had accepted an invitation to visit Africa—and there was no representative from the Guild to parry the comments of Joe Rauh, Washington counsel for Walter Reuther and the UAW, who said point-blank that he "would like to drive out the Lawyers Guild" and that it was "immoral to take help from communists." Rauh had served as counsel for the Freedom Democratic Party at the Atlantic City convention and had been hesitant to accept the compromise giving them only two at-large seats. It was his boss and personal friend, Walter Reuther, who had threatened to fire him if he didn't close ranks with the president's clumsy attempt to impose party unity from above.[63]

The Guild was a handy scapegoat for Rauh's disappointment, and he now insisted that Goodman and his fellow "Communists" were a liability for the movement. Al Lowenstein joined him in this appraisal, though the onetime ally of Robert Moses and SNCC at least recognized that local organizers and activists should have a say in whether Guild lawyers continued to represent the Council of Federated Organizations. Gloster Current of the NAACP, in contrast, showed little concern for the "Tom, Dick, and Harrys" at the "grass roots," as he put it. "The NAACP is a disciplined army," he said by way of metaphor. "No decision is made on the lower levels without authorization from the top," and the top leaders of the NAACP did not trust the Guild. Courtland Cox, representing SNCC in the absence of Moses and Foreman, insisted that "people on the scene" should make the decisions within COFO, and that "it so happens that most of the people on the scene are SNCC people." Anna Hedgeman, representing the National Council of Churches, and Andrew Young both tried to defuse the conflict by proposing a second meeting with Moses and Foreman (Hedgeman even offering "a good word" for the Lawyers Guild). But that fall the national NAACP, which had contributed little to COFO in the first place, persuaded its Mississippi affiliate to officially withdraw support, and Moses resigned as COFO director before the end of the year. Organizing would continue, but it would now be pushed forward by groups that were united in name only.[64]

The most important of these continuing efforts was the Freedom Democratic Party's campaign to prevent the Mississippi congressional delegation from taking its seats in the U.S. House of Representatives. Here again the Guild, led by Goodman and Arthur Kinoy, would play a crucial role. Following the Atlantic City convention, the FDP had fired Rauh as chief counsel and replaced him with a triumvirate of Kinoy (the Guild's vice president), Ben Smith (now cochairman of the Guild's southern campaign following Goodman's elevation to president), and William Kunstler. Anticipating that the Regular Democrats would win the official—and effectively whites-only—election to the U.S. House of Representatives that November, FDP leaders wanted to challenge the legitimacy of the outcome. Kinoy found the vehicle for doing so in an obscure federal statute dating from the Reconstruction era. The law would allow the FDP to serve formal notice of its challenge on the clerk of the U.S. House and then, armed with federal subpoena power, collect depositions on the forcible exclusion of black voters. The Guild would provide lawyers to collect sworn testimony, and it was this anticipated role that persuaded Goodman and Crockett to reopen the Jackson office after a brief shutdown at the end of the summer.[65]

Crockett would no longer staff the Jackson operation, however. His steady leadership and unruffled manner, along with the impeccable white

suit and Panama hat he wore on many occasions, had become the trade-
mark of the Guild's presence in Mississippi. But by the fall of 1964,
Goodman's law partner and friend was worn out. The stress of the summer campaign had taken its toll and the mounting tension and organizational chaos in the COFO office added further exasperation. In August,
Crockett wrote Goodman that the lack of effective coordination and communication from the COFO office made him "downright sore" and he
was afraid he had vented his anger on COFO staffer Hunter Morey. "I
told him that the Guild (and I) were damn fed up with being treated like
step-children whose efforts during the summer seems hardly to have been
noticed, let alone appreciated by the top COFO leadership." In a further
comment that would have surprised Jack Greenberg and the leaders of the
NAACP, Crockett anticipated that COFO's leaders would not ask the Guild
for continuing assistance because of their "subservience" to the Legal
Defense Fund. Crockett was wrong on this score, and both the Guild and
the LCDC would be asked to continue their Mississippi operations. But his
legendary patience was clearly wearing thin, and the prolonged absence
from Detroit weighed heavily on his thinking. At around the same time that
he was expressing his frustrations to Goodman, he wrote another colleague
coming to Jackson that his presence would be welcome "if only for the sake
of stimulating companionship in this 'hell-hole.'"[66]

In casting about for a replacement, Goodman and Crockett went
no further than their immediate circle of allied lawyers in Detroit. One
obvious candidate was fellow law partner Robert Millender. As an African American lawyer and a gifted political strategist, he would be a natural choice for leadership in one of the most important campaigns of the
black liberation struggle. But these qualities also made him indispensable
in Detroit, where he had already established himself as a preeminent coalition builder. Joining with UAW leaders Horace Sheffield and Buddy
Battle, the cofounders of the Trade Union Leadership Council (TULC),
Millender had served as chief counsel in campaigns to integrate jobs and
promote black leadership in the city's unions. In the 1961 mayoral election,
amid charges of police brutality against African Americans, Millender had
helped guide the get-out-the-vote campaign that carried the Irish Catholic
challenger, Jerome Cavanaugh, to victory over incumbent Louis Miriani.
Millender had gone from there to become the campaign manager for
Guild member John Conyers in his 1964 bid to win election to Congress.
Goodman and Crockett could not ask him to abandon these commitments
in mid stride.[67]

The next-best alternative was equally close at hand. Claudia Shropshire Morcom did not have the political savvy and experience of Millender,

but she was well suited to the job on her own merits. Her parents came from Mississippi and still had family and land in the state. She had already spent a week in Jackson and Greenwood during Freedom Summer and knew the dangers firsthand—a small-caliber bullet had cracked the windshield of her car and a firebomb later damaged the house where she and Anna Diggs had stayed. She was personable and hard working, and Goodman trusted her abilities after working with her on several criminal cases. Morcom had also gained a modest notoriety after *Jet* magazine featured her and Diggs in a cover story, "Women Lawyers to Aid Mississippi 'Freedom Corps.'" Pictured with Goodman in the firm's offices before her departure, Morcom was described in terms reserved for women professionals—a "chic divorcee" of thirty-one years "combining beauty and brains." There was no stereotyping of her role within the Goodman firm, however. In the few other law firms that hired women, they "traditionally just did the domestic work and maybe had some probate," as Morcom recalled. "But I did everything. . . . I did criminal law and I did tort cases."[68]

Like Crockett, Morcom would continue to draw pay from the Goodman firm during her work in Mississippi, a salary that in her case (as an associate) came to something less than $100 a week, as she recalled, plus rent and car expenses. Goodman would also take over her pending cases while she worked in the Jackson office. The rented house she settled into that November was anything but "chic." "I lived in Tougaloo, right across the railroad tracks from Tougaloo College, in a little two-and-half bedroom home . . . [that] had slat floors, and the mice and little bugs would come up." It was a ten-mile drive to the Farish Street office in the old station wagon she used to transport the volunteer lawyers (nearly a dozen arriving in her first months on the job) who came to help with the substantial docket she inherited from the summer campaign: forty-five cases on file with 315 defendants, plus twenty-four new cases added since her arrival, the defendants charged with everything from distributing leaflets without a permit to trespass to assault with a deadly weapon. With no regular schedule of volunteer arrivals, as during the summer, Morcom at times had to call Detroit and beg for additional help. "I called Ernie and it was a holiday, it was like a Monday, and I called up the firm and he was the only one there. And so I said, 'Ernie, I got trouble, I got all these people in jail and I don't have any lawyers. . . .' So Ernie . . . calls Damon Keith's office and that's where Mike Wahls was at the time, and Mike came down." Wahls (a future judge, like Keith and Morcom) joined the lengthening list of Guild volunteers who made their way to Mississippi that fall and winter. The neighbor lady who cleaned Morcom's house thought she was running a brothel, Morcom remembered, "because all these men, white and black were coming there."[69]

The number arriving spiked dramatically in January of the new year with the opening of the newly elected Congress and the simultaneous effort by the Freedom Democratic Party to block the seating of Mississippi's House delegation. In a historic moment on 4 January 1965, Congressman William Fitts Ryan of New York City (whose constituents included the parents of Andrew Goodman) rose during the swearing-in of members and objected to the seating of the Mississippi delegation. He was seconded by California's representative James Roosevelt, son of the late president, who urged his fellow congressmen to send a message that Mississippi's segregationists "cannot win 'elections' from a system based on murder and then claim the right to govern free men." Hoping that a few dozen congressmen would support Ryan and Roosevelt, the FDP members crowded into the House gallery were stunned when 149 House members (including the newly elected John Conyers) voted to prevent the seating of Mississippi's five representatives. A majority of 276 voted to swear them in, but the House leadership agreed to submit the contested election to the hearing process provided for in the statute Kinoy had unearthed.[70]

Goodman had already sent out the call in late December for volunteers who would go south to collect depositions from "Freedom Fighters and county officials," as he put it (the latter subpoenaed to cooperate). "We will do everything to help," he wrote Kinoy, though "financial considerations will be something of a barrier at this time." The Guild, in fact, was out of money and unable to pay travel expenses for those who responded to the call. More than 150 lawyers volunteered anyway, half of them from California and most of the rest from New York, Michigan, and Illinois. Many made their way to the FDP's Jackson offices on Farish Street, across the hall from the Guild, where Morcom and FDP attorney Morton Stavis (a Guild member from New Jersey) coordinated the intensive six-week campaign that collected depositions from more than four hundred African Americans. Goodman and Crockett, meanwhile, coordinated the collection of depositions from student volunteers and ministers who had returned home to Detroit and eight other northern cities after Freedom Summer.[71]

Goodman found several opportunities to go himself to Mississippi, scheduling executive board meetings in Jackson and traveling south on his own account when the occasion presented itself. The contrast with his visit in 1951 must have been striking, the helplessness of the night Willie McGee died now replaced with the hopeful mood of a movement on the offensive. Segregationists were giving ground in a slow and tenacious retreat, fending off the advancing movement with halfway measures and ad hoc arrangements. When Goodman and the Guild's executive board insisted on desegregating the restaurant at the airport hotel, management politely complied—and then put up partitions to segregate the racially mixed Guild members from other diners. Morcom also recalled that during lunch at the recently desegregated Sun 'n' Sand Motel, "people would get up and move from where our table was."[72]

Being shunned by local whites was no more agreeable in 1965 than in 1951, but unlike in the McGee campaign, when demonstrators came and went within a matter of days, the movement of the 1960s was a liberating force digging in for the long haul. Goodman's recollection of one night in Mississippi captures the lived routine of the combatants:

> I was coming back from some trip somewhere and decided to stop and see how [Claudia] was getting along. That evening she had the staff and other people over just to sit around and talk and dance. . . . I said, "Where can I buy some whiskey? We're gonna have a fun time, enjoy ourselves." It was illegal in Mississippi [but] they got all the whiskey they needed from the brother of the sheriff. I remember going there in the dark . . . and somebody drove me to this place, it was a beaten down little farmhouse somewhere, and knocked at the back door and he looked at the fellow who was with me, he knew him and he said okay.
>
> While we were enjoying ourselves and having snacks and dancing to the radio, a call came in, a number of people were arrested in southern Mississippi. Everything stopped. "Who's gonna go? Who has a car? Who can accompany?" Everyone knew what they had to do, it was a serious business. They went out, and . . . [the rest of us] finished our celebration.[73]

There was much to celebrate as the Freedom Democratic Party made unexpected headway in Washington and the Guild won historic new ground in the fight for civil liberties. Just weeks after the initial challenge to the Mississippi House delegation that January, the Supreme Court finally heard arguments on the suit brought by James Dombrowski, Ben Smith, and Bruce Waltzer against Louisiana's Subversive Activities and Communist Control Act. Noting that the three were arrested during the Guild's New Orleans conference and that Smith was a vice president of the organization, Goodman and David Rein argued in their amicus brief that the arrests were an act of "state vengeance" for the role these men had played "in attempting to translate into living reality this court's decisions as to the meaning of the 14th Amendment as a barrier to racial discrimination." As with the Trucks Act ten years before, waiting for the state courts to first adjudicate the matter would cause irreparable harm to the defendants and allow Louisiana, in the meantime, "to preserve its unconstitutional system of white supremacy in defiance of this Court's opinions." Arthur Kinoy amplified these points in his argument before the Court, emphasizing that Louisiana, having also declared both SNCC and the SCLC "subversive" for their advocacy of voting rights, was seeking the high court's "sanction to use its anti-subversive statutes to outlaw and undermine these voter registration and equality movements." Kinoy turned the cold war rhetoric of national security to a different use. The arrest of dissidents who promoted equal rights was, he stressed, "in direct conflict with the essence of national security, a free people functioning in a democratic society."[74]

The Court's decision three months later represented a landmark victory for the civil rights movement, and for the Guild. With only two dissenting votes, the justices in *Dombrowski v. Pfister* declared the subversive activities statute unconstitutional on its face and ordered the federal district court in Louisiana to issue an injunction forbidding further prosecution of Dombrowski, Smith, and Waltzer. Lacking any clear definition of what constituted "subversive" activity, the law was deemed to be a mechanism for harassing and punishing the opponents of racial segregation. "The chilling effect upon the exercise of First Amendment rights," Justice William Brennan wrote for the majority, would "derive from the fact of the prosecution, unaffected by the prospects of its success or failure." Brennan set aside the time-honored principle of "abstention" by which the Supreme Court had usually refrained from ruling on the constitutionality of state law until tested in state courts. On this occasion, at least, a state law could be challenged on constitutional grounds before it was used to further stifle dissent and do irreparable harm to dissenters. The practical consequences for the movement were underlined that spring when Kinoy, Kunstler, Smith, Waltzer, and Stavis, joined by Melvin Wulf of the ACLU, won a Supreme Court ruling that ordered the federal district court in Mississippi to review the constitutionality of the state's antipicketing statute. The contention that the law was being used "for the purpose of discouraging . . . civil rights activities" had to be recognized, the Supreme Court ruled, "in light of *Dombrowski v. Pfister*."[75]

The Guild's high-profile leadership in these cases and its prominent role in the FDP's congressional challenge inspired varied responses across the political spectrum. On the right, Mississippi representative Jamie Whitten delivered a back-handed compliment by publicly complaining on the floor of the U.S. House that the Guild's "well-organized, well financed national effort" to collect depositions to unseat him was creating "dissension and turmoil."[76]

On the left, FDP chairman Lawrence Guyot was equally impressed with the work of the Guild. In May 1965, he formally invited Goodman to "recruit attorneys in the North who will come South and volunteer their time, effort and expenses in assisting local attorneys to enforce Title III of the [Civil Rights] Act." The summer campaign in 1965 would entail the same kind of omnibus suits that Len Holt and the Guild had brought to desegregate local government facilities in Virginia and North Carolina, a strategy now made all the more potent by the Civil Rights Act of 1964. Goodman accepted the invitation on behalf of the Guild and immediately began to solicit support. Unlike the previous summer, however, when individual lawyers were urged to travel south, this time the Guild would assign teams of lawyers from the same firm or city to work directly with county leaders in the Freedom Democratic Party. They would help the FDP bring suit, county by county, to desegregate everything from libraries to hospitals to public swimming pools. "The promises inherent in the 1964 Civil Rights Act have yet to be fulfilled," Goodman pointed out in the "Attorney's Brochure" for Guild volunteers. With no self-enforcing provisions in the act, there was the danger that it would "become a dead letter, much as the 13th, 14th, and 15th Amendments did for 100 years." Goodman was confident the Guild could muster upward of twenty legal teams to launch omnibus suits in a dozen counties by summer's end.[77]

The response of cold war liberals to the Guild's high-profile role was heralded by a front-page story in the *New York Times* on 8 February. Under the headline "Leading Lawyers Join Rights Drive," the article announced the plans of the President's Committee (the body convened by John F. Kennedy in 1963) "to recruit 150 volunteers from the leading law firms of the nation to represent civil rights workers in Mississippi." To coordinate their efforts, the committee announced that it would open an office in Jackson and raise $200,000 for its support. Goodman was quick to send Bernard Segal, cochairman of the President's Committee, "a warm welcome into the legal arena of Mississippi" and a congratulatory note on winning the endorsement of the project from the Mississippi Bar Association. Goodman was well aware that this endorsement by the state bar had special implications for the Guild. The *Times* also recognized its significance. "The approval of the Mississippi Bar Association," the paper reported, "seemed to reflect an effort to undermine the legal monopoly that the left-wing Lawyers Guild has had so far in the Mississippi civil rights movement." Berl Bernhard, executive director of the President's Committee, confirmed this supposition by publicly declaring, "I am not a radical." If, as he explained, "responsible" Americans did not join the struggle, then "somebody else will, and their motives won't be as good." Sherwood Wise, president-elect of the Mississippi Bar Association, minced no words regarding the left-wing lawyers already in his state. "If you can keep these zealots off our neck," he said in welcoming the President's Committee, "you will have done Mississippi a great favor."[78]

"The Farish Street Crowd"

Notwithstanding the claims of the *New York Times*, the National Lawyers Guild had no monopoly in representing the civil rights movement in Mississippi. Carsie Hall, Jack Young, and R. Jess Brown had long provided legal counsel for the state NAACP, and the Legal Defense Fund supported their efforts with funding and staff, including a young intern, Marian Wright, who came to Jackson in 1964 to open an LDF office on Farish Street. The Lawyers Constitutional Defense Committee had been sending attorneys to Mississippi since the summer of 1964, and in the early spring of the following year the LCDC also opened an office on Farish Street, one block north of the Guild. With the arrival of the President's Committee in June of 1965, "the Farish Street Crowd," as Judge Harold Cox derisively called the civil rights bar in Jackson, grew yet again. "In no other southern state," wrote civil rights attorney and legal historian Frank Parker, "did so many national civil rights legal organizations have full-time, staffed offices."[79]

Inevitably, personal and organizational conflicts within this expanding Farish Street community would coexist with the shared goal of advancing the movement. Claudia Morcom recalled an especially tense relationship with the LDF's Marian Wright. "Two black women down working on the same cause, we should be really good friends," she remembered. "All I knew was Marian Wright wouldn't have anything to do . . . with us." Her staff, on the other hand, "used to come over and hang out" in the Guild office, and lawyers from both organizations ate at the same neighborhood restaurants. LCDC attorney Henry Aronson, serving as staff counsel for the Council of Federated Organizations, reportedly had a falling-out with Guild attorneys in early 1965, but as late as April he was collaborating with Morcom on a response to Judge Cox's demand for higher court fees to discourage appeal of his decisions. That same month, Bruce Waltzer reported to Goodman that the "LCDC is now firmly established in Mississippi and welcomes Guild participation." He covered his bets by adding that "if we find the LCDC starts to hedge" on such collaboration, the Guild could continue its own program. The wariness between the national leaders of these organizations was evident in Waltzer's cautionary note. More often, however, the urgent needs of the local movement drew the Farish Street attorneys into an operational alliance.[80]

This was especially evident in June 1965, when nearly one thousand supporters of the Freedom Democratic Party were arrested while protesting proposed amendments to the state's voting laws. The changes, on their face, represented an astonishing concession to the strides made by the civil rights movement, Governor Paul Johnson recommending that prospective voters no longer be required to interpret the state constitution or be judged "of good moral character" before registering. Johnson made it clear, however, that these changes were intended to put the state in the "most advantageous position possible" to resist the Voting Rights Act (then making its way through Congress) and the threat of federal registrars coming to Mississippi. His proposed concessions to the slow-moving but relentless pressure from all three branches of the federal government might also persuade the congressional majority to seat, for now, the state's still-disputed representatives in the U.S. House. Doing the right thing for the wrong reasons, the governor convened a special session of the Mississippi legislature to vote on his amendments.[81]

It was precisely the seating of this legislature, however, that the FDP now opposed, and for the same reason it was challenging the state's congressional delegation: both were elected by a whites-only electorate. When five hundred FDP protesters marched toward the capitol building, walking in silence on the sidewalks, they were arrested for parading without a permit and jailed in livestock barns at the state fairgrounds. This "concentration camp," as the National Council of Churches called it, received hundreds of additional prisoners over the following days, many of them held inside the city's makeshift stockade for over a week. Sixty would later sign affidavits that they were beaten by officers who had taped over their badge numbers. The city later admitted that officers had, indeed, taped their badges since 1961, claiming this was to "keep any one man from getting picked out" by civil rights groups for "retaliation."[82]

The crisis galvanized the entire Farish Street bar. Goodman came to Jackson and served as a legal observer during the continuing arrests (his presence duly noted by the FBI), and Claudia Morcom went to the fairgrounds with Carsie Hall and other local NAACP lawyers to win the release of those arrested. The LCDC's lawyers raised $45,000 for bail, and attorney John Honnold from the President's Committee joined Melvyn Zarr of the Legal Defense Fund in a federal suit that finally blocked the city from further use of its parade ordinance to suppress dissent. By so aligning itself with the movement, the President's Committee would lose the endorsement of the Mississippi Bar Association.[83]

In the months that followed, the Farish Street bar defended these and other protesters in state court, filed hundreds of removal petitions to move their cases to federal court, and pressed ahead with lawsuits to desegregate public facilities, school districts, and private accommodations. The Guild recruited nearly a dozen law firms at the start of the summer to take responsibility for the omnibus suits it hoped to file, and the Legal Defense Fund, the President's Committee, and the Lawyers Constitutional Defense Committee were also planning court injunctions against segregation of public facilities. As part of the Guild's collaboration with the Freedom Democratic Party, the Goodman firm took on the city of Jackson in August, filing suit in federal court on behalf of Hazel Palmer and "thousands of fellow Negro citizens" protesting discriminatory policies that included the closing of public swimming pools and the removal of benches from city parks to prevent court-ordered desegregation. Dick Goodman joined Crockett and Morcom on the case of *Palmer v. Thompson*, along with Leonard Rosenthal of Jackson.[84]

There was a growing difference in scale, however, between the Guild's efforts and those of its liberal counterparts in the Farish Street bar. The annual budget for the Guild's southern office came to $34,000 in 1965 (the equivalent of $170,000 in inflation-adjusted dollars forty years later). This was a sizeable burden for an organization that still counted fewer than a thousand members, but it was dwarfed by the resources that the mainstream liberal bar now brought to the table. The $200,000 that the President's Committee budgeted for its Jackson office—nearly six times greater than what the Guild could muster—was enough to pay for four staff lawyers, compared to the Guild's single full-time attorney. The Guild managed to transfer some of its operating costs onto the eleven firms (eight from the Midwest, including the Goodman firm) that volunteered to take responsibility for litigating particular desegregation suits. But the President's Committee subsequently mimicked this approach and their contributing firms (with a corporate clientele concentrated in New York, Philadelphia, and Washington) were bigger and richer.[85]

The Guild could squeeze only so much from its repeated rounds of fund-raising. "If it is to be 'freedom now,' it must be 'funds now'!" Bruce Waltzer proclaimed in one of several emergency appeals that summer. Even with these efforts, the office could not keep up with bills, and basic needs were postponed. At one point Morcom threatened (only partly in jest) to "go on strike" if the Guild didn't find the money to install an air-conditioner in her sweltering office. This particular issue was promptly addressed, but at various points during the summer she and Goodman had to cover current expenses with their own money. The President's

Committee suffered no comparable distress over finances. With leaders recruited from Wall Street and the U.S. Department of Justice (Burke Marshall, former assistant attorney general, becoming cochair in 1965), and with funding from the Ford Foundation in 1966, it was the most lavishly endowed legal representative in the South. In 1965, Claudia Morcom put an estimated eighty thousand miles on the used station wagon the Guild provided its staff; by the following year, lawyers for the President's Committee were crisscrossing Mississippi in brand-new cars donated by the Big Three automakers.[86]

With its modest resources, the Guild would struggle to achieve the ambitious goals that Goodman had articulated for the summer of 1965. The Freedom Democratic Party had formally requested the Guild's assistance in launching omnibus desegregation suits across the state, but the FDP's primary focus that summer was the continuing campaign to unseat the Mississippi delegation in the U.S. House of Representatives. The mass demonstrations in Jackson that June, together with the ongoing effort to establish a statewide independent party, left little time or energy for the campaign to desegregate public facilities. "It seems to me," Crockett finally observed, "that the FDP is not interested in and lacks the broad local leadership essential to working up the factual basis and arousing local support for desegregation suits." Even in cases in which the FDP's county-level organizers were able to muster plaintiffs and collect affidavits documenting discrimination, the cost of the litigation proved to be more than the Guild's participating firms had anticipated, particularly when added to the bills from Freedom Summer and the FDP's congressional challenge.[87]

For all these reasons, the results of the summer's campaign would be a disappointment in terms of both the number and the progress of omnibus suits. At the start, Goodman had anticipated that the blatantly segregationist laws and practices of local officials would so obviously be at odds with the Civil Rights Act that judges might dispense with prolonged wrangling over evidence and issue "summary judgments" in favor of desegregation. "In most cases," he had predicted, "the amount of time required for such litigation will not exceed three months and hence, we are hopeful that several counties can be desegregated by the end of the summer." His characteristic optimism had previously carried the Guild into uncertain but ultimately successful ventures in the South, but this time Goodman's zeal for action had outrun the organization's limited resources. In late August he reported to the executive board that nine county desegregation cases "have already been instituted or will be within the next several weeks," but more than half of these were never submitted and the final total was just three omnibus suits—well short of the dozen anticipated at the start of the summer.[88]

Of this handful, none would lead to quick settlements. *Palmer v. Thompson*, the suit the Goodman firm pursued against the City of Jackson, was a case in point. Here, city officials did not invoke explicitly segregationist arguments for closing public swimming pools, but claimed it was merely a matter of cost: the anticipated decline in revenue from whites who would shun integrated swimming pools made their continued operation economically unfeasible. Judge Cox predictably upheld the city's rationale for closing facilities to *both* blacks and whites, ignoring the fact that the pools had never paid for themselves and that one of them (previously leased by the city) was subsequently reopened by the YMCA on a whites-only basis. The appeal to the Fifth Circuit Court in New Orleans would prolong the case well beyond the summer, eventually bringing it— five *years* later—before the U.S. Supreme Court.[89]

By the late summer of 1965, it was evident that the Guild was gradually being eclipsed. Mississippi was no longer the focal point of civil rights activism—the struggle in Selma, Alabama, had shifted attention eastward in the spring, and the ghetto rebellion that summer in Los Angeles opened an entirely new chapter in race relations. Within Mississippi, the liberal bar was meanwhile settling in on Farish Street. "There are presently four legal groups operating in Mississippi and all are located in the capital city of Jackson," reported Morcom, who recommended moving the Guild office to the Delta region, where legal aid for the poor was scarce. The Guild, in effect, was being crowded out by the success of its campaign to galvanize the wider bar. Goodman would later take justifiable pride in the role he had played in this mobilization, but in the midst of the Guild's financial and programmatic crisis he drew far more negative conclusions. The 1965 summer program was overly ambitious, as he later conceded, and the organization's debts were approaching $10,000. The exclusive focus on the South no longer seemed necessary given the belated arrival of the liberal bar, and the Guild's local chapters had, in the meantime, been starved of resources and support from the national office.[90]

None of this was easy for Goodman to absorb. He had never imagined that the focus on the South would be a permanent strategy, but recognition that it had run its course was difficult for him to separate from his prominent role in promoting the policy. To rethink the strategy, as now seemed imperative, was to rethink his leadership. As the summer of 1965 came to a close, he arrived at the somber conclusion that he should decline to run for reelection as president and step down at the Guild's November convention in San Francisco. He urged the executive board to consider new officers, "particularly someone who will replace me, since I cannot be a candidate again." He cited "other commitments," but gave no hint what these might be.[91]

It must have been gratifying for Goodman that in the chorus of opposition to his stepping down, it was members of the New York chapter who were especially emphatic in supporting his continued leadership. "Your suggestion that you might not be a candidate for reelection came as something of a shock," wrote Victor Rabinowitz in a hurried reply, "and I urge most vigorously that you reconsider." He could not know what "other" commitments beckoned, but he was certain it would be "disastrous" for Goodman to leave. Rabinowitz had concluded, as he later wrote in his memoirs, that the turn south in 1964 had worked—"perhaps not perfectly, but it worked"—particularly in the boost it gave to the morale of the Guild. Goodman's old friend Martin Popper was equally insistent. "It must be perfectly obvious to you but, nevertheless, I believe it worthwhile saying that I think you are doing a wonderful job and that you have my complete confidence and respect. When added to that is my great affection, the combination is too great to allow you to resist my plea."[92]

Guild vice president Arthur Kinoy also chimed in with words of encouragement regarding the FDP challenge to Mississippi's congressional delegation. House leaders from both parties backed a move that September to dismiss the challenge without holding public hearings, and the motion to do so passed with 228 votes. The opposition, however, had been substantial: 143 representatives had voted against the motion to seat Mississippi's "whites only" delegation without hearings. Guild lawyers had collected the depositions that gave substance to this historic challenge, and Goodman had mobilized Guild members to lobby their representatives. "I cannot tell you," Kinoy wrote Goodman several days after the vote, "how much Bill [Kunstler] and I . . . appreciate the wonderful way you responded at every turn of the game to our frantic calls for help. Without your help and assistance it would have been very difficult, if not impossible, to have the results which actually occurred."[93]

By the opening of the San Francisco Guild convention two months later, Goodman had regained his customary optimism and self-confidence. The proceedings would give a further boost to his morale, and that of the delegates. The Guild had garnered considerable prestige over the previous two years, and while the national office in Detroit had neglected the local chapters, national membership had grown steadily to 950, nearly doubling the number at the start of the decade. "Our program in the South has highlighted that growth," Goodman wrote in the convention call, "but we must move on." Among those giving testimony to the organization's newfound stature was John Conyers Jr., the Guild's national executive board member and newly elected congressman. Conyers had played a key role in opposing the summary dismissal of the FDP challenge, delivering a speech from the House floor that Kinoy found "particularly impressive." As a featured speaker at the San Francisco convention, Conyers commended the Guild's contribution to this historic struggle. The congratulatory comments of the keynote speaker, Father Robert Drinan of Boston College Law School, were doubly significant since this leading figure in the liberal bar was not a member of the Guild. Writing to Goodman after the convention, Drinan thanked him for the opportunity to participate in the "inspiring" occasion and commended him "for the consistency and courage of the Guild under your leadership." Included was his application for membership and a check for his dues.[94]

Goodman was clearly moved by these and other testimonies to the prominence and importance of his role. After two decades of internal exile at the margins of acceptable practice, these were ample grounds for a feeling of vindication. "After you have been knocked about on the head for a while," he said in reply to Drinan, "it is good to have somebody tell you that it was all for the best, especially when you suddenly realize that probably this is an historically valid judgment." He wrote Popper that he felt "tremendously encouraged" by the convention, which had established new programs for the development of legal aid offices under President Johnson's antipoverty program. He had to also feel encouraged by his reelection without opposition, as well as the hefty sum of $20,000 the delegates had pledged toward recuperation of the Guild's finances.[95]

When the Guild's national executive board voted the following spring to close the Jackson office and transfer its remaining cases to the LCDC, it was time for a summing up. "It can be said," as Ben Smith wrote in the report Goodman read to the board, "that the Guild through its efforts furnished the earliest and most effective legal assistance (other than that provided by the Department of Justice) to the civil rights movement in Mississippi; that by its energy and example it stimulated the formation of the LCDC and the President's Committee and their programs in the South; that the work the Guild performed in 1964 and 1965 was of high quality, imaginative, and responsive to the real needs of the Movement." He might have added that the Guild's pivotal role in Freedom Summer and the FDP congressional challenge also helped put the issue of voting rights before the public and helped pave the way for the Voting Rights Act of 1965. "This is a high professional achievement for our bar association," Smith concluded, "and it is with this note that we can properly bring the program, as it has been conducted up to the present, to a close."[96]

The federal government was equally aware of the Guild's vital role in the South, though J. Edgar Hoover would not have described it in such complimentary terms. On 12 May 1965, the FBI director had sent a letter to Marvin Watson, special assistant to the president, at the White House. "There is enclosed a copy of a memorandum from Ernest Goodman, president of the National Lawyers Guild, to the executive board of the NLG, on the subject 'the 1965 Guild Program in the South for desegregation of public facilities.' I thought the President would be interested in the enclosed memorandum." The several postscripts indicated that Hoover also sent the memo to the attorney general "and to the military agencies by separate communications." The FBI was at the same time monitoring Goodman's correspondence with Martin Luther King regarding legal representation for those arrested in the Selma demonstrations.[97]

The FBI director's understanding of Goodman and the Guild was always distorted by his cold war obsessions, and he would have little to say about either in public. In his private communications with the president, however, he never doubted the Guild's importance to the civil rights movement. It was the one thing he got right.

11

Rebellion and Reaction

He was apprehensive, more so than he'd expected. It was, he assured himself, a familiar room, the auditorium on the second floor of Central Methodist Church, the massive stone building on lower Woodward Avenue where he had spoken many times before. Just the same, he felt the tension this December evening in 1966 as he stepped to the speaker's rostrum. Perhaps it was the intense lights of the cameras of all three national networks, their crews crowded into the front of the room, waiting for Goodman to address the closing rally of the daylong "Conference on the Draft." Perhaps it was the intense scrutiny that he knew would follow his call for legal resistance to the war in Vietnam, especially to the forced conscription that was sending thousands of young men to fight in Southeast Asia. Or perhaps it was the menacing presence in the back of the room of a half dozen men in suits and ties, sullen and quiet, their close-cropped hair and conservative dress setting them apart from the larger crowd of students and old leftists.

"The great question that young men face today," said Goodman, holding the rostrum with both hands, "is how far can an individual go in carrying out, in good conscience, the will of the state in conducting an immoral and illegal war? Is a moral choice possible?" It was a question he had been addressing since the fall of the previous year, when he agreed to serve as defense counsel for twenty-nine young men and women arrested in nearby Ann Arbor for a draft board sit-in. The protesters had not disputed their technical violation of the laws of trespass, but Goodman, in appealing their conviction through state and federal courts, had turned the case into a public forum on the higher laws that justified their civil disobedience. Citing the judgment of the allied tribunals at Nuremberg following World War II, Goodman had asserted that individuals not only had the right to resist the illegal actions of their government, they had the obligation to do so under international law. The Nuremberg tribunals had explicitly ruled that German officials guilty of crimes against humanity could not absolve their role by invoking the orders of their government. "It is no longer enough," Goodman had argued in his brief, "to hold only the government as an abstract entity or its ruling officials responsible for the violation of international law. Each individual, in accordance with his own ability and awareness, must act." The state court had refused to allow Goodman to make this argument to the jury, but antiwar activists had distributed thousands of copies of Goodman's brief across the country. Nuremberg, Goodman now explained to the draft-age students at Central Methodist Church, had established the individual's responsibility for opposing aggressive war, and the United Nations had made these principles a matter of international law.[1]

Once again, Goodman was at odds with prevailing opinion. As with the defense of Communists during the McCarthy era and of civil rights protesters in the South, he and his fellow critics would have to contest a broad consensus that supported official government policy. U.S. military action in support of the Republic of South Vietnam was legal, the American Bar Association had declared earlier that year, because article 51 of the United Nations Charter justified a "defensive" war against the aggressive actions of the North Vietnamese Communists, led by Ho Chi Minh. This justification for U.S. support of South Vietnam still commanded a nearly unanimous following in the media and both major parties, all the more so after President Johnson announced that on 4 August 1964, North Vietnamese torpedo boats had launched unprovoked attacks on U.S. ships in the Gulf of Tonkin. The public would learn later that the government had misrepresented these events to win support for bombing North Vietnam. In the meantime, Goodman and other critics of the war struggled to make the case against this escalating military intervention. The conference at Central Methodist Church was an opportune moment to do so, for by targeting the forced conscription that made every young man a potential casualty of the spiraling violence, the meeting had drawn the interest of the national media.

Goodman turned his audience's attention to the ABA's flawed rationalization for war. Article 51 of the UN Charter, as the National Lawyers Guild had pointed out that spring, justified defensive war only when *a member of the United Nations* was the victim of aggression, and neither North nor South Vietnam was a nation-state recognized by the UN. They existed only as temporary demarcations established after the Vietnamese Communists had defeated the French colonial army in 1954; by the terms of the Geneva Agreement that ended French rule, these provisional governments were to be dissolved after national elections had determined the leadership of a unified Vietnam. Fearing that the Communists would win the plebiscite in a landslide, the United States had backed South Vietnam's refusal to hold the elections. (Years later, President Eisenhower acknowledged that Ho Chi Minh would have won 80 percent of the vote if the election had been held during the French occupation.) Vietnamese nationalists in the North and South, Goodman explained to the audience at Central Methodist, were now fighting to overthrow the U.S.-backed regime in Saigon in what amounted to a civil war. It was neither the first nor would it be the last time, he pointed out, that the government's global crusade against Communism had promoted "democracy" only so long as it favored leaders acceptable to the United States.[2]

As Goodman was finishing these remarks he could see, squinting into the bright lights of the TV cameras, that the men dressed in coats and ties in the back of the room were now standing and edging forward. Police or thugs? Would they rush the stage? Were they armed? Suddenly, the lead man in the group took a long stride in Goodman's direction, pulled a bundle from under his overcoat, and hurled a heavy piece of folded fabric at the stage. It came partially open as it arced over the heads of the startled audience, revealing a large hammer and sickle on a red banner. "*Traitor!*" the man screamed at Goodman, the veins standing out on his neck as he repeated the cry, joined by the half dozen others who followed, all of them pointing at the stage as they rhythmically chanted "*Traitor! Traitor! Traitor!*"

As the *Detroit Free Press* reported the next day in a front-page story on the "School for Draft Dodgers," the hecklers left "when the conference members responded by applauding Goodman." The newspaper also reported that Frank Joyce, a white community organizer and draft resister, denounced the war as racist, citing the fact that "a disproportionately large share of American Negroes [are] dying on behalf of the most affluent society the world has ever known." The front-page coverage in the *Detroit News* included the words of Paul Booth, former leader of Students for a Democratic Society, who announced he would refuse to serve in Vietnam if so ordered. When he asked fellow draft resisters to stand, thirty-five in the crowd of two hundred rose to identify themselves, "apparently unintimidated," the *News* reported, "by the glare of national publicity."[3]

Both newspapers identified the hecklers who had disrupted Goodman's speech as members of the right-wing group Breakthrough. They were half right. Breakthrough was a small group of ideologically committed anti-Communists who frequently hectored left-wing personalities in Detroit, focusing particular attention on Goodman and Crockett. By December of 1966, however, Breakthrough had become something more than just a right-wing fringe group. Unknown even to its members, it had a very powerful and hidden sponsor. "In view of the activist nature of this organization and their lack of experience," the Detroit office of the FBI had written to J. Edgar Hoover two months before, "Detroit is proposing as a Counterintelligence technique that efforts be made to take over their activities and use them in such a manner as would be best calculated by this office to completely disrupt and neutralize the MDCP [Michigan District Communist Party]." To carry out this plan, an agent would pose as one Lester Johnson, presenting himself to Breakthrough as "an elderly, well-to-do individual who was in the past in some manner harmed by the Communists." Mr. Johnson would suggest targets and offer financial support. This "takeover," as the Detroit office called it, would "of course be accomplished without Breakthrough becoming aware of the Bureau's interests in its operation."[4]

With the partial opening of the FBI's files in the 1970s, the public would learn the breathtaking scope of this "Counter Intelligence Program," or COINTELPRO, as it was known to bureau insiders. Goodman, it turned out, was among the thousands of people targeted in a campaign to punish the political opponents of J. Edgar Hoover and the presidents he served in the 1950s and 1960s. Beyond the wiretaps, the electronic bugs, the opening of mail, the planting of informants, and the illegal break-ins and searches without warrants, the bureau would also attempt to sabotage the personal and political lives of leaders large and small, from Martin Luther King to Ernie Goodman and George Crockett. The campaign was as relentless as it was malicious. Days after the conference at Central Methodist, the Detroit FBI sent a memo to Director Hoover that proposed "a further step" in the effort "to influence the activities of Breakthrough"—in this case a letter from Lester Johnson congratulating the group for "the action you took to discredit and unmask Ernest Goodman to the people of Detroit." It was important, the letter continued, to make people aware of the "scum like Goodman who are hindering the efforts of our brave soldiers in Vietnam." To fortify Breakthrough's resolve, Johnson would send them a four-page review of Goodman's career, from the Civil Rights Congress to the Smith Act trial to Goodman's role as national president of the Lawyers Guild.[5]

J. Edgar Hoover would find further reason to question Goodman's patriotism in the years to come. In addition to his continuing support of the antiwar movement, Goodman in a few short years would become known for his courtroom defense of the Black Panther Party, a radical group that Hoover loathed and even Goodman would have found hard to defend in 1966. There was much else he would soon be forced to rethink in his political and professional life. Detroit was on the verge of the most violent civil unrest in the city's history, a cataclysmic upheaval that would forever change its political and social terrain.

In the meantime, the FBI was already exploiting every opportunity to vilify Goodman and disrupt, if not destroy, his law firm. Breakthrough was not the only weapon in this campaign. Other means were at hand, some already in play.

Exodus

The anonymous letters had arrived that fall in plain white envelopes. The one addressed to Goodman was short and blunt: "The scandalous conduct of one of the employees of your firm with the wife of another one should be called to your attention for action since it is becoming the talk of the town. HARRY PHILO is having an affair with Mrs. ROBB." The note to George Crockett arrived during his campaign to win election to Recorder's Court. "You should check into a situation which may affect your firm unfavorably from a publicity standpoint," the letter writer counseled, in feigned concern for the potential "adverse affect on your chance in the election. I refer to the affair between HARRY PHILO and Mrs. ROBB." A handwritten note on different stationery went to Philo's home, urging his wife to "talk sense" to her husband "and save your marriage and his career." The final note was the shortest of the four, addressed to Dean Robb: "Check on your wife and Philo."[6]

The FBI agent who supervised the sending of these messages assured his Washington superiors that "every precaution will be taken to insure that the foregoing anonymous letters cannot be traced back to the Bureau." The FBI director gave his hearty approval, noting that "since a member of the firm is a philanderer," the fraudulent notes might cause the desired "disruption within the firm." In November 1966, the Detroit bureau reported the apparent success of the operation. Philo's decision to quit the firm and leave the Detroit area, the report claimed, was the "tangible result of our counterintelligence program."[7]

The FBI's self-congratulation on this score was undeserved. Not only did the members of the firm know of the affair between Harry Philo and Barbara Robb long before the bureau hatched its clumsy attempt at gossipmongering, but Philo had already left the firm before the arrival of the anonymous notes. There was ample disruption within the partnership, but it was of the partners' own making, not the FBI's.[8]

Philo's departure was, in fact, a defining moment for the firm. The partners had survived the 1950s on the basis of their shared political principles and a camaraderie forged in the long struggle against the Red Scare. Having weathered the storm, they hoped the partnership would grow with the new movements for social change that were surging forward after 1960, the year Philo entered the firm. Goodman knew Philo through the moot court competition at the Detroit College of Law, an award that Goodman had established in the mid-1950s as a memorial to Ben Probe, the fellow Guild activist and deer hunter who had died of a heart attack at the age of forty-five. Philo had returned to law school while working at the Ford Rouge plant, and from the moment Goodman honored him at the backyard barbecue he hosted every summer for the winner of the Probe competition, Philo had seemed like a perfect candidate for the partnership: working class, a leader of the left-wing caucus in Local 600, and passionately committed to the struggle. Mentored by Robb, Philo had quickly come up to speed working with Dick Goodman, George Bedrosian, and Paul Rosen in developing the firm's unique expertise in personal injury law. Publication of the highly regarded *Lawyers Desk Reference* in 1965, coauthored by Robb, Philo, and Dick Goodman, established the firm as a national leader in the field, particularly in the use of expert witnesses and scientific data to establish the link between personal injury and economic loss. Success in these civil suits had, in turn, financed the political work of Crockett and the senior Goodman, as well as that of the newcomers Robert Millender and Claudia Morcom.[9]

There had been strains, however. Philo's quarrelsome style had needlessly sharpened the conflict between the Detroit and New York chapters over the Guild's future. Now, his blunt manner and barely concealed affair with Barbara Robb had plunged the firm into a profound crisis in the summer of 1966. Goodman himself had a complicated personal life, but it had remained private and separate from the partnership; Philo, in contrast, had personally wounded a founding partner, Dean Robb, the man who had mentored him as a successful lawyer. He had crashed the barrier between the personal and the professional, making his actions impossible to ignore. The FBI had been too slow moving to exploit the situation, but it had recognized a genuine vulnerability in the internal life of the Goodman partnership.[10]

Philo, as it happened, was one of three members of the firm who departed that summer. George Crockett had already taken a leave to focus his time and energies on running for public office. The legal work he had taken on in the 1950s defending immigrant leftists against deportation had declined along with the Red Scare, and he had never warmed to the personal injury law that financed so much of the firm's operations. Mississippi had deepened his commitment to political activism and he now wanted to turn his efforts northward. In his first campaign in 1965, he had placed dead last in a field of fourteen running for city council, but in the following year he won a convincing victory as a candidate for judge on Detroit's Recorder's Court. Few voters were swayed by the leaflets from Breakthrough—distributed covertly by the FBI—calling him an "Enemy Collaborator" with Vietnamese Communists.[11]

Claudia Morcom also left the firm in the summer of 1966. Like Crockett, Morcom was uncomfortable with what she saw as the growing emphasis on catering to the income-generating clientele in the firm's personal injury practice. After the long months in Mississippi representing activists and poor people, she wanted to return north and do the same kind of community-based law in Detroit. She found her opportunity in the city's newly organized Neighborhood Legal Service Centers (NLSC). With funding from President Johnson's War on Poverty, the NLSC provided legal services for indigent clients in landlord-tenant court, in disputes over credit and repossessions, and in the entire gamut of misdemeanor cases for which the poor could afford neither counsel nor bail. Morcom took the job as the NLSC's first director that summer and immediately hired James Lafferty, national secretary of the Lawyers Guild, to head the project's civil division.[12]

The simultaneous departure of these three members of the firm marked a turning point. Goodman would have little to say in the coming years about the unhappy circumstances of Philo's banishment, particularly the emotional damage the entire episode must have done to the remaining partners. Crockett's parting was obviously different. It was, above all, the happy consequence of his campaign for public office, and he and Goodman would remain friends long after. But they were no longer collaborators in the political and professional battles that had defined their relationship over the previous twenty years, from the time Crockett had arrived at the Sugar firm. His departure, along with Morcom's, meant that the cast had changed dramatically by the late summer of 1966.

Dick Goodman would bear the immediate brunt of this shakeout. The firm had scaled back its commitment to Mississippi after 1965, but the case of *Palmer v. Thompson* had taken on a life of its own. In response to the original suit challenging the city of Jackson's decision to close its swimming pools rather than submit to court-ordered desegregation, the city's lawyers had argued that cost rather than prejudice was the deciding factor. Few were surprised when Judge Archibald Cox accepted this transparent rationalization and dismissed the suit. The appeal to the Fifth Circuit Court in New Orleans had been filed in June of 1966 and the brief was due two months later. It did not arrive. Dick Goodman sent the court a belated "motion to extend time" that September, explaining that the departure of Crockett and Morcom had left him solely responsible for writing the brief, which he had begun in early August. But at this exact moment, he added, "one of the members of [the] firm resigned" (Philo), and Dick "was compelled to take over his entire case load." The unfinished brief for *Palmer v. Thompson* had been put aside.[13]

The Fifth Circuit agreed to extend the time limit and allow the appeal to go forward, but the public swimming pools in Jackson stayed bone dry and padlocked through the summer, a symbol of the scorched-earth defense of racial segregation that still dominated Mississippi politics. They would remain closed for the next five years as Paul Rosen, Dick Goodman's successor on the case, pressed on through a protracted appeal process. By the time the Supreme Court agreed to review the case in 1970, the liberal majority had disappeared with the retirement of Chief Justice Earl Warren and the resignation of Abe Fortas. Their successors, Chief Justice Warren Burger and Justice Harry Blackmun, both nominated by President Nixon, were far less sympathetic to the argument that closing the swimming pools had been motivated by neither cost nor safety but by a desire to avoid racial desegregation. By a 5-4 majority, the Supreme Court ruled in 1971 that a city could act "for any reason, sound or unsound," and the courts would have to ignore *motivation* and focus solely on the *outcome* of such actions. Even when that outcome might be construed as a public statement that blacks were inferior to whites and could not swim in the same water, the closing of the pools to *both* races had satisfied the claims of equal protection under the law.[14]

The gains of Freedom Summer and the Voting Rights Act of 1965 were also compromised by the resistance of Mississippi's segregationists. In the first two years under new federal standards eliminating registration tests, some 235,000 African Americans added their names to Mississippi's voter rolls, boosting the percentage of voters among black adults from 7 to 60 percent. Segregationists were in retreat on this front, but it was a grudging withdrawal to a new line of defense. To ensure that white votes still prevailed, the legislature eliminated the Second Congressional District along the Mississippi Delta, where black voters were a potential majority, and divided it among districts with white majorities. This gerrymandering would bury the black vote for the next twenty years, postponing the election of a black congressman until 1986.[15]

Progress in school desegregation had likewise been thwarted by Mississippi's white majority. Black parents who opted to send their children to previously all-white schools under the state's "freedom of choice" plan risked being fired from their jobs, evicted from their homes, or denied credit for their businesses. The threat of violence also discouraged many black parents from sending their children to the overtly hostile environment of white schools, limiting the number of such transfers to just 2 percent of all school-age African Americans in the spring of 1966. When more black parents began to press ahead that fall with freedom of choice in the town of Grenada, a crowd of white adults attacked the new students on the first day of school, beating the African American children with ax handles and pipes. Several students were hospitalized after the attack, one with a broken leg. A Memphis newspaper described a group of white men whipping a girl in pigtails, then chasing after her, "whooping and leaping up and down like animals." The police and FBI agents on the scene had done nothing to stop it, and the men later charged with the assaults were acquitted by an all-white jury.[16]

At moments like this, an unwavering commitment to nonviolence was difficult to sustain. After years of taking their lumps, a growing number of black activists were claiming the right to self-defense against a terror campaign that still targeted local leaders in Mississippi—Vernon Dahmer among them, murdered in January of 1966 by the Klan, and James Meredith, wounded five months later by shotgun fire. Armed self-defense seemed especially warranted when the police were not just indifferent to the violence but initiators of it. "I know *I'm* gonna stay non-violent no matter what happens," Martin Luther King said after a police riot that summer in Canton, Mississippi, in which state troopers teargassed and clubbed defenseless demonstrators. "But a lot of people are getting hurt and bitter," King acknowledged, "and they can't see it that way anymore." Among them were the members of the Lowndes County Freedom Organization in Alabama, who adopted a policy of armed self-defense after four activists were murdered in the voting rights struggle of 1965 (one of them, Viola Liuzzo, from Detroit). They soon adopted a bold symbol, the black panther, to represent their independent political party and to convey a new kind of power. The politics of the civil rights movement had reached a turning point by 1966, and not only in the South.[17]

Another Country

You didn't have to go to Mississippi to find segregated schools and black frustration with the slow pace of change. As Goodman and Crockett well knew from their Detroit experience, racial segregation was nearly as extreme in the Motor City as it was in the Deep South.

Even some of the tactics were the same. "The drawing and redrawing and the gerrymandering of school district lines," Goodman and Crockett had argued in a 1962 court suit, was designed by the Detroit Board of Education "to create and maintain a school system under which Negro children were segregated in and confined to public schools located in . . . all-Negro areas." With funding from the Trade Union Leadership Council, parents of children from the Sherrill Elementary School—where the student population had recently shifted to predominantly black—had brought the suit in federal court when administrators decided the graduating eighth graders would no longer be sent, as before, to predominantly white high schools in the outlying districts. The issues at stake went far beyond this particular case, as Goodman and Crockett made clear in their brief for "all other persons similarly situated." The suit was really about the citywide policy of confining African American students in central-city districts where the buildings were old, the classrooms overcrowded, and the curriculum pared of the college-prep and apprenticeship programs found in outlying districts. Even as black families had moved out of the central city, the gerrymandering of attendance boundaries channeled their children back into a "separate and unequal" system providing, as Goodman and Crockett argued, "a second rate education . . . contrary to Federal statutes and the 14th Amendment."[18]

Unlike Mississippi, where segregation had been imposed by state law, Michigan had prohibited racially segregated schools since 1869. Nevertheless, segregated schools were the norm a century later. Also unlike in Mississippi, defense of this de facto color line did not rely on violence or on overtly racist arguments, at least not in recent years. Detroit's school board was dominated by liberals after 1955, when candidates from the Serve Our Schools slate won election with backing from the UAW, the NAACP, and the Detroit Federation of Teachers. Publicly disavowing racial discrimination, the new board had hired hundreds of black teachers and begun construction of new schools in the inner-city districts. Over time, however, it became evident that even a liberal school board was reluctant to redraw attendance boundaries in ways that challenged neighborhood segregation. White voters might tolerate more black teachers in black schools, but the majority was vehemently opposed to racial integration in "their" neighborhood schools.[19]

Goodman recognized that the issue of school segregation was intimately tied to the shifting boundaries of residential segregation in the city. He knew firsthand from his childhood days how passionately these boundaries were contested by rival ethnic groups, the already-settled incumbents pitted against the newly arrived strangers. "I am not prepared to say that school segregation is *more* of a cause of housing segregation than vice versa," Goodman wrote to a colleague almost a year after the Sherrill suit was filed. But "these two developments interact," and changes in one had an immediate effect on the other. Many white parents, Goodman believed, feared that the quality of education would decline in any school where black enrollment was climbing, a fear that "has a rational basis," he acknowledged, so long as the schools failed to address "the different cultural and economic backgrounds of the two groups." The system hardly had time to make these adjustments, however, before whites fled to outlying districts where they could avoid integration altogether. Therefore, Goodman argued, any redistricting plan that distributed black and white students evenly across the system would at least slow the pace of white flight since white parents would know that "there was an integrated school in the area to which they might move," including the outlying districts. "There is no escape but for them to work toward a solution to the problem."[20]

Goodman was articulating the very argument that would, ten years later, define the debate over cross-district busing in Detroit and the rest of the nation. In the mid-1960s, however, these proposals for a citywide commitment to school integration were considered radical beyond consideration. It was enough, in the judge's estimate, that the liberal members of the school board elected in the fall of 1964 had pledged their opposition to segregation. With this promise of a new beginning, the judge declared the suit by the Sherrill School parents to be "moot."[21]

School segregation would grow worse nevertheless, and for reasons no school board could reverse without the aid of a comprehensive urban policy at all levels of government. Absent such a public commitment, deindustrialization and white flight would continue to accelerate at precisely the moment when black migration from the South was gathering new momentum, driven by the automation of cotton picking and the mounting backlash against the civil rights movement. The city's black population had jumped from 300,000 to 482,000 during the 1950s, the new arrivals crowding into a city that was, despite its reputation, less and less able to provide them with jobs: between 1947 and 1963, Detroit had actually *lost* 134,000 factory jobs as Packard, Hudson, and independent parts makers closed their plants and the Big Three shifted production to suburban and rural locations. Automation, meanwhile, replaced workers with machines, and the job ladder that had lifted previous waves of job-hungry workers out of the ghetto lost many of its lower steps.[22]

African Americans who tried to escape the inner city and move to outlying districts still had to run a gauntlet of abuse from whites who feared that even a single black family in their neighborhood would cause a wholesale collapse in property values. From the 1940s to the early 1960s, as historian Thomas Sugrue found in his study of housing segregation, "white Detroiters instigated over two hundred incidents against blacks moving into formerly all-white neighborhoods, including harassment, mass demonstrations, picketing, effigy burning, window breaking, arson, vandalism, and physical attacks." When these efforts failed to intimidate black home buyers, white resistance gave way to white flight. Even for those who recognized that the fear of sudden property loss became self-fulfilling when it inspired panic selling, it was hard to resist the logic of getting out early before your neighbor undersold the market. Some blocks changed from white to black within three years.[23]

Nowhere did the color line move faster than in Goodman's old neighborhood centered on Twelfth Street. Dick Goodman recalled that 75 percent of his classmates were Jewish when he graduated in 1951 from Central High School, located two blocks west of Twelfth; ten years later, 97 percent of the school's students were African American. Most Jewish residents did not welcome this black "invasion," but unlike other whites, Jews did not violently resist. Jewish leaders were supportive of the civil rights movement, and the mobility of Jewish institutions—particularly compared to Catholic parishes—made it easier to flee than fight. Since many more Jewish households were renters, it was easier to pull up stakes in any case. The resulting mass exodus flipped the Twelfth Street area from 99 percent white in 1940 to 96 percent black in 1960.[24]

By then, more of those fleeing the neighborhood were continuing northward across Eight Mile Road into suburban Southfield, adding their numbers to the more than three hundred thousand whites who left the city in the 1950s—equivalent to the entire population of the city of Toledo. Among those exiting the city was Goodman's mother, Minnie, who left her changing neighborhood near Dexter Avenue in 1956 and moved to California to live near her daughter Rose. Those who fled to Detroit's suburbs redrew the color line at the border with restrictive zoning (in Dearborn against apartment buildings), with physical attacks (in Warren against black home buyers), and with "steering" by real estate agents (in Grosse Pointe against everyone but white Anglo Saxon Protestants). Opposition to a metropolitan system of mass transit further isolated black Detroiters from the growing proportion of jobs located in the suburbs.[25]

The middle-class blacks who moved into the Twelfth Street area had about "five good years," as one recalled, before the poverty they'd left behind caught up with them. Highway construction and urban renewal projects were destroying much of the old housing in the lower east side ghetto, driving the poor outward. As landlords subdivided apartments in their overcrowded buildings, the Twelfth Street area soon became one of the highest-density and poorest neighborhoods in the city. In the summer of 1967, a time of economic boom in the suburbs, black unemployment in Detroit was officially measured at 8 percent; in the Twelfth Street area it was somewhere closer to 15 percent, and among blacks aged eighteen to twenty-four, a staggering 25 to 30 percent were unemployed. Among them were young men who had decided, much like the Purple Gang toughs of Goodman's youth, that "proper channels" were rigged and that crime, rather than school, was the more realistic alternative for getting ahead. News of the surrounding prosperity of white America came to them from a distant place, another land where the police, when you crossed the border, pulled you over for questioning. Goodman would later come to know something of the anger this enforced poverty could inspire in the ghetto's young men and women; in a few short years, the angriest among them would be his clients. For them, the urban ghetto felt like another country, "the name of which," wrote LeRoi Jones, "the rest of America has pounded into our heads for four hundred years, *Black.*"[26]

It was not just a separate nation but an occupied one. Of a police force numbering 4,400 men in 1963, Detroit had only 144 African American officers—barely 3 percent in a city that was already more than 30 percent black. For reasons unique to their job and the city's racial polarization, the white police officers who dominated this force had an especially prejudicial view of blacks. In any big city, it was common for police to have a low opinion of the drug pushers, juvenile delinquents, pimps, and brawlers that their job, by definition, compelled them to deal with on a daily basis. In white working-class neighborhoods where poverty was less extreme and where the police were the same race as the people they arrested, the inevitable antagonism between policemen and "the street" was leavened by ties of family, school, and church. Not so when race and extreme deprivation separated black street life from what was, in fact, an alien police force. White officers saw the worst of the ghetto and, with only superficial links to the law-abiding majority, thought it confirmed the prevailing stereotypes of black inferiority. In the eyes of virtually all these officers, the extralegal use of force and arrest without cause was justifiable in any black neighborhood, as were the words "nigger" and "boy" when these harsh measures were applied.[27]

Restraining the prejudicial use of police power against African Americans had been a concern of Goodman's stretching back to the 1940s, when he and Crockett led the investigation of the police killing of fifteen-year-old Leon Mosley. In the late 1950s, Goodman and the local Guild chapter had led the campaign to eliminate the common practice of "arrest for investigation," in which the police detained people without warrants or probable cause. The potential for abuse was obvious in unwritten rules calling for investigation of "all blacks west of Woodward Avenue after sundown," as one police official acknowledged in court. Goodman's campaign helped persuade the police commissioner to order patrolmen to submit written reports on suspicious people rather than take them into custody. In the first half of 1959, as Goodman's Civil Liberties Committee reported to the Detroit Bar Association, these measures had reduced the rate of arrest for investigation from thirty thousand to twenty-two thousand. But during a media-driven crusade against crime in December 1960, the police had again swept up hundreds of African Americans— middle class and poor—because the arresting officer saw them as "criminal types." In most cases, the only grounds for their public humiliation had been the color of their skin.[28]

Mayor Cavanagh, the long-shot challenger who won election in 1961 with the support of black voters, had pledged to change all this. His appointment to police commissioner, George Edwards, recalled that his job "was to teach the police they didn't have a constitutional right to automatically beat up Negroes on arrest." Opposed at every turn, it seemed, by the police department's entrenched bureaucracy, he had to admit there was still a long way to go when he left the job to become a federal judge two years later. The force was still only 5 percent African American by 1967, and Edwards, for one, believed that 90 percent of the white officers were "bigoted," some of them with "strong tie-ins" to organized crime. The best and worst among them had their own grievances with an underfunded police department that overworked its officers and refused to negotiate the conditions of work. But there was little sympathy in black Detroit for a police system that, as the head of Michigan's Civil Rights Commission concluded, "recruits a significant number of bigots . . . and puts them on duty in the ghetto, where the opportunity to act out prejudice is always available."[29]

As in Mississippi, it was hard under these conditions to maintain an unbridled faith in the liberal prescription for racial integration. Among those advocating a new emphasis on black self-determination was the Reverend Albert Cleage, founder of the Central Congregational Church on Linwood Avenue, a few blocks west of Twelfth Street. A former member of the NAACP's local executive board and a past admirer of the Reverend Charles Hill, Cleage had led the Sherrill School's parents in the civil suit that Goodman and Crockett had taken to federal court in 1962. He had since come to regard the NAACP and its liberal allies as too willing to settle for token gains and too timid to lead the movement. If they could not integrate the school system, then Cleage would call for local control of schools and urge black voters to reject the next millage with the slogan

"No Taxation for Discrimination." Likewise, if liberal Democrats would not fight for open housing or curb police abuses, then Cleage would urge African American voters to support the all-black slate of the Freedom Now Party, which he led in 1964 as candidate for governor. Too often, Cleage now insisted, integration had represented the aspirations of a black middle class eager to make itself a "replica of the white community," when the urgent need of most African Americans was for power—*Black Power*—to rebuild their community.[30]

Cleage's rhetoric scandalized the aging Reverend Hill, who urged Detroit's churches to close their doors to Cleage and the Freedom Now Party. "I don't want anything to do with organizations which want all-black," Goodman's longtime colleague told a meeting of fellow Baptist ministers. "There are white people suffering and dying for civil rights, too." For now, most black Detroiters agreed with this assessment, and Cleage received fewer than five thousand votes in his bid for governor. Yet his words resonated with a younger generation of militants who were calling for Black Power and armed self-defense, some gravitating even further to the left and calling for socialism as an alternative to white colonialism. Even as "flyspecks" compared to the mainstream civil rights organizations of the early 1960s, these militant voices were important, historian Angela Dillard has written, "as markers of slow but steady ideological shifts within the city's civil rights movement. By the late 1960s, this new generation of activists would have a decisive impact on the course of political mobilization in Detroit." Their impact on Goodman's political and professional life would be no less significant.[31]

In the meantime, the *Saturday Evening Post* was not alone in predicting that the call for Black Power would inspire "a new white backlash." In a candid admission of the thinking that predominated among whites, the *Post* went on to acknowledge, "We are all, let us face it, Mississippians. We all fervently wish that the Negro problem did not exist, or that, if it must exist, it could be ignored." It could not be ignored, of course, but the candor of the *Saturday Evening Post* echoed the sentiments of Detroit's new generation of radicals. At a Black Power rally on Twelfth Street in the summer of 1966, one student leader went so far as to describe Detroit as "Upper Mississippi." True liberation, he told the crowd, would come only when you "get this white man off your backs."[32]

Fire Storm

The city was burning, a nightmare landscape of fire visible from every side of the Cadillac Tower except the southeast, which looked to Canada.

Goodman had gazed out these windows from the thirty-second floor for decades, contemplating the city that sprawled westward toward the setting sun and the suburbs along the horizon. It was now a foreign and terrifying scene beneath him in July 1967, a lunatic's collage of blazing buildings and black smoke billowing upward. Two or three miles to the northwest, where the fires had been thickest—not far, Goodman reckoned, from his parents' old house on Burlingame near Twelfth Street—a collapsing roof sent a burst of cascading sparks into the darkening sky. Tracer shells from the heavy machine guns of the National Guard arced along a nearby street. He could see the pulsating lights of fire engines blinking in the gathering night. He could smell the city burning.

Surreal as this was, it was harder still to comprehend what was happening inside the office where he stood. The local executive board of the Lawyers Guild had convened an emergency meeting in the Cadillac Tower at the urging of Bernie Fieger, a past president of the local chapter and a national officer during Goodman's presidency. Even with the police roadblocks and surrounding chaos, a half dozen board members in addition to Fieger and Goodman had managed to make their way downtown, including Goodman's son Bill and Abdeen Jabara, a recent graduate of Wayne State Law School who served as secretary for the local chapter. To their mutual astonishment, Fieger now ignored the tragic events unfolding in the streets below and insisted, instead, that the group focus its attention on his proposed emergency resolution: that the Guild immediately go on record condemning the Soviet Union for arming the Arab states against Israel. The younger Goodman and Jabara would both later recall that Fieger, anxious to defend the Israeli military's victory the month before in the Six Days' War, turned aside their efforts to refocus on Detroit. "We were thunderstruck that he would insist on debating this issue," Jabara recalled years later.[33]

The debate over Israel would take on a special prominence in left-wing circles, but for now it was the streets of Detroit that dominated Goodman's thinking. The tragic scale of the upheaval was truly daunting: forty-three people would die in four days of violence and an estimated twelve hundred would be injured. This human catastrophe had followed on a police raid of an after-hours bar on Twelfth Street, a sharp encounter that tapped the explosive magma of black frustration. Some three thousand people had gathered to protest the mass arrest of the bar's patrons, their anger stoked by the double standard that many saw in the city's treatment of blacks and whites. The preceding month, when a white gang shouting "Niggers, keep out of Rouge Park" attacked a black Vietnam veteran and his pregnant wife, shooting and killing the unarmed man, the police had released all but one of the six suspects. Black Detroiters had good reason to believe that if the roles had been reversed, all of the blacks involved would have been jailed and beaten in the process. Now, the police had descended on Twelfth Street to arrest people as they celebrated the return of two black servicemen, men who had "paid their dues" in Vietnam.[34]

Sparked by the bottle-throwing protest against the police department's biased priorities, the rebellion had spiraled outward from Twelfth Street in two overlapping riots. The first was a destructive riot of arson and looting as crowds of mostly young men attacked area stores but rarely people; unlike in 1943, there was little racial violence between black and white civilians, some of the latter even joining the crowds that were "shopping for free." Among the many storeowners at risk was Freda Goodman, who had expanded her antique business by opening a showroom in an old carriage house in the Wayne State area. George Jordan, her sole employee and an African American, tried to protect her property by painting "soul brother" across the garage doors, a strategy that worked in her case but failed elsewhere: of the twenty-five hundred stores burned or looted, nearly one-third were black owned.[35]

The second "riot" occurred among the police and National Guardsmen who fired indiscriminately into crowds and buildings, killing thirty-three African Americans. Officials justified this deadly force by claiming that police were the frequent targets of sniper fire, but subsequent investigation confirmed that virtually all of the reported fire came from the wild shooting of nearby police and guard units. A sizable minority of policemen, as historian Sidney Fine summarized the evidence, "subjected blacks and some whites to verbal and physical abuse, used excessive force in making arrests, mistreated and sometimes brutalized riot prisoners, behaved improperly in conducting searches, and may have engaged in some looting themselves."[36]

The breakdown in police and Guard discipline was matched by the court system's virtual suspension of due process for more than seven thousand people arrested during the crisis. There simply was no precedent for handling such a massive influx of defendants, particularly at a time when five thousand paratroopers and eight thousand National Guardsmen were still patrolling the streets with tanks and heavy machine guns. In response to the Detroit Bar Association's call for help, nearly seven hundred lawyers from across the state volunteered to provide representation without fee, Goodman among them. "Going into the court building was a devastating experience," he recalled a year later. "It was surrounded by armed guards with machine guns. The building was practically a tomb and prisoners were being processed by some method I couldn't fathom." The normal method for processing prisoners had, in fact, been abandoned by Recorder's Court in response to the county prosecutor's request that the court impose the highest possible bail on thousands of people swept up in the mass arrests. The intent, the court's executive judge acknowledged in an extraordinary public statement, was "to keep these people off the streets" by imposing bail bonds of $10,000 to $50,000 on people who could not afford a tenth of that amount. The largest number of "these people," roughly three thousand by Crockett's estimate, had been arrested for violating the emergency curfew—a misdemeanor offense the equivalent of a traffic violation. Among them, Crockett later noted, was a very sizable number of "bystanders, the curious and those who were just too dumb to move on." In the fear and apprehension of the moment ("[W]e had no way of knowing," one judge later explained, "whether there was a revolution in progress"), the thousands arrested were treated as guilty until proven innocent and locked for days in overcrowded jails or city buses parked in the summer heat. In the process, the thirteen judges in the Recorder's Court were expected to ignore the Bill of Rights and its prohibition of "excessive bail" and "cruel and unusual punishment."[37]

There was also, as Goodman recalled of his experience, "no real effort to comply with the elementary right of a defendant to see his lawyer. You couldn't find your client at all except by blind luck. When I did find somebody, I couldn't get to him as there was no procedure by which a lawyer could interfere with the administrative procedures of the police. It was futile to try anything." In an eerie reprise of court practices in Danville and Mississippi, Detroit's court convened with soldiers in the courtroom, "rifles held at the ready." Judges brazenly harassed defense lawyers who had been denied previous access to their clients and who often hadn't been able to learn what the charges were. Goodman went on television to denounce the court for abdicating its role as an intermediary between police and defendant and becoming, instead, an extension of the prosecutor's office. "He got a lot of negative feedback," his son Bill recalled years later, "from so-called leaders within the community over his position on that."[38]

Only later would a postmortem of the system's failings vindicate Goodman and other critics. The study published in the University of Michigan's *Law Review* was especially damning of the court's assembly-line methods, in which fifteen to twenty unrepresented prisoners had been herded into the courtroom at a time, the judge pronouncing all of them subject to the same prohibitive bail without distinguishing between innocent bystanders and suspected looters. "The notable exception," the study emphasized, "was Judge Crockett, who attempted to individualize the bail procedure and adhere to the statutory guidelines." Whereas most other judges refused the assistance of Claudia Morcom's Neighborhood Legal Service Centers, Crockett enlisted the help of NLSC attorneys in gathering the information necessary to identify curfew violators who had no prior criminal record. He then released these individuals on their own recognizance and otherwise set bail at far lower levels for all but the more serious offenders.[39]

Some in the media took note. "Judge Crockett proved that even under trying circumstances it was possible for the courts to be what they ought to be," the *Detroit Free Press* editorialized. "Consideration of the suspects' rights at the beginning of the court process actually turned out to save time and prevented the necessity of back-tracking." Only after a tenuous peace had been restored to the city did other judges reconsider the unconstitutional bails they had set during the crisis. For many in the black community, it was too late. "The hardships imposed on the guilty and innocent alike by being kept in primitive lockups," the *Free Press* acknowledged a year after the rebellion, had already resulted "in savage resentments that still fester."[40]

It had been an anxious time for anyone living in Detroit, Goodman included. For the second time in his life he had seen the destructive forces of racial conflict devour his city, and on both occasions the focal point of violence had been neighborhoods he knew well. In 1943, it had been the Hastings Street area where he had spent the first years of his life in Detroit; in 1967, it was Twelfth Street, the neighborhood where he had met Freda and where his first son was born. Dozens of other cities in the United States would experience similar riots, but none matched the Detroit rebellion—the nation's worst civil disorder in the twentieth century. The city would carry the physical scars for decades to come, the burned-out buildings and abandoned homes of people fleeing the city, the empty lots turning to weed trees and wild grass.

The political terrain was likewise transformed. The liberal coalition that had severed its left wing in the 1950s and briefly returned to power in the 1960s now collapsed, as centrist unions and civil rights groups lost supporters to both political extremes. Many white workers in the North gravitated to the right-wing politics of George Wallace, the Alabama governor who carried his independent campaign for president to Detroit in 1968. "Both national parties have kowtowed to every group of anarchists that have roamed the streets of Michigan," the pro-segregationist governor announced to a packed house at Detroit's Cobo Arena. His pledge to "restore law and order in this country" was all too familiar to Goodman, who had heard Gerald L. K. Smith rally the city's hate groups in the 1940s with the same slogan. As before, the mixture of resentment and prejudice that Wallace now preached found an audience among whites who had their own economic worries, who feared the inevitable blight they associated with black neighbors, and who could not afford to move again or find private schools for their children. Exploiting these anxieties, Wallace's third-party campaign captured 10 percent of the vote in Michigan's general election that year. In Detroit's outlying neighborhoods and near suburbs, Breakthrough (the recent target of the FBI's "takeover") was meanwhile drawing crowds of four hundred to a thousand people to rallies urging whites to arm themselves and prepare for civil war.[41]

Across the racial divide, the political center of gravity in Detroit was also shifting. "The simple truth," George Crockett wrote in 1968, "is that Detroit's black community has no confidence in the administration of justice in their city. They believe that the temple of Criminal Justice is sagging, is tottering. They feel the beams resting on their necks." Those who bore the heaviest burden, the poor and the unemployed, focused their resentment on middle-class blacks as well as whites. Congressman John Conyers had been the target of their wrath at the very start of the rebellion when, as he tried to discourage rioters on Twelfth Street, he was shouted down by young men asking why he was "defending the cops and the establishment." As a community organizer on Twelfth Street later observed, "[T]hese people down here don't see any difference between them [middle-class blacks] and white folks." Many middle-class blacks returned the hard feelings. "We must stop cloaking our criminals in civil rights garments," wrote one reporter for the *Michigan Chronicle*. "The 12th Street crowd," she continued, "has been waiting a long time for a chance to loot the city." Middle-class black families that could afford to move were crossing 8 Mile Road into Southfield, abandoning Detroit and its spiraling crime.[42]

The "12th Street crowd" they left behind had little reason to expect better days. Detroit's principal employers had extended their hiring programs into the ghetto, but New Detroit, the corporate-community alliance that came together after the rebellion, fell far short of the extravagant promises that accompanied its formation. The overall trend, in fact, was continued disinvestment, as corporations shifted facilities and headquarters to suburban locations. Even New Detroit president William Patrick, the first African American elected to the city council, was forced to conclude that private sector capital could not reverse the city's decline. Only a massive program of federal investment could rebuild Detroit, but the mounting cost of the war in Vietnam foreclosed any prospect of such a commitment.[43]

New Left

The war was cutting a wide swath through Detroit and its old political alliances. On the left, an entire generation was turning against the liberal coalition that had championed the anti-Communist crusade in Vietnam, and Goodman was with them from the beginning.

The UAW and the NAACP still supported the president and his war aims long after many of their constituents (joined by Martin Luther King) had come to oppose the war's cost and its mounting death toll. A massive protest of over one hundred thousand at the Pentagon in the fall of 1967 marked the growth of antiwar sentiment, and Goodman's support for this burgeoning peace movement once again drew the attention of the FBI. The bureau took special interest in his trip to Vietnam in 1967 to defend a GI who had refused to go into combat. "He stayed there for several months interviewing all the persons directly and indirectly involved in the case," the Detroit bureau reported to the Secret Service and the FBI director. In a context where the military's desertion rate was soaring, the government feared that Goodman and other opponents of the war were contributing to the widening disaffection within the ranks. This particular case, however, turned out to be less compelling than either Goodman or the military had initially believed. The GI involved had refused combat but not out of opposition to the war or, for that matter, cowardice: he had refused to go on patrol because of an ankle injury. After an extended trial in Saigon, Goodman won acquittal on the charge of cowardice, but the court-martial sentenced the soldier to two years at hard labor for refusing an order.[44]

At home, the gathering momentum of social protest was taking on insurrectionary hues that red-baiters in the 1950s had only been able to imagine. Now, unlike the previous decade, there actually was a mass movement taking to the streets in opposition to U.S. foreign policy, and among the thousands of protesters there were many who called for defiance of military conscription. The FBI strove mightily to link these dissenting voices with a secret cabal of foreign agents, but it was a vain effort. It was universal conscription that forced millions of people to question the war, and the determined resistance of the Vietnamese persuaded many more that the United States either could not, or should not, prevail. "The fact that this small nation has succeeded in bringing the mighty U.S. war machine to a standstill is having far-reaching effects,"

Goodman told an overflow crowd of sixteen hundred at the University of Michigan in March of 1968 (his remarks dutifully transcribed by an FBI agent). "The sons of the middle class citizen are being sent to Vietnam, the resources of the country are strained, and the dollar is being seriously undermined by overspending."[45]

Opposing this "war machine" was no simple matter, as Goodman's fellow speaker that day, William Sloane Coffin Jr. of Yale University, could attest. A former CIA officer who resigned in the 1950s to become a Presbyterian minister, Coffin had joined with Dr. Benjamin Spock and others in signing "A Call to Resist Illegitimate Authority" the previous fall. As a result of this public act of defiance, Coffin and Spock were now under indictment by a federal grand jury for "conspiracy to counsel, aid and abet draft resistance." The stakes were rising along with the scale of protest. "Now is the time for those who propose social change to make their weight felt," Goodman told the standing-room-only crowd in Ann Arbor, "knowing that at this particular moment in history a greater segment of the United States population will be ready to listen to the need for change."[46]

More would be ready to listen, but as these new recruits moved leftward they would also transform the movement that Goodman and Crockett had known from years past. Students, antiwar activists, and black nationalists were just as likely to condemn the "old Left" as they were the Establishment, questioning long-standing alliances and the assumptions that sustained them. Among the oldest of these historical alliances was the bond that linked Jewish leftists with African American activists in the freedom struggle. The two groups had long been united by the shared experience of discrimination, but there was a growing tension in many big cities between Black Power advocates calling for local control of schools and teacher unions representing a disproportionate number of Jewish members.[47]

Overshadowing this and other points of tension was the issue of Israel and its occupation of the West Bank and Gaza after the Six Days' War. Goodman and his generation of leftists had welcomed the UN resolutions of 1947–49 calling for both a Jewish and an Arab state in Palestine, but Arab opponents of partition had objected to such a settlement, arguing that atonement for a European crime—the Holocaust—was being imposed on the non-European people displaced by the new state of Israel. The Israeli conquests of 1967 had dramatically intensified this conflict. Israeli protests over terrorist attacks from the surrounding Arab states had inspired Bernie Fieger's condemnation, at the height of the Detroit rebellion, of Soviet military support for the Arabs. Abdeen Jabara and Bill

Goodman had argued against the diversionary nature of Fieger's resolution, which ignored not only the streets below but also the fact that one of Israel's enemies, Jordan, had been armed by the United States. "Ernie was very troubled by the whole issue," Jabara recalled years later. The elder Goodman probably voted with the minority against Fieger's resolution, but he was "not nearly so clear about the rights and wrongs of it as Bill," Jabara remembered.[48]

In that regard, Ernie Goodman was not unlike many other Jewish leftists of his generation, confused and alarmed by events that had made the once quasi-socialist Israel into a military occupier. When Arab delegates to the International Association of Democratic Lawyers submitted a resolution to a conference in Helsinki declaring that the state of Israel had no legal basis for statehood, Goodman spoke against the resolution and (with the rest of the U.S. delegation) abstained from the vote that adopted this view. "Unfortunately none of us was in a position to adequately present the arguments for Israel," Goodman wrote to a friend in Jerusalem, "and I doubt whether many of us would have wanted to support Israel's present position in the face of numerous actions taken by the United Nations," all opposing Israeli occupation of the lands seized in 1967. He had to admit that the Arab standpoint "would be difficult to answer in terms of international law," but he probably was not prepared to embrace the position of the Student Nonviolent Coordinating Committee, which denounced Israeli Zionists for using "terror, force, and massacres" to conquer Arab lands from 1948 onward.[49]

SNCC would collapse and disappear soon after, eclipsed by the rise of an entirely new constellation of groups with explicitly revolutionary goals. Rebellion was in the air: 1968 was the year when a nationwide general strike nearly toppled the French government, when democratic socialists briefly overturned Soviet rule in Czechoslovakia, and when a massive wave of ghetto rebellions swept across the United States after Martin Luther King's assassination. For many activists, King's murder was the final proof that nonviolent protest was no match for the brutal reaction that awaited any movement for social change. It was no longer enough to hold teach-ins and debate the system's flaws. "Our view of the old Left," recalled Mike Hamlin, a Korean war veteran and leader of the new Left, "was that they had good ideas but they didn't do anything but talk." Militant action and armed self-defense were the bywords of the radical organizations that now emerged in Detroit, led by the in-plant radicals who organized the Dodge Revolutionary Union Movement (DRUM). Wildcat strikes over working conditions and the failure to promote black workers into the skilled trades elevated DRUM to citywide prominence and inspired others to join the League of Revolutionary Black Workers, led by Hamlin and a burly young militant from the Dodge plant named General Baker. They were joined by the group's charismatic leader, Ken Cockrell, an air force veteran and Wayne State Law School graduate soon to gain notoriety as one of Detroit's leading radical lawyers.[50]

Two other groups that appeared in 1968 would also gain considerable notoriety, and both would figure prominently in the futures of Goodman and Crockett. One took its defining symbol from the Lowndes County Freedom Organization in Alabama, which had organized the Black Panther Party in 1966 before fading from the scene. Revived by Huey Newton in the urban setting of Oakland, California, the Black Panthers had organized chapters across the country on the proposition that possessing firearms—a right protected by the Second Amendment to the Constitution—and using them in self-defense were the only effective means to deter racist police. In contrast to the League of Revolutionary Black Workers, the Panthers had no factory-based organization and drew most of their members from the black community's most disaffected young men and women. League organizers had little patience for the undisciplined and confrontational bluster of Panther members, who seemed to invite arrest, but they gave grudging support to the "breakfast for children" and other social programs the Panthers developed over time.[51]

There was less sympathy among League supporters (and certainly none among the NAACP's middle-class members) for the program of the Republic of New Africa (RNA). Founded in Detroit by attorney Milton Henry and his brother Richard, the RNA called for nothing less than the establishment of an independent black nation comprising the states of Mississippi, Louisiana, Alabama, Georgia, and South Carolina. The self-described socialists in the League regarded the RNA's program as an escapist flight from the hard realities of racism and the ghetto. Even so, a loose united front linked these quarreling groups in their shared opposition to police brutality and liberal tokenism.[52]

All of this ideological ferment would percolate into the Guild and dramatically alter its internal dynamics. Neither Goodman nor Crockett would entirely welcome the changes to come, but both men had played key roles in the process that drew young radicals into the organization and inspired them to transform it. Crockett's work in Mississippi had attracted students and young lawyers who saw the Guild as an alternative to the American Bar Association, while Goodman, in his last year before stepping down as Guild president, had hired Ken Cloke to organize law school students into campus-based chapters. When Victor Rabinowitz became national Guild president in 1967 (at Goodman's urging), he redoubled these efforts by adding a second recruiter to the campus campaign, a recent graduate of the University of Chicago Law School named Bernadine Dohrn. A dedicated activist in the Students for a Democratic Society, Dohrn "spent half her time organizing antiwar demonstrations," Rabinowitz later recalled, "and the other half organizing Guild chapters to defend the demonstrators." Associate membership in the Guild's student chapters grew dramatically, to the consternation of older members who regarded Dohrn and the new recruits as "ultraleftist." Rabinowitz, however, welcomed the energy and dedication Dohrn brought to the national office as he moved the Guild's headquarters back to New York City and embarked on a comprehensive campaign to rebuild local chapters.[53]

The success of Dohrn and Cloke's organizing campaign was evident by July of 1968, when the Guild convention in Santa Monica, California, hosted a delegate body that was visibly younger than previous gatherings. What these new recruits lacked in organizational experience and practical understanding of the law they compensated for with an exuberant dedication to radical social change and an impatience with any obstacle that prevented the Guild from aligning itself with "the movement." Goodman found himself in the middle of a heated generational debate during the convention. He favored, on the one hand, expanding the Guild's role in providing legal representation for the millions of young men drafted into the armed forces and the thousands now caught up in its system of military justice. He went before the delegates to argue for an initiative that would be modeled after "our Jackson, Mississippi, experience," as he later described it, with the Guild opening "legal offices in the Far East to advise and assist members of the armed forces in the protection of their rights." The convention adopted Goodman's proposal and the Guild—some twenty years after the close of the Lemas Woods case—opened an office in the Philippines to provide civilian counsel for servicemen facing military tribunals.[54]

On the other hand, Goodman was opposed to any proposal that would have the Guild open its ranks to students and paralegal workers as full members rather than nonvoting associates. Advocates of this proposition saw little value in the Guild continuing as a bar association open only to lawyers, and argued that the organization should redefine itself as "the legal arm of the movement." What this meant in terms of day-to-day practice was hard to know, since the "movement" encompassed a dizzying array of organizations and competing agendas. As a bar association, Goodman argued, the Guild had been able to recruit attorneys to the cause of civil liberties and civil rights without establishing a political litmus test. Admittedly, most of the members had been on the left during the McCarthy era, but the Guild had also enlisted civil libertarians who were not radicals. Goodman's argument that attorneys would abandon an organization that expanded its membership beyond the bar probably struck younger activists as elitist. But among attorneys of his generation, Goodman was not alone in questioning the viability of an organization that subordinated itself to something as diffuse as "the movement."[55]

Gray-flannel professionals like Rabinowitz and Goodman had a hard time identifying with the sloppy dress and profane language of the younger members, and they were especially troubled by youthful denunciations of the law as nothing more than a tool of the rich and powerful. "We must cut through this hypocrisy," Goodman later wrote in response. "We can't both talk about the Constitution as if it had no value and at the same time say we are demanding our constitutional rights." He simply could not accept the argument of the young radicals that the practice of law in a capitalist society was inevitably severed from the struggle for justice. He was well aware that legal systems could evolve in that direction, but determining whether such a moment had arrived required thought and analysis, not formulaic sloganeering. Goodman offered as evidence his experience in visiting South Africa. There he had watched two lawyers, Graham Fisher and Albie Sachs, defend antiapartheid activists in 1961 in court proceedings that were clearly stacked against the defense. "They knew very well that it was going to be tough. . . . They were fighting as fast as they could go and it was useful and very dangerous work." Any success they had in delaying or thwarting the actions of the state was still worth the effort. When Goodman had next visited in 1964, however, Fisher was on trial for his life and soon went underground; Sachs was in solitary confinement and was later exiled to Mozambique (where South African police agents nearly killed him years later in a car bomb attack). "There was no chance for a lawyer there. But until that time comes [here], or until it is clear it is coming, lawyers can do an immense amount of useful, constructive work for the movement, for the people, for the cause of democracy, and we would not denigrate that possibility."[56]

Even winning a case on technicalities, Goodman believed, was no less important than fighting it out on matters of political principle. Some in the new Left felt otherwise and pointed in disapproval to the case of Dr. Spock, in which defense attorneys had not only challenged the legality of the war but had also contested technical flaws in the selection of the grand jury that issued the indictments. Goodman no doubt agreed with David Rein, his colleague from the McCarthy era, who argued in defense of the strategy used in the Spock case. "Every time a political case is won," Rein had written in response to his critics, "the government is defeated in its attempt to punish someone for engaging in political dissent." Whether acquitted on technical grounds or matters of principle, the defendants would be free to fight on.[57]

Goodman and Crockett, however, were losing these arguments within the Guild. The debate, in fact, was becoming more acrimonious and more sharply defined along generational lines as the 1968 convention proceeded. "Where were those thirty- to forty-five-year-old lawyers needed to bridge the gap?" Rabinowitz asked years later, referring to the generation of members lost during the McCarthy era. The generational rift was especially evident in the debate over the politics of race and the role of black lawyers in the Guild. For all concerned, it was evident that the Guild was an overwhelmingly white organization. This had something to do with the fact that African Americans made up only 1 percent of the profession nationally, and that law schools had long enrolled only token numbers of black students. Even with a recent increase in enrollments, many of those who entered the bar may have felt they had enough difficulties ahead without adding the potential stigma of membership in a dissident organization. For any black lawyer, the National Bar Association provided an alternative point of allegiance to the profession, one that competed directly with the Guild. George Crockett, who was active in both organizations, believed that these objective difficulties called for a greater recruitment effort and warned against the perils of a diminished black presence. Because the national Guild "has never really made a serious and sustained effort to get and to keep black lawyers," he wrote in the immediate aftermath of the convention, "it finds now that it lacks sufficient black members to really understand black America's point of view. So the convention concludes that every black man who speaks long enough and loud enough must be speaking 'for the Negro.' "[58]

Crockett had in mind the convention speech of Milton Henry, the lawyer from Pontiac, Michigan, who spoke on behalf of the Republic of New Africa and its call for an independent black nation in the South. Henry was a graduate of Yale University Law School and an accomplished criminal lawyer. A friend and admirer of Malcolm X in the years immediately preceding the charismatic leader's assassination, he had taken the cause of Black Nationalism to its literal extreme. The law of nations, he argued in 1968, provided that with the emancipation of African Americans after the Civil War, the former slaveholders had the "duty to do justice and make reparation for past wrongs." Germany paid reparations to Israel for the death of 6 million Jews, and justice required a similar accounting for the kidnapping, murder, and uncompensated labor of 100 million blacks since 1619.[59]

The Reverend Cleage and others would also make the argument for reparations, but they would seek resources to support economic development and self-determination for black communities across the country. The RNA, in contrast, called for a separate, sovereign state to be carved out of the American South. It was, in effect, a revival of Marcus Garvey's Afrocentric separatism, with a change in destination. How the independent black nation would come into being was left unclear. Henry would later write that God "will show us the means," drawing on diplomacy, military tactics, and "the acquisition of political power within the area." A majority of the Guild delegates found this convincing enough to elect Henry a vice president of the organization and to call for the drafting of "a memorandum of law setting forth the legal authority for the establishment of the aforesaid separate black nation."[60]

Rabinowitz later described Henry's call for a complete separation of the races "demagogic and racist." He was not alone in this angry assessment. "Ernie Goodman and a few other senior members were livid with anger," Rabinowitz recalled. None of them was more enraged than George Crockett, who immediately declined his nomination to one of the Guild's vice presidencies. "Frankly, I had not thought that my fellow Guildsmen were so naïve and so out of touch with the mainstream of Negro life," he wrote Rabinowitz, "as to believe that the advocates of 'a separate black nation' really represent and speak for black Americans." He attributed the vote of the overwhelmingly white delegates to their "guilty conscience" for failing "to affirmatively seek black professional association." He would continue to "fight like hell" until white America recognized "that every state in this Union is as much ours as it is theirs, and that we don't intend to voluntarily surrender our right of mutual sovereignty over a single acre." Noting that he was not always in agreement with Malcolm X, he quoted his words with approval: "You let the white man know, if this is a country of freedom, let it be a country of freedom; if it is not a country of freedom, change it."[61]

Rabinowitz would eventually persuade Crockett to accept his nomination as an officer of the Guild and to fight the battle within the organization. The resolution on black nationhood, he argued, "is probably no worse than other mistakes the Guild has made and, if we handle ourselves intelligently, we shall survive it." Rabinowitz made good on this prediction by taking no action to fulfill the convention resolution.[62]

In the meantime, Goodman was coming to grips with the new political calculus from an entirely different direction. The starting point was the Soviet-led invasion of Czechoslovakia in 1968. In August of that year, Russian tanks had crossed the border to suppress the reform efforts of

Prime Minister Alexander Dubcek and others who had tried to democratize the Communist state. Dubcek and his followers in the Communist Party of Czechoslovakia had abolished press censorship, decentralized economic decision making, and announced an "Action Plan" calling for freedom of speech and movement. Soviet leaders, fearing that such reforms might spread to neighboring countries in the socialist bloc and threaten the monopoly power of Communist parties, sent troops into Czechoslovakia to forcefully end Dubcek's reforms. For Goodman, the invasion was no less a breach of international law than the far bloodier intervention by the United States in Vietnam. The National Lawyers Guild, he argued, was in a unique position to influence events. "While our organization is small," as he wrote to a colleague, "because of our long struggle against McCarthyism and our opposition to our country's invasion of Vietnam, our influence is considerable in all of the socialist countries." The Guild's condemnation of the invasion, he believed, might contribute in a small way to discouraging further repression of the Czechoslovakian reformers.[63]

There were still those in the "old Left," however, who believed that Soviet intervention was justified by the threat of Western intervention and the restoration of capitalism. In the debate that followed, Goodman had the advantage of knowing something of Czechoslovakia on a firsthand basis. Years before, during his 1961 visit to Prague, he had been heartened by the signs of reconstruction and concern for the "common welfare" that he found. Now, eight years later, he returned to Prague on behalf of the Lawyers Guild to investigate the circumstances of the Sovietled invasion. Goodman's interviews with lawyers, journalists, intellectuals, and Czechoslovakian leaders confirmed for him, as he later wrote, that the so-called Prague Spring was a popular movement to democratize socialism and had nothing to do with the restoration of capitalism. "Two points became clear to me in Prague. One was the amazing unity of the nation in the face of the common threat. This was underscored by the failure of the [Soviet-led invaders] to find a single leader, group or organization to support the invasion or give it any sanction or approval. The other point was the deep, emotional feeling I found and sensed everywhere that, whatever the consequences might be . . . , they would never give up their newfound freedom of expression and return to the days of repression and censorship."[64]

Goodman strongly identified with Dubcek's program for "Socialism with a human face," but there was considerable opposition within the Guild's Committee on International Law to his proposed resolution condemning the invasion. Opponents argued that "other mitigating considerations make it desirable for the Guild to take no action," citing among these the principle of "international proletarianism" and the possibility that Soviet intervention was warranted by reports of increased CIA activity in Czechoslovakia and secret talks between Dubcek and leaders of capitalist West Germany. Goodman rejected this claim that "socialist solidarity" justified the invasion. If socialist nations, he argued, could use armed force "to prevent internal changes in another socialist country . . . which they believe will result in capitalism, then capitalist countries would have the same right to prevent internal changes in other nations which they believe will result in socialist societies." In 1965, after the United States sent thirty thousand Marines to the Dominican Republic to suppress a popular uprising against the ruling military junta, President Johnson justified the invasion by citing the threat of Communist subversion. The Guild had condemned this action, Goodman pointed out, as it should now condemn the invasion of Czechoslovakia.[65]

He could not, however, convince a majority on the Committee on International Law, which deadlocked in a 3-3 vote on Goodman's proposed resolution. The executive board thereafter tabled the matter and Goodman's resolution was never issued. As he saw it, he had failed the many people he encountered in Prague who experienced freedom "as a living, breathing thing for which I think they would accept almost any sacrifice before losing it again." Invoking the murky principle of "international proletarianism" would not compensate these people for their loss. "I am conscious of my inability to convey the human aspect of the problem to my friends," he wrote to Alena Cepkova in Czechoslovakia. "I am afraid we tend to consider political or legal problems in terms of broad principles, detached from the people they affect."[66]

Goodman and Crockett were becoming harder to define as either "old" or "new" Left. Both men straddled the ill-defined boundary between these two poles, one rooted in the Popular Front and the cold war politics of the 1930s and 1940s, the other in the youthful rebellion against corporate culture and imperial aggression, whether U.S. or Soviet. For all the crosscurrents in this political tempest, Goodman and Crockett had staked out a consistent position: they would defend the equal application of the law, as well as the democratic right to change it.

New Bethel

The police would later insist that the two officers were on routine patrol when they stopped in front of New Bethel Church on Linwood Avenue, three blocks west of Twelfth Street. It was a coincidence, the police maintained, that the Republic of New Africa had rented the church for a meeting and that armed members of the group were standing outside when the squad car pulled up. The gunmen opened fire without provocation, according to the police. According to the RNA, the police arrived with guns drawn and fired first. Whichever account was closer to the truth, the shootout that Saturday night in March 1969 left one officer dead and another wounded. Minutes later, fifty policemen shot their way into the church, wounding 5 people inside and taking 142 persons into custody for the killing of Officer Michael Czapski.[67]

Much would be written about Judge Crockett's intervention in the case early the next morning, when he ordered the police to either bring charges against the people packed into the downtown jail of the First Precinct or release them immediately. The patrolmen's union later picketed his courthouse and circulated petitions calling for his removal from the bench, accusing him of protecting cop killers and coddling black revolutionaries. They had little understanding of what actually motivated the judge. Far from favoring the RNA, Crockett had denounced its call for a separate black nation as an "insult" to African Americans and their "inalienable right of citizenship" in the United States. The Detroit FBI had even reported to Director Hoover after the Guild's 1968 convention that Crockett's "disapproval of militant black extremist groups" made him a "responsible" and "civic minded Negro leader." The FBI would soon revert to its previous antagonism toward Crockett; in the meantime, only fellow Guild members knew the full extent of his distaste for the RNA. "What I think few people understand about Judge Crockett," Goodman wrote to the *Michigan Chronicle* in defense of his friend's actions, "is the strength of his attachment to the Bill of Rights and the Constitution."[68]

As Crockett had written a few months before the New Bethel shootout, he was determined to "change the habits, the thinking, and the practices of those who are charged with implementing the law." With passage of the Civil Rights and Voting acts, "we have all the laws we need," he had argued, "but we have too many police and government officials who do not live by the laws we have." Evidence of the police department's continuing tolerance for the abusive treatment of African Americans had been underlined in 1968 when police attacked peaceful demonstrators during a downtown rally for the Poor People's Campaign. An observer from the U.S. Department of Justice told reporters that he had seen "officers ride horses into a crowd which I judged to be under control," clubbing the demonstrators "for no apparent reason." When he urged local police officials to pull their officers back, the commanders tried and failed, one of them knocked to the ground by a patrolman.[69]

Changing the attitudes of these white officers would be difficult, Crockett recognized. "How do you get people to discard 350 years of believing that Negroes are property, that they have no rights, that they are inferior?" For that matter, he asked, "how do you change the thinking of that Black nationalist whose despair has turned to bitter hatred of all white people?" The answer, Goodman argued on Crockett's behalf in the *Chronicle*, was for the judge "to act as an independent administrator of justice and not, as has too often been the case, as an adjunct of the police and prosecutor's office." This meant, Goodman wrote, that the Constitution had to apply with equal force "for every person—rich or poor, black or white, those charged with serious as well as minor crimes." It was that equal application of the law that Crockett had found lacking in the New Bethel case. "Can any of you imagine," the judge later told the press, "the Detroit police invading an all-white church and rounding up everyone in sight to be bused to a wholesale lockup in a police garage?" Someone in the crowd outside the church had shot Officer Czapski, but was there "reasonable cause," as the law required, for rounding up *every* man, woman, and child in the building?[70]

Called to the downtown jail by community leaders, Crockett found upon arrival that there was no list of those arrested, no phone calls permitted for those jailed without charges, and no counsel provided for those being interrogated. The police argued that they needed time to process all of the detainees, but to Crockett it had the feel of July 1967, particularly with regard to the right to counsel. Whether one favored or opposed the Supreme Court's *Miranda* ruling, it was the law of the land regarding the right to effective counsel during an accusatory investigation. The *Miranda* rule was "drastic," Crockett later told reporter William Serrin of the *Detroit Free Press*, but necessary to "stop the police from running roughshod over the rights of the accused." To guarantee those rights, Crockett immediately convened court in the precinct offices and began to release those who had not been charged with any crime. The county prosecutor agreed to release 130 of these individuals, but objected to releasing nine cases that included men with traces of nitrate on their hands, indicating they had recently fired a gun. Crockett did not rule out the possibility that one or more of them may have fired at the police. Milton Henry, now known as Brother Gaidi, later told the press that he feared assassination by enemies of the RNA, and the armed members of the organization's security detail may well have seen the police's arrival—at the very moment Gaidi was leaving the church—as something other than coincidence. They may have fired first. If the tests for nitrate had been properly conducted with counsel present, Crockett told Serrin, he would have held the men in jail.

But the police "just botched the investigation" and he was duty bound to set the tests aside and release all but two of the suspects.[71]

There was good reason, moreover, to wonder if the police had targeted the RNA. The group's public brandishing of weapons, though constitutionally protected, made them especially unpopular with a white police force that saw them as enemy insurgents. As it happened, squad cars from four precincts arrived on the scene within minutes of the first shooting, and the district inspector just happened to be in the area to take command of the assault on the church. Police said they were fired on from the building; witnesses who confirmed the preceding gunfire on the street said there was no firing from the church and that the police had stormed the building with guns blazing. William Serrin inspected the church the next day. "The walls opposite the entry doors that lie in the police line of fire are pockmarked by perhaps a hundred bullet holes," he reported. Several witnesses, including one who testified for the prosecution, reported being kicked and beaten by enraged policemen. "Blood spattered pews and one wall," the *Free Press* reported. Police found ten guns, but would not say whether ballistic tests indicated they had been fired.[72]

Four men would later be charged with the murder of Officer Czapski. As the case made its way to trial, critics of Crockett's intervention continued to call for his impeachment, led by the Detroit Police Officers Association, Breakthrough, and the *Detroit News*—the latter calling Crockett's actions "unwarranted leniency." To counter this campaign, an organization calling itself the Black United Front rallied support for Crockett from a coalition that included Christian churches and the factory-based militants of DRUM. Goodman summarized their sentiments in his letter to the *Chronicle*. "Those who talk so piously about the desirability of peaceful racial integration," he wrote, "but are unwilling to accept the minimum step which Judge Crockett insists upon—equality of Constitutional rights—should be prepared to accept the alternatives of violence and racial separation."[73]

Myrtle Street

The newspapers were a catalogue of upheaval that October of 1970. Canada's government invoked the War Powers Act and sent paratroopers to Montreal, declaring the country on the brink of insurrection after the separatist Quebec Liberation Front kidnapped a British diplomat and a labor minister. Bernadine Dohrn, "last seen at a New York meeting of the National Lawyers Guild," had dropped out of the organization and become a fugitive in Ontario following her indictment in Detroit for "conspiring to transport explosives"; as the reputed leader of the Weathermen, an underground group conducting a bombing campaign against government buildings, she was now on the FBI's "Ten Most Wanted" list. Chile was under martial law following the shooting of the nation's top general and the election of a Socialist president, Salvadore Allende. Across the United States, more than 350,000 UAW members were on strike against General Motors, the first nationwide shutdown of the company since 1946.[74]

Next to the breaking news of these events on Sunday, 25 October was the front-page headline in the *Detroit Free Press*: "Policeman Slain Near Home Reported as Panther Office." It was, again, a deadly confrontation between the Detroit police and armed black militants, this time near Myrtle Street on Detroit's west side. Again, the sole fatality was a Detroit police officer, though this time the officer was an African American hired the year after the 1967 rebellion. The fifteen young men and women arrested for the killing of officer Glenn Smith were all members of the Black Panther Party. According to early press reports, the altercation began when the police received "citizen complaints" that party members were "harassing" pedestrians and "forcing" them to buy their newspaper, the *Black Panther.* "The paper contains stories about black grievances such as slumlords, price gouging and police brutality," the *Detroit News* reported, "but it also devotes much of its space to calls for violent revolution." The most recent edition had no fewer than 306 references to "pigs," the *News* reported, as in "Death to the Fascist Pigs." Confronted by police at the corner of Myrtle and Fourteenth streets, the newspaper hawkers reportedly assaulted the officers and then fled to the nearby house on Sixteenth Street that served as headquarters for the Panther's National Committee to Combat Fascism. The "sniping death," as the *News* called the killing of officer Smith, occurred in front of that house, followed by a nine-hour siege, as upward of a hundred police officers prepared for a possible assault. Unlike the New Bethel incident, however, the police deferred to community leaders who began prolonged negotiations with the young men and women barricaded inside the house. Twelve of the young militants finally agreed to surrender to the police. The three remaining in the house returned police gunfire until they were teargassed into submission.[75]

"I'd read about it in the newspapers," Goodman recalled of his first awareness of the case. His initial impression of the seven men and eight women charged with first-degree murder was mixed. The press was full of praise for the police and the restraint they had shown during the siege, while the contrasting image of the defendants was confirmed in press photos showing police officers carefully removing two small pipe bombs and twenty-five sticks of dynamite from the Panther house. "These young Panthers didn't seem to have any political orientation," Goodman remembered. "I didn't know whether I wanted to be involved with a group of people who were acting like revolutionists without any political theory to guide them or ideas on how to bring it about, just hitting out." There was at least as much support in the black community for the family of the slain officer as for the defendants, three of whom were jailed without bail and the rest held on bonds ranging from $10,000 to $25,000. Some civil rights leaders said they saw no difference between the detrimental effects of the Panthers and the Ku Klux Klan.[76]

Goodman was well aware, on the other hand, that police accounts of what had happened near Myrtle Street had to be cross-examined. He knew that many white patrolmen harbored a prejudicial antagonism toward not only black militants but toward blacks of any political stripe, and that many African Americans feared and distrusted a police force whose members so often shot first and asked questions later. Armed self-defense appealed to a sizable and growing number in the black community, well beyond the membership of the Black Panther Party. Panther rhetoric could be toxic and their parading with weapons could be provocative, but the Detroit chapter also carried out the national party's programs of providing a free breakfast for inner-city children, organizing free medical care, and confronting slumlords and price-gouging merchants. Even critics in the black community praised the party for its vigorous opposition to hard drugs. "In certain instances the Panthers do a fine job," acknowledged UAW vice president Nelson Jack Edwards. "[I]n other instances they let vengeance take control."[77]

The Myrtle Street defendants already had a lawyer, Elliot Hall, a Wayne State law graduate who had previously been an associate in the Goodman firm. Millender had recruited him to work on what Hall later recalled as "second tier" cases—criminal, divorce, and real estate—that fell outside the Goodman firm's bread-and-butter focus on personal injury law. He left on amicable terms in 1970 to form his own partnership with Dennis Archer and to focus on criminal law, representing, among others, the Panthers in several misdemeanor cases. While he had misgivings about his clients' incendiary rhetoric, he respected their community commitment and their socialist politics. They were not, in any case, the kind of hard-nosed ex-cons featured in media accounts of the national organization. "These kids were not criminals," he said of them years later. "They were thinkers, they disagreed with the system. They had no criminal record except for minor misdemeanors related to police harassment for selling their newspaper." Hall wanted to represent them, but with so many defendants and complex legal issues, the case threatened to over-whelm the limited resources of his fledgling firm.[78]

For the time being, Goodman held back from any direct involvement in the Detroit case. He knew that the Panthers were in the cross-hairs of FBI director J. Edgar Hoover, who had denounced them as "hoodlum-type revolutionaries," and Attorney General John Mitchell, who called them "a threat to national security" and deserving of FBI scrutiny. It probably took little of the bureau's prodding for local police across the country to mount their own counterinsurgency campaigns against an organization that rhetorically called for the killing of "racist pig cops." In the wake of the ensuing police raids from New York to California, the Panthers claimed a growing list of martyrs, including (by their count) twenty-eight members killed by police action in 1969. There was ample evidence that in more than a few of these cases, the Panthers' claim of political victim-ization was justified. Just months before the shoot-out in Detroit, a federal grand jury investigating the killing of Panther leaders Fred Hampton and Mark Clark in Chicago had found that the police claim of self-defense was false and that they had not been fired on before they shot Hampton in his bed.[79]

Goodman found this and other cases "interesting as well as dramatic," acknowledging years later that he was "sort of anxious to have my fling at this." He was approaching his sixty-fifth birthday, the point that he and his original partners had established for removing themselves from the firm's payroll. Far from retiring, he had every intention of keeping his of-fice in the Cadillac Tower and taking cases of his choice, working without fee or salary. The wealth that he and Freda had accumulated over the years made this possible. "It seemed at that time," as he recalled it, "I didn't have much of any real consequence to be doing. I felt kind of lonely. I wanted to do something important, something useful."[80]

He was in this frame of mind when he got a phone call in the early winter of 1971. It was Huey Newton, national leader of the Black Panthers, calling from California to ask if Goodman would take over as lead coun-sel and work with Hall on the Detroit case. Goodman knew that the Pan-thers, unlike some black militant groups, collaborated with white radicals and that Newton had enlisted a white lawyer, Charles Garry, to represent him on charges of murdering a police officer. Goodman was willing to give it a go, but wanted assurance that neither Newton nor the defendants would dictate the legal strategy for trying the case. He would count on the defendants to contribute their ideas, but he wanted no repeat of the Smith Act trial seventeen years before, when half the defendants had broken ranks from a unified defense. He also made it clear that he would need to bring on a team of young lawyers to help. "I said, 'frankly, Huey, I've never yet tried a case with a group of lawyers. . . . I've always done it myself. But I can't do it anymore. I'm not able to physically.'" Defending fifteen individuals against six major indictments for murder, assault, and conspiracy was a daunting task, particularly for a man with chronic back problems and the occasional dizzy spell. Newton agreed to Goodman's stipulations and honored them thereafter. For his part, Hall was "ecstatic" when he learned that Goodman, already something of a legend on Detroit's left, had agreed to take the lead in the case.[81]

"We were a rather odd group," Goodman said years later of a defense team that was intergenerational as well as interracial. Goodman and Hall were certainly an odd pair: Goodman, the white-haired elder, barely topped five foot nine; Hall, half Goodman's age, towered over him at six foot three, with a full afro and muttonchop sideburns. The two of them would do most of the trial work, Goodman for no fee and Hall—who had nothing like the reserves Goodman had accumulated—for a nominal fee of $300 a week. They would need help combing though the evidence and, as Goodman remembered, there were "a lot of young lawyers coming out of law school who were just aching to get in this kind of a case." Goodman recruited two who had just passed the bar exam to serve as specialists on a volunteer basis: Tom Meyer on ballistics and scientific matters, and Neal Bush on legal issues and key witnesses. They brought along a friend, Jeff Taft, who was not yet a lawyer but who proved very effective as a "street guy" who could talk with the defendants, develop links with their parents, and help with public relations. Both Bush and Taft were heavily bearded and made a contrasting impression with Goodman's suit-and-tie conservatism—Bush somewhat unkempt, as Goodman recalled, "his shirt sticking out half the time," while Taft was "sort of a half-comic figure but a pleasant one, a teddy-bear kind of guy, big belly, that long beard."[82]

These new leftists were just the kind of members who were transforming the Guild and moving it away from the button-down professionalism that Goodman still favored. Matters of style must have seemed less relevant, however, as he worked with these young radicals and came to respect their abilities and political commitment. Rounding out the team were two of Goodman's oldest friends, both dating back to the 1940s: Sid Rosen, the chief fund-raiser for the defense committee, and Morrie Gleicher, who led the public relations campaign. The predominantly white and Jewish composition of the team may have drawn comment from some black nationalists, but Goodman and Hall did not recall it being a problem during the trial.[83]

For all their bellicose sloganeering, the defendants turned out to be for the most part "bright and intelligent" in Goodman's estimate, ranging in age from fifteen to twenty-two years old. The youngest among them would later be separated from the trial as a juvenile; a second defendant was separated because she was pregnant, and a third because he agreed (only temporarily, it turned out) to testify for the prosecution. Only one of the remaining twelve could have fired the shot that killed Officer Smith, yet all of them were charged with first-degree murder and with "wickedly, maliciously, and feloniously" conspiring to kill Detroit police officers. Goodman believed that there was reasonable doubt concerning the murder charge, particularly given the emerging evidence that there were other gunmen in the neighborhood at the time Smith was killed, and that gunfire was coming from other locations on the same block. As for the conspiracy charge, there was in Goodman's opinion no evidence to support the prosecutor's claims. Making that case to the jury, however, would require a concerted effort to counter the early press reports that made the defendants seem like soulless terrorists. The first task, Goodman believed, was to humanize the defendants by establishing that they were the children of the ghetto: that they sprang from the particular conditions of ghetto life and that they had parents and families who supported them in their efforts to change these conditions. This was to be the focus of Gleicher's public relations campaign, which would feature the parents' plea that Detroit take a second look at the evidence and give their children a fair trial.[84]

Goodman and his fellow lawyers meanwhile had to anticipate three major issues before the trial began: the nature of the conspiracy charge, the prospects for finding a jury of peers, and access to the secret evidence held by the prosecutor.

The first of these was in many respects the most difficult issue facing the defense team. Unlike the Smith Act trials in the 1950s, when prosecutors could find no evidence of a conspiracy to overthrow the government with force and violence, or even a conspiracy to *advocate* such methods, in this case there was ample evidence that the Panthers had, in fact, stockpiled a small arsenal of guns, ammunition, and dynamite. Combined with the Panther newspaper's repeated exhortation to "kill the pigs," there was an abundance of circumstantial evidence that could be seen as consistent with violent intent, well beyond self-defense. It would be no easy matter persuading jurors that the defendants had engaged in nothing more serious than rhetorical excess and an obsessive (though legal) preoccupation with firearms and explosives. Developing an effective strategy for doing so became a focal point of the planning sessions convened every Sunday morning at the house that Goodman now owned across the Detroit River, on the Canadian shore of Lake St. Clair. Over bagels and doughnuts, the five men would analyze the options and assign tasks for the following week.[85]

The effectiveness of their strategy would depend in large part on what kind of jury sat in judgment of their clients. Here, the Panther defense team would benefit from the work of Ken Cockrell and Justin Ravitz, both working as partners in the law firm that Harry Philo had established after his return to Detroit. As defense lawyers in the several trials related to the New Bethel case, Cockrell and Ravitz had already confronted the difficulty of selecting a jury of peers. Lawyers for both the defense and the prosecution had the right to question prospective jurors and oppose their seating in two ways: they could challenge "for cause" if they found obvious bias or prejudgment of the case, or they could exercise a limited number of "peremptory challenges" without stating their reasons if they had a hunch the juror would be hostile. Before they could even consider such challenges, however, Cockrell and Ravitz had to confront the fact that the jury pool was overwhelmingly white in a city fast approaching 50 percent black. It was also an older and decidedly conservative group as well, making it impossible—no matter how many challenges the defense used—to seat a jury of the defendants' peers. When the judge agreed to hear evidence on how the Jury Commission had selected candidates for the jury pool, the testimony confirmed, as the *Detroit Free Press* reported, "that many persons were excluded for service for such reasons as having a beard, wearing miniskirts, being on welfare, or chewing gum." The most frequent grounds for exclusion had been race and politics, and the irrefutable evidence of bias had forced the presiding judge of the Recorder's Court to issue an order that in future cases the Jury Commission could exclude people from the jury pool only for reasons specifically enumerated in the law.[86]

Prospects for assembling a jury of peers in the Panther case were further improved by the assignment of Judge R. John Murphy of Recorder's Court to the case. The son of a union business agent for the sheet metal workers, Murphy "was a remarkable young judge" in Goodman's estimate. "He knew how to handle a courtroom and knew how to handle people. It was a delight working in this case with him as judge." Goodman certainly had reason to appreciate Murphy's several rulings in his favor. Among the first things that the judge agreed to was the lengthy questioning of prospective jurors that Goodman and Hall intended to conduct under the rules of "voir dire," the pretrial examination that allowed defense and prosecution attorneys to probe the backgrounds and attitudes of those in the jury pool. The limit on the number of peremptory challenges that each attorney could normally use was irrelevant to this case, since the large number of defendants meant Goodman and Hall would be permitted a total of 560 such challenges. They would use only 53 of these over five days of questioning aimed not only at identifying jurors they favored, but also at educating the entire jury pool—as many as 150 at a time waiting and listening to the questioning—on issues Goodman and Hall would emphasize during the trial. "I have always believed," Goodman wrote to Ann Fagan Ginger concerning his strategy, "that a lawyer should have the essence of his final argument in his mind before the voir dire." In his questioning of one prospective juror, a former union organizer who had just retired from Ford after thirty-one years in the plant, Goodman reminded the entire jury pool what it had taken to win "Power for the People" (the Panther slogan) in the UAW's 1941 strike for recognition. "Juror Mantle" was a willing if somewhat hesitant participant in the seminar:

MR. GOODMAN: And do you remember that it was charged that the workers used violence?

JUROR MANTLE: They were always blamed.

MR. GOODMAN: So the question of violence, at least as you remember in connection with the efforts of the Ford workers to organize the Ford Motor Company, even under a law which permitted them to do so, is that while the workers may have been called the violent persons involved in the situation, actually the violence that occurred was the result of the conditions that caused it, is that right?

JUROR MANTLE: Sometimes.

MR. GOODMAN: After that the company recognized the union and as a result of the agreement which was entered into, the working conditions were changed as a result of the efforts of the workers?

JUROR MANTLE: That's true, after a period of time.

MR. GOODMAN: After a period of time the workers began to control to some extent the environment in which they worked, did they not?

JUROR MANTLE: That's true.

MR. GOODMAN: Do you consider that the process by which the workers achieved the right to organize and bargain collectively with their employers [was] one in which the workers obtained some of the power which the Ford Motor Company had held for itself?

JUROR MANTLE: For recognition, yes. . . .

MR. GOODMAN: . . . It's hard for some younger person to remember the struggle of the older people and the things that they went through.

JUROR MANTLE: That's right.

MR. GOODMAN: But at the time you engaged in this struggle in 1940, even some of your friends looked upon you with some trepidation as though you weren't the right kind of guy and you were called names sometimes, weren't you?

JUROR MANTLE: That's true.[87]

Mr. Mantle did not end up on the jury, but Goodman had achieved his educational goal, underscoring how easily society's rebels, in 1941 or 1971, could be stigmatized when protest over the conditions of work or life ended in violence. This was the question that Goodman and Hall returned to with every prospective juror: could they look beyond the provocative language of the Panthers and recognize that it was the extreme poverty of the ghetto and the unyielding racism of the surrounding society that made such rhetoric appealing to young people? By the time the jury box was filled, the defense team was confident that they had twelve jurors and two alternates who could understand this basic argument. Ten were African American, evenly divided between men and women. Four were white—the only male among them later excused when psychiatrists determined that the stress of the case had rendered him "borderline psychotic." The prosecuting attorney, Walter Gibbs, knew that Goodman and Hall would get the jury they wanted with their ample supply of peremptory challenges. "He correctly assessed the problem," Goodman recalled of Gibbs, "recognized it and took the position 'I want black people on the jury too, they are part of the community.' He was a very decent guy."[88]

Goodman had reason to temper this opinion, however, when it came to chief prosecutor William Cahalan and the secret evidence that he wanted Gibbs to use in court. Normally, in cases where the accused were charged in an arrest warrant brought by the police, there would be a subsequent preliminary examination to review the evidence. The judge in such a hearing would determine if there was probable cause for the case to go to trial, and the defense attorneys would be able to seek a full disclosure of the prosecution's evidence through "discovery" proceedings *before* the trial. The Panther trial would be different, however. Unknown to Hall or the defendants until nearly two weeks after the Myrtle Street siege and arrests, the prosecutor had convened a secret grand jury (as state law permitted) and had persuaded citizen jurors drawn from Wayne County to issue the indictments that would bring the defendants to trial.

It was a proceeding that was only occasionally used in major felony cases, and it gave the prosecutor a distinct advantage. Unlike the usual preliminary examination, in which defense lawyers were present and the evidence was reviewed in open court, the grand jury was a closed proceeding with no defense lawyers allowed and with all of the evidence put under lock and key until the moment it was introduced at trial. The defense, in short, would be flying blind unless it could persuade Judge Murphy to overturn the state law that kept grand jury testimony secret.

The vagueness of the conspiracy charge and the lack of a preliminary examination, Goodman and Hall argued in their motion for discovery, put the defendants at a distinct disadvantage. Denying them access to grand jury testimony until the moment it was brought against them in court would limit the effectiveness of both cross-examination and investigation, subverting the right to *effective* counsel under the Sixth Amendment. "Because reason requires it and because justice demands it," Goodman and Hall argued, "the Court should grant the discovery sought in this case."[89]

Judge Murphy ruled in favor of their motion, but his initial order granting discovery—in which he proposed to personally review the grand jury minutes and decide what was relevant to the defense—was subsequently overturned on appeal by the prosecutor. Goodman and Hall had to wonder what Cahalan had up his sleeve. In the meantime, the best Judge Murphy could do was to arrange for an awkward compromise: in cases in which a prosecution witness had previously testified before the grand jury, the judge would provide a transcript of that testimony to the defense team as soon as the witness testified in trial court; the defense could then search the transcript for omissions or discrepancies compared to the testimony given in Recorder's Court and recall the witness for cross-examination the same day. Under these unusual terms, the trial began in late May 1971.[90]

It soon became apparent how difficult this process would be for the defense. An early indicator involved the testimony of an African American police officer, Forest Harvey, who said that shortly before the shooting of Officer Smith, several of the defendants had thrown rocks at his patrol car and one of them, Victor Grayson, had shouted, "Let's kill them." Under cross-examination, Hall asked Harvey (who he happened to know as a teenage friend) to read from his grand jury testimony describing the same event. Harvey had to concede that he had previously said that Grayson only yelled, "Let's get them." It was a small point, but the first of many that could potentially undermine the embellished police account of what had happened. The difficulty for the defense, however, was immediately apparent when the prosecuting attorney established that immediately after the arrest of Grayson, Harvey had told two other officers—both of whom had testified before the grand jury—that Grayson had indeed said "Let's kill them." Hall objected that this was hearsay evidence, but he also approached the judge and pointed out that "if we had had this information, we wouldn't have made that attack [on Harvey's testimony]. That is the danger." The defense was indeed flying blind, with little knowledge of what surprise testimony the prosecution would spring next.[91]

Nevertheless, the relentless cross-examination of prosecution witnesses by Hall and Goodman began to slowly erode the credibility of the police. This was especially so with respect to the emerging evidence that the Panthers had been singled out for unwarranted harassment in the selling of their newspaper. Hall's cross-examination of Officer Harvey established a prior pattern of conflict between the patrolman and Grayson, who Harvey had twice arrested for selling newspapers on Woodward Avenue. The police, in fact, had issued twenty-four traffic tickets that year to Panther news hawkers, charging them with "impeding pedestrian flow." These charges, the police reported, had been brought in response to citizen complaints, but Goodman's cross-examination of Officer Frank Randazzo effectively undermined that claim.[92]

Randazzo was the white patrolman who had first confronted the Panther news hawkers at the corner of Fourteenth Street and Myrtle. He now testified that the young militants were blocking the sidewalk and pressuring two women to buy the paper. Under cross-examination, Goodman asked how the Panthers could block the sidewalk when a gas station occupied that corner of Myrtle and Fourteenth, providing a wide expanse of pavement for pedestrian traffic. Randazzo had to admit that there were, in fact, no citizen complaints regarding the sale of the newspaper and that he had actually seen no evidence that the women were being intimidated. He had intervened nevertheless and arrested two of the newspaper hawkers, provoking a small melee with a crowd of onlookers. After noting for the jury's benefit that only one of these cases had gone to trial, ending in acquittal, Goodman asked Randazzo if he were not hostile toward the Panthers and black people generally. Randazzo denied he was prejudiced, but Goodman's cross-examination had established the strong impression that it was the police who had provoked the incident at Fourteenth and Myrtle. Their allegation that the Panthers were "blocking the sidewalk" was no different in this respect from what the Dearborn police in 1940 and the Mississippi police in 1964 had claimed in their attempts to give aggression a legal coloring.[93]

It was Randazzo's contradictory testimony about the shooting of Officer Smith that proved most damaging to the prosecution's case. Among all the many police officers who had converged on the Panther house on Sixteenth Street, two blocks from the original altercation, Randazzo was the only one who gave eyewitness testimony that he had actually seen a rifle barrel come out of a lower window in the Panther house and fire the single "sniper" round that killed Officer Smith. Randazzo testified that Smith, a plainclothesman from another precinct, was right in front of him and that both were watching the Panther house from a point a few doors to the north when Smith was shot in the head. Without this testimony, there was no evidence that the bullet that killed Officer Smith actually came from the Panther house. After a two-hour recess to read Randazzo's grand jury testimony, Goodman began by asking Randazzo if he had not previously testified that he and Smith were in a very different location from what he now claimed. Randazzo said he could not recall having so testified, at which point Goodman produced not only the grand jury transcript but also two of Randazzo's original police reports, all indicating that he was directly west of the Panther house, not north as he now claimed. Goodman followed with a telling question: "Officer, would you say your memory is not very good?" "Yes," the officer sheepishly replied. "So that testimony that you gave here earlier," Goodman continued, "is also incorrect, isn't it?" "Yes," Randazzo admitted.[94]

Even more damaging was the fact that Randazzo's testimony was completely contradicted by his partner, Officer Patrick Murray, who had testified before the grand jury that Randazzo was not even at the scene when Smith was shot. Despite the repeated urgings of the prosecutor to change his testimony before the grand jury, Murray had insisted that just minutes before Smith was killed, Randazzo had moved down the block to join other officers in a pursuit of—and an ongoing gun battle with— two men firing rifles. Neither of these two gunmen were caught and neither had entered the Panther house. In the end, Murray's secret testimony before the grand jury turned out to be a surprise gift for the defense. "This," Goodman observed, "was the high point of our case."[95]

So it went, with many prosecution witnesses giving testimony that often did more to undermine than support the charges against the defendants. The prosecution rolled into the courtroom shopping carts full of revolutionary literature taken from the Panther house, but jurors had to wonder what it all meant when, as the defense pointed out, the Panther library included commercially available movies like *The Battle of Algiers* and *Thirty Days to a More Powerful Vocabulary*. The prosecution called reporter Nadine Brown of the *Michigan Chronicle* to testify on her role negotiating the Panthers' surrender, but under cross-examination she explained that the reason they initially refused to come out of the house was because they were afraid they would meet the same fate as Bobby Hutton, a California Panther who had been gunned down when he surrendered to police. There was "absolutely nothing" in their behavior, she testified, that indicated they thought they had killed a policeman. City Council president Mel Ravitz was equally forthcoming under cross-examination about the failure of the city or New Detroit to address the endemic poverty and despair in the inner city.[96]

After nearly a month of such testimony, Goodman was confident that the prosecution had failed to make its case and that there was no need for the defense to call its own witnesses. Above all, Goodman did not want to put the defendants on the stand. They had been disciplined and quiet throughout the proceedings, but there was every likelihood that the prosecuting attorney's cross-examination would provoke these youngsters into sullen denial or angry outbursts that would alienate most jurors. The defense would rely instead on the closing statements of Goodman and Hall to convince the jury that there was more than reasonable doubt concerning the prosecution's claims. Goodman's closing statement on 25 June would cover the murder and conspiracy charges against all twelve defendants, while Hall's following statement addressed the charge of assault with intent to commit murder against the last three defendants who resisted surrender. Goodman was acutely aware that he would have to bear the primary burden of summarizing the weaknesses that he and Hall had exposed in the prosecution case over the previous month. He also knew that he would be speaking to a packed house, the courtroom's public seating filled with family of the defendants and onlookers eager to see Goodman in his celebrated role as counsel to the militant poor.[97]

He would not disappoint their high expectations. In his opening, Goodman emphasized that the death of Officer Smith was unjustified and regrettable. He also reminded the jury that when he was shot, Smith was dressed in street clothes, a black man without a badge (unable to pin it on his denim jacket), with a gun in his hand, in the middle of a tense situation outside his home precinct, surrounded by police officers who would not have recognized him. These "may well have been factors in what ultimately happened to Officer Smith," Goodman suggested before moving on to the key issue: whether the shot that killed Smith came from the house where the Panthers were barricaded. Goodman reminded the jury of the discrepancies in the testimony of police officers who contradicted each other as well as the testimony they had previously given to the grand jury. Officer Randazzo, in particular, had given conflicting accounts of when he arrived at the scene and what he could have seen of Officer Smith and the shot that killed him. Goodman underlined the glaring discrepancies in the testimony of Officers Randazzo and Murray. "It's absolutely impossible, members of the Jury, to reconcile the testimony of Officer Murray and Officer Randazzo in this case. Either one or both of them are lying. It is a harsh word to use," he conceded, "but when the lives of twelve people are involved, I cannot use a kinder word—too much rests on their testimony. The whole case of murder rests on it."[98]

Goodman focused next on the fact that Randazzo had admitted under cross-examination that he and other officers had engaged in a running gun battle with two men carrying rifles on the same block as the Panther house. In light of Murray's testimony, Goodman added, this shooting would have occurred at roughly the time Smith was killed. "Is it really fair," he continued, "to ask you to convict these twelve people on the basis of this kind of testimony, given that we were able to bring these conflicts in the testimony to your attention only after we were given access to the Grand Jury minutes?" The prosecution had argued that even if only one of the Panthers had fired the fatal shot, all twelve defendants were guilty of aiding and abetting the shooter. But there was good reason to doubt the prosecution's claims that the shot even came from the Panther house. It had to be asked, Goodman emphasized, why people who were supposedly conspiring to kill police officers would have shot the only man on the street who didn't look like one.[99]

After a twenty-minute recess, Goodman took up the conspiracy charges against the defendants. It was, he explained to the jury, a notoriously difficult charge to defend against. Unlike a murder charge—decided on concrete grounds of who saw what and when—a conspiracy case could be embellished with innuendo and guilt by association. What any one of the defendants said or did might be attributed to all of them by their common membership in the Panthers. As Goodman well knew from the Smith Act trials, mere possession of revolutionary books could be construed as evidence that the alleged conspirators intended to carry out the revolutionary acts described in their pages. In the case of the Panthers, the possession of weapons and dynamite made it all the easier for the prosecution to argue that the defendants intended to use these weapons to kill police officers. The judge had instructed the jury that this question of apparent *intent* had to be kept separate from the question of whether or not there was an agreed-upon *plan* to carry it out. This, Goodman emphasized, is what made conspiracy charges so difficult to deal with, since jurors were being asked to "compartmentalize" their minds. This was no easy task. The emotional impact of seeing shopping carts of weapons rolled into the courtroom could easily lead one to conclude that there *must* have been a plan of action to use them, even if there was no evidence of such a conspiracy. Since the defendants were not being charged with illegal possession of these weapons, the only reason the prosecution brought them into the courtroom was to create this emotional response. It was for this reason, Goodman told the jury, that the famous appellate judge Learned Hand had called the conspiracy doctrine "the darling of the prosecution nursery." It could be so easily used against a despised minority with little evidence of an actual crime.[100]

Goodman continued with a peroration on how conspiracy charges had been used in American history against movements of protest. Conspiracy charges had often been brought against unions, he began, because "it was found to be a useful instrument for employers who sought to prevent the organization of labor." One of the more famous of these cases occurred in 1886, when union leaders in Chicago were charged with conspiracy in a bombing that killed a number of policemen. The union leaders were never accused of actually throwing the bomb in Haymarket Square, only of conspiring to incite others to commit the crime. "If the charge of murder had been brought against them," Goodman argued, "they would have been acquitted. But they were charged with conspiracy to murder, and convicted. Four of them were executed at one time in a famous, tragic, terrible scene." Likewise, in the long history of resistance to slavery, the charge of conspiracy had been brought against slaves who rebelled or attempted to flee. Examples included the well-known case of Denmark Vesey as well as lesser-known cases like the one in Winston County, Mississippi, in which thirty-five slaves and one white man were charged in 1816 with "conspiracy to obtain freedom."[101]

Goodman might have noted that in many of these slave rebellions there actually was a conspiracy, and that such conspiracies were justified against a tyranny so complete as the institution of slavery. He had apparently contemplated doing something along these lines by using a famous quote from Thomas Jefferson, written in 1787, that no country could protect its liberties "if their rulers are not warned from time to time that their people reserve the spirit of resistance." For Jefferson, this meant that "the tree of liberty must be refreshed from time to time with the blood of patriots and tyrants. It is its natural manure." Goodman decided not to use such a bold claim to the right to rebel, probably because it could so easily be construed as justification for stockpiling weapons. "I am not taking the position that people should have explosives in their homes," he would later tell the jury, and references to the necessity for "manuring" the ground with "the blood of patriots and tyrants" would only contradict that message.

Goodman decided to draw instead from Frederick Douglass, the abolitionist who had famously chastised those who "profess to favor freedom and yet deprecate agitation" as people who wanted "crops without plowing up the ground."[102]

The predominantly black jury could readily identify with Douglass's allegorical defense of agitation. They would not have identified so easily, however, with the plight of Communist leaders hounded by conspiracy charges during the Smith Act trials. Goodman made no mention of their victimization, staying away from an issue that the Red Scare had made so indelibly controversial. He stuck to examples the jurors would recognize as closer to home, of conspiracy charges used to defeat the labor movement and suppress slave rebellions. "This is the way peoples' organizations in our country and in other countries have been attacked and decimated: use the conspiracy doctrine, apply it to the group, thus getting away from individual guilt, attribute everything in the organization or attributed to the organization . . . to all the defendants and ask the jury to convict."[103]

It was in this light that Goodman asked the jurors to reconsider the inflammatory rhetoric of the Panthers. He reminded them of how often the prosecution had cited the chant "There is a pig upon the hill. If you don't kill him, the Panthers will." He recalled that Nadine Brown, under cross-examination, had testified that among black youth, the term *pig* applied to all oppressors, not just police. Goodman pointed out that chanting this little ditty in public, which the Panthers did often enough, was hard to square with conspiracy, which the prosecution had described as a secretive undertaking. Rather, Goodman argued, it was part of an emerging culture of resistance that now more urgently demanded liberation. As such, it was no more relevant to a conspiracy than the many nursery rhymes from white culture that also had violent references. "Fee, fi, fo, fum, I smell the blood of an Englishman," Goodman recited to the jury. "Be he alive or be he dead, I'll grind his bones to make my bread." This gruesome little offering was no doubt a product of people who hated the English ("and for good reason," Goodman opined), but its macabre threat to eat their bones had no relevance to an actual conspiracy to do so. "Is it right for us, for white people," Goodman asked, "to develop a culture based upon violence for our children, but wrong when young black people begin to develop their own culture to reflect life as they see it?"[104]

"And what do they see?" he asked near the close of his summation, now nearly two hours long. "They see the wealthiest nation in the world unable to provide the smallest things for people at the very bottom." They see that after the 1967 riot, despite all the promises of help by elected officials, "nothing happened, the basic conditions remained the same." Council president Ravitz had testified, in fact, to deteriorating conditions. The defendants knew that society could "if it really wants to, and if it is in the interest of those who run things, build great beautiful houses and wonderful buildings. It's been done in the last four years. . . . Out in the suburbs it's been done. Whole new cities have arisen there." Comparable investment in the black community, Goodman concluded, would come only when its residents acquired the power to make it happen, just as abolitionists and union supporters had struggled for the power to secure their dignity and a measure of freedom. The defendants were associated with weapons, with harsh rhetoric, and with many other questionable things, "some of which may be bad, some of which can be criticized." But were they to be "the first group in our society who sought change who must be perfect—who are not to make mistakes?"[105]

"I am not suggesting," he said in closing, "that the defendants or anybody else can kill and get away with it, of course not. But the charge of murder has not been proved," and the charge of conspiracy was being "directed at people at the bottom who seek power to change their lives." Goodman turned to the jurors and acknowledged that he could not have made these arguments if the jury had been drawn from the suburbs. They would not have understood. "We who work in the city, live in the city, know the city, have to assess the claims and charges against these defendants, against the background in which they live and work, with an understanding of the life toward which they aspire. . . . It's on this basis and for the reasons that I have presented, that I ask you to acquit these defendants."[106]

An excited murmur rose from the spectators before Judge Murphy gaveled it down. "I looked over at the prosecutor," recalled law professor Edward Littlejohn, "and his body language told you he knew he was whipped." Some in the crowd remembered jurors nodding in agreement as Goodman had spoken, but Hall recalled being less certain of their response. "They didn't show much emotion, less than we had hoped. We really couldn't read them at that point." He needn't have worried. It took the jury only a few hours to vote for acquittal on the counts of murder and conspiracy to commit murder.[107]

The remaining charge of assault with intent to commit murder was the more difficult issue. Hall had taken the responsibility for the closing argument on this charge, which applied only to the three defendants who had stayed in the house until teargassed. He reminded the jury that a majority of police officers on the scene had testified that shots had come out of the house only after the police had fired tear gas into it; if the three remaining Panthers had really intended to kill police officers, Hall argued, they could have found many targets in the long hours preceding that moment. Instead, it appeared they had not fired until the house was filling with gas. If they had been charged with reckless use of a firearm, Hall conceded, "it would be something for you to consider." But the far more serious charge of intent to commit murder, Hall argued, was not supported by the evidence. Juror Angeline Buchanan, a middle-aged black woman who worked in an industrial laundry, found this convincing and held out for acquittal until 30 June, when she finally joined the majority in finding the three defendants guilty. Judge Murphy sentenced them to prison terms of three to four years, but the conviction was overturned on appeal and sent back to Recorder's Court for retrial. Judge Murphy accepted the prosecutor's motion to drop the charges in 1974, the year after the election of Coleman Young as Detroit's first African American mayor. That same year, Young appointed Elliot Hall to become the city's corporation counsel.[108]

Many years later, Hall reflected on what had impressed him about Goodman's approach to the case. "He was always so well prepared, with almost a pathological attention to detail," he remembered. This applied to the exhaustive preparation of briefs, the careful planning of the voir dire, and the deliberate approach to cross-examination. "In court, Ernie was always even tempered, well balanced and reasoned," an approach Hall contrasted with his own relatively more emotional style. Hall also had to be impressed with Goodman's sustained concern for the defendants, whom he supported in numerous ways over the months and years that followed: representing the convicted defendants in a civil suit when prison authorities denied them basic rights; seeking counsel for the youngest of those arrested when she was held in a New Jersey juvenile home; writing letters of recommendation and seeking financial aid when several of the defendants later applied to college.[109]

Goodman had also learned something from his co-workers during the trial. He had often called on partners and colleagues for assistance in past cases, but with the exception of Crockett, the collaboration had usually been limited to help preparing briefs, pleadings, memorandums, motions, or the countless other documents that accompany a trial. He had generally shouldered most of the burden himself, especially the drafting of briefs and the courtroom conduct of the case. The exceptions included the Smith Act trial, when he lost control of strategy and had to share the defense with three obstreperous clients. That result had been dissatisfying from both a professional and political standpoint, and was no doubt a blow to his ego. Now, out of necessity in a case that would have overwhelmed a single lawyer, he had worked with a team through a difficult trial. To be sure, he had still been the leader of the team, but he had learned to collaborate on a far more extensive scale and to accommodate different work and lifestyles. He had also come to respect the contributions of legal workers who were not yet lawyers or who had not yet established their own practice.

All of this would serve him well in the near future, in little more than a year, when he stepped onto the national stage in the most publicized case of his career.

12
Attica

Tear gas was still hanging in the air at Attica when prison authorities gave their first reports of inmate atrocities. Under orders from Governor Nelson Rockefeller, the New York state police had just retaken control of the prison on 13 September 1971, in a bloody assault that left thirty-nine inmates and hostages dead. According to the official version of events, the rebellious inmates who seized control of Cell Block D four days before had, that morning, taken eight of the prison guards they held as hostages to the catwalk above the prison exercise yard and slit their throats. Even as the police were shooting their way into the prison to retake control, the inmate executioners had allegedly mutilated the bodies of dead hostages. At least one of the victims, it was understood, had been castrated and his testicles shoved into his mouth.[1]

None of this was true. Autopsies conducted the next day revealed that all of the ten hostages killed during the assault had died of gunshot wounds. There had been no fatal slitting of throats, no mutilation, no castration. State officials had already reported that the rebels, three-quarters of them African American and Hispanic, had no firearms. The conclusion was inescapable: police gunfire had killed the hostages, some shot five, ten, or twelve times as the all-white assault teams fired point-blank at the retreating rebels and their hostages.[2]

The mounting evidence pointed to rank incompetence in the planning of the police assault and a vengeful cruelty in its execution. The assault teams had been issued shotguns loaded with buckshot, ensuring that the spreading pattern of deadly slugs would indiscriminately kill inmates and hostages alike. In spite of explicit orders that only the state police and National Guard were to participate in the retaking of the prison, the assault force had included Attica prison guards, many of them enraged at the inmate rebels and seeking revenge. Wounded prisoners were left to bleed to death. Surrendering inmates were stripped naked, ordered to crawl through mud and broken glass, then forced to run repeated gauntlets of white corrections officers armed with clubs. Rebel leaders were tortured for hours. Many of those included in the final list of casualties, investigators confirmed, were injured long after the assault was over.[3]

Reading the headline news, Goodman could recognize the same deadly mixture of rebellion and reaction that had convulsed Detroit after 1967. The rebel inmates, he knew, were not harmless innocents. They had been convicted of felonies, two-thirds of them for violent crimes. During the initial uprising, inmates had assaulted the captured prison guards and beaten some of them severely. One guard had died of his injuries.

Even so, the rebels were nothing like the murderous barbarians portrayed in the initial media accounts. As state investigators later confirmed, it was not blood lust that drove them to rebellion but long-standing grievances that prison officials had done little to address. They had lived with extreme overcrowding, 2,250 men packed into a prison that its superintendent considered secure for no more than 1,600. Inmates were locked in their six-by-nine-foot cells for fifteen hours a day with no TV and only a three-channel prison radio to fill the hours. The daily ration of hot water was delivered to each cell in a bucket; inmates could shower only once a week. They worked in the prison shops for as little as 25¢ a day, then marched in funeral-like silence to the mess hall (some guards prohibited talking), where they forced down barely edible food. Prison censors routinely sent intercepted books and magazines to storage, and prison rules prohibited chewing gum, the wearing of hats indoors, moustaches, and unbuttoned shirts; violators of these petty rules could be sent to solitary confinement for days. The all-white guard force did nothing to protect newly arrived inmates from the gang rule and homosexual rape that shadowed the prisoners' lives. Living in rural New York, the guards knew only the narrow spectrum of criminal behavior they saw in African American and Puerto Rican inmates, fueling a racist contempt for the prisoners and a matching brutishness in how they were treated.[4]

The assertiveness that Goodman and Crockett had come to know in Detroit's Black Power movement had likewise emboldened Attica's inmates to join the Black Panthers, the Black Muslims, or the Young Lords, a Puerto Rican group centered in the East Coast. Their seizure of Cell Block D had not been planned—it hinged, literally, on a defective door bolt—but after the initial violence and chaos of the uprising, the competing militant groups had set aside their differences and organized a rough democracy in D yard. More than half of the inmates had joined the revolt, and while it was obvious that white inmates had been less inclined to join, the more than three hundred whites who did so found a surprisingly

egalitarian and nonracist self-government. A member of the hastily organized security detail later described the role of his group in sustaining the
uprising:

> Security was mainly responsible for the food, medical care, cloth-
> ing or what have you; to keep people from being ripped off sexu-
> ally or keep the water supply, to see that everyone have mattress,
> blankets at night. Mainly that everybody stay together and recog-
> nize one another as brothers, under the same roof, same condi-
> tions, being able to look above the 1/1000 of an inch difference
> such as skin, not to get hung up in the racial thing and not let it
> grow into a racial riot—this is one of the main things we tried to
> prevent.[5]

To strengthen interracial solidarity there had even been a kind of "affirmative action" to bring whites onto the security team in rough proportion to their numbers in the uprising. Although the color line continued to
shape the social interaction of the inmates, they were bound together by a
common recognition of their grievances. "WE are MEN!" the rebels declared
in their first list of five demands. "We are not beasts and do not intend to be
beaten or driven as such." In the tense negotiations with prison authorities
that followed, the rebels had made some headway with fifteen practical
proposals for reforming Attica. If there was any public sympathy for the
inmates, however, it was eclipsed by the gruesome threat to kill the hostages if the police attacked. It turned out to be a bluff, but the threat had
inspired a deadly police riot and the cover-up that followed.[6]

Goodman was alert to this unfolding story and, like many others, was
horrified by the loss of life and the brutal conditions that had produced
such violence. He had reason to hesitate, however, before volunteering his
help to the Guild activists who were already organizing the defense of
Attica's rebels. Coming only months after Goodman had won the acquittal of Detroit's Black Panthers on most counts, Attica represented something far larger and even more complex than the trial he had just completed. No state troopers or guards would be charged for their role in the
violent assault that killed so many men, but state prosecutors would eventually bring forty-two indictments against the inmates, charging them
with assaulting captured guards or with stabbing and killing two inmates
accused of betraying the rebellion. To handle this surge of litigation, the
Lawyers Guild would recruit volunteers from New York City to Chicago.
But for now, the Attica defense focused on getting the case moved from
rural New York to the city of Buffalo, where the defendants had a better
chance of finding a jury of peers.

As the Attica cases slowly inched toward trial over the next three years, Goodman could only guess at the role he might be called upon to play. In the meantime, it was perfectly obvious that the political and economic upheavals of the early 1970s were transforming the political terrain in Detroit and nationally, redrawing the color line in a polarized debate over race relations. Much of the controversy centered on the decision of District Judge Stephen Roth, ruling in the case of *Milliken v. Bradley* that school integration in Detroit could only succeed if busing were carried out on a metropolitan basis. Amplifying the same points raised ten years earlier by Goodman and Crockett in the Sherrill School case, Judge Roth argued in 1972 that the inclusion of fifty-two suburban school districts in a metrowide busing plan was the only way to send the message to Detroit's remaining whites that there was no escaping integration by fleeing to outlying towns. Roth's decision promised to lift Detroit out of its isolation from the metrowide dimensions of the problem, but the means for doing so—the forced busing of children to distant and potentially hostile schools—was something parents of any color were bound to have misgivings about. While the state Democratic Party gave a lukewarm endorsement to cross-district busing as "an imperfect and temporary mechanism to help erase imbalances in our educational system," rank-and-file Democrats in suburban Detroit were overwhelmingly hostile. An antibusing referendum in Warren carried every precinct with 80 to 99 percent of the vote, and in the Democratic Party primary that year, George Wallace won 51 percent of the statewide vote. Wallace opted not to run as a third-party candidate when he lost the Democratic nomination, but Warren's Democratic mayor promptly endorsed President Nixon's reelection campaign. In the general election of 1972, the Republicans carried Michigan in a landslide that included the blue-collar—and once solidly Democratic—districts of the near suburbs.[7]

Two years later, the Supreme Court's conservative majority ruled 5–4 against cross-district busing. It had not been shown, the majority reasoned, that the suburbs had any direct role in perpetuating the segregation of Detroit's schools, and they therefore should not be included in the Court's desegregation order. Cross-district busing was dead and court-ordered busing solely within Detroit had the predicted outcome, accelerating white flight. The events marked the consolidation of a new political era in which many blue-collar whites in the North and South were abandoning the Democrats and voting for Republicans. Emboldened by his landslide victory in 1972, Nixon would secretly turn a portion of the national security state against his weakened rivals, recruiting former FBI and CIA agents to burglarize the offices of the Democratic Party.

"The Nixon White House ran amok as no other has done," conservative columnist George Will conceded, "and its abuses were uniquely lurid and sinister." Even Nixon's impeachment and resignation over the Watergate burglary did not reverse the ebb tide of liberal and left-wing fortunes. With the severe recession of 1973–74 and the double-digit unemployment that followed among Detroit's autoworkers, shop-floor militancy and radical politics were fading.[8]

Only a few bright spots illuminated this bleak terrain in the months before Goodman joined the Attica defense. Coleman Young, his long-ago collaborator in the Progressive Party, won election in 1973 as Detroit's first African American mayor. At the same time, the antiwar movement that Goodman had joined in the mid-1960s was finally forcing the U.S. government to begin withdrawing troops from Southeast Asia. In January 1973, this phased withdrawal culminated in the Paris Peace Accords, which officially ended U.S. military intervention. Goodman returned to Vietnam a year later, traveling this time to the North as a guest of the Jurists Association of the Democratic Republic of Vietnam. The anniversary of the accords and the prospects for reunifying the country made for a celebratory mood, shadowed by recognition of the war's staggering cost over the previous fifteen years: upward of 3 million Vietnamese dead, another 1–2 million Laotians and Cambodians killed, cities and villages in ruins, and fifty-eight thousand U.S. soldiers buried in cemeteries across the United States.[9]

When Goodman returned from Vietnam that winter, the last great trial of his life awaited.

Shango

The defendant's birth name was Bernard Stroble, but after his incarceration at Attica he had abandoned this slave identity, as he termed it, and replaced it with an African one: Shango Bahati Kakawana (a name, Goodman later acknowledged, "I had difficulty remembering and pronouncing"). In November of 1973, Shango had been charged under a single indictment for the murder of another prisoner during the uprising. As the slow-moving case made its way toward trial, the Attica Defense Committee called Goodman in the summer of 1974 and asked if he would be willing to represent Shango. "I thought that was a simple, straightforward case I could handle by myself," Goodman recalled years later. "There wouldn't be a number of other defendants involved in it and it would be much less complex and easier to take care of. So I said yes." It would, in fact, be anything but simple, for Goodman was taking on the case that would define the entire outcome of the litigation over Attica. He was also about to meet a client who would become the most extraordinary, and tragic, of friends.[10]

There was little in Shango's past that would hint at the importance he came to play in Goodman's life. Unlike the youthful radicals in the Detroit Panther case, he had no history of political commitment or social activism in his thirty-one years before the Attica uprising. Bernard was only six years old when his father, a sometimes steelworker and a full-time alcoholic, abandoned the family in Philadelphia. A New York parole report in 1968 described the pathos of his early years: "He began to run away from home, sleeping on public transportation and on one occasion, when only nine, wandered as far as New York City . . . in search of his father." He was convicted of shoplifting at the age of twelve and sentenced to a term in training school. Upon his release two years later, he returned to his mother's home in Florida, where he became increasingly unruly. Bounced between delinquent detention houses and training schools, his youth was a shambles by the time he and his mother left Florida in 1956 and moved to Detroit.[11]

On Christmas Eve, 1965, Stroble and two companions held up a jewelry store, Joe the Jeweler's, on Grand River Avenue in Detroit. During the robbery, someone shot and killed the salesman and wounded the proprietor, who was subsequently unable to identify his assailants. Two weeks later, Detroit police officers John Brady and Paul Frantti followed Stroble's car to his mother's house to question him about unpaid traffic tickets. Stroble ended up in a struggle with one of the officers, who was shot with his own gun (accidently or otherwise), while another of Stroble's companions shot the second policeman. Both officers survived. Shango became a fugitive, ending up in New York City. Six months later he shot and killed a small-time drug dealer in a Bronx poolroom in a fight over a bag of marijuana. When the police finally arrested him at his girlfriend's apartment (which he set on fire during his attempted escape), they claimed that he voluntarily confessed to the Detroit jewelry store killing as well as the wounding of one of the Detroit policemen.[12]

Stroble's "one-man crime wave," as a New York assistant prosecutor called it, drew multiple felony charges in two states for murder, manslaughter, robbery, arson, and assault. Once in custody, Stroble also drew the attention of prison psychiatrists. Doctors at Bellevue Psychiatric Hospital noted that Stroble possessed "some leadership potential and an ability to conform when properly motivated." But after an apparent suicide attempt in November 1966, they transferred him to the Rikers Island infirmary. Stroble's case officer warned that he could be "engagingly friendly in demeanor," but that this masked a "shrewd, manipulative individual lacking a sense of social awareness." Stroble showed "a reckless disregard for the life and property of others," the officer concluded. "He seems capable of anything." As if to prove the point, during the November 1967 trial for the New York poolroom shooting, he smashed a chair through a courtroom window in an attempt to escape. It took eight guards to subdue him.[13]

Convicted the following year of manslaughter in the poolroom slaying, Stroble was sent to Attica to serve his sentence. There he found a level of alienation to match his own. As the official report on the uprising later put it, "the Attica rebels were part of a new breed of younger, more aware inmates, largely black," who were "unwilling to accept the petty humiliations and racism that characterize prison life." Stroble's violent reputation preceded him and probably helped him avoid being victimized by other inmates. He struggled to redeem himself by conforming to the contradictory disciplines of prison rule and political radicalism. Like many inmates, he became something of a jailhouse lawyer, immersed in the legal proceedings that took him, temporarily, back to Michigan for trial and conviction in 1968 for the jewelry store killing and the wounding of the Detroit police officer. Sent back to Attica to finish serving his New York sentence, he slowly gained a measure of self-control. He ate one meal a day and, standing six foot two, kept his body trim through a strict regime of exercise. He began reading about global events and the history of black people in the United States.[14]

Taking on an African name was a measure of Shango's effort to remake himself. Out of the utter chaos of his boyhood life he had acquired an acute intelligence that he now honed during the prolonged introspection that prison life forced upon him. By all accounts, he grew more contemplative and stoic as the same prison conditions that made him a rebel also made him a social being, instilling a sense of his shared fate with others and a matching self-esteem that called for something better. He was radically opposed to the status quo, but he disapproved of revolutionary posturing and did not indulge in the incendiary rhetoric that characterized several of the leaders at Attica. He had not sought a leadership role before the uprising, nor did he in the early hours of the takeover. It was his reputation as someone who was self-possessed, thoughtful, *and* capable of any level of violence that led his fellow inmates to seek him out. They asked him to help lead the security detail, and Shango agreed. Four days later he took multiple gunshot wounds during the police attack on D yard.[15]

Two years after the bloody assault of 1971, a New York grand jury indicted Shango for the stabbing death of inmate Barry Schwartz. According to the state prosecutor, rebel leaders had called a kangaroo court during the occupation and sentenced Schwartz and a second prisoner, Kenneth Hess, to death for betraying the uprising. Both victims were white and both had been scorned by fellow inmates before the rebellion. Hess had a reputation as an extreme racist and had vehemently objected to being held in the same cell block with black and Puerto Rican prisoners. Schwartz was known as an informer, a jailhouse "snitch." This may have made the two men suspect in the eyes of many inmates, but the specific charge against them was that they had told a local reporter (one of several admitted to D yard during the rebellion) the names of those who had led the initial takeover of the prison. Inmate leaders had encouraged fellow prisoners to talk to reporters about prison conditions, but not about the events that had led to the beating and death of one of the guards, William Quinn. At the hasty meeting convened in D yard, rebel leaders had questioned Schwartz and Hess about information they may have given to reporter Stewart Dan about Quinn's beating—information that might later be used to prosecute those involved. When Dan was also questioned, he emphasized that neither man had told him anything that he and other reporters didn't already know, but some inmates standing around the meeting table were shouting that Schwartz and Hess were traitors and should be executed. Rebel leaders assured Dan that nothing would happen to the two men, who were stripped and marched off to D block. Dan subsequently told state investigators that "he did not even consider the incident important enough to include in his news report."[16]

What happened next was the nub of the case. Shango insisted that there had been no trial or sentence of execution and that he had been told to take the two men to a secure area where they could be protected from hostile inmates; the state argued that the meeting in D yard had been a trial and that Shango and others on the security detail were taking the two men to their execution. Shango, it was charged, had carried out the sentence on Schwartz while another executioner, Jomo Omowale, had killed Hess. Both men died of multiple stab wounds.[17]

Goodman had only the sketchiest knowledge of these details in the late summer of 1974 when he boarded the plane for Buffalo, New York, where the trial would be held. Meeting Shango for the first time in jail, it soon became evident to Goodman that he was not dealing with the average convict. "He was a remarkable man, physically," he remembered, "tall, strong, handsome, well-built, very self-possessed. He spoke fluently and well, good vocabulary." Goodman was immediately struck by the fact that Shango, rather than accepting with unquestioning gratitude the offer of counsel that Goodman represented, was actually interviewing *him*.

"He was interested in knowing who I was, my background, and what I thought about the Attica uprising, what my political and social views were. So it was intriguing to go there to see if I wanted to represent somebody who had no money to pay in a case that could be very complicated and long, and he was interested in questioning me about what kind of a lawyer he was going to get and whether he was going to have me as his lawyer."[18]

They agreed to meet again in a week. "When I came back we spent some more time talking and he agreed that I could be his lawyer. And I agreed he could be my client." Goodman was too shrewd to be entirely convinced of his client's innocence after these initial encounters, but he saw in Shango a man of obvious abilities. His scorn of self-promotion, his commitment to exposing the truth about the routine violation of inmates' rights before and during the assault on the prison, and his desire "to put up the kind of fight that would bring out the crucial social and political issues"—all these qualities appealed to Goodman. As he became familiar with the gruesome evidence of the case, he was convinced of Shango's innocence. His client had been nearby when Schwartz was killed, that was clear. But Shango was not the murderer.[19]

Taking the Lead

What began as a "simple, straightforward case" in Goodman's estimate became far more complicated that fall when the presiding judge combined several cases into a single proceeding. In addition to the original murder indictments, the prosecution wanted to prosecute Shango and four other inmates for "felony murder"—that is, a separate felony linked to the murder. In this case, the accompanying felony involved the alleged kidnapping of Schwartz and Hess and their imprisonment inside Cell Block D before they were killed. The judge accepted the motion to combine these indictments during the pretrial hearings, but then ruled that each of the five defendants would be tried separately on the murder and felony-murder indictments.[20]

"So the question was," Goodman recalled, "which defendant was going to go first. I was hoping that it would be one of the others because I was already weary." He was spending four days a week in New York preparing for the case and returning to Detroit for a brief rest on weekends. "I was 68 years old at the time. Doesn't seem so old now," he noted twenty years later, "but at the time it did." He knew the first case would be the most important: if it ended in acquittal, the other cases would probably be dismissed; if it ended in conviction, it would be difficult for all those who followed. In either case, he would be working without fee. "So while I wanted the challenge, I realized it would be an enormous burden."[21]

That burden fell squarely on his shoulders when the prosecution decided that Shango's case would be the first of the five to go to trial. Even before this turn of events, it was obvious that no single attorney, no matter what his age, could handle the sheer number of witnesses the prosecution intended to call. Goodman would need help. He had learned how to work with a team of lawyers and researchers during the Black Panther trial, and he now turned to the far wider support network of the Attica Defense Committee. Drawing on the National Lawyers Guild, the committee had already recruited a sizeable number of lawyers to handle the anticipated prosecution of sixty-two defendants. The Goodman firm alone had pledged four attorneys, with Dick Soble, George Bedrosian, and Bill Goodman joining Ernie on the roster. At least four other Detroit lawyers had enlisted in the defense effort (Dick Skutt, Ken Mogill, Stu Cohen, and Neal Bush), joined by attorneys and legal workers from New York, Boston, and Chicago. Volunteers were assigned as needed to the many cases inching their way toward trial, with two leadoff cases taking center stage in late 1974. In the first of these, a pair of well-known lawyers would argue the defense: Ramsey Clark, the former U.S. attorney general, and William Kunstler, the veteran civil rights and antiwar attorney. They would defend two inmates charged with the beating death of William Quinn, the guard killed at the start of the uprising. The second case, Shango's, had no headliners at the defense table, but Goodman and his cocounsels could count on a team of sixty volunteers to research the law, interview witnesses, profile jurors, and develop a publicity campaign. Goodman's son Bill would help litigate the case, joined by two others at the attorneys' table. One, Haywood Burns, a law professor at the State University of New York at Buffalo, was already known to the inmates as the legal coordinator for all sixty-two Attica defendants. The other was Shango.[22]

In the Detroit Smith Act trials twenty years before, Goodman had opposed the idea of defendants representing themselves. He had some misgivings about Shango taking this "pro se" role in the Attica trial, but this was a different case in a different setting. Goodman had worried in the Smith Act trial that political sloganeering by the defendants would undermine the First Amendment defense he wanted the jury to hear. At the Attica trial, in contrast, the charge was murder in a case that involved black-on-white violence and a savage killing. By representing himself, Shango would be able to demonstrate to the jurors that his intelligence and loyalty to the rebellion were incompatible with such a crime. It would help that Judge Joseph Mattina agreed to Goodman's request that Shango not be

brought into the courtroom in handcuffs and prison garb. While the jurors would certainly know that he had been serving time at Attica, they
would not know his record or whether he was still even in prison. They
would have to judge him on the evidence and on their impression of him
as a man. And as Goodman knew, "[H]e made a great impression generally. His vocabulary was great, his diction was excellent. A fellow who
never had any formal education was able to develop so he could speak on
his feet with lucidity."[23]

Shango would also be able to play an effective role in cross-examining
inmates who had been persuaded to testify for the prosecution against
their former comrades. Coming right up to the witness stand and quietly
addressing the "Attica brother" as a fellow inmate ("as though," Goodman
later described it, "he were just carrying on a conversation in adjoining
cells"), he could call upon his familiarity with these men to crack their testimony. "I began to understand that when you're dealing with people who
are all prisoners, their life is so different from mine [that] . . . I couldn't
possibly know their mental and emotional makeup. And Shango did."[24]

There were difficulties as well. As Goodman got to know Shango, he
recognized that "he had some deep emotional volcano within him which
could explode on occasion and account for some of the things he had
done." At times Shango also had trouble trusting other defendants and
members of the defense team, and these moments of paranoia could make
it difficult to develop defense strategy. Shango was a prisoner who returned
to his cell after a full day in court, and some of the most important discussions took place in the claustrophobic environment of the Erie County jail.
Disagreements were resolved without anger, Goodman recalled, "except
for one or two occasions." It was "a process of mutual education that became very valuable."

> Sometimes I had strong ideas on one approach or strategy, and
> Shango would come up with an opposite idea. I tried consciously
> to keep my mind open. Shango not only spoke very well but was
> also very thoughtful. . . . I learned to respect his judgment . . . and
> we developed ideas I could not have developed on my own. When
> I felt I was right about something, I fought for my position. There
> were many things that Shango didn't know about trying lawsuits,
> of course. But I found that he, too, kept an open mind and could
> change his position.[25]

Shango had a hard time trusting anyone, but this aging white lawyer
from Detroit seemed worthy of his confidence. His growing bond with
Goodman was evident during the "Wade hearing," a pretrial procedure

that permitted defense lawyers to cross-examine witnesses whose testimony linked the defendant to the crime. The Wade hearing for Shango's trial began in January 1975, and one of the first witnesses Goodman questioned was Jack Mildy, a former New York City detective now serving as an investigator for the prosecution. Mildy was a large, rude, and uncooperative man who seemed to enjoy running roughshod over Goodman's mild questioning. "He would challenge me on the question and say, 'Now, Mr. Goodman, tell me what you mean by that.' Or, 'I've told you what I said and it seems to answer your question.'" Thinking well ahead of the immediate proceedings, Goodman hoped he could get Mildy to perform in the same ill-tempered way during the trial, when the jurors were seated. "I was hopeful the jury might like me as a person," he recalled. "If the state investigator was crude and unpleasant, it would not sit very well." To see how far Mildy would go, Goodman asked purposefully naive questions and, as hoped, the witness became increasingly quarrelsome. "Suddenly I hear a yell in the courtroom in back of me and it startled the hell out of me and everybody else in the courtroom. Shango stood up and he pointed at him [Mildy] and he said, 'You let my lawyer alone! Don't you browbeat that guy anymore,' or words to that effect. Everybody had just sat back down and he went on, 'You pig!'" Judge Mattina immediately silenced Shango and ordered him to sit down. But Goodman knew his back was covered.[26]

Goodman also knew he was lucky to have drawn Judge Mattina for his trial. In addition to tolerating Shango's occasional indiscretion during the Wade hearing, the judge allowed the defense considerable latitude in probing the prosecution's case. An already arduous discovery process would otherwise have been far more difficult. The grand jury proceedings that produced the indictments were secret (as in the Panther case), and state prosecutors generally refused to go beyond a minimal compliance with the rules of discovery. Judge Mattina, however, ordered the prosecution to provide Goodman at least some of the grand jury testimony that related to the identification of the defendant, and this would prove to be crucial to the defense. The state was otherwise uncooperative, and even when the prosecutor appeared to be forthcoming, there was a catch, as Goodman recalled. "We eventually got the names of *potential* witnesses whom we could interrogate but they wouldn't give us the [shorter] list of witnesses they were going to *call*." The longer list would take that much more time to cull. It included many convicts who had participated in the Attica uprising but who were now, for whatever reason, collaborating with the prosecution. Many of them were scattered across the New York prison system or already out on parole.[27]

Much of the work in tracking these witnesses down fell to Linda Borus, a staff member for the Guild's New York chapter who became Shango's court-appointed investigator. She found an anxious group of men. Some were up for parole and others faced the possibility that they themselves might be indicted. The state insisted that it had made no promises to witnesses and that there was no retribution for those who sided with the rebels. But there was the inescapable fact that any inmate who refused to cooperate with the state put himself at risk. Prosecutors with the power to punish inmate witnesses could solicit testimony that justified the indictment of rebel leaders, while the reckless homicide of the police assault went unquestioned. In the many cases where Borus found that there had been extensive coaching of witnesses (what Goodman called "sandpapering"), she reminded each inmate that even though they were witnesses for the prosecution, they had the right to refuse to give testimony if it were untrue or if they thought it might be self-incriminating. Some witnesses were reluctant to talk with Borus, but others, who resented the intense browbeating of state prosecutors, welcomed her counsel.[28]

The bonds were so strong among inmates who had faced the fury of the state's bloody assault that several witnesses changed their testimony during the Wade hearing. One, Flip Crowley, told the court that he had perjured himself before the grand jury and that the prosecution had beaten and threatened him. Another, former Attica inmate Bob Thomas, completely contradicted the testimony of Jimmy Ross, the witness who had immediately preceded him. Ross had testified that he saw Shango slit Schwartz's throat in the cell where he was being held. Thomas, however, testified that he had seen another inmate, Tommy Hicks, go into the same cell and stab both Schwartz and Hess to death. To everyone's surprise, Thomas was testifying that the sole murderer was Hicks, a violent man known for his psychopathic hatred of whites. Hicks was later killed in the police assault to retake the prison, and Thomas had not been called to testify before the grand jury. Goodman now wondered why the state had called such a witness to the Wade hearing, and prosecutors apparently asked themselves the same question. By the time the case went to trial, they had removed Thomas from their list of witnesses.[29]

The damage had already been done to their case, however, since it now appeared that the state was deliberately manipulating the evidence to convict Shango for the crime committed by Hicks. Goodman drew attention to this prosecutorial misconduct and the coercion of witnesses in a series of pleadings to dismiss the case. "In a real sense, the 'unclean hands' of the government in these prosecutions," read one of the reiterated motions to dismiss, "covers over the blood on the hands of the assault force." The judge turned this and other motions aside for the time being, but Goodman hoped to convince the jury that the state had corrupted the investigation of the case.[30]

Finding jurors who would give this argument a fair hearing was, as always, a key concern. Buffalo's Erie County was certainly more diverse than Attica's rural environs, but there were many in the city—particularly in the white majority—who would have a hard time siding with the Attica rebels. To plumb community sentiment on this score, volunteer members of the "jury project" conducted a survey and developed a profile of the ideal juror—a person who would have the strength, if necessary, to argue with other jury members who might want to convict Shango on the state's tainted evidence. The information would prove to be useful when the defense team began questioning prospective jurors for the trial. Caucusing in a nearby room, Goodman, Burns, Shango, Bill Goodman, and Linda Borus would decide which candidates they would accept, which they would challenge "for cause," and which they would excuse without explanation by using one of their "peremptory" challenges.[31]

From the start, the prosecutor gave every indication that he would use his peremptory challenges to secure an all-white jury. Of the first ten selected for the twelve chairs in the jury box, all were white. "The prosecution excused every black person, one after the other," Goodman recalled. "We raised hell in the courtroom and the community when that happened, it became a big issue." Near the end of this contentious process, two more jurors were called for questioning. One was African American, an especially strong candidate in Goodman's estimate. "He was the president of a local union, an independent guy, and we found out from our 'network' enough to decide he would be a very good juror." The other candidate, who was white, appeared to be more sympathetic to the prosecution, but there was no reliable information on what kind of juror he might turn out to be. The prosecutor had already conducted his voir dire of the two, and the defense had to decide how to question them. "At Shango's suggestion, we announced we would not put a single question to either juror. We were saying we would accept the white juror if the prosecutor would accept the black juror." This put the prosecutor in a bind, for he was under mounting public pressure to avoid the appearance of a racially stacked jury. Shango's "silent approach" was vindicated when the prosecutor announced he would accept both men. He subsequently also accepted as first alternate a black woman who was, in Goodman's view, "solid, strong, a church person." She became the second black member of the jury when one of the original jurors was excused to attend a wedding. Goodman regarded this as crucial to the outcome of the case, since these two jurors would be able to "translate" certain things about black consciousness and life that might otherwise be lost on white members of the jury.[32]

Goodman was now four months into a relentless grind of pretrial hearings, discovery, and jury selection, and the start of the trial was still weeks away. "It was physically and emotionally difficult for me not being able to have any time for relaxation, going from Buffalo to Detroit, coming back, preparing every day, working every night and having no time to do anything else." The stress was occasionally relieved in the amiable surroundings of "Auburn Spot," the house on Buffalo's Auburn Street where legal volunteers from out of town stayed during the week. Goodman enjoyed the communal dinners at the house, especially when the younger members of the defense team got him talking about the 1930s and 1950s, the sit-down strikes and the Red Scare. But Goodman did not stay the night at Auburn Spot. "I just couldn't. I had to sleep by myself and have privacy." The Statler Hotel rented rooms by the month and had a comfortable piano bar that Goodman liked, with a young folksinger playing guitar. Even at the Statler, however, he was not sleeping well and the accumulating stress of the proceedings was sapping his strength. "The pressures became enormous," he remembered.[33]

The strain of it finally caught up with him during the voir dire of prospective jurors. He was questioning a particularly rude member of the jury panel, trying to draw him out in anticipation of asking the judge to dismiss him from the panel for cause. "Suddenly I didn't realize where I was, my orientation suddenly gave out. I just sat down in the midst of a very bad voir dire, really. Shango and the others wondered what the hell was going on and I didn't know myself." As disquieting as this was to members of the defense team, Goodman had experienced the symptoms before in moments of high stress, including the long-ago episode during the Smith Act trial. Diagnosed as "transitory hemispheric amnesia," the condition could trigger an "out-of-body" state in which, as he described it, his consciousness seemed to leave the body and look back down upon himself from above. The condition incapacitated Goodman for three days. When he returned to the case, he asked his son Bill to take on more of the trial work.[34]

His spirits were no doubt boosted by the unexpected windfall that appeared in the *New York Times* during jury selection. It took the form of a long open letter to the chief judge in the Attica trials from an assistant prosecutor by the name of Malcolm Bell. The letter charged that during grand jury hearings, the chief prosecutor had failed to investigate misconduct by corrections officers during and after the storming of the prison. Bell was not exonerating the Attica defendants, but he was making the point that the grand jury indictments were lopsided and conveyed the mistaken impression that the blame for all the acts of violence at Attica rested with the defendants. The effect of this well-publicized defection from the prosecution was to further stain the reputations of both the leaders of the assault, who had allowed it to degenerate into a sadistic massacre, and the prosecutors who failed to punish any of the officials responsible.[35]

Another surprise followed when Mary Jo Cook, a volunteer member of the Attica defense team, confessed at a press conference in New York City that she had been working all along as an FBI informant. The main target of her activities had been the Buffalo chapter of the Vietnam Veterans against the War (VVAW), but as she and her friends in the VVAW began working with the Attica defense, she had widened her reports to include the Attica support network. The defense team immediately filed a motion to call Cook to testify, arguing that the government's unconstitutional spying on the defense team was grounds for dismissal. Judge Mattina suspended jury selection for a week, and Cook took the stand and testified "at great length," according to Goodman, about her activities as an informant. Her FBI handlers were also called to the stand, as was Special Prosecutor Anthony Simonetti, whom the judge wished to question about the relationship between the FBI and the Attica prosecution. Goodman's hopes soared that the hearing would "blow this case up and out of the courtroom." The issues that Judge Mattina raised with Simonetti were so minor, however, that Goodman suspected the judge was giving the prosecutor an opportunity to dispel the impression of wrongful dealings with the FBI.[36]

The Trial

The jury was finally called to the Erie County courtroom on 20 May 1975. In his opening statement to the twelve men and women seated before him, the state's assistant prosecutor, Francis Cryan, tried to prepare the jurors for the kind of evidence they would have to evaluate. "This is an unusual case," he acknowledged, because the state's main witnesses were "inmates themselves, men who are convicted felons." He argued that they could be believed. "Understand the witness's circumstances, consider his record," Cryan asked of the jury, "but when you evaluate the testimony of any of these witnesses, first and foremost consider whether or not, in your opinion, . . . is he telling you the truth?" In making this pitch, the prosecutor clearly meant to preempt Goodman's attack on the credibility of his witnesses.[37]

Goodman's approach, however, was not to impugn the witnesses directly but to present them as victims of a cynical prosecution that extorted their testimony in return for parole or lighter sentences. In his opening statement to the jury, Goodman described the surprise testimony during the Wade hearing that had implicated Tommy Hicks in the killing of Schwartz and Hess. The state, he explained, had withheld that evidence in violation of its legal obligation to seek the truth. He warned the jurors that the prosecution would try to withhold evidence from them as well, all in a calculated attempt to convict Shango and punish him for his leadership role during the rebellion.[38]

There followed, over the next month, a long train of prosecution witnesses testifying to the circumstances that led to the killing of Schwartz and Hess. Each defense lawyer took responsibility for cross-examining particular witnesses, with Goodman concentrating on what he thought to be the three most important inmates on the list: George Kirk, the only witness who said he had seen Shango participate in the alleged kangaroo trial of Schwartz and Hess; Johnny Flowers, the only witness who said he had heard Shango say he would execute the two men; and Jimmy Ross, the only witness who said he had seen Shango kill Schwartz.[39]

"I firmly believe," Goodman later said of these cross-examinations, "never ask a witness any significant question unless you know in advance what his answer has to be." He would not be the first lawyer to abide by this principle, but the sheer scale of the Attica trial made it a difficult mandate to follow. The case involved hundreds of potential witnesses, some of them testifying repeatedly to police investigators, the grand jury, the Wade hearing, and defense investigators. The key would be for Goodman to draw the jury's attention to important discrepancies between past and present testimony, but to do this he had first to develop a comprehensive knowledge of everything the witness had said on the record. This was a manageable task only because he was able to concentrate on the three prime witnesses and leave the cross-examination of other inmates to his son Bill, Haywood Burns, and Shango. Goodman also had the advantage, as he saw it, of being the out-of-town lawyer, something he had first discovered decades before in San Francisco and Germany. "When you're away," he recalled soon after the Attica trial, "you concentrate solely, entirely and only on the case," without the daily distractions of life at home. "It gives you a real advantage over the opposition. Something you can't do if you're in your own city with all the ties you have and all the other things you are doing."[40]

With this complete immersion in the case, Goodman felt he could immediately recognize any discrepancy in witness testimony:

So instantly, when a witness testifies to some matter which I know is not true, which I know is contradictory, I'm in a position to say, "Now witness, you testified here at the Wade hearing on such a date?"

"Yes."

"And you testified out of that same chair before the same judge, didn't you?"

"Yes."

"And you testified under oath, didn't you? Now, I'll call your attention to the following testimony. Did you testify to that?"

"Yes."

"Just a moment ago you testified to the contrary."

Goodman would be educating two audiences. First, the witness would learn to be on guard, to take care, because Goodman had demonstrated his complete knowledge of the witness's previous words, taken from hearings the witness probably couldn't remember in the blur of past testimony. Eventually, the witness might even speak to matters about which he had not given previous testimony, but which he assumed Goodman already knew. Second, the jury would see that Goodman had done his job well, "that I [had] prepared carefully and that what I say is accurate and fair and they can believe me."[41]

The first of the three witnesses Goodman cross-examined, George Kirk, was dispensed with easily. When confronted with the variance between his current testimony linking Shango to the alleged trial in D yard and the previous accounts he had given to the grand jury and the Wade hearing, Kirk became confused and uncertain. Goodman pursued every discrepancy, no matter how small, with the same raised eyebrows and repeated question, "Are you as sure of that now as you were of the previous statement?" Kirk's testimony was so unconvincing that Judge Mattina subsequently granted Goodman's motion to dismiss the felony-murder charge for kidnapping, reducing it to "improper imprisonment."[42]

Johnny Flowers, the next witness, was a more difficult case. An articulate witness, Flowers stated that as a member of an inmate medical team he had been called to Schwartz's cell on either Friday or Saturday night at about 2:00 a.m., where he found Schwartz bleeding from a cut to his upper arm. After a member of the medical team had sewed and bandaged the wound, the medics encountered Shango as they were leaving. He reprimanded them for not having a pass and, according to Flowers, he then declared that Schwartz had been tried and convicted of treason, that the penalty was death, and that he was prepared to execute Schwartz.

Goodman was well aware, however, that Flowers had testified to very different circumstances when Linda Borus had visited him before the trial, at his cell in New York City's Tombs prison. On that occasion, Flowers had written and signed a longhand statement in which he said that Shango had told him and the medical team that the reason they needed a pass was because he (Shango) was responsible for protecting Schwartz and all the individuals in that block of cells, and that meant keeping them segregated from the rest of the prison population. Flowers quoted Shango as saying, "Look, we don't want anybody to get at these people . . . and we're trying to safeguard them and we can't let anybody in here who might do something to them." Goodman had immediately recognized the importance of Flowers's written statement and had it locked in a safe deposit box until the trial.[43]

It would now come in handy, for Flowers's testimony at trial completely contradicted the statement he had given to Borus. During cross-examination, Goodman pointed out that Flowers's first statements to the police contained no reference to Shango's alleged words regarding a pending execution of Schwartz and Hess. This story had been added later, when Flowers went before the grand jury. Goodman confronted Flowers with all these different statements he had made over time, including the version he acknowledged giving to Borus. "He turned and he twisted but there was no place he could go in front of that jury," Goodman remembered. "You [could] just see the jury going through the drama of these inconsistent statements." With the weak claim that "I'm right now and I was wrong then," Flowers tried to stick with his current testimony implicating Shango. Goodman was confident the jury could see Flowers for what he was: a man so manipulated by the prosecution that he would lie under oath.[44]

Finally, the principal witness for the prosecution, Jimmy Ross, came to the stand. Like Flowers, his testimony had also changed over time. In his first statements to the police, he had denied any knowledge of the murder, but by the time he had arrived before the grand jury he claimed to have been an eyewitness to the killing. Ross was "a little weasel-like guy," as Goodman described him, sallow-faced and pockmarked, a weak man who "couldn't possibly withstand the enormous pressures that were exerted in any prison." He was such a sorrowful presence that Goodman worried the jury might not welcome a tough cross-examination. He would have to approach him in a sympathetic way, treating him as "a pitiful object of a terrible prison system," a man who had been bullied into changing his testimony. Goodman began by walking Ross through his testimony in the Wade hearing, before the prosecution had finished sandpapering his version of events. Ross had then admitted that he was afraid of his inter-rogator, state investigator Jack Mildy, and he acknowledged that Mildy had coached him on portions of his testimony. Goodman then established that in his successive "eyewitness" statements, Ross had each time placed himself closer and closer to the event, from the far end of the corridor to directly in front of the cell where Schwartz was killed. As Ross became distraught, Goodman several times brought him to tears. The jury, he was confident, "began to sense finally that this poor creature was filled with all kinds of contradictions," to the point where "he could no longer call his soul his own."[45]

When the prosecution had called its last witness, there was still the matter of Bob Thomas and the surprising testimony he had given in the Wade hearing. The prosecution had, for good reason, decided not to call him as a trial witness, but Goodman and his fellow attorneys were also reluctant to call him for the defense. Thomas was an unreliable witness and some of his testimony might prove to be damaging to their case. Good-man therefore moved to have the judge call Thomas as a "witness of the court," an arrangement that meant neither the defense nor the prosecu-tion had to vouch for new evidence from Thomas, but both sides could cross-examine him on previous testimony to the grand jury or Wade hear-ing. In Goodman's estimate, the prosecutor got some "good stuff" from Thomas, but the defense established the more fundamental point: that Thomas had seen Tommy Hicks, not Shango, kill Schwartz.[46]

The defense now had to make a key decision: whether to call its own witnesses and make an affirmative case for acquittal, or forgo witnesses and simply ask the jury to reject the state's tainted evidence. Goodman favored the second approach, as he had through most of his career. "It was perfectly obvious by the end of the trial," he observed some months afterward, "not only to us but to the jurors and everybody else, that every single [prosecution] witness was under strong compulsion or had a strong interest in cooperating with the state and there was a lot to lose poten-tially in not cooperating." Goodman wanted the jurors to focus on the ways in which the prosecution had compromised its case by withholding evidence and using its power to coerce witnesses. He did not want them thinking about anything else, as they might if the defense brought new evidence. "Then the jury stops looking at the prosecution's case, stops asking itself have they really proved a case." Instead, they would be scru-tinizing the defense's case, "asking the question, can we believe the defen-dant? Can we believe the defendant's witnesses?"[47]

Shango, in contrast, felt that because so many of the prosecution witnesses had lied, he wanted the chance to call witnesses who would tell the jury and the public the unvarnished truth. There was, he insisted, a political point to be made at this juncture in the trial. "I tried to convince him," Goodman remembered, "that the question at issue in a criminal trial was not for the defendant to prove the truth, although sometimes it was possible, but rather for the prosecution to prove guilt." The prosecution had failed to do so, in Goodman's estimate, and he was confident the jury would acquit on that basis alone. In mid-June, Goodman and Shango argued the question back and forth at a daylong meeting in the Erie County jail. Goodman found the hot and unventilated prison especially oppressive. "Just being in that small room with sheet metal walls and one small window," Goodman remembered thinking, "was enough to destroy the morale of anybody." At the end of the day, however, they had reached a compromise: the defense would call its own witnesses to round out the case, but would limit the number to three.[48]

Dr. John Edland, the county coroner who performed the autopsies after the police assault, was the first to go before the jury. Rigor mortis, he explained, is a condition that lasts only about thirty hours, and since he had not examined Schwartz's body until midnight on Monday, the day of the police assault, Schwartz could not have been killed before Sunday, 12 September. In light of the fact that Jimmy Ross had claimed that Schwartz was killed on Saturday, Edland's testimony represented another blow to the state's case. In response, the prosecutor cited several textbooks that seemed to refute Edland's calculations, but Edland, to Goodman's relief, responded effectively. He agreed that it was inexact science and went on to discuss the relationship of politics to scientific judgment, recalling that he had been the first medical examiner to make public the fact that gunshot wounds had killed the hostages, not knives, as state officials had publicly stated. Edland went on in an emotional vein, declaring that he had paid a heavy price for telling the truth about his findings. He had become an outcast in the conservative community of Attica because he had told the truth about misconduct by white law enforcement officials, refusing to go along with the conspiracy of silence over the butchery at Attica.[49]

After Edland's testimony, the defense called Albert Victory, a white inmate who testified that Shango had urged interracial solidarity among the inmates during the uprising. Finally, the defense called Jim Ingram, a columnist for the *Michigan Chronicle*, Detroit's African American newspaper. Ingram, who had been part of the observer team during the siege of Attica, testified about the conversations he had with Shango just before the assault. Although the judge refused to let him testify as an expert witness on prison conditions and rebellions, Ingram gave useful testimony on racism in prison. It was a note on which Goodman was happy to rest his case.[50]

The prosecution summarized its case to the jury as best it could in light of the compromising testimony of its own witnesses. Goodman thought Cryan did a "pretty good" job, "better than I expected." The only thing lacking "was a sense of being a concerned human being." The defense followed with a summation divided into three parts. Goodman began by addressing the murder charge against Shango, reviewing in detail the prosecution's withholding of evidence and its coercion of witnesses whose testimony, in the end, had contradicted the prosecutor's claims. Haywood Burns then talked about the reduced charge of improper imprisonment, arguing that Hess and Schwartz were quarantined to save their lives in the midst of a hostile crowd of prisoners who believed they were traitors. Finally, Shango spoke about prison life and what it does to the prisoner. Goodman thought he did "very well, didn't overextend himself, didn't over-emotionalize it." He and Shango had worked on his presentation at length, recognizing that it was the only time he would be able to address the jurors directly. "He had to make the jury feel he was a pretty good human being and he could not have committed the kind of brutal, horrible murder that he was accused of." Goodman wanted Shango to impress the jury the same way he had impressed the defense team: that whatever he had been in the past, he was now capable of becoming a responsible member of society.[51]

The judge then gave the jurors instructions on what crimes they were to consider in judging Shango. They could find him guilty or innocent of killing Schwartz, but they could also consider the possibility that he had *aided and abetted* the murder of Schwartz. This widening of the charge was certainly to the prosecution's liking. The judge emphasized that Shango's mere presence didn't indicate aiding and abetting, but his instructions invited the jury to deliver a guilty verdict despite the compromised evidence. "This knocked me back on my heels," Goodman remembered. It was as if the prosecution, in light of evidence implicating Tommy Hicks in the murder, had decided at the last minute to abandon Ross's unconvincing testimony and accuse Shango of being an enabler rather than the actual killer.[52]

Goodman had to worry that this would make it easier for the jury to arrive at a guilty verdict. The first of the Attica trials had ended just two months before, in April, when Kunstler and Clark rested for the defense and the jury found their clients guilty of beating guard William Quinn to death. "The case is too old," Kunstler had said of the slackening public interest in the trial. Goodman could only speculate on what this augured for Shango. His case was certainly different from the one tried by Kunstler, and so was the approach he took to the trial. Goodman had great respect for Kunstler's political skills and personal commitment, particularly for the role he had played during the Attica standoff, when the rebels asked him to facilitate their negotiations with prison officials. Goodman, however, did not share Kunstler's penchant for dramatizing the political features of the case or engaging the judge in sharp and angry exchanges. Both he and Kunstler were "movement lawyers," broadly defined, and both wanted to win the public to their side as well as the jury. Both were successful trial lawyers, but Goodman was less flamboyant than Kunstler and more of a "lawyer's lawyer" when it came to preparation. Whereas Kunstler tended toward the broad brush of a political trial, Goodman gravitated toward the detail work of the legal craftsman, focusing on brief writing, the questioning of prospective jurors, and the pinpoint cross-examination of prosecution witnesses. In the case tried by Kunstler and Clark, the defense had called for picket lines outside the courtroom. "That must be done in some cases," Goodman observed years later, "but we didn't do it that way. We approached the jury on the basis of our understanding of their backgrounds."[53]

Goodman's attention to detail made this approach especially effective. During the trial he made a point of bringing people from the community and the defense team into the audience so that during breaks the jury could see Shango interact with these visitors, "chatting on a friendly, personal basis to a lot of people, smiling and laughing," as Goodman described it. The very teamwork that had made the defense so successful had also created a favorable impression with the jurors, as Goodman later recalled. "We made every effort to show the jurors we were humane and concerned, that this wasn't a game to us, that we were personally, intimately, and fully committed to the defense of a person and a cause we believed in. At the end, some of the jurors commented on this distinction between the defense and the prosecution. They also noticed the young people working with us so intensely, and the spectators who came over to talk to Shango during recesses." Goodman would later maintain that it was this "set of behaviors *within* the courtroom not without that 'sold' the jury on Shango as a responsible participant in the Attica rebellion."[54]

Vindication came sooner than expected. After deliberating little more than half a day, the jury informed the judge that it had come to a verdict. Reporters and members of the defense team were already crowded into the public seating, Shango's mother in the front row, when the jurors filed into the wood-paneled chamber of the Erie County Supreme Court. Goodman was exhausted and emotionally drained, sitting at the lawyers' table with his head in his hands. It was the culmination of many months of hard work, long stints of tedious preparation stretched between moments of anxious drama. "I knew I couldn't look at the jury and not break down," Goodman later recalled. "So I just put my head in my arms and laid my head down on the table and waited to hear. I was almost in a trance at the moment. Although the reading of the verdict is always a highly emotional moment, it was more so, much more so." When the jury foreman read the first verdict on the murder charge, "Not guilty," pandemonium broke out. Shango's mother shrieked and collapsed, sliding out of her chair and onto the floor. Judge Mattina stood at his bench, yelling at the court officer to "get an ambulance." But Mother Stroble revived and refused to be removed from the courtroom until the verdict on the charge of improper imprisonment was read. Again, "Not guilty." Again, pandemonium. "I never felt such a surge of absolute happiness," Goodman remembered. "Such relief. . . . Suddenly all this just welled up in this one moment and tears came out of my eyes. I couldn't do anything for a few moments but just sit at the table with my head in my hands and cry myself out."[55]

Years later, Goodman recalled the scene that followed. Shango was taken back to his jail cell and Goodman had lingered as the courtroom emptied. The judge had said he wanted to see him, and Goodman went back to the judge's chambers to thank Mattina for conducting the trial in a fair manner. They talked for quite a while, and when Goodman came out again the courtroom was empty. He walked through the empty building to the front door at the top of the courthouse steps, and paused. It was a dark night and he couldn't see very well. Hearing something at the bottom of the steps, he was suddenly wary. The trial had been an emotional catharsis not only for those who believed in Shango's innocence, but for those who hated him and what he stood for. Perhaps someone was lying in wait for him. Then he heard a distant pair of hands clapping at the bottom of the stairs, followed by others: his defense team had waited to applaud him. "I put down my briefcase and in a manner I had learned in some socialist countries, I applauded them as they applauded me. It was one of those moments I will never forget."[56]

Requiem for Shango

As Goodman and many others had predicted, Shango's acquittal made a shambles of the prosecution's case against the defendants who followed. Early the next year, the state dropped virtually all of the remaining indictments, an acknowledgment that no court would accept the tainted testimony of its poorly coached witnesses. That left only the civil suit brought by inmates and family against the state of New York for its reckless suppression of the rebellion. The case would drag on for fifteen more years, ending in 2000 with a settlement that obligated the state of New York to pay $8 million in damages to five hundred inmates and their survivors.[57]

Shango, in the meantime, would win his freedom. By the time of his acquittal, he had served his minimum sentence for the New York manslaughter conviction and was eligible for parole. Upon his release, he was immediately sent to Michigan to serve time for the jewelry store killing and the wounding of the Detroit policeman, convictions that Goodman and his fellow volunteers challenged in federal court on procedural grounds. "He was in Jackson Prison during this time and I saw him frequently," Goodman recalled of his continuing relationship with Shango. Citing the multiple errors of the presiding judge in the state court, the defense team was able to overturn the Michigan convictions in late 1978 and Shango was released the following year. For the first time in thirteen years, he was neither a fugitive nor a prisoner. "We had a drink together," Goodman remembered, "which we promised we would do one day."[58]

Shango and Linda Borus had fallen in love during the prolonged trial in New York and they moved in together in Detroit after Shango's release. In 1980, they had a son, Marcus, who would later go on to attend Central Michigan University. They named Goodman as Marcus's godfather. Jim Ingram, the *Michigan Chronicle* reporter who had testified for the defense during the Attica trial, bore witness to Shango's transformed nature. "He changed his whole way of thinking about things while he was in prison. He didn't go back to his criminal ways." He did go back to the streets, however, becoming a vocal opponent of the drug trade that was ravaging Twelfth Street and Linwood, the area where he lived. He was in all these respects a man who had rehabilitated his social life, though he still bore the scars and disabilities of his violent past. Borus believed he suffered from a kind of post-traumatic stress syndrome related to his life in prison, evidenced by reflexively paranoid reactions to "any unexpected touch," as she told a reporter years later. Two years after the birth of their son, she and Shango separated. He lived thereafter with his mother on Calvert Street and worked in the shoe repair shop she owned on Linwood. Mozie Stroble operated a nearby mission for the poor and owned both the building where the shoe shop was located and the restaurant across the street. Responding to the many down-and-out neighbors who lived in the area, she rented the apartment above the shoe store to an alcoholic man who, it turned out, was also a drug addict. According to later newspaper reports, drug dealers moved in on the man and turned the apartment into a shooting gallery, with a steady stream of junkies coming and going twenty-four hours a day.[59]

It was more than Shango could stand. He was already convinced, according to friends, that the government was abetting the drug trade as part of an effort to undermine the black community. Drug addicts now loitered in his mother's restaurant and broke into the shoe shop, burglarizing it on several occasions. Drug dealers linked to the notorious gang Young Boys, Inc., meanwhile, plied their trade immediately above Shango's workplace. He chased them out of his mother's restaurant on more than one occasion and tried to talk the newcomers into leaving the apartment. One day he went upstairs again and, according to press reports, physically assaulted three men he found there. "In less than an hour, young men driving Mercedes-Benzes and Cadillacs converged on the block," the *Detroit Free Press* reported, "brandishing handguns and long guns and swearing revenge." A lone killer ambushed Shango two days later in front of his mother's house, killing him at close range with three shotgun blasts to the head. Shango had been a free man for a little less than four years.[60]

"The phrase came to me, 'the short unhappy life of Shango,'" said Morrie Gleicher of the moment he learned of the shooting. Gleicher had been a fund-raiser for the Attica defense and had come to respect Shango's potential. "It was a terrible waste," he told a reporter. "There was a nobility of character about him. . . . Given the right circumstances, he could have been a productive human being." John Brady was less sure. Seventeen years before, when Brady was a Detroit policeman, Shango had nearly killed him with a pistol shot to the head at a spot about a mile away from where Shango was murdered. Brady still suffered headaches and the left side of his face was perpetually numb from nerve damage. "He lived a life of violence with no regard for human life," Brady said when a reporter for the *Free Press* sought him out. "The Good Book says, 'You live by the sword, you die by the sword.' It was inevitable." The reporter failed to ask what scripture applied in a case like Shango's, where the man who lived by the sword had apparently put it down, though not his fists.[61]

Goodman attended the funeral and mourned the sudden loss of his friend. The two had become emotionally intertwined through years of courtroom strategizing and long jailhouse discussions about Shango's case, the law, the politics of both, and the wider world. "I've never worked for a client . . . who contributed so much," Goodman would later say, "and was such a remarkable person that I learned not only to like him as a human being but to respect him as a co-counsel—because he was a co-counsel." When Shango was a prisoner in Michigan, Goodman sent him postcards when he traveled abroad, one from each country he visited. They were "real beautiful cards," Shango wrote in a letter to Sid Rosen, who had joined the defense team as a fund-raiser. "Each had a political note about the structure of the country and its scene. You can imagine how much these cards mean to me." In a life constrained not only by prison walls but his own history of deprivation, Shango found that Goodman filled a void. "He's a real wonderful and strong person whom I care an awful lot about," he confided to Rosen. "I can honestly say without reservation, I think more of him than any man I have personally known in all my life. I realize that's saying a whole lot, but it's true. He, Ernie, have [sic] given me more life and affection than my own father. . . . He's an unmatchable friend and comrade."[62]

Goodman also placed a special importance on his friendship with Shango, for reasons grounded in his own history. He had many African American friends and allies, but Shango was entirely different from his other clients and colleagues. He was not a lawyer like Crockett, or a political person like Millender, or an organizer like Len Holt, or a soldier like Lemas Woods, or an innocent like Willie McGee. He was a convicted killer whose life nevertheless confirmed Goodman's fundamental optimism about human potential. Shango had gone from low to high. A victim of circumstance—born black and poor to a one-parent family in a racist world—he also had an innate spark of redemption that made him stand out among the victims around him. Goodman would marvel years later at the unknowable mix of nature and nurture. "How does a person end up in prison rather than being a lawyer, let's say? What causes that? Is it the environment, heredity, a combination of both? Could society have prevented it? All these questions are involved in what you see here in Shango. The potential in what he really was and the potential for overcoming what he really was." In the end, he did not overcome the disabilities of his early life, but he had come a long way, and Goodman believed that Attica and the rebellion had crystallized the transformation. "When I met him, he was not the same kind of person he must have been 10–15 years ago."[63]

13
The Longer View

It was only a three-hour drive northeast of Detroit, but Stratford, Ontario, seemed a world away. There were several routes to the Shakespeare Festival that Ernie and Freda knew well, crossing the river into Canada at Detroit or Port Huron, often traveling with friends, usually the Crocketts. This summer it was just Ernie and Freda, celebrating their forty-third wedding anniversary. "I'm sitting at the banks of the Avon River here," Ernie said into the cassette recorder he had brought along, "a lovely grassy area looking out on the festival site and it's quiet and peaceful with ducks and swans around, people in little boats."[1]

It was only a few weeks after the Attica trial and Goodman wanted to make sense of what he had been through. The tape recorder was a first step, and he had already filled seven cassettes with his impressions of the trial as he traveled about, from his office in the Cadillac Tower to the house on Lake St. Clair, and from there to Stratford, where he now sat by the river in Queens Park. Throughout his life, he had always had in the back of his head the idea of writing a book, something more complete and detailed than the summary accounts he had written for the *Civil Rights News* or the *Guild Practitioner*. He had a reputation among his friends and family as a good storyteller, but he had not been a persistent writer. "The way it usually happens with me," he confided to the tape recorder, "is that after the event which I wanted to write about, I soon start gaining interest in other matters and lose the real quality which would have made [the writing] more important, more useful." The next campaign had always seemed more compelling than the last, and so not only did the recollection of events quickly fade, so did a sense of their significance. He had also come to despair of the meaningfulness of any written account he might leave behind. "When I go to the libraries and see the millions of publications that are all around usually buried deep in some research establishment,

444

I wonder what the hell anybody's going to do with all this stuff except eventually get rid of most of it."[2]

This time, though, he was determined. He was approaching his seventieth birthday and it now seemed there might not be many more campaigns for him, at least not of the same importance as Attica. He could feel his age, especially in his back, where a persistent pain had put him in the hospital and nearly driven him to surgery before Dean Robb found him a chiropractor. He tired sooner and his dizzy spell during the Attica trial worried him. The year before, Maurice Sugar had died at his home on Black Lake. Sugar, too, had struggled in his later years to make some record of his life, but he had waited too long and left only a half-finished manuscript. Contemplating the life of his friend and mentor, Goodman could not help but think of his own foreshortened future. And so he carried the cassette recorder with him, and the hours of tape piled up.[3]

This time, Goodman produced something close to a finished manuscript, a detailed account of the Attica trial based on his hours of tape-recorded material. The book, however, still eluded him. Several publishers showed interest in Goodman's proposal for a collection of chapters by different authors, each presenting a personal perspective on the trial, but in the end he could not persuade Linda Borus and Shango to complete their contributions. Like the comparative study he had started writing years before on legal systems in socialist and capitalist societies, the Attica book fell by the wayside.[4]

It would be left to others to catalogue his achievements. In the meantime, he would go on living as a semiretired lawyer on a comfortable income, free to pursue the next challenge, the new point of interest that always took precedence, as he confessed to his tape recorder, over the dissecting of past accomplishments. There would be other court cases to help with, younger lawyers to mentor, and old friends and family members to revisit. And with Freda there would be a renewed intimacy.

She and Ernie had made the trek to Stratford for many years, but the time they now spent together was taking on a different meaning. Rekindling a loving relationship was no simple matter, given the many difficulties that had troubled their marriage from the beginning. Freda's early disputes with her mother-in-law had been compounded by Ernie's quarrelsome and unilateral turn to the left after 1935. This was a shaky start to a marriage that had become all the more precarious during Ernie's affair with Laicha Kravchik, an infidelity that could only have compromised his affection for Freda. The bad feelings generated by these multiple shocks had shadowed their relationship over the years. Her antique business had given her an independent standing and an alternative circle of friends in the 1950s, allowing her to detach herself to some degree from the contro-versy and risks of her husband's political undertakings. They had endured difficult times and outlasted the Red Scare, a feat of perseverance that Freda had commemorated on Ernie's fifty-sixth birthday by giving him a piece of sculpture titled *Survivor.* "I find the title rather appropriate," she had written on the accompanying note, "for our latter years together any-way. They weren't always 'survival' years and I hope for both our sakes that perhaps they can improve. I'm willing to *try* anyway. Love, Freda." It would be trial and error for both, and despite all their efforts, they nearly separated in the late 1960s.[5]

After surviving this last crisis, Ernie and Freda came to recognize the underlying affection they had for each other and the comfort they found in their life together. They had always taken a mutual pleasure in traveling, starting with their honeymoon drive across the United States. As their income grew over the years, so had the itinerary and the accommodations, the roadhouse restaurants and Chevy Cabriolet replaced by airliners and first-class dining, from Mexico to Paris to Iran to South Africa. Many of these trips had included a detour to the local law courts, along with visits to Freda's brother in London and her family near Capetown. Ernie had sometimes accompanied Freda on the twice-a-year trip to London to buy inventory for her antique business, and he became especially fond of the city. "I have followed all your instructions," he wrote back to his office partners on an early visit, "and done nothing but bask in the London fog and enjoy the chill of the lovely London winter." Freda would meanwhile prowl the Portobello market for the eighteenth-century porcelains, orna-mental mirrors, and copper pots she took back to her Coach House Stu-dio on East Kirby Street, across from the Detroit Institute of Arts. With her success as an "International Junk Dealer," as Dean Robb called her, Freda had moved her studio in 1973 to larger quarters in the Garden Court Apartments, establishing a "Graceful Setting for Antiques," ac-cording to press reviews. It all made for a remarkable contrast: in the same years Ernie was in the news as defense counsel to Black Panthers and prison rebels, his wife was featured in the style section as an antique dealer to the wealthy, known to fashion editors for "her brisk British ac-cent." She was still known to friends and family as "the Duchess."[6]

If this jarring contrast had once been a source of conflict between the two, it was now a source of comfort and, for Ernie, a sly fulfillment. He had cast his lot with the downtrodden, yet he and Freda had achieved the kind of economic success he had once aspired to as a young business lawyer. His law firm had acquired a well-deserved reputation as one of the leading practitioners of personal injury law, winning cases and earning fees that not only supported his political work but made him and his partners prosperous. He and Freda invested the money in a series of real estate projects that were simultaneously homes for them to live in and displays of her creativity. They had sold their home of thirty years on Warrington Drive in 1969 and moved to an apartment on East Jefferson Avenue, closer to downtown. They bought a townhouse in London, England, then bought the Canadian house on Lake St. Clair in 1970, then sold both of these at the end of the decade to focus their attention on the vacation home they bought in Jamaica. Along the way there was also a house in Stratford, Ontario, which they sold in 1985, and finally, a house in suburban West Bloomfield. Freda was usually the initiator of these relocations, the move to West Bloomfield prompted by her interest in gardening. It was, she soon decided, a mistake. "In the city," her son Bill recalled, "she had been able to go into any restaurant and people would know her. In West Bloomfield, no one knew her and she was always getting lost." Within several years they had moved back downtown, taking an apartment in the 1300 tower of Lafayette Park.[7]

Ernie readily adapted to these changes. There was little to quarrel with: he lived in beautiful surroundings and Freda took good care of him. "If Ernie had been left to his own devices," his son Dick observed, "he would have been living at the YMCA and eating at the Coney Island." Instead, he lived in grace and style, Freda organizing dinner parties and fund-raisers in their home for civil rights, famine relief, and other causes.[8]

As part of this settled routine, Ernie and one of his oldest friends, Leonard Grossman, would take their bikes to Belle Isle, Detroit's island park, and cycle around the perimeter road. Stopping at the island's northern tip, they'd sit on a bench looking out on Lake St. Clair and talk as old friends do, ruminating on politics and picking though an ample storehouse of memories. Over time, the talk turned more often to friends who had died, among them Mort Furay, Goodman's hunting companion and colleague of nearly forty years. At the memorial service for Furay in 1972, Goodman had recalled how often his friend spoke of death—not in fear, but in recognition that it was "a worthy foe to be watched and kept at bay." Over the last fifteen years of Furay's life, he had risen to prominence in the local labor movement as president of the Hotel and Restaurant workers, becoming politically and personally aligned with Myra Wolfgang, the fiery chief executive of the union. When she died in 1976, Goodman spoke at her memorial service as well, recalling the "vivacious, pugnacious young" organizer of the 1930s who had since, like Rosasharon in

The Grapes of Wrath, "shared the milk of her life fully and without personal reservation with the working people of her union."[9]

Goodman and Grossman would have many more occasions to reflect on fallen friends. The future still beckoned, however. There was always the next deer hunt to plan, the next fishing trip to prepare for, the next Buck Dinner to organize. And as always, there was a wider world to explore.

At Home Abroad

The heavy pounding on the hotel door stirred Goodman out of a deep sleep. He and his old friend from the Sugar firm, Ned Smokler, were sharing the room in Lima, Peru, where they had participated in a conference of progressive attorneys from North and South America. The host government was sympathetic to the anti-imperialist politics of the conference, but police repression of social unrest over inflation and food shortages made Goodman and his colleagues apprehensive. "The local political situation was delicate," Smokler later recalled, "and Ernie and I agreed that in case any security problem arose, we would go straight to the American embassy." In the small hours of the morning, with the persistent pounding on their door, it appeared that moment had arrived.[10]

"It's a raid!" Goodman shouted as the two men stumbled out of bed in the dark room, still groggy with sleep. "To the Embassy, to the Embassy!" Smokler remembered a few moments of "agitation, flurry and excitement" before they both realized it was the night porter carrying out his orders to wake them at 5:00 a.m. for the return flight to Detroit. As Smokler recalled the event years later, "[T]wo slightly chagrined but greatly relieved lawyers made their way to the early morning plane."[11]

Goodman's presence in Peru on that June morning in 1974 was a measure of his long-standing belief that domestic and international issues were inextricably linked, as they had been for him since 1935. In his view, this was especially so with regard to the struggle for economic independence in Latin America, where the U.S. government had repeatedly intervened to protect the domineering influence of United Fruit, Standard Oil, and other corporate giants. Goodman had taken the lead in organizing the conference as a way of uniting the hemisphere's progressive lawyers behind the sovereign right of Latin American nations to take control of their natural resources—oil, bauxite, land, or copper—when these were controlled by foreign capital. Meeting less than a year after the Nixon administration and the CIA had supported a military coup against Chile's elected socialist government, the gathering in Lima took on a special urgency, marked by the presence of Chile's former minister of justice, now in exile. Goodman had opened the meeting as one of six men serving as cochairs, but voluntarily withdrew so that Ann Fagan Ginger could replace him at the podium; Ginger could appreciate this gesture better than most, twenty-seven years after her exclusion from the all-male confines of the Sugar firm. Goodman believed that the people of North and South America (women as well as men) could make common cause against the corporate globalization that weakened national sovereignty and despoiled local economies. "The financial and industrial interests, represented primarily by United States multi-national corporations," he wrote shortly after returning from Peru, "have created the same economic distortions in the economy of the United States, although at a different level, as those that plague Latin American countries."[12]

Out of this conviction came the American Association of Jurists (AAJ), formally established in 1975. Goodman and Ginger would serve over the next decade as the principal organizers of Guild participation in the AAJ's biennial meetings, joined by George Crockett, Claudia Morcom, and other veterans of the civil rights struggle in the United States. The governments that hosted these periodic gatherings—Cuba, Jamaica, Nicaragua, and Grenada—were themselves on the front lines of the struggle for economic independence, and welcomed the AAJ's critique of the unequal trade that impoverished underdeveloped countries. Goodman focused particular attention at these meetings on the fate of lawyers who were jailed and tortured in Chile, Brazil, and elsewhere for their defense of economic liberation and human rights. There had been persecution of lawyers in the United States during the McCarthy period, as he noted in his speech to the AAJ's 1977 convention, but it never reached "the level of oppression to which our colleagues who live under the military dictatorships in Latin America have been exposed." The American lawyer "who lives and works in the heartland of imperialism," he stressed, "has a special role and owes a special duty to the tens of millions who suffer the consequences of its economic, military and political policies."[13]

Freed from the rigors of constant litigation, Goodman was settling into the role of international doyen, a dean of civil rights lawyers in the United States and an emissary to troubled lands around the world. It was not an altogether new role. In 1961 he had observed South Africa's trial of Nelson Mandela and eight years later he had gone to Czechoslovakia to report on the Soviet invasion. Now, in March of 1978, the National Lawyers Guild asked him to play a similar role in Israel, a country he had long admired but had also come to question.

The focal point of his role would be to observe the trial of a U.S. citizen accused by the Israeli state of associating with terrorists. In many ways it was the most difficult case he would encounter in the years following the Attica trial. Like most on the left, Goodman had supported the founding of Israel in 1948 and still felt an emotional attachment to the Jewish homeland, tempered by his recognition that much of the state's legal foundation, particularly with respect to family law and immigration, favored Jewish citizens over their Palestinian neighbors. Since the troubled time in 1967 when Detroit's Guild members had debated the circumstances of the Six Days' War and the occupation of the West Bank and Gaza, the controversy surrounding the Jewish state had become increasingly polarized. Many still saw Israel as an outpost of democracy and Western values victimized by the terrorism of its Arab opponents, while others, including many in the new Left, now viewed the same country as a Zionist intruder in the Middle East, backed by American power. Goodman had conflicted feelings and no doubt welcomed the chance, at the age of seventy-two, to take a firsthand look at Israel's system of criminal justice.

The defendant in the case was Sami Esmail, a twenty-three-year-old graduate student in engineering from Michigan State University. The son of Palestinian immigrants, Esmail had traveled to Israel in 1977 to visit his dying father, who had returned to the West Bank city of Ramallah several years before. The Israeli security police arrested the American-born student in the Tel Aviv airport, interrogated him for the next six days, and finally charged him with membership in an enemy organization, the Popular Front for the Liberation of Palestine (PFLP). At no point was Esmail charged with any specific acts of terrorism or plans to carry them out; Israeli authorities acknowledged that Esmail had traveled to Israel solely to visit his father. He was charged nevertheless under a unique law that made Israeli courts competent to try a person who had committed an act in another country that would be illegal if it had been committed in Israel. Esmail had supported the PFLP while a student at Michigan State and had distributed its literature on campus; since such activity was illegal in Israel, Esmail was liable to prosecution once he landed in Tel Aviv. He had also visited Libya for two weeks in 1976 and, it was alleged, had undergone military training in that fervently anti-Israel nation; he was therefore, the Israelis charged, guilty of contact with enemy agents. The police claimed that Esmail had voluntarily signed confessions to this effect; Esmail said he had done so only after nearly a week of sleep deprivation, threats, and physical stress, and that he had visited Libya only at the government's invitation, as a political tourist.[14]

Goodman's investigation of the case and his observation of the trial in Tel Aviv reinforced his long-held beliefs in the exceptional qualities of U.S. law. There was, he reported, no provision for trial by jury in Israel.

A panel of three appointed judges would decide Esmail's fate, and the presiding judge would take part in the cross-examination of witnesses, at times blurring his role with that of the prosecutor. Under Israeli law, the fact that Esmail had traveled to Libya *automatically* made him guilty of contact with enemy agents, and it was the defendant's responsibility to provide an alternative explanation that would prove his innocence. The testimony of security agents was taken behind closed doors, and there was no verbatim transcript of the proceedings. The only evidence brought against Esmail was his signed confession, and while there was conflicting testimony about whether or not he had been tortured, there was no doubting that he had not been allowed to speak to a lawyer until after he had signed the declaration of guilt—a point of special significance to Goodman. Even if the confessions were valid, Goodman reported, none of this would make Esmail liable for prosecution in the United States, where the precedents Goodman had helped establish during the 1950s protected individuals in their *beliefs* and *associations*—no matter how unpopular—as distinguished from illegal *acts* or *plans* to carry them out. The extraterritorial claims of Israeli law made Esmail liable for behavior that was perfectly legal in Michigan, and on these grounds alone he would ultimately be convicted and sentenced to fiftten months in prison for "membership in an illegal organization." He was acquitted, however, on the charge of "contact with enemy agents."[15]

Goodman's report on these proceedings immediately embroiled him in a sharp dispute with opponents on both sides of the conflict. Before he had even issued his findings, critics of Israel within the Lawyers Guild were already denouncing the Jewish state for torturing Esmail and forcing him to sign a confession written in Hebrew, a language he did not speak. Goodman had little patience with this rush to judgment and privately scolded the editors of *In the Struggle*, the Detroit chapter's newsletter, for statements that were either untrue (the initial confession was in English) or disputed (even Esmail later stated that his torture was "more psychological than physical"). By failing to ascertain the facts, Goodman counseled his fellow Guild members, "we undermine our own integrity and provide a ready-made stick for our critics and enemies to beat us down." It was also worth noting that even though Israeli practice fell short of the high standards that he and others might apply, it was no worse than the common practice in most socialist and Western European countries, which also permitted interrogation without counsel and trial without jury.[16]

Goodman and his colleagues on the left were in general agreement that the FBI had played a pivotal and unseemly role in Esmail's arrest.

Speculation on this score was later confirmed when the FBI acknowledged that it had, in fact, alerted the Israeli government about Esmail's political activities in Michigan and his trip to Libya. Some within the Guild believed that all such contact with foreign security police was unacceptable, but Goodman took a measured approach. "I should make clear," as he wrote in his draft report, "that I do not question the right or even the duty of the FBI . . . to exchange information with their counterparts in other countries concerning possible murder, hijackings, etc." There was, however, no evidence that Esmail was engaged in such activity; he had been targeted by the FBI and Israeli security for his political beliefs, not for his actions.[17]

On the other side of the debate were critics like Bernard Fischman, a Guild member in New York who sent an open letter to *Guild Notes* condemning the final, edited version of Goodman's report. Fischman had seen the initial draft, which included Goodman's statement "I am opposed, on political as well as humanitarian grounds, to terrorism as a means of achieving political changes." This sentence had been removed from the final report by members of the Guild's International Committee, who also excised Goodman's comments on the FBI's role. Their stated reason for doing so was to pare the document of first-person opinion and limit it to the immediate circumstances of the trial. Fischman objected to what he saw as a more sinister intent, an implicit endorsement of terrorism. In response, Goodman acknowledged that he wished he had been able to participate in the last-minute revision of his report, but he had already left the country on another trip (this time to China) and he had authorized the committee to make changes as it saw fit. He reminded Fischman that the committee had also deleted a long paragraph in which Goodman had noted that struggles for national independence and fundamental social change "have frequently been accompanied or supported by terrorist groups." Fischman had failed to note *this* deletion in his open letter, and Goodman wondered if it was because such a reference to the historical background of political terrorism "might have brought into focus Israel's early use of the tactic." Whatever Fischman's motivation, Goodman took him to task for the same offense Fischman had directed at the International Committee. Like the committee, he had selectively quoted from the draft report. "Where was *your* explanation?" he asked.[18]

In his younger days, Goodman might have waded into such a debate and fought it through to some kind of resolution. But no longer. "I am getting sick and tired of this type of controversy," as he put it in his letter to Fischman, "and I do not intend to use my limited energies on this kind of dirt scratching any further." He felt the debate over Esmail's case had failed to grasp an underlying reality to which he was, characteristically, sensitive. "In all this political controversy, we tend to forget that a human being is involved. I met Sami in prison. He is an extremely bright and obviously sincere man. He reminds me of the best and brightest of our own—those who became committed to the civil rights or the anti-Vietnam war movements of the 60s. As I talked to him, I thought how much the same in appearance, in intensity and their idealism, are the Jewish and Arab young people of our time."[19]

This human dimension was hard for Goodman to put aside. On the one hand, as he noted in his report, Esmail's trial occurred just three days after a terrorist attack on a beach north of Tel Aviv in which thirty-seven Israelis were killed, including women and children. Israelis could not help but be concerned for their physical safety and security. On the other hand, thousands of Palestinians had been driven from their homes over the years, many forced into refugee camps in the West Bank and Gaza where they lived under Israel's military occupation. They could not help but resent the terms of their expulsion and subjugation. Goodman believed that Israel would eventually have to recognize an independent Palestinian state in the occupied territories, though he saw little near-term prospect for such a resolution. "I am afraid," he wrote a colleague after his return, "that Israel is storing up the grapes of wrath."[20]

Goodman could at least find consolation in the fact that Israel, confronted by the publicity surrounding the case and the pressure brought by members of the U.S. Congress, had agreed to parole Esmail after ten months in prison. But as Esmail told the media on his return to Michigan, had he not been an American citizen, his case would have been hopeless.[21]

The Final Verdict

It was one thing to observe a trial, and another thing to serve as defense counsel. "So much in court depends on a tone of voice or a whispered conversation, or something you see out of the corner of your eye," Goodman told a reporter on one occasion. "I feel fine, but I just can't see things as sharply. I get tired. I don't hear so well. And you can't have an attorney cupping an ear and saying, 'Whassat you say, judge?'"[22]

He still had his moments. In 1977 he made the opening statement on behalf of African American plaintiffs who charged the American Automobile Association (AAA) with racial discrimination in hiring and promotion. The Reverend William Cunningham, director of Focus: Hope, the nonprofit group that helped bring the suit, recalled Goodman's presentation as "the most dramatic thing I've ever seen in my life." Rising slowly before the judge and a hushed audience, Goodman mounted a withering attack on AAA's history of discrimination that was, in Cunningham's estimate, "what Moses must have sounded like coming down from the Sinai." The auto club agreed to pay $4.7 million in damages six years later, but by then Goodman had been forced to dramatically reduce his courtroom participation. The most telling of several moments that led to this diminished role came in 1980, during the trial of his old friend Morrie Gleicher on the spurious charge of taking kickbacks from government contracts. With his friend's career on the line, Goodman rose from the defense table to deliver the opening statement on Gleicher's behalf. He had uttered only a few sentences before he suddenly faltered, overwhelmed by the acute stress of the moment, unsure where he was and unable to make out the voices echoing in his head. It was the onset of the same transient amnesia that had felled him twenty-five years before during the Smith Act trial and again during the Attica case. His son Bill helped him back to his seat and finished reading the opening statement. Goodman soon recovered and Gleicher was acquitted, but it was Bill and another colleague, Ken Mogill, who handled most of the trial work in the case.[23]

Months later, the Lawyers Guild and the ACLU organized a banquet honoring Goodman's half century of commitment to progressive causes. The majority of the six hundred people who attended the Tribute to Ernest Goodman at the Book Cadillac Hotel that December of 1980 could not have known the particulars of his medical condition, but it was obvious that at the age of seventy-four, Goodman was nearing the end of his career. Sponsors and attendees of the event included both U.S. senators from Michigan, more than two dozen judges, half the members of the Detroit City Council, former governor G. Mennen Williams, and more than six hundred colleagues, comrades, and clients from labor and civil rights struggles stretching back to the 1930s. The keynote speaker was Detroit mayor Coleman Young, Goodman's long-ago partner in the Progressive Party. It was a remarkable constellation of political and social leaders that Young addressed that night, incorporating centrist Democrats, civil libertarians, and left-wing socialists.[24]

There was much to acknowledge. In the formal invitation that went to members of the labor movement, the mayor and UAW president Doug Fraser evoked the early days of union organizing when few lawyers were willing to take on "the difficult, often hazardous" job of defending workers in the picket line battles of the 1930s and 1940s. "Ernie was a rock of strength in those days," Young recalled over his signature. At the event itself, Judges Damon Keith and Claudia Morcom called to mind Goodman's early efforts on behalf of the civil rights movement, Helen Winter summoned the memory of his role defending her and others during the Red Scare, and city council president Erma Henderson recalled Goodman's part in nearly five decades of struggle in Detroit. The many members of the National Lawyers Guild in attendance had special reason to honor Goodman for his pivotal role in reviving the organization after the Red Scare of the 1950s; from the low point of fewer than five hundred members, the Guild now boasted a roster of six thousand lawyers, law students, and legal workers. Testimonials from across the country filled the banquet book. "Our love and respect goes to Ernie," said one, adding that Goodman's "only fault is that he does not come from New York."[25]

Goodman was gratified by the high praise showered on him by old friends, but it was the day-to-day work he did mentoring a new generation of lawyers that gave him the most satisfaction in these years. "There were little things that Ernie did that were enormous insights for me in trying a case or writing a brief," Ken Mogill remembered of his work with Goodman during the Attica and Gleicher trials. One particular moment stood out during the Gleicher case. "I put my final argument together based on the facts of the record and the law, but when Ernie read it he urged me to present it not as a matter of legal reasoning, but as a matter of human relations that connects with the jury on that level." Another young lawyer, Jeanne Mirer, recalled how Goodman had gone out of his way to help her start her own practice. She had agreed to help train members of his firm in the employment law she was beginning to master, and in return Goodman sent her cases and helped edit briefs. "You've got to have a strong ego to work with me," he told her after "ripping apart" a first draft. In terms of training, she reminisced years later, "I don't know who got more out of this."[26]

Paul Rosen recalled the same support from Goodman years before, when a contentious debate erupted over who would make the final argument to the Supreme Court in the case of *Palmer v. Thompson*. Both Arthur Kinoy and William Kunstler wanted the honor, and both personally lobbied Goodman to have the younger and less experienced Rosen moved aside. Goodman, who felt Rosen had done the lion's share of the work preparing the appeal, sided with Rosen against his better-known colleagues from New York. "He told them," as Rosen recalled of Goodman's response, "that 'you can't ask young people to do civil rights work and then at the point it reaches the Supreme Court, you take it away.'" In the end, it was Kinoy who had to step aside and allow Rosen to join with Kunstler in making the final argument for integrating Jackson's swimming pools. Dick Soble was another young lawyer who had reason to appreciate the confidence Goodman showed in his younger attorneys.

A tenants' rights lawyer before he entered the practice, Soble found that once he had demonstrated that he could contribute to the firm's success in personal injury cases, there was considerable latitude in the kind of pro bono work he could take on for low-income clients. He appreciated as well the decent living he could make along the way. The Goodman firm was "a kind of nirvana," he remembered, "because it did political work but at the same time the partners were able to make a living, they had taken no vow of poverty."[27]

The Goodman firm still stressed the importance of political commitment, but the roster of attorneys who followed that mandate was changing dramatically. Dean Robb left the firm in 1971 and moved to Traverse City in Michigan's northland. Over the years, he had joined Goodman and some of his closest friends, Sid Rosen and Mort Furay, on trout-fishing trips to northern Michigan, with Robb learning along the way "that I wasn't fit to live in Detroit all my life, or any asphalt jungle." For the former farm boy from southern Illinois, moving north was his chance to finally escape the city and start his own law firm.[28]

The departure of Dick Goodman five years later had to be especially troubling for the elder Goodman, since it marked not only the exit of his first son but also the appearance of an undeniable fault line within the structure of the partnership. When Dick entered the firm in 1960, he told his father he had little enthusiasm for devoting the rest of his life to personal injury cases. Even so, he had become a willing apprentice under Robb's tutelage and went on to make a name for himself in the development of product liability law—with ever-higher fees to match. He was devoted to the firm's political goals, though with less fervor than his brother Bill, who was active in the Lawyers Guild and served as its national president in the mid-1970s. Dick focused more of his energy on the personal injury practice that supported the firm's political work. While he accepted this "rainmaker" role, he also saw a jarring disparity between the unequal revenue generated by each member of the firm and the "socialist" policy (as Rosen ironically called it) of equalizing the salaries of senior partners. The continuing dispute over this mismatch between the division of labor and the division of rewards drove Dick out of the firm in 1976.[29]

With the death of Robert Millender two years later, the roster of senior partners Ernie had worked with through the 1960s shrank another notch. Millender was widely known as the "King Maker" of African American politics in Detroit, the man who had managed the campaigns of congressmen, judges, city council members and, most recently, the mayor. He remained throughout the paragon of the honest political broker, known for his integrity and his aversion to publicity. "He never took anything from his political work," Rosen recalled of his fellow partner. "No contracts or paid appointments. That was his power: 'They can't buy me.' "[30]

There was no shortage of applicants to fill these vacancies at the firm, which now enjoyed a national reputation for its personal injury practice and its continued support of cases brought on behalf of the United Farm Workers, the NAACP, and neighborhood legal services in southeast Michigan. Ernie was still the titular head of the firm, but with the day-to-day details of administration handled by others, he had settled into semi-retirement. He went to his office every day and sat at the head of the table at the monthly meeting of senior partners, though he didn't necessarily chair the proceedings. Based on a long-standing rule established by the original partners, he had stopped taking a regular salary after his sixty-fifth birthday. He did, however, share in the year-end bonuses distributed to the partners, even though he was no longer a significant contributor to the firm's income stream. Paul Rosen, whose success in negligence cases generated a growing share of that income, recognized the trade-off that accompanied his role. "We knew it was important to have [Ernie] beyond the economics, because your own stature was enhanced by working in the Goodman firm. To enter the courtroom as a member of the Goodman firm meant you had integrity."[31]

Goodman's peers in the State Bar of Michigan agreed. In 1992, they awarded him their Champion of Justice Award, given annually to lawyers or judges whose "extraordinary professional accomplishments have benefited the nation, state, or their local community." It was a measure of the unique qualities of his law firm that over the years, another five of his former partners and associates would also receive the award—Dean Robb, George Crockett, Claudia Morcom, Victoria Roberts (a ten-year veteran of the firm appointed to the federal bench in 1998), and Elizabeth Gleicher (daughter of Morrie Gleicher, appointed to the state appeals court in 2007). No other law firm could match their collective achievement. Goodman, the *Detroit Legal News* reported, "has defended those considered indefensible, not because of what they did, but because of who they were, reflecting the prejudices of their times." Three years later, the *Legal News* named Goodman one of Detroit's sixteen "Legal Legends of the Century."[32]

The times had certainly changed since the 1950s, when Goodman had been driven to the margins of acceptable practice. The political environment within the bar had come full circle, and there was no better measure of this than the selection of George Crockett for the Champion of Justice Award in 1996. It was a bittersweet moment. He had won election to Congress in 1980 and retired a decade later, but for all the honors

heaped upon him, he had not returned to a function of the state bar
since 1954—when he and Goodman had stood in silent rebuke of Judge
Medina's presence before that body. Forty years after being nearly disbarred for his role in the first Smith Act trial, Crockett joined Goodman
again at the annual dinner, the past and present recipients of the state bar's
highest award.[33]

There was vindication of another sort in the profound changes forced
on the FBI and police "Red Squads" in the years following the Watergate
crisis. Of particular relevance to Goodman and the Lawyers Guild were
two court suits that came to a conclusion in 1989 and 1990, one focusing
on the federal government, the other on Michigan and Detroit. Both followed from the congressional hearings in 1975 that exposed the government's massive campaign of illegal surveillance and harassment of U.S.
citizens, implicating both Republican and Democratic administrations.
"We have seen segments of our Government adopt tactics unworthy of a
democracy," the Senate Select Committee had concluded, "and occasionally reminiscent of the tactics of totalitarian regimes." The activities of the
FBI had drawn the special attention of investigators, revealing a campaign
of disruption that matched the worst fears of Goodman and others in the
Lawyers Guild. "The Government," Senate investigators concluded,
"operating primarily through secret informants, but also using other intrusive techniques such as wiretaps, microphone 'bugs,' surreptitious mail
opening, and break-ins, has swept in vast amounts of information about
the personal lives, views, and associations of American citizens." The
government's illegal activities, they found, went beyond mere surveillance. Between 1956 and 1971, the FBI's Counter Intelligence Program—
COINTELPRO—had initiated 2,370 covert actions against citizen groups
that represented no threat to national security but were perceived by J.
Edgar Hoover as threats to the status quo. The aim of these clandestine
actions had been to sabotage and disrupt the constitutionally protected
activities of government opponents. Clarence Kelly, the new director of
the FBI after Hoover's death in 1972, apologized for past abuses that
"were clearly wrong and quite indefensible," and President Gerald Ford's
attorney general, Edward Levi, announced new guidelines that expressly
prohibited investigation of organizations engaged in First Amendment
activities.[34]

Many of the FBI's covert operations had been directed against the
National Lawyers Guild, and more than a few against Goodman. After
the Senate investigations, the Guild sued the attorney general in 1977
seeking disclosure of the FBI's campaign against the organization and an
injunction against future persecution. Michael Krinsky of New York was

the lead lawyer in the suit and Goodman was his enthusiastic supporter. The results of the discovery process were staggering: over the next twelve years, the FBI was forced to produce more than four hundred thousand pages from its files related to the prolonged investigation and harassment of the Guild's *legal* activities. More than one thousand informants had been used to collect this political dossier, some of them working their way into leadership positions in the national organization and its local chapters. FBI agents had repeatedly broken into the Guild's offices, stolen documents, disrupted meetings, and done their best to sabotage the jobs and political careers of Guild members. Goodman and other national leaders of the organization had been singled out for special attention, the government going so far as to notify the CIA of Goodman's itinerary when he and Freda traveled abroad.[35]

The federal government fought the discovery process in the Guild's case every step of the way, prolonging it over years of litigation. The Reagan administration even claimed in 1983 that the court should dismiss the suit altogether because the forty-year investigation of the Guild, even if constitutionally invalid, had been carried out on the basis of "national security" and should therefore be exempt from judicial review. The court rejected this claim, but the government continued to resist full disclosure until the final settlement of the suit in 1989.[36]

Paralleling this welcome exposure of the FBI's political spying was an equally revealing exposé of police misconduct in Michigan. Since the Roosevelt administration, local Red Squads across the country had served as the frontline agencies of the FBI and the national security state, with both the Michigan state police and the Detroit police conducting surveillance and covert operations against those deemed a "potential" problem. The extraordinary reach of this political surveillance was revealed in 1974 when the Michigan Association for Consumer Protection (MACP) discovered that it had been secretly targeted for investigation by the state police solely because it was lobbying for a consumer protection bill. The Goodman firm took the MCAP case to court, with Dick Soble serving as the main courtroom attorney and George Corsetti, a legal advisor to MACP, the principal author of the brief calling for an end to such spying.[37]

As the case gained additional plaintiffs and expanded its scope to include Detroit's Red Squad, the discovery process revealed the extent of the secret surveillance conducted against Michigan citizens: the state police had compiled some thirty-eight thousand case files over the years and the Detroit police between fifty thousand to one hundred thousand files (depending on varied estimates of duplication). Together, the state and local police had collected an estimated 1.5 million names. With the initial round of court-ordered discovery, Goodman learned that his file alone contained over three hundred documents, many of which had been forwarded to the FBI. Police files had also been shared with Chrysler and other large corporations to identify—and blacklist—union activists and radicals, punishing them for political beliefs deemed unacceptable to government and business leaders. Mere attendance at an antiwar rally or a political forum had been enough to trigger investigation. Judge James Montante (a Guild member and past president of the Detroit chapter) issued a declaratory judgment against the unconstitutional laws that had authorized the surveillance and ordered the state and city police forces to open their files to those illegally targeted. It would take until 1990, however, to sort out the procedure for full disclosure of Detroit's files.[38]

Goodman knew better than most that the settlement of these cases hardly ended the threat to civil liberties and rights. As he had learned over a lifetime, there was an unrelenting pressure on public leaders to wield their power on behalf of privilege, and this corrupting influence was especially potent when there was no countervailing pressure for social equality. The abuse of power was nonpartisan in this respect, all the more so when Democrats and Republicans were united in support of the global expansion of U.S. power, military and corporate. As Goodman knew from hard experience, the national security state had long enjoyed the bipartisan support of liberals and conservatives, from Presidents Franklin Roosevelt and Lyndon Johnson to Richard Nixon and Ronald Reagan. The result could only be a continuing tension between the Bill of Rights—itself a legacy of the revolutionary struggle against British imperialism—and the "emergency powers" invoked so often against foreign enemies and domestic subversion, real and imagined. So long as the United States was preparing for global war, hot or cold, the challenge to civil liberties and rights would be ongoing.

It was a challenge that could be met. Those who drafted the Constitution may have thought of the courts only as an independent check on the other branches of government, "but after 200 years of conflict and development," as Goodman had written in the mid-1970s, "the judiciary now holds firmly in its hands not only the power to restrain excesses . . . , but the power to compel the executive and legislature to adopt and carry out measures designed to conform to what . . . is required by the Constitution." He had seen the positive side of such judicial activism throughout his life, from the court decisions that outlawed deliberate segregation to judgments that, however belatedly, overturned the worst abuses of the Red Scare. Judicial activism, of course, could also advance conservative causes. "For better or worse," as Goodman put it to his friend and fellow lawyer Edward Littlejohn in a 1996 interview, "a lawyer can actually participate in, even initiate, the legal process by which these social changes can be effected."[39]

He had also come to know the limits of that legal system. "How do you deal with the fundamental gap that has arisen in the last 20–30 years between the rich and the poor?" he had asked in the same interview. "The courts are not supposed to tamper with that question. The Constitution doesn't apply to those things." Only a mass movement could force a change in the balance of economic power between social classes, and without such a movement there was little a lawyer could do. Goodman had learned that lesson in the 1950s, when he lost the civil suit to block the dispersal of jobs from the Ford Dearborn plant. The city's mayor, even a onetime radical like Coleman Young, was also powerless to stem the economic tide that impoverished Detroit's workers. Joseph Hudson, owner of the department store chain that bore his name, had said as much in 1972. "The black man has the feeling he is about to take power in the city," Hudson had said little more than a year before Young's election. "But he is going to be left with an empty bag." For years, white business owners had been abandoning the city, the state, and, often enough, the country. Young could implement needed reforms in police practices and affirmative action in hiring, but he alone could not change the economic facts of life under global capitalism. "Business Exodus Withers City," the *Detroit Free Press* headlined a report two years *before* Young's election. "In many respects," the report began, "Detroit is like an old, worn out boxer with everything but the heart beaten out of him." The same could have been said of Young after his twenty years in office. In the end, his long tenure was characterized by the increasingly bitter denunciations he directed at suburban white leaders.[40]

There had been dramatic changes in personal injury law during these same years. By the 1980s, the dramatic rise in settlements and attorney fees had put lawyers on the defensive, charged with bringing frivolous suits that enriched themselves and drove up the cost of doing business or practicing medicine. Lawyers had brought some of this on themselves, Goodman had to acknowledge. He still believed that unless there were unions and government regulations to protect workers and consumers, and unless there was a social safety net to care for the victims of negligence, then civil suits to punish abusive business or medical practices were the last best defense for the ill treated. But he also believed, as he said in 1996, that there were "a lot of greedy lawyers who were just interested in getting a hell of a lot of money," and that these attorneys paid little heed, as he and his partners had, to the underlying conditions that endangered workers and consumers. Even so, he felt the pendulum in "tort reform" had swung too far in the direction of protecting corporations, particularly when Michigan's legislature passed a statute in 1995 exempting pharmaceutical companies from personal injury suits for drugs approved by the Federal Drug Administration. Given that many of these same companies were rushing poorly tested drugs to market while also lobbying for *weaker* FDA oversight, the net result was that Michigan was giving negligent pharmaceutical companies a "Get out of jail free" card. The burden of supporting the inevitable victims of such deregulation would now be forced on taxpayer-funded Medicare and Medicaid budgets rather than the companies responsible for their injuries.[41]

The pro-business bias in tort reform, he believed, would also make it difficult for younger lawyers to duplicate his firm's success in personal injury law. Corporations were prepared to invest massive amounts of money in the courtroom defense of their products and practices, but because of the legislative limits on awards and the unfriendly rulings of conservative judges, attorneys for the plaintiff would have a harder time recovering the cost of meeting this challenge. Inevitably, they would have less time and income to support pro bono work. "You can do it for a while because you're young," said Goodman of volunteer lawyers who hadn't yet started a family, "but you couldn't do it for long." Barring a change in political climate, the pressures would grow to turn away from clients who had little or no money.[42]

The Last Arrest

It was a late winter morning in 1996 and Goodman had been up since before dawn. He was eighty-nine years old and he was about to do something he had never experienced before. After witnessing countless arrests over the years, on this last occasion he would play a new role: this time, *he* was the one the police would take into custody.

Thousands of newspaper workers were on strike against Gannett and Knight Ridder, the two nationwide chains that ran Detroit's morning and evening newspapers as a single government-sanctioned monopoly. After union leaders had reluctantly accepted the joint ownership of the *Detroit News* and the *Free Press* some years before, they had not expected management to subsequently demand the elimination of hundreds of jobs and wage cuts for many of the workers who remained. By March of 1996, the strike against these unilateral demands had already gone on for eight months. Despite a readers' boycott and mass picketing to prevent the distribution of the Sunday edition, the companies sustained their curtailed operations with the replacement workers they had recruited before the strike began. Seeing this as an attempt to break the unions, strikers were asking supporters to escalate their efforts by blocking access to the downtown offices of the *Detroit News* on a weekly basis, an act of peaceful civil disobedience that would highlight public support for the striking unions.

Goodman's firm would represent many of those arrested, but Goodman himself would no longer serve as defense council. He was now the rank-and-file activist, the consumer, the union supporter on the picket line. That morning, he joined the contingent of protesters who walked past the cheering picketers outside the *News* building to sit down in front of the doors, knowing the police would haul them away. The arrest itself was a gentle affair. After the "sit-downers" refused to move aside, the police escorted Goodman to the bus that would carry him to police headquarters along with city council president Maryann Mahaffey, Bishop Thomas Gumbleton, and more than thirty others arrested that morning. The two officers who walked Goodman to the bus were African American. The photo in the *Detroit Sunday Journal*, the strikers' newspaper, showed Goodman walking between them, smiling broadly.[43]

He was no longer a practicing attorney. More often, he was now "Grandpa Ernie," a term of endearment he had come to relish over the previous twenty-five years. The oldest of Dick's children, Carlos, recalled that he always felt special for being Ernie Goodman's grandson. As a boy and a young adult, he had developed a close bond with his grandfather, a man he remembered as attentive and enthusiastic, never one to be admired from a distance as a remote figurehead. There was nothing distant about Ernie. "He was engaging, magical, silly, playful and spirited," Carlos recalled. It was the fishing trips to Black Lake that stood out in Carlos's memory as the times when Ernie was happiest. "We would go trout fishing in the morning, we would come back and he would make us lunch, then he would take his nap." In the afternoon, it was back out onto the lake, Ernie teaching the grandkids the finer points of fishing for pike. They took to his love of angling, but never warmed to the hunt. "Neither my sons or grandchildren have inherited my 45-year interest in hunting deer," Ernie wrote in one of his many letters to Carlos. "I appear to be an aberration in our family line, if not the entire Jewish population." Heart disease and, in 1996, the need to implant a pacemaker slowed him only by a step or two. His younger grandchildren could recall Grandad's continued readiness to play in the snow or go down the backyard slide.[44]

He had time to revisit old friends and relatives, and went to some lengths to establish a bond with the children of his sister Rose after she died. "We all got to know each other a little better," he wrote her sons after a weekend visit in the summer of 1992, "and what we learned was good." Enclosed with his note were copies of Rose's letters to Ernie and their parents. "They will help round out your image of your mother. As the years pass since her death I realize how unusual a person she was: soft, tender, loving and utterly without malice or hate."[45]

The most remarkable of his efforts to plumb the past had come in the spring of the same year, when he reestablished contact with Laicha Kravchik Gellman. Many decades after their affair had ended, Goodman found her in New York, an eighty-one-year-old widow who had just retired from her work at the Jewish community center in Brighton Beach. He visited her in 1993 and they established a frequent correspondence until her death from leukemia three years later. "Suddenly the whole turbulent period of my life came alive," she had written him in response to his first letters. "All these thoughts and memories rushing at me. Forty years vanished and I am remembering every moment of it fondly." Goodman must have felt the same, but it is hard to know. Neither of his sons were aware of Laicha's existence while Ernie was alive, though Laicha's daughter, Aviva, believed that Freda knew. In his letters, Ernie reminded Laicha how important she had been to the turning point in his life in 1935. She reminded him of a day spent years before in Greenwich Village, a moment known only to the two of them. "The important thing," she emphasized, "is that it did happen and the memories will grow and linger." Aviva later remembered that on her daily visits to the hospital while her mother was dying, she often found her on the phone with Ernie. It was an enormous comfort to Laicha. "After all our marches and demonstrations, dreams and aspirations, the world has not changed," she had written him. "If anything it's gotten worse. But I still haven't given up hope."[46]

Neither had Ernie, though he might have stressed how much the world *had* changed. Perhaps the most stunning of recent transformations was the collapse of the Soviet Union in 1991. The events of that year would have been impossible for Goodman to have imagined a half century before, in 1944, when he still believed the Soviet Union was a potential land of freedom. He had long ago abandoned his wartime exuberance for the Soviets and their defeat of Nazi Germany, but in the 1980s he had harbored the hope that Mikhail Gorbachev, the last president of the Soviet Union, would be able to reform and democratize socialism as Alexander Dubcek had tried years before in Czechoslovakia. Instead, Gorbachev's reforms had unleashed the centrifugal forces of nationalism in an empire built on military conquest. An attempted coup in 1991 effectively ended Gorbachev's rule, and the Soviet state thereafter splintered into fifteen separate nations. There would be no socialism with a human face.

Goodman could at least take some satisfaction in seeing Alexander Dubcek elected chairman of Czechoslovakia's Federal Parliament after the collapse of the Communist states in Eastern Europe. He would be happier still to see Nelson Mandela released from prison in 1990 to lead the final campaign against apartheid. With Mandela's election as president of the new South Africa in 1994, two of the defining poles of the world Goodman had known after 1945—Soviet Communism and South African apartheid—were gone.[47]

Detroit had been dying all along, garroted by the new rules of global capitalism. The middle-class wages of a union workforce had become a "disincentive," as it was politely labeled, to corporate investors. Goodman's hometown had become one of the most segregated metropolitan areas in America, with a core city riven by underemployment and crime. Even so, Goodman remained hopeful. He had seen the resurrection of a movement for social change twice in his own lifetime, in the 1930s and again in the 1960s. He never abandoned hope for the next unexpected spark, the next revival of a movement that would unite progressive people across the racial divide. He had known the women and men who had made that leap before, and he revered them still.

In 1996, he visited one of these stalwarts in Grand Rapids during the annual gathering of the state bar. Goodman took the opportunity to meet with Robert Williams, the onetime leader of the NAACP in Union County, North Carolina, who had come to Detroit thirty-five years before at Goodman's invitation to speak about the southern struggle. Williams had since paid dearly for his advocacy of armed self-defense against Klan violence, framed on trumped-up charges of kidnapping in 1961 and subsequently self-exiled to Cuba and China to avoid prosecution. He had returned to the United States in the late 1960s and settled in western Michigan after North Carolina dropped the kidnapping charges. He and Goodman had subsequently gotten to know each other during Ernie's successful defense of Ruby Nelson, a neighbor of Williams who had wounded a sheriff during the forcible attempt to remove her to a state mental hospital. In 1996, Williams was dying of Hodgkin's disease, but he still carried himself well on the evening he met Goodman and Claudia Morcom for dinner.

"He looked so wonderful," Goodman said of Williams in one of his last recorded interviews.

> He reminded me of a vision of Frederick Douglass coming down the hall. White hair on his head and a heavy shaped beard. A look of tranquility, of having seen everything and he's satisfied with

how his life looks to him. Some people have a look of sadness at that point in their lives when they know that they can't live much longer. Some people have a feeling of discomfort and unhappiness about an unfulfilled life, but his was one where "I've done everything I can and wanted to do and I'm satisfied with that."[48]

Ernie Goodman died the following year, felled by a stroke in March of 1997 at the age of ninety. He had described Williams as he would have described his own life in that moment. He had done everything he could and wanted to do in a life spanning the twentieth century, and he was satisfied with that.

Notes

Note on Sources

The single most important source of documentary material on Ernie Goodman's life is the collection of papers he left at the Walter P. Reuther Library of Labor and Urban Affairs, located at Wayne State University in Detroit. Documents drawn from the portion of the collection that was processed at the time this book was published are noted as "processed," followed by the series number, box, and folder. Documents from the unprocessed portion of the collection are listed by box and folder only. As the remainder of the collection is processed, these markers will change.

In citations where no interviewer is indicated, the session was conducted by the authors.

Abbreviations

CRCC   Civil Rights Congress Collection, Walter P. Reuther Library of Labor and Urban Affairs, Wayne State University, Detroit
EG   Ernest Goodman (in correspondence)
EGC   Ernest Goodman Collection, Walter P. Reuther Library of Labor and Urban Affairs, Wayne State University, Detroit
TAM   Tamiment Library, Collection 191, New York University, New York City
WRL   Walter P. Reuther Library of Labor and Urban Affairs, Wayne State University, Detroit

Chapter 1

1. *Attica: The Official Report of the New York State Special Commission on Attica* (New York: Praeger, 1972), 350–52, 372–73.
2. David Langum, *William M. Kunstler: The Most Hated Lawyer in America* (New York: New York University Press, 1999), chapters 2–3.
3. Showtime, *The Killing Yard*, directed by Euzhan Palcy, written by Benita Garvin (2001).
4. Maurice Isserman, *If I Had a Hammer: The Death of the Old Left and the Birth of the New Left* (Urbana: University of Illinois Press, 1993), xiii.
5. Hannah Arendt, *Men in Dark Times* (San Diego: Harcourt Brace, 1995), viii–ix. Arendt borrowed "when there was only wrong and no outrage" from the poem "To Posterity" by Bertolt Brecht.
6. Ernest Goodman, interview by Edward Littlejohn, 5 June 1996, 2, Oral History Project, Damon Keith Law Collection, WRL; Frederick Schauer, "The Exceptional First Amendment," in *American Exceptionalism and Human Rights,* ed. Michael Ignatieff (Princeton: Princeton University Press, 2005), 48.

7. Ignatieff, *American Exceptionalism and Human Rights*, 11; Ernest Goodman, interview by Edward Littlejohn, 24 June and 11 July 1996, 13, Oral History Project, Damon Keith Law Collection, WRL.

8. Goodman, interview by Littlejohn, 24 June and 11 July 1996, 20.

9. Ibid., 2; Ira Katznelson, *When Affirmative Action Was White: An Untold History of Racial Inequality in Twentieth Century America* (New York: Norton, 2005), 23.

10. Judge Keith, quoted in Norman Sinclair, "Lawyer, Activist Goodman Leaves Large Footprints," *Detroit Sunday Journal*, 30 March 1997.

11. "The arc of the moral universe is long, But it tends towards justice"— abolitionist Theodore Parker, c. 1850s, quoted in Kevin Boyle, *Arc of Justice: A Saga of Race, Civil Rights, and Murder in the Jazz Age* (New York: Henry Holt, 2004), frontispiece.

Chapter 2

1. The emphasis on drawing blood is Goodman's: "It was a bloody thing. . . . There were plenty of people who got injured and there was blood all over the place." His observations here and in much of this chapter are taken from a transcript of six oral history tapes, 205 double-spaced pages. The interviewer and the date of the tape recordings are not known. The transcription is located in EGC, box 13, folder "Transcript of Tape of Ernest Goodman Oral History." The quotes here are from pages 18–19. At some point after this interview, Goodman edited the first twenty-one pages into a narrative called "Background" that filled in some of the ellipses in the interview. These small amendments are sometimes incorporated into the material cited from the oral history, which will be referred to hereafter as "Goodman OH."

2. Elaine Latzman Moon, ed., *Untold Tales, Unsung Heroes: An Oral History of Detroit's African American Community, 1918–1967* (Detroit: Wayne State University Press, 1994), 61; Goodman OH, 11; Sidney Bolkosky, *Harmony and Dissonance: Voices of Jewish Identity in Detroit, 1914–1967* (Detroit: Wayne State University Press, 1991), 78.

3. Goodman OH, 15–20.

4. Bolkosky, *Harmony and Dissonance*, 42; Goodman OH, 5–6.

5. Beth Wenger, *The Jewish Americans: Three Centuries of Jewish Voices in America* (New York: Doubleday, 2007), 87–90; EG to "Freda, Dick, and Billy," 3 December 1949, EGC, box 4, folder "Goodman Book."

6. EG to "Freda, Dick, and Billy," 3 December 1949.

7. Goodman OH, 2. The death certificate for Minnie listed her birth date as 4 March 1886; the application to the Social Security Administration for death benefits in 1976 indicated her marriage to Harry Goodman occurred "Approx. 1903." Both documents are in the family's private collection.

8. Goodman OH, 3.

9. Steve Babson with Ron Alpern, David Elsila, and John Revitte, *Working Detroit: The Making of a Union Town* (Detroit: Wayne State University Press, 1986), 23–27; Bolkosky, *Harmony and Dissonance*, 19–23.

10. Moon, *Untold Tales*, 60; Goodman OH, 21.

11. Moon, *Untold Tales*, 60–61.

12. Bolkosky, *Harmony and Dissonance*, 20; Olivier Zunz, *The Changing face of Inequality: Urbanization, Industrial Development, and Immigration in Detroit, 1880–1920* (Chicago: University of Chicago Press, 1982), 392–93; Goodman OH, 7–9.

13. Bolkosky, *Harmony and Dissonance*, 23–25, 106–9, 229; Goodman OH, 4, 6–7, 12–13, 23; interview with Dick Goodman, 14 June 2006.

14. Goodman OH, 6–7.

15. On the role of public education, see Jeffrey Mirel, *The Rise and Fall of an Urban School System: Detroit, 1907–1981* (Ann Arbor: University of Michigan Press, 1999), 18–19. On the role of advertising and popular culture as a solvent of immigrant culture, see Stuart Ewen, *Captains of Consciousness: Advertising and the Social Roots of the Consumer Culture* (New York: McGraw Hill, 1976), 43–44, 62–65.

16. Goodman OH, 24.

17. Ibid., 26, 35; Neely Tucker, "The Trials of Ernie Goodman," *Detroit Free Press Magazine,* 8 December 1991, 10. Among the photographs in the family collection is one depicting the studious members of the Philomathic Debating Club.

18. Goodman OH, 28–29; Wayne State University Law School, "Ernie Goodman, Class of 1928, Remembers How It Was . . . ," *Wayne Lawyer* 6, no. 1 (1987): 7.

19. Lawrence Friedman, *A History of American Law* (New York: Simon and Schuster, 2005), 473–74.

20. Louis Anthes, *Lawyers and Immigrants, 1870–1940* (El Paso, TX: LFB Scholarly Publications, 2003), 173–216; Jerold Auerbach, *Unequal Justice: Lawyers and Social Change in Modern America* (New York: Oxford University Press, 1976), 94–95, 107, 118, 329; Albert Harno, *Legal Education in the United States* (San Francisco: Bancroft-Whitney, 1958), 102–8, 116.

21. Friedman, *A History of American Law*, 467–72, 545–46; Goodman OH, 36.

22. Goodman OH, 37–38. On Murphy cultivating links to immigrant lawyers, see Sidney Fine, *Frank Murphy: The Detroit Years* (Ann Arbor: University of Michigan Press, 1975) 34, 82.

23. Goodman OH, 30–34, 38–39.

24. Ibid., 36–37, 41, 50.

25. Ibid., 53–55; interview with Bill Goodman, 7 June 2007; interview with Dick Goodman, 14 June 2006.

26. Kevin Boyle, *Arc of Justice: A Saga of Race, Civil Rights, and Murder in the Jazz Age* (New York: Henry Holt, 2004), 105–18; Norman McRae, "Detroit in Black and White," in *Detroit Perspectives: Crossroads and Turning Points,* ed. Wilma Wood Hendrickson (Detroit: Wayne State University Press, 1991), 367.

27. August Meier and Elliot Rudwick, *Black Detroit and the Rise of the UAW* (New York: Oxford University Press, 1979), 12 (Ford quote), 19; Jean Madden

Pitrone, *Myra: The Life and Times of Myra Wolfgang, Trade-Union Leader* (Wyandotte, MI: Calibre, 1980), 51.

28. Babson et al., *Working Detroit*, 41–45; Boyle, *Arc of Justice*, 116–17.

29. Kenneth Jackson, *The Ku Klux Klan in the City, 1915–1930* (Chicago: Ivan Dee, 1992), 127–43; Boyle, *Arc of Justice*, 140–43.

30. Robert Rockaway, *The Jews of Detroit: From the Beginning, 1762–1914* (Detroit: Wayne State University Press, 1986), 133; Robert Conot, *American Odyssey* (Detroit: Wayne State University Press, 1986), 209–12; Bolkosky, *Harmony and Dissonance*, 78–79, 173; Goodman OH, 22. For a detailed history of Ford's anti-Semitism, see Neil Baldwin, *Henry Ford and the Jews: The Mass Production of Hate* (New York: Public Affairs, 2001).

31. Goodman OH, 42–44, 48–49; "By Way of Explanation," *Barrister of Alpha Theta Kappa* 1, no. 1 (1928): 2 (editorial quote), and *Barrister of Alpha Theta Kappa* 3, no. 1 (1930): 2 (on clubroom), Ernest Goodman's personal letter file, private collection.

32. "History of Michigan State University College of Law" (DCL affiliated with MSU in 1995), MSU College of Law Web site, www.law.msu.edu/history .html (accessed 7 August 2008); Anthes, *Lawyers and Immigrants*, 189; Jane Cleo Marshall-Lucas, "Breaking New Ground with Grace: The University of Michigan's First Black Woman Law Graduate," in *Rebels in Law: Voices in History of Black Women Lawyers*, ed. J. Clay Smith Jr. (Ann Arbor: University of Michigan Press, 1998), 86–89; Mona Harrington, *Women Lawyers: Rewriting the Rules* (New York: Alfred Knopf, 1994), 15; "Ernie Goodman, Class of 1928, Remembers," 8; Isadore Berger, "Women as Lawyers," *Barrister of Alpha Theta Kappa* 3, no. 1 (1930): 6.

33. "History and Goals," Wayne State University Law School Web site, www.law .wayne.edu/prospective/history_goals.html (accessed 7 August 2008); Wayne State University Law School, *Wayne Lawyer* 6, no. 1 (1987): 6–9.

34. Melvyn Dubofsky, *The State and Labor in Modern America* (Chapel Hill: University of North Carolina Press, 1994), 24–25, 44–47.

35. David Ray Papke, *The Pullman Case: The Clash of Labor and Capital in Industrial America* (Lawrence: University of Kansas, 1999), 65; Boyle, *Arc of Justice*, 228–339.

36. Goodman OH, 51–52.

37. Ibid., 49–50, 56.

38. Ibid., 57–58.

39. These details are taken from ibid., 57; and from Goodman's personal correspondence of 1927–30 with his cousin, sister, and girlfriend, private collection.

40. Irving Bernstein, *The Lean Years: A History of the American Worker, 1920–1933* (Boston: Houghton Mifflin, 1960), 255; Richard Ortquist, "Unemployment and Relief: Michigan's Response to the Depression during the Hoover Years," *Michigan History* (Fall 1973).

41. Fine, *Frank Murphy: The Detroit Years*, 247–48, 327–28, 339.

42. Goodman OH, 59–61; Bernstein, *The Lean Years,* 294 (Schwab and Hoover quotes).

43. Ernest Goodman, "Humanizing the Law," *Barrister of Alpha Theta Kappa* 3, no. 1 (1930): 11–12.

44. Fine, *Frank Murphy: The Detroit Years,* 218 (quote), 216–23, 235–39, 265–76, 284–85.

45. Carbon of letter from EG to "Sylvia," 3–4 November 1930, EG's file of general correspondence, private collection.

46. Interview with Freda Goodman, 25 January 2007; Marriage License 411302, Wayne County, Michigan, and Certificate of Marriage, 21 August 1932, private collection.

47. Goodman OH, 63–64; "Honeymoon Trip," handwritten diary, ruled notebook, unpaginated, private collection. Page numbers added to photocopy: 11, 30–25, 50, 54, 89–95, 102–4, 147–62.

48. "Honeymoon Trip," 105–12, 120–21, 135–39.

49. Ernest Goodman's personal letter file, private collection. Freda and her son stayed for weeks at a time with the extended family in the town of Macatawa, north of Saugatuck on the Lake Michigan shore. The quotes are taken from an undated letter in which she references her age as twenty-two years, making it 1935.

50. Moon, *Untold Tales,* 61.

51. Goodman OH, 67.

52. Ibid., 68.

53. Ibid., 63.

54. James Lorence, *Organizing the Unemployed: Community and Union Activists in the Industrial Heartland* (Albany: State University of New York Press, 1996), 28, 30.

55. Ibid., 29, 50.

56. Bert Cochran, *Labor and Communism: The Conflict That Shaped American Unions* (Princeton: Princeton University Press, 1977), 12; Roger Keeran, *The Communist Party and the Auto Workers Unions* (Bloomington: Indiana University Press, 1980), 16; Chris Johnson, *Maurice Sugar: Law, Labor, and the Left in Detroit, 1912–1950* (Detroit: Wayne State University Press, 1988), 122; Lorence, *Organizing the Unemployed,* 29–30, 32; *Detroit Times,* 6 and 7 March 1930; *Detroit Free Press,* 7 and 8 March 1930.

57. Maurice Sugar, *The Ford Hunger March* (Berkeley, CA: Meiklejohn Civil Liberties Institute, 1980), 25 (Ford quote), 30–39; Johnson, *Maurice Sugar,* 120–23.

58. Sugar, *The Ford Hunger March,* 42; Goodman OH, 86–87.

59. Goodman OH, 67–69.

60. Ibid., 69–71. When the state legislature finally passed an occupational disease law, Goodman wrote a series of articles identifying its strengths and weaknesses. Ernest Goodman, "Lawyer Explains Michigan Occupational Disease Act," *United Automobile Worker,* 26 June 1937.

61. Goodman OH, 82–83.

62. Moon, *Untold Tales*, 64; Goodman OH, 84.

63. Johnson, *Maurice Sugar*, 154–64 (quote on 163), 313–14.

64. Details of Sugar's family life are taken from Johnson, *Maurice Sugar*, 23–38.

65. James Weinstein, *The Decline of Socialism in America, 1912–1925* (New York: Vintage, 1969), 145–59, 173–76; Johnson, *Maurice Sugar*, 38–50, 71–73, 78.

66. James Jacobs, "The Conduct of Political Intelligence" (PhD diss., Princeton University, 1977), 43; Robert Murray, *Red Scare: A Study in National Hysteria, 1919–1920* (New York: McGraw Hill, 1955), 13–14, 210–22; Ronald Kessler, *The Bureau: The Secret History of the FBI* (New York: St. Martin's, 2003), 13–20.

67. Johnson, *Maurice Sugar*, 73, 98–108; Sugar, *The Ford Hunger March*, 19.

68. There is a vast and contentious literature on the schism in the Socialist Party and the emergence of the CP-USA. For a sampling of this scholarship, see Weinstein, *The Decline of Socialism in America*; Cochran, *Labor and Communism*; Theodore Draper, *The Roots of American Communism* (New York: Viking, 1957).

69. Johnson, *Maurice Sugar*, 131–35.

70. Lorence, *Organizing the Unemployed*, 33, 50; Keeran, *The Communist Party and the Auto Workers Unions*, 74, 97–98; Fine, *Frank Murphy: The Detroit Years*, 399–400, 432–40, 557.

71. Johnson, *Maurice Sugar*, 99.

72. For two contrasting views of the 1935 change in strategy to the Popular Front, see Harvey Klehr, *The Heyday of American Communism* (New York: Basic, 1984), 97–100, 167–90; and Fraser M. Ottanelli, *The Communist Party of the United States: From the Depression to World War II* (New Brunswick: Rutgers University Press, 1991), 83–105. In contrast to Klehr, Ottanelli stresses (97–98) that there was independent support within the CP-USA for the strategic shift.

73. Ottanelli, *The Communist Party of the United States*, 55–56, 96–98; Fernando Claudin, *The Communist Movement from Comintern to Cominform* (New York: Monthly Review, 1975), 1:182–99; C. V. Daniels, *A Documentary History of Communism* (New York: Vintage, 1962), 2:114–17.

74. Johnson, *Maurice Sugar*, 102–3.

75. Nick Salvatore, *Eugene V. Debs: Citizen and Socialist* (Urbana: University of Illinois Press, 1982) draws attention to Deb's articulation of socialist politics in a democratic-constitutional idiom.

76. Goodman OH, 79.

Chapter 3

1. Sidney Fine, *Sit-Down: The General Motors Strike of 1936–1937* (Ann Arbor: University of Michigan Press, 1969), 155 (Murphy quote).

2. For a detailed account of the Midland sit-down, see Steve Babson, *Building the Union: Skilled Workers and Anglo-Gaelic Immigrants in the Rise of the*

UAW (New Brunswick: Rutgers University Press, 1991), 171–78; and Wyndham Mortimer, *Organize: My Life as a Union Man* (Boston: Beacon, 1971), 120–22.

3. Ernest Goodman, interview by Edward Littlejohn, 5 June 1996, 3, Oral History Project, Damon Keith Law Collection, WRL; "Counsel for the Common People, Part 1," videotaped interview with Ernest Goodman, produced by William Bryce, WRL.

4. Affiliation forms, letterhead listings, and membership rosters for the CPCR are found in CRCC, box 1, folders "Conference for the Protection of Civil Rights—1935–1937" and "Affiliated Organizations, 1939–1940." Angela Dillard, in her excellent study of progressive religious leaders in Detroit's left movements of the 1930s through the 1960s, places too great an emphasis on the "strong religious underpinnings" of the CPCR and its successor organizations. *Faith in the City: Preaching Radical Social Change in Detroit* (Ann Arbor: University of Michigan, 2007), 87–88. A handful of Protestant ministers did play an important role as public leaders, but the underpinnings of the conference and its successor organizations were decidedly secular: union members predominated, the staff was disproportionately Jewish and socialist, the meetings were held in union halls, the funding came primarily from labor organizations, and the offices were located in the Hoffman Building, well known as a center of left-wing and labor activity.

5. Elaine Latzman Moon, ed., *Untold Tales, Unsung Heroes: An Oral History of Detroit's African American Community, 1918–1967* (Detroit: Wayne State University Press, 1994), 62 (quote).

6. Ibid.

7. Ibid., 65; Chris Johnson, *Maurice Sugar: Law, Labor, and the Left in Detroit, 1912–1950* (Detroit: Wayne State University Press, 1988), 160.

8. Johnson, *Maurice Sugar*, 159–61, 171–76; vertical file, "LeBron Simmons," WRL; C. LeBron Simmons, oral history interview by Norman McRae, circa 1969, 1–8, Blacks in the Labor Movement Collection, WRL.

9. Glenda Elizabeth Gilmore, *Defying Dixie: The Radical Roots of Civil Rights, 1919–1950* (New York: Norton, 2008), 118–28; Fraser Ottanelli, *The Communist Party of the United States: From the Depression to World War II* (New Brunswick: Rutgers University Press, 1991), 95–96, 144. On the importance of the Scottsboro case in establishing the CP-USA's standing among left-wing African Americans, see Mark Naison, *Communists in Harlem during the Depression* (New York: Grove, 1983), 57–94.

10. Jeremy Brecher, *Strike!* (San Francisco: Straight Arrow, 1972), 150–77.

11. Robert Zieger, *The CIO, 1935–1955* (Chapel Hill: University of North Carolina Press, 1995), 83–85. The "Committee" became the "Congress" in 1938.

12. Melvyn Dubofsky, *The State and Labor in Modern America* (Chapel Hill: University of North Carolina Press, 1994), 119 (Wagner quote).

13. "Counsel for the Common People, Part 1."

14. Bert Cochran, *Labor and Communism: The Conflict That Shaped American Unions* (Princeton: Princeton University Press, 1977), 97.

15. Peter Irons, *The New Deal Lawyers* (Princeton: Princeton University Press, 1982), 243–44; Robert Conot, *American Odyssey* (Detroit: Wayne State University Press, 1986), 274–75, 351–52; Neil Baldwin, *Henry Ford and the Jews: The Mass Production of Hate* (New York: Public Affairs, 2001), 312, 283–85.

16. Baldwin, *Henry Ford and the Jews*, 275–77; Charles Tull, *Father Coughlin and the New Deal* (Syracuse: Syracuse University Press, 1965), 11, 177, 180, 190–96.

17. Peter Amann, "Vigilante Fascism: The Black Legion as an American Hybrid," *Comparative Studies in Society and History* 25, no. 3 (1983): 497, 520; Thomas Jones, "The Murder That Brought Down the Black Legion," *Detroit News*, 5 August 1997; Johnson, *Maurice Sugar*, 181–86.

18. Maurice Sugar, "Memorandum on the Black Legion," undated typescript, 16–17, Sugar Collection, box 18, folder 1, WRL; Johnson, *Maurice Sugar*, 181–86.

19. Moon, *Untold Tales,* 65; CPCR, "Pickert Must Go!" leaflet, CRCC, box 1, folder "Conference for the Protection of Civil Rights, 1935–1937"; Bollens to Roger Baldwin, 28 May 1936, CRCC, box 16, folder "Correspondence with American Civil Liberties Union, 1936."

20. "CPCR. Financial Statement, Apr. 27th–July 27th, 1936," CRCC, box 1, folder "Conference for the Protection of Civil Rights, 1935–1937"; CPCR, "Civil Rights Guardian, GM Strike Number," pamphlet, CRCC, box 1, folder "Conference for the Protection of Civil Rights, 1935–1937"; oral history transcript, 198, EGC, box 13, folder "Transcript of Tape of Ernest Goodman Oral History" (hereafter "Goodman OH").

21. Detroit Police Department, Special Investigation Squad, Detective Division, "Conference for the Protection of Civil Rights," report dated 3 April 1936, Detroit Red Squad Files, folder 2a. Following litigation that began in 1974, the files of the Detroit Red Squad were released in 1990 to individuals named in the reports. The complete collection is held in the Burton Collection at the Detroit Public Library and is currently closed to the public. A partial collection is held by the authors. These documents are referenced henceforth as "Detroit Red Squad Files" according to the folder numbers in this partial collection.

22. Tom Klug, "Labor Market Policies in Detroit: The Curious Case of the 'Spolansky Act' of 1931," *Michigan Historical Review* 14, no. 1 (1988): 13–20; Sidney Fine, *Frank Murphy: The Detroit Years* (Ann Arbor: University of Michigan Press, 1975), 66–67, 396–403; James Jacobs, "The Conduct of Political Intelligence" (PhD diss., Princeton University, 1977), 107–12.

23. Jacobs, "The Conduct of Political Intelligence," 111; Fine, *Sit-Down*, 38; Jerold Auerbach, *Labor and Liberty: The LaFollette Committee and the New Deal* (New York: Bobbs-Merrill, 1966), 110–14.

24. "National Defense Report, Ernest Goodman," 18 November 1941, incorporating Detroit Police Department report of 18 April 1941 referencing "Hebrew Race" and "dark complexion," 1, 3, TAM, box 164, folder 10; "Civil Rights Federation, 2-11-40" and "Civil Rights Federation Rally, 2-22-40," 2 ("dark, Jewish appearance"), Detroit Red Squad Files, folder 30; Detroit Police Department, Office of the Special Investigation Squad, "Report on Communist Activities," 1 October 1936, 3 ("Liberty Ball"), Detroit Red Squad Files, folder 86.

25. Detroit Police Department, Office of the Special Investigation Squad, "Report on Information Obtained of Meeting of the Conference for the Protection of Civil Rights," Detroit Red Squad Files, folder 86.

26. CPCR, "To All Organizations and Individuals Who Wish to Maintain American Civil Liberties," 17 August 1936, Detroit Red Squad Files, folder 86.

27. Moon, *Untold Tales*, 63–64.

28. Goodman OH, 79.

29. Ibid., 80.

30. The summary of Kravchik's background is based on Goodman's personal correspondence, private collection; and on a phone interview with Aviva Gellman, Kravchik's daughter, 12 January 2008.

31. EG to Laicha Kravchik, undated letter fragment quoted in FBI report on Ernest Goodman by Mortimer Watson, 26 April 1947, 2, TAM, box 164, folder 7; Laicha Kravchik to EG, undated, Goodman's personal correspondence, private collection.

32. See Fine, *Sit-Down*, for the most complete account of the Flint sit-down strike.

33. Ibid., 338 (Fortune quote); Steve Babson with Ron Alpern, David Elsila, and John Revitte, *Working Detroit: The Making of a Union Town* (Detroit: Wayne State University Press, 1986), 80–86; Irving Bernstein, *Turbulent Years: A History of the American Worker, 1933–1941* (Boston: Houghton Mifflin, 1970), 641–46.

34. Gabriel Jackson, *The Spanish Republic and the Civil War, 1931–1939* (Princeton: Princeton University Press, 1965), 248–49, 349–52; George Hills, *The Battle for Madrid* (New York: St. Martins, 1976), 61; George Esenwein, "The Spanish Civil War," in *Spanish History since 1808,* ed. José Alvarez Junco and Adrian Schubert (New York: Oxford University Press, 2000), 245.

35. "Counsel for the Common People, Part 1"; Ottanelli, *The Communist Party of the United States*, 165–68; Jackson, *The Spanish Republic*, 277–83; Goodman OH, 120–21.

36. Jackson, *The Spanish Republic*, 286–90, 303–9, 333–34, 510–18; Esenwein, "The Spanish Civil War," 243.

37. Peter Carroll, *The Odyssey of the Abraham Lincoln Brigade: Americans in the Spanish Civil War* (Palo Alto: Stanford University Press, 1994), 12–19.

38. Adolph Ross, introduction to *American Volunteers in the Spanish War, 1936–1939* (Adolph Ross, 1993); Carroll, *The Odyssey of the Abraham*

Lincoln Brigade, 15–16; Saul Wellman, oral history transcript, interviewer unknown, authors' possession, 56. Years later when Goodman applied for a visa to visit the People's Republic of China, he described his efforts on behalf of Norman Bethune, the Canadian doctor who pioneered the use of blood plasma to treat battlefield wounds in Spain. When the Detroit police, citing Bethune's membership in the Canadian Communist Party, pressured the Art Institute to cancel Bethune's use of its auditorium for a fund-raiser to support the Spanish Republic, Goodman assisted in bringing a lawsuit that forced the city-owned facility to permit the program to go ahead as scheduled. EG to Liaison Office of the P.R.C., 11 April 1975, 2, EGC, box 23, folder "China Trip, June 1978."

39. "Minutes: Anti-Vigilance Conference, Sat. Aug. 14, 1937," 3 (number of local unions, CIO and AFL), and Detroit Police Department, Office of the Special Investigation Squad, "Information on the Conference for the Protection of Civil Rights Monthly Meeting," 30 June 1937, 1, Detroit Red Squad Files, folder 46.

40. Zieger, *The CIO*, 60–63; Auerbach, *Labor and Liberty*, 121–28.

41. Johnson, *Maurice Sugar*, 228–29; Conot, *American Odyssey*, 366–67.

42. "Police Will Continue Illegal Arrests, Pickert Tells Our Delegation," *Civil Rights News* 2 (November 1938), CRCC, box 10, folder "Civil Rights News—1938"; "$3,000 Suit Filed against Officers," *Detroit Free Press*, 21 October 1938, clipping, EGC, box 4, folder "Dies Committee 1938 (Detroit)." On Taylor's status as veteran, see Ross, *American Volunteers in the Spanish War*, 109.

43. "Police Will Continue Illegal Arrests."

44. James Petterson, *Congressional Conservatism and the New Deal: The Growth of the Conservative Coalition in Congress, 1933–1939* (Westport, CT: Greenwood, 1967), 184, 195.

45. David Caute, *The Great Fear: The Anti-Communist Purge under Truman and Eisenhower* (New York: Simon and Schuster, 1978), 100–101.

46. "Police Witness Supplies Name," *Detroit News*, newspaper clipping, undated, EGC, box 4, folder "Dies Committee 1938 (Detroit)."

47. Frank Murphy, "Living Democracy," *Civil Rights News* 2 (November 1938); EG to "Laicha," letter postmarked 8 November 1938, intercepted by the FBI and included in files turned over to the National Lawyers Guild, currently held in Tam, box 164, folder 6; EG to Frank Murphy, carbon, 10 November 1938, personal correspondence of Ernest Goodman, private collection; Sidney Fine, *Frank Murphy: The New Deal Years* (Chicago: University of Chicago Press, 1979), 508–9.

48. "Persons Attacked by Dies Committee," twelve-page typescript with entries for 115 names, CRCC, box 32, folder "Dies Committee, Persons Attacked"; *Civil Rights News* 2 (November 1938): 4; "Police Witness Supplies Name"; "Mayor Probing Aid Given Reds," *Detroit Free Press,* 14 October 1938, clippings, EGC, box 4, folder "Dies Committee 1938 (Detroit)."

49. "Counsel for the Common People, Part 1."
50. Martin Lewis, "Americanized Medicine," clipping circa 1938, EGC, box 4, folder "Dies Committee 1938 (Detroit)"; Ernest Goodman, "Summary of the Doctors' Cases," typescript, 7, EGC, box 37, folder "Doctor's Case."
51. "Dies Witness Links Reds to Picketing," *Detroit Times*, 12 October 1938, EGC, box 4, folder "Dies Committee 1938" (article is mislabeled "November 12"); "Statement of Dr. Eugene Shafarman to Henry Schweinhaut, Special Assistant to the Attorney General," 1, EGC, box 37, folder "Doctors Case"; "Statement of Doctor Eugene Shafarman, M.D.," on letterhead of same, Dr. Eugene Shafarman Collection, box 1, folder 1-12, WRL.
52. Dr. Harry Vaughan to Dr. Eugene Shafarman, 18 October 1938, Dr. Eugene Shafarman Collection, box 1, folder 1-11, WRL; "More Doctors Face City Ax," *Detroit News*, 20 October 1938, EGC, box 4, folder "Dies Committee 1938 (Detroit)."
53. Goodman, "Summary of the Doctors' Cases," 8–10; "Counsel for the Common People, Part 1."
54. "Dr. Shafarman's Appeal Debated," *Detroit Times*, 8 February 1939, "Board Hears Doctor's Plea," *Detroit News*, 8 February 1939, "Doctor Denies City's Charges," *Detroit Free Press*, 8 February 1939, EGC, box 4, folder "Dies Committee 1938 (Detroit)"; Goodman, "Summary of the Doctors' Cases," 10; Professional League for Civil Rights, "Second Report of Committee Investigating Peremptory Dismissal from the Accredited City List of Physicians . . . ," 2, CRCC, box 31, folder "Dies Committee Witnesses."
55. Professional League for Civil Rights, "Second Report of Committee," 3; Jacobs, "The Conduct of Political Intelligence," 116; EG to Eugene Shafarman, 16 November 1940, Dr. Eugene Shafarman Collection, box 1, folder 1-21, WRL; Ernest Goodman, "The Spanish Loyalist Indictments," sixteen-page typescript, 1, Dr. Eugene Shafarman Collection, box 1, folder 1-21, WRL.
56. "Statement of Dr. Eugene Shafarman to Henry Schweinhaut," 2–10.
57. Goodman, "The Spanish Loyalist Indictments." The balance of this account of the arrests is taken from this typescript memoir, together with Sidney Fine, *Frank Murphy: The Washington Years* (Ann Arbor: University of Michigan Press, 1984), 126–27.
58. Goodman, "The Spanish Loyalist Indictments," 2–3.
59. "Statement of Dr. Eugene Shafarman to Henry Schweinhaut," 14–19; Goodman, "The Spanish Loyalist Indictments," 3–4.
60. "U.S. Jury Indicts 16 Here in Spain War Drive, 12 Held," *Detroit Times*, 6 February 1940; "G-Men's Chain Gang: Held in Recruiting Plot," *Detroit Times*, 7 February 1940; "High Bonds Set for Alleged Spanish War Recruiting Agents," *Detroit News*, 7 February 1940; "U.S. Jails 12 in War Quiz Here," *Detroit News*, 6 February 1940; Goodman, "The Spanish Loyalist Indictments," 4–6; Fine, *Frank Murphy: The Washington Years*, 127.
61. Goodman, "The Spanish Loyalist Indictments," 7.
62. Ibid., 6–9; Fine, *Frank Murphy: The Washington Years*, 127.

63. Goodman, "The Spanish Loyalist Indictments," 8.
64. Fine, *Frank Murphy: The Washington Years*, 116–18.
65. Ibid., 124–25; Ernest Goodman, "Frank Murphy and the Spanish Loyalist Indictments in Detroit," *Detroit Legal News*, 17 July 1996, 6.
66. Fine, *Frank Murphy: The Washington Years*, 99, 102–12.
67. Jacobs, "The Conduct of Political Intelligence," 116.
68. Ronald Kessler, *The Bureau: The Secret History of the FBI* (New York: St. Martin's, 2003), 58–63, 66; Fine, *Frank Murphy: The Washington Years*, 128.
69. Report by S. A. William R. LaFlure, "Ernest Goodman," 12 June 1942, Detroit File 100-1512, 2, referencing the 27 May 1940 report, and memo from J. J. Stark, FBI, to Mr. Nichols, 6 September 1943, reporting on the 1940 correspondence between Hoover and Walter Winchell, TAM, box 164, folder 6; "National Defense Report, Ernest Goodman," 18 November 1941, incorporating Detroit Police Department report of 18 April 1941 comparing Sugar and Goodman, 1, 3, TAM, box 164, folder 10; "Civil Rights Federation Rally, 2-22-40," undated report in Red Squad Files, 2, folder 30.
70. Michael Krinsky et al., "FBI Operations, 1940–1941," in *The National Lawyers Guild: From Roosevelt through Reagan*, ed. Ann Fagan Ginger and Eugene Tobin (Philadelphia: Temple University Press, 1988), 36; EG to Walter Winchell, 21 June 1940, EGC, box 1, file "Correspondence."
71. Goodman, "The Spanish Loyalist Indictments," 11–14.
72. Ginger and Tobin, *The National Lawyers Guild*, 3–11.
73. Irons, *The New Deal Lawyers*, 125, 236; Ginger and Tobin, *The National Lawyers Guild*, 23, 34. The immediate context of the NLG's founding was President Roosevelt's attempt to pack the Supreme Court with additional appointees who would outvote the conservative ABA-supported justices who opposed New Deal legislation. See Ernest Goodman, "'Which Side Are You On?'" Detroit chapter of the NLG, annual dinner booklet, 2 June 1979, 19–20, EGC, box 3, folder 3-18.
74. Moon, *Untold Tales*, 64; Ann Fagan Ginger, "The Third Annual Convention: 1939 in Chicago," in Ginger and Tobin, *The National Lawyers Guild*, 32–33; Goodman OH, 133–34.
75. Goodman OH, 190–91.
76. Maurice Sugar to R. J. Thomas, 24 April 1939, 11, Sugar Collection, box 4, folder 4-17, WRL.
77. Ernest Goodman, foreword to *The Ford Hunger March*, by Maurice Sugar (Berkeley, CA: Meiklejohn Civil Liberties Institute, 1980), 23.
78. Johnson, *Maurice Sugar*, 239–40, 245; Sugar to R. J. Thomas, 24 April 1939.
79. For a summary of the "Beck" decision of 1898 and examples of its application, see Maurice Sugar, "The Good Old Days," typescript of a speech to the Detroit chapter of the National Lawyers Guild, 16 September 1960, 5–9, EGC, box 27, folder "Sugar Memorial." On Murphy's ruling in *Thornhill v. Alabama*, see Fine, *Frank Murphy: The Washington Years*, 169–79.
80. Goodman, foreword to *The Ford Hunger March*, 21–22.

81. "Counsel for the Common People, Part 1"; Dubofsky, *The State and Labor in Modern America*, 139 (Lewis quote), 163–64; Christopher Tomlins, *The State and the Unions: Labor Relations, Law, and the Organized Labor Movement in America, 1880–1960* (Cambridge: Cambridge University Press, 1985), 156.

82. Sugar to Thomas, 24 April 1939, 5; Johnson, *Maurice Sugar*, 239–40.

83. The description of Goodman's approach to deer hunting is based on the recollections of coauthor David Riddle.

84. Johnson, *Maurice Sugar*, 32; Jane Sugar to Sidney Rosen, undated note following Maurice's death, indicates that the first hunting group at their Black Lake cabin was in 1928, two years after they had finished construction. Sidney Rosen Collection, box 1, folder 1-52, WRL.

85. Ernest Goodman, "Defense of What?" typescript of radio address sponsored by the Civil Rights Federation, station WJBK, 8 June 1941, 1, CRCC, box 3, folder "Goodman Radio Speeches."

Chapter 4

1. Steve Babson with Ron Alpern, David Elsila, and John Revitte, *Working Detroit: The Making of a Union Town* (Detroit: Wayne State University Press, 1986), 77–79; Jean Madden Pitrone, *Myra: The Life and Times of Myra Wolfgang, Trade-Union Leader* (Wyandotte, MI: Calibre, 1980), 5–6, 23–28, 45, 51–52.

2. Chris Johnson, *Maurice Sugar: Law, Labor, and the Left in Detroit, 1912–1950* (Detroit: Wayne State University Press, 1988), 243.

3. Ibid., 244.

4. Fraser Ottanelli, *The Communist Party of the United States: From the Depression to World War II* (New Brunswick: Rutgers University Press, 1991), 114–15, 193, 198–99; Harvey Klehr, *The Heyday of American Communism: The Depression Decade* (New York: Basic, 1984), 397, 400–401.

5. Klehr, *The Heyday of American Communism*, 402–3; Ottanelli, *The Communist Party of the United States*, 200–201; Bert Cochran, *Labor and Communism: The Conflict That Shaped American Unions* (Princeton: Princeton University Press, 1977), 147; Ann Fagan Ginger and Eugene Tobin, eds., *The National Lawyers Guild: From Roosevelt through Reagan* (Philadelphia: Temple University Press, 1988), 31–36.

6. Roger Keeran, *The Communist Party and the Auto Workers Unions* (Bloomington: Indiana University Press, 1980), 210–11; Nelson Lichtenstein, *The Most Dangerous Man in Detroit: Walter Reuther and the Fate of American Labor* (New York: Basic, 1995), 157, 192–93; Cochran, *Labor and Communism*, 145–46; Ottanelli, *The Communist Party of the United States*, 200–203.

7. *Civil Rights News* 2–3, CRCC, box 10, folders "Civil Rights News—1938" and "Civil Rights News—1939." The Reverend Owen Knox's column, "I Believe," is in *Civil Rights News* 3 (October 1939). Goodman signed a letter to

"Friends" on CRF letterhead, 11 January 1940, as chairman of the Editorial Board, CRCC, box 1, folder "Conferences and Rallys—1940." The *Civil Rights News* was discontinued in 1940 and the *Civil Rights Newsletter* appeared the following year. In February of 1941, an inside article titled "CRF Denounces Lend Lease Bill" echoed the CP-USA line opposing the bill permitting the president to deploy the armed forces in undeclared wars at his discretion. The article was the exception to the newsletter's focus on domestic issues of civil rights. See CRCC, box 4, folder "Civil Rights Newsletter Correspondence—1940," and box 10, folder "Civil Rights Newsletter, 1940–1950."

8. Robert Divine, *The Reluctant Belligerent: American Entry into World War II* (New York: Wiley, 1965), 86–88, 90–91, 98; Mae Ngai, *Impossible Subjects: Illegal Aliens and the Making of Modern America* (Princeton: Princeton University Press, 2004), 85–86.

9. EG to Alfred Stern, 27 February 1940, EGC, box 35, folder "Civil Rights Congress and Federation"; Civil Rights Federation, "Minutes of the Monthly Conference—May 6, 1940," CRCC, box 4, folder "Steering Committee Meetings 1940."

10. Ngai, *Impossible Subjects*, 88; Michael Belknap, *Cold War Political Justice: The Smith Act, the Communist Party, and American Civil Liberties* (Westport, CT: Greenwood, 1977), 22–27, 39.

11. Ottanelli, *The Communist Party of the United States*, 191–92, 204; Johnson, *Maurice Sugar*, 244.

12. Carl Rudow, "10,000 Listed as 'Enemies,'" *Detroit News*, 7 February 1941; EG to Murray Van Wagoner, 15 August 1940, CRCC, box 96, folder 96-3.

13. Geoffrey Stone, *Perilous Times: Free Speech in Wartime* (New York: Norton, 2004), 285; Ronald Kessler, *The Bureau: The Secret History of the FBI* (New York: St. Martin's, 2003), 60; memorandum from J. E. Hoover to L. M. C. Smith, 29 March 1941, TAM, box 164, folder 6.

14. Johnson, *Maurice Sugar*, 243.

15. Dan Gillmor, "Ford's Fascism: Proof, Part 2," *Friday*, 31 January 1941, 5, 7; NLRB case no. C-199, Ford Motor Co., United Automobile Workers, decisions of 22 December 1937, Bureau of National Affairs, *Labor Relations Reference Manual* 1A, 360–68, and of 9 August 1939, *Labor Relations Reference Manual* 4, 438–45.

16. "Shop Laughter Upheld," *Detroit News*, 8 February 1941; Johnson, *Maurice Sugar*, 247–48; Keeran, *The Communist Party and the Auto Workers Unions*, 219.

17. NLRB, decisions of 22 December 1937, BNA, *Labor Relations Reference Manual* 1A, 362; Johnson, *Maurice Sugar*, 189; Maurice Sugar, *The Ford Hunger March* (Berkeley, CA: Meiklejohn Civil Liberties Institute, 1980), 113.

18. On CFR campaigns against the Detroit "Literature Licensing Ordinance," see "Your Steering Committee in Action," *Civil Rights News* 2 (December

1938): 4, CRCC, box 10, folder "Civil Rights News—1938." See also "Civil Rights Guardian/Issued by the Conference for the Protection of Civil Rights/ General Motors Strike Number," 7 (1937)(unnumbered), which references a 1935 campaign against a Detroit City Council antileafleting law. CRCC, box 1, folder "Conference for the Protection of Civil Rights, 1935–1937."

19. The mortgage note and the sales agreement for the lot ($800) and construction of the house ($7,230) are in the private collection of the Goodman family. The neighbors are indicated in *Polk's City Directory* (1940); interview with Dick Goodman, 14 June 2006.

20. Associated Press, "NLRB Bares Formula to Settle Ford Cases," *Detroit Free Press*, 24 June 1941; Washington Bureau, "Ford-Union to Arbitrate 4,020 Cases," *Detroit News*, 21 June 1941; "Counsel for the Common People, Part 1," videotaped interview with Ernest Goodman, produced by William Bryce, WRL. The NLRB had issued orders or completed hearings in nine cases by June of 1941 covering nearly two thousand firings; nearly the same number of discharges were under investigation in six other cases. Together with the above clippings, the Sugar Collection includes a typescript summary of "Labor Board Cases" in box 7, folder "Ford Organizing Drive."

21. Johnson, *Maurice Sugar*, 246–47; EG to Milton Kemnitz, 25 February 1941 and 18 April 1942, EGC, box 34, folder 4.

22. Johnson, *Maurice Sugar*, 225–26.

23. Judith Stepan-Norris and Maurice Zeitlin, *Talking Union* (Urbana: University of Illinois Press, 1996), 12–13; Johnson, *Maurice Sugar*, 246; William Allen, "UAW Defeats Ford on Handbills," *Daily Worker*, 9 December 1940; "Court Divided in UAW Case," *Detroit News*, 2 November 1940.

24. "Ford Rehires Union Group," *Detroit News*, 13 October 1941.

25. Johnson, *Maurice Sugar*, 245.

26. Jerold Auerbach, *Labor and Liberty: The LaFollette Committee and the New Deal* (New York: Bobbs-Merrill, 1966), 18–19, 25–28.

27. Ibid., 214–15; EG to David Saposs, 4 March 1940, EG to Carol King, 6 March 1940, and "Civil Rights Group Scans Ford Case," unidentified newspaper clipping, EGC, box 35, folder "Civil Rights Congress and Federation."

28. *NLRB v. Ford Motor Co.*, Sixth Circuit Court of Appeals, 8 October 1940, F.2d. 114, 905–16.

29. *Ford Motor Co. v. NLRB*, 312 U.S. 689 (1941); Sugar, The *Ford Hunger March*, 113; Sidney Fine, *Frank Murphy: The Washington Years* (Ann Arbor: University of Michigan Press, 1984), 300–303.

30. "Rehire 1,021, Ford Is Told," *Detroit News*, 18 January 1941; William Allen, "CIO Wins Jobs Back for 1,200 Ford Workers," *Daily Worker*, 21 March 1941; Adam Lapin, "'Stab in Back,' Murray Brands Green's Aid to Ford," *Daily Worker*, 4 February 1941; Arthur McPhaul, oral history, no date, no indication of interviewer, Talking Union Collection, WRL; Stepan-Norris and Zeitlin, *Talking Union*, 19, 135–38, 221, 225.

31. Stepan-Norris and Zeitlin, *Talking Union*, 152–53; Keeran, *The Communist Party and the Auto Workers Unions*, 218; August Meir and Elliot Rudwick, *Black Detroit and the Rise of the UAW* (New York: Oxford University Press, 1979), 103; Coleman Young and Lonnie Wheeler, *Hard Stuff: The Autobiography of Coleman Young* (New York: Viking, 1994), 41–42.

32. Meir and Rudwick, *Black Detroit and the Rise of the UAW*, 82–92.

33. Ibid., 88; "CIO Hearing Set for Today on Injunction," *Detroit Times*, 4 April 1941; "CIO Leaders Present Subpoena to Force Ford's Appearance," *Detroit News*, 4 April 1941; "CIO Fights to Bring Fords into Court," *Detroit News*, 4 April 1941. For the five volumes of testimony in the injunction hearing, see *Ford Motor Co. v. United Automobile Workers of America . . . and the Communist Party of the United States, Defendants*, District Court of the United States, Eastern District, April 3, 8, 9, 10, 11, 1941, Maurice Sugar Collection, box 55, WRL.

34. "Union Chief Presses for Immediate Talks," *Detroit Free Press*, 23 May 1941; Meir and Rudwick, *Black Detroit and the Rise of the UAW*, 92–94, 99–100; Archie Robinson, "1,800 Win Claims for Back Pay," *Detroit News*, 21 June 1941.

35. Johnson, *Maurice Sugar*, photo following 249; Adam Lapin, "120,000 Get Wage Boost," *Daily Worker*, 21 June 1941.

36. *Detroit Free Press*, 2 April 1941; "Union Opens Road and Cuts Pickets, Disorders Subside," *Detroit Free Press*, 3 April 1941; "CIO Fights to Bring Fords into Court."

37. American Social History Project, *Who Built America* (New York: Pantheon, 1992), 2:433 (FDR quote); Lichtenstein, *Labor's War at Home* (New York: Cambridge University Press, 1982), 39; Steven Fraser, *Labor Will Rule: Sidney Hillman and the Rise of American Labor* (New York: Macmillan, 1991), 462 (Summers quote).

38. Ernest Goodman, "Defense of What?" typescript of CRF-sponsored broadcast on station WJBK, 8 June 1941, CRCC, box 3, folder "Goodman Radio Speeches."

39. Ibid.

40. Johnson, *Maurice Sugar*, 244.

41. "Statement of Policy Proposed by the Steering Committee," EGC, box 35, folder "Civil Rights Congress and Federation." The role of Goodman and Zier in "polishing up" this statement is referenced in the handwritten minutes, "Spec. St. Comm. Mtg. Sun Nov. 2, 1941," CRCC, box 4, folder "Steering Committee Meetings July–December, 1941."

42. "October Steering Committee Report," CRCC, box 4, folder "Steering Committee Meetings July–December, 1941." The report was prepared for the following month's delegate conference. The jury refused to convict the defendants of "seditious conspiracy," finding no evidence of an actual plot. See Belknap, *Cold War Political Justice*, 38–39.

43. Belknap, *Cold War Political Justice*, 41; Art Preis, *Labor's Giant Step: Twenty Years of the CIO* (New York: Pathfinder, 1972), 141.

44. "October Steering Committee Report"; Belknap, *Cold War Political Justice*, 38–39.

45. Divine, *The Reluctant Belligerent*, 122, 158; Belknap, *Cold War Political Justice*, 38; John Edgar Hoover to Special Agent in Charge, Detroit, 23 February 1942, TAM, box 164, folder 6.

46. "Steering Committee Report for December, 1941," typescript, CRCC, box 4, folder "Steering Committee Meetings July–December, 1941."

47. Alan Clive, *State of War: Michigan in World War II* (Ann Arbor: University of Michigan Press, 1979), 61; Keeran, *The Communist Party and the Auto Workers Unions*, 231.

48. EG to Maurice Sugar, 9 November 1942, "Re: UAW Unemployment Compensation Department," Maurice Sugar Collection, box 76, folder 76-5, WRL; "Memorandum of Relationship between Maurice Sugar and Attorneys in the General Division," 14 March 1942, EGC, box 27, folder "Inter Office Memos."

49. Harold P. Woertink, Federal Bureau of Investigation, "Key Figure Summary Report, Ernest Goodman," Detroit file no. 100-1512, 15 December 1943, 22, and Earl Shuford, Federal Bureau of Investigation, "Ernest Goodman Alias Ernie Goodman" (100-6963), Detroit file no. 100-1512, 28 February 1945, 8, TAM, box 164, folder 6; Lichtenstein, *Labor's War at Home*, 92; Clive, *State of War*, 37, 44–45, 114; EG to Maurice Sugar, 1 October 1943, 3, EGC, box 27, large folder "Sugar File," file folder "Inter Office Files."

50. Lichtenstein, *Labor's War at Home*, 52–53, 133–35.

51. Clive, *State of War*, 70–71 (WLB quote).

52. Robert Zieger, *The CIO, 1935–1955* (Chapel Hill: University of North Carolina Press, 1995), 230 (CIO quote).

53. Gilbert Gall, *Pursuing Justice: Lee Pressman, the New Deal, and the CIO* (Albany: State University of New York Press, 1999), 161–63.

54. "Counsel for the Common People, Part 1."

55. Ibid.

56. Ibid.

57. "Labor Law Violator Will Be Arrested, Sheriff Says," *Houston Chronicle*, 22 September 1943; "Counsel for the Common People, Part 1."

58. "R. J. Thomas, CIO Leader, Arrested After Union Plea," *Houston Post*, 24 September 1943; "Counsel for the Common People, Part 1."Goodman remembered the subject's name as Tim O'Halloran. The reporter for the *Houston Post* said it was a Pat Sullivan and a third writer called him O'Sullivan.

59. United Press International, "Manford Act Flayed by J. Frank Dobie," *Houston Post*, 24 September 1943.

60. "Counsel for the Common People, Part 1."

61. "Court Hears Argument in Thomas Case," *Houston Chronicle*, 21 October 1943; "Texas Supreme Court Overrules Attorney General in UAW Free Speech Case," *Federated Press*, 26 October 1943.
62. Gall, *Pursuing Justice*, 77, 163–67.
63. These arguments were summarized by Maurice Sugar in "Texas and Thomas," *[UAW] Ammunition*, undated, EGC, box 19, folder "R. J. Thomas," WRL.
64. "Counsel for the Common People, Part 1"; *Thomas v. Collins*, 323 U.S. 516 (1945); Gall, *Pursuing Justice*, 171–73; Gilbert Gall, "Rights Which Have Meaning: Reconceiving Labor Liberty in the 1940s," *Labor History*, August 1998.
65. Gall, *Pursuing Justice*, 172, 175.
66. "U.S. Supreme Court Outlaws Texas Gag Statute," *United Automobile Worker*, 1 February 1945; "Counsel for the Common People, Part 1"; Gall, *Pursuing Justice*, 171.
67. "Counsel for the Common People, Part 1"; Gall, *Pursuing Justice*, 171, 335.
68. "Minutes of Steering Committee Meeting," 4 August 1941, 11 August 1941, and 18 August 1941, CRCC, box 4, folder "Steering Committee Meetings July–Dec., 1941."
69. Ngai, *Impossible Subjects*, 175–201, 325–26; Stone, *Perilous Times*, 283–96.
70. Clive, *State of War*, 145–49; Meir and Rudwick, *Black Detroit and the Rise of the UAW*, 177–82; Norm McRae, "The Michigan Civil Rights Congress and the Struggle for Negro Civil Rights," 87–99, loose-leaf draft, no date, authors' possession. Goodman's role as one of four defense attorneys, along with Lebron Simmons, Elvin Davenport, and Joseph Caigen, is noted in the Civil Rights Federation's mimeo sheet, the *Sojourner Truth Daily News*, 8 March 1942 and 26 April 1942, CRCC, box 67, folder "Sojourner Truth News." Goodman and his colleagues were featured speakers along with the Reverend Charles Hill at the mass meeting held two weeks after the riot at Ebenezer AME Church, as advertised in the flyer "Sojourner Truth Mass Meeting," CRCC, box 67, folder "Sojourner Truth—printed material."
71. Ginger and Tobin, *The National Lawyers Guild*, 48–51; Meir and Rudwick, *Black Detroit and the Rise of the UAW*, 125–33.
72. "Minutes of Emergency Conference on the Fifth Column in Detroit's Plants," 26 June 1942, CRCC, box 96, folder 19; Ernest Goodman, "Negroes and Jews Must Unite against Fascism," *Michigan Chronicle*, 9 January 1943; Civil Rights Federation, *Smash Detroit's Fifth Column*, 19–23, saddle-stitched pamphlet, thirty-six pages, undated, authors' collection. The pamphlet describes the National Workers League and the Highland Park meeting in March 1942.
73. Civil Rights Federation, *Smash Detroit's Fifth Column*, 35–36; Milton Kemnitz to "Jack and Jordan," cc to Ernest Goodman, 9 June 1942, EGC, box 34, folder "Sojourner Truth"; "Minutes of Emergency Conference on the Fifth Column in Detroit's Plants," 26 June 1942, CRCC, box 96, folder 19.
74. Woertink, "Key Figure Report, Ernest Goodman."

75. Ibid.; taps, mail intercepts, wastepaper coverage, etc., referenced in "Correlation Summary, Main File No. 100-6963, 30 October 1968, Subject: Ernie Goodman," 7, 13, 16, 22, 25, TAM, box 164, folder 8; memo from Lawrence M. C. Smith, War Division, to J. Edgar Hoover, "Recorded" 30 June 1942, and memo from John Bugas to director, FBI, 5 March 1943, TAM, box 164, folder 6.

76. Clive, *State of War*, 156.

77. Jack Raskin, oral history interview by Norm McRae, 1970, 14, WRL; interview with Rollo O'Hare, 31 January 2008; Meir and Rudwick, *Black Detroit and the Rise of the UAW*, 109–10, 129 (Packard quote), 191–92 (R. J. Thomas quote); Clive, *State of War*, 139; Glen Jeansonne, *Gerald L. K. Smith, Minister of Hate* (New Haven: Yale University Press, 1988), 26–28, 40–42, 68.

78. Jeansonne, *Gerald L. K. Smith*, 64–89.

79. Clive, *State of War*, 156 (quote from *Life*).

80. Ibid., 158; Janet Langlois, "The Belle Isle Bridge Incident: Legend, Dialectic and Semiotic System in the 1943 Detroit Race Riots," *Journal of American Folklore* 96 (1983): 183–99.

81. Meir and Rudwick, *Black Detroit and the Rise of the UAW*, 204; Clive, *State of War*, 163–64.

82. Selig Harrison, "The Political Program of the United Automobile Workers" (BA thesis, Harvard University, 1948), 117–18, HD 8076.H3, WRL; Frank Semperger, "Direct Political Action by Labor in Wayne County, 1941–1946" (MA thesis, Wayne State University, 1948), 49–51, HD 8076.S42, WRL; Russ Cowans, "Blast Report of Committee to Study Riot," *Michigan Chronicle*, 18 September 1943.

83. "Statement Unanimously Adopted by the Executive Board, Detroit Chapter, National Lawyers' Guild, on the Recent Disorders in Detroit," 26 June 1943, EGC, box 29, folder "1943 Detroit Race Riot."

84. EG to Francis Biddle, 20 July 1943, and Wendell Berge to EG, 6 August 1943, EGC, box 29, folder "1943 Detroit Race Riot."

85. EG to George Marshall, 10 July 1944, EGC, box 34, folder "Civil Rights Congress #4"; program, "Institute on Race Relations: The Common Struggle for Full Integration of the Negro People into American Life, Sponsors," 4, and Institute on Race Relations, "Sixth Session," 3 April 1944, 2–5, EGC, box 34, folder "Civil Rights Congress #2."

86. Institute on Race Relations, "Sixth Session," 6–8.

87. Ibid.

88. Peter Irons, *A People's History of the Supreme Court* (New York: Penguin, 1999), 270–72; EG to George Marshall, 10 July 1940, EGC, box 34, folder "Civil Rights Congress #4."

89. Stone, *Perilous Times*, 243–44, 254–58, 272–75.

90. Harold P. Woertink, Federal Bureau of Investigation, "Ernest Goodman Alias Ernie Goodman" (100-6963), Detroit file no. 100-1512, 9 March 1944, 4–5 (Goodman on Bugas), and memo from Attorney General Francis Biddle to J. Edgar Hoover and Hugh B. Cox, 16 July 1943, TAM, box 164, folder 6.

91. Woertink, "Key Figure Report, Ernest Goodman," 17; Frank W. Mulderig, Federal Bureau of Investigation, "Ernest Goodman Alias Ernie Goodman" (100-6963), Detroit file no. 100-1512, 6 February 1946, 10, TAM, box 164, folder 6.

92. Woertink, "Key Figure Report, Ernest Goodman," 2, 5–7; Mulderig, "Ernest Goodman Alias Ernie Goodman," 3, 5–8, 10–11; Shuford, "Ernest Goodman Alias Ernie Goodman," 3.

93. Memo from Biddle to Hoover and Cox, 16 July 1943; Stone, *Perilous Times*, 250.

94. Shuford, "Ernest Goodman Alias Ernie Goodman," 6; Stone, *Perilous Times*, 254–55.

95. Institute on Race Relations, "Sixth Session," 19–23.

96. Ibid., 11–14, 18.

97. Angela Dillard, *Faith in the City: Preaching Radical Social Change in Detroit* (Ann Arbor: University of Michigan Press, 2007), 210–11; "Minutes of the Executive Board Detroit Branch NAACP January 14, 1946," and "Minutes Detroit Branch N.A.A.C.P. 1944," hardcover ledger book, 103, in Charles A. Hill Family Collection, box 1, Bentley Historical Library, University of Michigan, Ann Arbor. The executive board minutes indicate that Baltimore had the second largest chapter with fifteen thousand members.

98. Institute on Race Relations, "Sixth Session," 11.

99. Ibid., 17–18.

100. Anthony Beevor, *Stalingrad: The Fateful Siege, 1942–1943* (New York: Penguin, 1998), 38, 106, 388–94, 428. Like many on the left, Goodman must have taken a special pleasure in noting that the Soviet general who accepted the Nazi surrender at Stalingrad, Marshal Nikolay Voronov, had been a military advisor to loyalist Spain during the siege of Madrid, directing republican artillery from Retiro Park.

101. Institute on Race Relations, "Sixth Session," 9.

102. Melvin Small, "How We Learned to Love the Russians: American Media and the Soviet Union during World War II," *Historian* 36, no. 3 (1974): 470 (quote), 455–78.

103. Joseph Starobin, *American Communism in Crisis, 1943–1957* (Berkeley: University of California Press, 1975), 61; editorial, "We Salute Our Russian Allies," *Detroit News*, 11 November 1943; "Jane R." to Jane Mayer, 9 December 1944, on the letterhead of Detroit Council of American-Soviet Friendship, EGC, box 21, folder "Buck Dinner, 1939–1954." The list of sponsors of the council is printed on the back of the letter.

104. Institute on Race Relations, "Sixth Session," 25.

Chapter 5

1. EG to Maurice Sugar, 5 December 1946, "Re: Allis-Chalmers Case," 3, "Expenses Incurred," Maurice Sugar Collection, box 76, folder 76-7, WRL.

2. Marion Wilson, *The Story of Willow Run* (Ann Arbor: University of Michigan Press, 1956), 6–9, 51, 56, 70, 76, 84–85; John McManus, "Willow Run Village: Up by Its Bootstraps," *Detroit News*, 16 October 1956; "Eleven Mile Route Serves Willow Run," *Detroit Free Press*, 31 January 1943.

3. EG to Sugar, 5 December 1946.

4. Curtis MacDougall, *Gideon's Army* (New York: Marzani and Munsell, 1965), 5–21; Stephen Fraser, *Labor Will Rule: Sidney Hillman and the Rise of American Labor* (New York: Free Press, 1991), 530–35. On the ritual obeisance within the Democratic Party to southern opinion on race matters, see Ira Katznelson, *When Affirmative Action Was White: An Untold History of Racial Inequality in Twentieth Century America* (New York: Norton, 2005).

5. MacDougall, *Gideon's Army*, 24–27 (*Tribune* quote on 27).

6. On the GM strike and Reuther quotes, see Nelson Lichtenstein, *The Most Dangerous Man in Detroit: Walter Reuther and the Fate of American Labor* (New York: Basic, 1995), 227–47; John Barnard, *American Vanguard: The United Auto Workers during the Reuther Years, 1935–1970* (Detroit: Wayne State University Press, 2004), 212–19.

7. Lichtenstein, *The Most Dangerous Man in Detroit*, 230 (Romney quote).

8. B. J. Widick and Irving Howe, *The UAW and Walter Reuther* (New York: Random House, 1949), 143.

9. EG to Maurice Sugar, "Re: OPA Protest against Automobile Price Increase," 4 November 1946, Maurice Sugar Collection, box 76, folder 76-7, WRL; Lichtenstein, *The Most Dangerous Man in Detroit*, 246 (prices).

10. EG to Maurice Sugar, "Re: UAW Radio Matters," 12 January 1946, Maurice Sugar Collection, box 76, folder 76-6, WRL.

11. EG to Maurice Sugar, "Re: National Health Bill," 24 June 1946, EGC, box 76, folder 76-7; Jennifer Klein, "The Politics of Economic Security: Employee Benefits and the Privitization of New Deal Liberalism," *Journal of Policy History* 16, no. 1 (2004): 37–47 (NAM quote on 47).

12. Klein, "The Politics of Economic Security," 48–52.

13. Lichtenstein, *The Most Dangerous Man in Detroit*, 232, 235, 288 (auto wages).

14. Chris Johnson, *Maurice Sugar: Law, Labor, and the Left in Detroit, 1912–1950* (Detroit: Wayne State University Press, 1988), 284; *Social Security Board v. Nierotko*, 327 U.S. 358 (1946); *Trailmobile Co. v. Whirls*, 331 U.S. 40 (1947); EG to Maurice Sugar, "Re: Nierotko Case," 10 June 1946, Maurice Sugar Collection, box 76, folder 76-7, WRL.

15. "Counsel for the Common People, Parts 3–4," videotaped interview with Ernest Goodman, produced by William Bryce, WRL; Johnson, *Maurice Sugar*, 285; Barnard, *American Vanguard*, 267.

16. EG to Frances Williams, 19 April 1944, EGC, box 34, folder "Civil Rights Congress #4."

17. "Summary, 1945 Fees," Maurice Sugar Collection, box 4, folder 4-19, WRL; *Historical Statistics of the U.S.* (Washington, DC: U.S. Bureau of the Census, 1975), 1:176; Maurice Sugar to George Addes, "Payments Made for Legal Services Rendered to the International Union and Region, UAW-CIO, 6/1/46– 5/31/47," and "Legal Fees, 6/1/46–5/31/47," Maurice Sugar Collection, box 4, folder 4-16, WRL.

18. "Counsel for the Common People, Parts 3–4"; "Memo of Mr. Sugar to the Staff," 5 August 1943, 13 July 1943, 11 November 1946, EGC, box 27, folder "Staff Memos (MS)"; "Memorandum on Relationship between Maurice Sugar and Attorneys in the General Division," 14 March 1942, and E. Wynn to Mr. Sugar, 20 November 1943, EGC, box 27, folder "Sugar File/Interoffice Memos."

19. Workplace Injury Litigation Group, "Hero" (obituary for Marcus), *Workers First Watch* 3, no. 2 (2003): 20–21; "Counsel for the Common People, Parts 3–4"; memo listing "Miscellaneous" expenses for 1944, Maurice Sugar Collection, box 4, folder 4-19, WRL.

20. George Crockett, oral history interview by Herbert Hill, 2 March 1968, WRL. All unattributed biographical information that follows comes from this source.

21. Ernie Goodman, "An Unofficial, Incomplete Biographical Sketch and a Few Personal Recollections of Congressman George W. Crockett, Jr.," Maurice Sugar Collection, box 118, folder 118:b, WRL. This appears to be a portion of an NLG annual dinner booklet.

22. Albert Deutsch, "Death Penalty against Negro GI Assailed by Prosecutor in Case," *PM*, 31 October 1946 (*PM* columns of Deutch are in clipping file, EGC, box 34, folder "Lemas Woods"); Ernest Goodman, "Lemas Woods," 1, undated manuscript, EGC, box 34.

23. "Counsel for the Common People, Parts 3–4"; Goodman, "Lemas Woods," 9, 26.

24. Morris MacGregor Jr., *Integration of the Armed Forces, 1940–1965* (Washington, DC: Center for Military History, U.S. Army, 1985), chapters 2, 3, 4.

25. Kevin J. Berry, "Military Commissions: Trying American justice," *Army Lawyer*, July 2003; "Counsel for the Common People, Parts 3–4."

26. Goodman, "Lemas Woods," 26.

27. EG to President Harry S. Truman, 23 September 1946, 2, EGC, box 34, folder "Lemas Woods."

28. Ibid.; Goodman, "Lemas Woods," 23.

29. "Counsel for the Common People, Parts 3–4."

30. Ibid.

31. Typewritten memo from "Hub" George, *Detroit Free Press*, undated, EGC, box 34, folder "Lemas Woods"; Albert Deutsch, "Negro Soldier Gives Own Version of 'Frame-Up,'" *PM*, 17 April 1947; Goodman, "Lemas Woods," 34–35.

32. Sherwin Wine, "Goodman Pleads for Justice: Pvt. Woods' Trial Tests Army Treatment of Negro Soldiers," *Jewish News*, 11 July 1947.

33. Lemas Woods Defense Committee, "For Immediate Release," 2 August 1947, EGC, box 34, folder "Lemas Woods."
34. Goodman, "Lemas Woods," 42.
35. Albert Deutsch, "Vital Mosquito Net Introduced at Retrial of Negro GI for Murder," *PM*, 29 July 1947.
36. Goodman, "Lemas Woods," 45; Albert Deutsch, "Range of Fatal Bullet Debated," *PM*, 30 July 1947.
37. "Counsel for the Common People, Parts 3–4"; Goodman, "Lemas Woods," 53.
38. Goodman, "Lemas Woods," 54–55.
39. Ibid., 56.
40. Goodman, handwritten notation, "Lemas Woods," 58.
41. "Agents Disagree on Source of Confession," *San Francisco Chronicle*, 3 August 1947, and J. Campbell Bruce, "Prosecution Witness Helps Defense in Second Trail of Soldier," *San Francisco Chronicle*, undated clipping, EGC, box 34, folder "Leams Woods."
42. Goodman, "Lemas Woods," 58.
43. "Pvt. Lemas Woods Jr. Home, Lauds Defense," undated clipping, EGC, box 34, folder "Lemas Woods."
44. MacGregor, *Integration of the Armed Forces*, chapter 12; *Uniform Code of Military Justice: Text, References and Commnetary Based on the Report of the Committee on a Uniform Code of Military Justice to the Secretary of Defense* (Washington, DC: U.S. National Military Establishment, 1949), articles 25, 27, and 38, pp. 35–56.
45. Paul Gardner, "Detroiters of Goodwill," *Pittsburgh Courier,* 15 November 1947.
46. William A. Williams, *The Tragedy of American Diplomacy* (New York: Dell, 1962), 203–73.
47. David Caute, *The Great Fear: The Anti-Communist Purge under Truman and Eisenhower* (New York: Simon and Schuster, 1978), 27; Williams, *Tragedy,* 210.
48. Williams, *Tragedy,* 240.
49. "Poll Shows Public Favors Ban on Communism in the U.S.," 19 April 1947, WRL, clipping in EGC, box 13, folder "Communism." Twenty-six percent opposed such a ban and 13 percent expressed no opinion.
50. Caute, *The Great Fear,* 89–90.
51. Ellen Schrecker, *The Age of McCarthyism: A Brief History with Documents* (Boston: St. Martin's, 1994), 167–71 (attorney general's list).
52. Kevin Boyle, *The UAW and the Heyday of American Liberalism, 1945–1968* (Ithaca: Cornell University Press, 1995), 24–28; Nat Ganley, oral history interview by Jack Skeels, 16 April 1960, 33–34, WRL.
53. Barnard, *American Vanguard,* 64, 212; Lichtenstein, *The Most Dangerous Man in Detroit,* 260; Johnson, *Maurice Sugar,* 294.
54. Clancy Sigal, *Going Away: A Report, a Memoir* (New York: Houghton Mifflin, 1962), 319–20.

55. August Meir and Elliot Rudwick, *Black Detroit and the Rise of the UAW* (New York: Oxford University Press, 1979), 213. Reports that Crockett was "dismissed" or "fired" are found in Barnard, *American Vanguard*, 239, and Boyle, *The UAW and the Heyday of American Liberalism*, 43. Crockett's persistent inquiries to Reuther and Reuther's responses regarding negotiations over a nondiscrimination clause are included in three folders of correspondence covering 1945 and the first quarter of 1946 in the George Crockett Collection, part 1, box 1, WRL. In the same box, see George Crocket, "Labor Looks Ahead," carbon of draft column for the *Michigan Chronicle* dated 27 April 1946.

56. Crockett recalled moving to the Sugar firm and working at the Canfield garage "in late 1947 or early 1948." He was off by a year. Reuther won the UAW presidency in 1946 and gained control of the executive board in November of 1947, foreclosing Crockett's hopes of returning. Crocket's first billings from the Sugar firm appear nine months earlier, in February 1947. His leave of absence and his tenure as garage janitor must therefore have begun in late 1946 or early 1947. For Crocket's billings, see Albert Abood, UAW Accounting Department, to Maurice Sugar, 22 August 1947, "Payments Made for Legal Services . . . June 1, 1946–May 31, 1947," Maurice Sugar Collection, box 4, folder 4-16, WRL.

57. Ernest Goodman, interview by Tom Lonergan, 20 May 1989, 1–3, authors' possession; Art McPhaul, oral history interview by Norman McRae, 5 May 1970, 5, Blacks in the Labor Movement Collection, WRL.

58. Sec. 28.343–44 of Michigan Statutes; Elaine Latzman Moon, ed., *Untold Tales, Unsung Heroes: An Oral History of Detroit's African American Community, 1918–1967* (Detroit: Wayne State University Press, 1994), 53; Goodman, interview by Lonergan, 20 May 1989, 3.

59. Stephen Meyer, *Stalin over Wisconsin: The Making and Unmaking of Militant Unionism, 1900–1950* (New Brunswick: Rutgers University Press, 1992), 150–57.

60. Ibid., 200.

61. Roger Keeran, *The Communist Party and the Auto Workers Unions* (Bloomington: Indiana University Press, 1980), 273, 279; Barnard, *American Vanguard*, 232–33.

62. Meyer, *Stalin over Wisconsin*, 13–14, 158, 197.

63. Barnard, *American Vanguard*, 228 (Reuther quote).

64. Meyer, *Stalin over Wisconsin*, 207–9; Maurice Sugar, "Analysis of the Taft-Hartley Act and Instructions to UAW-CIO Local Unions," twenty-six-page saddle-stitched pamphlet, section 7, and R. J. Thomas, "To Recording Secretaries of All Unions, UAW-CIO," 3 November 1947, and George Addes to Walter Reuther, "Subject: Poll of Board on Signing Taft-Hartley Affidavits," 31 October 1947, and press release of UAW-CIO Public Relations Department, 31 October 1947, all in Walter Reuther Collection, box 65, folder 2, WRL; stenographic record, "Board Meeting—Fort Shelby Hotel—Detroit,

Nov. 28–December 1, 1947," 235 (on Crockett), Maurice Sugar Collection, box 4, folder 4-20, WRL (hereafter cited as "steno record"); EG to Maurice Sugar, "Re: Taft-Hartley Bill," 22 August 1947, including worksheet indicating Goodman's appearance before the executive board on two occasions, 12 June and 9 July, "to explain the bill," Maurice Sugar Collection, box 76, folder 76-9, WRL; Johnson, *Maurice Sugar*, 295–96; *Proceedings of the Eleventh Convention, 1947, of the [UAW]*, 9–14 November 1947 (Detroit: UAW, 1948), 92.

65. Keeran, *The Communist Party and the Auto Workers*, 282–83.

66. "Counsel for the Common People, Parts 3–4."

67. Steno record, 315–17. A second charge, that Sugar and his associates were only moderately competent and that their radical reputation provoked adverse rulings from conservative judges, was obviously partisan invective; the record of Supreme Court victories and successful litigation at all levels of the legal system spoke for itself.

68. Steno record, 257, 259, 246–47, 249–50, 324.

69. Ibid., 231–35, 237–39.

70. Ibid., 275–76.

71. George Addes to Emil Mazey, 4 June 1947, Walter Reuther Collection, box 115, folder 115-6, WRL; Maurice Sugar to R. J. Thomas, 24 April 1939, "4/28/39 Proposal Accepted by Board," 10–13, Maurice Sugar Collection, box 4, folder 4-17, WRL; steno record, 264, 292–94. In addition to attaching a copy of the 1939 agreement, Addes provided Reuther and Mazey in 1947 with a timeline of subsequent board meetings, 1940–46, renewing the agreement. He also provided a detailed summary of the amendments made in 1944 regarding total compensation for "services and expenses of the legal department," the amount raised from $1,500 a month to $2,100 because of "the very substantial increase which has shown to exist in the expenses of the legal department by reason of the heavily increased rent, stenographers' salaries, and general office maintenance."

72. Steno record, 267.

73. Press release from Public Relations Department, UAW-CIO, 8 January 1948, Walter Reuther Collection, box 115, folder 7, WRL; Maurice Sugar to Walter Reuther, 26 January 1948, Maurice Sugar Collection, box 5, folder 5-3, WRL.

74. Harold Cranefield to Irving Levy, 15 October 1948, Walter Reuther Collection, box 115, folder 115-7, WRL; "Counsel for the Common People, Parts 3–4"; interview with Dick Goodman, 14 June 2006.

75. Maurice Sugar to Walter Reuther, 9 February 1948 and 26 February 1948, Maurice Sugar Collection, box 5, folder 5-3, WRL; steno record, 235, 239, 284, 288–89; "Matters Being Handled by Ernest Goodman for the International Union," Maurice Sugar Collection, box 5, file 5-1, WRL; billings and accompanying notes, EG to Emil Mazey, 5–9 April 1948, Maurice Sugar Collection, box 76, file 76-10, WRL.

76. "Counsel for the Common People, Parts 3–4"; Barnard, *American Vanguard*, 237–39; Keeran, *The Communist Party and the Auto Workers*, 284–85.

77. "Speech of Maurice Sugar at the Rogge Meeting Held on March 25, 1948," Maurice Sugar Collection, box 5, file 5-5, WRL.

78. "Counsel for the Common People, Parts 3–4."

79. Letter from Emil Mazey to UAW Region 1 and 1A local union presidents, Walter Reuther Collection, box 84, folder 8, WRL.

80. MacDougal, *Gideon's Army*, 44; Lichtenstein, *The Most Dangerous Man in Detroit*, 304.

81. Wine, "Goodman Pleads for Justice."

82. MacDougall, *Gideon's Army*, 66–67.

83. Ibid., 283.

84. William Muller, "Wallace Aims Parting Shot," *Detroit News*, 14 May 1948; Frank Morris, "Rally Puts $40,000 in Wallace Till," *Detroit Times*, 14 May 1948; FBI "Memo," 14 May 1948, describing Olympia event, TAM, box 119, folder 1; interview with Dick Goodman, 14 June 2006; Progressive Party of Michigan, "Draft Platform," 1948, Sidney Rosen Collection, box 1, folder 32, WRL; "Progressive Party: National and State Nominations," two-page legal-size mimeo, EGC, box 37, folder "Nat. Convention."

85. MacDougal, *Gideon's Army*, 157–58, 282, 303.

86. Joseph Starobin, *American Communism in Crisis, 1943–1957* (Berkeley: University of California Press, 1975), 60–70, 78–83, 107–20.

87. MacDougal, *Gideon's Army*, 268–71, 427.

88. Barnard, *American Vanguard*, 320; Robert Zieger, *The CIO, 1935–1955* (Chapel Hill: University of North Carolina Press, 1995), 267–72; MacDougal, *Gideon's Army*, 172–73, 249; *Ford Facts*, May 1948, Sidney Rosen Collection, box 1, WRL.

89. Stephen Sarasohn and Vera Sarasohn, *Political Party Patterns in Michigan* (Detroit: Wayne State University Press, 1957); John Fenton, *Midwest Politics* (New York: Holt, Rinehart, and Winston, 1966), 11–44.

90. James Jacobs, "The Conduct of Local Political Intelligence" (PhD diss., Princeton University, 1977), 122–24 (on Sigler); "Progressive Party: National and State Nominations."

91. "'Wall Street Runs Nation,' Says Goodman," *Iron Mountain News*, 20 October 1948; affidavit filed 21 October 1948 by James M. Demulling, EGC, box 37, folder "Progressive Party"; interview with Bill Goodman, 7 March 2006.

92. *Detroit News*, 24 March 1948, 25 March 1948; United Public Workers, "Press Release," 30 March 1948, Yale Stuart Collection, box 1, folder "Press Releases, December 1946–April 1949," WRL.

93. "Judge for Yourself," reprint of letters from Allen Sayler to Honorable Harry S. Toy, 9 March 1948, and Harry Toy to Allen Sayler, 11 March 1948, Maurice Sugar Collection, box 5, folder 5-5, WRL; "Toy Pistol Waved at Candidate," *Wallace Campaigner*, 12 April 1948, 4, Harold Norris Collection, box 13, folder 13-6, WRL.

94. Caute, *The Great Fear*, 161.

95. Progressive Party of Michigan, postelection analysis, Sidney Rosen Collection, box 1, folder 32, WRL. The author of this analysis noted that one of the "principal victories in the campaign" was the defeat of Governor Sigler. Vote totals are from the *Michigan Official Directory and Legislative Manual, 1949–1950* (Lansing: Secretary of State, 1949), 229–31, 244–46, 253.

96. Ernest Goodman to Thirteenth District Progressives, 28 March 1949, EGC, box 34, folder "13th D.C."

97. Edward Pintzuk, *Reds, Racial Justice and Civil Liberties: Michigan Communists during the Cold War* (Minneapolis: MEP, 1997), 20, 34; Coleman Young and Lonnie Wheeler, *Hard Stuff: The Autobiography of Coleman Young* (New York: Viking, 1994), 97, 104–5.

98. EG to Thirteenth District Progressives, 21 April 1949, EGC, box 34, folder "13th C.D."; Caute, *The Great Fear*, 339–40; Jacobs, "The Conduct of Local Political Intelligence," 125–27.

Chapter 6

1. "Counsel for the Common People, Parts 3–4," videotaped interview with Ernest Goodman, produced by William Bryce, WRL.

2. Paine was a favorite of Goodman's. Neely Tucker, "The Trials of Ernie Goodman," *Detroit Free Press Magazine*, 8 December 1991, 21.

3. "Memorandum of Agreement between Benjamin Marcus and Each of the Following Attorneys . . . ," 8 January 1948, and "Memorandum of Office Agreement," 24 December 1947, and "Memo from Ben Marcus to Office Lawyers," 6 September 1949, EGC, box 27, folder "Inter Office Memos"; interview with Dean Robb, 22 August 2005.

4. *Detroit Yellow Pages*, December 1949, Burton Collection, Detroit Public Library; interview with Dean Robb, August 22, 2005; Judith Stepan-Norris and Maurice Zeitlin, *Left Out: Reds and America's Industrial Unions* (Cambridge: Cambridge University Press, 2003), 19.

5. "Memorandum of Office Agreement," 24 December 1947, and "Note on Office Space," 4 October 1949, and Cadillac Tower lease, 3 May 1950, EGC, box 27, folder "Inter Office Memos"; interview with Dean Robb, 22 August 2005; *Detroit Yellow Pages*, 1950–53; National Lawyers Guild, Detroit chapter, *A Tribute to Ernest Goodman*, 13 December 1980, saddle-stitched banquet book, authors' possession. The rent in 1947 for the entire suite was $845. With inflation, the cost in 1949 would have been at least $900.

6. "Counsel for the Common People, Parts 3–4."

7. EG to "Freda, Dick, and Billy," letters of 3 and 4 December 1949, EGC, box 4, folder "Goodman Book." Case details are taken from "Counsel for the Common People, Parts 3–4"; and Ernest Goodman, interview by Edward Littlejohn, 31 May 1996 and 5 June 1996, Damon Keith Law Collection, Oral History Project, WRL.

8. EG to "Freda, Dick, and Billy," 4, 7, 10, and 17 December 1949, EGC, box 4, folder "Goodman Book."

9. "Counsel for the Common People, Parts 3–4."

10. Ibid.

11. EG to "Freda, Dick, and Billy," 26 December 1949, and the undated letter following, EGC, box 4, folder "Goodman Book."

12. EG to "Freda, Dick, and Billy," 26 December 1949, and the undated letter following.

13. "Counsel for the Common People, Parts 3–4."

14. Goodman, interview by Littlejohn, 5 June 1996, 12.

15. "Counsel for the Common People, Parts 3–4."

16. Ibid.

17. Interview with Dean Robb, 22 August 2005.

18. Interview with Ann Fagan Ginger, 18 November 2005.

19. Tom Lonergan, *It's in the Constitution* (Columbia College Chicago, 1993), videotape; interview with Dean Robb, 22 August 2005; interview with Dick Goodman, 14 June 2006.

20. "Counsel for the Common People, Parts 3–4"; interview with Dean Robb, 22 August 2005.

21. "Counsel for the Common People, Parts 3–4"; Lawrence Friedman, *A History of American Law,* 3rd ed. (New York: Simon and Schuster, 2005), 223.

22. Goodman, interview by Littlejohn, 5 June 1996, 5–6.

23. "Counsel for the Common People, Parts 3–4"; Ann Fagan Ginger and Eugene Tobin, eds., *The National Lawyers Guild: From Roosevelt through Reagan* (Philadelphia: Temple University Press, 1988), 110; interview with Dean Robb, 28 August 2007.

24. Edward Littlejohn and Donald Hobson, *Black Lawyers, Law Practice, and Bar Associations—1870 to 1970: A Michigan History* (Detroit: Wolverine Bar Association, 1987), 23–29; interview with Dean Robb, 22 August 2005. Governor Williams appointed Jones, McCree and Davenport to vacancies and McCree and Davenport won reelection.

25. George Crockett III, interview by Louis Jones, 5 May 2003, 8, Detroit African American History Project, WRL; interview with Dean Robb, 22 August 2005.

26. David Caute, *The Great Fear: The Anti-Communist Purge under Truman and Eisenhower* (New York: Simon and Schuster, 1978), 62–69; Ellen Schrecker, *Many Are the Crimes: McCarthyism in America* (New York: Little, Brown, 1998), 177–82; Thomas Powers, *Intelligence Wars: American Secret History from Hitler to Al-Qeda* (New York: New York Review Books, 2004), 83–92; Katherine Sibley, *Red Spies in America: Stolen Secrets and the Dawn of the Cold War* (Lawrence: University of Kansas Press, 2004), 92–95, 120, 180, 188, 280; Ted Morgan, *Reds: McCarthyism in Twentieth Century America* (New York: Random House, 2004), 225–29, 290–91.

27. Geoffrey Stone, *Perilous Times: Free Speech in Wartime* (New York: Norton, 2004), 404 (Vinson).

28. Michael Belknap, *Cold War Political Justice: The Smith Act, the Communist Party, and American Civil Liberties* (Westport, CT: Greenwood, 1977), 81–82, 140; Schrecker, *Many Are the Crimes*, 192–94; Stone, *Perilous Times*, 407.

29. Schrecker, *Many Are the Crimes*, 198; Stanley Kutler, *The American Inquisition: Justice and Injustice in the Cold War* (New York: Hill and Wang, 1982), 157–64. Quotes appear on 162 (Jackson) and 163 (Frankfurter).

30. Kutler, *The American Inquisition*, 156; George Crockett, interview by Tom Lonergan, 27–28 March 1987, authors' possession; Schrecker, *Many Are the Crimes*, 197.

31. George Crockett, *Freedom Is Everybody's Job! The Crime of the Government against the Negro People: Summation in the Trial of the 11 Communist Leaders* (New York: National Non-partisan Committee, circa 1949–50), 2, 16; Crockett, interview by Lonergan, 27 March 1987.

32. Ernest Goodman, interview by Tom Lonergan, 20 May 1989, authors' possession; Crockett, interview by Lonergan, 27 March 1987.

33. Kutler, *The American Inquisition*, 173; Crockett, interview by Lonergan, 27 March 1987; Goodman, interview by Lonergan, 20 May 1989.

34. Crockett, interview by Jones, 5; *Polk's City Directory* (1953); Goodman, interview by Lonergan, 20 May 1989; Crockett, interview by Lonergan, 27–28 March 1987.

35. George Crockett, "Labor Looks Ahead," typescript draft of column for *Michigan Chronicle*, 27 April 1946, George Crockett Collection, part 1, box 1, folder "Labor Looks Ahead, Jan.–July, 1946," WRL; Crockett, interview by Lonergan, 27 March 1987.

36. Ellen Schrecker, *The Age of McCarthyism: A Brief History with Documents* (Boston: St. Martin's, 1994), 18, 115; Morgan, *Reds*, 293 (quote), 375; Powers, *Intelligence Wars*, 109–13, 322–29, 405–11; Sibley, *Red Spies in America*, 2, 218; William C. Sullivan, *The Bureau: My Thirty Years in Hoover's FBI* (New York: Norton, 1979), 117–21, 203–4. Sullivan is quoted in Belknap, *Cold War Political Justice*, 175.

37. Powers, *Intelligence Wars*, 121.

38. Margaret Collingwood Nowak, *Two Who Were There: A Biography of Stanley Nowak* (Detroit: Wayne State University Press, 1989), 225; EG to John McManus, 31 January 1951, and "Statement of Reasons, Re: Charles Andrew Hill, Jr.," undated, and Captain Charles A. Hill Jr. to Commanding General, Continental Air Command, 10 January 1951, and Irving Richter, "How a Young Pilot Beat a Disloyalty Charge," *Courier Magazine*, 5 May 1951, all in EGC, box 35, folder "Charles A Hill Jr., Army Loyalty Case."

39. Captain Charles A. Hill Jr. to Commanding General, Continental Air Command; EG to McManus.

40. Caute, *The Great Fear*, 112, 592–93n15; Stone, *Perilous Times*, 345–51; Schrecker, *Age of McCarthyism*, 167.

41. "Minutes of Board of Directors Meeting, Civil Rights Congress, 28 June 1946," EGC, box 34, large folder "Civil Rights Congress," file folder #1; Stone, *Perilous*

Times, 344; Caute, *The Great Fear*, 168, 170. Attorney General Brownell finally issued new regulations to permit a hearing after a group had been listed. The first hearing wasn't granted until 1955, and it wasn't until 1958 that a group was actually removed.

42. "Initiating Committee" and "Sponsors" in "Urgent Summons to a Congress on Civil Liberties," 1946, 4, EGC, box 34, large folder "Civil Rights Congress," file folder #1;CRC, "America's 'Thought Police': Record of the Un-American Activities Committee," October 1947, forty-seven saddle-stitched pages, inside cover has list of officers, CRCC, box 5, folder "Research Material, 1947–1950; Gerald Horne, *Communist Front? The Civil Rights Congress* (Cranbury, NJ: Associated University Presses, 1988), 16, 106.

43. Horne, *Communist Front?* 141, 294; interview with Dean Robb, 22 August 2005; Edward Pintzuk, *Reds, Racial Justice and Civil Liberties: Michigan Communists during the Cold War* (Minneapolis: MEP, 1997), 105; Moon, *Untold Tales*, 154, 158–59 (Dillard quote). See CRCC, box 65, folder "Discrimination—Local, Clippings, 1950–1952" for clippings on efforts to desegregate restaurants, bars, and dance halls through enforcement of the Diggs Act.

44. Pintzuk, *Reds, Racial Justice*, 105; "Detroit Police Department, Special Investigation Bureau, Dec. 11, 1948 . . . Subject: Picketing at 8841 12th St . . . ," Detroit Red Squad Files, Miscellaneous.

45. Moon, *Untold Tales*, 260; Pintzuk, *Reds, Racial Justice*, 84–87; Michigan Committee on Civil Rights, "Leon Mosley Case," 5 January 1949, and Civil Rights Congress, "The Leon Mosley Case, Fact Sheet," and EG to Hon. Arthur Gordon, 28 December 1948, EGC, box 39, folder "Leon Mosley."

46. Art McPhaul, interview by Norm McRae, 5 May 1970, 8, Blacks in the Labor Movement Collection, WRL; Horne, *Communist Front?* 31–32, 141–43; Sarah Hart Brown, "Communism, Anti-Communism, and Massive Resistance: The Civil Rights Congress in Southern Perspective," in *Before Brown: Civil Rights and White Backlash in the Modern South,* ed. Glenn Feldman (Tuscaloosa: University of Alabama Press, 2004), 189–90, 195–97. Even during the Reverend Hill's 1946 presidency of the Detroit NAACP, some members of the executive board cautioned against the "communistic tendencies which are trying to creep in. . . . Let us as board members stand by the principles upon which the NAACP was built and not turn either to the right or to the left." "Minutes of the Executive Board Detroit Branch NAACP, September 16, 1946," hardcover ledger book, 165, Charles A. Hill Family Collection, Bentley Historical Museum, University of Michigan, Ann Arbor.

47. "Copy of Correspondence between the Un-American Committee and the NFCL," memo from George Marshall to board members, January 1946, and EG to George Marshall, 9 January 1946, EGC, box 34, folder "Civil Rights Congress #4"; "Obituaries: George Marshall," *Columbia College Today*, May 2001; George Marshall, "Salem, 1950," *Masses and Mainstream* 3, no. 7 (1950); Horne, *Communist Front?* 30, 240–44.

48. "Jewish Unit Assails Group," *Detroit News*, 2 August 1950, and "Civil Rights Congress Rejected by Council," *Detroit Jewish Chronicle*, 10 August 1959, and "Reds Smear City's Police," *Detroit Free Press*, 14 October 1951, clipping file, CRCC, box 1, folder "Attacks on CRCC"; James Jacobs, "The Conduct of Local Political Intelligence" (PhD diss., Princeton University, 1977), 126–27; Arthur McPhaul, "Report to the National Executive Board of the Civil Rights Congress, re: Labor, Its Relationship to the Civil Rights Congress in the Struggle for Civil Rights," seven-page typescript, undated, 1, CRCC, box 5, folder "Reports—1953–1954." For contrasting analyses of the CP-USA's role in the CRC, see Pintzuk, *Reds, Racial Justice*, which describes the CRC as an "arm" of the CP-USA, and Horne, *Communist Front?* which describes the organization at its founding as a genuine Popular Front of liberals and Communists.

49. Anne Shore to Aubery Grossman, 12 October 1950, CRCC, box 2, folder "CRCC Correspondence—1950"; Art McPhaul to "Dear Friend," 18 May 1954, CRCC, box 5, folder "Reports—1953–1954"; Jack Raskin, oral history interview by Norm McRae, 1970, 13, WRL. CRC addresses: May 1947, 609 Hammond Building; December 1948, 242 Reid Building, 140 Cadillac Square; November 1950, 1442 Griswold; July 1953, 918 Charlevoix Building.

50. Peter Irons, *A People's History of the Supreme Court* (New York: Penguin, 1999), 376.

51. Pintzuk, *Reds, Racial Justice*, 95–96.

52. "Statement of Mrs. Rosalee McGee," undated, CRCC, box 62, folder "Willie McGee—1948–1950"; "Exclusive: The Story of Willie McGee," eight-page tabloid by national CRC, reprinting series of articles from the *New York Daily Compass*, 14–19 June 1950, and "Fact Sheet on Willie McGee Case," 22 October 1949, and "Fifth Appeal to Save Willie McGee," CRC Press Release, 27 October 1949, 2, CRCC, box 62, folder "Willie McGee—1951"; Horne, *Communist Front?* 79–81; Pintzuk, *Reds, Racial Justice*, 119.

53. Anne Shore to Aubery Grossman, 17 November 1950, CRCC, box 2, folder "CRCC Correspondence—1950."

54. "Unionists Move," *Pittsburgh Courier*, 21 April 1951, and "The Case of Willie McGee: A Fact Sheet Prepared by the Civil Rights Congress," 2, CRCC, box 62, folder "Willie McGee—1951"; Art McPhaul to Aubrey Grossman, 21 March 1951, and Anne Shore to William Patterson, 13 March 1951, and Aubrey Grossman to Anne Shore, 16 March 1951, CRCC, box 63, folder "Willie McGee—Correspondence—'51"; Horne, *Communist Front?* 88, 90–91.

55. "Counsel for the Common People, Parts 3–4" (all Goodman quotes regarding the McGee case that follow are taken from this source); Horne, *Communist Front?* 75; "Circuit Court Denies McGee Appeal, Last Legal Hope in U.S. Supreme Court," CRC New York press release, 13 March 1951, and "To: All Chapter Secretaries, From: Aubrey Grossman," 15 March 1951, CRCC, box 63, folder "Willie McGee—Correspondence—'51"; "Losing Battle for McGee Fought to End," "Jones Sheriff Begins Moving McGee to Laurel," and

courtroom photo of Goodman and Abzug, *Jackson Clarion Ledger,* 8 May 1951, CRCC, box 63, folder "Willie McGee, 1948–1951—Clippings."

56. Horne, *Communist Front?* 82, 92–93; "The Case of Willie McGee: A Fact Sheet Prepared by the Civil Rights Congress," 2; carbon typescript of *Jackson Daily News* editorial, 7 July 1950, CRCC, box 62, folder "Willie McGee— 1948–1950."

57. "Troopers Jail 50 as Negro Seeks Reprieve," *Detroit Free Press,* 7 May 1951; Horne, *Communist Front?* 95–96.

58. "Counsel for the Common People, Parts 3–4."

59. Pintzuk, *Reds, Racial Justice,* 182.

60. Caute, *The Great Fear,* 166 (quote), 91; Stone, *Perilous Times,* 354–55 (quote).

61. Stepan-Norris and Zeitlin, *Left Out,* 96; McPhaul, "Report to the National Executive Board of the Civil Rights Congress," 3; "Memo from Ernest Goodman," handwritten list of clients and attorneys, EGC, box 4, folder "HUAC Detroit 1952."

62. "Counsel for the Common People, Parts 3–4"; Stepan-Norris and Zeitlin, *Left Out,* 97 (Rouge employment).

63. Stepan-Norris and Zeitlin, *Left Out,* 95–123; Kevin Boyle, *The UAW and the Heyday of American Liberalism, 1945–1968* (Ithaca: Cornell University Press, 1995), 76–77; Nelson Lichtenstein, *The Most Dangerous Man in Detroit: Walter Reuther and the Fate of American Labor* (New York: Basic, 1995), 313–15; John Barnard, *American Vanguard: The United Auto Workers during the Reuther Years, 1935–1970* (Detroit: Wayne State University Press, 2004), 243–44; "Washington Confab Didn't Bring Jobs," *Ford Facts,* 8 March 1952, EGC, box 4, folder "HUAC Detroit 1952"; "Counsel for the Common People, Parts 3–4."

64. "Un-American Committee Calls Two Local Officers," *Ford Facts,* 23 February 1952, EGC, box 4, folder "HUAC Detroit 1952."

65. "Complaint," *Local Union 600 et al. v. Ford Motor Company,* in U.S. Dist. Ct. for the Eastern Dist. of Michigan (1952) (quote on 7), EGC, box 13, folder "Local 600 vs. Ford Motor Company"; Stepan-Norris and Zeitlin, *Left Out,* 123.

66. Schrecker, *Age of McCarthyism,* 58; Caute, *The Great Fear,* 96.

67. Leonard Levy, *Origins of the Bill of Rights* (New Haven: Yale University Press, 2001), 189–201.

68. Schrecker, *Age of McCarthyism,* 58–60.

69. Boyd Simmons, "Ford Local Is Called Red-Tinged," *Detroit News,* 23 February 1952; "Ford Local's Chiefs in Quiz," *Detroit News,* 18 February 1952; "See Plot to Quiet Truman's Critics," *Detroit News,* 25 February 1952.

70. Stepan-Norris and Zeitlin, *Left Out,* 123–24.

71. McPhaul, "Report to the National Executive Board of the Civil Rights Congress," 3; *Detroit News* photos, 26 February 1952.

72. *Detroit News* photos, 26 February 1952; Roger Keeran, *The Communist Party and the Auto Workers Unions* (Bloomington: Indiana University Press,

1980), 253–55, 266; U.S. Congress, HCUA, *Communism in the Detroit Area,* 82nd Cong., 2nd sess., 1952, 2832.

73. HCUA, *Communism in the Detroit Area,* 2820–22.

74. "Rice Explains Committee Appearance," *Ford Facts,* 8 March 1952, EGC, box 4, folder "HUAC Detroit 1952"; HCUA, *Communism in the Detroit Area,* 2920–21.

75. "UAW Official Faces State Dept. Inquiry," *Detroit News,* 29 February 1952; "Reds Invoke Constitution," *Detroit News,* 27 February 1952; HCUA, *Communism in the Detroit Area,* 3010 (Nowak) and 3184 (Moore).

76. HCUA, *Communism in the Detroit Area,* 2832; "Four Subpoenaed by House Body," *Pittsburgh Courier,* February 1952, EGC, box 4, folder "House Un Comm., General Pamphlets."

77. "Grandmother Back in City for Quiz, Kept under Guard," *Detroit News,* 28 February 1952; McPhaul, interview by McRae, 5 May 1970.

78. Coleman Young and Lonnie Wheeler, *Hard Stuff: The Autobiography of Coleman Young* (New York: Viking, 1994), 113–16; Boyle, *The UAW and the Heyday of American Liberalism,* 108–13; Lichtenstein, *The Most Dangerous Man in Detroit,* 315–17.

79. HCUA, *Communism in the Detroit Area,* 2879–80.

80. Ibid., 2884–85.

81. Ibid., 2886, 2891.

82. "Counsel for the Common People, Parts 3–4"; Young and Wheeler, *Hard Stuff,* 132; interview with Esther Shapiro, 30 November 2006.

83. "Red Cell at Ford's to Be Aired," *Detroit News,* 9 March 1952; Arthur McPhaul, oral history, no date, no indication of interviewer, 28–29, WRL.

84. Judith Stepan-Norris and Maurice Zeitlin, *Talking Union* (Urbana: University of Illinois Press, 1996), 205; "Counsel for the Common People, Parts 3–4."

85. "400 Reds at Ford's Ex-Local Aid Says," *Detroit News,* 11 March 1952; "Names of Detroit Red Leaders Given at Quiz," *Detroit News,* 1 March 1952; HCUA, *Communism in the Detroit Area,* 3082, 3115 (Jackson quotes).

86. B. J. Widick, *Detroit: City of Race and Class Violence* (Detroit: Wayne State University Press, 1989), 133, 127–36.

87. Boyle, *The UAW and the Heyday of American Liberalism,* 80–81; Asher Lauren, "Red Purge Board Seizes Ford Local," *Detroit News,* 15 March 1952; Stepan-Norris and Zeitlin, *Left Out,* 112.

88. Ernest Goodman to Carl Stellato, 6 March 1952, and Ernest Goodman to Allen Rosenberg, 5 August 1952, and Ford Motor Company, "The Decentralization Story," twelve-page pamphlet, undated, 1, EGC, box 13, folder "Local 600 vs. Ford Motor Company"; Stepan-Norris and Zeitlin, *Left Out,* 125–26.

89. Stepan-Norris and Zeitlin, *Left Out,* 97.

90. Boyle, *The UAW and the Heyday of American Liberalism,* 79 (quote); Lichtenstein, *The Most Dangerous Man in Detroit,* 36–44.

91. EG to Professor Thomas Emerson, 31 March 1965, TAM, box 44, folder 13; "National Lawyers Guild Statement Opposing Investigation by the House

Committee on Un-American Activities of the Ku Klux Klan," 6 July 1965, TAM, box 19, folder 17.

92. Ginger and Tobin, *The National Lawyers Guild*, 94–96. The Lawyers Guild withdrew from the Soviet-backed International Association of Democratic Lawyers in 1951 to protest the previous expulsion of the Yugoslav Lawyers Association. See *Lawyers Guild Review* 11, no. 4 (1951) and related documents in TAM, box 5, folder 38.

93. Kutler, *The American Inquisition*, 181; Belknap, *Cold War Political Justice*, 219–21; "3,000 Face Unmasking in Quiz Here," *Detroit News*, 25 February 1952; Widick, *Detroit*, 132.

94. HCUA, *Communism in the Detroit Area*, 2878–79; Young and Wheeler, *Hard Stuff*, 128; "Four Subpoenaed."

95. Raymond Arsenault, "'You Don't Have to Ride Jim Crow': CORE and the 1947 Journey of Reconciliation," in Feldman, *Before Brown*, 21–67.

Chapter 7

1. Ernest Goodman, interview by Tom Lonergan, 20 May 1989, authors' possession; "Counsel for the Common People, Parts 3–4," videotaped interview with Ernest Goodman, produced by William Bryce, WRL.

2. Goodman, interview by Tom Lonergan, 20 May 1989, 17; "5 Days Only to Save Willie McGee," CRC Detroit flyer featuring Jackson newspaper quote, and "Save Willie McGee" petition, CRCC, box 62, folder "Willie McGee—1951"; *Clarion Ledger*, 5 August 1951, CRCC, box 63, folder "Willie McGee—1948–1951—Clippings"; "Counsel for the Common People, Parts 3–4"; interview with Dick Goodman, 14 June 2006; Neely Tucker, "The Trials of Ernie Goodman," *Detroit Free Press Magazine*, 8 December 1991 (Bill quote).

3. Interview with Dick Goodman, 14 June 2006 and 20 June 2007; interview with Bill Goodman, 7 June 2007.

4. Interview with Dick Goodman, 14 June 2006.

5. Interview with Bill Goodman, 7 March 2006.

6. George W. Crockett III, interview by Louis Jones, 5 May 2003, Detroit African American History Project, WRL; interview with Dick Goodman, 14 June 2006; Ernest Goodman, interview by Edward Littlejohn, 5 June 1996, Damon J. Keith Law Collection Oral History Project, WRL.

7. "Counsel for the Common People, Parts 3–4."

8. George Crockett, interview by Tom Lonergan, 28 March 1987, 6, authors' possession.

9. Art McPhaul, interview by Norm McRae, 5 May 1970, 18, Blacks in the Labor Movement Collection, WRL; interview with Dick Goodman, 14 June 2006; interview with Esther Shapiro, 30 November 2006; Gerald Horne, *Communist Front? The Civil Rights Congress* (Cranbury, NJ: Associated University Presses, 1988), 291.

10. Joseph Starobin, *American Communism in Crisis, 1943–1957* (Berkeley: University of California Press, 1975), 198–201 (quote on 200).

11. Edward Pintzuk, *Reds, Racial Justice and Civil Liberties: Michigan Communists during the Cold War* (Minneapolis: MEP, 1997), 74, 115; Horne, *Communist Front?* 291.

12. Invitation card, "We've Got a Buck and You're in Luck . . . ," for dinner on 29 January 1949, and letter from unidentifiable (perhaps "Martha") to Jane Mayer, 31 January 1939, on letterhead of the Medical Bureau and Committee to Aid Spanish Democracy, EGC, box 21, large folder "Buck Dinner, 1939–1954," loose, no file.

13. "Contributions at Buck Dinner by Tables, Feb. 4, 1950," and "Buck Dinner—1950," typescript list of tables and guests, and typed draft of 1946 program, "Buck Dinner. (Benefit of ~~Detroit Council of American Soviet Friendship~~ [penciled in:] Civil Rights Federation)," and Anne Shore to Jane Mayer, 2 April 1951, and "The Case of the Civil Rights Congress for the Buck Dinner," 1947, and Anne Shore to "Buck Dinner Committee Members," 25 February 1953, and Anne Shore to Jane Mayer, 9 February 1951, all in EGC, box 21, large folder "Buck Dinner, 1939–1954," loose, no file.

14. Interview with Dean Robb, 22 August 2005; "(1) Cranefield," six-page typescript carbon of verse, penciled year of '45, EGC, box 21, large folder "Buck Dinner, 1939–1954," small folder "Buck Dinner"; interview with Leonard Grossman, 8 August 2006; Ernest Goodman, "Reminiscences on the Life of Mort Furay . . . , March 17, 1972," Maurice Sugar Collection, box 16, folder 19, WRL; "In Memorium, Mort Furay, 1910–1972," *Hotel-Bar Restaurant Review* 6 (March 1972), and Toni Jones, "Union Leader Mort Furay Dies," *Detroit Free Press*, 13 March 1972, EGC, box 38, large folder "Mort Furay"; interview with Dick Goodman, 14 June 2006.

15. The annual list of headhunters for the 1940s through the 1960s are in EGC, box 21, large folder "Buck Dinner, 1939–1954," large folder "Buck Dinner, 1955 through 1958," and large folder "Buck Dinner, 1959–1964."

16. "Buck Dinner—1950," typescript list of tables and guests; Erma Henderson with Michael Kitchen, *Down through the Years: The Memoirs of Detroit City Council President Emeritus Erma Henderson* (Bloomington, IN: Authorhouse, 2004), 63–101; Coleman Young and Lonnie Wheeler, *Hard Stuff: The Autobiography of Coleman Young* (New York: Viking, 1994), 110–11; Anne Shore to Jane Mayer, 11 March 1952, has attached a typed list of headhunters with Coleman Young's name crossed out in pencil, EGC, box 21, large folder "Buck Dinner, 1939–1954," loose, no file.

17. "Buck Dinner" typed drafts of 1947 and 1949 programs, including "Appreciation for Head Cooks," and letter from Anne Shore to Jane Mayer, 11 March 1952, and "Draft of Introduction to Operetta," undated but attached to 1953 papers, EGC, box 21, large folder "Buck Dinner, 1939–1954," loose, no file; invitation cards, various years, EGC, box 21, large folder "Buck Dinner, 1939–1954," small folder "Buck Dinner."

18. Pintzuk, *Reds, Racial Justice,* 44; "McCarthy Was a Senator," single typed song sheet on yellow paper, undated but with penciled year of '54, EGC, box

21, large folder "Buck Dinner, 1939–1954," small folder "Buck Dinner"; invitation card for 1949 dinner, EGC, box 21, large folder "Buck Dinner, 1939–1954," loose, no file.

19. "Is It a Crime to Have a Garden Party?" CRCC, box 3, folder "Garden Party Case—1953"; "The Story of the Illegal Raid and Arrests at the Civil Rights Congress Garden Party," EGC, box 34, folder "Civil Rights Congress #4."

20. "Is It a Crime to Have a Garden Party?"; interview with Esther Shapiro, 30 November 2006.

21. Interview with Esther Shapiro, 30 November 2006; Mark Kahn, "Profile of a Labor Activist: Harold A. Shapiro," *Michigan Jewish History* 40 (Fall 2000): 37–43.

22. Boyd Simmons, "Defense Fails to Shake Testimony of Spy for FBI," *Detroit News*, 11 December 1953; interview with Dick Goodman, 14 June 2006.

23. Phone interview with Aviva Gellman Blaichman, 12 January 2008.

24. FBI report on Ernest Goodman by Mortimer Watson, file 100-1512, 26 April 1947, containing excerpts of letter from EG to Laicha Kravchik, 18 July 1938, TAM, box 164, folder 7, 2; EG to Laicha, letter postmarked 3 October 1938, TAM, box 164, folder 6, 1; FBI "Correlation Summary," main file 100-6963, 30 October 1968, "Subject: Ernie Goodman," 22, TAM, box 164, folder 8.

25. R. B. Shipley to Freda Goodman, 18 June 1953, private collection, Goodman family.

26. EG to Leonard Boudin, 12 October 1955, and Freda Goodman to R. B. Shipley, 15 July 1953, private collection, Goodman family.

27. FBI "Correlation Summary," 54; Freda Goodman to R. B. Shipley, 15 July 1953.

28. Interview with Esther Shapiro, 30 November 2006.

29. EG to Senator Burton K. Wheeler, 14 December 1955, private collection, Goodman family.

Chapter 8

1. "Cooling Off," *Detroit Free Press*, 14 February 1954, and Russell Harris, "Red Trial All Politeness; 'Michigan Six' Smile at Judge," *Detroit News*, 28 October 1953, and Boyd Simmons, "Goodman's Glasses Play Major Role in Court Drama He Enacts for Reds," *Detroit News*, 15 November 1953, EGC, box 38, folder "Publicity of Smith Act Trial."

2. Boyd Simmons, "Attorney for Reds Attacks Morals of U.S. Witness," *Detroit News*, 13 November 1953, and "Cooling Off," EGC, box 38, folder "Publicity of Smith Act Trial."

3. "Court Denies Traitor Heaven," *Detroit Times*, 31 July 1952, EGC, box 38, folder "Publicity of Smith Act Trial."

4. Peter Irons, *A People's History of the Supreme Court* (New York: Penguin, 1999), 335–36.

5. Irons, *A People's History of the Supreme Court*, 339, 350.

6. Ernest Goodman, "Defense of What?" typescript of CRF-sponsored broadcast on station WJBK, 8 June 1941, CCRC, box 3, folder "Goodman Radio Speeches."

7. James Sweinhart, "Insurrection Expert Tells How Takeover Could Work Out Here," no. 8 in ten-part series, *Detroit News*, 18 May 1952, EGC, box 19, folder "Trucks Act."

8. Carl Rudow, "Proof Sought of Subversion," *Detroit News*, 7 March 1952.

9. *House Bill No. 20*, Michigan 66th Legislature, 9 January 1952. Passed as Act 117 of Public Acts of 1952.

10. Owen Deatrick, "Socialist Workers Banned from Ballot under Anti-Red Law, *Detroit Free Press*, 18 April 1952; "Appeals Legality of Anti-Red Law," *Detroit Times*, 31 July 1952.

11. "Counsel for the Common People, Parts 3–4," videotaped interview with Ernest Goodman, produced by William Bryce, WRL; "Attorney Who Gave Legal Aid to Reds Defended as Non-member," *Detroit News*, 31 July 1952.

12. "Red Registry Ruling Waits," *Detroit News*, 21 May 1952.

13. "Counsel for the Common People, Parts 3–4."

14. "Communist Injunction Plea Fails," *Detroit News*, 30 July 1952.

15. Ibid.; "Red Listing Delayed by U.S. Court," *Detroit News*, 23 April 1952; "Trucks Act Still Held in Abeyance," *Detroit Free Press*, 2 August 1952.

16. Al Kaufman, "Williams to Sign Anti-Red Bill," *Detroit Times*, 10 April 1952; Owen Deatrick, "Williams Says He'll Sign Bill to Register Communists," *Detroit Free Press*, 10 April 1952; Ernest Goodman, interview by Edward Littlejohn, 21 February 1997, 18, Oral History Project, Damon Keith Law Collection, WRL.

17. "Trucks Act Still Held in Abeyance"; "Reds Offered Ally in Fight," *Detroit News*, 21 November 1952; Don Hoenshell, "2 Parties Lose Place on Ballot; Plan Red Roundup," *Detroit News*, 18 April 1952; "Form Group to Fight Trucks Act," *Detroit Free Press*, 18 December 1952; "Unite against Trucks Act: UAW Leaders on Committee," *Labor Defender*, 1 (January 1953): 1, EGC, box 19, folder "Trucks Act"; Frank Lovell and Genora Dollinger to "Dear Friends," 19 April 1953, Ernest Mazey Collection, box 8, folder 5, WRL; *Wage Earner*, quoted in "Dear Friend" letter, undated, of the Citizens' Committee against the Trucks Law, 3, EGC, box 19, folder "Trucks Act."

18. Michael Belknap, *Cold War Political Justice: The Smith Act, the Communist Party, and American Civil Liberties* (Westport, CT: Greenwood, 1977), 152–56; "Detroit Reds Seized by FBI," *Detroit Times*, 17 September 1952.

19. Goodman, interview by Littlejohn, 21 February 1997, 18.

20. "Counsel for the Common People, Parts 3–4."

21. Goodman, interview by Littlejohn, 21 February 1997, 17; "Counsel for the Common People, Parts 3–4."

22. James Haswell, "State Asked to Define Its Red Law," *Detroit Free Press*, 5 February 1953; Hub M. Greene, "High Court Tosses Back Trucks Act," *Detroit Free Press*, 17 March 1953; Jerry Ter Horst, "Anti-Red Act Changes Due,"

Detroit News, 20 March 1953; "Test Is Due for Red Law," *Detroit News,* 20 April 1953; "Amended Michigan Subversive Act Still Faces Court Challenge," *Federated Press,* 2 May 1953, EGC, box 19, folder "Trucks Act."

23. Clancy Sigal, *Going Away: A Report, a Memoir* (New York: Houghton Mifflin, 1962), 333; William Hundley, interview by unknown member of the Ron Aronson–Judy Montell documentary crew, 28 April 1999, 8–9, conducted for production of *1st Amendment on Trial: The Case of the Detroit Six* (DVD).

24. "Personal Biography, T.D.," four-page typescript, EGC, processed box 3, series 1, folder 13; Ernest Goodman's Opening Statement to the Jury, typescript, 15, EGC, processed box 1, series 1, folder 17.

25. "Background" (Schatz), "Vital Statistics" (Winter), and "Biography" (Ganley), EGC, processed box 3, series 1, folders 14, 16, 17.

26. Hundley, interview, 10, 14.

27. Ibid., 14–15, 10.

28. Frank A. Picard, "What Is This Menace Called Communism?" *Wayne Law Journal* 3, no. 1 (1954): 6–10, 16.

29. "Court of Appeals," "History," and "Judges Index," in "History of the Sixth Circuit," www.ca6.uscourts.gov (accessed 25 September 2008); "Bankers Promise 'Best' Program," *Cass City Chronicle,* 17 April 1931.

30. Letter from Jane R. to Jane Mayer, 9 December 1944, on letterhead of Detroit Council of American-Soviet Friendship, EGC, box 21, folder "Buck Dinner, 1939–1954." The list of sponsors of the council is printed on the back of the letter. See also Robert Lake to "Dear Friend" on letterhead of Detroit Council of American-Soviet Friendship, 1 February 1945, Sam Sweet Collection, box 1, folder 17, WRL.

31. "EG, 11-13-52, Memorandum," twelve-page typescript, EGC, processed box 3, series 1, folder 20; EG to station WJBK-TV, 1 October 1953, and Hon. Frank Picard to Dr. H. M. Pollard, 12 October 1953, and EG to Frank Picard, 14 October 1953, and Frank Picard to EG, 16 October 1953, EGC, processed box 5, series 1, folder 1; "Red Trial Opens; Judge Cautions Jury Prospects, *Detroit News,* 27 October 1953.

32. "See Reds Losing Dismissal Plea," *Detroit Times,* 30 September 1953.

33. Belknap, *Cold War Political Justice,* 67, 79–80, 92–109.

34. "Memo on Defense of Smith Act Cases," 2–4, 1 December 1952, twelve-page typescript, EGC, processed box 3, series 1, folder 21. The likely author is Crockett: Goodman is referred to in the third person, it shares stylistic elements with other memos in which Crockett is identified (particularly the opening line, "I propose to set forth"), and it reflects an intimate knowledge of both the Foley Square trial and the Detroit setting.

35. "Memorandum to Smith Act Defendants, Subject: Staff," 11 December 1952, five-page typescript, 2–3, EGC, processed box 3, series 1, folder 22.

36. "EG, 11-13-52, Memorandum."

37. Ibid.

38. "Memo on the Memos," December 1952, EGC, processed box 3, series 1, folder 23.

39. "Counsel for the Common People, Parts 3–4."

40. Joseph Starobin, *American Communism in Crisis, 1943–1957* (Berkeley: University of California Press, 1975), 190–213; Edward Pintzuk, *Reds, Racial Justice and Civil Liberties: Michigan Communists during the Cold War* (Minneapolis: MEP, 1997), 18–30; Ellen Schrecker, *Many Are the Crimes: McCarthyism in America* (New York: Little, Brown, 1998), 19–26.

41. "Counsel for the Common People, Parts 3–4."

42. *United States of America v. Saul Laurence Wellman et al.*, no. 33295, "Withdrawal of Appearance, Oct. 19, 1953" and "Notice of Appearance, Oct. 19, 1953," EGC, processed box 1, series 1, folder 15.

43. Interview with Saul Wellman, 1980, interviewer unknown, 150, authors' possession; "Counsel for the Common People, Parts 3–4."

44. Boyd Simmons, "12 Jurors Drawn for Trial of 6 Reds," *Detroit News*, 29 October 1953; Robert Perrin, "Jury Drawn for Trial of Six Reds," *Detroit Free Press*, 30 October 1953; "Opening Statement," typescript, EGC, processed box 1, series 1, folder 17.

45. Jack Crellin, "Tells Story at Opening of U.S. Trial," *Detroit Times*, 3 November 1953; Robert Perrin, "Statements Open Trial of Six Reds," *Detroit Free Press*, 3 November 1953.

46. Robert Perrin, "Threaten Contempt Action against Commie Defendant," *Detroit Free Press*, 5 November 1953; Harris, "Red Trial All Politeness"; Louis Tendler, "Picard Firmness Conquers Ordeal," *Detroit News*, 16 February 1954.

47. Hundley, interview, 14; Starobin, *American Communism in Crisis*, 216–19; Pintzuk, *Reds, Racial Justice*, 21–25; Belknap, *Cold War Political Justice*, 165–66; Jack Crellin, "Reveal Red Plan to Nab President," *Detroit Times*, 19 November 1953; Boyd Simmons, "Red Plot to Seize President is Told; Trial in Uproar," *Detroit News*, 19 November 1953; John Griffith, "Red Trial Witness Assailed," *Detroit Free Press*, 20 November 1953.

48. "Light Touch Enters Red Trial," *Detroit Free Press*, 5 December 1953; Boyd Simmons, "Red Moves Aired by Mrs. Baldwin," *Detroit News*, 21 November 1953; Boyd Simmons, "Jury Is Shown Red Order to Recruit Auto Workers," *Detroit News*, 25 November 1953; John Griffith, "U.S. Told to Hurry Its Case on Reds," *Detroit Free Press*, 25 November 1953.

49. Closing statement, "Mr. Goodman: May It Please the Court . . . ," forty-legal-page typescript, 18, 28–29, EGC, processed box 2, series 1, folders 1–2.

50. Boyd Simmons, "2 FBI Spies Roil Judge," *Detroit News*, 22 December 1953; Boyd Simmons, "FBI Aides' Testimony Is Studied for Perjury," *Detroit News*, 23 December 1953; John Griffith, "2 U.S. Witnesses Lied at Red Trial," *Detroit Free Press*, 23 December 1953; Jack Crellin, "Probe Perjury by FBI Spy," *Detroit Times*, 23 December 1953; closing statement, 22–26; Hundley, interview, 14.

51. "Red Defendant Given Jail Term," *Detroit Times*, 12 January 1954; Don Gillard, "Judge Gives Saul Wellman Sixty Days," *Detroit Times*, 29 January 1954; EG to Frank Donner, 7 January 1954, EGC, processed box 5, series 1, folder 3.
52. "Counsel for the Common People, Parts 3–4"; Boyd Simmons, "Fresh Surprises Due in Red Trial," *Detroit News*, 11 December 1953.
53. "Counsel for the Common People, Parts 3–4."
54. Closing statement; "Acquittal of 6 State Reds Asked," *Detroit Free Press*, 5 January 1954.
55. "Counsel for the Common People, Parts 3–4"; Boyd Simmons, "Act to Deport One of Reds in Trial Here," *Detroit News*, 17 February 1954.
56. "Text of Judge Picard's Lecture to Reds," *Detroit Times*, 19 February 1954; Boyd Simmons, "6 Reds Get Prison Terms, Spurn Russia Trip," *Detroit News*, 19 February 1954; Jack Crellin, "Reds Sentenced to 4–5 Years," *Detroit Times*, 19 February 1954; Frank Picard, "What Makes a Communist Tick," *U.S. News and World Report*, 19 March 1954.
57. Hundley, interview, 11–17.
58. Jack Crellin, "6 State Reds Face Five Years in Conspiracy," *Detroit Times*, 17 February 1954; Simmons, "Act to Deport One of Reds in Trial Here."
59. Conrad Komorowski, *The Strange Trial of Stanley Nowak* (Highland Park, MI: Stanley Nowak Defense Committee, 1954), 6–7; Margaret Nowak, *Two Who Were There: A Biography of Stanley Nowak* (Detroit: Wayne State University Press, 1989), 233.
60. Nowak, *Two Who Were There*, 129–43, 188–99, 234; David Good, *Orvie: The Dictator of Dearborn* (Detroit: Wayne State University Press, 1989), 109–18; "U.S. Drops Fraud Indictment against Senator Nowak," *Detroit Free Press*, 9 February 1943.
61. Louise Pettibone Smith, *Torch of Liberty: 25 Years in the Life of the Foreign Born in the U.S.* (New York: Dwight-King, 1959), 258–68, 401; David Caute, *The Great Fear: The Anti-Communist Purge under Truman and Eisenhower* (New York: Simon and Schuster, 1978), 230, 587; Mae M. Ngai, *Impossible Subjects: Illegal Aliens and the Making of Modern America* (Princeton: Princeton University Press, 2004), 237–39.
62. "Brownell Details Subversion Fight," *New York Times*, 18 March 1953; Caute, *The Great Fear*, 226; Nowak, *Two Who Were There*, 226–27. The Goodman firm's denaturalization and deportation cases take up four boxes in the unprocessed portion of the EGC, boxes 15–18.
63. Caute, *The Great Fear*, 241; Smith, *Torch of Liberty*, 331–33.
64. "Counsel for the Common People, Parts 3–4."
65. "Your Legal and Civil Rights: Defend Them," typescript for pamphlet with cover letter from Anne Shore to Gale Printing Co., Detroit, 31 March 1951, CRCC, box 24, folder "Correspondence, 3/12/1951"; Caute, *The Great Fear*, 225.

66. James C. Hawell, "An Objective Appraisal of Labor's Senator," *Detroit Free Press*, 25 April 1943; *Schneiderman v. U.S.*, 20 U.S. 118 (1943).

67. Stanton L. Smiley deposition with Ernest Goodman, EGC, box 15, folder C-646; Nowak, *Two Who Were There*, 242–43.

68. "Counsel for the Common People, Parts 3–4"; Caute, *The Great Fear*, 123–25; Nowak, *Two Who Were There*, 249–50.

69. Ernest Goodman and George Crockett, "Brief for Petitioner," 12 November 1957, *Stanley Nowak v. U.S.*, no. 72, 60–92, EGC, box 15, folder "Nowak, Stanley"; Nowak, *Two Who Were There*, 244–49; "Transcript of Proceedings," 7:877–923 (Zygmunt) and 9:1226 (Picard), *U.S. v. Stanislaw Novak*, Civil Action no. 12, 391, Stanley and Margaret Nowak Collection, box 7, WRL.

70. "Transcript of Proceedings," 5:554–67 (Hewitt) and 9:1225 (Picard quote), 1229–30; Nowak, *Two Who Were There*, 250–51.

71. "Transcript of Proceedings," 9:1221; Nowak, *Two Who Were There*, 254–55.

72. Irons, *A People's History of the Supreme Court*, 393–94, 401–4. Eisenhower's last appointment, Charles Whittaker, was an undistinguished corporate lawyer from Kansas City.

73. Goodman and Crockett, "Brief for Petitioner," 56–57, 59, 61.

74. Ernest Goodman and George Crockett, "Brief for Petitioner," 12 November 1957, *Rebecca Maisenberg v. U.S.*, no. 76, EGC, box 31.

75. *Pennsylvania v. Nelson*, 350 U.S. 497 (1956); *Albertson v. Millard*, 345 Mich. 519 (1956); "State Court Kills Trucks Anti-Red Act," *Detroit Free Press*, 15 May 1956.

76. *Yates v. U.S.*, 354 U.S. 298 (1957); Belknap, *Cold War Political Justice*, 236–51.

77. *Nowak v. United States*, 356 U.S. 660 (1958); *Mainseberg v. United States*, 356 U.S. 670 (1958).

78. Susan Siggelakis, "Advocacy on Trial," *American Journal of Legal History* 36 (1992): 505–6; Ann Fagan Ginger and Eugene Tobin, eds., *The National Lawyers Guild: From Roosevelt through Reagan* (Philadelphia: Temple University Press, 1988), 137, 158–59.

79. Belknap, *Cold War Political Justice*, 244; National Lawyers Guild, "National Executive Board Minutes, Report of the Secretary," 27 October 1957, 1, Harold Norris Collection, box 15, folder 19, WRL; Goodman, interview by Littlejohn, 21 February 1997; Jack Greenberg, *Crusaders in the Courts: How a Dedicated Band of Lawyers Fought for the Civil Rights Revolution* (New York: Basic, 1994), 350; Stanley Kutler, *The American Inquisition: Justice and Injustice in the Cold War* (New York: Hill and Wang, 1982), 181–82; Ginger and Tobin, *The National Lawyers Guild*, 136.

80. Caute, *The Great Fear*, 178–80, Gerald Horne, *Communist Front? The Civil Rights Congress* (Cranbury, NJ: Associated University Presses, 1988), 37–40, 49–50, 65–69, 354–58.

81. Ronald Kessler, *The Bureau: The Secret History of the FBI* (New York: St. Martin's, 2003), 106–7; Maurice Isserman, *If I Had a Hammer: The Death of*

the Old Left and the Birth of the New Left (Urbana: University of Illinois Press, 1993), 1–34.

82. "Notes on a Trip to Europe and Africa—March 1961," typescript diary, 6, 10, 15, 22–24, EGC, box 26, folder "Travelogue."

83. "Legends in the Law," *DC Bar,* Web site of the District of Columbia Bar, www.dcbar.org, "For Lawyers/Resources" (accessed 20 March 2007); Howard Ball, *A Defiant Life: Thurgood Marshall and the Persistence of Racism in America* (New York: Crown, 1998), 66–67.

84. I. F. Stone, *The Haunted Fifties* (New York: Vintage, 1969), 25–30, 219–20, 223–24; Kessler, *The Bureau,* 61–68, 127–31, 173–74, 184–89; Caute, *The Great Fear,* 112–14; James Jacobs, "The Conduct of Local Political Intelligence" (PhD diss., Princeton University, 1977), 65–69.

85. FBI "Correlation Summary," main file no. 100-6963, 30 October 1968, "Subject: Ernie Goodman," 58, TAM, box 164, folder 8; memo from SAC Detroit to Director, FBI, 22 June 1955, TAM, box 164, folder 7; Jacobs, "The Conduct of Local Political Intelligence," 67–68.

86. *Supplementary Detailed Staff Reports,* book 3, 23 April 1976, Senate Select Committee to Study Governmental Operations with Respect to Intelligence Activities; Kessler, *The Bureau,* 65–66, 77–80, 91–93, 107–8, 156–58, 174.

87. *NAACP v. Alabama,* 357 U.S. 449 (1958).

88. *United States Law Week, Supreme Court Opinions,* 15 November 1960, 4013–18.

89. The Henderson case and its various appeals are detailed in *People v. Henderson,* 343 Mich. 465, 72 N.W. 2d 177 (1955) and *Henderson v. Bannan,* 256 F.2d 363 (1958). In *Gideon v. Wainwright,* 372 U.S. 335 (1963), Justice Harlan's concurring opinion referenced the Henderson case.

90. EG to Carey McWilliams, 22 March 1957, EGC, box 5, folder "Detroit Bar and Guild Investigations."

91. Ibid.

92. "Detroit Bar to Back Flier," *Detroit Times,* 10 October 1953.

93. *Brown v. Board of Education,* 347 U.S. 483 (1954).

94. John White, "E. D. Nixon and the White Supremacists: Civil Rights in Montgomery," in *Before Brown: Civil Rights and White Backlash in the Modern South,* ed. Glenn Feldman (Tuscaloosa: University of Alabama Press, 2004), 198–221.

95. Dick's letter is dated 21 July 1959; Ernie's is undated. Ernest Goodman's personal letter file, private collection. The quotes that follow in the rest of this chapter are drawn from these letters.

Chapter 9

1. The events in Petersburg and Hopewell are described in "Ernest Goodman Reports on Trip to Hopewell, Virginia for Guild Special Committee," *Guild Lawyer* 20, no. 4 (1962): 3, EGC, box 1, folder "Hopewell, Va., March 1962."

2. Virginia Historical Society, the Center for Virginia History, *Annual Report for 2001*, 22, www.vahistorical.org/about/annualreport01.pdf (accessed 3 October 2008).

3. Interview with the Reverend Curtis W. Harris, 2003, *Voices of Freedom*, Special Collections and Archives, Virginia Commonwealth University, http://dig.library.vcu.edu/cdm4/item_viewer.php?CISOROOT=/voices&CISOPTR=4& CISOBOX=1&REC=9 (accessed 3 October 2008); Len Holt to Anna J. Diggs, 18 March 1962, EGC, box 1, folder "Hopewell, Va., March 1962." Holt described Harris in his letter to Diggs as "a wonderful guy with a lot of guts who has performed the miracle of organizing the plain folks of Hopewell into one of the South's most effective protest groups against segregation."

4. Len Holt, *An Act of Conscience* (Boston: Beacon, 1965), 188; Len Holt, *The Summer That Didn't End* (New York: William Morrow, 1965), 11.

5. Len Holt to Goodman, Crockett, Eden, Robb, and Philo, 1 March 1962, EGC, box 1, folder "Hopewell, Va., March 1962."

6. "Guild Spokesman Addresses Southern Christian Leadership Conference in Virginia," *Guild Lawyer* 20, no. 4 (1962): 4; "Detroit Lawyer Recalls Mandela Treason Trial Acquittal," *Detroit Free Press*, 30 July 1990.

7. "Guild Spokesman Addresses," 4.

8. Ibid.

9. EG to Mr. and Mrs. Sylvester James and Mr. and Mrs. Herbert Bowen, both of Hopewell, 4 April 1962, and Len Holt to Dr. Martin Luther King, 3 April 1962, EGC, box 1, folder "Hopewell, Va., March 1962."

10. Memo from SAC Norfolk (100-5602) to Director, FBI, 30 November 1962, "re Leonard Winston Holt, Jr.," TAM, box 164, folder 26. Holt had been under surveillance since the previous year. The various FBI reports in folder 26 indicate that as a young man, the son of a plumber, growing up in Chicago, he had joined the Communist Party in 1949 and been expelled five months later for "advancing a political line contrary to the line of the CP." Three years later he was convicted of illegally riding on a freight train in West Virginia while en route to Howard University to enroll in the law school.

11. George Lewis, *The White South and the Red Menace: Segregationists, Anti-communism, and Massive Resistance, 1945–1965* (Gainesville: University of Florida Press, 2004), 179.

12. Alan Draper, *Conflict of Interests: Organized Labor and the Civil Rights Movement in the South, 1954–1958* (Ithaca, NY: ILR, 1994), 19–27, 36, 158; Howard Ball, *A Defiant Life: Thurgood Marshall and the Persistence of Racism in America* (New York: Crown, 1998), 140–47.

13. Jeff Woods, *Black Struggle, Red Scare: Segregation and Anti-Communism in the South, 1948–1968* (Baton Rouge: Louisiana State University Press, 2004), 151–52; Lewis, *The White South and the Red Menace*, 73, 169.

14. Ernest Goodman, "The NLG, the FBI and the Civil Rights Movement: 1964—A Year of Decision," *Guild Practitioner* 38, no. 1 (1981): 1, EGC, box 25, folder "1964 Convention, Detroit."

15. Victor Rabinowitz, *Unrepentant Leftist: A Lawyer's Memoir* (Urbana: University of Illinois Press, 1996), 175; "NLG National Executive Board Minutes," 27 October 1957, 1, Harold Norris Collection, box 15, folder 19, WRL; "Plugs for the Loopholes," *Time*, 9 March 1959; "Report of the National Lawyers Guild on the Recommendations of the American Bar Association," in Ann Fagan Ginger and Eugene Tobin, eds., *The National Lawyers Guild: From Roosevelt through Reagan* (Philadelpia: Temple University Press, 1988), 165–66; "National Executive Board, National Executive Board Meeting," 22 March 1959, Harold Norris Collection, box 15, folder 19, WRL.

16. "Detroit Chapter Report, Build the Guild Panel," undated but sometime in 1958–59, 1, Harold Norris Collection, box 15, folder 16, WRL; "NLG National Executive Board Minutes," 8 October 1960, Harold Norris Collection, box 15, folder 20, WRL; "Detroit Chapter Active in New Members Drive," *Guild Lawyer* 18, no. 5 (1960), Harold Norris Collection, box 13, folder 13, WRL; "Executive Secretary's Suggested Substantive Program for 1960–1961," 3, Harold Norris Collection, box 15, folder 5, WRL; Correspondence between Ernest Goodman and police commissioner Edward Piggins, 1957–1958, EGC, box 2, folder "Correspondence"; "Detroit Chapter Election to Be Held Feb. 23," *Guild Lawyer* 17, no. 2 (1959): 1, 6, and "Detroit Chapter," *Guild Lawyer* 17, no. 4 (1959), Harold Norris Collection, box 13, folder 13, WRL; "Annual Chapter Meeting Honors Circuit Judge James Montante," *Guild Lawyer* 19, nos. 9–10 (1961): 9, Harold Norris Collection, box 13, folder 14, WRL; Ernest Goodman, interview by Edward Littlejohn, 24 June and 11 July 1996, 9, Oral History Project, Damon Keith Law Collection, WRL.

17. "New Member Drive Sparked in Every Chapter," *Guild Lawyer* 18, no. 4 (1960): 1, 6, and "Executive Secretary Tours Country—Reports That Guild is Thriving," *Guild Lawyer* 17, no. 8 (1959): 7, Harold Norris Collection, box 13, folder 13, WRL. Leadership positions of African Americans are indicated in "Annual Chapter Meeting Honors Circuit Judge James Montante," 9, and the letterhead roster in chapter president Don Loria's letter to "Dear Fellow Attorney," 29 April 1964, EGC, box 3, folder "Law Day," and in "National Lawyers Guild, Silver Anniversary Convention, 1962," program booklet, EGC, box 24, folder "NLG Conventions 1950 . . . 1967."

18. Rabinowitz, *Unrepentant Leftist*, 175; Goodman, "The NLG, the FBI and the Civil Rights Movement," 2; Leo Linder, "Selecting Priorities for Guild Work While under Attack: The Ginger Strategy," in Ginger and Tobin, *The National Lawyers Guild*, 149–50; "A Cry for Help: Norfolk to Berkeley to New York to Detroit," in Ginger and Tobin, *The National Lawyers Guild*, 185–87; "Counsel for the Common People, Parts 3–4," videotaped interview with Ernest Goodman, produced by William Bryce, WRL.

19. Rabinowitz, *Unrepentant Leftist*, 175–76; "National Lawyers Guild Twenty Fifth Anniversary Convention," program book, 24–25, EGC, box 24, folder "NLG Conventions"; Goodman, "The NLG, the FBI and the Civil Rights Movement," 3.

20. Ball, *A Defiant Life*, 150.

21. Holt, *An Act of Conscience*, 39, 82; Woods, *Black Struggle, Red Scare*, 95 (quote), 93–98, 131–42.

22. Ann Fagan Ginger to "Len, Ernie, George, Vic, Aryay," 3 April 1962, EGC, box 2, folder "Atlanta Ga. SNCC."

23. Holt, *An Act of Conscience*, 49; Holt, *The Summer That Didn't End*, 72; "Those Kennedy Judges," *Time*, 6 November 1964. The ABA's Standing Committee on the Federal Judiciary gave Cox its highest rating as "exceptionally well qualified." Ann Garity Connell, *The Lawyers' Committee for Civil Rights under Law: The Making of a Public Interest Group* (Chicago: Lawyers' Committee for Civil Rights under Law, 2003), 115.

24. Ira Kaye to National Lawyers Guild, Att. Ernest Goodman, 16 April 1963, and "Alabama Lawyers," typed list "Rec'd from Conley, 4/12/63," and Dion Diamond to EG and George Crockett Jr., 3 May 1962, and Jim Dombrowski to George Crockett, 25 May 1962, EGC, box 3, folder "Proof of Need for Attorneys"; EG to Dan McCullough, 23 April 1962, EGC, box 3, folder "Communications with Other Bar Associations."

25. "Interview with Robert Zellner," in *The Eyes on the Prize Civil Rights Reader*, ed. Clayborne Carson et al. (New York: Penguin, 1991), 127–30; William Kunstler, *Deep in My Heart* (New York: William Morrow, 1966), 62; Anne and Carl Braden to EG, 22 October 1962, EGC, box 3, folder "Southern Lawyers."

26. Eugene Rostow, "The Lawyer and His Client," *American Bar Association Journal* 48, no. 1 (1962): 25–30, and no. 2 (1962): 146–51; "Biographical Note," Department of Archives and Special Collections, Finding Aid for the John C. Satterfield/ABA Collections, University of Mississippi Libraries, http://dm.olemiss.edu/archives/collections/guides/latesthtml/MUM00685.html (accessed 3 October 2008); Douglas Blackmon, "Silent Partner: How the South's Fight to Uphold Segregation Was Funded Up North," *Wall Street Journal*, 11 June 1999 (*Time* magazine quote); "The FBI Intrudes on Guild-ABA Relations," in Ginger and Tobin, *The National Lawyers Guild*, 190; Dombrowski to Crockett, 25 May 1962; Benjamin Dreyfus to John Satterfield, 9 March 1962, EGC, box 3, folder "Communications with Other Bar Associations"; "Bar Group Chief's Reply to Bobby," *San Francisco Chronicle*, 2 October 1962.

27. "Assistance to Southern Lawyers, Resolution Adopted by 1962 Convention at Detroit, Michigan," EGC, box 3, folder "Law Day."

28. Herman Wright to Benjamin Dreyfus, 10 January 1964, EGC, box 25, folder "1964 Convention, Detroit."

29. Horace Julian Bond to EG and George Crockett, 4 May 1962, EGC, box 3, folder "Southern Lawyers"; SNCC, "High Court Hears Boycott Case," *Student Voice*, 25 February 1964, 4, www.crmvet.org/docs/sv/sv640225.pdf (accessed 3 October 2008); Dion T. Diamond to EG and George Crockett, 3 May 1962, EGC, box 3, folder "Proof of Need for Attorneys"; Michael Standard

to EG, 1 November 1962, EGC, box 1, folder "Hopewell, Va., March 1962"; Chester Bulgier, "2 Detroiters Lead Attorneys Aiding South's Integrationists," *Detroit News*, 7 October 1962.

30. Samuel Mitchell to Len Holt, 24 July 1962, EGC, box 3, folder "Communications with Other Bar Associations"; Victor Rabinowitz to George Crocket and EG, 15 October 1962, and George Crockett to L. E. Thomas, 20 September 1962, and Ben Smith to EG, 21 March 1962, EGC, box 3, folder "Southern Lawyers." Following the fatal bombing of the Sixteenth Street Baptist Church in 1963, Morgan condemned the "intolerance and bigotry" of Birmingham, which he called "a dying city." He moved to Atlanta and pursued a career in the ACLU. Diane McWhorter, *Carry Me Home: Birmingham, Alabama; The Climatic Battle of the Civil Rights Revolution* (New York: Simon and Schuster, 2001), 171–72, 534–35, 563.

31. Len Holt to Mr. and Mrs. Carl Braden, 27 September 1962, and EG to Anne and Carl Braden, 30 October 1962, EGC, box 3, folder "Southern Lawyers"; Kunstler, *Deep in My Heart*, 364; Carl Braden to EG, 16 September 1963, and EG to Edward Lynch, 17 September 1963, in EGC, box 3, folder "New Orleans Conference."

32. U.S. Dist. Court, Western Dist. of Va., Danville Div., "Civil Action," Plaintiffs: Rev. Alexander I. Dunlap et al. and . . . the Danville Progressive Christian Assn, an affiliate of the SCLC; National Lawyers Guild, "Memorandum of Law in Lynchburg, Virginia Omnibus Suit," U.S. Dist. Court, Western Dist. of Va., Lynchburg Div., Civil Action no. 535, EGC, box 1, folder "Danville, Va., Omnibus Suit, Oct-62"; Jack Greenberg, *Crusaders in the Courts: How a Dedicated Band of Lawyers Fought for the Civil Rights Revolution* (New York: Basic, 1994), 114–15, 118, 156, 164, 172–73, 275–78, 352–53 (quote); Holt, *An Act of Conscience*, 176; Ball, *A Defiant Life*, 63, 67, 73–75; Len Holt to Leonard Karlin, 6 October 1962, EGC, box 1, folder "Danville, Va., Omnibus Suit"; Len Holt to EG, undated (but after Bill Goodman's stay and before the Atlanta conference) said he expected the judge to divide the Danville suit, TAM, box 44, folder 7. Holt reported in the case of Danville, "Since the filing of the suit, the meetings of the City Council have been integrated, the Danville Technical Institute has been integrated and the police department is seeking Negro applicants." In *An Act of Conscience*, 62, Holt reports that the filing of the Danville suit led to the desegregation of courtroom facilities, the city cemetery, and the city armory. Guild members also raised concerns about the omnibus approach. See Leonard Karlin to EG, 1 October 1962, EGC, box 1, folder "Danville, Va., Omnibus Suit." Karlin asked if the scope of the Danville suit "was such that it is likely to take an inordinately long time in the nisi prius [trial] court." In several cases, the courts refused to grant standing to plaintiffs who were not directly impacted by discrimination, or dismissed portions of a suit where plaintiffs failed to identify defendants. *Thaxton v. Vaughan* (Lynchburg) 321 F.2d 474 (1963).

33. "What to Do," fourteen-page typescript for *Manual for Laymen*, together with related correspondence with Margolis and Julian Bond regarding its use, in EGC, box 1, folder "CLAS," and box 3, folder "Manual for Laymen."

34. William Goodman, "1962: My Summer Job," in the National Lawyers Guild, Detroit chapter, banquet book, Karen Sandlin, ed., In *Honor of the Legal Volunteers of the Civil Rights Movement*, 2 April 2004, 65, authors' possession; Rabinowitz, *Unrepentant Leftist*, 166–68; Bulgier, "2 Detroiters Lead Attorneys Aiding South's Integrationists." For the experience of Dennis Roberts, a student in the following year's program, see Ginger and Tobin, *The National Lawyers Guild*, 194–96.

35. "Report of the Committee on Offenses against the Administration of Justice," 6 January 1962, 5–9, EGC, box 1, folder "Hopewell, Va., March 1962"; *Jordan v. Hutchinson*, 323 F.2 597 (1963); "U.S. Court of Appeals for the Fourth Circuit, No. 8834, Brief for Appellants," 3, EGC, box 1, folder "Jordan v. Hutchinson, Norfolk Va., Oct. 1962."

36. Edward Dawley, "Black People Don't Have Legal Problems," in Ginger and Tobin, *The National Lawyers Guild*, 183–84; Len Holt to "Dear Everybody," cc'd to EG, Sam Sucow, and Aryay Lenske, 8 September 1962, and EG to Len Holt, 17 September 1962, EGC, box 1, folder "Jordan v. Hutchinson, Norfolk Va., Oct. 1962."

37. Dean Robb, "How the Mississippi Project Started," and Harry Philo, "The Beginning of the Guild Project," in Sandlin, *In Honor of the Legal Volunteers*, 24–26; interview with Dick Goodman, 20 June 2007; Detroit African American History Project, "Robert Millender," Biography Search Display, www.daahp.wayne.edu (accessed 4 April 2009); Coleman Young and Lonnie Wheeler, *Hard Stuff: The Autobiography of Coleman Young* (New York: Viking, 1994), 57. Robb has the dates wrong in his account of the southern campaign, recalling the events of 1962 as occurring in the following year. In EG to E. A. Dawley, 31 October 1962, EGC, box 3, folder "Southern Lawyers," Goodman indicates that the firm had just acquired a new associate, Robert Millender. Significantly, Dawley had written Goodman inquiring about the possibility of finding a place in the Detroit firm.

38. EG and George Crockett to members of CASL, 6 April 1962, EGC, box 1, folder "Hopewell Virginia, March 1962"; Len Holt to Samuel Mitchell, 10 July 1962, EGC, box 3, folder "Declaratory Relief for Racist Statute"; Robb, "How the Mississippi Project Started," 25.

39. George Crockett and EG to Rabinowitz Foundation, 1 November 1962, EGC, box 3, folder "Southern Conference 1962"; Robb, "How the Mississippi Project Started," 26; EG to Len Holt, 4 October 1962, TAM, box 44, folder 7

40. Jack Greenberg to George Crockett, 31 October 1962, and George Crockett to Don Hollowell, 21 November 1962, and note from "Ann" to "George and Ernie," undated, EGC, box 3, folder "Southern Conference 1962."

41. "National Lawyers Guild . . . Hold Historic Integrated Lawyers Conference on Civil Rights, Negligence Law," *Guild Lawyer* 20, no. 9 (1962): 1, 6–7; George

Crockett to Herman Wright, 5 December 1962, and report from Wyatt Tee Walker, cc'd to Hollowell, Crockett, et al., January 1963, EGC, box 3, folder "Southern Conference 1962."

42. Edward Cambridge, "N.Y. Guild Member Views Atlanta Lawyers Conference," *Guild Lawyer* 20, no. 9 (1962): 8; Rabinowitz, *Unrepentant Leftist*, 187; Aryay Lenske to EG and Crockett, 7 December 1962, EGC, box 3, folder "Southern Conference 1962."

43. "National Lawyers Guild . . . Hold Historic Integrated Lawyers Conference," 6; Ann Fagan Ginger to George Crockett and EG, 5 November 1962, and EG to Ginger, 9 November 1962, EGC, box 3, folder "Southern Conference 1962."

44. "National Lawyers Guild . . . Hold Historic Integrated Lawyers Conference," 6–7; program, "A Workshop Seminar for Lawyers on Civil Rights and Negligence Law," EGC, box 3, folder "Southern Conference 1962."

45. "Bobby Chides Lawyers on Dixie Crisis," *San Francisco Chronicle*, 30 September 1962; "Bar Group Chief's Reply to Bobby," *San Francisco Chronicle*, 2 October 1962; "Lawyers Guild Vows Support," *San Francisco Chronicle*, 1 October 1962; "Lawyers Guild Offers Aid in Meredith's Court Fight," *New York Times*, 2 October 1962; "Bar Association Rift over Ole Miss," *San Francisco Examiner*, 1 October 1962; Irving Dilliard, "The Constitutional Crisis," *York (PA) Gazette and Daily*, 9 October 1962; "Before the Bar," *St. Louis Post-Dispatch*, 2 October 1962.

46. "A Conference on Southern Civil Rights Litigation and the Northern Lawyer," brochure, 2 March 1963, and Ron Dorfman, "Lawyers Urged to Help Civil Rights," *Chicago Maroon*, 5 March 1963, EGC, box 3, folder "Chicago Conference."

47. Azza Salama Layton, *International Politics and Civil Rights Policies in the United States, 1941–1960* (Cambridge: Cambridge University Press, 200), 141–42; Robert Kennedy to George Crockett, 28 June 1963, EGC, box 3, folder "White House Conference"; Connell, *The Lawyers' Committee*, 77–85.

48. "Press Release, June 24, 1963," EGC, box 3, folder "White House Conference." Both Tweed (a Democrat) and Segal (a Republican) were corporate lawyers. Neither had previously worked with the civil rights movement, though Tweed did at least have a long history of supporting efforts to provide Legal Aid. Connell, *The Lawyers' Committee*, 18–22, 61–69, 85.

49. ABA Special Committee on Civil Rights and Racial Unrest, "Recommendations of the Board of Governors Adopted by the House of Delegates," 13 August 1963, 3, EGC, box 3, folder "Communications with Other Bar Associations"; Anthony Lewis, "Lawyers Acting in Racial Crisis," *New York Times*, 14 August 1963; Connell, *The Lawyers' Committee*, 88, 97, 108, 114, 119–31 (quotes on 88 and 114).

50. Ann Ginger to George Crockett and EG, 5 November 1962, and EG to Ginger, 9 November 1962, EGC, box 3, folder "Southern Conference 1962."

51. U.S. Dist. Ct., Western Dist., Danville Div., *Mrs. Mary Shirley Thomas, Plaintiff, v. Eugene McCain* (1963). Thomas sought compensatory damages of $15,000 and punitive damages of $35,000 for the beatings of 10 June, plus costs. William Kunstler, in his memoir, *Deep in My Heart*, 221, describes the court proceeding in which Thomas identified Chief McCain as her assailant.

52. SNCC, "Danville Virginia," saddle-stitched pamphlet, August 1963, EGC, box 1, folder "Danville Sitin, March 1963"; U.S. Dist. Ct., Western Dist., Danville Div., *Mrs. Mary Shirley Thomas, Plaintiff, v. Eugene McCain*; Holt, *An Act of Conscience*, 23–25, 36, 93–95, 142.

53. Kunstler, *Deep in My Heart*, 215–16; Holt, *An Act of Conscience*, 21, 35–40, 81–82, 85–86, 100, 113, 136, 190–91, 225, and the entire injunction and picketing ordinance quoted on 230–33; *Baines v. City of Danville*, 337 F.2d 5 585 (1963); U.S. Dist. Ct., Western Dist., Danville Div., *Julius E. Adams et al.* [13 others] *v. Archibald A. Aiken, Judge, Eugene McCain, Chief of Police, et al.*, civil action no. 584 (1963). According to Holt (198), one member of the Danville police told a SNCC organizer that "Chief's been talking to Chief Pritchett and you know what that means." Laurie Pritchett was the chief of police in Albany, Georgia, where the same strategy of massive detention but minimal violence had reduced publicity and dissipated local protests.

54. Holt, *An Act of Conscience*, 177.

55. Greenberg, *Crusaders*, 275–77, 306–11, 333–34, 347; Holt, *An Act of Conscience*, 19–20, 67–70, 157, 177, 197, 223.

56. Arthur Kinoy, *Rights on Trial: The Odyssey of a People's Lawyer* (Cambridge: Harvard University Press, 1983), 187–88; Holt, *An Act of Conscience*, 106–11, 115–16. Holt and Dawley became public critics of the Virginia NAACP in 1962 while representing black workers at the federal shipyard in Norfolk, Virginia. State NAACP president Robert Robinson testified for the government in the case, saying there was no discrimination. Robinson was a union representative for the cafeteria workers at the yard, and Holt and Dawley charged him with cultivating a sweetheart relationship with management. See "Tidewater Federal Employees Association, Press Release," undated, and "Complaint for Expulsion of Robert D. Robinson as President of Virginia State NAACP," 30 March 1962, addressed to "National Office, NAACP," EGC, box 1, folder "Hopewell, Va., March 1962."

57. Interview with Nate Conyers, 22 August 2007; interview with Dean Robb, 28 August 2007; Holt, *An Act of Conscience*, 40, 44, 117, 136, 175, 185, 202–16; draft, "Petition for Writ of Error," Supreme Court of Virginia, by Albert Best, Anna Diggs, and David Klein, all of Detroit, submitted 25 August 1963, concerning the January sit-in at the Howard Johnson restaurant in Danville, EGC, box 1, folder "Danville, Va., Trespass Convictions."

58. Timothy Minchin, *What Do We Need a Union For? The TWUA in the South, 1945–1955* (Chapel Hill: University of North Carolina Press, 1997), 37, 134–37; SNCC, "Danville Virginia," saddle-stitched pamphlet; Fred Findling,

"Separate, Not Equal," and Richard Goodman, "Memories of the Freedom Summer," in Sandlin, *In Honor of the Legal Volunteers,* 49–51.

59. Interview with Nate Conyers, 22 August 2007. The proceedings in Aiken's court are described in detail in the Department of Justice brief filed on behalf of the defendants in the federal hearing on these cases. The brief is quoted at length in Kunstler, *Deep in My Heart,* 219–21. See also Holt, *An Act of Conscience,* 144–54, 173, 179.

60. U.S. Dist. Court for Western Dist., Danville Div., *The Rev. Lendell W. Chase, Thomas Holt, and James Dixon, Plaintiffs, v. Honorable A. M. Aiken, Defendant,* C.A. no. 583, EGC, box 1, folder "Danville Sit In, March 1963."

61. Kinoy, *Rights on Trial,* 191–93; Kunstler, *Deep in My Heart,* 19, 148–49, 310–11; Holt, *An Act of Conscience,* 137.

62. Greenberg, *Crusaders,* 351–52; Kinoy, *Rights on Trial,* 193–95; Holt, *An Act of Conscience,* 8, 137–40, 147–48, 174–75.

63. *Baines v. City of Danville,* 337 F.2d 579 (1964), 583; *Baines et al. v. Danville* and related cases, 321 F.2d 643–45; Holt, *An Act of Conscience,* 52–53, 200–205, 216–18, 223; Kinoy, *Rights on Trial,* 201–6, 207 (quote); Kunstler, *Deep in My Heart,* 225–27, 231.

64. SNCC, "Danville Virginia"; Holt, *An Act of Conscience,* 1, 40–45, 190–92, 199, 201–15, 218, 221–25; Harry Lore to EG, 10 August 1963, and "The Pressure of Conscience," six-page typescript, 4–5, EGC, box 3, folder "Book on CLAS."

65. Holt, *An Act of Conscience,* 41; interview with Nate Conyers, 22 August 2007; interview with Dean Robb, 28 August 2007. The *New York Times* assessment appeared on 11 August and is quoted in Kunstler, *Deep in My Heart,* 232.

66. *Baines v. City of Danville,* 337 F.2d 579 (1964). Discussion of Michie's ruling without hearing the merits is on p. 583; on law regarding appeal of remand orders, pp. 596–97.

67. Holt, *An Act of Conscience,* 226 enumerates the campaign's modest gains: one black policeman hired, desegregation of Memorial Hospital, passage of a fair employment ordinance for city jobs, employment of several blacks in retail positions, and eight hundred black voters registered. Kinoy to EG, 13 September 1963, and EG to Kinoy, 27 September 1963, EGC, box 1, folder "Danville Sit In, March 1963."

68. National Lawyers Guild, Detroit chapter, "Press Release," 23 September 1963, EGC, box 3, folder "Ben Smith." Planning for the conference had proceeded over the summer: EG and George Crockett to Ben Smith, 10 July 1963, and EG to Ben Smith, 24 July 1963, and EG to Victor Rabinowitz, 30 August 1963, and Rabinowitz to EG and George Crockett, 7 September 1963, EGC, box 3, folder "New Orleans Conference."

69. Interview with Dean Robb, 28 August 2007; NLG, "Press Release," 23 September 1963; Douglas Martin, "John T. McTernan, He Fought for Freedom,"

New York Times, 16 April 2005; John Baker, Hilton Inn, to EG, 25 November 1963, and attached "Travel Agent" accounts with billings for 3–6 October 1963, EGC, box 3, folder "New Orleans Conference."

70. Kunstler, *Deep in My Heart*, 236; NLG, "Press Release," 23 September 1963; George Crockett to William Kunstler, 1 October 1963, describing his panel, including the title of Collins's presentation, in EGC, box 3, folder "New Orleans Conference."

71. *Dombrowski v. Pfister*, 380 U.S. 479nn1, 4; EG to "Dear Fellow Member," 28 October 1964, EGC, box 3, folder "Ben Smith"; Bruce Waltzer to David Finkel and Ben Margolis, 2 December 1963, and Benjamin Dreyfus to Burke Marshall, 21 October 1963, EGC, box 3, folder "New Orleans Conference"; I. F. Stone, "Eastland and Southwine Sued for $500,000 in Anti–Civil Rights Conspiracy," *I. F. Stone's Bi-Weekly*, 11 November 1963, 4; "Red Propaganda Aim of Bill," *Times-Picayune*, 12 May 1962. Frank Adams, *James A. Dombrowski: An American Heretic, 1897–1983* (Knoxville: University of Tennessee Press, 1992), 266, says that Waltzer and Smith were arrested at their homes. Goodman, Stone, Dreyfus, and (most telling) Waltzer himself all indicate in the citations above that the two lawyers were arrested at the conference.

72. Adams, *James A. Dombrowski*, 268; Kinoy, *Rights on Trial*, 217; Kunstler, *Deep in My Heart*, 243; Woods, *Black Struggle, Red Scare*, 44–47; EG to Ben Dreyfus, 19 March 1964, EGC, box 3, folder "Ben Smith." On changing CASL's name, see EG to "Dear Fellow Member," 28 October 1964. Guild leaders had concluded that a committee to "assist southern lawyers" suggested a potentially patronizing attitude.

73. Adams, *James A. Dombrowski*, 267–68.

74. Woods, *Black Struggle, Red Scare*, 182, 187–88; Kinoy, *Rights on Trial*, 228–32; Kunstler, *Deep in My Heart*, 238–40.

75. EG to Ben Smith, 17 October 1963, EGC, box 3, folder "Ben Smith"; John McTernan to EG and George Crockett, 8 October 1963, and Arthur Kinoy to EG and George Crockett, 9 October 1963, EGC, box 3, folder "New Orleans Conference."

Chapter 10

1. "Memorandum to Director FBI from SAC Detroit (100-6963), 13 March 1963, Subject: Ernest Goodman," and carbon of reply, to SAC Detroit (100-6963), from Director, FBI, 28 March 1963, "Subject: Ernest Goodman, Security Matter C," TAM, box 164, folder 7.

2. Carbon of memo to J. Walter Yeagley, Assistant Attorney General, from Director, FBI, 22 April 1963, "Subject: Ernest Goodman, Security Matter C, Internal Security Act of 1950 (Passport Section)," and attached memo of 24 January 1963, and FBI Report by SA John E. King, 22 March 1965, Detroit Field Office file 100-1512, on Ernest Goodman, Bureau file no. 100-6963, 3–4,

TAM, box 164, folder 7; FBI "Correlation Summary," main file no. 100-6963, 10/30/68, "Subject: Ernie Goodman," 75, TAM, box 164, folder 8; interview with Dick Goodman, 14 June 2006.

3. Correspondence with Lawyers Cooperative Publishing Co., 14 February 1963 through 22 March 1963, EGC, box 26, folder "Travelogue."

4. Carbon of memo to J. Walter Yeagley; FBI Report by SA John E. King, 13 March 1964, Detroit Field Office file 100-1512, re: Ernest Goodman, Bureau file no. 100-6963, pp. 3–4, TAM, box 164, folder 7.

5. Nick Kotz, *Judgment Days: Lyndon Baines Johnson, Martin Luther King Jr., and the Laws That Changed America* (Boston: Houghton Mifflin, 2005), 77, 167–68, 171–74; Taylor Branch, *Parting the Waters: America in the King Years, 1954–63* (New York: Simon and Schuster, 1988), 403; John Dittmer, *Local People: The Struggle for Civil Rights in Mississippi* (Urbana: University of Illinois Press, 1995), 217. Kotz (78) says there were five African American FBI agents; Ronald Kessler, *The Bureau: The Secret History of the FBI* (New York: St. Martin's, 2003), 172, says fifty-one.

6. James Jacobs, "The Conduct of Local Political Intelligence" (PhD diss., Princeton University, 1977), 67–68; Tim Weiner, "A 1950 Plan: Arrest 12,000 and Suspend Due Process," *New York Times*, 23 December 2007; Kotz, *Judgment Days*, 69–76, 236.

7. Branch, *Parting the Waters*, 908–15; Taylor Branch, *Pillar of Fire: America in the King Years, 1963–1965* (New York: Simon and Schuster, 1998), 207, 249–50; Kotz, *Judgment Days*, 83–86, 229–41, 246–49.

8. Adam Nossiter, *Of Long Memory: Mississippi and the Murder of Medgar Evers* (Cambridge, MA: Da Capo, 1994), 105–43, 243. In 1994, Beckwith was tried again on new evidence and convicted.

9. Dittmer, *Local People,* 109–10, 215.

10. Mississippi registration figures compiled from John Herbers, "A Louder Voice," *New York Times*, 22 November 1964; Kessler, *The Bureau*, 147; Morton Stavis, "A Century of Struggle for Black Enfranchisement in Mississippi," *Mississippi Law Journal* 57, no. 3 (1987): 602–7, 621–22; Dittmer, *Local People*, 52–54, 70–71, 137–38, 224; William Kunstler, *Deep in My Heart* (New York: William Morrow, 1966), 328–30; Len Holt, *The Summer That Didn't End* (New York: William Morrow, 1965), 150–53.

11. Clayborne Carson, *In Struggle: SNCC and the Black Awakening of the 1960s* (Cambridge: Harvard University Press, 1995), 46, 97–98; Holt, *The Summer That Didn't End*, 35–36, 153–54.

12. Holt, *The Summer That Didn't End*, 35; Carson, *In Struggle*, 98–100, 112.

13. "Report of the Committee to Assist Southern Lawyers to the National Executive Board," 8 November 1963, 2, TAM, box 5, folder 20.

14. Ernest Mazey to EG, 21 November 1963, and accompanying summary minutes, dated 14 November, of the 10 November 1963 meeting in New York, EGC, box 3, folder "Southern Law Office 1."

15. Mazey to EG, 21 November 1963, and accompanying summary minutes.

16. Ernest Goodman, "The NLG, the FBI and the Civil Rights Movement: 1964—A Year of Decision," *Guild Practitioner* 38, no. 1 (1981): 5–6, and Herman Wright to Julius Cohen, EGC, box 25, folder "1964 Convention, Detroit." On New York chapter activities, see the *Guild Lawyer*, published in New York, with frequent reports in 1962–63 on local chapter activities, including "Calendar of Events," February 1963, 2, EGC, box 2, folder "Material on Criminal Procedure."

17. "National Executive Board Meeting," 10 November 1963, minutes, and "Report of the Committee to Assist Southern Lawyers to the National Executive Board," 8 November 1963, TAM, box 5, folder 20; Goodman, "The NLG, the FBI and the Civil Rights Movement," 7.

18. Ernest Goodman, interview by Edward Littlejohn, 21 February 1997, 8, Oral History Project, Damon Keith Law Collection, WRL; Victor Rabinowitz to EG, 8 January 1964, EGC, box 25, folder "1964 Convention, Detroit." Unless otherwise indicated, all quotes and decisions of the meeting are taken from the transcript minutes, "National Executive Board Meeting, Sunday, November 10, 1963."

19. Goodman, "The NLG, the FBI and the Civil Rights Movement," 6.

20. Jeff Woods, *Black Struggle, Red Scare: Segregation and Anti-Communism in the South, 1948–1968* (Baton Rouge: Louisiana State University Press, 2004), 190–92; Arthur Schlesinger, *Robert Kennedy and His Times* (Boston: Houghton Mifflin, 1978), 641–44; C. David Heymann, *RFK: A Candid Biography of Robert F. Kennedy* (New York: Dutton, 1998), 359–61; Dittmer, *Local People*, 211.

21. New Cadillac Square Apartment Building, "History," www.newcadillacsquare.com/history.htm (accessed 6 October 2008).

22. Victor Rabinowitz, *Unrepentant Leftist: A Lawyer's Memoir* (Urbana: University of Illinois Press, 1996), 178; Goodman, interview by Littlejohn, 21 February 1997, 8; David Rynin to EG, 7 January 1964, EGC, box 25, folder "1964 Convention, Detroit"; "The Guild and the South," typescript carbon, undated, TAM, box 24, folder 26.

23. EG to Herman Wright, 6 January 1964, and Benjamin Dreyfus, "Statement to the Convention," 21 February 1964, and Dreyfus to EG, 9 January 1964, and EG to Dreyfus, 14 January 1964, EGC, box 25, folder "1964 Convention, Detroit."

24. "Report of John E. King, 22 March 1965, Detroit Field Office File No. 100-1512, Title: Ernest Goodman," TAM, box 164, folder 7; Goodman, "The NLG, the FBI and the Civil Rights Movement," 7–8.

25. EG to Ben Smith, 19 November 1963, EGC, box 3, folder "Notes and Memos"; Rabinowitz, *Unrepentant Leftist*, 180; Goodman, interview by Littlejohn, 21 February 1997, 8, 12.

26. Interview with Claudia Shropshire Morcom, 14 June 2007.

27. Dittmer, *Local People*, 230–34; Jack Greenberg, *Crusaders in the Courts: How a Dedicated Band of Lawyers Fought for the Civil Rights Revolution*

(New York: Basic, 1994), 351; Branch, *Pillar of Fire*, 273; Holt, *The Summer That Didn't End*, 90–91.

28. Ann Garity Connell, *The Lawyers' Committee for Civil Rights under Law: The Making of a Public Interest Group* (Chicago: Lawyers' Committee for Civil Rights under Law, 2003), 114, 124–27; Holt, *The Summer That Didn't End*, 88.

29. PBS, *Mississippi, America,* documentary written, directed, and produced by Judith McCray (Carbondale: Southern Illinois University, 1995) (quote at 28:35); Goodman, interview by Littlejohn, 21 February 1997; Goodman, "The NLG, the FBI and the Civil Rights Movement," 10–12; Branch, *Pillar of Fire*, 273. The ACLU apparently did not send a representative to this meeting with the FBI, but Rachlin, Leo Pfeffer of the American Jewish Congress, and Edward Lukas of the American Jewish Committee made it clear they wanted a continuing liaison with the FBI and some protection for the safety of their lawyers. Goodman had previously met with both Rachlin and Pfeffer to encourage their collaboration in a joint effort, and Pfeffer had participated in the Guild conference the previous fall in New Orleans. Goodman would have been chagrined to learn that these men were now seeking FBI protection while (in Rachlin's case) simultaneously heaping scorn on the Guild.

30. Dittmer, *Local People*, 78, 119–38; Branch, *Pillar of Fire*, 66–73, 438, 440; James Foreman, *The Making of Black Revolutionaries* (New York: Macmillan, 1972), 380–81.

31. Victor Rabinowitz to EG, 26 March 1964, TAM, box 44, folder 16; Connell, *The Lawyers' Committee,* 122, 130–31.

32. Holt, *The Summer That Didn't End*, 37–38, 281–85.

33. Dittmer, *Local People*, 215–18, 237, 240–41; Holt, *The Summer That Didn't End*, 30.

34. "Instruction Sheet," Guild mimeo for training attorneys, 3–4, EGC, box 2, folder "Mississippi Project 1964"; PBS, *Mississippi, America*; Greenberg, *Crusaders*, 348.

35. Greenberg, *Crusaders*, 348; PBS, *Mississippi, America*, 9:53 (Crockett); EG to Edward Currie, Mississippi Bar Association, 15 June 1964, EGC, box 3, folder "Misc. ABA"; "National Lawyers Guild Asks ABA Aid in South's Dearth of Responsibility," *Legal Chronicle,* 14 August 1964, 1, EGC, box 2, folder "Mississippi Project 1964." There were occasional cases in which the state practice was invoked. See CLAS press release, 1 July 1964, Jackson Field Office, EGC, box 1, folder "CLAS," protesting the challenge in the City Court of Columbus brought against Henry McGee Jr. of Chicago and Ralph Shapiro of New York.

36. David Rynin to EG, 7 January 1964, EGC, box 25, folder "1964 Convention"; EG to Holt, 28 August 1962, and Holt to EG, 15 August 1964, EGC, box 3, folder "Special Projects"; interview with Dick Goodman, 20 June 2007; interview with Bill Goodman, 7 June 2007.

37. Rabinowitz, *Unrepentant Leftist*, 189; interview with Dick Goodman, 20 June 2007; EG to Len Holt, 1 June 1962, TAM, box 44, folder 7. Six weeks later, Goodman wrote Holt again (12 June 1962, box 44, folder 7) to remind him of agreed-upon procedures for assigning volunteer attorneys to cases.

38. Holt to EG, 16 November 1962, EGC, box 3, folder "Southern Conference, 1962."

39. Interview with Claudia Shropshire Morcom, 14 June 2007; CLAS Report to the NLG Executive Board, "Re: Mississippi Summer Program," June 1964, and NLG, "For Immediate Release," 15 June 1964, EGC, box 2, folder "Mississippi Project 1964."

40. PBS, *Mississippi, America,* 15:47.

41. Ibid., 17:18; George Crockett, interview by Tom Lonergan, 15 May 1987, authors' possession.

42. National Lawyers Guild, "For Immediate Release," 15 June 1964; Lawrence Warren, "No One Should Have Stood Idly By," and Don Loria, "Loria's Mississippi Journal" and "Fighting for Civil Rights," in National Lawyers Guild, Detroit chapter, banquet book, Karen Sandlin, ed., In *Honor of the Legal Volunteers of the Civil Rights Movement,* 3 April 2004, 33–34, authors' possession.

43. Loria, "Loria's Mississippi Journal."

44. Goodman, "The NLG, the FBI and the Civil Rights Movement," 4; EG to Father Robert Drinan, 6 May 1964, EGC, box 1, folder "CLAS"; form letter from Donald Loria and Dean Robb to "Dear Fellow Attorney," 29 April 1964, EGC, box 3, folder "Law Day"; "Mississippi Summer Program," report of Committee for Legal Assistance in the South to the National Executive Board June meeting, and "Conference Call," 8 May 1964, EGC, box 2, folder "Mississippi Project 1964"; Robert Stein, "5 Days Scared Out of My Wits," in Sandlin, *In Honor of the Legal Volunteers,* 29; George Crockett to EG, handwritten and undated, estimating monthly expenses at $1,425 but probably closer to $2,000 given anticipated travel expenses, EGC, box 2, folder "Mississippi Project 1964."

45. Report of SA John E. King, Detroit, Field Office File 100-1512, 22 March 1965, 3, TAM, box 164, folder 7; FBI "Correlation Summary," main file no: 100-6963, 30 October 1968, "Subject: Ernie Goodman," 76–77, TAM, box 164, folder 8; Geoffrey Fieger, "1964: Fighting Injustice," in Sandlin, *In Honor of the Legal Volunteers,* 52. The right-wing group was probably Breakthrough, led by Donald Lobsinger. The flyer identified a second group on the "Punishment List" that included one of the coauthors of this book, David Elsila

46. PBS, *Mississippi, America,* 34:10 (quote); Crockett, interview by Lonergan, 15 May 1987, 6–7.

47. Branch, *Pillar of Fire,* 498–500, describes the Klan's central role in planning and carrying out the murders.

48. Anna Diggs Taylor, "It Was a Visit to Hell," 22, and Claudia Morcom, "The Summer That Lasted a Lifetime," 57, in Sandlin, *In Honor of the Legal Volunteers;* interview with Claudia Morcom, 14 June 1964; Holt, *The Summer That Didn't End,* 20–24, 189–91; PBS, *Mississippi, America,* 35:22; Dittmer, *Local People,* 247; Crockett, interview by Lonergan, 15 May 1987.

49. Holt, *The Summer That Didn't End,* 30; Dittmer, *Local People,* 251–52; Branch, *Pillar of Fire,* 399.

50. Goodman's letter to LBJ is reproduced in Holt, *The Summer That Didn't End,* 269–70. On Judge Clayton's more accommodating role, see Greenberg, *Crusaders,* 348. Dittmer, *Local People,* 404–6, says the differences between the judges were marginal, but notes Clayton's favorable (and "reluctant") 1966 ruling regarding school desegregation. Morcom, in her interview of 14 June 2007, recalls that Clayton permitted court staff to notarize documents for Guild lawyers, something Cox and Mize would not do. She recalled a moment when she and Rita Schwerner approached Clayton to sign a removal petition. "He was back in chambers and he . . . said to her, to Rita, 'My people have not been very kind to you, have they?' . . . He was a decent man."

51. "Senate Approves New Judgeships," *New York Times,* 1 July 1965; Foreman, *The Making of Black Revolutionaries,* 381–82.

52. Kotz, *Judgment Days,* 172; Branch, *Pillar of Fire,* 373; Dittmer, *Local People,* 250–51.

53. Woods, *Black Struggle, Red Scare,* 210–11; Doug McAdam, *Freedom Summer* (New York: Oxford University Press, 1988), 148; Kotz, *Judgment Days,* 164, 170; *Congressional Record—Senate,* 18 March 1965, 5284–88; "List of Guild Attorneys Participating in the Mississippi Project—1964," EGC, box 2, folder "Mississippi Project 1964." The federal government brought indictments against Sheriff Rainey, Deputy Sheriff Price, Sam Bowers, and ten others for violating the civil rights of the three dead men. Price, Bowers, and five others were convicted, while the remainder, including Rainey, were acquitted. Stavis, "A Century of Struggle," 620; Dittmer, *Local People,* 418, 510–11.

54. Carson, *In Struggle,* 117, 122; Dittmer, *Local People,* 251, 259; Holt, *The Summer That Didn't End,* 12; Stavis, "A Century of Struggle," 617.

55. Holt, *The Summer That Didn't End,* 207–42, reproduces the entire daily listing of arrests and assaults; Carson, *In Struggle,* 122.

56. Goodman, interview by Littlejohn, 21 February 1997, 9.

57. Myzell Sowell, "Hopscotching around Mississippi," 27, and Robert Stein, "5 Days Scared Out of My Wits," 29–30, in Sandlin, *In Honor of the Legal Volunteers.*

58. EG to John Caughlan, 3 August 1964, EGC, box 2, folder "1964 Mississippi Project"; Gordon Black, "Biographical Sketch of John Caughlan," *Communism in Washington State: History and Memory Project,* Harry Bridges Center for Labor Studies, University of Washington, http://depts.washington

.edu/labhist/cpproject/whoswho.htm#coughlan (accessed 7 October 2008); Allen Zemmol, "Intimidating the Intimidators," in Sandlin, *In Honor of the Legal Volunteers,* 44.

59. Oscar Baker to George Crockett, 23 July 1964, authors' possession.

60. Fay Stender to EG and George Crockett, 27 July 1964, and EG to Fay Stender, 31 July 1964, and Crockett to EG, handwritten, no date, but some time after 12 August 1964, EGC, box 2, folder "1964 Mississippi Project"; Kunstler, *Deep in My Heart,* 197–200.

61. EG to Walter Craig, President, ABA, 7 August 1964 (quote), and EG to Sidney Carlton, 24 July 1964 (quote to state bar), EGC, box 3, folder "Misc. and American Bar Association"; Connell, *The Lawyers' Committee,* 130–32; Greenberg, *Crusaders,* 348; Kunstler, *Deep in My Heart,* 313.

62. Carson, *In Struggle,* 117; Branch, *Pillar of Fire,* 72.

63. "Rough Minutes of a Meeting Called by the National Council of Churches to Discuss the Mississippi Project," 18 September 1964, EGC, box 1, folder "CLAS"; Nelson Lichtenstein, *The Most Dangerous Man in Detroit: Walter Reuther and the Fate of American Labor* (New York: Basic, 1995), 392–95.

64. "Rough Minutes"; Arthur Kinoy, *Rights on Trial: The Odyssey of a People's Lawyer* (Cambridge: Harvard University Press, 1983), 263–64; Carson, *In Struggle,* 137, 156; Dittmer, *Local People,* 315–18, 341–43; Foreman, *The Making of Black Revolutionaries,* 399–406; Branch, *Pillar of Fire,* 469. The rough minutes identify the chief spokesman for the NAACP as "Kerns," though there is no such name in the listing of those present. Foreman reproduces the minutes and identifies the speaker as Gloster Current, who is listed in the minutes and who was well known for his top-down manner and belligerence toward SNCC. "Kerns" would appear to be a phonetic rendering of his name by Mendy Samstein of SNCC, who took the notes.

65. Kinoy, *Rights on Trial,* 261–62, 268–69; Stavis, "A Century of Struggle," 627–32, 640–41; EG to Henry Aronosn, 7 October 1964, EGC, box 2, folder "1964 Mississippi Project."

66. George Crockett to EG, 20 August 1964, and Crockett to John W. Porter, 7 August 1964, EGC, box 2, folder "1964 Mississippi Project"; Rabinowitz, *Unrepentant Leftist,* 179–80. On chaos in COFO's Jackson office, see Carson, *In Struggle,* 150, and Dittmer, *Local People,* 324–30. A photo of Crockett in his white suit jacket is included in EGC, box 2, folder "Correspondence."

67. B. Pennie Millender, interview by Louis Jones, 29 August 2003, and Robert Millender, "Biography Search Display," Detroit African American History Project, Wayne State University, Detroit.

68. Interview with Claudia Morcom, 14 June 2007; Chester Higgins, "Women Lawyers to Aid Mississippi 'Freedom Corps,'" *Jet,* 9 July 1964, 16–19, EGC, box 2, folder "1964 Mississippi Project."

69. Interview with Claudia Morcom, 14 June 2007; EG to Claudia Shropshire, 9 November 1964, and Claudia Morcom, "National Lawyers Guild, Southern

Regional Office, Progress Summary," 5 February 1965, EGC, box 2, folder "1964 Mississippi Project."

70. Kinoy, *Rights on Trial*, 271–75; Kunstler, *Deep in My Heart*, 331–34; Stavis, "A Century of Struggle," 645.

71. Form letter from EG to "Dear Fellow Attorney," 30 December 1964, EGC, box 2, folder "Challenge Correspondence"; EG to Arthur Kinoy, 29 December 1964, EGC, box 2, folder "1965 Mississippi Project"; Kunstler, *Deep in My Heart*, 337–41; Kinoy, *Rights on Trial*, 280–82; Dittmer, *Local People*, 340. On Detroit depositions, see EGC, box 2, folder "Challenge Correspondence," especially "Press Release, National Lawyers Guild, Detroit, Mi.," undated, and letters between Rita Schwerner, working for Kunstler-Kinoy, and George Crockett, 15 March and 17 March 1965. Stavis, "A Century of Struggle," lists 153 participating attorneys in appendix A, 674–76.

72. Interview with Claudia Morcom, 14 June 2007.

73. Goodman, interview by Littlejohn, 21 February 1997.

74. Ernest Goodman and David Rein, "Brief of National Lawyers Guild Amicus Curiae in Support of the Appellants Benjamin E. Smith and Bruce Waltzer," U.S. Supreme Court, October Term, 1964, 4–5, 9; Kinoy, *Rights on Trial*, 278–79.

75. *Dombrowski v. Pfister*, 380 U.S. 479 (1965); *Cameron et al. v. Johnson, Governor of Mississippi, et al.*, 381 U.S. 741 (1965).

76. Woods, *Black Struggle, Red Scare*, 217; Kinoy, *Rights on Trial*, 294.

77. Lawrence Guyot to EG, 10 May 1965, and EG to Lawrence Guyot, 13 May 1965, EGC, box 2, folder "Mississippi Project 1964"; "Attorney's Brochure," 12 June 1965, and form letter from EG to [blank] soliciting volunteers, 14 May 1965, EGC, box 2, folder "1965 Mississippi Project."

78. Fred Graham, "Leading Lawyers Join Rights Drive" and "Civil Rights Lawyer," *New York Times*, 8 February 1965; Connell, *The Lawyers' Committee*, 132–35.

79. Greenberg, *Crusaders*, 341; Henry Schwarzschild to Irwin Gostin, 27 April 1965, EGC, box 1, folder "CLAS," references the case report from the LCDC office "for the first five weeks of its full-time operation." The letterhead address of the LCDC office was 603 North Farish Street. The Guild office was at 507 1/2 North Farish. Frank Parker, *Black Votes Count: Political Empowerment in Mississippi after 1965* (Chapel Hill: University of North Carolina Press, 1990), 80.

80. Dittmer, *Local People*, 335–36; typescript report of Morcom to "Dear Jim" (Lafferty, the Guild's executive secretary), undated but internal reference to 20 April, EGC, box 2, folder "1965 Mississippi Project"; Bruce Waltzer to EG, 25 April 1965, EGC, box 2, folder "1965 Mississippi Project, Correspondence."

81. Dittmer, *Local People*, 344.

82. *New York Times*, coverage on 8, 14–16, 18, 19, 23–26 June and 1 July 1965; *Jackson Daily News*, 14 June 1965; Dittmer, *Local People*, 345–46.

83. Bureau Main File, Ernest Goodman, "Correlation Summary," 77, reference 100-358684-81, TAM, box 164, folder 8; Connell, *The Lawyers' Committee,* 134–35, 158; interview with Claudia Morcom, 14 June 2007; *Guyot v. Pierce,* 372 F.2d 658 (1967). The FBI report cited here said its information covered activities between February of 1962 and March of 1965, but the reference to Goodman's presence "among a group of more than 1000 individuals who were arrested for participation in a demonstration on the Capital grounds at Jackson, Miss., protesting certain legislation" indicates the events of June 1965.

84. W. C. Shoemaker, "Suit to Open Pools, Parks Is Filed Here," *Jackson Daily News,* 5 August 1965, EGC, box 2, folder "1965 Mississippi Project"; Connell, *The Lawyers' Committee,* 135, 158; Greenberg, *Crusaders,* 342.

85. "Report to National Lawyers Guild Convention," 11–14 November 1965, EGC, box 24, folder "National Lawyers Guild 1968 [*sic*] Convention" indicates that $25,000 for the southern office came directly from the Guild, representing nearly half of the Guild's total budget of $53,000, and another $8,847 came from the Fund for Equal Justice, the tax-exempt foundation established by the Guild; "Operation 'Amicol' (Adopt a Mississippi County Legally), Lawyers and Assignments of Mississippi Counties," EGC, box 2, folder "Pleadings."

86. Bruce Waltzer to "Dear Fellow Guild Member," 22 June 1965, and Claudia Morcom to EG, 12 May 1965, and EG to Ben Smith, 8 October 1965, EGC, box 2, folder "1965 Mississippi Project"; interview with Claudia Morcom, 14 June 2007; Connell, *The Lawyers' Committee,* 140, 159–62, 166–67.

87. George Crockett to Claudia Shropshire, 11 January 1966, 5, EGC, box 1, folder "CLAS." Problems with funding the litigation are described in Hugh Manes to EG, 18 October 1965, and Harry Lore to EG, 6 May 1965, EGC, box 2, folder "1965 Mississippi Project."

88. "Attorney's Brochure," 12 June 1965, EGC, box 2, folder "1965 Mississippi Project"; EG to Members of Executive Board, 30 August 1965, and "Memorandum on the Guild Programs Present and Future, Claudia Shropshire," no date, 1, EGC, box 24, folder "National Lawyers Guild 1968 [*sic*] Convention." Shropshire's undated memo indicates only three suits had been filed "since mid-July" and Len Rosenthal's billing to the Jackson office at the end of August indicates suits for Humphreys County, Madison County, and Hinds County (Jackson). Leonard Rosenthal to "Dear Madam," 27 August 1965, EGC, box 2, folder "Correspondence"; Goodman, "The NLG, the FBI and the Civil Rights Movement," 15.

89. "Decision of Judge William Harold Cox, re Hazel Palmer et al v Allen C Thompson, Mayor, city of Jackson," 14 September 1965, U.S. District Court, Southern District of Mississippi, EGC, box 2, folder "Palmer v. Thompson."

90. "Memorandum on the Guild Programs Present and Future, Claudia Shropshire," 3; Goodman, "The NLG, the FBI and the Civil Rights Movement"; James Lafferty, "State of the Guild: Report and Recommendations of the

Executive Secretary to the National Lawyers Guild Convention, Nov. 10–14, 1965," 2, 4, EGC, box 24, folder "National Lawyers Guild 1968 [*sic*] Convention."

91. EG to unnamed executive board members, 25 August 1965, EGC, box 24, folder "National Lawyers Guild 1968 [*sic*] Convention."

92. Victor Rabinowitz to EG, 30 August 1965, and Martin Popper to EG, 7 October 1965, EGC, box 24, folder "National Lawyers Guild 1968 [*sic*] Convention"; Rabinowitz, *Unrepentant Leftist*, 178.

93. Arthur Kinoy to EG, 21 September 1965, EGC, box 2, folder "1965 Mississippi Project"; Stavis, "A Century of Struggle," 661–64.

94. Lafferty, "State of the Guild," 1; EG to "Dear Fellow Member," 14 September 1965, and Robert Drinan to EG, 15 November 1965, EGC, box 24, folder "National Lawyers Guild 1968 [*sic*] Convention"; *Congressional Record-—House*, 17 September 1965, 23399–401; Kinoy, *Rights on Trial*, 292–94.

95. EG to Robert Drinan, 17 November 1965, and EG to Martin Popper, 23 November 1965, and EG to Ed Lamb, 18 November 1965, and Hugh Manes to Members of the Committee on Guild Programs, 26 October 1965, EGC, box 24, folder "National Lawyers Guild 1968 [*sic*] Convention."

96. Ben Smith to EG, 20 April 1966, EGC, box 25, folder "NLG Natl. Executive Board Minutes, 1964–1968." Liberal commentators and historians largely ignored the role of the Guild in Freedom Summer and the Mississippi struggle, 1964–65. Daniel Pollitt, "Timid Lawyers and Neglected Clients," *Harper's*, August 1964, called attention to the President's Committee and the LCDC and made no mention of the Guild. For Goodman's reaction, see his letter to Pollitt, 3 August 1964, and Pollitt's reply, 13 August 1964, EGC, box 2, folder "Mississippi Project 1964." Ann Garity Connell's history of the President's Committee and its role in the South makes no mention of the Guild. Frank Parker in *Black Votes Count* highlights the role of the LCDC, the Legal Defense Fund, and the President's Committee (with which he was associated). "The standard accounts of the Mississippi Freedom Summer Project almost totally neglect the participation of these groups," he adds, all three of which "opened offices in Jackson in 1964 and 1965." Parker reproduces the "standard" neglect of the Guild, the lead group in Freedom Summer and the first to open an office in Jackson. John Dittmer's *Local People* is one of the few accounts of Freedom Summer that references all four legal groups (NLG, LDF, LCDC, and the President's Committee).

97. Goodman, "The NLG, the FBI and the Civil Rights Movement," 14–15.

Chapter 11

1. Goodman's remarks were paraphrased in detailed notes taken by a police informer, Detroit Police Department, Criminal Intelligence Bureau, "Conference on the Draft," 29 December 1966, TAM, box 164, folder 10. The Ann Arbor draft case and quotes from Goodman's brief are taken from Goodman's

draft essay, "The Ann Arbor Sit-in," no date, EGC, box 4, folder "Goodman Book."

2. "Statement of the National Lawyers Guild Criticizing the American Bar Association Resolution Supporting the Legality of U.S. Intervention in Vietnam," TAM, box 24, folder 25; Dwight Eisenhower, *Mandate for Change* (Garden City, NY: Doubleday, 1963), 337–38, 372.

3. William Serrin and George Walker, "City's Clergy Help to Form School for Draft Dodgers," *Detroit Free Press,* 29 December 1966; Morgan O'Leary, "Traitor! Cry Rings at Antidraft Parley," *Detroit News,* 29 December 1966.

4. Memo from SAC Detroit to Director, FBI, 18 October 1966, TAM, box 124, folder 8.

5. Ronald Kessler, *The Bureau: The Secret History of the FBI* (New York: St. Martin's, 2003), 107–8, 150, 158–59, 174; memo from SAC Detroit to Director, FBI, 3 January 1967, TAM, box 123, folder 7.

6. Memo from SAC Detroit to Director, FBI, 27 September 1966, and memo from Director, FBI, to SAC Detroit, 13 October 1966, TAM, box 113, folder 12.

7. Memo from SAC Detroit to Director, FBI, 18 November 1966, TAM, box 113, folder 12.

8. As per endnote 13, Dick Goodman notified the Fifth Circuit Court of Appeals on 22 September that the unexpected departure of a member of the firm (Philo) in August had delayed preparation of the brief for the *Palmer v. Thompson* appeal. As noted above, the Detroit bureau of the FBI did not seek authorization for sending the forged notes until one week later and did not receive that authorization until mid-October.

9. Interviews with Dick Goodman, 20 June 2007, Paul Rosen, 26 June 2007, and Dean Robb, 28 August 2007; "Death Takes Probe, Law Guild Head," *Detroit News,* 29 May 1954.

10. Interview with Bill Goodman, 7 June 2007.

11. "An Analysis of the Detroit 1965 Primary Election," typescript on legal paper, no date, George Crockett Collection, part 2, box 1, folder 1-27, WRL; "Memorandum" from SAC, Detroit, to Director, FBI, 30 September 1966, with Breakthrough flyer attached, and reply from Director, FBI, 13 October 1966, TAM, box 123, folder 7.

12. Interview with Claudia Morcom, 26 March 2008; interview with James Lafferty, 12 November 2008.

13. "Motion to Extend Time to File Brief," *Hazel Palmer et al. v. Allen C. Thompson, Mayor of City of Jackson,* U.S. Court of Appeals for the Fifth Circuit, 22 September 1966, EGC, box 2, folder "Palmer v Thompson."

14. Interview with Paul Rosen, 26 June 2007; Paul Rosen, "The Summer That Lasted a Lifetime," in National Lawyers Guild, Detroit chapter, banquet book, Karen Sandlin, ed., In *Honor of the Legal Volunteers of the Civil Rights Movement,* 3 April 2004, 31–32, authors' possession; Peter Irons and Stephanie Guitton, eds., *May It Please the Court: The Most Significant Oral Arguments*

Made before the Supreme Court (New York: New Press, 1993), 291–304; *Palmer v. Thompson*, 403 U.S. 217 (1971).

15. Frank Parker, *Black Votes Count: Political Empowerment in Mississippi after 1965* (Chapel Hill: University of North Carolina Press, 1990), 30–35, 50–55, 91, 140.

16. John Dittmer, *Local People: The Struggle for Civil Rights in Mississippi* (Urbana: University of Illinois Press, 1995), 390, 403–6.

17. Ibid., 395–401 (King quote, 401); Clayborne Carson, *In Struggle: SNCC and the Black Awakening of the 1960s* (Cambridge: Harvard University Press, 1995), 158–66.

18. Ernest Goodman and George Crockett, "Complaint," *Sherrill School Parents Committee v. The Board of Education of the City of Detroit*, U.S. Dist. Ct. for the Eastern Dist. of Michigan, Southern Div., civil action no. 22092, 22 January 1962, EGC, processed box 5, folder 14.

19. Jeffrey Mirel, *The Rise and Fall of an Urban School System* (Ann Arbor: University of Michigan Press, 1999), 222–75; Angela Dillard, *Faith in the City: Preaching Radical Social Change in Detroit* (Ann Arbor: University of Michigan Press, 2007), 257–59.

20. EG to Malcolm Burnstein, 4 December 1962, EGC, processed box 11, folder 14.

21. Hon. Fred Kaess, "Order of Dismissal," *Sherrill School Parents v. Board of Education*, U.S. Dist. Ct., civil action no. 22092, 3 May 1968, EGC, processed box 9, folder 7; Mirel, *Rise and Fall*, 266–69, 272–73. Goodman had a long history with many of the principals in the Sherrill School case. The judge, Fred Kaess, was the same man who, as a federal attorney, had prosecuted the Detroit Smith Act case ten years before. The liberal slate on the school board was led by attorney Abe Zwerdling, Goodman's UAW replacement in the long-ago purging of Maurice Sugar.

22. Thomas Sugrue, *The Origins of the Urban Crisis: Race and Inequality in Postwar Detroit* (Princeton: Princeton University Press, 1996), 23, 126–38.

23. Ibid., 211–18, 226–27, 233–71 (quote, 233); Dillard, *Faith in the City*, 278.

24. Interview with Dick Goodman, 14 June 2006; Sugrue, *The Origins of the Urban Crisis*, 242–45.

25. Sugrue, *The Origins of the Urban Crisis*, 23; Charles Abrams, *Forbidden Neighbors: A Study of Prejudice in Housing*, 2nd ed. (Port Washington, NY: Kennikat, 1971), 100–101; Louis Masotti and Jeffrey Hadden, eds., *Suburbia in Transition* (New York: New Viewpoints, 1974), 154–57; *Detroit Free Press*, 1 June 1981; *Detroit News*, 6 February 1960 and 19 April 1960; *New York Times*, 12 March 1967.

26. Sidney Fine, *Violence in the Model City* (East Lansing: Michigan State University Press, 2007), 4, 92, 333, 44; LeRoi Jones, "Black Is a Country," in *Home: Social Essays* (New York: William Morrow, 1966), 86.

27. Fine, *Violence in the Model City*, 99, 104.

28. "1959 Supplemental Report by the Civil Liberties Committee of the Detroit Bar Association on the Detroit Police Department Policy on 'Arrests for

Investigation,'" Ernest Goodman, Chairman, 17 December 1959, George Crockett Collection, part 2, box 3, folder 37, WRL; Fine, *Violence in the Model City*, 13–15; B. J. Widick, *Detroit: City of Race and Class Violence* (Detroit: Wayne State University Press, 1989), 151–52; Robert Conot, *American Odyssey* (New York: Bantam, 1975), 580.

29. Jack Kresnak, "City Police: A Past of Racism," in *Blacks in Detroit*, ed. Scott McGehee and Susan Watson (Detroit: Detroit Free Press, 1980), 74; Fine, *Violence in the Model City*, 95–118 (CRC quote, 95; Edwards quotes, 97, 101, 103).

30. Dillard, *Faith in the City*, 22, 204, 241–44, 252–60, 269–70; Mirel, *Rise and Fall*, 266–69, 330–31, 335; Peniel Joseph, *Waiting 'Til the Midnight Hour: A Narrative History of Black Power in America* (New York: Henry Holt, 2006), 83.

31. Dillard, *Faith in the City*, 234–35, 264 (Dillard quote), 264–66, 279–81 (Hill quote).

32. Joseph, *Midnight Hour*, 146 (*Saturday Evening Post* quote); Fine, *Violence in the Model City*, 29.

33. Phone interview with Abdeen Jabara, 24 March 2008; interview with Bill Goodman, 7 June 2007.

34. U.S Riot Commission, *Report of the National Advisory Commission on Civil Disorders* (New York: Bantam, 1968), 84–87; Fine, *Violence in the Model City*, 149–51.

35. U.S Riot Commission, *Report of the National Advisory* Commission, 87–96; Fine, *Violence in the Model City*, 156–66, 291–300, 330–34; interview with Freda Goodman, 25 January 2007.

36. U.S Riot Commission, *Report of the National Advisory Commission*, 97–106; Fine, *Violence in the Model City*, 235–50 (quote, 236).

37. "The Administration of Justice in the Wake of the Detroit Civil Disorder of July 1967," *Michigan Law Review* (May 1968), 1549–50, 1553n44 (Goodman quote), 1558; Fine, *Violence in the Model City*, 197, 204, 253–54, 254 (judge's quote), 260, 264; interview with John Philo, 18 June 2008; "U-M's Court Study Shows Value of Keeping Cool," *Detroit Free Press*, 7 October 1968; George Crockett, "Recorder's Court and the 1967 Civil Disturbance," *Journal of Urban Law* 45 (1968): 841–42; George Crocket to Charles Quick, 1 April 1968, George Crockett Collection, series 2, box 4, folder 5, WRL; U.S Riot Commission, *Report of the National Advisory Commission*, 339–40.

38. "The Administration of Justice in the Wake of the Detroit Civil Disorder," 1553n44 (quote); Fine, *Violence in the Model City*, 263–64; interview with Bill Goodman, 7 June 2007.

39. Fine, *Violence in the Model City*, 256–57; "The Administration of Justice in the Wake of the Detroit Civil Disorder," 1547–48 (quote), 1555.

40. "U-M's Court Study Shows Value of Keeping Cool," *Detroit Free Press*.

41. Conot, *American Odyssey*, 716–18; Widick, *Detroit*, 189–91.

42. Crockett, "Recorder's Court and the 1967 Civil Disturbance," 847; Fine, *Violence in the Model City*, 169, 304–6.

43. Fine, *Violence in the Model City*, 440–51.

44. Report of John E. King, "Ernest Goodman," U.S. Department of Justice, FBI, Detroit office, 3 April 1968, TAM, box 164, folder 8.

45. "Deliberation Day and Draft Teach-in, University of Michigan, 3/19–20/68," U.S. Department of Justice, FBI, Detroit office, 2 April 1968, 16, TAM, box 164, folder 11. This informant report paraphrases Goodman's comments.

46. Ibid.

47. Nathan Glazer, "What Happened to the Grand Alliance," in *Jews in Black Perspectives: A Dialogue,* ed. Joseph Washington Jr. (Cranbury, NJ: Associated University Presses, 1984), 105–12.

48. National Lawyers Guild, "Memorandum in Support of Resolution of the National Lawyers Guild Urging Establishment of an Arab Independent State in Palestine," 24 June 1949, TAM, box 69, folder 23; phone interview with Abdeen Jabara, 24 March 2008.

49. EG to Ed Gefner, 6 August 1970, EGC, box 23, folder "Arab-Israel"; Claybourne Carson Jr., "Blacks and Jews in the Civil Rights Movement," in Washington, *Jews in Black Perspectives*, 113–31, quote on 124.

50. Interview with Mike Hamlin, 20 May 2008; Dan Georgakas and Marvin Surkin, *Detroit: I Do Mind Dying; A Study in Urban Revolution* (Cambridge, MA: South End, 1998).

51. Interview with Mike Hamlin, 20 May 2008; James Geschwender, *Class, Race and Worker Insurgency: The League of Revolutionary Black Workers* (Cambridge: Cambridge University Press, 1977), 140–42; Georgakas and Surkin, *Detroit*, 50, 119, 131–32.

52. Milton Henry, "An Independent Black Republic in North America," in *Black Separatism and Social Reality: Rhetoric and Reason,* ed. Raymond Hall (New York: Pergamon, 1977), 33–39; interview with Mike Hamlin, 20 May 2008.

53. "Minutes," National Executive Board Meeting, 22 May 1966, 3, and 4–6 November 1966, 3, EGC, box 25, folder "NLG Natl. Executive Board Minutes, 1964–1968"; Victor Rabinowitz, *Unrepentant Leftist: A Lawyer's Memoir* (Urbana: University of Illinois Press, 1996), 183–85.

54. Ernest Goodman, "The NLG, the FBI and the Civil Rights Movement: 1964—A Year of Decision," *Guild Practitioner* 38, no. 1 (1981): 17. In 1972, after Philippine president Ferdinand Marcos declared martial law, the government raided the Guild's office, deported the staff, and turned the files over to U.S. Naval Intelligence. See Howard DeNike, "The Guild Military Office in the Philippines," and Bob Hilliard, "Government Spied on Guild Military Office," in Ann Fagan Ginger and Eugene Tobin, eds., *The National Lawyers Guild: From Roosevelt through Reagan* (Philadelphia: Temple University Press, 1988), 285–89; and Admiral Zumwalt Jr., Chief of Naval Operations, to Patrick Gray, Director, FBI, 12 December 1972, TAM, box 113, folder 12.

55. "Remarks of Ernest Goodman in Opposition to the Idea That the Guild Should Be a Guild of 'Left Lawyers,'" undated typescript, EGC, box 25, folder "Fall 1963 Correspondence, re The Future of the Guild." The folder date is a typo, as indicated by the internal evidence from the document.

56. Ibid.; "Broken but Unbroken, A Quiet Enemy of Racism," *New York Times*, 17 May 1988. Goodman remained in touch with Sachs over the years. See EG to Albie Sachs, 16 May 1979, EGC, box 39, folder "South Africa."

57. "Remarks of Ernest Goodman"; David Rein, "The Movement and the Lawyer," *Guild Practitioner* 28, no. 1 (1969): 1–2. For additional perspectives on the 1968 convention, see the other commentators appearing with Rein in the *Practitioner*, and the various authors of "The Confrontational Convention in Santa Monica, 1968," in Ginger and Tobin, *The National Lawyers Guild*, 261–66.

58. Rabinowitz, *Unrepentant Leftist*, 187; William Goodman, "The National Lawyers Guild as an All-White Organization," in Ginger and Tobin, *The National Lawyers Guild*, 309–14; William Patrick Jr., "The Integration of the Bar," 1964 Guild Convention, Detroit, 22 February 1964, EGC, box 25, folder "1964 Convention Detroit"; George Crockett to Victor Rabinowitz, 29 July 1968, EGC, box 24, folder "NLG Conventions."

59. Henry, "An Independent Black Republic in North America," 33–39.

60. Ibid.; "Resolution on Separate Black Nation," TAM, box 24, folder 40. Cleage opposed the RNA call for a separate black nation. Dillard, *Faith in the City*, 274.

61. Rabinowitz, *Unrepentant Leftist*, 189; Crockett to Rabinowitz, 29 July 1968.

62. Victor Rabinowitz to George Crockett, 22 August 1968, EGC, box 24, folder "NLG Conventions"; Rabinowitz, *Unrepentant Leftist*, 189.

63. EG to Robert Schmorleitz, 4 February 1969, EGC, box 10, folder "Czechoslovakia."

64. Ibid.

65. "Minutes of the National Executive Board Meeting, Detroit, 19–20 October, 1968, TAM, box 5, folder 36; "Minutes of the ... Committee on International Law," 11 April 1969, and "Minutes of the National Executive Board Meeting—April 26, 27, 28, Denver, 1969," TAM, box 5, folder 37. Quote of opponents is taken from Sam Rosenwien to Victor Rabinowitz, 12 April 1969 and attached "Dissenting Comments by Samuel Rosenwein," TAM, box 5, folder 37. Goodman wrote two statements on Czechoslovakia: the first was a long report attached to the letter sent to Schmorleitz in February 1969, the second a condensed two-page version submitted to the International Law Committee in April, both in EGC, box 10, folder "Czechoslovakia." His quotes are from the long report, 3–5.

66. EG to Robert Schmorleitz, 4 February 1969; EG to Alena Cepkova, 23 May 1969, EGC, box 10, folder "Czechoslovakia."

67. For summary accounts of the New Bethel incident, see Georgakas and Surkin, *Detroit*, 54–57, 161–64; Fine, *Violence in the Model City*, 418–23; Widick,

Detroit, 201–5; Heather Thompson, *Whose Detroit? Politics, Labor, and Race in a Modern American City* (Ithaca: Cornell University Press, 2001), 75–77, 129–35; "The Linwood Incident: A Detailed Report," *Detroit Free Press*, 31 March 1969.

68. Crockett to Rabinowitz, 29 July 1968; "Memorandum" to Director, FBI from SAC Detroit, 13 November 1968, TAM, box 229, folder 16; Ernest Goodman, "Justice Led to Hostility, Charges Goodman of ACLU," *Michigan Chronicle*, 26 April 1969, FBI clipping file, TAM, box 164, folder 10.

69. Philp Foner, ed., *The Black Panthers Speak* (New York: J. B. Lippincott, 1970), xii (Crockett quote); Georgakas and Surkin, *Detroit*, 158–59.

70. George W. Crockett Jr., "Racism in American Law," *Guild Practitioner* 27, no. 4 (1968): 176–84; Goodman, "Justice Led to Hostility"; Fine, *Violence in the Model City*, 422.

71. William Serrin, "Judge Crockett: The Man Behind the Controversy," *Detroit Free Press*, 6 April 1969; Gary Blonston, "RNA's Goal: Black Nation," *Detroit Free Press*, 31 March 1969.

72. William Serrin, "How Did It Begin?" and "Timetable of Events in Shooting," and Lee Winfrey, "Two Charged After Slaying of Policemen outside Church," and Roger Allaway, "How Police Responded," all in *Detroit Free Press*, 31 March 1969; Thompson, *Whose Detroit?* 133–34.

73. Georgakas and Surkin, *Detroit*, 55; Goodman, "Justice Led to Hostility."

74. "Canada Invokes War Powers Act," and "Ontario Hunts Weathermen," *Detroit News*, 16 October 1970; "Free Four, FLQ Tells Canada," and "Marxist Confirmed in Chile," *Detroit Free Press*, 25 October 1970.

75. "Policeman Slain Near Home Reported as Panther Office," *Detroit Free Press*, 25 October 1970;John Peterson, "Panther Newspaper—A Source of Friction," *Detroit News*, 27 October 1970; "15 Accused in Police Killing, Surrender After Long Siege," and Tom Ricke, "Reporter, Black Leaders Help End Confrontation," *Detroit Free Press*, 26 October 1970.

76. "Counsel for the Common People, Parts 5–6," videotaped interview with Ernest Goodman, produced by William Bryce, WRL; "Dynamite Is Found in Panther House," *Detroit Free Press*, 27 October 1970; Robert Pavich and John Nehman, "15 Are Charged in Slaying of Detroit Officer," *Detroit News*, 26 October 1970; *Detroit News*, 16 November 1970, quoting Rev. Ray Shoulders of Michigan Human Rights Council on BPP and KKK.

77. *Detroit News*, 16 November 1970, quoting Edwards.

78. Interview with Elliot Hall, 12 June 2008.

79. "For Panthers: Elliot Hall," *Sunday News Magazine*, 28 February 1971; Foner, *The Black Panthers Speak*, x, xxvi–xxvii, 137.

80. "Counsel for the Common People, Parts 5–6."

81. Ibid.; Ernest Goodman, interview by Edward Littlejohn, 6 June 1996, 4–5, Oral History Project, Damon Keith Law Collection, WRL. In his interview with Bill Bryce, Goodman said he took the call from Huey Newton in February 1971, but Tom Meyer was writing to him about details in the case on

11 January. See Meyer to EG, 11 January 1971, EGC, processed box 19, folder 24.

82. "Counsel for the Common People, Parts 5–6"; interview with Elliot Hall, 12 June 2008; "For Panthers: Elliot Hall"; handwritten and signed receipts to Elliot Hall, $300 a week, 5/10/71 thru 6/14/71, EGC, processed box 18, folder 19; Goodman, interview by Littlejohn, 6 June 1996. In his interview with Edward Littlejohn, Goodman said that Hall was paid $400 a week, but this does not square with the receipts found in the EGC.

83. "Counsel for the Common People, Parts 5–6"; interview with Elliot Hall, 12 June 2008.

84. "Counsel for the Common People, Parts 5–6"; State of Michigan, in the Circuit Court for the County of Wayne, "Indictment," EGC, processed box 12, folder 8.

85. Interview with Elliot Hall, 12 June 2008.

86. Thompson, *Whose Detroit?* 129–35; Georgakas and Surkin, *Detroit*, 162–64. There were two trials for the four men accused of murder in the New Bethel incident. Both ended in acquittal for the defendants.

87. "Counsel for the Common People, Parts 5–6"; "Introduction to the Voir Dire," typescript summary by Ernest Goodman, EGC, processed box 13, folder 14; State of Michigan, in the Recorder's Court for the City of Detroit, *People of the State of Michigan, Plaintiff, v. Erone DeSausseure et al., Defendants*, no. 70-07518, and "Voir Dire of the Jury by Mr. Goodman," 43, 36–40, EGC, processed box 13, folders 14–15; EG to Ann Ginger, 8 February 1972, EGC, processed box 19, folder 28.

88. "Jurors," typescript summary of jury members by occupation and personal history, EGC, processed box 19, folder 2; *Michigan v. DeSausseure et al.*, "Proceedings and Testimony Taken . . . May 24, 1971, Vol. VII," 1089; "Counsel for the Common People, Parts 5–6."

89. *Michigan v. DeSausseure et al.*, "Memorandum of Law in Support of Defendants' Motion for Discovery," 22 March 1971, 3–4, 6.

90. State of Michigan, in the Court of Appeals, no. 11452, 4/27/71, EGC, processed box 13, folder 12; *Michigan v. DeSausseure et al.*, "Proceedings and Testimony Taken . . . May 24, 1971, vol. VII," 1095.

91. *Michigan v. DeSausseure et al.*, "Proceedings and Testimony Taken . . . May 25, 1971," 43–48, EGC, processed box 14, folder 7; interview with Elliot Hall, 12 June 2008.

92. *Michigan v. DeSausseure et al.*, "Proceedings and Testimony Taken . . . May 25, 1971," 36–38, 63–67; Peterson, "Panther Newspaper—A Source of Friction."

93. *Michigan v. DeSausseure et al.*, "Proceedings and Testimony Taken . . . May 26, 1971," 1380–1400, EGC, processed box 14, folder 8.

94. Ibid., 1400–1412.

95. "Research, Closing Argument," EGC, processed box 18, folder 8; "Proceedings and Testimony Taken . . . May 26, 1971," 1415–20.

96. *Michigan v. DeSausseure et al.*, "Excerpt of Proceedings Taken . . . on May 4 [24?], 1971," 6–8, 11, EGC, processed box 13, folder 18; *Michigan v. DeSausseure et al.*, "Closing Argument to the Jury by Ernest Goodman," edited transcript, 24–25, 30, EGC, processed box 17, folder 16.

97. "Counsel for the Common People, Parts 5–6"; interview with Elliot Hall, 12 June 2008.

98. "Closing Argument by Goodman," 2–9.

99. Ibid., 9–11.

100. Ibid., 13–15, 17–18.

101. Ibid., 16–17.

102. Photocopy of pages 355–57, *Papers of Thomas Jefferson*, letter to William Stephens Smith, from Paris, 13 November 1787, with several quotations underlined, EGC, processed box 18, folder 8; "Closing Argument by Goodman," 32. The Jefferson quotes are collected in the same research file as the Douglass quote, together with options that included Tom Paine and Sam Adams.

103. "Closing Argument by Goodman," 21.

104. Ibid., 21–23.

105. Ibid., 30–31.

106. Ibid., 31–32.

107. Neely Tucker, "The Trials of Ernie Goodman," *Detroit Free Press Magazine*, 8 December 1991 (Littlejohn quote); interview with Elliot Hall, 12 June 2008.

108. *Michigan v. DeSausseure et al.*, "Proceedings . . . June 25, 1971," closing statement of Elliot Hall, 03686-03691, EGC, processed box 17, folder 1; "Introduction to the Final Argument," typescript, EGC, processed box 17, folder 16; "Jurors," 1; U.S. District Court, Eastern District of Michigan, *David Johnson v. Perry Johnson*, Warden, Civil Action, "Complaint, Jurisdiction," EGC, processed box 19, folder 28; EG to Darnell Cole, Dir. College of Osteopathic, E. Lansing, 16 February 1977, EGC, processed box 19, folder 29.

109. Interview with Elliot Hall, 12 June 2008; letters between EG and Leonard Weinglass in Newark, NJ, August 1971, EGC, processed box 19, folder 26; letters between EG and David Johnson in Ionia and later Jackson prison, October–December 1971, EGC, processed box 19, folder 27, over access to legal library and prisoners' rights; letter from EG to David Johnson, #129985, Cadillac Mi. [prison], 25 August 1972, regarding possible availability of funds in defense committee accounts for use in paying his tuition, EGC, processed box 19, folder 28; EG to Darnell Cole, 16 February 1977, recommending admission of Erone DeSausseure to college.

Chapter 12

1. *Attica: The Official Report of the New York State Special Commission on Attica* (New York: Praeger, 1972), 455–58.

2. Ibid., 458–60; Fred Ferretti, "Autopsies Show Shots Killed 9 Attica Hostages, Not Knives," *New York Times*, 15 September 1971; Joseph Lelyveld, "Findings Shock Families of Hostages," *New York Times*, 15 September 1971; William Farrell, "Rockefeller Lays Hostages' Deaths to Troopers' Fire," *New York Times*, 17 September 1971. Two guards were seriously injured by knife wounds.

3. *Attica: The Official Report*, 332–40, 358–59, 433–34, 456–58, 490; Fred Ferretti, "Doctors in Disagreement on Injuries to Inmates," *New York Times*, 17 September 1971; "Use of Shotguns in Attica Revolt Deplored in House Unit's Report," *New York Times*, 27 June 1973.

4. *Attica: The Official Report*, 33–40, 46–47, 50, 54–58, 65, 68, 75–81; Tom Wicker, *A Time to Die* (New York: Quadrangle, 1975), 7 (superintendent's estimate), 8–9, 13, 16.

5. The quote is from an interview with Jomo Omowale, EGC, box 8, folder "Attica Pleadings and Motions," WRL. See also *Attica: The Official Report*, 105–6, 195–200, 490; Wicker, *A Time to Die*, 7–8; Tom Wicker, "'Unity!' A Haunting Echo from Attica," *New York Times*, 15 September 1971.

6. *Attica: The Official Report*, 195–200; Wicker, *A Time to Die*, 315.

7. David Riddle, "Race and Reaction in Warren, Michigan, 1971–1974: *Bradley v. Milliken* and the Cross-District Busing Controversy," *Michigan Historical Review* 26, no. 2 (2000): 1–49 (state Democratic Party quote on 38); Elwood Hain, "Sealing Off the City: School Desegregation in Detroit," in *Limits of Justice: The Court's Role in School Desegregation*, ed. Howard Kalodner and James Fishman (Cambridge, MA: Ballinger, 1978), 223–308.

8. *Milliken v. Bradley*, 418 U.S. 717 (1974); George Will, "Up Front," *New York Times Book Review*, 11 May 2008, 4.

9. National Lawyers Guild, Detroit chapter, *A Tribute to Ernest Goodman*, 13 December 1980, saddle-stitched banquet book, authors' possession.

10. Ernest Goodman, interview transcript, interviewer unknown, "Subjects Covered: Shango Trial (Attica Prison)," 2, Damon Keith Law Collection, WRL (hereafter "Goodman interview, Damon Keith Collection").

11. Interview with Mozie Lee Smith, 27 September, 2000; interview with Linda Borus, 28 February, 2001; "Probation Investigation Report," New York State Supreme Court, First Judicial District, Bronx County, 1–4.

12. "Probation Investigation Report," 6; "Background and Shango's Story," EGC, box 8, folder "General File Evidence Collection"; *New York Times*, 6 August 1966; *Detroit Free Press*, 17 and 20 January 1966; *Detroit News*, 9 October 1968.

13. "Probation Investigation Report," 1, 10–12; *Detroit News*, 2 January 1966.

14. *Attica: The Official Report*, 105; Goodman interview, Damon Keith Collection, 3. For a summary of Stroble's Michigan convictions, see State of Michigan, in the Supreme Court, *Bernard Stoble v. Michigan Department of Corrections and Michigan Parole Board*, no. 21580, "Brief in Opposition to Application for Leave," Attorney General Frank Kelley, Nov. 27, 1974, 1–5.

15. Goodman interview, Damon Keith Collection, 3.

16. *Attica: The Official Report*, 284–85; Stewart Dan, interview by state police, "Dan G-1, 1/28/75," EGC, box 6, folder "Shango Case, Transcript of Cross-examination of Key Witnesses"; Ernest Goodman, oral history of Attica trial, transcript of tape 1, 6–15, transcript of tape 2, 1–4, and transcript of tape 9, 1–5, EGC, box 6, large folder "Shango Book." The fourteen tapes and accompanying transcripts are undated, but tape 1, p. 1 indicates that Goodman recorded this account of the trial a year after attending a 1974 conference in Peru.

17. *Attica: The Official Report*, 285–86.

18. Goodman interview, Damon Keith Collection, 3.

19. Ernest Goodman, "The Shango Trial: The Lawyer, the Client, and the Jury," in *The National Lawyers Guild: From Roosevelt through Reagan,* ed. Ann Fagan Ginger and Eugene Tobin (Philadelphia: Temple University Press, 1988), 294; Goodman interview, Damon Keith Collection, 3; Goodman oral history, tape 4, 17–18.

20. Goodman oral history, tape 1, 6–10.

21. Goodman interview, Damon Keith Collection, 3–4, 6.

22. Goodman, "The Shango Trial," 293; Goodman interview, Damon Keith Collection, 5–6; "Attica Verdict: Guilty," *Time*, 14 April 1975; interview with Bill Goodman, 28 October 2008.

23. Goodman, "The Shango Trial," 294–95; Goodman interview, Damon Keith Collection, 10.

24. Goodman interview, Damon Keith Collection, 9–11.

25. Goodman, "The Shango Trial," 293–94 (long quote), 297; Goodman interview, Damon Keith Collection, 9.

26. Goodman oral history, tape 2, 7–11 and tape 4, 1–2; interview with Ken Mogill, 18 August 2008. The New York state constitution called for grand jury indictments for persons charged with "a capital or otherwise infamous crime." Because the Attica indictments were issued by a citizens' grand jury that had already reviewed the evidence, state law did not require a subsequent hearing for probable cause. Established under federal rulings regarding witness identification of defendants, the Wade hearing provided an alternative forum for discovery.

27. "Notice of Motion and Affidavit in Support of Motion in People of the State of New York against Shango Bahati Kakawana," EGC, box 7, folder "Discovery-Logs and Witnesses Who Discovered Bodies," 4 February 1975, 1–7; Goodman oral history, tape 2, 7–8, 12–13.

28. Goodman oral history, tape 2, 8–9, tape 3, 12–13, tape 5, 5–6, tape 9, 16–17.

29. Ibid., tape 5, 6–13, tape 8, 15–16, tape 12, 8.

30. Motion to Dismiss, filed 7 April 1975 with State of New York Supreme Court, EGC, box 7, folder "Rehearing Motion to Dismiss"; interview with Linda Borus, 24 July 2000.

31. Goodman, "The Shango Trial," 295; Goodman interview, Damon Keith Collection, 5; interview with Richard Skutt, 4 December 2000; Goodman oral history, tape 7, 1–8.

32. Goodman, "The Shango Trial," 296; Goodman interview, Damon Keith Collection, 9; Goodman oral history, tape 8, 1–5.

33. Goodman interview, Damon Keith Collection, 10; Goodman oral history, tape 2, 18, tape 3, 1–4, tape 3, 14–16, tape 7, 14.

34. Goodman oral history, tape 7, 14–16; Goodman interview, Damon Keith Collection, 10.

35. "Cover-Up on Attica?" *Time,* 21 April 1975; Goodman oral history, tape 7, 8–9.

36. U.S. Senate, Select Committee to Study Governmental Operations with Respect to Intelligence Activities, *Hearings,* vol. 6, 2 December 1975, 110–14; Goodman oral history, tape 7, 10–12; EGC, box 7, folder "Mary Jo Cook, Prosecutorial Misconduct."

37. Assistant New York State Prosecutor Francis Cryan, "Opening Statement," 26–27, EGC, box 6, folder "Shango Case Trans. Cross-exam Key Witnesses."

38. Goodman oral history, tape 8, 10–13.

39. Ibid., tape 9, 8–10.

40. Ibid., tape 3, 5 (long quote), tape 9, 11–12.

41. Ibid., tape 9, 13–14.

42. Ibid., tape 9, 15–16; interview with Linda Borus, 13 November 2008.

43. Interview with Linda Borus, 13 November 2008; Goodman oral history, tape 9, 16–17, tape 10, 1–10.

44. Goodman oral history, tape 10, 4–11.

45. Ibid., tape 5, 9, tape 10, 13–17, tape 12, 1–5.

46. Ibid., tape 12, 8–11.

47. Ibid., tape 10, 3, tape 12, 13–14.

48. Interview with Linda Borus, 13 November 2008; Goodman oral history, tape 12, 14–18, tapes 13–14, 4.

49. Goodman oral history, tapes 13–14, 6–10.

50. Ibid., tape 12, 18, tapes 13–14, 5.

51. Goodman, "The Shango Trial," 297; Goodman interview, Damon Keith Collection, 11–12.

52. Goodman oral history, tapes 13–14, 11–12; interview with Bill Goodman, 28 October 2008.

53. Goodman, "The Shango Trial," 295; Goodman interview, Damon Keith Collection, 4; Goodman oral history, tape 4, 6–7; "Attica Verdict: Guilty."

54. Goodman interview, Damon Keith Collection, 11 (chatting); Goodman, "The Shango Trial," 295 (show jurors); Goodman to Beth Benora et al., 18 September 1975, Sid Rosen Collection, box 1, folder 5, WRL.

55. Goodman, "The Shango Trial," 297; Goodman interview, Damon Keith Collection, 12.

56. Goodman oral history, tapes 13–14, 19–20.

57. "Attica Verdict: Guilty"; Goodman, "The Shango Trial," 298; "Compensation Set on Attica Uprising," *New York Times*, 20 August 2000.

58. Goodman interview, Damon Keith Collection, 13. The successful appeal in federal court focused on Michigan's failure to prosecute Shango in 1968 within 120 days of his arrival from Attica, as required under the Interstate Agreement on Detainers. The U.S. Court of Appeals for the Sixth Circuit ruled for the plaintiff, 587 F.2d 830–40, and the U.S. Supreme Court denied certiorari in 1979, U.S. 440, 940.

59. Lisa Collins, "Shango's Story," *Metro Times Detroit*, 19 September 2001; Tim Belknap and Rick Ratliff, "Freed Killer Fought Drug Dealers, Paid with His Life," *Detroit Free Press*, 5 December 1982; undated draft for press release, Morris Gleicher Collection, box 1, folder 5, WRL; interview with Linda Borus, 13 November 2008.

60. "Freed Killer Fought Drug Dealers."

61. Ibid.; Sandy McClure, "Detroit's 'Meanest Man' Recalled by One of His Victims," *Detroit Free Press*, 5 December 1982.

62. Goodman oral history, tape 3, 17; Shango to Sid Rosen, no date, return address at Jackson prison, Sid Rosen Collection, box 1, folder 5, WRL.

63. Goodman interview, Damon Keith Collection, 13.

Chapter 13

1. Ernest Goodman, oral history of Attica trial, transcript of tape 8, p. 9, EGC, box 6, large folder "Shango Book."

2. Ibid., tape 1, 2.

3. Interview with Dean Robb, 22 August 2005; Chris Johnson, *Maurice Sugar: Law, Labor, and the Left in Detroit, 1912–1950* (Detroit: Wayne State University Press, 1988), 17–18.

4. Interview with Linda Borus, 13 November 2008. Goodman's correspondence with publishers can be found in EGC, box 6, folder "Shango Book."

5. Freda Goodman to EG, 20 August 1962, Ernest Goodman's personal letter file, private collection.

6. Ernest Goodman, "My Dear Friends, Associates and Loved Ones," 3220 Cadillac Tower, 21 January 1961, Ernest Goodman's personal letter file, private collection; interview with Freda Goodman, 25 January 2007; interview with Dean Robb, 22 August 2005; Yvonne Petrie, fashion editor, "Old Pub Sign Hails Antiques in Coach House," *Detroit News*, 24 May 1965; "Graceful Setting for Antiques," *Detroit Free Press*, 28 September 1973.

7. Interview with Bill Goodman, 28 October 2008; deeds, mortgages, and sales agreements for the various properties are in the Goodman family's private collection.

8. Dick Goodman, Memorial Service for Ernest Goodman, Birmingham Temple, 28 March 1997, CD recording, private collection (hereafter "Memorial Service").

9. Interview with Leonard Grossman, 8 August 2006; interview with Esther Shapiro, 30 November 2006; interview with Bill Goodman, 28 October 2008; Ernest Goodman, "Reminiscences on the Life of Mort Furay . . . , March 17, 1972," Maurice Sugar Collection, box 16, folder 19, WRL; "Memorial for Myra Wolfgang . . . April 19, 1976, Ernest Goodman, Remarks," EGC, box 5, folder "Myra Wolfgang."

10. Ned Smokler, "52 Years of Memories . . . ," in National Lawyers Guild, Detroit chapter, *A Tribute to Ernest Goodman,* 13 December 1980, saddle-stitched banquet book, authors' possession.

11. Ibid.

12. Ernest Goodman, "Inter-American Conference: Peru," *Guild Practitioner* 31, nos. 3–4 (1974): 126, 127–28. Goodman's leading role in organizing the conference is evident from the correspondence found in EGC, box 11, folder "AAJ 1st Conf. Peru, 1974."

13. Ernest Goodman, "The Role of Jurists in the Struggle against Imperialism," typescript, Third Conference of AAJ, Havana, Cuba, 24–29 October 1977, 3. Correspondence, agendas, and lists of participants for the meetings in Cuba, Jamaica, Nicaragua, and Grenada are found in EGC, boxes 10 and 11.

14. Details of the case are taken from two sources: "Ernest Goodman in Tel Aviv on Saturday, March 18, 1978," a twenty-nine-page typescript; and the "Report by Ernest Goodman to the National Lawyers Guild as Observer at the Trial of Sami Esmail in Israel," an eighteen-page typescript dated May 1978, with accompanying documents from the Israeli embassy and the U.S. Department of Justice. Both are found in EGC, box 13, folder "Sami Esmail."

15. "Ernest Goodman in Tel Aviv"; "Report by Ernest Goodman"; Polk Laffoon, "Sami Esmail Back in the U.S., Calls Trial in Israel Unfair," *Detroit Free Press,* 22 October 1978; "The Case of Sami Esmail," single page, two-sided typescript, Abdeen Jabara Collection, box 5, folder "Litigation, State of Israel v. Sami Esmail, Correspondence and Political Action," Bentley Historical Library, University of Michigan, Ann Arbor. The Israeli embassy in Washington, DC, issued a statement defending the government's extraterritorial claims by likening them to the U.S. practice of prosecuting aliens whose actions in another country affected persons or property within the United States and were illegal under U.S. law. (Embassy of Israel, "The Case of Mr. Sami Esmail," 27 March 1978, Abdeen Jabara Collection, box 5, folder "Litigation, State of Israel v. Sami Esmail, Correspondence/FOIA Request," Bentley Historical Library, University of Michigan, Ann Arbor.) Goodman was well aware of such cases involving counterfeiting, antitrust, and narcotics. These were, he pointed out in his report, specific crimes "designed to create harm" and those who commit them "know in advance they will suffer the consequences if caught. But those who visit a country for personal reasons should not be trapped into criminal proceedings because of their hostility or organizational opposition to the government of that nation or its policies." "Report by Ernest Goodman," 16–17.

16. EG to the Detroit chapter, National Lawyers Guild, Att: Struggle Staff, 30 March 1978, EGC, box 13, folder "Sami Esmail"; "Ernest Goodman in Tel Aviv," 26; Laffoon, "Sami Esmail Back in the U.S."

17. "FBI Chief Said His Agency Gave Israel Information on Esmail," *JTA [Jewish Telegraphic Agency] Daily News*, 21 November 1978, Abdeen Jabara Collection, box 5, folder "Litigation, State of Israel v. Sami Esmail, Correspondence and Press Releases," Bentley Historical Library, University of Michigan, Ann Arbor; EG to Bernard Fischman, 31 August 1978, EGC, box 13, folder "Sami Esmail."

18. EG to Bernard Fischman, 31 August 1978; EG to Mary Alice Theiler, 27 June 1978, EGC, box 13, folder "Sami Esmail."

19. EG to Bernard Fischman, 7 April 1978, EGC, box 10, folder "Czechoslovakia."

20. "Report by Ernest Goodman," 10; EG to Mi-chael [*sic*] Frishberg, 27 June 1978, EGC, box 13, folder "Sami Esmail"; interview with Dick Goodman, 20 June 2007.

21. Laffoon, "Sami Esmail Back in the U.S." Esmail's case continues to figure in debates over Israel's criminal justice system. For two more recent and opposing views on the Esmail trial, see Alan Dershowitz, *Chutzpah* (Boston: Little, Brown, 1991), 237–38, and Norman Finkelstein, *Beyond Chutzpah: On the Misuse of Anti-Semitism and the Abuses of History* (Berkeley: University of California Press, 2005), 152. The introduction to Finkelstein's book was written by Felicia Langer, Esmail's attorney and for many years the only lawyer in Israel who would defend Palestinians in security cases.

22. Neely Tucker, "The Trials of Ernie Goodman," *Detroit Free Press Magazine*, 8 December 1991.

23. Ibid. The case files for the Gleicher trial are found in EGC, box 12, folder "M.G. & Casey."

24. "Tribute Sponsors," typescript document with longhand title listing over 350 individuals, and "Planning Meeting," typescript notes dated 27 August 1980, Morris Gleicher Collection, box 4, folder 12, WRL; Tucker, "The Trials of Ernie Goodman."

25. "Dear Brother and Sister," typescript invitation from Coleman Young, Morris Gleicher Collection, box 4, folder 12, WRL; "Program," centerfold in *A Tribute to Ernest Goodman*; Ann Fagan Ginger and Eugene Tobin, eds., *The National Lawyers Guild: From Roosevelt through Reagan* (Philadelphia: Temple University Press, 1988), 341.

26. Interview with Ken Mogill, 18 August 2008; interview with Jeannie Mirer, 12 March 2008.

27. Interview with Paul Rosen, 26 June 2007; interview with Bill Goodman, 7 June 2007; interview with Dick Soble, 2 June 2008.

28. Interview with Dean Robb, 22 August 2005.

29. Interview with Dick Goodman, 20 June 2007; interview with Paul Rosen, 26 June 2007; interview with Bill Goodman, 7 June 2007. Paul Rosen left the

firm in 1989 for reasons that included the policy of equalizing income while the division of labor remained unequal. The same disputes contributed to the dissolution of the firm after Ernie's death. George Bedrosian, the firm's managing partner, declined to be interviewed on these matters.

30. Interview with Paul Rosen, 26 June 2007.

31. Interview with Dick Soble, 2 June 2008; interview with Dick Goodman, 20 June 2007; interview with Paul Rosen, 26 June 2007.

32. "State Bar Honors 5 Lawyers as Champions of Justice," *Detroit Legal News*, undated clipping, Ernest Goodman's personal file, private collection; "Newspaper Picks 16 Lawyers as Legal Legends of the Century," *Detroit Legal News*, October 1995; "Champion of Justice Award," www.michbar.org (accessed 16 December 2008).

33. Ernest Goodman, interview by Edward Littlejohn, 17 October 1996, 5–8, Oral History Project, Damon Keith Law Collection, WRL.

34. Quotes are taken from "Introduction and Summary," in *Intelligence Activities and the Rights of Americans, Final Report*, book 2, 26 April 1976, Senate Select Committee to Study Governmental Operations with Respect to Intelligence Activities. The FBI's COINTELPRO activities are documented in book 3, *Supplementary Detailed Staff Reports*, 23 April 1976. Geoffrey Stone, *Perilous Times: Free Speech in Wartime* (New York: Norton, 2004), 496–97 (Kelly quote 496).

35. Michael Krinsky, "National Lawyers Guild v. Attorney General," in Ginger and Tobin, *The National Lawyers Guild*, 336–38; Michael Krinsky to EG, 19 December 1978, noting Goodman's "extraordinary support of the litigation," TAM, box 113, folder 12; Director, FBI to Legat Madrid, 24 February 1971, regarding notification of CIA on Goodman's travel plans to Europe, TAM, box 164, folder 8.

36. Krinsky, "National Lawyers Guild v. Attorney General," 337. The FBI materials obtained by the Guild are deposited in boxes 145–239, Tamiment Library, New York University. The estimate of four hundred thousand pages is taken from the abstract to the Guild collection.

37. Interview with Dick Soble, 2 June 2008; interview with George Corsetti, 19 September 2008.

38. "Court Authorizes Release of Red Squad Files," press release, 10 May 1990, Morris Gleicher Collection, box 5, folder 24, WRL; EG to Michael Krinsky, 22 October 1976, TAM, box 119, folder 1.

39. Goodman, interview by Littlejohn, 5 June 1996, 3 (quoting from an article titled "Prospectus"), and 24 June and 11 July 1996, 19–20.

40. Ibid., 24 June and 11 July 1996, 19–20; Coleman Young and Lonnie Wheeler, *Hard Stuff: The Autobiography of Coleman Young* (New York: Viking Penguin, 1994), 197 (Hudson); Susan Holmes and Edward Shanahan, "Business Exodus Withers City," *Detroit Free Press*, 27 June 1971.

41. Goodman, interview by Littlejohn, 17 October 1996, 14; Robert Raitt, "Don't Buy into Tort Reform's Promises," *Detroit Free Press*, 7 September 2007. For

alternative views on tort reform in Michigan, see www.michiganjustice.org and www.protectpatientsnow.org (accessed 15 December 2008).

42. Goodman, interview by Littlejohn, 17 October 1996, 15; interview with Dick Soble, 2 June 2008; interview with Paul Rosen, 26 June 2007.

43. Norman Sinclair, "Lawyer, Activist Goodman Leaves 'Large Footprints,'" *Detroit Sunday Journal*, 30 March 1997; Julie Hurwitz, Memorial Service.

44. Carlos Goodman, Memorial Service, reading from letters; Goodman, interview by Littlejohn, 24 June and 11 July 1996, 4.

45. EG to "Hank and Bob," 19 August 1992, Ernest Goodman's personal letter file, private collection.

46. Laicha Kravchik Gellman to EG, 19 April 1992, and 30 July 1993, Ernest Goodman's personal letter file, private collection; phone interview with Aviva Gellman Blaichman, 12 January 2008.

47. E-mail from Bill Goodman, 23 February 2009.

48. Goodman, interview by Littlejohn, 17 October 1996, 3.

Index